FEMALE PSYCHOLOGY

The Emerging Self

I am a woman giving birth to myself

SECOND EDITION

FEMALE PSYCHOLOGY

The Emerging Self

SUE COX
*University of California,
San Francisco*

ST. MARTIN'S PRESS
New York

LIST OF EXPERIENTIAL EXERCISES

Library of Congress Catalog Card Number: 80-52382
Copyright © 1981 by St. Martin's Press, Inc.
All Rights Reserved
Manufactured in the United States of America
54321
fedcba
For information, write St. Martin's Press, Inc.,
175 Fifth Avenue, New York, N.Y. 10010

artist: Marta Thoman

cloth ISBN: 0-312-28742-9
paper ISBN: 0-312-28743-7

Acknowledgments

Acknowledgments and copyrights continue at the back of the book on page 488 and following pages, which constitute an extension of the copyright page.

ARTICLES

"The Context and Consequences of Contemporary Sex Research: A Feminist Perspective" by Leonore Tiefer. Published in *Sex and Behavior: Status and Prospects*, McGill, W., Dewsbury, D., and Sachs, B. © 1978 by Plenum Press. Reprinted by permission of Plenum Press.

"Woman's Place: A Critical Review of Anthropological Theory" by Susan Carol Rogers, from *Comparative Studies in Society and History*, Vol. 20, No. 1, excerpts from pp. 137–153, © 1978. Reprinted by permission of the author and Cambridge University Press.

"Summary and Commentary" by Eleanor Emmons Maccoby and Carol Nagy Jacklin, from Chapter 10, pp. 349–366, in *The Psychology of Sex Differences* by Eleanor Emmons Maccoby and Carol Nagy Jacklin, with the permission of the publishers, Stanford University Press. © 1974 by the Board of Trustees of the Leland Stanford Junior University.

CONTENTS

PREFACE

Female Psychology: The Emerging Self provides a feminist interpretation of the psychology of women that emphasizes the social and political, rather than the biological, bases of women's behavior. Collected here are some of the major empirical and theoretical papers from the feminist psychological literature.

Since the first edition of this book, several important developments have taken place: the subject of the psychology of women has become an established academic discipline; the number of courses in it, as well as in the field of women's studies, has grown; and many new theories have been advanced and old ones reconceptualized. There was a great need for a new edition to reflect the evolution of the discipline. Thus, many new articles appear in this collection; but classic papers, valuable for their theoretical contributions, have been retained from the first edition.

The second edition, like the first, begins with a General Introduction, which outlines the themes of the book. Following are the articles, arranged in seven sections. Introductions to the sections relate the articles to each other and to the themes set forth in the General Introduction. The first section reviews "Biological and Cultural Perspectives" on the psychology of women. The second, "Psychological Sex Differences," surveys some of the outstanding work in sex-difference research. "The Ethnic Diversity of Female Experience" focuses on the experiences of women who are Black, Asian, Chicana, and Native American. Following, "Psychological Oppression" reinterprets sex differences and offers a sociopolitical analysis of the psychology of women. "Relationships: Sexuality and Intimacy" is new to this edition and reflects advances in the field. "Mental Illness or Social Problem?" explores the relation between emotional disorder and sex role. The final section, "Toward Change and Liberation," discusses possibilities for individual and social change.

Many kinds of illustrations enliven and add depth to the text: reproductions of paintings and sculpture, photographs, drawings, and cartoons; poetry and quotations; and experiential exercises designed to increase the reader's awareness of ideas explored in the text. References for further reading at the end of the section introductions will help readers to pursue various topics further.

This book would not have been possible without the women's movement and the work of many feminists. I feel particularly indebted to *Signs: Journal of Women in Culture and Society* and to the *Psychology of Women Quarterly,* not only because several of the articles published here first appeared in these journals but because the journals provide a forum for the presentation and discussion of feminist theory and values in the behavioral sciences.

I am also grateful to the many feminist psychologists who responded to my requests for suggestions about the contents of the second edition. It is heartening that the feminist values of sharing, cooperation, and support continue to permeate our work. In selecting, editing, and arranging the articles that appear here, one aim was to produce "our" book of readings on the psychology of women.

I especially want to thank the women who wrote articles for this edition: Saundra Rice Murray, Reiko Homma True, Marjorie Whittaker Leidig, Kristiann Mannion, Ellyn Kaschak, and Donna Moore. I would also like to thank everyone whose work illustrates this book. My special thanks go to Marta Thoman for the drawings that open each section and for the cover and the frontispiece.

My critic readers, Irene Hanson Frieze, Leonore Seltzer, Marjorie W. Leidig, and Jean-

Emerging Light by Remedios Varo. Reprinted by permission of Walter Gruen.

nette Fiss provided much appreciated advice, and I thank them for their support.

Without the spirit of feminism, this book could not have existed. Since it is "our" book, I feel that "we" should share the royalties. To this end, any royalties in excess of expenses and labor for both editions will be given to the women's movement.

General Introduction

Since the first edition of this book, the psychology of women and women's studies as a whole have continued to expand and have become established as enduring, creative, and valued academic disciplines. In 1975, during the production of the first edition, *Psychology of Women Quarterly* and the interdisciplinary journal *Signs* were just beginning, as were many other women's studies journals. (See listing of these at the end of the Introduction.) At present, several years of publication of these journals have given us a body of feminist scholarship of extremely high quality in terms of feminist academic standards which include but are not limited to traditional ones. Feminist scholarship has gained legitimacy by successfully demonstrating the value of challenging the traditional (male) perception of reality by critiquing existing theory, reconceptualizing core concepts, and expanding empirical knowledge. This collection of readings contains only a sample of what academic feminist psychologists and related feminist social scientists have to offer on the psychology of women from a Female* (and human) perception of reality.

In the past, more so than currently, an issue plaguing psychology of women courses was the extent of their relationship to feminism. Various degrees of feminism† are and have been apparent in the personal views of instructors and students involved in these courses, in the materials used to teach these courses, and in the basic approach to the sub-

ject matter. It is true, however, that historically the impetus for women's studies was generated by the women's movement, and many women's studies classes were, in part, outgrowths of consciousness-raising (CR) groups. The activities of CR groups generated self-awareness and sociopolitical awareness. These insights usually brought about personal transformations and eventually led to efforts to change the larger society. (For further discussion, read Nassi and Abramowitz on CR groups and Polk on the women's movement in the section "Toward Change and Liberation".)

One relationship of CR groups to women's studies has been described in a report on their effectiveness in producing change (Brush, Gold and White, 1978):

> Women's studies courses and programs are a rapidly growing and innovative addition to college curricula. Partially an outgrowth of consciousness-raising groups, they attempt to bring the atmosphere of self-discovery and the excitement of the women's movement to the college campus. Two sets of goals are stressed by many teachers and students: (1) traditional academic goals of intellectual mastery of subject matter and the imparting of a substantial amount of information, and (2) less traditional goals of personal change, analogous to those changes attempted by consciousness-raising groups. The courses try to challenge basic self-concepts and sex-role beliefs and to encourage women to adopt more positive attitudes toward themselves and women in general. (pp. 870–871)

It is the process of personal change that can make women's studies courses different from others, and the continuing integration of these changes into the approach to and involvement with the intellectual subject matter that ac-

---

*Use of upper case here distinguishes reality based on women's experiences from that based on men's view of women's reality (female).
†See Appendix B for a description of these.

Representation of the world, like the world itself, is the work of men;
they describe it from their own point of view, which they confuse with
absolute truth.

Simone de Beauvoir, *The Second Sex*, 1953

---

counts for their genuine success in both personal and intellectual terms.

Certain aspects of personal change in CR groups and women's studies courses also involve the development of feminist consciousness, as the unconscious becomes conscious. As indicated above, feminist consciousness involves increased awareness on many levels—the societal, the interpersonal, and the personal. There can be increased spiritual awareness as well. A description of this more personal and spiritual side of feminist consciousness is found in a discussion of the heroine of Margaret Atwood's recent novel, *Surfacing*, contained in a special issue of *Signs* on "Women and Religion" (Christ, 1976):

> *Surfacing* exemplifies two structural elements of female quest which can be isolated for comparison with the quests of other heroines, in literature and in life. Awakening from a male-defined world to the greater terror and risk, and also the great potential healing and joy, of a world defined by the heroine's own feeling and judgment, is one of the stages or moments of the female quest which may have important spiritual implications. Often this requires a heroine to return to the past to redefine her relation to it—exchanging his story for her story, as feminists sometimes put it. This awakening is especially poignant for women who, like Atwood's protagonist, having suppressed their own feelings in order to acquiesce to male value systems. Rejection of a male-defined world may also open a woman to a full experience of the great powers, as happens to the heroine of *Surfacing*. This

awakening could be called a "conversion" to a new religious world view, in conventional religious terminology. However, "awakening" or "surfacing" seem to be better metaphors for describing this spiritual experience, which is more the emergence of what is known but suppressed than the radical turning around or adopting of an alien world view implied by the conventional term. A second stage of the female quest which often has profound spiritual implications is moving from victimhood to power. This movement is especially important for woman who have previously been identified as powerless. Correlative to awakening or surfacing, this movement may also open the protagonist to the experience of great cosmic powers which ground her newly felt sense of her own power. (p. 325)

The two notions of (a) change in self-concepts, sex-role beliefs, attitudes, and values, and (b) awakening or surfacing are related. In Jungian terms (more about Jungian theory below), the first of these could be seen as intellectual and emotional changes making way for changes in the self; the second as spiritual transformations leading to the Self. The subtitle, "The Emerging Self," is intended to include both changes in the self and transformations of the Self.

A parallel distinction between female and Female is also introduced occasionally with the former based on society's (men's) perception of reality, while the latter is based on women's experience and reality. It is Female experience and reality, attained through the

Women have no means of coming to an understanding of what their experience is, or even that it is different from male experience. The tool for representing, for objectifying one's experience in order to deal with it, culture, is so saturated with male bias that women almost never have a chance to see themselves culturally through their own eyes. So that finally, signals from their direct experience that conflict with the prevailing (male) culture are denied and repressed.

Shulamith Firestone, *The Dialectic of Sex*,
1970

process and content of feminism, with which this book is concerned. As in the first edition, one of the major premises of this text is that a significant relationship exists between the psychology of women and the principles of feminism and that, through feminism, we can discover aspects of this psychology not found in the traditional approach to the subject. Although the subtitle "The Emerging Self" bears close relation to the content of this book, "A Feminist View," would be an equally appropriate subtitle.

Another aspect of this edition which has not changed from the previous one is the definition and value of both the content and process of feminist scholarship. Some qualities of feminist scholarship noted in the first edition also characterize the work contained in the present volume. While valuing the objectivity and analytical abilities intrinsic to scientific work, academic feminists tend to be aware of limitations inherent in the extremes of these and feminist scholarship tends to be more interdisciplinary and aware of ethnic and class differences among women (and men). There is more of an emphasis on the sociopolitical context of the psychology of women combined with an explicit awareness and concern with values in their own work and the work of others. As feminists value women and Female experience, feminist scholars value cooperation and interdependency, in contrast to the more competitive, individualistic style of the male experience and value system.

There is one further note regarding values and feminist scholarship. Feminists have criticized traditional academic disciplines for their claim to "objectivity" and being value free, particularly as they affect women. Values are always present in scientific research, and feminist scientists advocate making them explicit. Linda Gordon, a feminist historian, expresses this well:

Of course there are dangers in being partisan scholars. But there are worse dangers in posing as objective. The first is that since no one can achieve real political neutrality, those who claim it are misleading people. In the academic world, we still need to repeat that those who accept the traditional academic assumptions are in fact as political as those who reject them. The second danger is that those who seek neutrality will not be able to understand anything. To claim neutrality is to surrender any critical distance on one's own culture, to accept as permanent and natural traditions which are in fact disintegrating. (1975, p. 565)

A Feminist Approach to the Psychology of Women

As stated earlier, the approach to the psychology of women taken in this collection of readings is a feminist one. It assumes that the present subordinate status of women is not intrinsic to nature but is a product of culture and is, therefore, changeable. It further argues that

The right to vote, or equal civil rights, may be good demands, but true
emancipation begins neither at the polls nor in courts. It begins in
woman's soul.

Emma Goldman, "The Tragedy of Woman's
Emancipation," *Anarchism and Other*
Essays, 1911

---

much of what is presently regarded as the psychology of women is the result of subordinate status and therefore sociopolitical in origin.

There are actually several feminist conceptualizations of women's subordinate status. (See Polk's article for more on this subject.) One of these has to do with the arbitrary division of human attributes into "female" and "male," with the male attributes having higher status. Another concerns the dichotomization of values based on arbitrary sex role definitions. Such differences in values create a "female" and a "male" culture with "male" values and culture having higher status and being the dominant culture. A third has to do with domination of females by males through institutional and personal means. And, finally, an economic conceptualization sees the subordinate status and role of women originating in economic development and being maintained by the current economic structure.

These views are not mutually exclusive, of course, and while all are assumed in the present collection of readings, primarily the first three are drawn upon for interpretations of the psychology of women.

Sociopolitical Relation of the "Feminine"/"Masculine" Duality on Many Levels

Many theorists have dealt with the "Feminine"/"Masculine" dichotomy. While some theorists have reified these concepts and assumed that they are reflected (or even originate) in the psychological "natures" of women and men, feminist theorists have assumed instead that they are sociopolitical in origin and that they are the result of unequal power. The sociopolitical relationship of "femininity" and "masculinity" is apparent on many levels—the societal, the interpersonal, and the intrapsychic. This is another theme that is developed in this text and will be elaborated further in this section.

Jungian theory describes intrapsychic structures and processes and is an example of a theory that reifies "Feminine" and "Masculine." According to this theory, the anima and the animus are archetypal and therefore unconscious figures representing the inner "feminine" personality in men and the inner "masculine" personality in women. Although Jungian theory has gained partial acceptance among feminists because it acknowledges both "feminine" and "masculine" in each person and places a relatively high value on the "feminine" component (in men), this theory essentially links the outer "female" and "male" personalities to the presumably innate psychological "natures" of women and men.

Jungian theory can be criticized on many grounds. Goldenberg (1976), for example, notes that the concept of the anima is developed more fully than that of the animus and that men are encouraged to develop their contrasexual personality whereas women either are not or are encouraged only within certain limits. And, according to Goldenberg, archetypes are, by definition, unchanging and un-

---

changeable, so Jungian theory ultimately supports "feminine" and "masculine" (inner and outer) stereotypes as the status quo.

In place of Jungian theory as it is now, Goldenberg (1976) suggests recovering the lost, buried images of women but *not* establishing these images as archetypes. In her view, imaginal activities can be understood as archetypal to the degree that they move inner psychological processes: *"Archetypes therefore would refer to the imaginal or religious process itself rather than to past documents of that process"* (p. 449). This represents both a negative and a positive relation to Jungian theory. While acknowledging the patriarchal myopia of Jung, by removing it, Goldenberg returns to the spiritual essence upon which Jung's work is based.

Shulamith Firestone (1970) was one of the first feminists to analyze the basic duality of "Masculine" and "Feminine." The dialectic of sex is to be understood in terms of the sexual dualism in nature based on the biological-material reality of women's reproductive functions. According to Firestone, it is because of this biological difference that the reproductive family unit contained within it the first division of labor and the historical basis for the sexual imbalance of power. It is from this sexual imbalance of power that "masculinity" and "femininity" were derived. To Firestone, psychological "maleness" and "femaleness" are the direct result of power dynamics and once established, are maintained by social conditioning and power differences.

These "masculine" and "feminine" dynam-

ics are apparent on a cultural level as well. According to Firestone, "culture is the attempt by man to realize the conceivable in the possible" (p. 172). Two modes of accomplishing this are the idealistic, aesthetic mode, in which the limitations of reality are denied through the creation of an alternate reality, as in art; and the scientific, technological mode, in which the contingencies of reality are overcome through the mastery of reality's own workings, the laws of nature. Culture, then, is the dialectic between these two modes.

The correspondence of these two different cultural modes with the two sexes respectively is unmistakable.... the aesthetic response corresponds with "female" behavior. The same terminology can be applied to either: subjective, intuitive, introverted, wishful, dreamy, or fantastic, concerned with the subconscious (the id), emotional, even temperamental (hysterical). Correspondingly, the technological response is the masculine response: objective, logical, extroverted, realistic, concerned with the conscious mind (the ego), rational, mechanical, pragmatic, and down-to-earth, stable. Thus the aesthetic is the cultural recreation of that half of the psychological spectrum that has been appropriated to the female, whereas the technological response is the cultural magnification of the male half. (p. 175)

In a more empirical and scientific way, psychologists have also reified "masculinity" and "femininity," linking them with the left and right hemispheres of the brain, although the research in this area is somewhat controver-

So dualism resides in the very brain. The ways of perceiving that came to be grouped in the left hemisphere are the tools men used to take control of the planet. Linear thinking, focused narrowly enough to squeeze out human or emotional considerations, enabled men to kill . . . with free consciences. Propositional thinking enables men to ignore the principles of morality inherent in all the earth's systems, and to set up instead their own version of right and wrong which they could believe as long as its logic was internally consistent. . . . All ways of perceiving that threatened the logical ways with other realities were grouped together on the other (right) side of the brain and labeled "bad."

gina, *Amazon Quarterly*, 1974

---

sial. The left hemisphere has been associated with linear, sequential, and "propositional" thought; the right hemisphere with simultaneous, Gestalt, and "appositional" thought (Bogen, 1969). Whether these two apparent modes of functioning are actually located in each of the two hemispheres, the point is that they are described as gender related.

The association of alleged hemispheric qualities with those of the male and female are grounded in Western and Eastern thought. From a Buddhist doctrine:

> The Chinese Yin-Yang symbol neatly encapsulates the duality and complementarity of these two poles of consciousness. . . . Note that one pole is in time, the other in space; one is light, one dark; one active, one receptive; one male, one female. (Ornstein, 1972, pp. 65–66)

From American college students during the 1950s on the Osgood Semantic Differential Test:

> The Left was characterized as bad, dark, profane, female, unclean, night, west, curved, limp, homosexual, weak, mysterious, low, ugly, black, incorrect, and death, while the Right meant just the opposite—good, light, sacred, male, clean, day, east, straight, erect, heterosexual, strong, commonplace, high, beautiful, white, correct. (Domhoff, 1973, p. 146)

Feminist critique (Star, 1979a, 1979b) of the scientific work on hemispheric lateralization is that it contains interpretations that reify psychological "maleness" and "femaleness" and supports the values and conditions of patriarchy. Star finds untested assumptions and faulty methodology employed which she feels are rarely questioned because the results or their interpretations support cultural assumptions about "maleness," "femaleness," and male superiority. Sometimes, researchers interpret similar findings in opposite ways in order to justify the same conclusion regarding these myths. Similarly, she notes that research findings can lead to very different conclusions when interpreted in a Female-positive way.

In view of the complex and contradictory nature of research findings in this area, Star suggests that men's social and economic dominance have been linked too simplistically to left hemispheric dominance and to men's assumed greater capacity for linear (left-brain)

Where left handedness is present, the character pertaining to the opposite sex seems more pronounced. This sentence is not only invariably correct, but its converse is also true; where a woman resembles a man, or a man resembles a woman, we find the emphasis on the left side of the body. Once we know this we have the diviner's rod for the discovery of left handedness. This diagnosis is always correct.

Wilhelm Fliess, *Der Ablauf der Lebens,* 1923

---

thinking. The following excerpt is from Star (1979b):

> The existence of a social system which encourages competitiveness between different modes of thought, and often emphasizes linearity at the expense of holism, does not imply that this system must derive from brain structure; nor need we assume that the system that exists supports or interacts smoothly with extant brain structures. The brain is so much more overwhelmingly labile than static, individual than standard, and state dependent rather than constant over time, that we must find language that reflects this when talking about brain-society interactions—whether on the level of metaphor or actual function. For feminists, I suggest that we take the *corpus callosum* as our metaphorical and functional ideal locus—the always-changing, time-independent, inter-hemispheric conductive tissue, which connects the two hemispheres and hence cannot be separated analytically or physically from either. (pp. 126–127)

There has been much speculation regarding the nature and origin of the apparent difference in cognitive styles of the two hemispheres, which leads to further descriptions (or examples) of the possible hemispheric differentiations of the "masculine" and the "feminine." Jaynes (1976), for example, posits that the ancient mind was without hemispheric specialization, humans lacked self-consciousness and their behavior was guided by hallucinations. Through evolution, the left hemisphere specialized, humans acquired a self-consciousness and a sense of responsibility for their actions, and their behavior became self-controlled. The right hemisphere was "left to the gods." Galin (1974) attributes hemispheric lateralization with conscious and unconscious processes. According to him the less than total integration of the two hemispheres accounts for the dissociation of experience where the individual's unconscious emotional or somatic reactions are independent of the conscious thoughts and awareness. Finally, in a recent review of the evidence, Corballis (1980) decides that modern interpretations of cerebral asymmetry emphasizing a basic duality of cognitive processing between two hemispheres are based on ancient myths regarding left and right handedness.

Differences in left and right hemispheric functioning have also been linked to the experiential styles of the obsessive-compulsive and

Feminine/Masculine: Yin/Yang

Purpose: To experience the Female and Male points of view (the feminine and masculine) in ourselves; to reclaim, own, and value both parts and attempt to integrate them; to see how these two parts manifest themselves in our lives presently.

Directions:

1. Without identifying with either the masculine or feminine, list the essential qualities of both Male and Female points of view. The following is the beginning of such a list. The group may want to add to the list so that everyone feels clarified as to what these two are and to distinguish them from male and female (since every male and female contain both masculine and feminine).

Male Point of View *(masculine, yang)*	**Female Point of View** *(feminine, yin)*
The creative, arousing, generating, phallic element. The begetter.	The receptive, yielding, containing, gestating element. The bearer.
Sun, light, penetration.	Earth, darkness, womb.
Active, aggressive, assertive, initiating and moving toward a conscious goal.	Passive, waiting, letting nature take its course, in tune with the repeating cycles of nature.
Conscious knowledge, discrimination, meaning, law, order. Directness, to the point.	Dark instinctive earth wisdom, not consciously thought out. Indirect, serpentine.
Understanding, meaning, essence.	Experience, being, existence.
Objective, Head-centered, Linear, Invulnerable, Penetrating, Definite, Analytical.	Subjective, Heart-centered, Round, Vulnerable, Yielding, Mysterious, Intuitive.

2. Close your eyes and relax (you may either sit comfortably in a chair or lie down).
3. Imagine a blank screen in front of you. Have someone slowly read the list of items for feminine and allow these words to evoke the feminine.
4. After the list is read, let an image appear on the screen. Don't try to censor or change it; take whatever appears.
5. Interact with the image as follows:
   (a) Talk to it by saying "hello" and have it say "hello" back. You may wish to speak out loud if you are doing the exercise with one other person.
   (b) What are your feelings toward the image? Get in touch with them and note them to yourself (or out loud if there is only one other person present).
   (c) What do you want or need from it? Get in touch with this and note it.
   (d) Become the image. As you become it, look back and see yourself standing there.
   (e) What does it feel like to be this image?
   (f) Find out what it wants and needs.
   (g) Now become you again.
6. Open your eyes and, without disturbing your mood, write a description of your experience.
7. As soon as you have finished writing, close your eyes again.
8. Imagine a blank screen in front of you. Have someone slowly read the list of items for the masculine and allow these words to evoke the masculine.
9. Let an image appear on the screen [repeat steps 4 through 6].
10. As soon as you have finished writing, close your eyes again.
11. Imagine a blank screen. Let the images for both the feminine and masculine appear on the screen. Watch them. See how they interact. Let them talk with each other.
12. Come into the situation yourself, talk with them and try to improve the relationship between them.
13. Imagine a mountain in the background that the three of you are going to climb. Go to the base of the mountain and begin the ascent, observing how all three go up the mountain.
14. When you get to the top, look around at the setting and each other. Feel the sunshine; smell the air.
15. Look up at the sun and see a beam of sunshine come from it and end at a spot on the ground in front of you. Down the sunbeam comes a wise old person. Ask this person anything any of you would like to know. Perhaps problems have come up among the three of you that the wise old person may be able to offer comments or advice about.
16. When you have finished talking with the wise old person, thank her/him, say goodbye, and let her/him return up the sunbeam.
17. Rest for a few moments and then open your eyes. Write a description of what happened.

What happened in this exercise? What did you learn? What did you experience? How do these images manifest themselves in your present life? Share your experiences with the group.

hysterical personality disorders (to be described below) respectively (Allen, 1977):

> It would seem that the thinking styles described for the hysteric and for the obsessive-compulsive in many ways correspond respectively to the thinking functions of the right and left cerebral hemispheres of the brain that have been reported by some investigators.... The right is global, holistic, impressionistic, and aesthetic in its apperception; the left deals in details, verbal memory, logic, discrete recall, linearity, and time sequence.... Both these left-right hemisphere modes of functioning have obvious adaptive value, and each complements the other. One is tempted to speculate that when a clearly defined hysteric or obsessive style of thinking exists, it may have resulted from a suppression or repression of the functions of the complementary or that the functions of the complementing hemisphere were not fully activated at some critical time in a specific maturational period. (pp. 315–316)

To carry this a step further, it is generally well accepted that there is a similarity between the obsessive-compulsive personality disorder and "masculinity" and between the hysterical personality disorder and "femininity." (See Shapiro, 1965, for a more complete description of these disorders.) Though there may be systematic biases in the diagnostic process, it seems to be empirically well established that more men than women have the diagnosis obsessive-compulsive personality disorder, while the reverse is true for the hysterical personality disorder (DSMIII, 1980).

Personality disorders are a fairly mild type of disturbance, different only in degree from personality. According to the *Diagnostic and Statistical Manual of Mental Disorders* (1980) of the American Psychiatric Association a personality disorder is defined as follows:

> Personality traits are enduring patterns of perceiving, relating to, and thinking about the environment and oneself, and are exhibited in a wide range of important social and personal contexts. It is only when personality traits are inflexible and maladaptive and cause either significant impairment in social or occupational functioning or subjective distress that they constitute Personality Disorders. (p. 305)

Personality disorders are pervasive and have been conceptualized as the disorder of our times comparable to the neuroses of Freud's era. (Giovacchini, 1975).

The diagnostic criteria for hysterical and obsessive personality disorders appear in Table 1. Also contained in this table are the traits which differentiate the "healthy male" from the "healthy female," as judged by clinicians according to the classic study by Broverman, et al. (1970).

In surveying the characteristics of the two psychiatric definitions of the disorders, the reader should be reminded that the psychiatric profession is a heavily male dominated one, in its group membership and its ideology, so that the labelling and describing of these disorders are affected accordingly. To be specific, the definitions may be interpreted as a male (obsessive) view of the obsessive and the hysteric. One might postulate that these definitions may be at least slightly distorted favorably toward obsessives and unfavorably toward hysterics.

One can also see how some of the traits of the obsessive may even generate some of the qualities of the hysteric. For example, the obsessive's "insistence that others submit to [their] way of doing things" and a "lack of awareness of the feelings elicited by this behavior" can generate in the hysteric "over-

TABLE 1

Interpersonal Level

Obsessive-Compulsive Personality Disorder[1]	Healthy Male[2]	Healthy Female[2]	Hysterical Personality Disorder[1]
			behavior that is overly dramatic, reactive, and intensely expressed as indicated by at least three of the following:
restricted ability to express warm and tender emotions	not as emotional not as excitable in a minor crisis	more emotional	self-dramatization, e.g., exaggerated expression of emotion
unduly conventional, serious, formal and stingy	liking math and science	less competitive (?)	incessant drawing of attention to self
perfectionism that interferes with the ability to grasp "the big picture"	more competitive	disliking math & science	craving for activity and excitement
preoccupation with trivial details, rules, order, organization, schedules, and lists	more objective	more excitable in a minor crisis less aggressive (?)	overreaction to minor events irrational, angry outbursts or tantrums
insistance that others submit to (their) way of doing things	more aggressive more dominant		characteristic disturbances in interpersonal relationships as indicated by at least two of the following:
lack of awareness of the feelings elicited by this behavior	more independent	more submissive less adventurous	perceived by others as shallow and lacking genuineness, even if superficially warm and charming
excessive devotion to work and productivity	more adventurous		
exclusion of pleasure and the value of interpersonal relationships	feelings not as easily hurt not conceited about appearance	less objective more conceited about appearance	egocentric, self-indulgent, and inconsiderate of others vain and demanding
indecisiveness; decision-making avoided, postponed, or protracted perhaps because of an inordinate fear of making a mistake	not as easily influenced	less independent more easily influenced more easily hurt	dependent, helpless, constantly seeking reassurance prone to manipulative suicidal threats, gestures, or attempts

Intrapsychic Level

The "Masculine": Left Hemisphere:	The "Feminine": Right Hemisphere:
details, verbal memory, logic, discrete recall, linearity, time sequence, sequential	global, holistic, intuitive, impressionistic, aesthetic, spatial, simultaneous
self-consciousness, sense of responsibility for actions, self-control	"left to the gods"
Patriarchal Mode of Consciousness; "Male Principle":	Matriarchal Mode of Consciousness; "Female Principle":
dualistic, dichotomous with shifting inferior and superior valuations assigned to either pole	inclusive, all-encompassing, communion among all the disparate elements
conscious	unconscious and supraconscious
identifies itself with superior and other as inferior	positive and negative aspects of all elements

Cultural Level

Scientific, Technological	Aesthetic

[1]According to the DSMIII, Compulsive Personality Disorder and Histrionic Personality Disorder (1980), pp. 315, 327–328.
[2]According to Broverman, et al. (1970), pp. 4–5.

reaction to 'minor' events" and "irrational, angry outbursts or tantrums" (as interpreted by the obsessive). The "restricted ability to express warm and tender emotions" of the obsessive can create in the hysteric behavior which is "dependent, helpless, constantly seeking reassurance" (from the obsessive perspective). "The exclusion of pleasure and the value of interpersonal relationships" of the obsessive can produce in the hysteric "incessant drawing of attention to self" and "craving for activity and excitement" (again, as seen by the obsessive). The reader can probably make other connections or see other relationships between these two sets of characteristics.

Of course, the hysteric's dynamics may also be seen as inducing those of the obsessive, though not equally so according to this presentation. As conceived, the characteristics of the obsessive and hysteric are characteristics of an unequal power distribution in which the obsessive attempts to maintain power and control and the hysteric reacts to a relative lack of same. While each of these styles of defense may have been developed originally in response to external (and internal) threat, one style is more compatible with establishing and maintaining higher status, more power and control, congruent with the male sex role and "masculinity"; the other with lower status, less power and control, congruent with the female sex role and "femininity."

The hysterical personality disorder has recently been understood as an exaggeration of the ("normal") feminine sex role (Belote, this volume; Brodsky, 1980; Wolowitz, 1972). Similarly, it could be argued that the obsessive personality disorder is an exaggeration of the ("normal") masculine sex role. In fact, if there is a great deal of overlap among the "healthy male," "masculinity," the obsessive personality, and the obsessive personality disorder, then these may be loosely combined so that various aspects of each of these may be seen as merely adding dimensions to one another. Similarly so for the "healthy female," "femininity," the hysterical personality, and the hysterical personality disorder. Finally, the two of these, denoted as "masculine" (obsessive) and "feminine" (hysterical) may be shown in relationship to each other. These terms will be used occasionally in the introductions to the various sections of this book as the concepts they represent, taken singly and in relation to each other, become developed.

Descriptions of hemispheric functioning constructed from work cited previously have also been included in Table 1. Again, whether these two modes of functioning are located in each of the two hemispheres or exist independently of any particular spatial location, they seem accurate in describing differences in our subjective experience of some aspects of psychological functioning. In sociopolitical context, the functioning attributed to the left hemisphere is more highly valued by our society than that attributed to the right hemisphere. In Firestone's (1970) terms, the scientific, technological mode of culture and consciousness is more highly valued than is the aesthetic mode.

Finally, patriarchal and matriarchal modes of consciousness are also included. It is not clear how these relate to the sociopolitical context. One possibility is that the two Principles coexist and the Male Principle is currently the one in ascendence. Another is that the Male Principle by its very nature creates power differences and therefore may be the source of the sociopolitical context in which

There are an almost infinite number of polarities by means of which one can differentiate between the two cultures. The old culture, when forced to choose, tends to give preference to property rights over personal rights, technological requirements over human needs, competition over cooperation, violence over sexuality, concentration over distribution, the producer over the consumer, means over ends, secrecy over openness, social forms over personal expression, striving over gratification, Oedipal love over communal love, and so on. The new counterculture tends to reverse all of these priorities.

Now it is important to recognize that these differences cannot be resolved by some sort of compromise or "golden mean" position. Every cultural system is a dynamic whole, resting on processes that must be accelerative to be self-sustaining. Change must therefore affect the motivational roots of a society or it is not change at all.

Philip Slater, *The Pursuit of Loneliness*, 1970

---

the Male Principle is dominant. Though there may be others, these are the two basic possibilities offered by feminist matriarchal theorists (Newton and Webster, 1973; Webster, 1975).

In summary, Table 1 illustrates the duality of "Masculine" and "Feminine" at many levels—the interpersonal (obsessive and hysterical), the intrapsychic (hemispheric and modes of consciousness), and the cultural (scientific, technological and aesthetic modes). Feminist consciousness involves sociopolitical awareness at all of these levels and provides a context with which to understand the psychology of women in the readings which follow.

Organization of Contents

The selection of readings in this book reflects a sociopolitical awareness of the psychology of women. In the introductions to each section further interpretations are offered, and connections are made between the various sections. This may be especially useful when an

article could easily have been placed in more than one section. An example of this occurs in the first section, "Biological and Cultural Perspectives." The first article offers critiques of the study of the biological basis of psychological sex differences and of the investigation of sexuality. As an example of the more sociopolitical emphasis of this book, the other article on cross-cultural perspectives summarizes current work on female status and power rather than behavioral sex differences.

Following the biological and cultural background for assessing the "nature" of the psychology of women, the next section summarizes some of the psychological research on this topic. "Psychological Sex Differences" presents some of the outstanding work in this area with critiques of this work as well. While race and socioeconomic class are two important variables mediating the psychology of women, they have not received the attention they deserve in the literature. By focusing on the psychology of Black, Asian, Chicana, and Native American women in the next section,

It is often argued that it is useless to change social institutions until the mentality of the individual has changed, and the argument has too often been a convenient justification for the indefinite postponement of necessary changes. But have we, in fact, done what lay in our power to change the individual human unit, while we tried to change society? Did we carry on the two tasks together as we should have done, so that they intermingled and supported each other?

Léon Blum (1872–1950)

"Ethnic Diversity of Female Experience," we attempt to compensate for this and provide more of an understanding of the psychology of all women.

The fourth section, "Psychological Oppression," presents a theory of the psychology of women and "femininity" in terms of psychological oppression. Women as a minority group, the informal expressions of power in daily interactions, and the role of male violence toward women in keeping women in their place—both in the world and in their own psyches—are discussed.

"Relationships: Sexuality and Intimacy" are the topics of the next section. An interesting theory by Chodorow is presented which seems to account for difficulties in female-male relationships as well as the cultural devaluation of women based on the fact that women mother. Women's potentially inordinate sexual drive, the female-female relationship of lesbianism, and women's relationship to motherhood and the family throughout the life cycle are also further explored in this section.

Although a separate section on the important topic of women and work is not included, it is interesting to note how many references to work are found in this section on relationships, from labor force statistics with regard to women and motherhood, to the notion of the emotional work women do in their relationships with men. Other articles in this section emphasize the importance of work to women, although stereotypically, despite the high participation of women in the labor force, they have been defined in terms of their relationships to other people instead of to work, a fact corroborated by the articles in the section on ethnic diversity. The section on psychological oppression suggests the importance of economic independence for women, as do the sections on mental "illness" and change and liberation.

The sixth section, "Mental Illness or Social Problem?" explores the basis of "mental illness" as related to sex roles and the sociopolitical context. The similarity of "femininity" to masochism and hysteria are exfrom **Kathe Kollwitz**

What would happen if one woman told the truth about her life?
  The world would split open.

Muriel Rukeyser

Emerging Ones by Leonor Fini; reprinted by permission of the artist

plored and "learned helplessness" as one basis of depression in women is presented. Treatment issues are also raised regarding feminist and traditional approaches to psychotherapy.

In the final section, "Toward Change and Liberation," some suggestions for change are presented in terms of consciousness-raising groups, feminist psychotherapy, and assertiveness training. There is an analysis of sex-role change and androgyny, and, finally, an article that provides an analysis for personal, interpersonal, and societal change in terms of the sociopolitical context.

At the end of each section is a list of books and articles for further reading on the subject presented.

Since Female psychology depends not only on the intellectual content of the study of women, but on awareness and "surfacing," experiential exercises are provided in each section to facilitate this process. (See complete list on p. iv.) The instructor may use these exercises as preferred, either as large class, small group, or outside activities, or students may simply pursue the exercises on their own.

Students may also benefit from keeping a journal, even if it is not a course assignment. In this journal they may record the results of the experiential exercises, and insights, realizations, awarenesses, thoughts, and feelings about the content of the book or about the entire course. The journal could serve as a medium for observing connections among intrapsychic, interpersonal, and societal aspects of the psychology of women. Students might also record for example, dreams, appropriate quotations from others, reactions to their own internal processes, and interactions with other people. This journal can, by the end of the course, provide a vivid account of each student's change and growth throughout the year. It can reflect one's successes and peaks as well as one's difficulties and struggles.

Journals

Feminist Studies

Psychology of Women Quarterly

Sex Roles: A Journal of Research

Signs: Journal of Women in Culture and Society

Women's Studies

Women's Studies Abstracts

Women's Studies International Quarterly

Biological and Cultural Perspectives

Questions regarding the biological and cultural bases of the psychology of women remain unanswered by traditional science, since the nature-nurture question and the issue of women's presumed "inferiority" are inextricably bound. According to the articles in this section, male bias has pervaded both the content and process of scientific activity.

Leonore Tiefer examines how male values and male reality affect scientific research on sexuality and biological theories of psychological sex differences (portions of this paper will be discussed further in the introduction to "Relationships: Sexuality and Intimacy"). According to Tiefer, the narrowness and rigidity of the scientific model represent "an unfortunate confounding of the norms of science with the masculine behavioral role in Western society." She notes the similarities between the values of science and the characteristics of the male sex role: being independent, analytic, unemotional, and in control. Attention to detail to the exclusion of the whole could also be suggested as a characteristic of both science and the "masculine" (obsessive) personality. (See Table 1 of the Introduction to this book.)

Specifically, the effects of male-dominated science are demonstrated with regard to research on sexuality, particularly its focus on genital sexuality to the exclusion of other variables that are culturally so much more a part of women's experience of sexuality than men's. Tiefer's main argument is not that these aspects of human sexuality are excluded because the methods of science do not permit their investigation, though this may also be true. Instead, she argues that both the methods of science and the content of what is studied reflect the narrowness and rigidity of masculinity.

In relation to psychological sex differences, Tiefer points to the potential danger in "biologizing" them. In surveying research on prenatal hormonal effects, particularly that of androgenization, she finds numerous examples of this. Data are overinterpreted, and there is in general a reluctance to consider social mediating factors. There are, of course, other biological sex differences which have been studied in relation to psychological sex differences—variations in chromosomes, gonads, internal reproductive organs, external reproductive organs, and pubertal hormones. The above considerations would apply to research in these areas as well. The concern advanced by Tiefer and shared by many feminists is that by falsely attributing a biological explanation to a given behavioral sex difference, the psychological "nature" of women becomes fixed and unchangeable. Furthermore, women's presumed "nature" is often used to justify women's culturally defined inferiority.

Tiefer continues the discussion of possible outcomes were there to be clearly demonstrated behavioral sex differences that were biologically determined. The "inferior" group could be denied full membership in society, a basis of patriarchy. Or resources and experiences could be provided to develop abilities and increase capacities to the level of the other group, a more feminist proposal (though based on a superior/inferior dichotomy, characteristic of a patriarchal mode of consciousness). Another feminist possibility might be to permit equal access to resources and then to allow whatever differences there may be to exist without attaching a difference in valuation to them (characteristic of a matriarchal mode of consciousness).

Romanticism develops in proportion to the liberation of women from their biology. *As civilization advances and the biological bases of sex class crumble, male supremacy must shore itself up with artificial institutions, or exaggerations of previous institutions, e.g., where previously the family had a loose, permeable form, it now tightens and rigidifies into the patriarchal nuclear family. Or, where formerly women had been held openly in contempt, now they are elevated to states of mock worship. Romanticism is a cultural tool of male power to keep women from knowing their condition. It is especially needed—and therefore strongest—in Western countries with the highest rate of industrialization. Today, with technology enabling women to break out of their roles for good—it was a near miss in the early twentieth century—romanticism is at an all-time high.*

Shulamith Firestone, *The Dialectic of Sex,*
1970

Of course, we may never know what psychological sex differences are in fact innate since we can never hold constant the social and cultural conditioning each sex group receives. Furthermore, what is crucial is not whatever possible differences there may be, but the meaning the culture makes of these differences and the value and worth accorded to each individual on the basis of group membership.

The discussion so far has assumed that it is women who are potentially regarded as inferior. It should be noted that a theory of the biological or psychological superiority of women is rarely considered.

Scientists' opinions vary, of course, about the degree to which biological sex differentiation contributes directly to psychological sex differences. However, one's belief in the matter may be as much an indication of one's political view as of the "objectivity" with which the data are assessed. Tiefer refocuses on the issue of the "sociology of psychological knowledge" and urges the psychological profession to renew an emphasis on the humanitarian concern of improving the quality of human life.

Another approach to the "nature" of behavioral sex differences is a cross-cultural one. If there is a broad range of behavior and temperament of women and men in various cultures, then it would seem likely that the extent to which biological sex differences determine psychological differences is minimal or nonexistent. Such is the conclusion reached by Margaret Mead in the study of three different cultures:

If those temperamental attitudes which we have traditionally regarded as feminine—such as passivity, responsiveness, and a willingness to cherish children—can so easily be set up as the masculine pattern in one tribe, and, in another, be outlawed for the majority of women as for the majority of men, we no longer have any basis for regarding aspects of such behavior as sex linked." (1935, pp. 279–80)

According to Susan Carol Rogers, feminist anthropologists among whom there is a diversity of perspectives have currently been more concerned with female status and forms of power and less with behavioral sex differentiation. Although her original article also examines cross-cultural behavioral differences as well as female status, the excerpted portion is concerned only with the latter.

It is not nature, but class society, which robbed women of their right to participate in the higher functions of society and placed the primary emphasis upon their animal functions of maternity. And this robbery was perpetrated through a two-fold myth. On the one side, motherhood is represented as a biological affliction arising out of the maternal organs of women. Alongside this vulgar materialism, motherhood is represented as being something almost mystical. To console women for their status as second-class citizens, mothers are sanctified, endowed with halos and blessed with special "instincts," feelings and knowledge forever beyond the comprehension of men. Sanctity and degradation are simply two sides of the same coin of the social robbery of women under class society.

Evelyn Reed, *The Myth of Women's Inferiority*, 1954

In her presentation of female status and power, Rogers includes data and theories that assume universal female subordination and those that do not. Theorists assuming the former attribute such conditions to economic and political factors, to the domestic social locus of women, and to restricted personal autonomy. Rogers points out the male bias in the data upon which these theories are based and the further bias of defining status in such a way that precludes assumed female subordination. She also suggests the limitations of seeking measures that can be applied in all cultures. In the second section of her paper, Rogers presents theories that assume the relative importance of the domestic sphere over the public sector of society and of formal and legitimated forms of authority. However, as the author states, most of these analyses are based on data from peasant societies, and may be of limited applicability to our own.

Another theory deserving special emphasis is based on women's closer relationship to and association with nature (Ortner, 1974). It has been used to account for behavioral sex differentiation, though it has also been used to account for the universality of female subordination. Woman's link to nature stems from her

Stellar Food by Remedios Varo; reprinted by permission of Walter Gruen

Were there actually such things as the fabulous nations of maidens, the mounted demons, galloping from the edges of the world to make ice and golden sand splash to all sides? Was there ever a "man-hating army" with changing tresses and awesome customs? ... In time and reality the Amazon kingdoms not only comprise an extremist end of matriarchy but also are a beginning and a purpose in themselves. ... In the mother clan, there was a constant progression of great mothers begetting more great mothers. Amazons however, reproduced the daughter type, which practically skips a generation and is something altogether different. They were conquerers, horse tamers, and huntresses who gave birth to children but did not nurse or rear them. They were an extreme, feminist wing of a young human race, whose other extreme wing consisted of the stringent patriarchies.

Helen Diner, *Mothers and Amazons*, 1965

---

body and its functions, the social roles she occupies as a result of these, and her psychic structure, which is a further outcome of her reproductive body and social roles. That women compared to men spend more of their lives involved in their bodily and reproductive processes seems obviously to associate women more closely with nature. The social role of confinement to the domestic family group for the caretaking and socialization of children also places women closer to nature and at a lower order of culture. In domestic/public structural conflicts, the domestic, with which women are linked, is subsumed by the emergent unit, society, which is a higher level than the domestic units of which it is composed. As a further result of this, psychically, women seem pan-culturally to be involved more with concrete feelings, things, and people than with abstract entities, and tend more toward relative subjectivity than toward objectivity.

Ortner draws from this further implications relevant to the psychology of women. In addition to women occupying more of a middle status between nature and culture, women are also seen as mediating between the two, converting nature to culture. As one example,

women transform animal-like infants into cultured beings. Women's intermediate position then has greater symbolic ambiguity:

> The psychic mode associated with women seems to stand at both the bottom and the top of the scale of human modes of relating. ... Thus we can account easily for both the subversive feminine symbols (witches, evil eye, menstrual pollution, castrating mothers) and the feminine symbols of transcendence (mother goddesses, merciful dispensers of salvation, female symbols of justice and the strong presence of feminine symbolism in realms of art, religion, ritual and law). (Ortner, 1974, p. 86)

It is interesting that this may also be seen as paralleling the two aspects of the matriarchal mode of consciousness—the unconscious (primitive and potentially destructive) and the supraconscious (spiritual and transcendent).

In an earlier portion of Rogers' paper on behavioral differentiation, Ortner's analysis is criticized on several bases. First, it is uncertain whether "nature" and "culture" are universally recognized or important distinctions. The hierarchical relationship of the two with "culture" in the superior position is not universally accepted. And Rogers provides coun-

AND GOD CREATED WOMAN IN HER OWN IMAGE

And God Created Woman in Her Own Image by Ann Grifalconi, 124
Waverly Place, New York, N.Y. 10011. © 1971 Ann Grifalconi

terexamples to Ortner's schema from our own
culture:

> The ideology of the American western frontier
> includes the notion of women as "culture"-bear-
> ing or civilizing agents, who eventually subdued
> those rowdy anti-social males who had tended to
> revert to nature before the arrival of the "gentler
> sex." American sexual imagery portrays man
> with his "natural" animal lust channeled by
> more responsible and civilized women. (Rogers,
> 1978, p. 134)

If the duality of nature and culture is of limited explanatory use, it may be of descriptive
value. For example, it describes both the
(male) cultural devaluation of women and the
transcendent position of women vis à vis culture (men). Another theory that attempts to account for men's fluctuating valuation of
women will be presented in the section "Relationships: Sexuality and Intimacy." Briefly,
Chodorow (1971) asserts that developmentally
the emotional and psychological separation
from the mother is more difficult for males
than for females due to the differences in gender identity that must be achieved. Men's denigration and devaluation of women, then, arise
in order to achieve separateness and betray

the underlying recognition of maternal omnipotence. Both extremes in valuation of
women exist in men, and women are associated with both the primitive unconscious, and
the transcendent supraconscious. Again, it is
interesting that such formulations coincide
with the modes of consciousness described in
Table 1 of the "General Introduction."

In conclusion, although Rogers does not discuss the issue of the occurrence of matriarchies, it seems relevant to the discussion
here. While the majority opinion in anthropology is against their past existence, several interesting theories of matriarchies have been
proposed (Newton and Webster, 1973; Webster, 1975). It would seem difficult to disen-
tangle the effects of male bias and patriarchal
attitudes from an "objective" assessment of
prehistoric conditions. The existence of matriarchies in the past has been used to justify
the superiority of patriarchy in the present. Alternatively, it has provided hope that patriarchy is not inevitable and that present
conditions can change. The past occurrence of
matriarchies is not necessary for conditions to
change and regardless of whether they actually existed they do provide useful images
with which to imagine conditions other than

what they are now. Such images can allow one to break the mental and emotional "set" of externally imposed limitations that women have psychologically internalized as a result of their psychological oppression as described in that section of this book.

For Further Reading

Burstyn, J. E. 1978. Women, science, and society (Special issue). *Signs: Journal of Women in Culture and Society, 4* (1).

Friedl, E. 1975. *Women and Men: An Anthropologist's View.* New York: Holt, Rinehart and Winston.

Hubbard, R., Henifin, M. S., and Fried, B. (Eds.). 1979. *Women Look at Biology Looking at Women.* Cambridge, Mass.: Schenkman.

Hubbard, R., and Lowe, M. (Eds.). 1979. *Genes & Gender: II.* New York: Gordian Press.

Kessler, S. J., and McKenna, W. 1978. *Gender: An Ethnomethodological Approach.* New York: Wiley.

Lamphere, L. 1977. Review essay: Anthropology. *Signs: Journal of Women in Culture and Society, 2,* 612–627.

Matthiasson, C. J. (Ed.). 1974. *Many Sisters.* New York: Free Press.

Money, J., and Ehrhardt, A. A. 1972. *Man &* *Woman Boy & Girl.* Baltimore: Johns Hopkins University Press.

Quinn, N. 1977. Anthropological studies on women's status. *Annual Review of Anthropology, 6,* 181–225.

Rapp, R. 1979. Review essay: Anthropology. *Signs: Journal of Women in Culture and Society, 4,* 497–513.

Reiter, R. R. (ed.). 1975. *Toward an Anthropology of Women.* New York: Monthly Review.

Rosaldo, M. Z., and Lamphere, L. (Eds.). 1974. *Woman, Culture, and Society.* Stanford: Stanford Univ. Press.

Stack, C. B., Caulfield, M. D., Estes, V., Landes, S., Larson, K., Johnson, P., Rake, J., and Shirek, J. 1975. Review essay: Anthropology. *Signs: Journal of Women in Culture and Society, 1,* 147–159.

Tobach, E., and Rosoff, B. (Eds.). 1978. *Genes & Gender: I.* New York: Gordian Press.

Leonore Tiefer

The Context and Consequences of Contemporary Sex Research: A Feminist Perspective

1. Introduction

Practicing scientists rarely take the opportunity to reflect on the philosophies—scientific, political, and personal—which guide our work. Moreover, sophistication in such analysis is neither part of our training nor is it an expected or rewarded part of our professional competence.

Nevertheless, it is a valuable exercise, from time to time, to attempt to recognize the philosophical context that guides and defines day-to-day work in science. This conference and celebration, with its emphasis on assessing the contemporary state of our knowledge about sexual behavior and projecting current research trends into the future, provide a signal opportunity for such philosophical reflection.

Trained as a scientist, I do not pretend expertise in the forms of analysis I shall attempt, although the insider's point of view provides illumination not available to other analysts. I see this as a first attempt to step back from practical professional activities to survey some of the contextual features that define sex research.

I would like to consider some of the current aspects and future directions of sex research from the perspectives offered by contemporary feminism. In recent years, feminist analyses have illuminated our understanding of a variety of social institutions and processes. I propose to focus on some of our research on animal and human sexuality, and on biological theories about behavioral differences between the sexes.

The feminist perspective allows exploration of the ways in which ideologies of a variety of types serve to perpetuate a patriarchal vision of social institutions, sex roles, and human nature. I believe that one can use this point of view profitably to examine both the underlying assumptions about scientific research and particular examples of research and theory.

I hope to develop two distinct lines of argument. First, with regard to research on animal, and more particularly, on human sexuality, I will suggest that there is a certain narrowness plaguing our research. Our considerations of female sexual behavior, male reproductive physiology, the subjective aspects of sexuality, and the nonerotic components of sexuality have been impoverished, it seems to me, by both excessive reliance on one rigid scientific model, and on the masculine experience as the primary point of reference. Furthermore, I will suggest that to some degree our excessive reliance on one definition of legitimate scientific research stems from an unfortunate confounding of the norms of science with the masculine behavioral role in Western society.

Second, feminists note with concern a growing imbalance in contemporary psychology toward biological explanations of mental phenomena and suggest that, whereas such a research focus has considerable value and promise, its political consequences require careful analysis and cautious extrapolation of results beyond the particular experimental conditions utilized. Failure to observe such caveats seems to me to disregard the two-way connections between social ideology and scientific research.

Finally, taking into account the merits of these various criticisms as well as the strengths of contemporary lines of research, I hope to educe some positive suggestions for future research and theory.

2. Feminist Perspectives on the Crisis in Contemporary Science

Making use of its specialized methodologies, science made enormous advances in understanding natural phenomena. Those very methodologies, however, have come under intense criticism in the last few decades as being inappropriate for the comprehension of complex interactions and as being unable to fulfill the promise of a value-free orientation. Among the allegations frequently made are that science forces the investigator to fractionate whole systems into isolated parts (Ovenden, 1975); to conduct experiments in artificially controlled settings that cannot duplicate natural interactions (Cronbach, 1975); and to enforce an illusion of objective, impersonal observation (Bruner, 1970).

Many critics point out, in particular, that the hard-nosed approaches exemplified in the physical sciences can be especially inappropriate for psychology (Maslow, 1966; Farson, 1965; Sanford, 1965; Koch, 1965). For example, Farson (1965, p. 3) warns, "To force the data of human experience into a mold copied from the exact sciences seems to me to be inappropriate, even crippling."

One of the key norms of science has traditionally been its separation from social and political pressures, its reliance on an objective, consensually determined set of methods and values. If there were one word to sum up the unique contribution of science as a way of obtaining knowledge about the world (as opposed to the methods of art or religion, say), that word would be "objectivity." Jesse Bernard (1950, p. 273), for example, concludes a broad discussion of the relationship between the conduct of science and the cultural context in which it is conducted, "Scientific techniques, both physical and social, then, contain their own correctives for class, cultural, or any other kind of bias. Rich man, poor man, beggerman, thief; doctor, lawyer, merchant, chief; Zuñi, Dobuan, Eskimo—all, using scientific techniques, get the same results if they ask the same questions.... Science is objective, beyond culture."

But sociologists of science have long been skeptical of this claim, pointing out the interdependence of science and social ideology in

The basilar region of the female head is also smaller, the occipital more elongated, and the frontal developed in a minor degree, the organs of the perceptive faculties being commonly larger than those of the reflective powers. The female cerebral fibre is slender and long rather than thick. Lastly, and in particular, the organs of philoprogenitiveness, of attachment, love of approbation, circumspection, secretiveness, ideality, and benevolence, are for the most part proportionately larger in the female; while in the male those of amativeness, combativeness, destructiveness, constructiveness, self-esteem, and firmness predominate.

G. Spurzheim, M.D., *Phrenology*, 1826

---

the generation of research questions, the methods used, and especially in the choice of alternative explanations for one's findings (Merton, 1963; Barber, 1952; Blume, 1974; Schumpeter, 1949). Gunnar Myrdal (1970, p. 157) comments, "The ordinary social scientist believes that his analysis and inferences are simply founded upon his observation of facts.... Now we all know that when we look back at any earlier era, we regularly find that not only popular discussion but also the work of the social scientists were biased in the sense that their approach was influenced by dominating national or group interests in the society they were part of. However, like contemporary social scientists today, they were firmly convinced that their analysis and inferences were founded simply upon their observations of facts."

The current attacks on science emphasize that knowing about the social structure of science—who does it, how do they learn, where do they do it, who pays for it, what are the explicit and implicit demand characteristics of the business, what are the interrelations between the scientific "establishment" and other institutions in society, what are the codes of conduct for scientists, what are the rewards and how are they gotten—predicts inevitable dependence of scientific behavior on the values of the dominant ideology and reinforcements of the dominant sectors of society.

These various sorts of criticism have not

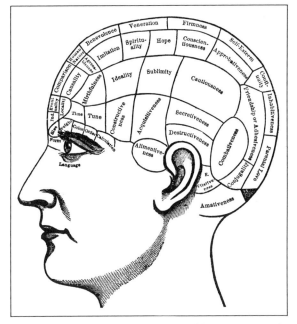

From Phrenology: A Practical Guide to Your Head by Orson Squire Fowler and Lorenzo Niles Fowler. Design by J. Steinberg and U. McGeehan. Copyright © 1969 by Chelsea House Publishers, a Division of Chelsea House Educational Communications, Inc. By permission.

Phrenology, a 19th century precursor of psychology, drew conclusions about the psychological nature of women based on "scientific" measurements. Today, on the basis of more advanced and sophisticated techniques, the same "discoveries" are made about the psychology of women. In both cases, the scientific conclusions reached reflect social norms and are used to justify women's position in society.

gone unanswered by the scientific community. Too often, however, the scientific response has focused only on the element of irrationalism in the critiques, and the responses have merely restated faith in the ultimate self-correcting properties of science (Frankel, 1973; Hebb, 1974; Pirages, 1975). Falsely claiming that "the objectors to modern psychology do not want an objective science, but a sort of self-contemplation" (Hebb, 1974, p. 73), the defenders of the faith have failed to isolate the constructive elements of the criticism.

Many feminist scholars concur with the criticisms of science. Their critique, like that from other ideological perspectives, focuses on two major points: the ultimate inadequacy of the scientific method as currently understood and developed to answer the most interesting questions of nature, and the unacknowledged relationship between scientific behavior and the political and ideological surround.

Feminist scholars note the similarity between the questioned values of science and some characteristics of the Western model of masculinity. The glorification, for example, of efforts to be independent, analytic, unemotional, and in control in both arenas seems a coincidence not to be disregarded (Carlson, 1972; Nash, 1975; Feldman, 1975). Observations about the similarity of scientific norms and masculine, heterosexual norms have been made before (e.g., Snow, 1956; Maslow, 1966). They do not necessarily say that science evolved its peculiar emphasis because the people doing it were men. Rather, this focus points out that science, like other institutions in society, takes its values from the prevailing patriarchal ethos (Kanter, 1975; Lorber, 1975; Bakan, 1966).

Acceptance of the feminist opinion does not deny the usefulness of research as it is now conducted. Rather, it suggests that *excessive reliance* on traditional methods precludes comprehensive understanding. As Maslow (1966, p. 5) expressed it, "I believe mechanistic science ... to be not incorrect but rather too narrow and limited to serve as a *general* or comprehensive philosophy."

Second, feminists are acutely aware of the influence of powerful institutions on maintaining the social status quo in society and see the scientific establishment and scientific research as forces that too often in the past have been used to oppress rather than promote the interests of women. These issues will receive greater discussion in a later section of this paper, but suffice it to say here that, whenever the "nature" of people is discussed, especially in the context of a discussion of sex differences, feminists are keenly concerned about the potential for abuse of scientific data. In the nineteenth century, during the birth of both the scientific study of sex differences and the first wave of the feminist movement, this potential for abuse was made manifest by the activities of Francis Galton. "Galton's legacy to the psychological study of sex differences is that he established the field within the broader context of differential psychology, and gave ample evidence that one's attitudes, values, and ideologies may infiltrate one's interpretation of data" (Buss, 1976, p. 285).

Excessive confidence in the traditional methods of science to encompass the complexities of nature and humanity, inattention to the cultural values determining research content and methodological approach, and insensitivity to the role of science in providing material for social policy decisions—these are the elements of the feminist critique of science. Let us see how aspects of our contemporary science of sex research look from this critical vantage point.

3. Masculine Biases in the Study of Sexual Behavior

The current theories and data in the area of mammalian sexual behavior, especially human sexual behavior, suffer from a biased and inadequate vision, a state of affairs I tentatively attribute to the narrow definition of sexuality plaguing the research area.

Most sex research in psychology has utilized animal subjects, tested under controlled laboratory conditions, in brief heterosexual pair tests. Usually the animals will be placed together in a relatively small test enclosure. Sometimes one will be tethered, or enclosed in the goalbox of a T maze, or given access to a partner only after performance of some operant response. The traditional measures utilized in the pair test include the timing and frequency of mounts, intromissions and ejaculations by the male, and of lordoses* by the female. Occasionally, some measure of "proceptive" behavior by the female (approach, solicitation, darting, or some species-appropriate behavior) will be tabulated. Based on research, theories about the physiological control of sexual behavior, environmental conditions supporting or inhibiting sexual behavior, and the influence of early life experience on adult sexual behavior are drawn.

The "meaning" of sexual activity in such animal studies is limited to genitally oriented copulation. The only acts considered sexual are genital contacts. Necessarily, but sadly for our understanding of sexuality, no relevance is made of the partners' past histories with one another, enjoyment of the various moves, subjective involvement in the processes, reminiscences of previous erotic experiences, fantasies, etc. Likewise, the most prominent studies of human sexuality (Kinsey, Pomeroy, and Martin, 1948; Kinsey, Pomeroy, Martin, and Gebhard, 1953; Masters and Johnson, 1966) also adopt a genital definition for sexual expression in their observations, tabulations, and discussions of the vicissitudes of human sexual processes.

For example, examine the conclusions, widely cited, that males and females are differentially sexually responsive to psychological experiences and stimuli in the arousal of sexual desire and the achievement of sexual satisfaction. In the 1953 volume, Kinsey and his coauthors declare:

> The sexual responses and behavior of the average male are, on the whole, more often determined by the male's previous experience, by his association with objects that were connected with his previous sexual experience, by his vicarious sharing of another individual's sexual experience and by his sympathetic reactions to the sexual responses of other individuals. The average female is less often affected by such psychological factors. (p. 687)

What are the data which substantiate such conclusions and how were they collected? Kinsey's conclusions were based on the differential response of sampled males and females in our society to questions administered in a personal interview such as, "How often are you aroused by commercial movies, burlesque shows, seeing others engaged in sex acts, your own fantasies about the opposite sex, writings or drawings about sexual activity, etc.?"

---

* *lordosis*: the position of arching the back and elevating the haunches so as to receive the male in intercourse, typical of most mammals.

School of Humans by Ann Leda Shapiro. Reprinted by permission

Data so collected, showing differential responses by the two sexes, seem to me to warrant a conclusion like, "More males than females report being aroused by observing in real life or in symbolic depiction certain sexual acts involving either other humans or animals." To claim, however, that these data warrant a conclusion like "the sexual responses of males are more often determined by their previous experience" seems totally *unwarranted*. Perhaps Kinsey's careful choice of words, "The average female is less often affected by *such* psychological factors" should be taken to mean that he felt women were affected by *other* psychological factors. Unfortunately, Kinsey's failure to specify any other psychological factors resulted in his original qualification being overlooked.

One might suggest assessing, for example, the nature of the romantic involvement and commitment of the partner, the presence of overt reassurance and reinforcement by the partner, the woman's own body image, the woman's feelings of self-worth both within and independent of the particular relationship, the woman's previous experience with forced sexual activity, the woman's attitudes toward sex in exchange for advantages, etc. Studying the involvement of such factors as these requires both the development of new techniques of study and a broader definition of what is a sexual stimulus and a sexual sit-

uation than we see in Kinsey's questions or Masters and Johnson's observations.

In fact, recent studies directly measuring sexual arousal through some sort of vaginal plethysmograph or on-the-spot self-report suggest no differences in rate and frequency of female arousal in response to pictures and stories depicting sexual activities as compared with similar measures made in men (Schmidt and Sigusch, 1973). But such research, too, focuses on genital reaction as *the* measure of sexual involvement and offers less illumination than would research on what men and women themselves consider sexual stimuli, and their responses (overt and covert) to such stimuli.

We do have intimations that nongenital elements in the definition of sexuality may be appropriate in studying women's experience. Some women contend that sex without orgasm can be perfectly satisfying, that extravaginally induced orgasm may be more intense than intravaginally induced orgasm although the latter may in some ways be more pleasurable, and that looking at the beloved or anticipating a reunion or recalling an emotionally intense interaction can be erotically, though not genitally, ecstatic.

We could simply not define such phenomena as "sexual," and relegate them to the scientifically inaccessible world where reside such other elusive phenomena as "love." But

Even though she may think otherwise consciously, the idea that what is masculine is in itself more valuable than what is feminine is born in her blood. This does much to enhance the power of the animus. What we women have to overcome in our relation to the animus is not pride but lack of self-confidence and the resistance of inertia. For us, it is not as though we had to demean ourselves (unless we have been identified with the animus), but as if we had to lift ourselves. In this, we often fail for lack of courage and strength of will.

Emma Jung, *Animus and Anima*, 1957

that would be wrong, because what is sexual ought to be for the scientist what a person calls sexual, and people will continue to call nongenital experiences sexual except when they are filling out questionnaires or answering questions in situations in which the demand characteristics are such that the definitions are made by others.

Rossi (1973) points out how the "phallic fallacy" of male sex researchers demeans nongenital sexuality. Oftentimes, women are labeled "immature" because for them the greatest pleasure in sexual encounters comes from what is labeled "foreplay," rather than what is labeled "sexual intercourse." The genital intercourse bias of sex research has precluded study of the psychological and physiological roles and functions of such "foreplay" acts. Perhaps such behaviors even affect phenomena like luteal hormone (LH)* release or sperm transport, effects overlooked by otherwise zealous researchers!

A recent survey of knowledge concerning the behavioral coordination of male and female animals during sexual encounters attempted to identify the interactional elements in the situation (Larsson, 1973). The three sections in the review were titled: (1) behavioral

coordination between the male and the female during coitus; (2) reproductive function of the female as determined by exteroceptive stimulation from the male; and (3) the behavior of the male as determined by the physiological condition of the female. The survey, extensive as it was, had little discussion of behavioral variables in the female and their effect on physiological functions in the male.

Although Larsson concludes, "The behavior exhibited by one partner thus generates physiological changes in the other, and an organized pattern of behavioral and physiological responses emerges" (Larsson, 1973, pp. 48–49), the concern of sex researchers with male behavior and female physiology results in less being known about the interactional elements than if the assumptions governing earlier research had been more carefully scrutinized. Not only does this bias weaken our theories, it has practical consequences. For example, it contributes to the imbalance in applied research on contraceptive methods toward those affecting females. I do not deprecate animal research on sexuality, although I believe that the evidence is overwhelming that sociocultural forces not relevant for animals definitively determine human expectations, definitions, and patterns of behavior and sexual experience (Petras, 1973). This inevitably limits the generalizations derived from animal sexuality research.

---

*luteinizing hormone (LH): one of the gonadotropic hormones of the pituitary gland. It induces release of the egg from the graafian follicle and transformation of the latter into a corpus luteum.

Man differs from woman in size, bodily strength, hairiness, etc. as well as in mind.

Charles Darwin (1809–1882)

To increase their value, animal studies of the future must attempt a greater balance than before, with emphasis being placed on a careful analysis of female patterns of behavior. Beach's (1976) recent attention to the "proceptive" components of female sexual behavioral patterns is an important step in this direction. He asserts:

> The female's tendency to display appetitive responses finds little opportunity for expression in laboratory experiments which focus exclusively on her receptive behavior, or upon the male's execution of his coital pattern. The resulting concept of essentially passive females receiving sexually aggressive males seriously misrepresents the normal mating sequence and encourages a biased concept of feminine sexuality. (p. 115)

We need to remedy the imbalances of the past with studies of the female experience of the Coolidge effect, criteria for individual preferences in choice of sexual partners, the forms of situational inhibition and facilitation to which female mammals are responsive, the aspects of sexual activity that are reinforcing for female mammals, the existence of anything remotely resembling the human orgasm in either male or female nonhuman mammals, etc.

In the last section of this paper I will suggest some new approaches to the study of human sexuality, but suffice it to say here, as McCormack (1975) has done in a study of political behavior, that sex differences may not be differences in degree, they may well be differences in kind. So long as sex as men experience it is the only kind of sex deemed worthy of study, so long will we deprive ourselves of true understanding.

4. Biology and Research on Sex Differences in Humans

4.1. Biological Theories about the Origins of Group Differences in Humans

Because of the tremendous influence of science on social attitudes and social policy, feminists are particularly concerned with research alleging biological bases for human sex differences. Bardwick (1976) correctly claims that "Radicals seem generally opposed to the idea of physiological determinism and [are] angered at the idea that physiological differences between the sexes might be significant in accounting for psychological and social differences between women and men" (p. 95), but she fails to credit the realistic sources of the misgivings.

In controversial areas, areas in which social policy decisions will have important effects on individual lives and opportunities, the impact of scientific data is an ingredient in policy making not to be underestimated. History suggests that our society has two responses available to the demonstration of differences in capacity between social groups. The first is to exclude from certain social and political opportunities those considered unfit to bear the responsibilities of full citizenship. This choice is adopted when the differences are seen to result from the inexorable consequences of biological givens, to be "natural," and, therefore, predominantly immutable. This is the reason given why 10-year olds may not now vote, and it used to be the reason given why women were not permitted to vote.

The second response is to provide a variety of compensatory, affirmative experiences for those demonstrating lesser abilities to render them more competitive with the higher-achieving group. This choice is adopted when the original differences are seen to result from the inequities of opportunity or encouragement.

There is an interesting relationship, historically, between those advocating one or the other of these positions, a relationship that will take us a bit further into the connection between science and social phenomena. As Eisenberg (1972, p. 124) expresses it, "Some readers may object to 'politicizing' what should be a 'scientific' discussion. My contention is that it is necessary to make overt what is latent in treatises on the 'innate' nature of man."

Pastore (1949) has shown, in a most interesting and undercited study of 24 prominent scientists who published in the field of nature-nurture differences, the almost perfect correlation between the advocacy of liberal or radical philosophies and an environmentalist outlook on group differences on the one hand, and political conservatism and support for a hereditarian explanation for group differences on the other. "This inner relationship suggests that it would be as reasonable to classify the nature-nurture controversy as sociological in nature as to classify it as scientific in nature." (Pastore, 1949, p. 177).

Pastore observes that the period providing his data, the latter part of the nineteenth century and the first half of the twentieth, was marked by widespread social and political changes. He notes, "In this atmosphere of impending social change, the position of the hereditarian would be to favor the status quo

since he would contend that the essential incorrigibility of man's inherent nature was at the basis of social evils" (1949, p. 2). Pastore then concludes, "It is probable . . . that in most cases the scientists were not aware of the specific impact of their political loyalties upon their scientific thinking" (p. 182) but that the connection cannot be fortuitous. He attempts to analyze whether the scientific statements preceded the political advocacy of a particular position or vice versa, but whether such a chicken-and-egg question can ever be answered, the striking correlation for 22 of his 24 scientists is noteworthy.

The political aspect of biological theories of the causation of human differences has been made stunningly manifest in the recent controversy over the book by Edward O. Wilson (1975) titled *Sociobiology* (Wade, 1976). The social policies that follow from an acceptance of Wilson's position are apocalyptically laid out by a study group formed of Wilson's colleagues at Harvard (Sociobiology Study Group, 1975). They allege that the "biological determinism" advocated by Wilson is a position where "Aggression, competition, extreme division of labor, the nuclear family, the domination of women by men, the defense of national territory, individualism, are over and over again stated to be the result of 'human nature' [and that] present social arrangements are either unchangeable or if altered will demand continued conscious social control because the changed conditions will be 'unnatural' " (p. 1).

Feminists, striving to "free the human personality from the restricting prison of sex-role stereotyping and to develop a conception of

It is as if in the evolution of sex a particle one day broke away from an X-chromosome, and thereafter in relation to X-chromosomes could produce only an incomplete female—the creature we now call the male! It is to this original chromosomal deficiency that all the various troubles to which the male falls heir can be traced.

Ashley Montagu, *The Natural Superiority of Women,* 1970

mental health that is free from culturally imposed definitions of masculinity and femininity" (Bem, 1975) understandably regard, therefore, scientific trends supporting theories about the biological bases of sex differences and sex roles with alarm, and with skepticism.

4.2. The Biologizing of Contemporary Psychology

For years I have watched a developing trend in contemporary psychology. As Carlson (1972) puts it, "The biologizing of general psychology is well under way" (p. 27). In every field it seems that physiological models and research strategies are held to offer the best route to understanding the traditional subjects of psychological inquiry.

Differences in cognitive processing strategies are attributed to differential functioning of the right and left cerebral hemispheres (e.g., Hellige, 1975). Differences in dietary habits are thought to result from variations in ventromedial hypothalamic functioning (Schachter, 1971). Efforts to alter patterns of emotional responsiveness emphasize biofeedback techniques, asserting that the autonomic foundations of emotion make direct biological intervention the most efficacious route to altered mental experiences (Brown, 1974). The presence of an extra Y chromosome in some men is purported by some to have a direct influence on later development of criminal behavior (Owen, 1972). The most exciting developments concerning the etiology and treatment of psychopathology focus on bio-

chemical theories and research (e.g., Friedhoff, 1976). Other psychological phenomena, too, from attention to intelligence, from childhood behavioral irregularities to nonverbal communication of emotion are alleged to be most usefully understood from the perspective of underlying biological contributions.

Let us look, then, at some research in the area of human sex differences and explore the implications of the current "biologizing."

4.3. Prenatal Contributions to Human Psychological Sex Differences

The commanding paradigm in the study of animal sex differences has been, for the last 20 years or so, the relationship of prenatal hormone influences to later sexual dimorphism. Originating from the powerful studies of embryonic sexual differentiation reported by Jost in the 1950s, hundreds of experiments have been conducted on a multitude of species to elaborate the extent to which prenatal androgenization contributes to the development of behavioral sex differences in copulation, aggressiveness, activity patterns, feeding behavior, learning capacity, emotionality, and, recently, a variety of human behaviors as measured by observation or self-report.

Thousands of words have been devoted to creating finer and finer distinctions between organizational and activational effects of hormones, to ascertaining precisely the neural mechanisms affected by critical period androgens, to defining the temporal parameters

The male is a biological accident: the Y (male) gene is an incomplete X (female) gene, that is, has an incomplete set of chromosomes. In other words, the male is an incomplete female, a walking abortion, aborted at the gene stage. To be male is to be deficient, emotionally limited; maleness is a deficiency disease and males are emotional cripples.

Valerie Solanis, *SCUM (Society for Cutting Up Men) Manifesto*, 1967–1968

of the androgenic effect, to identifying which androgens are involved in various species, to revealing the contributions of postnatal hormonal interactions with the earlier critical androgens, to clarifying whether the primary effect is on those tissues that will mediate later hormonal effects or will directly process stimulus input and direct particular behavioral output in response, and so forth. It is a classic example of research begetting more research and more hypotheses than ever could have been imagined.

One recent statement of the presumed effects of prenatal hormones on human psychological development derives from the work of Anke Ehrhardt and her colleagues (Ehrhardt and Baker, 1974a,b). Ehrhardt compares the behaviors of girls prenatally androgenized to some degree by the excessive output of their abnormal adrenal glands with the behaviors of their presumably unaffected female siblings. She also looks at boys suffering from the adrenogenital syndrome* and compares them with

their presumably unaffected female siblings. She also looks at boys suffering from the adrenogenital syndrome and compares them with their presumably unaffected brothers. She concludes that statistical differences are observed between unaffected and affected girls in energy expenditure, sex of preferred playmates, fight initiation, daydreams about wedding and marriage, outlook toward career possibilities, outlook toward pregnancy and motherhood, interest in dolls and infants, and interest in functional versus dressy feminine clothing, jewelry, and cosmetics. She interprets the "boyish" behavior and identification of the adrenogenital girls as being a result of the prenatal androgenic stimulation, and unlikely to be due to parental attitudes or other mediating psychological factors.

Although Ehrhardt states her conclusions carefully and takes great pains to qualify their implications, nevertheless her interpretation of her own work requires that she believe, "If prenatal exposure to androgen modifies behavior in genetic females and in the described clinical conditions, one may assume that similar hormonal factors contribute to the development of temperamental differences between males and females in general" (Ehrhardt and Baker, 1974a, p. 49). Ehrhardt and Baker go on to emphasize, "If prenatal hormone levels contribute to sex differences in behavior, the effects in human beings are subtle and can in no way be taken as a basis for prescribing sex roles" (1974a, p. 49), a disclaimer which sug-

adrenogenital syndrome: a condition produced by a genetically transmitted enzymatic defect in the functioning of the adrenal cortices of males or females, which induces varying degrees of insufficiency of cortisol and aldosterone and excesses of adrenal androgen and pituitary adrenocorticotropin. Abnormal function of the adrenal cortex starts in fetal life and, unless treated, continues chronically after birth. Females born with the syndrome have ambiguous genitalia and, if they survive without salt loss and dehydration, undergo severe virilization. Males are usually not recognized at birth, but if they survive, will prematurely develop sexually during the first years of life.

Until now it has been thought that the level of testosterone in men is normal simply because they have it. But if you consider how abnormal their behavior is, then you are led to the hypothesis that almost all men are suffering from testosterone poisoning.

Testosterone poisoning is particularly cruel because its sufferers usually don't know they have it. In fact, when they are most under its sway they believe that they are at their healthiest and most attractive. They even give each other medals for exhibiting the most advanced symptoms of the illness.

Alan Alda, "What Every Woman Should
Know About Men," *Ms.* (Oct. 1975)

---

gests that they, like contemporary feminists, perceive the connection between biological explanations and social policy prescriptions. But, because of an overemphasis on the alleged direct behavioral consequences of the biological treatments underlying the research, they are led to conclude that the observed group differences in behavior are due to the biological differences in treatment.

By contrast, I believe that there are alternative explanations for their results. I begin by assuming that biological influences can cause behavioral consequences by circuitous routes, the endpoints of which relate only indirectly to the original biological interventions. The first factor to consider is the potential continuing ambivalence by the parents as to the results of the adrenogenital excesses. Bing and Rudikoff (1970), for example, focus on two sets of parents of adrenogenital girls and show how their behavior toward their daughters is profoundly altered by the medical problem, albeit in very different ways.

The second factor to consider is the likely possibility that prenatal androgen does have some direct effect on factors contributing to increased activity level and energy expenditure, but not on any behaviors more complex than these. Were this true, the adrenogenital girls would likely ally themselves with other chil-

dren with the same high energy levels and identify with their (culturally imposed boyish) norms of fantasies about adult careers, "boys" toys, and clothing preferences. The effects of peer pressure and identification, with no countermanding by the parents (and it is important to note here that "there was usually very little parental pressure toward more femininity" (Ehrhardt and Baker, 1974a, p. 49) would be sufficient to account for the differences in behavior, fantasy, and expectations for adult roles.

To allege that hormones have a direct effect on desire for functional clothes, intention to have a career, choice of playmates, engaging in fights, etc., makes little sense when one looks at the behavior of boys in cultures where male role behavior is very different than in our own. Are we to think that the androgens found in these other cultures are of different types, or that their effects are somehow thwarted or that the effects of socialization are somehow greater in those other cultures?

The only significant difference between boys with the adrenogenital syndrome and their unaffected brothers is a greater expression of energy expenditure (Ehrhardt and Baker, 1974a). The lack of any differences in play, fantasy, or adult aspirations suggests that their behavior is adequately predictable from

BECAUSE OF THEIR
RAGING HORMONAL
IMBALANCES,
WOMAN MAKE BETTER
MOTHERS THAN MEN

© Ellen Levine, from *All She Needs . . .*, Quadrangle, 1973

a knowledge of the socialization rules, and thus that the only behavioral influence of the prenatal androgen (either in normal or excess amounts) is on energy expenditure and socially mediated consequences of external genital morphology.

In a recent review of the literature on prenatal hormone effects on human behavior, Reinisch (1976, p. 82) observes, "IQ is raised only in children whose genitalia are also affected by hormones and not in children who show no genital masculinization." Although the enhanced IQ levels in prenatally androgenized subjects is not thought to be a reliable finding (Ehrhardt and Baker, 1974b), Reinisch's observation is consistent with my hypotheses, unless of course she is suggesting that people think with their genitals! That is, those individuals whose response to the prenatal hormone exposure includes genital masculinization are somehow treated differently and therefore behave differently from those not so affected.

Although my major concern in this section is to point out the failure to consider nonbiological explanations for human sex differences in clinical research where biological variables are manipulated, it is not amiss to mention that some aspects of my alternative explanation may be appropriate even for our under-

standing of the effects of prenatal androgen on behavior development in the rhesus monkey. Although some studies detail ways in which the mother's behavior cannot completely account for sex differences in monkey play behavior (e.g., Rosenblum, 1974), nevertheless differences in behavior toward male and female offspring on the part of the parent can go a long way toward explaining the sex differences in outcome (Jensen, Bobbitt, and Gordon, 1967; Mitchell, 1968).

A careful analysis of data recently presented with regard to the necessary dosage and duration of prenatal androgen treatment given rhesus monkeys in order to masculinize their behavior reveals that no androgenic treatment over and above that necessary for masculinization of the genitalia is required for "masculinization" of play behavior (Phoenix, 1974). Conceivably, the mothers' differential treatment of offspring, dependent on observations of the external genitalia, is responsible in large part for the sex differences in their subsequent behavior.

In the published excerpts of the discussion following Phoenix's and Ehrhardt's papers (Friedman, Richart, and Vande Wiele, 1974), Ehrhardt asked Phoenix whether he thought maternal behavior might have been influenced by the presence of male genitalia in the

I'M WORKING HARD
AT THINKING LIKE
A MAN

pseudohermaphroditic* offspring. He agreed that it might well have been, but the discussion then turned in a different direction, and it is unclear to what extent Phoenix would have been willing to attribute the changed offspring behavior to changed maternal behavior (Friedman et al., 1974, p. 79). I raise this alternative interpretation of the animal data mostly to show that researchers who manipulate biological variables seem at times blind to nonbiological interpretations of their own results, and that whereas such "linear" thinking might have no particular harm in animal experimentation, it clearly is to be avoided in theorizing about human beings.

4.4. Summary of Biologizing Comments

Postulating and investigating biological contributions to the genesis and expression of human behavior is obviously an important scientific activity, and I am advocating neither its cessation nor its curtailment. I am, however, advocating extreme caution in drawing conclusions about the impact of physiological fac-

---

* *pseudohermaphroditism*: hermaphroditism. The prefix was once used to denote the fact that the gonads were not hermaphroditically mixed (ovarian plus testicular tissue) as in true hermaphroditism, but were either testicular (male pseudohermaphroditism) or ovarian (female pseudohermaphroditism). In modern usage, the preferred terms are male, female, and true hermaphroditism. Agonadal hermaphroditism is a fourth form.

tors at our present state of inadequate knowledge, because of the politically conservative uses to which such conclusions may be put.

Roberts (1974) suggests that the rejection of a true hypothesis regarding genetic contributions to race differences is socially a far less severe error than erroneously accepting a false hypothesis regarding such contributions, and he therefore advocates using the nonscientific values to set the statistical parameters for such research. I doubt if this suggestion will catch on, but I present this as one way in which one might come to terms with this social–scientific interface.

Our thinking about the causes of human behavior profoundly affects the ways in which we attempt to assign roles to people and the ways in which we attempt to alter people's behavior. Adams (1964) documents the tremendous changes that occurred in the treatment of mental patients in the nineteenth century as professionals adopted a medical model of interpersonal disturbance. "What we choose to believe about the nature of man has social consequences. Those consequences should be weighed in assessing the belief we choose to hold, even provisionally." (Eisenberg, 1972, p. 124).

It seems that many currently recognize the uses to which biologically based information can be put. I cited Ehrhardt to that effect ear-

from **Stepping Westward**

*If woman is inconstant,
good, I am faithful to
ebb and flow, I fall
in season and now
is a time of ripening.*

Denise Levertov

lier (Ehrhardt and Baker, 1974a,b). Gastonguay (1975) attempts to ride both sides of the same fence in his proposal for a sociobiology unit in high school science. Erring in overstating what is known, drawing far too broad conclusions, he suggests, "It appears that most higher societies depend on some form of hierarchy. This is a natural outcome of species variation; individuals possess differing strength, leadership ability and so on" (1975, p. 484). But his article concludes with this caveat: "However, as we attempt to quantify human behavior in this way, we must use extreme caution, for there are always those who would use such knowledge in order to promote a social stratification of opportunity" (p. 486). He seems to have waived his own opportunity to display such caution.

Alone, such caveats are insufficient when not supplemented by environmental-based hypotheses about the development of the behavior in question. If the only information supplied, and the only interpretations offered focus on physiological determinants, then the warning to exercise caution will go unheeded. Mary Brown Parlee (1973) shows, for example, how assumptions about the physiological etiology of the premenstrual syndrome in women dictated many early attempts to "cure" the problem, caveats about alternative possibilities to the contrary notwithstanding. As long as science holds the unquestioned respect of people

in control of policy making, scientists must bend over backward not to provide premature or erroneous prescriptions, especially in controversial areas such as those I have been discussing.

5. Suggestions for Future Sex Research

Even a partial acceptance of the foregoing comments indicates the need for an expansion of the methods we employ in the study of human sexuality, in terms of choosing questions for research, designing our studies, and drawing sensible and sensitive conclusions. Following the structure of earlier sections, let me first discuss the area of sexuality, and then consider research on sex differences.

5.1. Toward a Nonsexist Understanding of Human Sexuality

The need to encompass the whole of human sexuality in our theories requires development of methods for understanding the subjective side of sexuality, both for the affective and cognitive domains. Gagnon (1975, p. 140), for example, has recently predicted that future sex research will have to deal with "the calculus of pleasures" as well as more traditional observations and tabulations.

The thought of returning to reliance on introspection in our studies strikes dismay into psychologists aware of the failures of early

Structuralist attempts, but several authors have recently pointed out that we can avoid the early errors without abandoning the method altogether. Radford (1974) suggests that introspection as a scientific method has its problems, but that they are not insurmountable, and that information garnered through this method can be of inestimable value in complementing other data.

Levine (1974) notes that students of perceptual processes have managed to incorporate qualitative self-report into a viable scientific methodology by the use of multiple cross-checks and overlapping intersecting indicators of particular pieces of behavior and states of awareness. The scientific necessity for control does not only mean the use of control groups as part of an experimental design. He encourages a compilation and classification of the various types of data-collection methods and the inferences one may legitimately draw from each. Instead, then, of always using the same style research for each interesting question, one would be able to choose the best research technique for each particular question.

Carlson (1971, p. 208) has proposed such a classification for personality research, enumerating the strengths of "experimental methods of laboratory psychology, the correlational methods of differential psychology, and the clinical methods stemming from the tradition of French psychiatry and Viennese psychoanalysis." She claims that previous discussions of the various psychological methods have seen them as competing, whereas "the three approaches presented here are conceived of as complementary.... Tentative knowledge gained from any one approach must ultimately be weighed by alternative methods" (p. 209).

It is important to incorporate our own experiences as sexual human beings into the hypotheses we generate, recognizing of course the limitations introduced by such bias. Nevertheless, each of us would probably attest to the fact that our experiences of sexual arousal and pleasure have undergone numerous changes throughout our lives, yet our current literature seems oblivious to this common experience. Studying the changes in one's perception of sexuality and oneself as a sexual being from childhood through adolescence and the phases of adulthood will open vast regions of insight heretofore neglected.

There have been some studies attempting to incorporate subjective emphases. Hessellund (1976) included quotations about sexual fantasies along with quantitative data in his report about masturbation habits of married persons. Vance and Wagner (1976) had college students write their subjective descriptions of orgasm and then asked raters to try to separate those written by males from those written by females. Kanter, Jaffe, and Weisberg (1975) include numerous quotes of personal feelings and recollections in their study of intimate relationships in communal households. Other recent quasianthropological studies of homosexuals, pederasts, and transsexuals have attempted a balance of objective and self-report data.

Others have advocated this sort of research without exploring precise methods. Hochschild (1975, p. 284), for example, suggests that we "should attend to the actor's own definition of his or her feelings in order to find out how emotion vocabularies are used, what inner experiences they refer to, and what social situations or rules call them forth or squash them out." Bell (1975) recommends that researchers involve themselves more in the lives of their homosexual research subjects in order to more fully appreciate the meanings of sexuality in their subjects' experience.

Some specific methods described by Carlson (1971) include short-term longitudinal studies, soliciting anonymous brief introspective accounts of selected constructs during data-collecting situations organized entirely for other purposes, and the reporting of much phenomenological data now incidentally collected but rarely appearing in the literature.

In addition to the introduction of subjective emphases in sex research, we need to begin to see sexuality as encompassing behaviors and attitudes that are profoundly influenced by classes of social rules which are themselves nonerotic. For example, Blumstein and Schwartz (1974) have taken great care to explore the impact of group identification on both self-labeling and sexual activity participation in bisexual women. Moyle (1975) shows how the functions of sexuality in a society (Samoa, in his example) are illuminated by a study of sexual themes in art, poetry, games, and stories. Similarly, studies in our own culture of graffiti, song lyrics, motion picture themes, styles of social dancing, fashion, cosmetic and jewelry adornments, etc., will illuminate our understanding of sexuality.

How we define "sexuality" is one of the critical elements in the decisions about what and how we research. "To label nude scenes of coitus as sexual but scenes that do not expose the genitals as romantic may be to reveal a phallic fallacy to which male researchers are particularly prone" (Rossi, 1973, p. 164). A genitally oriented definition is, according to some writers (e.g., Francoeur and Francoeur, 1974), consistent with and reflective of a particular "hot" sex (in the McLuhan sense of "hot")

framework, which may well be inappropriate to describe the experiences and values of future generations.

The challenge of sexuality research in the future is exploring the multiple meanings for sexual expression, and the ways they reflect individual and societal needs. A feminist perspective will broaden and increase the value of sex research by encouraging attention to a wide spectrum of aspects of sexuality, and by reminding us of our ultimate obligation to contribute to the enrichment of human sexual experience.

5.2. Toward a Nonsexist Study of Sex Differences

The inappropriate extrapolation of scientifically studied sex differences is of great concern to feminists. We are particularly "concern[ed] that any evidence of physiological influences will be taken as grounds for the perpetuation of sex inequalities in family, political, and occupational roles" (Rossi, 1973, p. 151). For example, Kinsey and his colleagues (1953), having demonstrated to their own satisfaction that the sexuality of males and females is differentially affected by "psychologic stimuli" continue: "Since there are differences in the capacities of females and males to be conditioned by their sexual experience, we might expect similar differences in the capacities of females and males to be conditioned by other, nonsexual types of experience" (p. 712).

I would like to suggest a number of directions for future research on sex differences that ameliorate some of these problems. The first suggestion is to do less research specifically designed to explore differences between the sexes. As Michael Lewis (1975) notes, "It seems to me that research in sex differences . . . is probably motivated by implicit variables

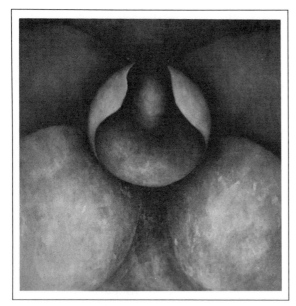

Birth of the Form by Miriam Brumer. Reprinted by permission

having more to do with sociopolitical than scientific issues. Remember that for any important psychological variable there is greater within-group than across-group variance" (p. 333).

Moving beyond the study of sex differences to a true study of individual differences can enable us to discover more about the intrasex variation in abilities and predispositions, and perhaps to begin tracing some biological contributions for intrasex differences. Ehrhardt and Baker (1974a, p. 50) look forward to a time when "it can be documented that prenatal hormone levels are among the factors that account for the wide range of temperamental differences and role aspirations within the female, and possibly also within the male sex." I am not sure why such factors are more likely to contribute to female than to male intrasex differences, but such a research focus would be a useful direction.

Maccoby and Jacklin (1974) point out the reluctance of editors to publish studies showing the absence of sex differences, a reluctance that obviously must recede if our ultimate understanding of the range of sex similarities and differences is not to be severely impaired. Those studies that do focus on sex differences would do well to heed Block's (1976) analysis of Maccoby's and Jacklin's book. Block suggests that differences in the "pattern" of performance and traits are likely to be obtained, and that considering sex (or gender) as a moderating variable may be most fruitful for future research and theory.

As a second contribution, I feel that psychologists must gain a greater awareness of cross-cultural differences in sex-role behaviors before tendering any generalizations regarding the origins of sex differences. It seems absurd to claim that some set of behaviors is importantly influenced by male hormones when that same set of behaviors may represent the epitome of femininity in some other culture. It is no accident that Women's Studies, that branch of scholarship infused with a feminist perspective, is determinedly interdisciplinary. We have seen how the narrowness of vision suffered by one discipline can result in serious oversimplification of complex issues, a situation remedied by a focus on interdisciplinary cross-checking and cross-fertilization. I am not suggesting that the psychological point of view, that perspective which emphasizes intraindividual processes and determinants of behavior and mental life, is inappropriate or socially regressive, only that the individual perspective, uninformed by insights from the other social sciences, is likely to err repeatedly.

Finally, the issue of the social responsibility of the scientist is an important one in the area of sex differences research. The unfortunate use of biological theories of group difference to justify inequitable social treatment stands as a large signpost urging caution in the generation and generalization of biologically based hypotheses. I am not recommending that a board of feminist scholars ought to pass on the ideological legitimacy of every research study proposing to investigate biological variables and sex differences. That would be an undemocratic outrage. Rather, I am recommending that an awareness of the uses to which scientific conclusions are put in contemporary society ought to encourage a redoubling of efforts to produce careful observations, well-designed studies, theories that take into account the nature of the present state of evidence, and the likelihood of practical misuse. Attending to the "sociology of psychological knowledge" (Buss, 1975) will prevent the excesses of the past while encouraging sensitivity to the consequences of scientific research in the present and future.

6. Conclusion

In her 1973 presidential address to the American Psychological Association, Leona Tyler (1973) discusses many of the reasons why the original hope that society would benefit importantly from psychological research has dimmed during the last decades. She suggests that the choice of research projects has come to depend more on "such things as the availability of a new technique or instrument, the recognition of an unanswered question in a report of previous research, a suggestion from a friend or advisor, or just the fact that a federal program has made grant funds available" (p. 1025) than on commitment to a research issue because of its potential theoretical or humanitarian importance. She urges us to reconsider our research directions, and devote ourselves to making choices that will illuminate our understanding and enrich the quality of human life.

Studies of sexuality and of maleness and femaleness are potentially of great moment both for our understanding of what it is to be human and for enriching our experience of what it is to be human. But before we can provide such research, we have to analyze more carefully the factors underlying our choice of method, of conceptual definitions, of research population, our theoretical assumptions, and the potential uses of our data and conclusions. The feminist perspective provides one angle from which to attempt such analysis.

Susan Carol Rogers

Woman's Place: A Critical Review of Anthropological Theory

Current Work on Female Status: Universal Female Subordination

By far the majority of work now being done on women centers on female forms of power and female status. Sexual differentiation per se either is not treated, or taken as one of several indications of low female status. There is considerable diversity within this body of work, both in regard to its rootedness in earlier research, and to the degree of political motivation evident. While some anthropologists explicitly state that their work is motivated by a desire to mobilize direct action to change the contemporary power structure in our own and other societies, others are more modestly attracted to the problem of rethinking the roles of women in society.[1] Still others are simply interested in understanding the female experience in various societies, and in opening up a formerly neglected area of study.

All of the scholars to be considered here have a feminist perspective in the sense that they reject "the view of women as passive victims of their sexual constitution . . . or as formless lumps shaped by their environment."[2] They assume instead that women are social actors, with goals of their own, and means to achieve them. To the extent that women have low status, this is considered the result of social or cultural arrangements, not of inherent female inferiority. Beyond this, however, the feminism of these scholars reflects the diversity of contemporary American and British feminists. For some, it is inextricably bound up with neo-Marxist thought. Others, rejecting this kind of doctrine, believe in integration: the breakdown of sexual differentiation. Still others may be termed segregationists, emphasizing the differences between men and women, and the superiority of women. This diversity of political orientation, together with variations in the extent to which it is incorporated into anthropological analysis, results in a number of different interpretations of data, and the subsequent development of varying theoretical or analytical schemes. The greatest dividing line between these scholars centers around the question of whether or not women may be assumed to be universally subordinated to men. Both views will be discussed here.

One of the most important strategies of American feminism, particularly in the late 1960s, was "consciousness-raising," an institutionalized process by which neophyte feminists learned first, that they are subordinated, and second, how and in what forms this subordination occurs. The development of this kind of awareness was seen as an essential first step to political awareness and to the mobilization of women to effect reasoned political, social, and personal change.

A number of feminist anthropologists have continued this process by demonstrating that women are universally subordinated. To them, the notion that women in other societies may not be, or do not believe themselves to be,

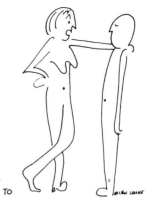

I SOMETIMES WONDER
IF YOU'RE THE RIGHT ONE
FOR ME TO BE SUBMISSIVE TO

subordinated, is evidence of "false-consciousness."[3] They assume that the sex groups are universally related hierarchically, and focus, in their research, on the female group. They maintain that unless women can be demonstrated to be dominant, they must be subordinate. The criteria they choose for measuring female power and status are such that women may never be shown to be dominant. This is not, however, taken to indicate that women are submissive. On the contrary, it is held that women often have at their disposal important means of wielding power and influence. Because of the nature of all social or cultural systems, however, men simply have more power. The key to understanding and criticizing these scholars, then, is the criteria they use for measuring female status or power. It should be pointed out that they superficially resemble the nineteenth-century evolutionists in their attempt to demonstrate the cross-cultural subordination of women. They differ, however, in not assuming women to be passive or submissive, and in not taking the status of women in their own society as an ideal to be thrust upon other women. Our society is a model only in the sense that criteria applicable to female status here are assumed to be applicable elsewhere. These criteria used for measuring female status can be described as follows.

Economic. Women's contribution to the economy of a society has been the focus of a great deal of attention. Reversing the assumption

---

Experiencing Culture from the Male Point of View

Purpose: To assist you in experiencing that we live in a culture in which the male point of view predominates.

1. Role Reversal

   Directions: With any of the following items—magazine article, advertising, school textbooks, movie or television scenarios, song lyrics, romance story:

   a. Reverse the pronouns by actually crossing out the words *she, he, him, her* and write the opposite above the space.
   b. Re-read the piece again with the pronouns reversed as you have pencilled them in.
   c. What are the direct and indirect messages about women (and men)?

   Another version of this exercise is to change the pronouns to all of one gender, that is, change the characters to be all males or all females. Then re-read the piece and see what messages you get.

---

made by some nineteenth-century evolutionists, it has been argued that female status increases with women's contribution to the subsistence economy.[4] This notion is implicit in Brown's analysis,* and feminists have placed a great deal of emphasis on the importance of extradomestic economic activity as a means of raising women's status.

---

*Ed. note: Judith K. Brown, "A Note on the Division of Labor by Sex," *American Anthropologist*, 72 (1970).

In every known society, the male's need for achievement can be recognized. Men may cook, or weave, or dress dolls, or hunt hummingbirds, but if such activities are appropriate occupations of men, then the whole society, men and women alike, votes them as important. When the same occupations are performed by women, they are regarded as less important.

Margaret Mead, *Male and Female*, 1948

This view is problematic, however, unless further qualified. In some societies, after all, slaves may perform most of the subsistence labor without enjoying especially high status. Dorothy Remy argues that the status of women should be measured by their capacity to obtain economic security or autonomy within the structural constraints of the total economy. Superior female status would result from a division of labor in which women contribute more than men to the subsistence economy, and a system whereby women have control over both their own labor and its fruits.[5] She argues that a careful distinction must be made between the value or prestige assigned to economic activities and their actual importance. For instance, in hunting and gathering societies, (male) hunting is often the most highly valued activity, while (female) gathering provides up to 90 percent of the caloric intake. Women's status in this situation is higher than an exclusive focus on the ideological aspects of the economic system would suggest. However, the fact that male activities are given higher ideological value gives men an edge over women.[6] Women's labor, moreover, is virtually always ultimately controlled by men. Remy cites two indications of this. First, marriage and bridewealth arrangements are made independently of the desire of women, and second, women commonly develop close relationships with their sons and fight for the latters' economic success, because they are dependent upon their sons for economic security.[7]

Thus, although women may be politically or economically active in traditional societies, they are still subordinated. With capitalist development, Remy argues, women's status further deteriorates, because the relative economic importance of subsistence activities decreases, and because women are systematically barred from, or discriminated against, in wage employment.[8] The status of women may therefore be raised only by restructuring the economy and adopting a socialist system. Also "women must liberate themselves to gain control of their economic potential and therefore their autonomy."[9]

Sanday also reacts to the notion that women's participation in subsistence activities may be used as a simple measure of their status. Unlike most of the others, she defines exactly what she means by "status," making explicit the usually implicit equation of status and power.[10] She specifies four measures of female status:

I. Female control over produce
II. External and internal demand or value placed on female produce
III. Female participation in at least some political activities
IV. Female solidarity groups devoted to female political or economic interests.[11]

She selects twelve societies from Murdock's *Ethnographic Atlas*, scores them on the basis of presence or absence of these four factors, and then compares these scores with the percentage of female contribution to subsistence

The primitive woman is independent because, not in spite of her labor. Generally speaking, it is in those societies where women toil most that their status is most independent and their influence greatest; where they are idle, and the work is done by slaves, the women are, as a rule, little more than sexual slaves....

Robert Briffault, *The Mothers*, 1927

in each society. Virtually no direct correlation was found between the two, indicating that access to resources does not necessarily result in control over them.

Political. Female participation in political activities becomes a focal point in many studies of female status. In most of these, it is maintained that females virtually never have formal political power.[12] This assumption is commonly found in anthropological literature.[13] In the work here considered, however, a distinction is drawn between power ("the ability to gain compliance") and culturally legitimated authority ("the recognition that [such ability] is right").[14] It is demonstrated that women may have considerable amounts of informal power or influence, and that this has been underestimated in the ethnographic literature. This type of power is regarded by these scholars, however, as less important or desirable than legitimated authority. If men control political offices and other positions of authority, they ultimately dominate women. That women have only informal, manipulative power at their disposal, it is argued, is demeaning and indicative of low status. Although the importance of female informal power—and, as a result, female status—is assumed to vary from society to society, males are held to be universally dominant by virtue of their universal monopolization of formal or legitimized power.

Social Loci. This belief in the preeminence of formal political power is further underlined

Mother and Child of the Kalahari Bushman Tribe, sculpture by Malvina Hoffman, reproduced through the courtesy of Field Museum of Natural History, Chicago

by those scholars who focus on the arenas in which men and women operate. Implicitly or explicitly, the definition of formal political power used in these analyses includes the specification that it be operative in a public sphere. A distinction is often drawn between the private "domestic" or familial, on the one hand, and the public, social, or political, on the other. The former are defined as the fundamental mother-child units of a society, while the latter include those "activities, institutions, and forms of association that link, rank, organize, or subsume" the former.[15]

It is held that women are always relatively more tied than men to the domestic because of their childbearing and rearing functions. The importance of the domestic unit may vary somewhat in different types of societies, with subsequent implications for women's status and power. It is always, however, molded by higher level arrangements in the extradomestic arenas, so that, although women may be dominant in the domestic unit, they are ultimately subordinated if men control extradomestic activities. For instance, Lamphere, like Sanday, sees female solidarity as an important indication of female power within a subordinated situation. Assuming that this female solidarity necessarily has a domestic base, she suggests that it will arise where male authority structures allow for it, or where male authority is weak or absent in relation to the domestic scene.[16] Rosaldo suggests that female solidarity—whether informal or institutionalized—"add[s] social and moral value to an *otherwise* domestic role"[17] (emphasis mine). The domestic role, however, even when thus "enhanced," is still the domestic role: "women will seem to be oppressed or lacking in value and status to the extent that they are confined to domestic activities, cut off from other women and the social world of men."[18] Female subordination will disappear only when women are no longer identified with domestic life. The sexual distinction between the domestic and extradomestic arenas must be blurred, so that women may participate equally in social and political activities, and men participate in the domestic life of the home.[19] The domestic arena is thus seen as a kind of albatross, universally weighing women down, and preventing them from participation in valued male spheres.[20]

Autonomy. Another measure of female status, found for example in the work of Michaelson and Goldschmidt, is the degree of personal autonomy enjoyed by women. Marriages which are arranged, rather than based on personal choice and love, as well as difficulty of divorce, are seen as indications of male dominance: women are subordinated in a male system and unable to make their own life choices.[21] It will be noted that Remy pointed to women's lack of control over marriage arrangements as indicative of low female status. Blumberg[22] also sees freedom to marry as an important criterion for measuring female status. She further generalizes the notion, however, when she adds the criterion of "life choice freedom"; that is, the amount of personal choice a woman has in deciding what she will do, quite beyond marriage arrangements. The (unwarranted) assumption here is that men always have this kind of choice, and if women do not, it is because they are male dominated.

The above are a number of ways of defining female status. Various characteristics of female roles are taken as indicative of subordinate status. Although these indications are most often presented as criteria by which female status may be measured, the fact that women are assumed from the outset to be subordinated introduces considerable tautology. The first problem with these analyses, then, is that whether or not the notion of universal female subordination is justified, all of these analyses demonstrate its existence because the criteria for measuring female status are chosen and defined with this conclusion in mind. Furthermore, these "criteria" are often only descriptive statements about female roles, improperly put forth as analytic tools appropriate for the measurement of female status. Secondly, because attempts are being made to find "objective" criteria applicable to all societies, variations in the contextual meaning of particular institutions are often overlooked, and their value or function in our society tends to be reified and generalized. Finally, because these analyses are all based on cross-cultural data from a variety of sources, a great deal of the data base is biased.

Sources of Cultural Valuations of Women. For example, let us examine the argument "that male, as opposed to female activities are always recognized as predominantly important, and cultural systems give authority and value to the roles and activities of men."[23] It is almost always "culture" which is portrayed as the actor in this argument: for example, as well as *giving* authority and value, culture is said to *devalue* women,[24] or *assign* dominance to males.[25] I would argue that "culture" cannot do anything; it is the members of a society or culture who may act. The question to be posed then, is *who* is devaluing, assigning, and so on. Leavitt, Sykes, and Weatherford suggest that it is the androcentrism of anthropologists themselves, reflecting, often unconsciously, the male bias of their own personal and professional socialization, which leads to consistent assertions and assumptions of high cultural valuation of males and male activities throughout the ethnographic record.[26] Although the cultural baggage of anthropologists is undoubtedly an important factor, we may assume that these assertions also have some empirical basis in the expressed values and beliefs of the members of societies studied by anthropologists. If Ardener is correct in arguing that ideological systems are not necessarily generated by a society as a whole, the question of which members express such beliefs and their values becomes a crucial one. That is, *men* might regard their activities as predominantly important, and *their* cultural systems might give superior value to the roles and activities of men. As Ardener* points out, most ethnographic data focus on male cultural perceptions, assuming them to be representative of the society as a whole. But might not women in some societies perceive *their* activities as predominantly important and more highly valued than those of men?

Perhaps the best statement of such a dichotomy is found in the following comments made by female and male informants respectively, and quoted in Kaberry's study of the Nsaw (Cameroon):

> Important things are women. Men are little. The things of women are important. What are the things of men? Men are indeed worthless. Women are indeed God. Men are nothing. Have you not seen?

> Yes a woman is like God, and like God she cannot speak. She must sit silently. It is good that she should only accept.[27]

---

*Ed. note: Edwin Ardener, "Belief and the Problem of Women," in Jean LaFontaine, ed., *The Interpretation of Ritual* (London, 1972).

In a number of societies, it is reported that men and women perceive themselves as "separate entities" or "different breeds."[28] Undercurrents of mutual antagonism between the sexes, and verbal belittling of each other are by no means limited to the Nsaw.[29] This antagonism is often reported, especially in West African societies, to erupt in collective action of one sex group against the other, by means of institutionalized mechanisms of a type which suggest that in these cases at least, the two sex groups may indeed be viewed as separate entities, with different interests and goals.[30] In other cases, the expression of such differences takes less disruptive forms. Separate prestige systems, based on different criteria, by which each sex group ranks its own members, sex-based differences in ranking the value of resources or the attractiveness of various kinds of work are mentioned in diverse ethnographic studies, and may be indications of separate male and female ideologies.[31] Oppositions between ideological systems and material reality, such as that pointed out by Remy, may in fact be completed or mediated in some cases by the existence of two ideological systems. Finally, in a number of situations in which the male role is largely defined or asserted by men in terms of its sacred or ritual content, women are reported to exhibit considerable skepticism, "merely going along with the game"[32] or "remain[ing] regrettably profane in their attitudes toward the men."[33]

Kaberry, in noting this phenomenon among Australian aborigines, questions whether male anthropologists are correct in reporting that Australian men and their rites represent the sacred element in the community, in view of her observation that Australian women do not seem to "be cognizant of the fact and accept it."[34] I would argue that it is possible for quite different ideologies regarding the place or value of males and females in the social order to exist side by side in the same society. Furthermore, discovering or reporting only one or the other ideology will result in serious distortion of the social reality. The argument that males are universally dominant because their activities are universally more highly valued thus dissolves. More information is needed about female perceptions of themselves and their cultures. In the meantime, statements about low cultural valuation of women may be assumed to be, at least in some cases, only public male valuations of women. While important to consider, such valuations are rather lopsided grounds on which to base theories about women, if women in the same societies do not accept them, and have their own counter valuations.

Sexual Segregation. In view of this possibility, the equating of sexual segregation with discrimination against women—an assumption found in older ethnographic sources, as well as in those under discussion—is particularly spurious. On the contrary, marked social and economic segregation is conducive to the development of separate ideological systems and of two contrasting valuations of the importance and attractiveness of each sex group and its activities. In this case, the barring of one sex group from the domain of the other does not necessarily have negative implications for the excluded group. Furthermore, it may not be legitimate to consider one group as more excluded than the other, if neither has access to the other's domains.

Where sexual segregation exists *without* this kind of duality, so that the resources, activities, and so on of one sex group are more valued by both, while members of the other sex group are consistently denied access to them, then sexual discrimination is present. In other words, sexual segregation per se is neither discriminatory, nor a sign of discrimination. Only in the presence of other factors may the two be associated. Because these factors are clearly present in our society, the tendency is to facilely associate all segregation with discrimination. A closer look at the evidence indicates that this is not justified in all cultural contexts.

Distribution and Meaning of Social Loci. Finally, data on the social loci of men and women are no less male-biased than are those on cultural valuations. Because anthropologists have tended to assume that women are primarily and narrowly involved in domestic and family activities,[35] virtually all of the available data on female roles are analyses of marriage practices and descriptions of domestic life. In attempting to synthesize these data, and make cross-cultural generalizations about women, one is led to the conclusion that women everywhere do little but marry men and run (or get run by) households. It is unclear, however, how much information on nondomestic aspects of female roles has gone undiscovered or unreported because anthropologists have failed to ask the proper questions. For instance, expressing his surprise on learning of the role played by women in the formal state hierarchy of precolonial Ashanti, Rattray states:

> I have asked the old men and women why I did not know all this. . . . The answer is always the same: "The white man never asked us this; you have dealings with and recognize only men, we supposed the European considered women of no

account, and we know you do not recognize them as we have always done."[36]

In many West African societies, women traditionally played active economic, social, and political roles in extradomestic spheres, including a variety of institutionalized positions of formal authority in such state systems as Dahomey and Nupe, as well as Ashanti. Tilly and Scott demonstrate that in Europe a large percentage of nineteenth-century working-class women worked outside of the home.[37]

Clearly, women are not universally identified exclusively with the domestic, nor do men always monopolize positions of legitimized power. Nevertheless, as far as one can tell from available data, women are generally more closely identified with the domestic than are men, and societies in which women regularly have access to formal power appear to be relatively rare. In our society, as many contemporary feminists point out, relegation to the domestic sphere means isolation from most important seats of power. Furthermore, great value is placed on formal authority, and our lives are shaped, to a considerable extent, by decisions at least overtly made by the "authorities."[38] Feminists have argued effectively that barring women from positions of formal authority leaves them prey to ultimate male dominance.

It may well be asked, however, if "household" and "formal power" have the same significance in other societies as in our own. Is the status of a peasant woman and a contemporary American urban middle-class woman identical, given that both center their activities in the household and have little or no access to formal power? The scholars here under discussion would argue that the same criteria should be applicable to both women, and that

Though it appears that both men and women live together within the institutions of society, men really define and control the institutions while women live under their rule. The government, army, religion, economy, and family are institutions of the male culture's colonial rule of the female. . . . A female culture exists. It is a culture that is subordinated and under the male culture's colonial, imperialist rule all over the world. Underneath the surface of every national, ethnic, or racial culture is the split between the two primary cultures of the world—the female culture and the male culture. . . . Crossing national boundaries often awakens a woman's understanding of her position in society. We cannot, like James Baldwin, even temporarily escape to Paris or another country from our caste role. It is everywhere—there is no place to escape.

Fourth World Manifesto, Jan. 13, 1971

---

they have comparable statuses: both play subordinate roles. Another group of anthropologists, however, takes a more cultural relativist stance; they argue that power in the household, in certain sociocultural contexts, may indeed be more significant than formal or extradomestic forms of power. Some have even suggested that the very selection of formal political power as a basis of analysis for all types of societies is a projection of the androcentric bias in our own. In Australian aboriginal societies, for example, "although the men play a more important political role in intergroup relationships, political institutions are not highly developed and are geared to economic survival, in which women play a central role."[39] This perspective is considered below.

Female Status: Variable Female/Male Power Distribution

Virtually all of the scholars so far considered assume universal male dominance. In this respect, the feminist anthropologists discussed above have not completely broken rank with conventional anthropology. They do depart from convention by insisting that women are important actors in social and cultural processes. Another group of scholars shares this conviction, but takes it further, by rejecting, categorically or provisionally, the notion of universal male dominance. These scholars are primarily interested in addressing themselves to the paucity of ethnographic information on women, without explicit recourse to particular political doctrines. They thus free themselves from commitment to proving universal female subordination and instead seek appropriate ways of assessing female status in particular types of societies, rather than attempting to find universal criteria.

Obviously, because the status of women is a politically loaded issue in our society, their work does have political implications, whether or not they are made explicit. The set of analyses which follows is based on particular assumptions about female nature. . . . Furthermore, it at least implicitly addresses itself to, or obviates, a number of important questions left open by the work discussed in the section above: if women are truly not passive, incapable, stupid, or inherently inferior to men, how is it that they have allowed themselves in all times and all places to be subordinated by men? How is it that late nineteenth-century and contemporary feminists are the first women in the world to feel their subordination and try to do something about it? If women have never before succeeded in ridding themselves of the yoke of male dominance, why should we believe we can?

Much of this literature is characterized by an insistence on examining the position of men and women vis-à-vis each other. If it is

Bronze Figure of the Woman Mud Carrier of Hong Kong, sculpture by Malvina Hoffman, reproduced through the courtesy of Field Museum of Natural History, Chicago

assumed at the outset that males are dominant, then one need not examine male roles. These may, in effect, be held constant, while women's roles may be examined and compared for explanations or degrees of subordination (hence the need for universal criteria). In this view, it is pointless to discuss the relative position of men and women within a culture: it will always be fundamentally the same. If, on the other hand, one assumes that the power relationships between men and women are cross-culturally variable, then what is of interest is the relative power of each.[40] In this case, criteria appropriate to particular cultures or types of societies are more important than universal criteria. Also, in this less global view, it becomes irrelevant that men may be dominant outside of a particular sociocultural context (e.g., that urban men often control institutions affecting peasant life).[41] What is of interest is the power distribution between those men and women who share daily life. Finally, in rejecting universal male dominance, it can no longer be assumed that male spheres of activity are by definition the most important. The relative significance of male and female spheres must vary with the relative status of each sex group in the society under study.

Public/Domestic Spheres. The notion that males universally monopolize public spheres is found in many of these analyses. The meaning of the public sphere, however, is radically revised. For example, it has often been demonstrated that peasant societies are domestic-centered; that is, the family is the key economic, political, and social unit in this type of society.[42] In view of this characteristic, several scholars argue that one need not look beyond the domestic sphere to measure the relative status of male and female peasants; power in the private, not the public, sphere is of greatest real importance. Friedl, for instance, demonstrates that male monopolization of prestigious public roles gives an appearance of male dominance in the Greek village she studied.[43] This public prestige, however, gives men no advantage in the private sphere, where the "realities of power" are to be found. Here, men and women play complementary roles, and neither enjoy higher prestige. Furthermore, because women bring dowries of land into the household, and remain in control of this property, they sometimes upset the balance of domestic power by controlling not only their own realms, but encroaching on those of their male counterparts as well.[44]

Dubisch adopts Friedl's argument, but broadens this last notion by pointing out that contributions to a household may take non-property forms (e.g., having children, being a good parent, standing up for the family). She suggests that the relative contribution of each spouse will shape their power relationship.[45] Drawing on her study of a Greek peasant village, she proposes the following criteria for measuring male/female power distribution:

1. respect accorded one spouse by the other, publicly and privately;
2. interference of one spouse in the sphere of the other;
3. decision-making in regard to allocation of family resources;
4. arranging plans for children.[46]

Friedl points out that because the household is the crucial unit in peasant society, female power here implies considerable control over "secondary" extradomestic functions.[47] Nelson further develops this point, although she does not give priority to the household as a seat of power. She suggests that the frequently drawn contrast between the female social world, which is said to be private, "domestic, narrow, and restricted," and the "political, broad, and expansive" public world of men, represents, in the Middle Eastern context she examines, an inappropriate imposition of Western social scientists' own categories.[48] She demonstrates that the sharp sexual segregation found in the Middle East means, not so much that women are relegated to restricted private realms, but that they have a wide range of contacts among themselves, from which men are excluded. The crucial role women play as structural links between kinship groups (fundamentally important in these societies), as well as the potent social control wielded by female solidarity groups,[49] suggest that the Middle Eastern woman's "domestic" world is, in its own way, political, broad, and expansive.

Formal/Informal Power. Riegelhaupt's study of the public nature of female roles among Portuguese peasants brings to the fore the distinction between formal and informal power. She contrasts the realities of peasant political and economic life with the formal inferiority of women stemming from Portuguese laws barring them from participation in formal political processes and limiting their economic activities. It is demonstrated that peasant men, as structured inferiors in an authoritarian state, gain virtually nothing from their political rights.[50] In the economic realm, the productive roles of men and women in the household (the primary productive unit) are complementary and equally interdependent. Furthermore, as household directresses, women control farm budgets, making or participating in all marketing and agricultural decisions.[51]

Riegelhaupt maintains that the crucial dimension to be examined in determining power distribution in peasant societies is the way in which information is gained, and the means by which subsequent decisions are implemented.[52] A number of factors place women at a significant advantage here. Men spend most of their time working in isolation in outlying fields. Their manifest mistrust of each other, resulting in brittle social relationships, further limits contact between men.[53] Women, on the other hand, divide their time between domestic-based work in the village proper, and marketing produce in urban centers. In the former arena, they are in frequent contact with each other, and develop considerable sex group solidarity. In the markets, they have access to communication with non-local potential patrons in positions of power vis-à-vis the State.[54] Women are thus in a better position than their male counterparts to control information dissemination, to be cognizant of village needs, and to aid in the accomplishment of individual and community goals.[55] In this cultural context, this informal power is considerably more significant than the formal privileges of men.

Formal/Informal Public/Private Roles. Chiñas synthesizes all of these considerations in her development of an analytical framework from which to view women. She begins by asserting that one sex or the other is not necessarily dominant, but may be in a complementary relationship in terms of economic roles and all other aspects of the social system.[56] She maintains that this possibility implies that women's roles cannot necessarily be evaluated in terms of men's roles: conclusions based on a comparison of dissimilar things are logically invalid. Like Ardener, she makes explicit and rejects two assumptions commonly found in anthropological literature: (1) "the sexes perceive their culture and their own sex's place in it in essentially the same way." (2) "men and women share a common culture on similar terms."[57] Because most ethnographic literature takes a male point of view, she proposes to explore the female view, by setting up a series of opposing pairs. She first distinguishes between formalized and nonformalized roles: those bundles of rights and duties which are clearly defined and publicly recognized, and those which are not so clearly perceived or rigidly defined, respectively. Secondly, she distinguishes between private and public domains: the family or domestic group, on the one hand, and everything else, on the other. To understand the power relationship between the two sexes, the distribution of all four types of roles—formalized public, formalized private, nonformalized public, and nonformalized private—must be examined.

She maintains that, virtually universally, males monopolize formalized public roles (e.g., mayor, priest), and that formalized private roles are most often distributed complementarily between men and women (e.g., mother/father, wife/husband).[58] In the Mexican peasant society she studied, women play public nonformalized roles which are complementary to the public formalized roles of men. Within this cultural context, she suggests that the former are as crucial both to the understanding, and to the operation, of the system, as are the latter.[59] Women also play a variety of nonformalized private roles; these, as well as their public roles "function to maintain the integrity of the household, to avoid conflict and violence, and more generally to add oil to the social machinery in a system where there exists a high level of fear and anxiety."[60] Women are able to play these roles largely because they "operate in a social universe separate from men and therefore are privy to information which men either do not or may not circulate among themselves, and [because] certain types of movement and courses of action are open only to women."[61]

Perhaps because nonformalized roles are extremely important in peasant societies, Chiñas suggests, female status in these societies is apt to be relatively high. She maintains that there are no societies where women completely dominate men. However, in some societies, as among Mexican peasants, neither group is dominant. The power relationship between males and females varies cross-culturally, from this situation, to one in which women are very subordinated to men. She leaves unanswered the question of how sex-group status is determined in particular societies. She rejects the notion that it is determined on the basis of contribution to subsistence, or that female status improves along social evolutionary lines. She tentatively suggests that there may be some relationship between the relative status of the sexes and the value placed on nonformalized roles, or the importance of sex as a social marker.[62]

Cross-Cultural Variations in Female Role Analysis. Most of these analyses are based on work in peasant societies. In noting this tendency, Chiñas suggests that it may be because nonformalized roles seem to be of particular importance among peasants, so that male dominance does not exist in this cultural context.[63] It should be clear, however, that concepts developed for analysis of peasant societies are not applicable to all types of societies. The results of such projection would be as unsatisfactory as the general application of concepts developed for analysis of sex-group relationships in our own society. Although little work of this sort has been done in other types of societies, work by Denise Paulme underlines this point.

In her review of some of the more common themes in sex-role definition in sub-Saharan Africa, Paulme rejects the assumption found in much of the ethnographic literature on African women, that divergence from the Western ideal implies lower female status. She asserts that the picture often drawn of the subservient African woman "merely expresses a fondly entertained masculine ideal which does not tally with the realities of everyday life."[64] She notes that in many African societies, women have no rights over their husbands' property, but that they often have their own property, over which their husbands have no jurisdiction.[65] In many cases, women have full (formalized) authority over a considerably wider area than the household (e.g., voluntary associations, marketplace).[66] Women also often have a wider network of interpersonal relationships than do men. Particularly in patrilineal societies, "men never seem to conceive of ties other than those of kinship linked with common residence ... [whereas] among women the mere fact of belonging to the same sex is enough to establish an active solidarity."[67] Finally, she points out that insofar as familial orientation is strong in particular African societies, it is most frequently directed toward the natal, rather than the conjugal family. Thus, the parent/child bond is likely to be stronger, and to entail more (or more important) rights and duties than, for instance, the husband/wife bond.[68] All of these factors suggest that theories of women based upon "women's attachment to the domestic" (in the Western sense of the domestic), their exclusion from activities in the larger world, their lack of economic autonomy, and their paucity of public, formalized roles, will have only limited applicability.

This set of analyses, then, differs from the previous one primarily in the rejection of the conventional notion of universal male dominance, and also in the lack of a search for universal criteria for measuring sex-group status. As a result, the projection of American cultural values and conceptions is avoided to a greater extent: to these scholars, such projection is invalid and promises little illumination of female status or roles in other societies. Therefore, they also reject a number of other culture-bound notions common in the ethnographic literature, which appear in the work of the first group of feminist anthropologists considered. For instance, "power" is most often used in ethnographic literature to mean primarily, or most importantly, legitimized formal authority.[69] The insistence upon informal expressions and channels of power as integral parts of the social system, often as important or more important than formalized power, is a radical departure, having implications especially, but not exclusively, for the study of sex-group power relationships. Their work establishes that such informal behavior is hardly more random, arbitrary, or individualized, than formal behavior, and is thus as open to the scrutiny of social scientists.[70] A second common assumption which is challenged is the notion that the domestic sphere is necessarily of secondary importance. While the first group of feminist anthropologists sees woman's "relegation" to the domestic sphere as evidence of subordinated status, the second group maintains that, in some cultural contexts, the domestic sphere is a key seat of power. Also, it may have decisive impact on activities and relationships beyond it. The African analyses further suggest that the double association of domestic/woman, extradomestic/man is not necessarily an accurate one. In sum, what distinguishes this group of scholars is that they do not assign a priori a negative valuation to characteristically female aspects of social life.

The major problem with much of this work is the distortion resulting from overemphasis on women. Because the problem is defined, for the most part, as one of understanding the relationship between male and female roles (particularly in terms of power distribution), one would expect more balanced information on both sex groups. It might, of course, be argued that it is information on women which is missing from the ethnographic record: we already have information on men, so it is appro-

Pigmies of the Ituri Forest in Central Africa, sculpture by Malvina Hoffman, reproduced through the courtesy of Field Museum of Natural History, Chicago

priate to emphasize data on women. Exclusive focus on female forms of power, however, may give the impression that women are relatively more powerful than they are: it is possible to overstate the case. Particularly if one is arguing that a complementary or dialectical relationship exists between the two sex groups, overemphasis on one or the other makes it impossible to adequately understand the relationship between the two.

Psychological Sex Differences

Issues regarding the biological basis and cultural backdrop for psychological sex differences were explored in the previous section. Similar issues pertaining to biases inherent in the psychological research are again relevant as are biases of a predominately white, middle-class, and college student subject population. Experimenter bias may also influence the outcome of sex difference research since virtually every investigator has expectations regarding sex differences. Additionally, the search for sex differences leads one necessarily to a theory of behavior based on specific traits an individual may possess (trait theory of personality) rather than to a theory about how the social context or situation can predict or explain behavior (context theory of personality).

Many of these biases pervade psychological research in general and are of concern to feminists as they specifically affect the psychology of women. The articles contained in this section are based on data not immune to these criticisms. To complicate matters further, different conclusions regarding some of the psychological sex differences have been reached even among reviewers whose work appears here. Rather than regarding this section as providing definitive answers to the question of what *are* the psychological differences between females and males, the articles included are intended to present some of the outstanding work in this area along with its problems. This is, after all, a more accurate reflection of our present state of knowledge.

Eleanor Emmons Maccoby and Carol Nagy Jacklin's *The Psychology of Sex Differences* (1974) is considered the most complete reference on the recent psychological sex difference literature. As a result of their

---

Woman/Man: Word Associations and Images

Purpose: To explore some of our attitudes and feelings about women and men.

Directions: Read the following questions and write your responses. Be aware of your experiences as you do the exercises.

1. What are your associations to the word *woman*?
2. What do you like about women? What do you dislike about them?
3. What do you expect of women? What do you expect to get from and give to them?
4. What do you actually give to and get from women?
5. What do you want and need from women?
6. What fears do you have about women? [May be repeated, substituting other emotions for "fears."]
7. What other feelings do you have about women?

Repeat the above questions substituting *man* and *men* for *woman* and *women*.

What were your experiences? What did you learn about yourself? About your relationships with women and men?

---

exhaustive review of the developmental sex differences literature extending an earlier summary by Maccoby (1966), these two feminist researchers have been able to draw certain conclusions. According to a set of explicit criteria, they have established psychological sex differences that are "real" and those that are "myths," as well as those for which no conclusions may yet have been reached. These are summarized in the excerpt that appears here.

Untitled drawing by Melissa Mathis

Maccoby and Jacklin also discuss the degree of confidence we may have in the conclusions reached. This discussion is based on problems endemic to developmental research—problems in validity and reliability of measurements, limits of generalizability to only certain situations, differences between the laboratory and the real world, and the measurement of theoretical constructs varying with age as the infant becomes an adult. In addressing the question of the origin of psychological sex differences, the possible role of biological factors in aggression and visual-spatial abilities is proposed as a readiness to learn. Otherwise, three processes of socialization affect the learning of sex roles. These are praise and encouragement, in which parents and significant others reinforce the child for appropriate sex-typed behaviors; imitation, in which the child learns spontaneously through imitation of a role model of the same sex; and self-socialization, in which the child develops a concept of maleness and femaleness, adjusting his or her behavior to match the appropriate concept.

Maccoby and Jacklin's results and conclu-sions are not without problems, however, according to the next article by Jeanne Block. A more extensive though similar review of hers appears in the *Merrill-Palmer Quarterly* (1976). In Block's opinion, sex difference conclusions may be premature. She presents evidence that alternative decision criteria can be applied, yielding different conclusions, and that various "slippages" have occurred in the cataloging and analyzing of the data, distorting some of the conclusions.

Both Maccoby and Jacklin's frequently cited work and Block's extensive critique deserve careful attention. Together, they speak to the enormity of the task of establishing unequivocally the existence of psychological sex differences.

An additional problem, however, is that any psychological sex differences now observed, even if we could be sure what they were, would be open to the dual interpretation of "nature versus nurture." That is, any differences we measure are within a social context in which there are differing expectations regarding the two sexes. Within the so-

Psychologists must realize that it is they who are limiting discovery of human potential. They refuse to accept evidence, if they are clinical psychologists, or, if they are rigorous, they assume that people move in a context-free ether, with only their innate dispositions and their individual traits determining what they will do. Until psychologists begin to respect evidence, and until they begin looking at the social context within which people move, psychology will have nothing of substance to offer in this task of discovery. I don't know what immutable differences exist between men and women apart from differences in their genitals; perhaps there are some other unchangeable differences; probably there are a number of irrelevant differences. But it is clear that until social expectations for men and women are equal, until we provide equal respect for both men and women, our answers to this question will simply reflect our prejudices.

Naomi Weisstein, "Psychology Constructs
The Female," 1971

---

ciopolitical context, sex differences would be seen as the result of power differences between the two sexes inherent in patriarchy.

Aggression, for example, is a variable for which the evidence is in dispute, though even if the data permitted the conclusion that men are more aggressive than women, this could be the result of differences in social expectations for the two sexes within a patriarchal context in which women mute their aggression. According to Maccoby and Jacklin, aggression is a variable for which there is a "real" sex difference. It is presumed to have a biological substrate and is therefore assumed to be an innate psychological sex difference. Other scientists, however, do not agree that the existence of a biological basis for a sex difference in aggression has been demonstrated (Bleier, 1979; Salzman, 1979). Furthermore, in a recent review of the experimental psychology literature on adult sex differences in aggression it was found that the common assumption that men are physically and verbally more aggressive than women was not justified (Frodi, Macaulay, and Thome, 1977). Cross culturally, an innate sex difference in aggression has been theorized as a major determinant in the universality of patriarchy in either its establishment or maintenance (Quinn, 1977; Webster, 1977), although the nonuniversality of patriarchy has been argued (Rogers, 1978), as well as the past existence of matriarchies (Newton and Webster, 1973; Webster, 1975). (See the previous section on biological and cultural perspectives.) Even so, psychological sex differences in aggression as measured in the U.S. today are the result of the combined effects of cultural patriarchy, differing social expectations for the two sexes, and possible innate (biologically based) differences. This would apply to the study of other psychological sex differences as well.

Obviously, there are many more psychological topics other than sex differences to which feminist scholarship has been and could be applied. Current research issues and trends in these areas have been reviewed in the next article by Martha T. Shuch Mednick. Acknowledging the relationship of feminism to the new psychology of women, Mednick pre-

Like all sciences and all valuations, the psychology of women has hitherto been considered only from the point of view of men. It is inevitable that the man's position of advantage should cause objective validity to be attributed to his subjective, affective relations to the woman, and . . . the psychology of women hitherto actually represents a deposit of the desires and disappointments of men. An additional and very important factor in the situation is that women have adapted themselves to the wishes of men and felt as if their adaptation were their true nature. That is, they see or saw themselves in the way that their men's wishes demanded of them; unconsciously they yielded to the suggestion of masculine thought.

Karen Horney, "The Flight from
Womanhood," 1926

sents fundamental questions posed by feminist analyses. These, then, form the basis for current research and theory. While the study of psychological sex differences may be useful, it can be and has been used to justify women's inferior status, according to Mednick. Feminist critiques of psychology and its methodology have also been a trend.

According to Mednick, areas in which feminist research is beginning include achievement, sex roles, sexuality, the reproductive cycle, power, creativity, and women in groups, among others. The author then covers in depth two areas—sex roles and identity, and achievement—while forgoing a third—mental health and therapy. It is interesting to note how many of these topics are also included in this collection of readings. The main activity

in the first of these has been androgyny. (See Garnets and Pleck's discussion of androgyny.) In relation to achievement, recent work has been concerned with how this motive is defined by women's experience, fear of success, and expectancy and causal attribution; it is indeed unfortunate that these topics cannot be presented more fully in this collection of readings. Topics for future research are women and power, aspects of women's lives aside from reproductive events, the interpersonal and intimate lives of women (see the section on relationships), and more on black women and other minority women (see the next section on ethnic diversity). Finally, Mednick suggests further study of sex-role change (see the section on change and liberation).

For Further Reading

Frieze, I. E., Parsons, J. E., Johnson, P. B., Ruble, D. N., and Gail L. Zellman (Eds.). 1978. *Women and Sex Roles: A Social Psychological Perspective.* New York: W. W. Norton.

Maccoby, E. E. (Ed.). 1966. *The Development of Sex Differences.* Stanford: Stanford Univ. Press.

Maccoby, E. E. and Jacklin, C. N. 1974. *The Psychology of Sex Differences.* Stanford: Stanford Univ. Press.

Mednick, M., Hoffman, D., and Tangri, S. 1977. *Women and Achievement.* Washington, D.C.: Hemisphere.

I have pointed out that characteristics and inferiority feelings which Freud considered to be specifically female and biologically determined can be explained as developments arising in and growing out of Western woman's historic situation of underprivilege, restriction of development, insincere attitude toward the sexual nature, and social and economic dependency. The basic nature of woman is still unknown.

Clara Thompson, "Cultural Pressures in the
Psychology of Women," 1942

O'Leary, V. 1977. *Toward Understanding Women.* Monterey, Calif.: Brooks/Cole.

Sherman, J. A. 1971. *On the Psychology of Women.* Springfield, Ill.: Charles C. Thomas.

Sherman, J. A. 1978. *Sex-Related Cognitive Differences.* Springfield, Ill.: Charles C. Thomas.

Sherman, J., and Denmark, F. 1978. *Psychology of Women: Future Directions of Research.* New York: Psychological Dimensions.

Spence, J. T., and Helmreich, R. L. 1978. *Masculinity and Femininity: Their Psychological Dimensions, Correlates, and Antecedents.* Austin, Tex.: University of Texas Press.

Unger, R. K. 1979. *Female and Male: Sex and Gender.* New York: Harper & Row.

Unger, R. K., and Denmark, F. L. 1975. *Woman: Dependent or Independent Variable?* New York: Psychological Dimensions.

Williams, J. H. 1977. *Psychology of Women: Behavior in a Biosocial Context.* New York: W. W. Norton.

Williams, J. H. 1979. *Psychology of Women: Selected Readings.* New York: W. W. Norton.

Eleanor Emmons Maccoby and Carol Nagy Jacklin

Summary and Commentary

Summary of Our Findings

Unfounded Beliefs About Sex Differences

1. *That girls are more "social" than boys.* The findings: First, the two sexes are equally interested in social (as compared with nonsocial) stimuli, and are equally proficient at learning through imitation of models. Second, in childhood, girls are no more dependent than boys on their caretakers, and boys are no more willing to remain alone. Furthermore, girls are not more motivated to achieve for social rewards. The two sexes are equally responsive to social reinforcement, and neither sex consistently learns better for this form of reward than for other forms. Third, girls do not spend more time interacting with playmates; in fact, the opposite is true, at least at certain ages. Fourth, the two sexes appear to be equally "empathic," in the sense of understanding the emotional reactions of others; however, the measures of this ability have so far been narrow.

Any differences that exist in the "sociability" of the two sexes are more of kind than of degree. Boys are highly oriented toward a peer group and congregate in larger groups; girls associate in pairs or small groups of age-mates, and may be somewhat more oriented toward adults, although the evidence for this is weak.

2. *That girls are more "suggestible" than boys.* The findings: First, boys and girls are equally likely to imitate others spontaneously. Second,

the two sexes are equally susceptible to persuasive communications, and in face-to-face social-influence situations (Asch-type experiments), sex differences are usually not found. When they are, girls are somewhat more likely to adapt their own judgments to those of the group, although there are studies with reverse findings. Boys, on the other hand, appear to be more likely to accept peer-group values when these conflict with their own.

3. *That girls have lower self-esteem.* The findings: The sexes are highly similar in their overall self-satisfaction and self-confidence throughout childhood and adolescence; there is little information about adulthood, but what exists does not show a sex difference. However, there are some qualitative differences in the areas of functioning where the two sexes have greatest self-confidence: girls rate themselves higher in the area of social competence; boys more often see themselves as strong, powerful, dominant, "potent."

Through most of the school years, the two sexes are equally likely to believe they can influence their own fates, rather than being the victims of chance or fate. During the college years (but not earlier or later), men have a greater sense of control over their own fate, and greater confidence in their probable performance on a variety of school-related tasks that they undertake. However, this does not imply a generally lower level of self-esteem among women of this age.

4. *That girls are better at rote learning and simple repetitive tasks, boys at tasks that re-*

quire higher-level cognitive processing and the inhibition of previously learned responses. The findings: Neither sex is more susceptible to simple conditioning, or excels in simple paired-associates or other forms of "rote" learning. Boys and girls are equally proficient at discrimination learning, reversal shifts, and probability learning, all of which have been interpreted as calling for some inhibition of "available" responses. Boys are somewhat more impulsive (that is, lacking in inhibition) during the preschool years, but the sexes do not differ thereafter in the ability to wait for a delayed reward, to inhibit early (wrong) responses on the Matching Familiar Figures test (MFF) or on other measures of impulsivity.

5. *That boys are more "analytic."* The findings: The sexes do not differ on tests of analytic cognitive style. Boys do not excel at tasks that call for "decontextualization," or disembedding, except when the task is visual-spatial; boys' superiority on the latter tasks seems to be accounted for by spatial ability (see below), and no sex differences in analytic ability are implied. Boys and girls are equally likely to respond to task-irrelevant aspects of a situation, so that neither sex excels in analyzing and selecting only those elements needed for the task.

6. *That girls are more affected by heredity, boys by environment.* The findings: Male identical twins are more alike than female identical twins, but the two sexes show equivalent amount of resemblance to their parents.

Boys are more susceptible to damage by a variety of noxious environmental agents, both prenatally and postnatally, but this does not imply that they are generally more influenced by environmental factors. The correlations between parental socialization techniques and child behavior are higher for boys in some studies, higher for girls in others. Furthermore, the two sexes learn with equal facility in a wide variety of learning situations; if learning is the primary means whereby environmental effects come about, sex equivalence is indicated.

7. *That girls lack achievement motivation.* The findings: In the pioneering studies of achievement motivation, girls scored higher than boys in achievement imagery under "neutral" conditions. Boys need to be challenged by appeals to ego or competitive motivation to bring their achievement imagery up to the level of girls'. Boys' achievement motivation does appear to be more responsive to competitive arousal than girls', but this does not imply a generally higher level. In fact, observational studies of achievement strivings either have found no sex difference or have found girls to be superior.

8. *That girls are auditory, boys visual.* The findings: The majority of studies report no differences in response to sounds by infants of the two sexes. At most ages boys and girls are equally adept at discriminating speech sounds. No sex difference is found in memory for sounds previously heard.

Among newborn infants, no study shows a sex difference in fixation to visual stimuli. During the first year of life, results are variable, but neither sex emerges as more responsive to visual stimuli. From infancy to

adulthood, the sexes are highly similar in interest in visual stimuli, ability to discriminate among them, identification of shapes, distance perception, and a variety of other measures of visual perception.

Sex Differences that Are Fairly Well Established

1. *That girls have greater verbal ability than boys.* It is probably true that girls' verbal abilities mature somewhat more rapidly in early life, although there are a number of recent studies in which no sex difference has been found. During the period from preschool to early adolescence, the sexes are very similar in their verbal abilities. At about age 11, the sexes begin to diverge, with female superiority increasing through high school and possibly beyond. Girls score higher on tasks involving both receptive and productive language, and on "high-level" verbal tasks (analogies, comprehension of difficult written material, creative writing) as well as on the "lower-level" measures (fluency). The magnitude of the female advantage varies, being most commonly about one-quarter of a standard deviation.

2. *That boys excel in visual-spatial ability.* Male superiority on visual-spatial tasks is fairly consistently found in adolescence and adulthood, but not in childhood. The male advantage on spatial tests increases through the high school years up to a level of about .40 of a standard deviation. The sex difference is approximately equal on analytic and nonanalytic spatial measures.

3. *That boys excel in mathematical ability.* The two sexes are similar in their early acquisition of quantitative concepts, and their mastery of arithmetic during the grade-school years. Beginning at about age 12–13, boys' mathematical skills increase faster than girls'. The greater rate of improvement appears to be not entirely a function of the number of math courses taken, although the question has not been extensively studied. The magnitude of the sex differences varies greatly from one population to another, and is probably not so great as the difference in spatial ability. Both visual-spatial and verbal processes are sometimes involved in the solution of mathematical problems; some math problems can probably be solved in either way, while others cannot, a fact that may help to explain the variation in degree of sex difference from one measure to another.

4. *That males are more aggressive.* The sex difference in aggression has been observed in all cultures in which the relevant behavior has been observed. Boys are more aggressive both physically and verbally. They show the at-

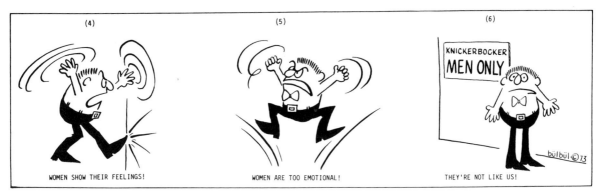

tenuated forms of aggression (mock-fighting, aggressive fantasies) as well as the direct forms more frequently than girls. The sex difference is found as early as social play begins—at age 2 or 2½. Although the aggressiveness of both sexes declines with age, boys and men remain more aggressive through the college years. Little information is available for older adults. The primary victims of male aggression are other males—from early ages, girls are chosen less often as victims.

Open Questions: Too Little Evidence, or Findings Ambiguous

1. *Tactile sensitivity.* Most studies of tactile sensitivity in infancy, and of the ability to perceive by touch at later ages, do not find sex differences. When differences are found, girls are more sensitive, but such findings are rare enough that we cannot have confidence that the difference is a meaningful one. Additional work is needed with some of the standard psychophysical measurements of tactile sensitivity, over a range of ages. Most of the existing studies in which the data are analyzed by sex have been done with newborns.

2. *Fear, timidity, and anxiety.* Observational studies of fearful behavior usually do not find sex differences. Teacher ratings and self-reports, however, usually find girls to be more timid or more anxious. In the case of self-reports, the problem is to know whether the results reflect "real" differences or only differences in the willingness to report anxious feelings. Of course, the very willingness to assert that one is afraid may lead to fearful behavior, so the distinction may not turn out to be important. However, it would be desirable to have measures other than self-report (which make up the great bulk of the data from early school age on) as a way of clarifying the meaning of the girls' greater self-attribution of fears and anxiety.

3. *Activity level.* Sex differences in activity level do not appear in infancy. They begin to be seen when children reach the age of social play. During the preschool years, when sex differences are found they are in the direction of boys' being more active. However, there are many instances in which sex differences have not been found. Some, but not all, of the variance among studies can be accounted for by whether the measurement situation was social. That is, boys appear to be especially stimulated to bursts of high activity by the presence of other boys. But the exact nature of the situational control over activity level remains to be established. Activity level is responsive to a number of motivational states—fear, anger, curiosity—and is therefore not a promising variable for identifying stable individual or group differences. More detailed observations

What are little girls made of?
What are little girls made of?
Sugar and spice
And all that's nice.
That's what little girls are made of.

Nursery Rhyme

---

are needed on the vigor and qualitative nature of play.

4. *Competitiveness.* When sex differences are found, they usually show boys to be more competitive, but there are many studies finding sex similarity. Madsen and his colleagues find sex differences to be considerably weaker than differences between cultures and, in a number of studies, entirely absent. Almost all the research on competition has involved situations in which competition is maladaptive. In the Prisoner's Dilemma game, for example, the sexes are equally cooperative, but this is in a situation in which cooperation is to the long-run advantage of both players and the issue is one of developing mutual trust. It appears probable that in situations in which competitiveness produces increased individual rewards, males would be more competitive, but this is a guess based on commonsense considerations, such as the male interest in competitive sports, not upon research in controlled settings. The age of the subject and the identity of the opponent no doubt make a difference—there is evidence that young women hesitate to compete against their boyfriends.

5. *Dominance.* Dominance appears to be more of an issue within boys' groups than girls' groups. Boys make more dominance attempts (both successful and unsuccessful) toward one another than do girls. They also more often attempt to dominate adults. The dominance relations between the sexes are complex: in childhood, the sex segregation of play groups means that neither sex frequently attempts to dominate the other. In experimental situations

in which the sexes are combined, the evidence is ambiguous on whether either sex is more successful in influencing the behavior of the other. Among adult mixed pairs or groups, formal leadership tends to go to males in the initial phases of interaction, but the direction of influence becomes more sex-equal the longer the relationship lasts, with "division of authority" occurring along lines of individual competencies and division of labor.

6. *Compliance.* In childhood, girls tend to be more compliant to the demands and directions of adults. This compliance does not extend, however, to willingness to accept directions from, or be influenced by, age-mates. Boys are especially concerned with maintaining their status in the peer group, and are probably therefore more vulnerable to pressures and challenges from this group, although this has not been well established. As we have seen in the discussion of dominance, it is not clear that in mixed-sex interactions either sex is consistently more willing to comply with the wishes of the other.

7. *Nurturance and "maternal" behavior.* There is very little evidence concerning the tendencies of boys and girls to be nurturant or helpful toward younger children or animals. Cross-cultural work does indicate that girls between the ages of six and ten are more often seen behaving nurturantly. Within our own society, the rare studies that report nurturant behavior are observational studies of free play among nursery school children; sex differences are not found in these studies, but the setting normally does not include children

A little girl is as a rule less aggressive, defiant, and self-sufficient; she seems to have a greater need for being shown affection and on that account to be more dependent and pliant.

Sigmund Freud, "The Psychology of Women," 1933

much younger than the subjects being observed, and it may be that the relevant elicitors are simply not present. Female hormones play a role in maternal behavior in lower animals, and the same may be true in human beings, but there is no direct evidence that this is the case. There is very little information on the responses of adult men to infants and children, so it is not possible to say whether adult women are more disposed to behave maternally than men are to behave paternally. If there is a sex difference in the tendency to behave nurturantly, it does not generalize to a greater female tendency to behave altruistically over varying situations. The studies of people's willingness to help others in distress have sometimes shown men more helpful, sometimes women, depending on the identity of the person needing help and the kind of help that is needed. The overall finding on altruism is one of sex similarity.

... [Earlier] we raised the question of whether the female is more passive than the male. The answer is complex, but mainly negative. The two sexes are highly similar in their willingness to explore a novel environment, when they are both given freedom to do so. Both are highly responsive to social situations of all kinds, and although some individuals tend to withdraw from social interaction and simply watch from the sidelines, such persons are no more likely to be female than male. Girls' greater compliance with adult demands is just as likely to take an active as a passive form; running errands and performing services for others are active processes. Young boys seem more likely than girls to put out energy in the form of bursts of strenuous physical activity, but the girls are not sitting idly by

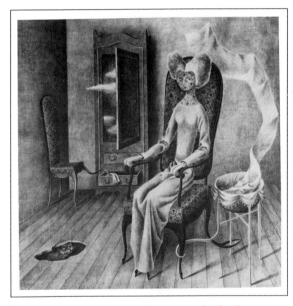

Mimicry by Remedios Varo; reprinted by permission of Walter Gruen

while the boys act; they are simply playing more quietly. And their play is fully as organized and planful (possibly more so), and has as much the quality of actively imposing their own design upon their surroundings as does boys' play. It is true that boys and men are more aggressive, but this does not mean that females are the passive victims of aggression—they do not yield or withdraw when aggressed against any more frequently than males do, at least during the phases of childhood for which observations are available. With respect to dominance, we have noted the curious fact that while males are more dominant, females are not especially submissive, at least not to the dominance attempts of boys and girls their own age. In sum, the term "passive" does not accurately describe the most common female personality attributes.

I HAD THIS TERRIFIC SHRINK

HELPED ME FIND THE REAL ME.

TOLD ME I HAD TO WORK AT MY WOMANHOOD.

WHO WOULD HAVE THOUGHT BEING PASSIVE COULD BE SO ACTIVE.

© Ellen Levine, from *All She Needs . . .*, Quadrangle, 1973

Superdik by Gladys Nilsson. Permission of artist

Returning to one of the major conclusions of our survey of sex differences, there are many popular beliefs about the psychological characteristics of the two sexes that have proved to have little or no basis in fact. How is it possible that people continue to believe, for example, that girls are more "social" than boys, when careful observation and measurement in a variety of situations show no sex difference?

Of course it is possible that we have not studied those particular situations that contribute most to the popular beliefs. But if this is the problem, it means that the alleged sex difference exists only in a limited range of situations, and the sweeping generalizations embodied in popular beliefs are not warranted.

However, a more likely explanation for the perpetuation of "myths," we believe, is the fact that stereotypes are such powerful things. An ancient truth is worth restating here: if a generalization about a group of people is believed, whenever a member of that group behaves in the expected way the observer notes it and his belief is confirmed and strengthened; when a member of the group behaves in a way that is not consistent with the observer's expectations, the instance is likely to pass unnoticed, and the observer's generalized belief is protected from disconfirmation. We believe that this well-documented process occurs continually in relation to the expected and perceived behavior of males and females, and results in the perpetuation of myths that would otherwise die out under the impact of negative evidence. However, not all unconfirmed beliefs about the two sexes are of this sort. It is necessary to reconsider the nature of the evidence that permits us to conclude what is myth and what is (at least potentially) reality.

How Much Confidence Can Be Placed in These Conclusions?

Having gone through the often tedious process of summarizing and analyzing existing research, we must ask ourselves about the adequacy of this method as a way of knowing the truth about sex differences. We have tallied studies—the number showing higher scores for boys, the number favoring girls, and the number showing no difference—knowing, of course, that the studies differ widely in the rigor of their design and procedures, the number of subjects used, the definition of variables, etc. It is not uncommon to find a "box score" in which the majority of studies find no difference, but where the studies that do find a difference favor one sex by a considerable margin (say, two or three to one). We have interpreted such an outcome as a weak trend in the direction indicated by the largest number of studies, but recognize that it is quite possible that the minority of studies might turn out to have more than a kernel of truth. With stereotypes and biases being as common as they are in the field of sex differences, it is quite possible that the majority of studies were all distorted in the same direction. We think it equally likely, however, that the appearance of a sex difference often depends upon detailed aspects of the situation in which behavior was studied—details that have so far gone unrecognized, but that interact with the more obvious aspects of a situation to change the way in which it is perceived.

We have repeatedly encountered the problem that so-called "objective" measures of behavior yield different results than ratings or self-reports. Ratings are notoriously subject to shifting anchor points. For example, if a parent is asked, "How often does your daughter cry?," the parent may answer "Not very often," meaning "Not very often _for a girl._" The same frequency of behavior might have been rated "quite often" for a son, from whom

Mother and Child by Mary Cassatt; reprinted by permission of National Gallery of Art, Washington; Chester Dale Collection

the behavior was less expected. Ratings, then, if they are made against different subjective standards, should minimize sex differences where they exist. Where they do not exist, ratings might produce them, but in the opposite direction from stereotypical behavior. It is puzzling that ratings so frequently yield sex differences in the stereotypical direction. For example, in one study, teachers rated each child in their class on activity level; the boys received higher average ratings; but "actometer" recordings for the same group of children

One might consider characterizing femininity psychologically as giving preference to passive aims. This is not, of course, the same thing as passivity; to achieve a passive aim may call for a large amount of activity.

Sigmund Freud, "The Psychology of
Women," 1933

did not show the boys to be engaging in more body movement. Obviously, the possibility exists that teachers are noticing and remembering primarily the behavior that fits their stereotypes. There is another possibility, however: that teachers are analyzing clusters or patterns of behavior that a simple single-attribute measurement such as an actometer score does not capture. If this is so, however, and the teachers are reporting something real about sex differences, the cluster that they are attending to should not be named "activity level," for the label implies that the behavior is simpler than it is.

The problems of shifting anchor points for ratings, selective perceptions of raters, and unclear definitions of what is being rated are not the only problems that beset the student of sex differences. It matters how large a "chunk" of behavior is chosen for analysis. This point has been nicely illustrated in work by Raush (1965), in which he compared the social interactions of a group of clinically diagnosed "hyperaggressive" boys with a group of normals. The sequences of aggressive behavior were monitored. The two groups of boys were similar in the frequency and kind of response the victim first made. They were also similar in the aggressor's response to the victim's response. It was only in the fourth and fifth actions in the sequence that the groups diverged—the "hyperactives" continued to respond intensely; the normals "let it go" without continuing the sequence. It may be that sex differences, too, emerge at only certain points in a sequence, and the results of a study

will depend upon how detailed and continuous the measurements are. Often, of course, an experimental situation is arranged in such a way that only single responses are recorded, and then summed across trials. Such a procedure makes it nearly impossible to detect either sequences or other patterning of behavior.

We have found a number of instances in which sex differences are situation-specific. For example, although boys and girls do not differ in their attachment to their parents in early childhood (that is, their tendency to remain close to them, interact with them, and resist separation from them), or in the amount of positive interaction with nonfamily adults, boys do interact more with same-sex agemates. Unfortunately, many studies tally social behavior without specifying the "target" of this behavior. Similarly, studies of "nurturance" behavior (rare in the first place) have usually not identified the beneficiary of the behavior. Clearly, if a child brings a glass of water to his mother, the behavior is subject to different interpretations than if he does the same helpful act for a younger sibling. Furthermore, it makes a difference who is watching. We suspect, for example, that a man may behave more dominantly toward his girl friend and she more submissively when other men are present than they would do in private. It is possible, too, that marriage partners are especially likely to become more equal in dominance with time if there are children—that it is the need to maintain a united front before the children and to support one an-

> *The passivity that is the essential characteristic of the "feminine" woman is a trait that develops in her from the earliest years. But it is wrong to assert a biological datum is concerned; it is in fact a destiny imposed upon her by her teachers and by society.*
>
> Simone de Beauvoir, *The Second Sex*, 1953

---

other's disciplinary moves that is a primary factor producing a change in the dominance relations of a married pair. These situational subtleties have gone largely unnoticed in existing research; we have had no choice but to report the data that researchers have obtained, but we think findings will be much clearer when these distinctions begin to be introduced.

We have attempted to understand the relationship of sex differences to age; we have wanted to know at what age a particular difference first manifests itself, whether it is temporary, whether it increases or decreases with development. We have been able to make only a tantalizing beginning to a genuinely developmental analysis. It is reasonably clear that differences in "temperament" and in social behavior emerge much earlier than differences in specific intellectual abilities. Furthermore, there are a few instances in our review where a difference was evident only briefly, during a limited age period. This appears to be true, for example, on certain measures of "impulsivity," where boys are more impulsive only during the preschool years. On the whole, however, our efforts to understand developmental change have been frustrated by two things: (1) the fact that certain ages are overrepresented, others underrepresented, in research on a given topic; and (2) the fact that the methods of measuring a given attribute change so drastically with age that cross-age comparison becomes virtually impossible. Newborn infants in the first two or three days of life, nursery school children, and college students are the groups most frequently studied. In addition, extensive data are available for school-age children on attributes that are clearly relevant to school success (e.g., intellectual aptitudes and achievement scores), with much less information available on social behavior. Very little is known about age changes during adulthood with respect to either cognitive or social measures.

The problem of changing measures over ages is a ubiquitous one in developmental psychology. One can learn something about a young child's attachments and fears by tallying the frequency with which he literally hides behind his mother's skirts; to attempt to do so with an adult would be absurd. One may measure quantitative skill in a preschooler by finding how accurately he can count, and of a fifth- or sixth-grader by asking him to do percentages; but by college age, subjects must be asked to solve differential equations before stable individual differences can be identified. There are great shifts with age not only in *what* is measured buy in *how* measurement is done. Behavioral observation is fairly frequent with young children. From the time children become literate through adulthood, however, observational studies in naturalistic settings are very rare, and scores are based either on questionnaires or other self-reports, or on experimental situations using a deliberately restricted set of eliciting conditions and behavioral measures.

It is to be expected that results of experiments may yield quite different results than "real life" observations. It is possible, for ex-

The girl's nature as biologically conditioned gives her the desire to receive, to take into herself; she feels or knows that her genital is too small for her father's penis and this makes her react to her own genital wishes with direct anxiety; she dreads that if her wishes were fulfilled, she herself or her genital would be destroyed.

Karen Horney, "The Dread of Woman," 1932

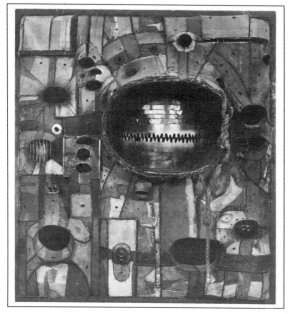

Lee Bontecou. *Untitled.* 1961. Canvas and welded metal. 72 × 66¼ × 26 inches. Collection of Whitney Museum of American Art.

ample, that if a girl is put into a foot race, she will be as competitive and active as a male. But she might be much less likely to enter such a race spontaneously, and naturalistic observation would show her to be less frequently engaged in competitive behavior, whereas the foot race "experiment" would not. The conclusions of both kinds of studies are correct, but they have rather different implications. The shift from naturalistic observation in early childhood to experimental studies at later ages may mean that sex differences in self-selection of activities have had a better chance of being detected in the early years, rather than that there has been any decline in the importance of motivation and interest with growth.

In a certain sense it is reasonable to make the shift from observational data to questionnaires or self-reports. If one is sampling behavior in a nursery school, it may be meaningful to record simply that a child moved across the room. If one looked out the window at a college student walking down the sidewalk just before the bell rang, however, what is meaningful to record about his behavior? The fact that he was walking? The fact that he was going to class? The fact that he was taking a course in psychology? The fact that his attendance at this class was part of his four-year program to obtain a bachelor's degree? Elements of an adult's behavior are usually part of a nested set of organized action sequences (i.e., "plans"). Judging by the data we collect about people at different ages, researchers implicitly assume that a young child's behavior is less so. This is probably correct, although there are probably many more nested sequences in children's behavior than have been detected with the usual techniques of time sampling and frequency tallies of individual behavior elements. If plans of varying duration and complexity do assume more and more control of behavior as the individual develops, it would be reasonable to ask about the plans, rather than to spend so much time enumerating specific responses, as is done for young children. However, the value of observational data surely does not decline to zero with increasing age. We can point out here only that, reasonable though the shift in methods may be, it makes the meaning of measured age changes quite ambiguous. We hope there will be an increase in observational work in naturalistic settings with sub-

The boy, on the other hand, feels or instinctively judges that his penis is much too small for his mother's genital and reacts with the dread of his own inadequacy, of being rejected and derided. Thus his anxiety is located in quite a different quarter from the girl's, his original dread of women is not castration anxiety at all, but a reaction to the menace to his self-respect.

Karen Horney, "The Dread of Woman," 1932

jects beyond nursery school age, so that a few more cross-age comparisons will be possible.

One interesting age trend emerged in our survey that is probably *not* a reflection of changes in methods of measurement: this is the tendency for young women of college age to lack confidence in their ability to do well on a new task, and their sense that they have less control over their own fates than men do. These trends are not seen among older or younger women. Age 18–22 is the period of their lives when many young adults are marrying or forming some other kind of relatively enduring sexual liaison. In the dating and mating game, women traditionally are expected to take less initiative than men. Perhaps it is at this period of their lives more than any other that individuals define themselves in terms of their "masculinity" and "femininity," and when greater sex differences may therefore appear than at earlier or later ages, with respect to any attribute considered central to this definition.

This brings us to a related point: that sex differences may be greater among certain subgroups of men and women than among others. In a recent paper, "On Predicting Some of the People Some of the Time," Bem and Allen (1974) suggest that an individual's behavior is likely to be stable across situations and across time with respect to only those attributes that are central to his self-definition. If the individual thinks of himself as a "friendly" person, and considers it important to be as friendly as possible, then he should be consistently friendly in many situations, partly because he will continually monitor his own behavior to take note of how friendly he is

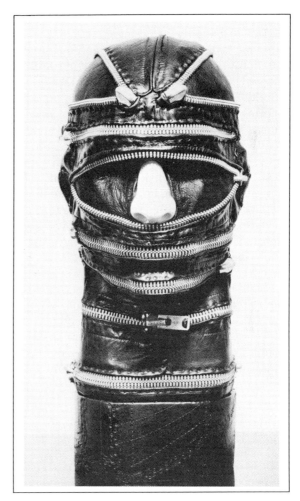

J.G. 1969 by Nancy Grossman. Collection of Gilbert and Lila Silverman

being and will correct his own behavior if he is not behaving in ways that are consistent with his self-definition. For other individuals, however, friendliness is not a defining attribute; self-monitoring activity will not be directed toward maintaining consistency with

*No matter how friendly and obliging a woman's Eros may be, no logic
on earth can shake her if she is ridden by the animus. Often the man
has the feeling—and he is not altogether wrong—that only seduction or a
beating or rape would have the necessary power of persuasion.*

Carl G. Jung, "Aion: Phenomenology of the
Self," 1951

respect to friendly behavior, and hence such behavior will vary greatly depending on the situation in which the person finds himself. In this vein, it is reasonable to believe that "masculinity" and "femininity" are essential self-defining attributes for some people but not for others. If the studies summarized in previous chapters of this book* had been based on selected subsamples of subjects, including only those women who consider it important to be feminine and those men for whom masculinity is central to their self-concept, the chances are that greater sex differences would have been reported and the findings would have been much more consistent than we have found them to be. The variations in findings from one study to another probably reflect, in part, the relative concentration of people of this type in the subject population, as well as subtle variations in experimental situations that would signal to the subjects whether the tasks they were called on to perform had any relevance to masculinity or femininity.

On the Etiology of Psychological Sex Differences

In previous chapters* we have discussed three kinds of factors that affect the development of sex differences: genetic factors, "shaping" of boylike and girl-like behavior by parents and other socializing agents, and the child's spontaneous learning of behavior appropriate for his sex through imitation. Anyone who would hope to explain acquisition of sex-typed behavior through one or two of these processes alone would be doomed to disappointment. Not only do the three kinds of processes exert their own direct influence, but they interact with one another.

Biological factors have been most clearly implicated in sex differences in aggression and visual-spatial ability. We have argued that the male's greater aggression has a biological component, citing in support the fact that (1) the sex difference manifests itself in similar ways in man and subhuman primates; (2) it is cross-culturally universal; and (3) levels of aggression are responsive to sex hormones. We have also found, surprisingly, that there is no good evidence that adults reinforce boys' aggression more than girls' aggression; in fact, the contrary may be true. Here, however, there are questions about the adequacy of our information. Direct observational studies of parental reactions to aggression have been carried out in settings in which only the responses to a child's aggression *toward the parents* (or sometimes toward siblings) could be observed. When it comes to permissiveness for fighting among unrelated children, we must rely on parent interviews. Parents *say* they encourage daughters to defend themselves as much as they do sons, and that they attempt to teach non-aggression to the same degree to both sexes. Serbin et al. (1973) found that in the case of aggressive or destructive behavior by one child toward another child in nursery

*Ed. note: *The Psychology of Sex Differences* by Eleanor Maccoby and Carol Nagy Jacklin (Stanford: Stanford University Press, 1974).

In general, it can be said that feminine mentality manifests an underdeveloped, childlike, or primitive character; instead of the thirst for knowledge, curiosity; instead of judgment, prejudice; instead of thinking, imagination or dreaming; instead of will, wishing.

Emma Jung, *Animus and Anima,* 1957

school, teachers were more likely to intervene (and perhaps scold the guilty child) if the aggressor was a boy. It is possible that mothers react in an opposite way when they are supervising groups of children in neighborhoods and parks. We doubt it, but we do not know. Meanwhile, the available evidence is that adults do not generally accept or approve aggression in either sex. Either their reaction is equally negative for the two sexes, or they react somewhat more strongly to boys' aggression, on the grounds that boys are stronger and more given to fighting and therefore must be kept under closer control. Although strong negative reactions by parents and teachers may actually be "reinforcing" to some children, this is not usually what is meant when it is alleged that parents shape the aggressive behavior of the two sexes differently. What is usually meant is that they allow, accept, or encourage the behavior more in boys, and this we have not found to be true. The negative evidence on differential socialization has strengthened the case for biological origins of the sex differences in aggression. This does not mean that we believe aggressive behavior is unlearned. There is plentiful evidence that it *is* learned. We argue only that boys are more biologically prepared to learn it.

Does the male predisposition toward aggression extend to other behavior, such as dominance, competitiveness, and activity level? Probably yes, to some degree, but the case is not strong. Among subhuman primates, dominance is achieved largely through aggression, and an individual's position in the dominance

Women

Women   Or they
  should be   should be
  pedestals   little horses
    moving   those wooden
    pedestals   sweet
    moving   oldfashioned
    to the   painted
      motions   rocking
      of men   horses

the gladdest things in the toyroom

          The   feelingly
          pegs   and then
        of their   unfeelingly
        ears   To be
      so familiar   joyfully
      and dear   ridden
    to the trusting   rockingly
  fists   ridden until
To be chafed   the restored

egos dismount and the legs stride away

Immobile   willing
  sweetlipped   to be set
  sturdy   into motion
    and smiling   Women
    women   should be
      should always   pedestals
      be waiting   to men

May Swenson

hierarchy is related to levels of sex hormones. However, there is no direct evidence that

Relationships

The legal children of a literary man
Remember his ugly words to their mother.
He made them keep quiet and kissed them
  later.
He made them stop fighting and finish their
  supper.
His stink in the bathroom sickened their
  noses.
He left them with sitters in lonesome houses.
He mounted their mother and made them
  wear braces.
He fattened on fame and raised them thin.

But the secret sons of the same man
Spring up like weeds from the seed of his
  word.
They eat from his hand and it is not hard.
They unravel his sweater and swing from his
  beard.
They smell in their sleep his ferns and roses.
They hunt the fox on his giant horses.
They slap their mother, repeating his
  phrases,
And swell in his sight and suck him thin.

                              Mona Van Duyn

tial ability rests primarily with genetic studies. There is evidence of a recessive sex-linked gene that contributes an element to high spatial ability. Present estimates are that approximately 50% of men and 25% of women show this element phenotypically, although of course more women than this are "carriers." This sex-linked element is not the only genetic element affecting spatial ability, and the others appear not to be sex-linked. There is so far little evidence for sex linkage of any of the genetic determiners of other specific abilities such as mathematical or verbal ability. The existence of a sex-linked genetic determiner of spatial ability does not imply that visual-spatial skills are unlearned. The specific skills involved in the manifestation of this ability improve with practice. Furthermore, cross-cultural work indicates that the sex differences can be either large or small, or may even disappear, depending upon cultural conditions affecting the rearing of the two sexes. Where women are subjugated, their visual-spatial skills are poor relative to those of men. Where both sexes are allowed independence early in life, both sexes have good visual-spatial skills.

Our review of the socialization pressures directed at the two sexes revealed a surprising degree of similarity in the rearing of boys and girls. The two sexes appear to be treated with equal affection, at least in the first five years of life (the period for which most information is available); they are equally allowed and encouraged to be independent, equally discouraged from dependent behavior; as noted above, there is even, surprisingly, no evidence of distinctive parental reaction to aggressive behavior in the two sexes. There *are* differences, however. Boys are handled and played with somewhat more roughly. They

dominance among adult human groups is linked either to sex hormones or to aggressiveness. The fact that "dominance" in most human groups is called "leadership" provides a clue to the fact that adult human beings influence one another by persuasion, charisma, mutual affection, and bargaining, as well as by force or threats thereof. To the extent that dominance is *not* exercised by coercion, the biological male aggressiveness is probably not implicated in it.

The case for biological control of visual-spa-

also receive more physical punishment. In several studies boys were found to receive both more praise and more criticism from their caretakers—socialization pressure, in other words, was somewhat more intense for boys—but the evidence on this point is inconsistent. The area of greatest differentiation is in very specifically sex-typed behavior. Parents show considerably more concern over a boy's being a "sissy" than over a girl's being a tomboy. This is especially true of fathers, who seem to take the lead in actively discouraging any interest a son might have in feminine toys, activities, or attire.

Is the direct socialization pressure from parents sufficient to account for known sex differences? For some behaviors, probably so. In some areas, clearly not. Aggression is a case of the second kind. Also, we see nothing in the socialization of the two sexes that would produce different patterns of intellectual abilities. In the area of sex typing as narrowly defined, there is clear parental pressure, particularly on boys; nevertheless, children seem to adopt sex-typed patterns of play and interests for which they have never been reinforced, and avoid sex-inappropriate activities for which they have never been punished. Observations of parental behavior may not have been detailed enough to pick up the more subtle pressures exerted, but it is our impression that parents are fairly permissive where many aspects of sex typing are concerned, and that direct "shaping" by parents does not, in most instances, account for the details of the behavior that is acquired. Parents seem to treat a child in accordance with their knowledge of his individual temperament, interests, and abilities, rather than in terms of sex-role stereotypes. We suspect that others who do not

know the child well as an individual are more likely to react to him according to their stereotyped views of what a child of a given sex is likely to be like. Although this conclusion runs counter to common sense, it appears possible that relative strangers exert more stereotyping pressure on children than their own parents do. In any case, we believe that socialization pressures, whether by parents or others, do not by any means tell the whole story of the origins of sex differences.

How then does psychological sex differentiation come about? The psychoanalytic theory of identification would have it that the child identifies with the same-sex parent and learns the details of a sex role through imitation of this parent. Social-learning theory also emphasizes imitation, but argues that children are more often reinforced when they imitate a same-sex than an opposite-sex model, so that they acquire a generalized tendency to imitate not only the same-sex parent but other same-sex models as well. The distinction between acquisition and performance of a given item of behavior is stressed. A child may learn how to do something by watching an opposite-sex model, but may seldom do it because he learns (through observation or otherwise) that such action would probably be punished if performed by a person of his own sex.

We have found several reasons to be dissatisfied with these theories. The first is that children have not been shown to resemble closely the same-sex parent in their behavior. In fact, the rather meager evidence suggests that a boy resembles other children's fathers as much as he does his own, at least with respect to most of the behaviors and attributes measured so far. The same applies to girls' resemblance to their mothers. When people believe they see parent-child resemblance, we suspect they are often noticing physical resemblance rather than behavioral resemblance.

A second problem is that when offered an opportunity to imitate either a male or female model, children (at least those under age 6 or 7) do not characteristically select the model whose sex matches their own; their choices are fairly random in this regard. Yet their behavior is clearly sex-typed at a much earlier age than the age at which choice of same-sex models begins to occur. A final problem is that children's sex-typed behavior does not closely resemble that of adult models. Boys select an all-male play group, but they do not observe their fathers avoiding the company of females. Boys choose to play with trucks and cars, even though they may have seen their mothers driving the family car more frequently than their fathers; girls play hopscotch and jacks (highly sex-typed games), although these games are totally absent from their mother's observable behavior.

To recapitulate briefly: we have been discussing the biological factors and the learning processes that have been alleged to underlie the development of behavioral sex differences. It is tempting to try to classify the differential behaviors as being either innate or learned, but we have seen that this is a distinction that does not bear close scrutiny. We have noted that a genetically controlled characteristic may take the form of a greater *readiness to learn* a particular kind of behavior, and hence is not distinct from learned behavior. Furthermore, if one sex is more biologically predisposed than the other to perform certain actions, it would be reasonable to expect that this fact would be reflected in popular beliefs about the sexes, so that innate tendencies help to produce the cultural lore that the child learns. Thus he adapts himself, through learning, to a social stereotype that has a basis in biological reality. (Of course, not all social stereotypes about the sexes have such a basis.) It is reasonable, then, to talk about the process of acquisition of sex-typed behavior—the *learning* of sex-typed behavior—as a process built upon biological foundations that are sex-differentiated to some degree.

So far we have discussed two learning processes that have been presumed to account for the development of socially defined sex-appropriate behavior. The first emphasizes direct parental reinforcement. We have seen that, although differential reinforcement of boys and girls may account for some sex typing as narrowly defined (e.g., the fact that boys avoid wearing dresses and playing with dolls), there are large areas of sex-differentiated behavior where parental sanctions and encouragement seem to play only a very minor role. A second process widely believed to be crucial in differentiation is the child's identification with (and imitation of) the same-sex parent and, by generalization, other same-sex models. The weaknesses of this process in accounting for the evidence have been delineated above.

We turn now to a third kind of process—the one we entitled "self-socialization" in Chapter 1. This process has been most explicitly enunciated by Kohlberg (1966). Kohlberg stresses that sex-typed behavior is not made up of a set of independent elements acquired by imitating actions the child has seen same-sex people perform. It stems from organized rules the child has induced from what he has observed and what he has been told, and these rules are in many ways a distortion of reality. They are based upon a limited set of features that are salient and describable from a child's point of view (e.g., hair styles and dress); the child's sex-role conceptions are cartoon-like—oversimplified, exaggerated, and stereotyped. He fails to note the variations in the sex-role behavior of his real-life models. A compelling example of this is seen in the case of a 4-year-old girl who insisted that girls could become nurses but only boys could become doctors. She held to this belief tenaciously even though her own mother was a doctor. Hers was a concept clearly not based upon imitation of the most available model. It represented an induction from instances seen and heard (in fiction as well as fact), and like most childish rule inductions it did not easily take account of exceptions.

The child's problem in behaving in ways appropriate to his sex is two-fold: he not only must have some conception of what boylike and girl-like behavior is, but also must have a clear conception of his own sex identity so that he knows which kind of behavior to adopt. Kohlberg notes that neither a child's conception of his own sexual identity nor his notions of what it means to be "masculine" or "feminine" are static. Both change with intellectual growth. Initially a child might know only what his or her own sex is without understanding that his own gender is unchangeable. When sex constancy has been achieved, the child then seeks to determine what behavior is appropriate for his own sex. Early in development, he may not know precisely which other people share a sex category with him; a boy of four may know, for example, which other children are also boys, but he may class all adults together as "grown-ups" and fail to make consistent distinctions between men and women or to realize that men and boys are similar in

the sense of all being males. When sex groupings have been understood, the child is then in a position to identify what behavior is appropriate for his sex by observing what kinds of things males, as distinct from females, do and to match his own behavior to the conceptions he has constructed.

There is a problem with the Kohlberg view: sex typing of behavior occurs much earlier than gender constancy normally develops. We do not question that the achievement of gender constancy may accelerate the process of sex typing. Indeed, R. G. Slaby (1974) has found that those kindergartners who have come to understand that gender is constant choose to observe same-sex models (as compared with opposite-sex models), whereas other children of the same age do not. But we would like to argue that gender constancy is not necessary in order for self-socialization into sex roles to begin. Children as young as 3, we suggest, have begun to develop a rudimentary understanding of their own sex identity, even though their ability to group others according to sex is imperfect and their notion about the permanence of their own sex identity incomplete. As soon as a boy knows that he is a boy in any sense, he is likely to begin to prefer to do what he conceives to be boylike things. Of course, he will not selectively imitate male models if he does not yet know which other people around him are in the same sex category as himself. But he will nevertheless try to match his own behavior to his limited concept of what attributes are sex-appropriate.

We believe that the processes of direct reinforcement and simple imitation are clearly involved in the acquisition of sex-typed behavior, but that they are not sufficient to account for the developmental changes that occur in sex typing. The third kind of psychological process—the one stressed by cognitive-developmental theorists such as Kohlberg—must also be involved. This third process is not easy to define, but in its simplest terms it means that a child gradually develops concepts of "masculinity" and "femininity," and when he has understood what his own sex is, he attempts to match his behavior to his conception. His ideas may be drawn only very minimally from observing his own parents. The generalizations he constructs do not represent acts of imitation, but are organizations of information distilled from a wide variety of sources. A child's sex-role concepts are limited in the same way the rest of his concepts are, by the level of cognitive skills he has developed. Therefore the child undergoes reasonably orderly age-related changes in the subtlety of his thought about sex typing, just as he does with respect to other topics. Consequently, his *actions* in adopting sex-typed behavior, and in treating others according to sex-role stereotypes, also change in ways that parallel his conceptual growth.

Jeanne H. Block

Debatable Conclusions About Sex Differences: A Review of Maccoby and Jacklin

In a time of intense, polarized debate on the issue of the equality of the sexes, it is an awesome responsibility to undertake a distillation of available research findings regarding the extent and nature of sex differences. Eleanor Maccoby and Carol Jacklin have not been intimidated by this consequential challenge. Their book, *The Psychology of Sex Differences*, has already become a frequently cited reference because of the reputation of the authors, the contemporary interest in the topic, the scope of the book's coverage, and the extensive documentation provided. The authors' conclusions about sex differences have ramifications both for psychological theorizing and for political-social decision-making. Because of its potential influence as a statement of what psychologists have found out about sex differences, the work requires close scrutiny and careful evaluation as to its conceptual and empirical adequacy.

The book, a sequel to Maccoby's *The Development of Sex Differences* published in 1966, assays the results of approximately 1,600 studies (published, for the most part, between 1966 and 1973) for inclusion in their 233-page Annotated Bibliography. Studies are organized around eight broad topical areas and, within areas, studies are classified for their relevance to particular psychological dimensions or constructs. Eighty-three tables summarize analyses in which means and/or standard deviations were evaluated for sex differences. Each table includes information about the investigator(s), ages of subjects, sample sizes, specific variables analyzed, and the results of the between-sex statistical comparisons. Each table is extensively discussed.

Maccoby and Jacklin, on the basis of their evaluation of the empirical literature, conclude that there are a number of "unfounded beliefs about sex differences" (p. 349): that (1) girls are more "social" than boys, (2) girls are more "suggestible" than boys, (3) girls have lower self-esteem, (4) girls excel at simple repetitive tasks while boys are superior on tasks requiring more complex cognitive processing and the inhibition of previously learned responses, (5) boys are more "analytical," (6) girls are more affected by heredity and boys by environment, (7) girls are less motivated toward achievement, and (8) girls are more auditorially oriented while boys are more visually oriented.

"Sex differences that are fairly well established," according to the authors, are the following: that (1) girls excel in verbal ability, (2) boys excel in visual-spatial ability, (3) boys excel in quantitative ability, and (4) males are more aggressive.

With respect to seven additional areas, the authors conclude the evidence is equivocal: (1) tactile sensitivity, (2) fear, timidity, and anxiety, (3) activity level, (4) competitiveness, (5) dominance, (6) compliance, and (7) nurturance and "maternal" behaviors.

Further, their evaluation of sex-differentiated parenting behaviors revealed "... surpris-

But no one can evade the fact, that in taking up a masculine calling, studying, and working in a man's way, woman is doing something not wholly in agreement with, if not directly injurious to, her feminine nature.... [Female] psychology is founded on the principle of Eros, the great binder and deliverer; while age-old wisdom has ascribed Logos to man as his ruling principle.

Carl G. Jung, "Aion: Phenomenology of the Self," 1951

---

ingly little differentiation in parent behavior according to the sex of the child" (p. 338) and led them to conclude that "the reinforcement contingencies for the two sexes appear to be remarkably similar" (p. 342).

Earlier assessments of sex differences by Maccoby and others (e.g., Terman & Tyler, 1954; Tyler, 1965) also evaluated the empirical literature and reached conclusions quite different from those embodied in the current Maccoby and Jacklin appraisal. The erosion in the evidence for sex differences over the past decade raises questions both puzzling and profound.

Although a monumental work, *The Psychology of Sex Differences* is nevertheless a controversial portrayal of the field. Broadly stated, three sources of weakness or disputation can be said to characterize the book: (1) sex difference research to date often does not permit sensible conclusions of any kind yet to be drawn; (2) Maccoby and Jacklin have employed various moot decision principles that importantly shape the conclusions drawn; and (3) in a sequence of surveying the literature, abstracting findings, tallying results, and then formulating conclusions, various "slippages" have occurred that sometimes are of appreciable consequence. Each of these points will be developed briefly here; an extended and documented critique is available elsewhere (Block, J. H. "Assessing sex differences: Issues, problems, and pitfalls." *Merrill-Palmer Quarterly*, 1976, *22* (4).)

Attenuating Factors Affecting the Empirical Base on Which Conclusions About Sex Differences Depend

Maccoby and Jacklin included all studies uncovered in their bibliographic search because "... there was no reasonable basis for selecting some studies and excluding others" (p. 11). Accordingly, there is wide variation in the quality of the data base. The statistical power of studies contributing to their conclusions ranges widely; more than one-third of the comparisons between the sexes are based on total samples of 60 or less and about one-fifth of the comparisons involve total samples of less than 40. In many studies, unreliability of measures is an attenuating factor; to the extent that sex differences are assessed using undependable scores, true differences between the sexes will go undetected. The conceptual quality of psychological measures used to assess sex differences has often been ignored; the absence of sex differences when evaluated by casually constructed, construct-invalid measures does not mean that differences would not emerge when appropriate measures are used. The inconsistency characterizing findings in many areas is often a function of these psychometric and methodological deficiencies.

Empirical inquiry into sex differences has often been essentially unfocused and accidental, investigators being less interested in sex differences per se than in the interrelation-

from *I'm Not for Women's Lib ... But,* copyright bülbül 1976, Arachne
Publishing, Mountain View, CA. 94040

---

ships among variables. In such studies, measures often are selected precisely because they have controlled for sex or have not demonstrated sex differences in other research contexts. Sex differences are tested with the hope that their *absence* will justify merging samples of males and females and will simplify analysis and reporting of results. In the absence of a conceptual rationale for expectable divergence, these studies burden the literature with null findings of inconsequential import. Maccoby and Jacklin note the incidental quality of many sex differences and suggest that the time has come for studies guided by explicit hypotheses derived from considered conceptual schemas. However, in the meantime, it must be recognized that the empirical data base with respect to sex differences is unrepresentative in ways that cannot be well assessed.

The empirical literature on sex differences also reflects great unevenness in the representation of various age groups. Of the studies contributing to the Maccoby and Jacklin conclusions, 75 percent are based on research participants 12 years old or younger; almost 40 percent derive from studies of preschool children. Other investigators have reported evidence for increasing sex differentiation with age and, guided by this insight, I examined the Maccoby and Jacklin conclusions from this perspective. When the studies cited by the authors are sorted according to the age of the participants into three categories—infancy through age 4, ages 5 through 12, and age 13

and over—the percentage of comparisons showing clear and significant sex differences shows marked increase over time, from 37 percent in the earliest period, to 47 percent in the middle period, and to 55 percent in the oldest age group. This trend is even more striking if studies based on small samples are excluded. Conclusions about the existence of sex differences thus depend upon the age mix in the set of studies being examined, a recognition that importantly tempers the Maccoby and Jacklin evaluations based predominantly on samples of preadolescent children.

The Evaluational Framework of Maccoby and Jacklin

The authors have taken pains to indicate the decision rules and methodological values guiding their evaluational and integrative effort. But other decisions and values might as reasonably have been applied, resulting in very different summary conclusions. It is instructive to indicate how the reasonable but debatable decisions of Maccoby and Jacklin may have contributed to their conclusions.

In organizing research data, the conceptual rubric or classification scheme employed by the research collators takes on critical significance. When research results achieved with a variety of instruments tapping different phenomena are brought together in order to assess the coherence of the empirical evidence surrounding a particular construct such as impulsivity or empathy or achievement emphasis or breaking set, what conceptual criteria shall be used to categorize the existing studies? Categories can be defined too broadly as, for example, in the achievement domain where Maccoby and Jacklin bring together some twelve indicators of parental pressures for achievement, such as praise, criticism, parental standards for intellectual performance, expectations of household help, educational goals set for the child, anxious intrusions into the child's performance, and so on. Although many of these measures clearly relate to the achievement dimension, others, lacking both construct and discriminant validity, are readily challengeable. Anxious interference and criticisms, for example, could be construed readily as indicators of maternal anxiety or impatience or intrusiveness rather than as indices of achievement emphasis. With such heterogeneous measures, it is not surprising that Maccoby and Jacklin found little difference between the sexes in the socialization pressures experienced.

Organizing rubrics also can be defined in ways that may be too limited. Thus, for example, Table 3.9 (Impulsivity, Lack of Inhibition) consists of 37 between-sex comparisons of which 28 are accounted for by the Matching Familiar Figures Test (or its variant, the Design Recall Test), Delay of Gratification tasks, and the Motor Inhibition Test. Although Maccoby earlier defined impulsivity more broadly to include distractability, activity level, lack of persistence, temper tantrums, and aggressiveness, here the authors have chosen a more restricted, cognition-emphasizing definition. Many personologists would consider their present definition too limited and would conceptualize impulsivity more broadly to encom-

pass noncognitive aspects as well. With a broader view of impulsivity, the conclusions of Maccoby and Jacklin would change.

Finally, classification rubrics can be established that combine conceptually disparate behaviors. For example, in evaluating sex differences with regard to the ability to "break set" or restructure, the authors consider together *both* responses to problems requiring insight for solution (e.g., the Luchins' water-jar problem) *and* responses to the word game Anagrams, a "... task calling for breaking set in a verbal context ..." (p. 103). Although both insight problems and anagrams require a recombination of stimulus elements for solution, the cognitive task demands involved in classical insight problems are fundamentally different from those involved in anagram solution. Combining these two measures enables Maccoby and Jacklin to conclude that "... it is by no means demonstrated that boys excel on tasks calling for restructuring or breaking set ..." (p. 132). Had they kept separate the two kinds of studies, it would be noted that males score significantly higher on insight problems (12 of 14 comparisons; no significant differences on two) while females score higher on 4 of 10 comparisons involving anagram task performance (with the remaining 6 comparisons showing no significant sex differences). By combining these two conceptually disparate tasks, Maccoby and Jacklin arrive at a different conclusion about sex differences in breaking set than are suggested by the task-separated data.

Obviously, theoretical preferences guide one's choice of a conceptual rubric and I do not mean to suggest that Maccoby and Jacklin have been wrong in their selections. I do mean to emphasize that other, no less rigorous, classification schemata would result in a different organization of the available empiricism and issue conclusions of a very different sort.

A second consequential decision was to "emphasize the null hypothesis." The inferential inadequacy of the null hypothesis approach and its tendency to mislead interpretation of data have long been recognized. To avoid the "hopeless inconsistency" generated by the significant-nonsignificant dichotomy (a strategy central to the Maccoby and Jacklin analysis), such statisticians as Cronbach recommend the reporting of descriptive data and the use of confidence intervals to provide a proper interpretative perspective. The interpretative perspective is distorted also when Maccoby and Jacklin enter the word "None" in the "Difference" column of their tables and use expressions like "unfounded beliefs" and "myths" in their summary evaluations of data bases yielding inconsistent findings with respect to sex differences. In these several ways, inconclusive results are transformed into strongly stated negative results.

A methodological preference running through the Maccoby and Jacklin volume is a preference for "objective" data and a disenchantment with ratings because of their vulnerability to stereotypes. In their concluding chapter, they note:

> We have repeatedly encountered the problem that so-called "objective" measures of behavior yield different results than ratings or self-reports. Ratings are notoriously subject to shifting anchor points.... For example, in one study, teachers rated each child in their class on activity level; the boys received higher average ratings; but "actometer" recordings for the same group of children did not show the boys to be engaging in

more body movement. Obviously, the possibility exists that teachers are noticing and remembering primarily the behavior that fits their stereotypes. (p. 356).

Their interpretation of this study is worth close inspection. In this research, Loo and Wenar found that teacher ratings of activity based on long-term observations of children in many different contexts were sex discriminating while a *single* mechanical recording of activity in the classroom situation was not. The low reliability of actometer scores is well

known and, indeed, was acknowledged by the investigators. For this reason, most actometer studies use several different time samplings of activity and, under these conditions, the more reliable activity scores typically reveal sex dif-

ferences. Further, Maccoby and Jacklin's stereotype interpretation of the rating results is directly challenged by a study cited in their Annotated Bibliography (Halvorsen & Waldrop) in which composited actometer scores correlated highly with teachers' ratings of activity-related variables. So, the example introduced by Maccoby and Jacklin to support their view has a more parsimonious explanation.

The second study construed by the authors as evidence for stereotypes (Meyer & Sobieszek) provides no such support since the critical analysis of variance issued *no* differences even approaching statistical significance.

Certainly, stereotypes are a problem in the scientific evaluation of sex differences and their influence must be carefully weighted. Rather than giving precedence to one kind of data over another, however, the inferential adequacy of *all* kinds of data must be evaluated closely. The preferences of Maccoby and Jacklin have led them to minimize or even to dismiss findings that would importantly modify some of their conclusions.

Slippages in the Evaluational Sequence

It is inevitable, in so extended and complicated an effort, that errors, omissions, and other deficiencies will occur. Inevitability accepted, it is nevertheless imperative that such inaccuracies be few and of small import. It is therefore a most unhappy responsibility to have to report finding more flaws in the documentation and interpretation of Maccoby and Jacklin than are, I believe, acceptable in a reference volume. Only a sampling of the "slippages" I happen to have encountered can be presented here.

Some studies published within the designated time span of the search for studies of sex differences were not included in the Annotated Bibliography. Errors of this kind are inescapable and difficult to estimate or to evaluate for their significance. More immediately serious is the question of the sufficiency of the research summaries in the Annotated Bibliography. These summaries are sometimes erroneous and with some frequency fail to include mention of significant interactions with sex, do not recognize the existence of consistent trends over several studies conducted by an investigator, and do not record clear differences in the patterning of relationships as a function of sex. Thus, a study by Cruse of children at four ages is summarized as finding significant sex differences at only two age levels. In fact, the original article reveals a significant main effect for sex; between-sex comparisons at each of the separate age levels are *not* reported and are not inferrable from the data. A study on childhood accidents (Manheimer & Mellinger) is tersely summarized with the statement, "boys' accident rate was higher than girls" (p. 533). The original article reveals that, in a sample of almost 9,000 successive admissions to an emergency room, boys had significantly more accidents at *every* age level between 4 and 18 years and that accident frequency *increased* with age for boys and *decreased* with age for girls. Such information adds immeasurably to the power and implicativeness of these findings. A study by Staub is reported as showing no sex differences; the original article reveals strikingly significant differences between boys and girls in the *pattern* of relationships among variables.

A second source "slippage" is the omission

of relevant studies included in the Annotated Bibliography from the tables organized according to topical areas. Thus, I happened to encounter nine studies pertinent to Activity Level that were not tabled; in *each* of these nine studies, males were significantly more active.

Omissions were found to be a consequential problem in other tables as well. Table 7.5, Compliance with Adult Requests and Demands, omits eight studies from the Annotated Bibliography and Table 4.5, Curiosity and Exploration, also omits eight studies related to environmental exploration that I noted in the Annotated Bibliography. Inclusion of these studies changes the nature of the conclusions to be drawn about sex differences in activity level, compliance, and curiosity. There does not appear to be a rationale for these, and other exclusions since, in most instances, the omitted studies employed dependent measures similar (or even identical) to those tabled. Obviously, the clerical work involved in sorting and tabling studies was enormous and some error was unavoidable. What is unfortunate, however, is that the overlooked studies in some cases seem to change importantly the tenor of the conclusions.

Discrepancies between discussion in the text and tabled results represent a third source of "slippage" in the Maccoby and Jacklin volume. For example, the authors conclude that differences found in general intellectual abilities between ages 2 and 7 usually favor girls but urge caution in interpreting this finding since "the higher scores of girls tend to be found in studies of 'disadvantaged' children" (p. 65). The data referenced (Table 3.1) contain 18 between-sex comparisons in the 2 to 7 years age range. Six of these 18 studies involved "disadvantaged" samples and of these, 2 or 33 percent found girls scoring significantly higher. Twelve of the 18 studies were based on middle-class samples and of these, 4 or 33 percent found girls scoring significantly higher. Since these percentages are identical, the attribution of the observed trends to the "disadvantaged" origin of some samples is quite unjustified.

In summarizing the findings on task confidence and locus of control, Maccoby and Jacklin note "... a tendency for young women of college age to lack confidence in their ability to do well on a new task, and their sense that they have less control over their own fates than men do. These trends are not seen among *older or younger women*" (p. 359; italics added). Reference to the relevant tables for the basis of this implicative relationship raises some disconcerting questions. Table 4.8, Task Confidence, suggests that the sex difference noted at college age extends downward as well since 2 of the 3 between-sex comparisons at younger ages (7 to 14 years) find boys more confident. Table 4.9, Locus of Control, includes 12 comparisons of younger subjects; no sex differences were found in 8 of these 12 studies, suggesting that conclusions about locus of control at younger ages are, at best, equivocal. Now, consider the evidence for the assertion that differences in confidence and perceived control are not sex differentiating among adults beyond college age. Neither of the two tables includes *any* comparisons of adult men or women over the age of 21. Thus, there are no empirical grounds for the authors' assertions that "these trends are not seen among older or younger women."

Variation in the standards of evidence used to evaluate the aggregated findings surrounding a particular data base represents a final kind of "slippage" affecting conclusions about sex differences. Maccoby and Jacklin use a "box-scoring" approach to tally the results of studies within a domain according to those favoring males, favoring females, and finding no significant sex differences. Depending upon the balance of significant/nonsignificant findings, conclusions about sex differences are drawn. Thus, for sex differences said by Maccoby and Jacklin to be "well established," females score higher in 28 percent of the studies of verbal ability, males score higher on 9 percent, and the remaining 63 percent of the studies yield no significant sex difference. For spatial abilities, males score higher in 39 percent of the studies and females in 5 percent; for quantitative ability, males score higher in 46 percent of the studies and females in 11 percent; and for aggressivity, males score higher in 55 percent of the studies and females in 5 percent. But compare these percentages for "well-established" findings to the percentages characterizing "equivocal" results—for example, activity level where, including the omitted studies, males score higher in 41 percent of the studies and females in 5 percent; or dominance where, including studies omitted, males score higher in 42 percent of the studies and females in 4 percent; or compliance where females score higher in 50 percent of the studies and males in none. Shall we conclude with Maccoby and Jacklin that sex differences are "unfounded with respect to self-esteem when males score higher in 73 percent of the tabled studies of task confidence and females in none; or in insight problems requiring restructuring where males score higher in 86 percent of the studies and females in none? And what shall we conclude about curiosity when, including omitted studies, males score higher in 48 percent of the studies and females in 14 percent? As this sampling indicates, there is wide variability in the criteria Maccoby and Jacklin used to evaluate sex differences.

Tracking a Conclusion Back to the Original Data

In previous sections, examples of "slippage" have been reported more or less in isolation. But errors can compound, their cumulative effect thus distorting seriously our understandings of sex differences. Consider, for example, the authors' comment in their summary chapter regarding "instances in [their] review where a difference was evident only briefly, during a limited age period. This appears to be true, for example, on certain measures of 'impulsivity' where boys are more impulsive only during the preschool years" (p. 357). What is the basis for this assertion regarding male impulsivity during the preschool period?

This summary statement was heralded in an earlier interpretation, this time employing a more restricted notion of 'impulsivity": "The reader may recall that this is the age [i.e., preschool] at which boys were found to be more 'impulsive' in the sense that they were less able than girls to wait for a delayed, more attractive reward" (pp. 144–45).

This interpretation in turn may be traced back still further to the authors' discussion of the tabled evidence for sex differences in impulsivity: "As may be seen in Table 3.9, there is *some* [italics added] evidence that boys are more impulsive on this measure [delay of gratification] during the preschool years ..." (p. 101).

Reference to Table 3.9 reveals three studies employing the delay of gratification paradigm with preschool children, two studies based on samples of largely black, lower SES children yielding no significant sex differences and one study by Mischel and Underwood (1973) in which a significant sex difference was found.

The original article by Mischel and Underwood cites three other investigations conducted by Mischel and his associates studying preschool children with a similar experimental paradigm. Mischel and Moore (1973) found no significant sex differences; two remaining studies made no mention of testing for sex differences. The Mischel and Moore study should have been picked up by the research scan of Maccoby and Jacklin but was neither tabled nor included in the Annotated Bibliography.

Thus, Maccoby and Jacklin's willingness to attribute greater impulsivity to boys during the preschool years is predicated upon the results of only one study together with neglect of the findings from three other studies. A single, unreplicated result based upon a specific and narrow experimental paradigm (waiting time for a preferred reward) has, through an erosion of qualifications, been converted to a positive conclusion about age-limited sex differences in "impulsivity." More substantial standards of evidence would seem to be required before such a conclusion is warranted.

In Summary

This is a monumental yet ambivalence-inducing book. The authors' discussion of problems besetting research on sex differences is perceptive; their identification of areas of psychological functioning that have been underresearched or where findings appear especially inconsistent should encourage investigators toward fruitful new studies; their developmental perspectives, embodied in their discussion of the acquisition of sex-role concepts, extend previous theorizing. By systematizing and ordering, by raising questions both incisive and intriguing, Maccoby and Jacklin have generated new and provocative hypotheses about sex-role development and have helped move the study of sex differences toward the necessary next stage of scientific investigation, by hypothesis testing. These are consequential contributions.

But insofar as the book is viewed as a reference work, large problems surround it. The long, arduous, complicated evaluation process undertaken by the authors in their effort to impose organization upon a sprawling, unruly body of data is vulnerable to error and reasonable argument at every step along the way. Readers seeking the state of knowledge regarding sex differences will find the book a valuable entry point into the literature, but they will need to be selective in accepting its conclusions.

Martha T. Shuch Mednick

Psychology of Women: Research Issues and Trends

I would like to remind you that the theme of this lecture series was Psychology: The State of the Art. The speaker was requested not to do a typical review or survey, but to be critical and evaluate the discipline "in terms of the basic premises of research and theory, where current approaches are leading and how they could be extended or changed in order to improve the state of research." The task is to organize and integrate, to climb the mountain of reprints, preprints, technical reports, books, and other accumulated wisdoms, look at the vista, and prepare a map or guide for the future. Maybe the analogy of a forest would have been better, or even a jungle, because that is how it has seemed as the literature has accumulated. Everyone and her brother is tossing the sex variable into the data-eating machines, and the task of selecting and assessing the significant themes is indeed a formidable undertaking.

My first point about the state of the art is that it is young and at a developmental stage, in which important elements of the big picture may not be visible. I also think some disorder and conceptual untidiness can be tolerated at this stage, simply because lack of orthodoxy and a freedom from pressure to conform to any particular mold can stimulate new ideas and set directions that investigators would not otherwise take.

Another point is one that is an intrinsic part of our area of study, one I value and would not want to lose. We are composed of a variety of fields. Everyone working in this area was trained or is being trained in one of the well-established fields of psychology and has chosen to apply her or his expertise to the study of women. Thus the diversity of the work in this field reflects interest and training in most of the conceptual and methodological domains of the discipline. Moreover, it is basic as well as applied and academic as well as professional. This makes us very rich and enhances productivity and creativity but makes any state of the art assessment unusually challenging.

What follows then is simply my view of what has happened, what is happening, and some hopes for future happenings.

Psychology of Women and Feminist Thought

There is a new psychology of women. It has developed hand in hand with political feminism, and the intellectual concerns of the field continue to reflect feminist thought. Of course the atmosphere of the movement made women's issues salient. However, more important and of greater significance for the study of women, and for psychology, is that feminist ideology has led to a reevaluation of existing theory and research, to a questioning of basic assumptions, and to analyses that have demonstrated how each aspect of our discipline has supported a functional social mythology about women.

The major questions raised by feminist analyses are the following.

1. What are the fundamental assumptions that a discipline has concerning the *true* nature of women and how have these assump-

For by her unconsciousness, woman exerts a magical influence on man, a charm that lends her power over him. Because she feels this power instinctively and does not wish to lose it, she often resists to the utmost the process of becoming conscious. . . . Many men take pleasure in woman's unconsciousness. They are bent on opposing her development of greater consciousness in every possible way, because it seems to them uncomfortable and unnecessary.

Emma Jung, *Animus and Anima*, 1957

---

tions affected methodology, conceptualization, and application of knowledge?

2. What substantive areas have been neglected and how has this affected our knowledge of women—and of men?

3. How has neglect of the study of women affected the discipline in general?

The explicit agenda of feminist research on women also includes a specific set of changes in the personal and social arena. Therefore such research must not merely generate new knowledge but also focus on how to use this knowledge to attain the sociopolitical and personal changes that are congruent with feminist goals.*

Feminist scholarship is no longer tied to political feminism; the intellectual movement has acquired functional autonomy. The evidence of this is in the wealth of scholarly work that is appearing in numerous disciplines.[1-3] Many references are available, and anyone who has had a chance to read the first issues of the new journal *Signs*[4] has had a taste of this healthy, productive scholarship.

It has been documented by feminist scholars in many fields that women have been either studied very selectively, i.e., in domains that are defined as those of women, or that they are entirely ignored. Each field has its euphemism for the study of women: in psychology it has been Sex Differences, in sociology it is Marriage and the Family, and Sex Roles. Jean Lipman-Blumen and Ann Tickamyer's[5] analysis of fifteen years of research on Sex Roles concludes that it was in fact only the study of the female role, and that this has been sociology's female ghetto. In history and literature women were rendered invisible. Even histories of families were written without any attention to their women members.[6] For example, a recent book on the Jewish immigrant talks only about fathers and sons; the women, as is well known, were not part of the real action. Philosophy is explicit in its *exclusion* of women from theories of "human nature."[7, 8] It is shocking to discover that even Sartre was not enough affected by his alliance with de Beauvoir to include women in his grand theory.

George Bernard Shaw in *An Intelligent Woman's Guide to Socialism and Capitalism*[9] said, "All books on socialism are addressed to men. You might read a score of them without even discovering that such a creature as a woman ever existed." He would probably say the same about our esteemed APA journals— even today, in 1976.

---

*If anyone has problems about this as being unscientific, unpsychological, or too political, let me note that every psychological theory talks about change, any model of "adjustment" implies personal change, and a vast amount of recent psychological research has been oriented toward trying to propose ways of changing people's attitudes and behaviors. This is political.

Being an incomplete female, the male spends his life attempting to complete himself, to become female . . . by constantly seeking out, fraternizing with, and trying to live through and fuse with the female, and by claiming as his own all female characteristics—emotional strength and independence, forcefulness, dynamism, decisiveness, . . . etc.—and projecting onto women all male traits—vanity, frivolity, triviality, weakness, etc. It should be said, though, that the male has one glaring area of superiority over the female—public relations. (He has done a brilliant job of convincing millions of women that men are women and women are men.)

Valerie Solanis, *SCUM Manifesto*, 1967–1968

I refer to the work in other disciplines to show that similar feminist critiques have appeared in numerous intellectual areas and that the themes and goals outlined above are apparent in all of these. How these themes have affected the research in our own field will become clearer as we discuss some of our general and specific concerns.

Defining the New Psychology of Women

As I suppose is usually true of developing fields, the matter of definition is in and of itself an issue.[10,11] How has the new psychology of women been defined? In a review appearing in the second volume of *Signs*, Reesa Vaughter[12] states:

> The psychology of women is concerned with the construction of a psychology that is relevant to women, as well as to men; that studies women, as well as men; that employs methodology that is appropriate, meaningful, and congruent with the lives of women as well as men's; that develops theories that predict female, as well as male, behavior; and that studies questions that are of interest to women as well as to men. In brief, the goal of the psychology of women is the development of a non-sexist science, a psychology of human behavior.

It sounds like an eventual self-destruct, but not a bad way to go. Indeed this is very apt as a description of the concerns of many who are at work in the field.

Psychology of women is to some extent being defined pragmatically, its boundaries determined by what is being done. In line with my earlier comments, I think we should avoid overly restrictive definitions so that the psychology of women can continue to serve as an umbrella and catalyst for a diverse group of investigators, theoreticians, and practitioners. However, some more specific definitions can be and have been proposed. These focus forthrightly on the point that we are concerned with the study of *women*, on intragroup and life-cycle variations, and on the study of uniquely female experiences.[13-16] Women have always been studied as a reflection of man, from a masculine point of view, and in the service of the study of man's world. We are changing this androcentric bias, looking at woman in her own right and not as "other"; as more than a satellite revolving around the male personification of the universe. Moreover, since most of the work is pursuing directions stimulated by questioning of social institutions, i.e., of the environment that has fostered the neglect and distortion, the field is social-psychological in the broadest sense of that term. This means a shift from the theoretical models that focus only on intrapsychic variables.

A few comments are in order about the relationship of this field to traditional research on sex differences. Sex comparisons are, of course, not to be ignored, and are in fact being made in numerous new areas. Those who wish to avoid controversy, fear sex-segregation and so-called ghettoization, or, for other reasons, deny that there is a separate field, argue that this is "just" sex-difference research. If that is the case, then every question we ask about girls and women would be answerable only by a comparison with boys and men. Apart from what I have already said about the need to focus on intragroup variations and on the unique female experience, an underlying assumption of the study of sex differences is that biological sex is a variable that carries with it certain fixed properties and that these comparative studies will tell us the *true* nature of the male and female of that species.

In her historical analysis of the psychology of women, Stephanie Shields[17] has shown the origin of concerns about comparing the sexes, in efforts to document myths about woman's inferiority, and hence to justify her inferior social status and unequal treatment. The eyes that examined these "differences" just as those that examined race "differences" were not those of value-free, objective scientists. They at least wore blinders—if they were not "aware" of their bias, all the worse since this postponed urgently needed questioning of the basic assumptions of their science.

The data on sex differences continues to be used unjustifiably to make policy decisions about women, particularly with regard to education and employment. The perilous nature of such a course has been discussed by Tangri,[18] who notes that the sex-difference literature is replete with methodological problems and numerous contradictions. This is further attested to by Sherman's[19] and Block's[20] critical analyses of the Maccoby and Jacklin[21] summary of sex-difference research. While both agree that the summary and bibliography are useful, the conclusions and inferences drawn in this widely referenced book are open to serious question. In any event, such research can be only one of various approaches to the psychology of women.

Current Issues and Research

Turning to a very general and selective view of what is now happening with regard to the psychological study of women, I detect three broad classes of work. These can be ordered on a continuum of opportunism. The first category—and although I can't provide hard data, it is my impression that this is the most productive and influential aspect of the field, and the least opportunistic—is that directly or indirectly stimulated by concern with feminist issues.[22]

The second set includes studies that involve information-gathering expeditions in a variety of areas. This is not entirely opportunistic, because the research may reflect practical needs. For example, there are questions concerning personnel psychologists in this era of affirmative action,[23,24] or those in the military: what are we going to do with those women once they get here, what if they cry? Or, some psychologists have simply become interested and curious about what does happen when women are added into the little behavior equations they have been fiddling with for all these years. In some areas, e.g., achievement motivation research, there is now a big scramble to see who can answer the puzzle first.

Finally, and several of my students have

noted this as they've helped me search the literature, there is a class of work that is blatantly opportunistic, and it's called "Let's see if everything we always knew about people applies to women." So under the continuing publish-or-perish pressure and the "hot topic" "get in on the fad" mentality, everyone is doing it.

As you may have guessed, I am most interested in the first category of work. I won't argue that useful information cannot be generated in the other contexts, but I am willing to argue that the value of the work will be inversely related to this little continuum.

Feminist Critiques

The study of the new psychology of women has produced an important series of critiques that attack the status quo and demand revision.[25-28,30] The sum of this work is that psychology has been a weapon for keeping woman in her place; it has perpetuated the myth of woman as a victim of her biology. If you think this view has changed in recent years, I urge you to pick up a delightful opus by David McClelland.[29] He has brought us Power—a whole bookful of it, including a chapter on Power and the Feminine Role—forced, I imagine, by the publisher, who highlights it in his blurb (and made *me* buy the book). The chapter is a slight update of an oldie he wrote in the sixties for a pre-revolutionary—that is, 1776—compendium of women. This is all a prelude to saying that the more it changes, the more they stay the same. I won't tell you what he says about women and power. He talks a lot about his mother-in-law and other female relations. What I do want to tell you is that this is the only chapter in

which biology is mentioned. And the last chapter is one about why men make war, and everyone knows that biology has nothing to do with that.

Psychology has also depicted women as incompetent, incapable of abstract thinking, passive, inferior—in short, deservedly powerless victims. None of the areas of psychology has escaped this discouraging assessment. Weisstein's[25] classic piece focused on the work of personologists and clinicians. Miriam Kieffer[26] has written in a similar vein about social psychology. She offered a compelling example of the wipe-out of women by the "liberals" in this field from the work of Gordon Allport. In the one paragraph devoted to women in his book *The Nature of Prejudice,* "Allport indicates that sex-grouping remains important throughout the life of such people as misogynists, but says '. . . for many people this "war of the sexes" seems totally unreal. They do not find in it ground for prejudice.' (p. 33)." Kieffer also notes that a chapter in Allport's book is titled "Traits Due to Victimization" and mentions blacks, Jews, and homosexuals, but *not* women. Although Hacker wrote about women's marginality in an attempt to close this conceptual gap in the classic work on prejudice, her effort did not have much impact when it first appeared. Kieffer describes several early efforts to develop antiwoman attitude measures, but such work received very little attention prior to 1970.

Helson's[27] review of research on attitudes about women who pursue careers serves a similar critical function. She noted that the professional and popular opinion that career women were maladjusted, unhappy creatures was bolstered by biased interpretations of biased data, and had a tenacious grasp on the thinking of many researchers in the field. A book published in 1968 was characterized by her as illustrative of psychologists' views of career women. The main purpose of this book, called *Developing Woman's Potential*, was to "document the restrictions placed on women's intellectual and vocational aspirations. However, the author, Edwin C. Lewis,[30] persists in the belief, presumably based on evidence, that girls who aim for careers are likely to be frustrated and dissatisfied with themselves, less well adjusted, and have poorer self-concepts than those who choose to become housewives" (p. 36). It is noteworthy that Lewis reveals his blatant bias in his own prefatory remarks:

> I believe I have an advantage, as a man, in writing about women. Most books and articles about women have been written by women, and many have been justifiably criticized for being too emotional and biased. It is difficult, and perhaps impossible, for a female writer to be objective in discussing women's roles. In many cases, their views and arguments are in support of their own role, and perhaps are an attempt to justify it. The result may be interesting but not *objective* [italics added]. In any case, . . . I wish to emphasize . . . that my being a man should be of secondary concern. I am writing as a psychologist and I hope my views will be judged on that basis. (preface, p. viii).

Can anyone imagine a woman making a similar statement in her preface to her book "Psychology, the Study of Man"?

Helson* provides us with another useful analysis in her review of creativity research.[28]

In no other area has woman been rendered more invisible, and this is a most literal illustration of the effects of a belief in an immutable biological imperative. Women, it was said, have no need to be creative, since they perform the ultimate creative act. Her review of this area goes right to the heart of the problem. She indicts the phallocentrism of the field and demonstrates how investigators concerned themselves only with creative men and masculine areas of interest, or with the question of why women are *not* creative. Helson found creative women—her own creativity is reflected in her description of her hunt for these invisible persons. She attacks social mythology, presents a perspective analysis of the influence of social climate on an entire field of research, and demonstrates that data are simply ignored when they fly in the fact of cherished belief.

Critiques have also focused on methodology. McKenna and Kessler[31] surveyed several hundred articles published on "attraction" and "aggression" which had used only male or only female subjects. They demonstrated how bias in design placed limits on the type of knowledge acquired. Women and men used in these "objective" experimental studies were treated in dramatically different ways. The independent variables used with women were less likely to involve active treatment or arousal (e.g., no shock). Furthermore, the dependent measures were unlikely to involve active responding. In a related study, Prescott and Foster[32] interviewed experimenters and found that choice of sex of population was related to the subject matter of the study and reflected sex stereotyping. Thus, psychologists study physical aggression between men, attraction between men and women, and hesitate to use women in arousal studies because

---

*I must note that Helson is one of the few women who has done research in this area and the only psychologist who has conducted programmatic research on creative women. Since she has done this for at least fifteen years, she must have found a few.

"I frankly could not bring myself to do this with college girls." They assert that females are too variable and thus mess up the research (they call it noise) and attribute it to hormones, no doubt! They say it is unethical to expose females to aversive stimulation. But not for men? It is thus apparent that we have biased knowledge in many areas of psychology because of stereotypic beliefs that affect our seemingly objective methodology.

A series of papers originally prepared for a workshop and to be published in a volume of which Julia Sherman and Florence Denmark[33] are coeditors, were addressed to a wide range of women's research topics and generated questions for future research in each area. In addition to content specific themes, common issues emerged. First of all, each of the writers talked about the *absence* of research addressed to what they saw as important issues for women. This was true in heavily discussed and researched areas such as achievement,[34-37] sex roles,[38] female sexuality,[39] and the reproductive cycle,[40] as well as in those which have received less attention such as power,[34,41] creativity,[28] and the study of women in groups.[41]

A second common theme was that research in these substantive areas had not been viewed in a social, political, and cultural context and that this was needed. Third, in each area it was shown how assumptions about the role of women had guided theory, empirical thought, and methodology.

Review of Recent Research

With respect to the current substantive concerns of the field, the results of my unscientific scan of recent literature, of papers delivered at meetings and those that appear out of thin air via the informal network, indicate that the most heavily researched and discussed area continue to be sex roles and sex identity, the study of achievement, and mental health and therapy. Reesa Vaughter's[12] more systematic survey of the research of 1975 confirms this. I will discuss only some aspects of two of these areas as illustrations of attempts to close the knowledge gap.

The psychological study of sex roles and sex identity is the general rubric under which I classify all the work on sex-role stereotyping and sex bias and its effects, sex identity, studies of masculinity, femininity, and psychological androgyny, and sex-role attitudes, values, and behavior.

Psychologists have talked and theorized and researched for years about what is variously termed gender or sex identity. Somewhere along the line a jump was made from the notion that the sexes develop a core sense of male or female identity to the idea that "masculinity" and "femininity" were traits that could be measured by asking for self-descriptions of various sorts. Fundamental to the development of these measures and concepts was the assumption that women and men and also femininity and masculinity are opposites and not mutually exclusive, and MF emerged as a unidimensional concept, of course to be measured on a single scale.

The superb methodological critique by Ann Constantinople[42] and theoretical discussions by Alice Rossi,[43] Rae Carlson,[44] and Ravenna Helson[45] presaged the work of Sandra Bem,[38,46] Jeanne Block,[47,48] Janet Spence et al.,[49] and several others[50] who in the past few years have begun to explore the notion that masculinity and femininity are separate dimensions. We now have a psychological conceptualization of a new kind of sex identity, androgyny. Coleridge said, "The truth is, a great mind *must* be an-

If, as the girls always said, it's never too early to think about whom to marry, then it could certainly not be too early to think about who to be. Being somebody had to come first, because, of course, somebody could get a much better husband than nobody.

Alix Kates Shulman, Memoirs of an Ex-Prom Queen, 1972

---

drogynous," and, as Ravenna Helson[45] has noted, a balance of feminine and masculine intellectual and personal qualities appears basic to creative endeavor.

At least four new approaches[38,46,49,50] to the measurement of sex identity have been generated by this work, each gracing us with a new scale or a variation of an old one. As is usual when new measures are developed in psychology, people have begun the not very fruitful, at least for purposes of shedding light on the concept, business of churning out correlations with one or another of the scales and everything else. We will, in the next few years, have a lot of sorting out to do in this area.

Serious research on the meaning of the concept for male and female behavior in a wide range of situations is also undergoing intensive exploration. Sandra Bem[38] sees the androgyne as the "ideal personality" and has explicitly stated that her research interest stems from her feminist conviction that liberated sexual identity is an ideal goal for women and men.

I am concerned that the popular connotative meaning of the term androgyny is not the same as its intended meaning—that the best of female and male traits, values, and behaviors are available to both women and men, thus broadening their repertoire of competencies, behavioral options, and varieties of emotional and intellectual responsivity. Rather, it has been commonly interpreted in terms of women becoming like men. In this connection I have too often seen the slip in spelling where the "y" in gyn is changed to an "e" and the word becomes androgenous. Whatever we call it, however, this work does challenge the idea that men and women and masculinity and femininity are opposites, it clearly reflects a feminist perspective, and it is a topic that is now attracting great interest.

Another very significant issue in this area is with the absence of effort to spell out the process and implications of change. Most of these studies have demonstrated that androgynous types are better adjusted, have higher self-esteem, and have a broader range of competencies than those who are sex-typed, particularly the feminine types.[46-50] Some researchers have begun to look at antecedents of androgyny.[51] However, although all of the theoretical work and discussions of studies concur on the desirability of psychological androgyny or a balance of the masculine and feminine, a model for change has not been proposed.[52]

Of direct relevance to this issue of change are the numerous studies of sex-role attitudes and ideology, as well as those on stereotyping and sex bias. There is continued interest in how sex-role concepts, attitudes, and behav-

Have you got a doll that plays like Billie Jean King, thinks like Margaret Mead and talks out like Barbara Jordan?

from *Sugar Daddys a Sticky Myth*, copyright bülbül 1976, Arachne Publishing, Mountain View, CA. 94040

iors are socialized, developed, and maintained, and how these affect many areas of the behavior of women and of men.*

Although attitudes about selected aspects of women's roles have changed in recent years, the tenacity of sex-typed behaviors has been demonstrated again and again. Recent work has shown the subtlety of the socialization process. An example of this is revealed in a study by Rosenfeld, cited by Vaughter.[12] She demonstrated that toys played with by boys and girls, apart from being sex-typed in the usual sense, require children to engage in very different types of behaviors while playing. Boys' toys elicit a wider range of competencies than girls' toys, and both girls and boys showed greater response frequencies to boys' toys than to girls' toys. Other studies have shown that girls and boys tend to choose sex-typed toys when given a free choice. Taken together, this work demonstrates how the environment reinforces passivity, a narrow response repertoire, and fewer competencies in the girl. Such subtleties in the socialization process must be fully analyzed in order for an adequate model of role-change to be developed.

*See Vaughter's[12] review for a comprehensive summary of recent work in these areas.

The fascination and interest in the study of women and achievement also continues unabated. It stems from the question of why women do not fully utilize their intellectual potential. The area is broad and includes the study of achievement motivation and the whole gamut of achievement behavior such as the development of various competencies, educational attainment, career and occupational aspiration and development, and creativity.[53,54]

In a paper integrating and applying a wide array of research and theory on achievement to women and work, Judith Long Laws[37] demonstrated how stereotypic assumptions about women who work has produced a body of information that merely reinforces these beliefs. For example, the assumption is generally made that women are not serious workers, they are not "attached" to the labor force, not "motivated," and "work intermittently." This leads to different interpretations of the same *behavior* for women and men. Thus, when women leave jobs it is assumed that they are working intermittently and that this behavior is unrelated to career concerns; when men leave jobs it is assumed that they are pursuing career goals and it is seen as part of a normal process of career development.

Laws also notes that the usual assumption is that women who work are deviant. This leads

The creativity of woman finds its expression in the sphere of living, not only in her biological functions as mother but in the shaping of life generally, be it in her activity as educator, in her role as companion to man, as mother in the home, or in some other form. The development of relationships is of primary importance in the shaping of life, and this is the real field of feminine creative power.

Emma Jung, *Animus and Anima*, 1957

to an emphasis on the *why* of their deviance rather than to studies of factors that lead to success, satisfaction, and advancement in careers and jobs. Biases such as these pervade career interest and motivation literature. It is consciousness raising to note that girls and women are always asked if they plan to work, and if so, why; boys and men are never asked these questions. The finding, congruent with sex-role demands, that young girls say they don't plan to work and that if they do it will be temporary and at traditional jobs, leads directly to policies such as denying girls a full program of vocational education.[55] It also denies the facts, i.e., that most women will work because they have to and that they will do so during most of their adult years and, moreover, that the biased practice generated by biased research insures that they will be at an economic disadvantage for the rest of their lives.[56,57,92]

Research on the achievement motive reveals another instance of blunders based on such biases. Florence Denmark, Sandra Tangri, and Susan McCandless[34] have, in a survey of research and theory on the achievement motive, outlined the numerous problems of motivational research. When McClelland and Atkinson began their program of research on achievement motivation, they focused on intellectual competition, organizational skills, and *military* leadership ability. The measure they devised, and which has been since used to explore achievement motivation, was based on the themes of imaginative stories written in response to these instructions.

It quickly became apparent that the measure was not valid for women, although the issue of the irrelevance of the arousal instructions was not reflected upon until very recently.[34] Their attempts to study women in such a framework produced results that were so inconsistent and difficult to explain that a conscious decision was made to omit them. In 1958 Atkinson, McClelland, and their colleagues published the massive volume, *Motives in Action, Fantasy and Society*,[58] in which they summarized all the work done to that date. Here women were relegated to the often-quoted footnote reflecting the investigators' conclusion that women should not be studied, since they need approval and not success.

Let me say right now that I believe that everyone needs approval as well as all kinds of success, and to relegate one "need" or "motive" to women and another to men is patently ridiculous. Indeed, in an excellent review of the child development research in this area, Aletha Stein and Margaret Bailey[59] point out that the real issue has to do with the behaviors that receive social rewards. Of course, men don't seem to need approval for achievement, because by the time they have reached their college years, they have been approved of and indeed loved to pieces for their successful achievement endeavors; nor does it ever stop. After a while people start to pay them.

Women, on the other hand, have received less, or at best, inconsistent approval for independence, for competence, indeed for most achievement-related behavior. So at the point in life when one is thinking about a major

They have an extraordinary need of support when engaged in any activity directed outward, but are absolutely independent in such feeling and thinking as related to their inner life, that is to say, in their activity directed inward. Their capacity for identification is not an expression of inner poverty but of inner wealth.

Helene Deutsch, *The Psychology of Women,*
Vol. I, 1944–1945

field, of career choice, of what one will do for the rest of one's life, men and women have developed very different expectations about what is likely to happen for behaving in intellectually competent or achieving ways.

The research that began in the context of the new surge of interest has approached various aspects of achievement and has done so in a variety of ways. One that has attracted continuous attention is the fear of success (FOS). There continues to be an outpouring of studies on this concept. It also has "pop" popularity. The phenomenon of fear of success—its pervasion of the media and people's minds—is in itself worthy of some thought; in one day recently I read about it in the newspaper *and* heard it discussed on two TV shows and on the radio. It is an attractive idea because it is a simple explanation that fits very well with others' and self-conceptions of why women do not pursue success. Thus women and others can say: well, women avoid success because of these fears that are rooted in a disposition learned in early childhood, and it's very hard to change. Moreover, with an intrapsychic emphasis of this sort, the need for change in the social system, a more radical and difficult process, is deemphasized. Two recent reviews have stressed this as well as other conceptual and methodological problems in FOS research, and anyone contemplating research in this area should look at these.[60,61]

The usefulness of the concept is very much unresolved. There is no doubt that people express negative imagery about certain types of success,[60-62] that sex differences are not as

The Loge by Mary Cassatt; reprinted by permission of National Gallery of Art, Washington; Chester Dale Collection

clear-cut as they initially seemed,[53,62] and that these vary with such factors as sex-role attitudes,[63,64] type of school attended, scorer characteristics,[62] and race.[65,66] Moreover, how this type of verbal expression of negative attitudes and feelings about success is related to any aspect of achievement *behavior* is unclear.[67]

An approach that is generating almost as much interest and that appears to me to have greater potential for arriving at a model for

change in achievement behavior is the work on expectancy and causal attribution about success and failure. This approach regards expectancy level and causal attribution as mediators of the effects of success and failure on achievement behavior. Girls and women have generally shown a pattern of low expectancy and external attribution for success,[35,68] an apparent reflection of stereotypic views of females as less intelligent and less competent than males.

Expectancy level affects achievement behavior in a very direct way. For example, Gurin and Pruitt[69] examined the effect of expectancies on labor-market behavior. In an analysis of data on national samples, they found that, just as in the laboratory or with academic performance, women have much lower expectancies in the job situation than do men. What is most interesting and practically significant about these findings is that these low expectancies lead directly to less and also nonfunctional job-seeking behavior; women, for example, make fewer efforts than men to change jobs for the sake of advancement. This suggests that expectancies must be changed in order for more functional behavior to be learned.

However, attributions also appear to play a role in this process. If a successful accomplishment is followed by an attribution to an external factor such as "a lucky break," it is not likely to lead to increased expectancy levels or to *functional* achievement behavior. This low expectancy-negative attribution cycle has been discussed by Irene Frieze and her colleagues.[35,68]

In recent work, investigators have begun to stress the importance of examining how factors in the immediate situation and the larger social context affect the person. For example, studies have examined others' expectancies and attributional biases, how these influence reward allocation,[70] and how changes in such biases affect attributional patterns and, consequently, achievement behavior.[34] Individual differences, particularly in sex identity, sex-role attitudes, and achievement motivation also appear to moderate attributional patterns.[71,72] The model developing in this area is thus reflecting the social-psychological perspective I have stressed.

There is, of course, more that is happening in these and in other specific substantive areas. There are new approaches to the study of the reproductive process,[40] of fertility behavior,[22,73] of female sexuality,[39] of women's health issues,[74] and, of course, of therapy and mental health.[75,76] It does appear that in all of these areas we are moving to the revision demanded by the critiques, that there has been an expansion of what we know, and that interest continues to be high. Moreover, the spirit is one of excitement and furious activity, a marked contrast to the jaded quality of many of the agonized reappraisals we are hearing from other corners of psychology these days.[77-79]

Concerns for the Future

The last part of this article concerns hopes for future happenings. There are three items on my agenda. The first concerns women's issues that have been discussed in other contexts but that have not received adequate attention in our field. The second item has to do with suggestions for theoretical and empirical direction for the continued study of change in woman's role and status. Finally, I will say a few words about the impact of all of this on psychology.

Neglected Areas

I can actually generate a long list of missing data, but some stand out as particularly significant. The first concerns the psychological study of power. Chesler and Goodman[91] have said that women need power and money but that they will not even talk about either of these; these topics are more taboo to them than sex. Indeed, women in this field are extremely reluctant to come to grips with this issue, and it has not received the attention commensurate with its importance. There has been little study of the power structures within which we live and work and of modes of in-

fluencing the public world. In two major literature summaries, Unger[41] and Denmark et al.[34] discussed the relevance of psychological research on power to women and concluded, in part, that research on power and power motivation has focused on men and masculine spheres of activity. Moreover, studies of women and power have looked at the family and couple relationships.[41]

In her unique study of reactions to power strategies used by men and women, Johnson[93] found that the power styles women tend to use simply reinforce their helpless status; if a woman uses an effective style, she is called masculine, pushy, and aggressive. A double bind of this sort clearly precludes the development of behavior that might increase control and influence in the public arena.

As Denmark et al.[34] note in their discussion of power motivation, power is associated in our minds with evil and masculinity, and this may be why it is avoided by women. This does not, however, free women from the effects of power, since they are generally in submissive and powerless roles. We should bear this in mind when we raise questions about the values implicit in the suggestions I am making.

Turning to a totally different area, there has been surprisingly little attention to research on women's lives. I am referring here to life beyond the adolescent years, to the study of women's life cycle. The obvious biological

The Difference

It involves a simplicity,
the difference between men and women.
Women render from complexity
A simpler face.
For that, men think her simplistic.
But she is not.

It's a matter of living:
living equals people.
That is what you will find
when a woman draws the lines.

But do not think it stops there.
The lines are only possible
in the round
that holds them, buoying,
like a mother holds a child.

Grace Wade

events associated with reproduction have been studied only incompletely, and almost not at all in a sociocultural context. The misconceptions that thus direct research in these areas have been documented by Mary Parlee.[40] There is apparently no event between pregnancy and menopause, unless there are postpartum "problems." The focus on clinical populations has led to many misconceptions. This is illustrated in the research on menopause and the postmenopausal years. The studies that *have* been done reflect the attitudes of the professionals, virtually all of whom are men who see women as patients, as much as perhaps more than anything about the women themselves. The few studies of nonclinical populations, and cross-cultural research, indicate that the menopause per se is not a "problem" for most women, and that the biology of the occasion is far less important than other factors that characterize life at this time.[80–82] Certainly, this suggests that associating woman's psychological existence only to the biology of reproductive events cannot tell the whole story.

We also know very little about women's interpersonal lives. A book by Esther Harding[83] written in 1933/1975 is special in this regard. Her work has remained relatively obscure, perhaps because she is a Jungian as well as a woman writing about women. One does not have to accept her concepts to see the value of her work, particularly in terms of charting some directions in this area. She has a nonjudgmental posture about what is "right" or "wrong" as a way of life for women, and she attends to the varieties of intimate relationships that are possible. Her discussion of sources of satisfaction via various life styles and throughout the life cycle is a fruitful source of hypotheses for research and might well be read by therapists, too. Her focus is on intimacy and private life, and her view is cultural and abiological. Clearly, this too is an area that must be part of a psychology of women.

Finally, I must draw attention to the lack of research on black and other minority women. What is available is not based on data. When my student Saundra Murray and I[84] set out to look for a "literature" we encountered a vacuum. If women have been invisible in our field, these women may as well be said not to exist. At this point I will say only that it is clear that racism and sexism victimized these women[69] and placed them lowest on the scale of almost any social indicator that has been examined.

The Study of Sex-Role Change

Turning to some not very systematic thoughts on how to proceed with the study of sex-role change, my own work and, in particular, my reading of a broad range of research in many disciplines on women and achievement have convinced me that sex-role change is indeed at the heart of the matter. We are only beginning to examine the consequences of sex-typing from a psychological point of view, but many of these have long been visible in data from other disciplines and from cross-cultural studies. For example, we knew from sociological, anthropological, and economic analyses that women always worked, that the occupational world is rigidly sex-typed, that women's work, traits, and tasks are devalued and have little prestige, and that this is true everywhere in the world.[54,85,86]

The intransigence of sex-role behaviors has been anecdotally observed and also confirmed in cross-cultural research. We have learned from the kibbutz[87] and from the Scandinavian and Soviet[88] experiences that ideological commitment to equality and emancipation, long-term government-sponsored public campaigns, and institutional rearrangements such as day care are necessary but not sufficient effectors of lasting change.

We can understand why this is the case by realizing that many indicators of sex-role change are more apparent than real. Changed behaviors, such as more women working outside the home, or women doing "masculine" jobs, have usually been the result of contemporaneous factors that have created societal needs for women to assume these roles. Thus, during national crises[89,90] or when, as was the case in Finland and the Soviet Union, there is a drastic change in the sex ratio, or if anti-natalism becomes serious public policy, women are cycled into the work setting. In the context of a study of sex roles in the kibbutz,[89] I found that the performance of masculine work by women under "crisis" conditions was quite acceptable. But it was also clear that such events were temporary and did not reflect changed assumptions about the true nature of the role of men and women, nor about the relative value of the masculine and feminine domains. These observations have led me to conclude that a model for role change must include a description of a social-psychological process in which the important mediators are changed assumptions about sex-role behaviors and their value—i.e., the rewards associated with these behaviors.

I discussed earlier the issue of the subtle ways in which sex-typed behaviors are socialized. We need attention to such factors not only with respect to childhood socialization, but also with regard to how these behaviors continue to be maintained throughout life. For example, we hear a great deal about role models and the need for them. How much do we know about how this process operates and what the factors are that determine who will serve as a role model for any particular individual, for what class of behavior, and in what kind of situation?

We must also learn how and which aspects of the feminist movement have affected personal change. There has been much discussion about consciousness-raising groups and their effects on individuals, but we know very little about how involvement in such groups leads to and sustains personal change. The question has to be framed in terms of how the individual moves from a changed set of beliefs

BREAK IT TO HER GENTLY, RUFFLES AND LACE ARE NOT THE REAL ME.

Ms Meg series, copyright bülbül 1980, Arachne Publishing, Mountain View, CA. 94040

about her personal condition, to taking actions, and to developing a sustained pattern of new behaviors.

Breathes there in psychology a theoretical orientation that might provide the broad framework for this model?

Of course, I have a preference for a point of view that is free of assumptions about sex-related constraints on behavioral possibilities. A model involving reinforcement, expectancies, and attributions about reward or punishments, and a focus on behavioral outcomes seems most tenable. The behavior of those who control the rewards must also be systematically examined. This, it seems to me, is what is generally left out of behaviorists' formulas. But any model that does *not* include this as part of any analysis ultimately places total responsibility for change in the wrong place—on the victim.

Psychology and the New Psychology of Women

With respect to our relation to and impact on our discipline, I believe that what we are learning is indeed relevant to all people and can improve the discipline in the many ways suggested by the critiques. Adding women to psychology doesn't seem like a bad idea, nor does the elimination of sexism. At this time I do not see much evidence that we have made

a resounding impact. Scanning Annual Review of Psychology since 1973 was sobering; 1975 was a big year because that was the year of the first review of the psychology of women. I think the term "women" was in the index for the first time that year. However, even looking under "sex role," "sex differences," "mother," or "maternal" doesn't add a great deal for the previous years, or for 1976.

There has been little impact on those who are writing the texts or on the "big thinkers" in the field. For example, Buss,[77] in a recent paper on the sociology of psychological knowledge, argues that knowledge and theory arise within a social context and are conditioned by social forces. He notes, and provides numerous examples of this, that there is a growing army of psychologists who implicitly practice the sociology of knowledge. Maybe it was the army metaphor that helped him to ignore all of the feminist criticism of psychology, a body of work that would have made his case a good deal stronger. Moreover, in contrast to other criticism it is not passive and nihilistic, it is optimistic and provides suggestions for growth, development, and radical change.

We need to develop tactics for imposing our findings, our critiques, our analyses on psychology. I would also like to suggest, on the other side of the coin, that male psychologists

... Much of the current focus on being liberated from the constraints and protectiveness of the society which is proposed by Women's Liberation groups has never been applied to Black women, and in this sense, we have always been "free," and able to develop as individuals even under the most harsh circumstances. This freedom, as well as the tremendous hardships from which Black women suffered, allowed for the development of a female personality that is rarely described in scholarly journals for its obstinate strength and ability to survive. Neither is its peculiar humanistic character and quiet courage viewed as the epitome of what the American model of femininity should be.

Joyce Ladner, *Tomorrow's Tomorrow*, 1971

---

begin a study of their own sexism and of their misogynistic attitudes and behavior. Knowledge in this area would certainly advance the discipline. At the same time, I am not concerned about the new psychology of women being a separate field, as long as it is voluntary separatism and well rewarded, and we don't forget both sides of the agenda.

Ethnic Diversity of Female Experience

Although there may be some universalities of women's experience, there are also differences. One important diversity is that of ethnicity or race. The focus of this section will be the psychology of women with emphasis on Black, Asian, Chicana, and Native American women, although these major racial and ethnic groupings oversimplify the cultural diversity within each group. For example, there are seventeen distinct ethnic groups for Asian women and over five hundred different groups for Native women, according to the articles in this section.

The papers in this section reveal that relatively little is known about most of these groups of women in terms of the psychological literature, although this seems somewhat less true for Black women. And in addition to the problem of scarcity of research in these areas, it is quite possible that what does exist should raise questions similar to those voiced by Mednick in the last section. By making appropriate substitutions, these would be:

1. What are the fundamental assumptions that a discipline has concerning the true nature of racial minorities and how have these assumptions affected methodology, conceptualization, and application of knowledge?
2. What substantive areas have been neglected and how has this affected our knowledge of minorities—and of whites?
3. How has neglect of the study of minorities affected the discipline in general?

Many of these issues appear directly or indirectly in the papers that follow. As research activities in these areas increase, we can hope that new conceptualizations will emerge and that further exchange with studies on the psychology of white women may prove enriching to all.

The interdisciplinary approach taken in many of these articles is due only in part to the scarcity of data. To understand the psychological lives of these women, a broader perspective of the cultures of origin and the relationships of these to the dominant (white) society must be attempted. If universal female subordination is assumed, then all of the cultures from which these groups of women came were patriarchal, though the relative status of females and males within each culture probably varied. If universal female subordination is not assumed, then some Native American tribes may be seen as having been matriarchal. Certainly, each culture has had a unique set of beliefs regarding the "nature" of women and men and its own set of values regarding human relationships. These then probably affect the psychology of these women to varying degrees depending on the strength of connection with the culture of origin.

In relation to the dominant society, there are numerous effects. Feminist anthropologists have observed the depressive effect on women's status and a decrease in the relative status of women in cultures affected by Western colonialism, including Western practices and attitudes regarding women (Quinn; 1977). Although these observations are of cultures outside the United States, it is possible that there has been a similar effect on minority cultures within the U.S.

As members of racial minority groups, these women have experienced both institutional and psychological oppression (see the next section for more about psychological oppression) unknown to white women. They may have experienced additional institutional and

---

Experiencing Various Points of View

Purpose: To develop awareness of sexual and ethnic experiences other than our own.

Directions: Close your eyes, find a comfortable position, and relax while someone reads the following instructions out loud for you.

1. *Sex* Imagine that your sex is reversed. If you are a male, you are now a female; if you are a female, you are now a male.... How is your body different now? ... Become really aware of this new body, particularly the parts that have changed.... If you don't want to do this, that's O.K. But don't say to yourself "I *can't* do this." Say "I *won't* do this," and then add whatever words come to you next. By doing this you may get some idea of what it is that you are avoiding by refusing to do this reversal.... How do you feel in this new body? ... And how will your life be different now? ... What will you do differently, now that your sex has changed? ... And how do you feel about all these changes? ... Continue to explore your experience of being the opposite sex for awhile....

    Now change back again and get in touch with your real body and your real sex.... Silently compare the experience of being yourself with being the other sex.... What did you experience as the other sex that you don't experience now? ... Were these experiences pleasant or unpleasant? ...

Continue to explore your experience for a little while....

2. *Race* Now imagine that your skin color is reversed: If you are black or dark-skinned, you are now white. If you are white-skinned, you are now black or dark-skinned.... Become really aware of your new body.... How is your body different now? ... And how do you feel in this body? ... How will your life be different, now that your skin color has changed? ... And how do you feel about these changes? ... Continue to explore your new existence for awhile....

    Now change back to your own skin color and your own body.... Silently compare the experience of being yourself with the experience of having a different skin color.... What differences do you notice between the two, and how did you feel in each? ...

Try this exercise by imagining that you are a Black, Chicana, Asian, Native American or white woman. After each exercise, open your eyes and record your experiences. If possible, have members of the class (or women from outside the class) of various ethnic backgrounds share with each other their experiences arising from the exercise, giving feedback on the basis of real experience as compared with the imagined experiences.

---

psychological oppression as women, although there is some evidence that because of their racial minority status they have escaped to some extent the luxury and the liability of "femininity," which may be a major component of the psychological oppression of women. The psychological implications of these experiences and the relevant psychological dimensions for each of these groups of women have not yet been determined.

At present, the least that may be inferred is that the psychological lives of these women are quite complex when compared with white women, for example. Many of these women have bicultural identifications, though the kind of identifications may vary with the degree of assimilation and acculturation to the dominant society. Psychologically integrating a complex and perhaps sometimes contradictory set of identifications, norms, and values must be an emotionally difficult task. On the more positive side, by developing internal capacities and resources, these women may also be more ingenious and creative. As one of the authors states, "to move between these two worlds can be a feast of appreciation for human ingenuity, or it can be the bitterest trap."

Many of these themes are apparent in the papers that follow, though the content of each is unique. Saundra Rice Murray's paper deals with images and roles of Black women. Images of Black women as they appear in the media and Black women's self-perceptions are presented and then the roles of mother, wife, student, and labor force participant are examined. Some of the topics noted by Murray have also been studied in relation to white women, as mentioned by Mednick in the last section. These are sex roles and androgyny, and achievement and fear of success. Of course, the limitations regarding available knowledge about Black women are highlighted as are directions for future research.

Comparatively less is known about Asian women. Reiko Homma True provides profiles of pioneer immigrant, new immigrant, and U.S.-born Asian women. From the historical and demographic backgrounds of these groups of women, some psychological aspects of their lives may be deduced. Although few, the known psychological studies on Asian American women are reported in her paper. In conclusion, True gives a description of the newly emerging Asian woman and relates some of

Lift Every Voice and Sing, sculpture by Augusta Savage, 1939. Photo © Estate of Carl Van Vechten. Printed by permission of Beinecke Rare Book and Manuscript Library, Yale University.

the issues relevant to change for these women.

Maria Nieto Senour provides some of the traditional cultural background of Chicana women by describing the psychological aspects of Mexican women and Mexican American women. A synopsis of the psychology of women in the dominant culture is given followed by a discussion of its relationship to the Chicana with regard to acculturation. Based on the research that exists, Senour then summarizes female and male differences in the areas of personality characteristics, social dimensions, and academic achievement. She then draws conclusions based on the research and offers some of her own and others' findings on androgyny.

Although probably the least is known about Native American women, they may have the greatest cultural diversity of any of the groups presented thus far. Shirley Hill Witt presents briefly an historical and cultural background of Native American women and then, some recent data on the topics of work and educa-tion. In concluding, Witt reminds the reader of the potential contributions of these women to the larger society.

Indeed, to the extent that *any* minority group is excluded from full participation, it may be the dominant society's loss which is greater.

For Further Reading

Asian American Women. 1976. Palo Alto, Calif.: Stanford Univ.

Asian Women. 1971. Berkeley: Univ. California Press.

Blicksilver, E. (Ed.) 1978. *The Ethnic American Woman: Problems, Protests, Lifestyles.* Dubuque, Iowa: Kendall/Hunt.

Diaz-Guerrero, R. 1975. *Psychology of the Mexican: Culture and Personality.* Austin: Univ. Texas Press.

Gridley, M. E. 1974. *American Indian Women.* New York: Hawthorn.

Hernandez, C. A., Haug, M. J., and Wagner, N. N. (Eds.). 1976. *Chicanos: Social and Psychological Perspectives.* (Second ed.) St. Louis: C. V. Mosby.

Huston, P. 1979. *Third World Women Speak Out.* New York: Praeger.

Ladner, J. 1971. *Tomorrow's Tomorrow.* New York: Doubleday.

Landis, R. 1971. *The Ojibwa Woman.* New York: W. W. Norton.

Lerner, G. 1972. *Black Women in White America.* New York: Random House.

Martinez, J. L. (Ed.). 1978. *Chicano Psychology.* New York: Academic Press.

Medicine, B. 1975. (Bibliography on Native American women.) *The Indian Historian, 8,* 51–53.

Mirande, A., and Enriquez, E. 1979. *La Chicana: The Mexican-American Woman.* Chicago: Univ. Chicago Press.

Murray, S. R., and Scott, P. B. (Eds.). 1981. (Special issue on Black women.) *Psychology of Women Quarterly.*

Reid, P., and Puryear, G. R. 1981. *Minority Women: Social and Psychological Inquiries.* New York: Holt, Rinehart and Winston.

Stimpson, C. (Ed.). 1979. Women in Latin America (Special section). *Signs: Journal of Women in Culture and Society, 5* (1).

Sue, S., and Wagner, N. N. 1973. *Asian-Americans: Psychological Perspectives.* Palo Alto: Science and Behavior Books.

Terrell, J. U., and Terrell, D. H. 1974. *Indian Women of the Western Morning: Their Life in Early America.* New York: Dial.

Trejo, A. D. (Ed.). 1979. *The Chicanos: As We See Ourselves.* Tucson: Univ. Arizona Press.

Waltrip, L., and Waltrip, R. 1964. *Indian Women.* New York: David McKay.

Saundra Rice Murray

Who Is That Person? Images and Roles of Black Women

She is one of a population whose adult female members number some eight million. She has probably experienced some form of discrimination on the basis of sex or race. In all likelihood, her ancestors were American slaves. She is a black woman.

But her identity is more complex than the features of race and sex conveyed by her label. To draw a more complete profile of the black woman, we will in this paper look at her, the roles she plays, and the images of her—both those held by others and those held by the black woman of herself. First, we will consider the topic of images, contrasting the mammy/matriarch of the media with black women's own conceptions. We will then discuss the roles of mother, wife, student, and worker, focusing on expectations for behavior in the various roles, actual behavior in those roles, and the interplay of image and role.

Data sources for this inquiry include empirical studies from psychology, sociology, and anthropology. The multidisciplinary focus is deliberate, guided by two considerations. The first is practical, and stems from the fact that in any social-scientific field, empirical data on black women are scarce. The second consideration is conceptual. Quite simply, it is impossible to draw a realistic portrait from only one disciplinary perspective.

We might note at this point the source of our title, which comes from Bronfenbrenner's recent (1979) theoretical commentary on roles:

Operationally, a person's social position and hence her role label can be defined as a reply to the question, "Who Is That Person?" from the perspective of someone acquainted with both the person and the social context in which the person is located. (p. 85)

Images

Image is a convenient label for the mental representations we make of real things or persons. Sometimes the term may refer to stereotypic qualities of a group; in other contexts, images may be of specific individuals. The sources of our images are varied. We may glean them from face-to-face social interaction, from conventional wisdom, even though the subjects of that wisdom are seldom or never part of our own existence, and from various forms of communication (e.g., books, electronic media).

Both of these aspects—the content and the source of images—have been examined in recent inquiries about black women (Harley & Terborg-Penn, 1978; King, 1973). We address these two themes in the paragraphs that follow.

Media Images

Psychologists have recognized for some time that stereotypes often serve to maintain and justify the inferior status of certain groups. It

Untitled drawing by Irmagean. By permission of the artist, © 1974

thus comes as no surprise that black women, who are victims of both racial and sexual bias, are often characterized in negative ways.

One important source of images of the black woman is the media. At first glance, this seems paradoxical because black women are so often missing from the pages of newspapers or from the lineup of television programs. But the very invisibility of the black woman conveys a message: she is not worthy of any sort of regard—positive or negative.

The usual invisibility of the black woman has another impact. When she is featured, the image stands out because it is not an aspect of our daily fare. Think for a moment of recent newspaper articles about black women. In all likelihood, you will recall stories about one or two black women appointed to high govern-

ment positions, or about a welfare recipient who has managed to outwit the system in some significant, perhaps illegitimate, fashion.

These women have their counterparts in stereotypes of black women: the ambitious achiever, who makes it in the real world because of the double virtues of femaleness and blackness, and the lazy, unemployed black woman who prefers reportedly huge welfare sums to steady employment.

In films, the images are no less stereotypic. "Mammy" stands as the most memorable. She is, as described by Rawles (1977), "calm, smiling, and completely sexless" and a source of comfort to the whites for whom she works. While maintaining an appropriately servile face to the world, within her own home, however, she is the matriarch, holding men and children under a stern and domineering thumb.

The matriarch image may also be found in scholarly writings. Frazier (1966) used the term to describe a type of black family, often female-headed. Moynihan and his associates (U.S. Department of Labor, 1965) borrowed the concept and subsumed all manner of ills affecting the black family under its banner. But critics (Bond & Peery, 1970; Dill, 1979; Harrison, 1977; Jackson, 1973; Staples, 1970) have been thorough in their analyses of the Black Matriarchy as a myth, a distorted image. The enormity of the distortion will become apparent in subsequent portions of this paper.

The ways in which television portrays black women and how these media images are viewed by various audiences have been the subject of some empirical study. Black female characters in television comedies are viewed as low in achievement, self-recognition, and succorance and as high in dominance and nurturance (Reid, 1979)—exact fits to the matriarch/mammy image. Black female characters have also been perceived as nonaggressive, nonaltruistic, low in self-control, and inclined to use explanations of actions and feelings to promote understanding, resolve conflicts, or reassure others (Donagher, Poulos, Liebert, & Davidson, 1975). Again the image of mammy is evoked; but now she is less concerned with helping others, perhaps as a response to the "me" generation.

An added twist concerns the roles in which black women are cast. A report of the U.S. Commission on Civil Rights (1977) indicated that, in 1973, the fourteen black females in a sample of dramatic prime time television programs were depicted as nurses (two), prostitutes (two), maids (two), and—with one in each category—cook, student counselor, welfare office worker, secretary, and student. The occupations of three characters could not be classified. Thus, black women are free to exhibit negative characteristics in the subordinate roles that often are stereotypically associated with black women.

How do black women—who are by definition closest to the real thing rather than to the image—view these distortions? We know from at least one study (Darden & Bayton, 1977) that black women tend to view black female characters less favorably than men do. Perhaps more importantly, black women view themselves in a different light from that emitted from the television screen.

Self-Images

While variations of the mammy/matriarch image dominate the media, other—more positive—images of black women exist. These images are found in literary works and depict the black woman as strong, independent, and competent—qualities that she often uses in self-descriptions.

The images are embodied in the models of womanhood that black adolescents emulate. Ladner (1971) has identified these as the resourceful, hard-working woman, one whose responsibility often includes keeping the family intact; the carefree woman; and the upwardly mobile and educated middle-class woman. From other studies we find that black women perceive themselves as more instrumental and task-capable (Scanzoni, 1975a) and more self-confident (Epstein, 1972; Fichter, 1967) than white women.

Although black women rate themselves relatively high on these characteristics that are often considered masculine, they also rate themselves as more expressive than white women (Scanzoni, 1975a, 1975b; Kane et al., 1971). This is consistent with O'Leary and Harrison's (1975) finding that black men and women, in comparison to whites, make few distinctions between men and women on the basis of sex-typed personality traits. Black women's equal endorsement of expressive and instrumental qualities lends support to Harrison's (1977) observation that black women are androgynous. (See Young, 1970 and Lewis, 1975 for discussions of the antecedents of this quality.)

We find little in these self-images to support the assumption that black women hold themselves in low esteem. This may be because they evaluate themselves according to standards of the black, rather than of the white, community (Harrison, 1977; Gurin & Epps, 1975; Owens, 1975). But black women's self-images may also be derived from their own experiences in various roles.

Untitled drawing by Irmagean. By permission of the artist, © 1975

Roles of Black Women

By several accounts (Beale, 1970; King, 1973; LaRue, 1976; Lewis, 1977), black women have been denied the deference, care, and eco-

nomic security accorded many middle-class majority women. The images we have described suggest that black women have also escaped the negative aspects of conventional womanhood—for example, sex role stereotypes that depict women as helpless, passive, and intellectually weak persons. In the following sections we review these themes from the perspective of roles.

The Black Mother

It is difficult to separate image from reality when we speak of the black mother's role, because, for many black people, motherhood has a special meaning that transcends conventional definitions. In literature, "mama's" importance is derived not only from the daily care she gives to her children, but also from her significance as a symbol of black people. Rushing (1978) writes: "Afro-American attitudes toward mother are extremely complex, but in almost all other poems, mother is above criticism, the almost perfect symbol of black struggle, suffering, and endurance" (p. 76). In novels of the black experience, the black mother has also been condemned for repressing her son's "normal masculinity and aggressiveness" (Dance, 1975) in order to prepare him for his subordinate position.

Because the images of black mothers are antithetical and, as we noted earlier, often unattractive, we might expect that black women assume the role with ambivalence. The few data that bear on attitudes toward motherhood suggest that, for lower-class women, it is pre-

Look at my arm! I have ploughed and planted and gathered into barns,
and no man could head me—and ain't I a woman? I could work as much
and eat as much as a man—when I could get it—and bear the lash as
well! And ain't I a woman? I have born thirteen children, and seen most
of 'em sold into slavery, and when I cried out with my mother's grief,
none but Jesus heard me—and ain't I a woman?

Sojourner Truth, abolitionist and feminist,
speech before Woman's Rights Convention,
Akron, Ohio, 1851

ferred over the role of wife (Bell, 1971) and viewed as an important step toward womanhood (Ladner, 1971). Studies of class-related differences in childrearing have been conducted (Hess & Shipman, 1965; Kamii & Radin, 1967; Zegiob & Forehand, 1975), but little is known about how middle-class black mothers evaluate their role (Reid, 1978).

However, the expectations for the black mother's role are clear and are reflected in black women's views concerning motherhood. Black women endorse traditional role expectations that women are to be concerned primarily with the care and well-being of their children and spouses (Bonner, 1975; Gump, 1975), and see their role as one requiring a balance between self- and other-direction (Steinmann & Fox, 1970). Men and older women tend to express traditional views more than younger women (Scanzoni, 1975b).

It has been suggested that role prescriptions for black women also include the expectation of work outside the home (Gump, 1978; Gump & Rivers, 1975; Harrison, 1977). About 58 percent of black women with children are employed (Minority Women Workers, 1977), and studies of the career patterns of black women indicate that they return to full-time work following the birth of a child sooner than white women (Mott, 1978). Black women tend to have greater labor force participation after, rather than before, they have children (Gump, 1978; Vetter & Stockburger, 1974).

The dual responsibility of black mothers—to raise *and* provide economic support for their children—thus assures black women's place in two realms: the home and the marketplace. Some of the behaviors of black women in the mother role reflect the strategies she uses to balance the demands of the two spheres. Abrahams (1975) describes strategies used by black women to assert their respectability as mothers; for example, the black mother may use testimonies to publicize her adherence to a standard of maternal excellence. An illustrative testimony is from a mother whose daughter had neglected her children: "I'm not gonna have those babies out in the street. They're gonna stay here even if (their mother) moves out. I'll not have it, not knowing who's taking care of them" (Rainwater, 1970, p. 205, quoted in Abrahams, 1975).

Working mothers use several strategies to cope with the difficulties of enacting multiple roles. When wife-worker conflicts arise, black women try to change others' demands. Mother-worker conflicts are handled by establishing priorities and eliminating roles, while mother-wife conflicts are reduced by the use of combined strategies (Harrison & Minor, 1978).

The fact that their spouses and children accept the notion of the working wife and mother (Axelson, 1970; Entwisle & Greenberger, 1972; King, Abernathy & Chapman, 1978) perhaps ameliorates some of the strain that inevitably accompanies the continual juggling of roles and responsibilities. Gump (1978) writes from clinical experience of one psychological cost, the "deficit of caring," from which

Nikki-Rosa

childhood remembrances are always a drag
if you're Black
you always remember things like living in
    Woodlawn
with no inside toilet
and if you become famous or something
they never talk about how happy you were to
    have
your mother
all to yourself and
how good the water felt when you got your
    bath
from one of those
big tubs that folk in chicago barbecue in
and somehow when you talk about home
it never gets across how much you
understood their feelings
as the whole family attended meetings about
    Hollydale
and even though you remember
your biographers never understand
your father's pain as he sells his stock
and another dream goes
And though you're poor it isn't poverty that
concerns you
and though they fought a lot
it isn't your father's drinking that makes any
    difference
but only that everybody is together and you
and your sister have happy birthdays and
    very good
Christmasses
and I really hope no white person ever has
    cause
to write about me
because they never understand
Black love is Black wealth and they'll
probably talk about my hard childhood
and never understand that
all the while I was quite happy

                                    Nikki Giovanni

black women themselves suffer even as they care for and provide support for others.

Black Wives

Two related themes dominate the literature on the black wife. One is the economic contribution she makes to the family through her work outside the home. Labor force data indicate that married black women living with their husbands are more likely to be in the labor force than their counterparts who are single, widowed, divorced, or separated (Minority Women Workers, 1977). In comparison to white wives, black wives cite economic more than personal reasons for working (Landry & Jendrek, 1978). In fact, if there is one role expectation unique to black wives, it is that they will work. Thus, Fichter (1967) found that black female college graduates believed, more than white females, that their prospective husbands expected them to work regularly. Similarly, black males expected prospective mates to work regularly, a finding consistent with the greater emphasis that black men, in comparison to white men, place on instrumental qualities of potential mates (Melton & Thomas, 1976).

Given the expectation that the wife should work and the actual and historically high level of labor force participation of black wives, it comes as no surprise that a second theme in studies of black wives focuses on the marital power black women derive from their economic contribution. The power of black wives has been thought to be so great that common

She said that I must always be intolerant of ignorance but understanding of illiteracy. That some people, unable to go to school, were more educated and even more intelligent than college professors. She encouraged me to listen carefully to what country people called mother wit. That in those homely sayings was couched the collective wisdom of generations.

Maya Angelou, *I Know Why the Caged Bird Sings*, 1969

lore, aided by some social-scientific analyses, holds that black women are more powerful than their husbands.

Several studies have explored the power relationships in black families (Blood & Wolfe, 1969; Hyman & Reed, 1969; Mack, 1974; Middleton & Putney, 1960; Scanzoni, 1971, 1975a; TenHouten, 1970) and in general, the data indicate that black marriages tend to be egalitarian, often more so than those of whites (Willie & Greenblatt, 1978). However, other factors, such as social class and the decision-making context, affect the patterns of spouse dominance.

But the egalitarian nature of the marriage does not assure marital satisfaction, and some evidence indicates that many black women, particularly lower-class women, are far from being in a state of bliss (Brown, Perry, & Harburg, 1977; Staples, 1973; Bell, 1971; Scanzoni, 1971). For example, in a recent study (Scanzoni, 1975a), black wives and husbands scored lower than whites on marital satisfaction indicators of empathy, sex, and companionship.

Several factors affect the level of satisfaction black wives have in their marriages. Among these factors are lack of economic security, alcoholism, extramarital affairs, educational incompatibility, and the frustration—directed outwardly at the spouse—that stems from racial oppression (Staples, 1973). However, the black woman's marital satisfaction is relatively high when she views herself as capable or instrumental (Scanzoni, 1975a). Fu-

ture research on wives might examine the factors that seem to enhance or erode this sense of competence, which, though apparently needed within the marriage, may be particularly valuable if the marriage ends.

Black Women as Students

The student role is one that we generally associate with childhood and adolescence. Although we refer to female college students as women, and much of what we know of the psychology of women comes from studies of college populations, we rarely consider data collected on this group as aspects of the behavior and attitudes of women as students.

We have good reason to look at black females in college. In 1973, some 56 percent of black females between the ages of sixteen and thirty-four were enrolled full- or part-time in college. For these women, college has an important impact on their economic futures. College-educated black females tend to improve their relative income advantage over their noncollege-educated counterparts up to retirement (Institute for Educational Policy, 1976). Moreover, black females with one or more years of college have a higher rate of labor force participation (68.8 percent) than that (59.7 percent) of black women who have completed four years of high school (Lee, 1977).

Unfortunately, we have few data bearing on the prescriptions for black women's behavior in the role of student, the meaning of the college experience as an opportunity for intellec-

Realization by Augusta Savage; by permission of The Schomburg Center for Research in Black Culture, The New York Public Library; Astor, Lenox and Tilden Foundations

tual and social growth, and the ways in which the status of student affects relationships with and perceptions of others. We fare somewhat better when we consider specific attitudinal and motivational patterns. We know, for example, that the career choices of black women reflect sex role constraints. Thus, black women aspire to careers that are traditional for women—for example, elementary and second-ary school teaching, social work, and nursing (Fichter, 1967; Gurin & Katz, 1966, Gurin & Epps, 1975). It is questionable whether these aspirations are related to the actual careers that these women subsequently enter, but the occupational categories in which black women are found most frequently are strikingly similar to the choices made by college women.

Not all black women aspire to traditional careers, and those who intend to pursue an innovative career are different in some respects from their more traditional sisters. For example, traditionals tend to be more feminine in sex role identity, attribute their academic failures to lack of ability, and have low expectancies for success (Mednick, 1979). Innovators are more likely than traditionals to say that their career choices are ideal ones (Mednick & Puryear, 1975).

The achievement-related motivation of black college women has also been examined in some depth (Fleming, 1978; Murray & Mednick, 1975; Mednick & Puryear, 1976; Okediji, 1971; Petty, 1968; Schroth, 1976). However, the picture that emerges is one of conflicting findings from which general patterns cannot be described. This perhaps reflects the problems associated with applying constructs tested on men to the behavior of women. Another possibility suggested by Gump and Rivers (1975) is that an extrinsic factor, sense of responsibility, may be more important than achievement motivation in explaining black women's strivings. This notion has not been examined, but Turner and McCaffrey (1974) found that black women's career involvement plans were influenced by others' (e.g., parents) expectations.

The fact that the adult American Negro female emerges a formidable character is often met with amazement, distaste and even belligerence. It is seldom accepted as an inevitable outcome of the struggle won by survivors, and deserves respect if not enthusiastic acceptance.

Maya Angelou, *I Know Why The Caged Bird Sings,* 1969

Several researchers have turned to the fear of success construct to resolve some of the discrepancies encountered in studies of achievement motivation in women. As defined by Horner (1968, 1972) fear of success is a tendency to become anxious about achieving success. This avoidance motive is presumed to be most strongly aroused in highly able and motivated women because of their expectations for negative consequences. Early studies of black women's fear of success imagery indicated that this group exhibited a lower incidence than comparable white groups (Bright, 1970; Mednick & Puryear, 1976; Weston & Mednick, 1970). Despite the low frequency of imagery in black women, fear of success is related to differences in black militancy attitudes (Puryear & Mednick, 1974) and locus of control (Savage, Stearns, & Friedman, 1979). Fleming (1978), who used an updated scoring procedure, found that fear of success inhibited nontraditional achievement striving in working-class black women. Because measures of the motive tap concerns about the negative impact of success on affiliation and other aspects of feminine identity, the studies cited suggest that, for some black women, success in achievement-related situations may be perceived as incompatible with femininity.

In general, studies of college women highlight the differences among black women on dimensions of sex-role traditionality. However, with regard to career orientation, the simultaneity of traditional and nontraditional elements that characterizes black women's mother and wife roles is apparent: black college women expect to work outside the home,

Niki de Saint Phalle. *Black Venus.* 1967. Painted polyester. 110 × 35 × 24 inches. Collection of Whitney Museum of American Art. Gift of the Howard and Jean Lipman Foundation, Inc.

but they also expect to fulfill traditional functions in their private lives. As we shall see in

Poem for a Lady Whose Voice I Like

so he said: you ain't got no talent
   if you didn't have a face
   you wouldn't be nobody

and she said: god created heaven and earth
   and all that's Black within them

so he said: you ain't really no hot stuff
   they tell me plenty sisters
   take care better business than you

and she said: on the third day he made chit-
   terlings
   and all good things to eat
   and said: "that's good"

so he said: if the white folks hadn't been under
   yo skirt and been giving you the big play
   you'd a had to come on uptown like everybody else

and she replied: then he took a big Black
   greasy rib
   from adam and said we will call this woe-
   man and her
   name will be sapphire and she will divide
   into four
   parts
that simone may sing a song

and he said: you pretty full of yourself ain't
   chu

so she replied: show me someone not full of
   herself
   and i'll show you a hungry person

Nikki Giovanni

the following section, black women at work also must deal with expectations for traditional behavior.

Labor Force Participant

We have seen that employment and the expectation of a lifetime of work are central to the roles of mother, wife, and student. That black women work is evident from labor force participation statistics: in 1976, for example, half of all black women over sixteen years of age were in the civilian labor force (Minority Women Workers, 1977). Compared to other race/sex groups, black women have the highest unemployment rates, the lowest earnings (although the gap between black and white women is closing), and tend to be in low-status, low-mobility occupations. Among black professionals, women are represented most frequently in traditionally female areas, such as elementary and secondary school teaching, social work, and nursing.

Beyond analyses of participation rates, studies have focused on family background and other personal characteristics as determinants of the continued low status of black women in the marketplace (see, for examples, Gump, 1978; Gump & Rivers, 1975; Gurin & Pruitt, 1977; Jackson, 1973). A small number of studies have provided experimental data on the discrimination (racial or sexual) that black women face (Fugita, Wexley, & Hillery, 1974; Haefner, 1977; Hamner, Kim, Baird, & Bigoness, 1974), but as Allen (1979) commented: "Meanwhile, established societal practices and norms which systematically deny black women equal opportunity to achieve at levels commensurate with their abilities are ignored" (p. 686).

Inquiries of the type recommended by Allen may reveal that images, role expectations, and institutional constraints together have an impact on working black women. Dumas (1978) described how these factors affect black women executives, who often are expected to function as the organization's "mammy":

> There is general resistance to having black women perform competently in formal high status positions. Rather, the preference is to have the black woman assume a variety of functions that resemble those described for the black mammy during the plantation era.... For example, the black woman in leadership is expected to comfort the weary and oppressed, intercede on behalf of those who feel abused, champion the cause for equality and justice—often as a lone crusader.... She is called upon to fill in for her boss in dealing with problems of sex and race, to mediate in situations of conflict, quiet the "native," curb the aggression of black males, dampen the impact of other aggressive black women, and to maintain stability or restore order in the organization or one of its sectors. (pp. 6-7)

The woman who takes on these functions often suffers negative consequences. Her competence and value to the organization may be questioned if her informal role is enacted at the expense of performance in her formal position. She may feel exploited or find the dual roles so demanding of time and energy that she "burns out."

Although Dumas notes that her data are drawn from her own experiences and those of her associates, she has provided a view that suggests directions for the study of black women at work. The obvious parallels between the home-centered (mother and wife) roles and the worker role may be of particular interest, because they offer a clue to why black women tend not to consider work in self-fulfillment terms. Being all things to all people—at home and on the job—leaves little time for being oneself.

Conclusion

We conclude this paper with the point well made in many efforts to view black women from an empirical perspective: employment and care of others are central to the black woman's definition of herself and her roles. Beyond this, many unanswered questions may be explored. Among them are the institutional arrangements that restrict black women's access to and mobility in certain occupations, the changes in role expectations over the life cycle, and differences among black women in personal styles, skills, attitudes, and motivations.

As we begin to look more closely, we must do so realizing that a focus on work and responsibility to others may limit our view. Other aspects of black women's experience (racism, religion, artistic creativity, athletic achievement, political activism, and sexuality—to name just a few) have been considered in too few social-scientific studies. In large measure, the limits and possibilities of other images, other roles remain unexamined.

Reiko Homma True

The Profile of Asian American Women

when I was young
kids used to ask me
what are you?
I'd tell them what my mom told me
I'm an American
chin chin Chinaman
you're a Jap!
flashing hot inside
I'd go home
my mom would say
don't worry
he who walks alone
walks faster

Joanne Miyamoto
(Asian Women, 1971)

Asian American women have lived in the United States for nearly 150 years and there are now fifth and sixth generation Asian American women. Yet, an attitude frequently encountered in the United States is to view them as if they are new immigrants and treat them with stereotyped racism. They are seen as "reserved, quiet, shy, humble" (Fujitomi and Wong, 1973), or as "exotic, feminine, sexy" (Lott and Pian, 1979). Other stereotyped images applied to them are: "treacherous like a dragon lady" and "hard working neuter gender, who work as competent aids and tools, without faces and personality" (Lott and Pian, 1979). These are traditional characteristics attributed to women in Asia, as if the century of life experiences in the United States has had little impact.

Although some Asian American women may fit these stereotypes, as a group, they are far more complex and represent a rich and diverse background and character. Their life in the United States has been a difficult one, fraught with the double injustices of racism and sexism. Until recently very little has been written about them and the available literature has been not only limited, but often distorted. For this reason, the general population of Americans know little about them except for these stereotypes.

While their mothers and grandmothers tended to be silent backbones of their families and preferred not to attract attention to themselves, a growing number of Asian American women are becoming concerned and are beginning to challenge the myths and stereotypes about themselves. They are now working to collect relevant data and to articulate their needs and concerns (Asian American Women, 1976; Asian Women, 1971; Lott and Pian, 1979). The purpose of this paper is to review the current data available on Asian American women and to discuss their status and the critical issues confronting them at this time.

Historical Background

The term "Asian American women" refers to a diverse group of women representing as many as seventeen ethnic-cultural groups such as Chinese, Guamanians, Japanese, Koreans, Pilipinos (this is the contemporary spelling for those from the Philippines, who were previously referred to as Filipinos), Samoans, and Vietnamese (Lott and Pian, 1979). In terms of population and history in this country, the major groups are considered to be Chinese, Japanese, Koreans, and Pilipinos. For this reason, the data available on Asian American women is limited generally to these groups at this time.

Chinese women were the first group to enter the United States. As early as 1848 they followed their men who sought new opportunities in gold mining, the railroads, and other work which required workers willing to work for cheap wages (Lee, 1960). However, their population over the next several decades became limited in contrast to the large number of Chinese men who entered the United States. Several factors cited as contributing to this imbalance include the cultural tradition of leaving wives behind to care for elderly parents, the enactment of the Chinese Exclusion Act in 1882, and the expectation of some husbands to be temporary workers with plans to return to China as soon as they were able (Pian, 1976). The small number of Chinese women who came into the U.S. included wives and daughters of merchants who were given a special exemption status, and prostitutes who were mostly illegally smuggled into this country. Only now are the many tragedies and the exploitation of these prostitutes being written about (Louie, 1971). Many were stricken with diseases and died young; others persevered through adversity and, after their servitude, married to raise families of their own.

The second group of Asian women to immigrate were Japanese. They were sent for by Japanese male workers who preceded them as laborers. The Japanese were recruited as replacements for the Chinese laborers who were by then experiencing intense hostility because of their threat to the economic security of

Chinese Lady, 1880's. Courtesy the Bancroft Library

white men. Most of the Japanese workers were young bachelors from economically hard-pressed farming communities in Japan. Although hostilities were to develop rapidly against them also, Japanese men were not subjected to the exclusionary immigration law which would have severely restricted the immigration of Japanese women. So, after they were able to save enough money, they sent for brides carefully selected through arranged marriages by family go-betweens. They exchanged photographs but knew little of each other. These women were known as "picture brides" and were generally strong, young women selected from the farming commu-

One hundred women are not worth a single testicle.

Confucius (551–479 B.C.)

nities where the men were originally recruited (Gee, 1971).

Between 1900 and 1920 was the peak period for the entry of Japanese women into the United States, after which they encountered many hardships. They accompanied their husbands into the rural farming communities and labor camps, where their back-breaking double and triple duty life as wife/mother/field worker began. When their lives barely began to stabilize, they were hit by mounting anti-Japanese sentiments of whites which culminated with their incarceration after the outbreak of World War II.

Korean and Pilipino laborers were the next group to replace the Chinese and Japanese workers. But only a small number of women would follow their men during the early period of their immigration. The traditional cultural pattern of women staying behind to take charge of family obligations is cited as the critical factor for this phenomenon. The few women who chose to accompany their husbands came for personal reasons. For example, in the case of Korean women those who came were generally Christians who were anxious to leave religious discrimination behind and to start a new Christian community (Navarro, 1976; Sunoo and Sunoo, 1977). Like their predecessors these women were also confronted with adversities and racism, but stayed on to support their men and to raise their children.

While Asian men far outweighed the number of Asian women in the early immigration, a significant increase in the number of Asian women began to take place after the end of World War II and after the liberalization of

the immigration law in 1965. Since then, the trend has been reversed, and more Asian women are entering the United States than men. One significant factor is the large number of Asian women who married American servicemen and related military personnel. They are popularly referred to as "war brides" and have immigrated from Japan, Korea, the Philippines, and Vietnam in successive waves (Pian, 1976). Moreover, the changes in the immigration law in 1965 liberalized the eligibility for immigration and allowed the entry of wives and children of the older Asian immigrant males. Also professional women and other women who qualified as new immigrants came with their husbands and children. The most significant groups of women who are immigrants are Koreans, Chinese, Pilipinos, and Vietnamese refugees, and their number is rapidly increasing (Pian, 1976).

Current Status as Reflected in Statistics

Statistical data available on Asian and Pacific American women are based on an analysis of 1970 census (DHEW, 1974), the 1975 Survey of Income and Education (U.S. Department of Labor, 1975), immigration data (U.S. Immigration and Naturalization Services, 1950–1975), and preliminary findings from a DHEW field survey (1976). Although they are mostly limited to the Chinese, Japanese, Korean, and Pilipino groups, they provide some indication of the current status of Asian American women. Some of the profiles that emerge from these data are as follows:

The current population of Asian Americans is estimated to be nearly 4 million, of which

The five worst infirmities that afflict the female are indocility, discontent, slander, jealousy, and silliness. . . . Such is the stupidity of her character that it is incumbent upon her, in every particular, to distrust herself and obey her husband.

Confucian marriage manual

approximately 50 percent are women. Nearly two-thirds of all these women are residing in the Western region of the country, primarily clustered around California, Hawaii, and Washington. However, sizable groups have also settled in major cities in other areas as well. Although they represent several generations and diverse age groups, the majority are foreign born, of whom at least sixty percent have immigrated since 1970.

Their educational profile seems to indicate that they are somewhat better educated than the total U.S. population. The median level of educational attainment is 12.7 years for Asian women compared to 12.1 years for the total U.S. women's population. Many of them have obtained a college education or other professional training. This is particularly striking among Pilipino women who include a recent influx of highly trained women from the Philippines with 27 percent of them having a college education compared with 15 percent for Pilipino males, and 8 percent for the total of U.S. women. These statistics do not reveal the status of some of the subpopulations, however, for example, elderly immigrants, wives of U.S. servicemen, and Indochinese refugees, for whom educational opportunities have been limited.

The majority of Asian American women are married and maintaining their families with a relatively low rate of family break-up. However, this trend is gradually changing, and now 9 percent of the women are classified as heads of households. There are also substantial numbers of women who live alone, and many of them are elderly widows.

Although the traditional image of the Asian woman is that of housewife, a large number of them are in the work force. While 41.4 percent of all U.S. women are working, the rate for Asian women is well over 50 percent. The past ten years have shown a dramatic increase with this trend continuing. Despite their relatively high educational attainments, however, most are employed at lower level occupations and are making considerably less money than their white female or white or Asian male counterparts with comparable education (DHEW, 1974; Fong & Cabazas, 1976).

In terms of their occupational status, preliminary analysis in the San Francisco-Oakland area (Fong and Cabazas, 1976) shows that they are largely concentrated in a restricted labor market including the garment industry, banking, insurance, hotels, and telephone communications. Moreover, within these industries they occupy low-status, and low-paying jobs such as clerks, operatives, food servicers, and cleaners. They are virtually absent from the management ranks and other leadership positions.

Profile of Asian American Women

As the history of their immigration to the United States may suggest, there is now a diverse group of Asian American women in the United States. In addition to the expected ethnic differences, there are also distinct generational and socioeconomic differences among them. For this reason, they can best be described by clustering them in several major groupings, which share similar identity, background, and experiences. Following is a brief profile of some of these groups.

This character, pronounced "onna" in Japanese and "niu" in Chinese, is the symbol for woman.

Pioneer Immigrant Women

Although many of the pioneer immigrant women are now dead, a substantial number of them are still alive and are in their seventies and eighties. Most of these women are from China and Japan and came here as wives of laborers and merchants. Except for their courage and determination to persevere, most of them had little educational and language preparation and were ill equipped to survive in a vastly different culture. However, most have survived through years of strenuous work in field, factory, and so forth, and have withstood severe racial discriminations.

As young girls growing up in Asia, particularly in China, Japan, and Korea during the early 1900s, these women were socialized to value the traditional old world definitions of the woman's role as secondary to that of men. According to the Confucian tradition which originated from China and greatly influenced the social and moral structure of other Asian countries, women were regarded as the handmaiden of men, to help maintain the patriarchal, authoritarian social structure. As women, they had no rights of their own. As children, they were taught to follow the dictates of their fathers, and in their growing years to serve their husbands and sons. They could be divorced at any time, by the whim of their husbands, but they had no right to initiate divorce on their own. Care was taken to mold them into quiet, subservient women to be at the behest of their men (Benedict, 1946; Yang, 1959).

However, the oral history of the early immigrant women reveals they were often much stronger, co-equal partners with their husbands (Gee, 1971). Those who were willing to take the risk of venturing to a strange country for an unknown life were probably much more strong willed, atypical women. Another often neglected fact is that some of these women were from areas where women had a much greater role and power than usual or where remnants of an earlier matriarchal social system had been maintained (Takamure, 1972).

The role played by these pioneer women within the Asian family system is eloquently described by one of their daughters:

> She was a peasant, . . . as with the masses of the Chinese people, she was born into poverty, subjugated by a feudal system which had outlived its time. . . . She was a female, the victim of feudal traditions. After four years of school, she was withdrawn because her family could not pay the tuition of two children; her younger brother replaced her. On her marriage she was consulted, but the decision was made by Grandfather. Her life was patterned on the Confucian ethic, to serve her father in youth, to serve husband, and then to serve her sons in old age.

Yet in spite of these oppressive experiences, she was also a matriarch:

Difficult as it is to deal with realities, some Vietnam veterans have been able to speak about their experiences in Vietnam, because they began to understand the nature of sexual violence in an aggressive, colonialist war. The roots of this violence come from deep within our own culture and take their toll on women all over the world, including ourselves.

Jane Fonda and Nancy Dowd, Vietnamese
Women's Slide Show, 1972

My mother was the center of our family, her strong character dominated most of our young world. Her role as an Asian woman was that of a living "vessel of culture." She carried out the rites of ancestor worship, taught us Chinese etiquette, observed the traditional holidays with tantalizing delicacies—in essence, she taught us that we were Chinese and that all things Chinese were best. (Jen, 1971)

New Immigrants

While the early group of immigrant women are relatively homogeneous within their own ethnic groups, the recent immigrant women come from much more heterogeneous backgrounds. Those often singled out as having the greatest difficulty and needing better understanding are women who married American servicemen and other related personnel. It is estimated that they number as many as 200,000 at this time and are widely distributed throughout the country. Because of the negative community attitude toward interethnic marriages and the circumstances surrounding many of the war-time liaisons, there has been tremendous hostility toward them within the military establishment. Often they have been rejected by their adopted in-laws and by their own families as well. Many of them had limited educations, had difficulty with English, and were often ill prepared to cope with the demands of American society. Although there were many family break-ups among these marriages, other women have survived

Stop Bombing by Mitsu Yashima. Copyright, 1980, Mitsu Yashima.

through all adversities, sometimes with the support of understanding spouses, in-laws, and other support groups advocating for the welfare of these women (Kim, 1975; Kim, 1977).

Another group of new immigrants are those who have immigrated from Hong Kong, Taiwan, Korea, the Philippines, and, more recently, refugees from Vietnam, Cambodia, and Laos. Although refugees are having special problems in dealing with traumatic losses and the transition into a new country, many new immigrant women are also experiencing a number of adjustment problems. Those who came with limited educational, language, occupational, and cultural preparation are forced to work now to help support the generally marginal income of their husbands. In spite of the fact many of them have young children, they are unable to secure appropriate child care arrangements for their children, who are left to roam the streets and become easy prey as recruits into the youth gang structure.

While poorly educated working-class women are more tradition-bound in terms of their sex role orientation, there is a considerable number of new immigrant women who are students and professionals. They come from middle- or upper-class backgrounds and do not necessarily adhere to old world norms. This is partly a reflection of the social change taking place in their own Asian countries, where the status of women is changing considerably (Lebra, 1976; Navarro, 1976). In addition, those who chose to seek new opportunities away from their country are more likely to be atypical and questioning, and sometimes rebellious against the traditional norms.

This hypothesis was tested by Fong and Peskin (1969) in their study of China-born college students in California. Using the California Personality Inventory designed to assess various sub-areas of personality, they found female students to be significantly less inclined than their male counterparts to be accepting of traditional norms and responsibility, which may also relate to a tendency to be deviant and rule breaking. Among the female students, this tendency was more prominent for students who came to the U.S. on a visa status than for students who were naturalized citizens. As most of the naturalized students came to the U.S. with their parents as immigrants and could depend on them for support and protection, the researchers speculated that they were more influenced by their parents' values than visa students, who had to leave their families behind and were forced by circumstances to be more independent and self-reliant.

Another study focusing on the changing attitude of foreign born Chinese students was conducted by Braun and Chao (1978) in Michigan. Using the Spence-Helmreich Attitudinal Scale, designed to measure liberal and conservative tendencies in individual attitudes toward women, they found contemporary foreign born Chinese male and female students to be quite liberal. While Caucasian female students scored highest on most subscales and Caucasian males consistently lowest on all subscales, Chinese male and female students scored differently relative to each other. Chinese male students were found to be more liberal in their attitudes toward behavioral areas such as freedom, dating, courting, etiquette, drinking, swearing, telling jokes. Chinese female students were more liberal than Chinese male or Caucasian male students in more substantive areas involving socioeconomic issues such as vocation, education, intellectual roles, marital relationship and obligations.

U.S.-born Women

Like their immigrant sisters, there is a wide range in the age and the social background of the U.S.-born Asian American women. The older group of women who are second or third

In the Chinese family system, there is superficial quiet and calmness and quarreling is frowned upon, but in reality all is in conflict.

Helen Foster Snow, Ting Ling, in *Women in Modern China*, 1967

---

generation Americans—the Asian community's method for enumerating generations in the U.S. is different from that of the white, European-descended community's; they call the immigrant generation the first generation and the first U.S.-born generation the second generation—are mostly of Chinese and Japanese descent and are now in their forties and fifties. Their immigrant parents were generally mindful of the old world traditions and tried to mold their daughters into the dutiful, compliant wife/mother role (Kingston, 1976; Sone, 1953; Wong, 1950). Duty, responsibility, family obligation, modesty, acceptance of the status quo, and so forth, were some of the traits stressed by their parents. For the most part, they appeared on the surface to have accepted this role. Instead of pursuing college educations, most have married and raised children. They have managed also to work outside the home as clerks and service personnel to supplement the family income. Some who obtained college educations are working as teachers and nurses. They are known as hardworking, competent, reliable workers, but they are relegated to the subservient, helper role and are rarely promoted to leadership positions (Conference Discussions, 1979).

There are indications that many of these women have not fully accepted such roles and that they have been experiencing a great deal of frustration and turmoil within themselves. Such conflicts were studied by Caudill and DeVos (1956) with Japanese Americans in the Chicago area immediately after World War II. Through the analysis of TAT, Rorschach, and psychotherapy records of three groups of men and women (immigrants, known as Issei; those

who were born in the U.S. but grew up in Japan; and second generation Japanese Americans, generally referred to as Nisei), they found that the Nisei women showed signs of the greatest amount of internal conflict. The investigators felt these women were caught between two oppositional forces: the need to break away from family and the guilt over feeling such need. They also noted that the few professional women studied were experiencing the greatest strain in this respect. The limitation of this study is that the findings are based on the application of nonobjective instruments and fail to take into account the psychological impact of concentration camp experience on these subjects. For this reason, the findings should be interpreted with caution. Nevertheless, they provide interesting observations.

Although many of these women felt conflicted about their educational and occupational aspirations and the demands of their families, most did settle into a dual career life of a housewife and a wage earner/worker, placing their priority in raising their children. Although their occupational and educational interest took a secondary status in their lives, they are faced with the need to deal with a mid-life crisis when their children are grown, in much the same manner as Anglo middle-aged housewives must deal with the empty-nest syndrome and redefine their purpose in life (JACL, 1977). Although comparable data are not available for other middle-aged Asian American women, impressions among professional human services workers are that they are also experiencing similar problems.

Although there is much less information on

the younger U.S.-born women in their twenties and thirties who are children of immigrant parents, they seem to be experiencing the same types of conflict as their older sisters. While social attitudes among immigrant parents with relatively high educational and social status are thought to be less traditional, a large number of the immigrant parents are from more traditional, working-class backgrounds and have limited understanding and acceptance of permissive Western attitudes toward women. For this reason, their values and expectations of their daughters often clash with those of young Asian American women, who expect the same liberal privileges as their American peers. Their experience is described by a student who participated in an Asian American Women's course at her college:

> The daughter of a first generation mother in White America, I was frustrated into tears when prohibited from the dates, dances, and parties of my seemingly "freer" classmates.... I was discouraged from participating in any activity which would take me out of the safe circle of my family.... I remember the jealous anger I would feel when my brothers would be allowed to do things denied me because "I was a girl." (Jen, 1971)

In spite of these generational clashes, there seems to be an interesting change taking place in the Asian American community in terms of the roles played by their women. While first generation women were seen to have played a generally submissive, but often substantively strong role within their own family structure, their daughters seem to be assuming a much more central role in the family decision-making processes. According to the study conducted among Seattle Japanese American families concerning their kinship network, Yanagisako (1976) noted that the authority of the fathers and eldest sons had been dramatically eroded. While in Asia the traditional family ties were maintained by males in the extended family system's corporate clan relationship, here the link between the families was maintained by Nisei women. Some of the factors contributing to this change are thought to be the shift away from the extended family to nuclear family structure in the Japanese American community, the relegation of fathers to the external role of wage earners and providers, and the strong need for a more actively supportive female within the household as a protection against external threats of racism. Although the study was limited to the investigation of the Japanese American families, it appears that such changes are taking place among other Asian American families as well.

Emerging Asian American Women

The younger generation of Asian American women is beginning to emerge. An increasing number of these women are questioning the

Mountain Moving Day

The mountain moving day is coming
I say so yet others doubt it
Only a while the mountain sleeps
In the past all mountains moved in fire
Yet you may not believe it
O man this alone believe
All sleeping women now awake and move
All sleeping women now awake and move

Yosano Akiko, 1911

traditional role of Asian women and challenging the second class citizen role accorded them within and outside their communities. Several social scientists have noted such indications in the women's struggle to define their own identity, roles, and positions in society. For example, using psychotherapy cases as illustrations, Fong (1968) and Yamamoto (1968) discuss the problems and conflicts faced by Chinese and Japanese American women and the process for dealing with the pressures of traditional family values and peer and community expectations.

Similarly, in a study of Sansei (third generation) Japanese American male and female college students in northern California, Maykovich (1972) also noted their struggle to reconcile traditional family values and contemporary social pressures. She interviewed 508 Sansei college students, including 248 female subjects, and found considerable heterogeneity among them. On the basis of their attitude toward traditional values and involvement in social issues, she identified four types of Sansei: *liberated,* who are actively involved in political issues, but subscribe to the traditional values of diligence and conformity; *militants,* who are not satisfied with evolutionary changes and advocate a revolutionary change; *conformists,* who accept traditional values and are detached from social issues; and the *anomic,* who reject traditional values but are not involved in social action. In spite of the heterogeneity among the Sansei, she identified one commonality among them—the search for a new ethnic identity.

Although Maykovich's study did not identify significant differences between Sansei male and female students, another study in Hawaii by Arkoff, Meredith, and Dong (1963) suggests an emerging difference between them. Using the Jacobson Scale, which measures male dominant and egalitarian attitudes toward marriage, they compared Japanese American and Caucasian American students. While they found Japanese American male students to be male dominant in their attitude, Japanese American female and Caucasian male and female students were more in agreement concerning the egalitarian nature of marital roles.

More recently, stimulated by the third world and feminist movements of the 1960s and 1970s, many women are beginning to take more active roles in the community and to demand equal status for themselves (Lott and Pian, 1979). In spite of their ethnic and socioeconomic diversity, many of the women are convinced now that there is a greater purpose and need to unite as Asian American women. They feel their past division among themselves played a part in perpetuating their marginal status within the United States. They strongly believe that the only way to fight against the persistent racism and sexism against themselves is to establish a unifying identity as Asian American women, emphasiz-

Too Much to Require

Fathers
required me
to split my tongue

to learn the silent
graces
of womanhood
like sweeping
cobwebs from family relics

                        and so i am gentle

to taste
that guilt for not being
 'what you should be'
and working harder/for/everything

                        and so i am gentle

to remember the ease
of instant omission
and the necessity for
assimilation

                        and so i am gentle

to forget hiroshima
to ignore vietnam
to accept tule lake
to enjoy chinatown

            o yes, daddy,
            very gentle i am

            when i clean my gun.

                        Janice Mirikitani

small and limited among women with higher educational background and college students, an increasing number of working-class women and semiprofessional women are joining their ranks. Most of these women are young women in their twenties and thirties and include both foreign born as well as second, third, and fourth generation women. However, there are some older women who are part of this movement and they provide support and leadership to the younger women as role models. Many of these women have taken part in ethnic studies at colleges and universities, or have been involved in community organization efforts to create needed services within the Asian American community (Asian American Women, 1976; Asian Women, 1971). In addition, several Asian American women's organizations have been established within the past few years with the specific purpose of advocating for their concerns (Lott and Pian, 1979). The most exciting and dramatic movement in this regard is the nationwide effort currently being mounted to organize national and regional networks of Asian and Pacific Island women. Their plan is to carry out regional conferences in key cities and to convene a national forum in Washington, D.C. to highlight their concerns.

However, such growth and change cannot take place without some resistance and negative repercussions, and there are still many obstacles for Asian American women. The resistances may come from any of several sources: internal psychological fear and self-doubt among the women themselves, disapproval from their families, from their ethnic communities, and from the outside world of schools and work. Such difficulties, for example, have been highlighted in an article de-

ing their shared concerns. They are also sympathetic to the similar concerns expressed by their third world sisters and believe there is a need to establish linkages with them.

Although the number of Asian American women who shared such ideology was initially

scribing the application of assertiveness training techniques with an Asian client (Yanagida, 1979).

Conclusion

Although Asian American women have generally been portrayed as subservient, complacent individuals, content with their life and family, this brief review of the literature and available data indicate that they lead very different lives. One commonality, however, is that their lives are often difficult ones, full of frustration and pain and often fraught with the injustices of sexism and racism. The issues confronting Asian American women are many but include racism and sexism, inequities in income and employment, problems of dual responsibility as workers and mothers, and uncertainties involved in conflicting cultural demands. While Asian American women have been relatively silent in the past, there is a growing recognition among them that they will need to forge ahead in partnership with other minority women in order to advocate for their concerns.

Maria Nieto Senour

Psychology of the Chicana

Psychological literature relating directly to the Chicana (Mexican-American woman) is extremely limited. This undoubtedly reflects the lack of interest, on the part of social scientists, in both Mexican-Americans and women until recent years. The scant data on Chicanas that do exist are generally to be found within studies focusing on other issues. Moreover, the validity of these data is not beyond question. However, the purpose of this chapter is not to present a definitive Chicana psychology, but rather to initiate an exploration of the topic by reviewing the literature on the psychology of women, Mexican, and Mexican-American cultures and experience, a limited amount of research on Chicanos, and some recent studies on the relationship between sex roles and ethnicity.

Traditional Mexican-American Culture

The Mexican family is purportedly founded on the supremacy of the father and the corresponding total self-sacrifice of the mother (Diaz-Guerrero, 1955). Literature on the Mexican family indicates that the wife must devote herself to the satisfaction of everyone else's needs by the complete denial of her own. As a child, she is groomed for her destiny at home and school by encouragement to acquire the appropriate feminine skills. Generally, any attempt to achieve academically or professionally is seen as unfeminine and is discouraged.

If this is indeed an accurate reflection of the Mexican woman's role in the family, there must also be rewards for the woman in this system, such as the devotion of her children. However, in terms of her mental health, there may be a price as well. Diaz-Guerrero (1975) estimated that 44 percent of the female population of Mexico City over eighteen years of age is "neurotic." This neurosis is manifested mostly in self-belittlement and depression.

Three studies by Mexican psychoanalysts indicate the existence of conflict between Mexican males and females (Aramoni, 1961; Gonzalez, 1959; Ramirez, 1959). Men are shown to assert their dominance by wielding economic power over their women or by using even cruder means such as physical abuse. They are described as demonstrating little tenderness or affection for their wives. Women are described as feeling exploited, as experiencing pressure to respond lovingly to men who treat them like personal property. These perceptions of their status leave Mexican women feeling vengeful so that they deliberately undermine the father's relationship with his children. They are said to frequently raise boys who doubt their masculinity and are compulsively *machos* while attempting to mask feelings of dependence on the mother and fears of impotence. Their daughters are raised to be distrustful of all men and consequently unable to love men genuinely. While this Freudian image of punishing men and passively resistant women can by no means be considered the norm in Mexican families. Aramoni, Gonzalez, and Ramirez report the existence of such traits in numerous individuals seeking therapy.

In a continent-wide study of sex roles, San Martin (1975) found notions of the inferiority of women and superiority of men alive and well throughout Latin America. Women are expected to be gentle, mild, sentimental, emotional, intuitive, impulsive, fragile, submissive, docile, dependent, and timid. Men are hard, rough, cold, intellectual, rational, farsighted, profound, strong, authoritarian, independent, and brave.

The literature indicates that within the Mexican-American family are also found clearly defined sex roles to govern behavior. The older have authority over the younger, and the men have authority over the women (Madsen, 1969). Women, in traditional Mexican-American culture, are said to devote themselves totally to their families, allowing their entire lives to revolve around husband and children. They are the primary source of nurturance and maintain a close relationship with their children throughout life. Traditional Chicanas have few contacts with individuals outside the family, so their affectional ties with those in the family, especially with other females, are very strong (Murillo, 1971). In comparison with people of other cultures in the United States, Chicanos are said to dominate their wives, overprotect their daughters, and expect passive compliance in return (Padilla & Ruiz, 1973). Derbyshire (1968) suggested that this male dominance exists only because females choose to play a subordinate role. He finds Chicanas attempting to bolster a *machismo* at home that is threatened by the Chicano's lack of status in the dominant culture.

Other writers have attacked these portrayals of Chicano males and females as stereotyped. Inappropriate research tools, methodologies, and examiner bias are accused of perpetuating destructive myths about the Chicano family which need to be disproved by adequate research (Cotera, 1976). Nevertheless, Jaco (1957) found that Spanish-surnamed women in Texas exhibit higher incidences of manic-depressive, involutional, and schizophrenic psychoses than men. In Fabrega, Rubel, and Wallace's (1967) study of Mexican-American outpatients, women reported a greater number of psychiatric symptoms than men. The authors attributed their finding to notions of masculinity and femininity in Mexican-American culture. In a recent study of Chicano acculturation, Go (1975) found females between the ages of 13 and 18 reporting significantly higher anxiety levels than men on the manifest anxiety scale.

Psychology of Women of the Dominant Culture

The Chicana is a product of two cultures; traditional Mexican-American culture, which she experiences at home, although frequently in diluted forms, and dominant American culture, which she experiences almost everywhere else, especially at school.

Therefore, a look at recent research in the psychology of American women will give information on the other half of the Chicana's feminine experience.

Since most of these data were gathered on American, white, middle-class undergraduates, their applicability to Mexican-American women must be viewed with caution. It is also appropriate to remember that while these studies emphasize the differences between

Curandera by Carmen Lomas Garza. Color etching, © 1977. Reprinted by permission of the artist.

men and women, there are many more similarities than differences between the sexes and the differences that do exist are not absolute; there is a distribution of all traits within both sexes. Finally, it should be noted that the dominant culture is not without its contradictions regarding sex roles and contains more than one model of behavior.

Keeping these things in mind, it can nevertheless be said that real psychological differences exist between men and women of the dominant culture. These differences are reflected in lifestyles, ego organization, personality qualities, motives, and goals. The sources of these differences include (a) infant differences in gross activity level and sensitivity to stimuli, (b) parental responses that are sex linked, (c) social pressures to identify with appropriate models of the same sex, (d) the physiology of the mature reproductive system, and (e) the internalized concepts of masculinity and femininity by which individuals evaluate

themselves (Bardwick, 1971).

The main personality characteristics that Bardwick (1971) says separate women from men are passivity, dependence, and lack of self-esteem. Some of these differences are apparent at birth. Female infants are less active and more introverted, more sensitive to stimuli, and more responsive to greater numbers of stimuli than male infants. At thirteen months, females show a greater preference for high complexity stimuli and demonstrate earlier language development and greater field dependence than males.

Middle-class girls of the majority culture, unlike traditionally raised Mexican-American girls, are encouraged to achieve, especially in academic and affiliative areas. They frequently develop motives to achieve and self-concepts rooted in successful achievement while remaining dependent on the reactions of others and pursuing popularity. After puberty, the stress on social success decreases the need for academic success as a means of acquiring self-esteem. This trend continues until academic-vocational success is perceived as a threat to success as a woman. Because the dominant culture applies masculine criteria to the evaluation of the performance of females as well as of males, the greatest esteem is given to women who distinguish themselves professionally. Yet such women also run the risk of being perceived as failures as women. Hence, the development of fear of success in career-oriented women and a selection of such nurturing fields as nursing, teaching, and counseling for those who pursue a career. It seems, then, that the Chicana receives many more ambivalent messages regarding sex-role expectations from the dominant culture than she does from traditional Mexican-American culture. Rewards for conformity with cultural expectations are also more uncertain from the dominant culture.

Acculturation

The Chicana is influenced by two cultures and appears to be in transition between the two. Some social scientists see Mexican-Americans as an insulated group which continues Mexican customs despite residence of several generations in the United States (Kiev, 1972). Others say that Mexican-American cultural isolation is on the wane because of a decline in educational segregation, exposure to military service, changes in housing patterns, employment, and political movements. As a result, these social scientists predict that traditional sex roles are changing and will continue to change (Padilla & Ruiz, 1973).

Murillo (1971) believes in the existence of a good deal of conflict among Chicanos regarding the Chicana's role. He maintains that fewer women are accepting the traditional role. Many are struggling for greater equality and a greater range of personal and vocational choice within both the dominant society and Mexican-American culture.

The effect of acculturation on Chicanas is not fully understood. Some data suggest that individuals who either retain their cultural values or wholly ascribe to the value system of the majority culture manifest less psychopathology than those in the midst of assimilation (Fabrega & Wallace, 1968; Fabrega, Swartz, & Wallace, 1968a, b).

Demographic data on the Chicana indicate that she is not isolated from the institutions of the dominant culture. There are currently over 3 million Chicanas in America. Of these, 85 percent live in the Southwest; the remainder reside throughout the country; and 85 percent are urban dwellers. Their median age is 19.6 years, 10 years younger than the median age of all American women (Cotera, 1976). Census data (U.S. Bureau of the Census, 1973) for 1970 reveal that 87.2 percent of Spanish-surnamed women in the 5 Southwestern states between the ages of 14 and 17 are enrolled in school, and 21.9 percent of Chicanas over the age of 16 are high school graduates (as opposed to 31.5 percent of Chicanos). They have attained a median educational level of 9.1 years, which is 3 years below that of the entire female population in the United States but only .3 years behind the 9.4-year level of Mexican-American males. Of Chicanas over the age of 16, 36.7 percent are currently employed, including 29 percent of married Chicanas. In contrast, 39 percent of all married women in the United States work. Chicanas earn a mean income of $2,515; only 1 percent earn $10,000 a year or more (77.2 percent of Chicanos are employed, and their mean income is $5,424; 10 percent earn $10,000 a year or more).

The effects of these contacts of Mexican-American women with the dominant society are not altogether clear. Kiev (1972) stated that women, old people, and adolescents experience particular difficulty during such transitions because new economic demands and employment opportunities conflict with the traditional values that require women to remain in the home. According to Derbyshire (1968), Mexican-American adolescent girls experience less conflict over their own identities and social roles than boys. He found girls

The Black Latin & the Mexican Indian

When I grew up on New York streets
And fought my way thru knee deep garbage
My Mama sewed stars on Amerikkkan flags
At the Brooklyn Navy Yard
Like all the other Mamas
And I was lonely

When you grew up in California fields
And listened to the fat greasy patrones
Call your Papa a Wetback Greaser
Your Mama worked in the packing houses
Worked for pennies—so that white ladies could
   wear silk stockings
Paid for with your daily hunger
Were you lonely too?

While you grew callouses on your hands
I grew a callous on my heart
And, somewhere, we lost what little laughter
   we'd known
And the loneliness grew

While you picked tomatoes
I picked pockets

And we both learned how to lie and steal and
   fight
Some call it survival
I call it loneliness

But, one day the smog lifted
The city and the country smiled at each other
And so did we
The Mariachi met the Mambo
And so did we
And like the frozen snow in Spring
We melted
And like the warm winds of Summer
We were gentle
And no matter how the rain falls
And if time stops dead in its track tomorrow
I will praise the Gods for your existence
I will dance to your rhythms
Even as the sun grows cold
And I'm not lonely anymore

Avotcja

identifying more closely with Anglo females and their maternal roles, while boys identify more closely with *machismo* and the husband roles of the traditional Mexican culture. In a comparison of Anglo and Chicano responses to sex-role related verbal stimuli, Martinez, Martinez, Olmedo, and Golman (1976) found that Chicana responses resembled those of Anglos while Chicano males differed from other groups. In a study of Mexican-American acculturation, Go (1975) arrived at findings that appear to conflict with those of Derbyshire. She found adolescent Chicanas under eighteen years of age to report higher levels of anxiety than young Chicanos. She also found that highly acculturated Chicanas reported higher anxiety than highly acculturated Chicanos. The more acculturated Chicanas became, the greater the anxiety they reported. This was not true for Chicanos. While these studies on acculturation yield somewhat contradictory results, they seem to indicate that acculturation pressures are experienced differently by Mexican-American males and females.

Male-Female Differences

In addition to apparent dissimilarities in response to acculturation, research indicates a number of other psychological differences between Chicano males and females, but studies that look at sex differences are extremely limited. They are also scattered over a variety of topics with findings which, at times, appear contradictory. Therefore, it is difficult to compose either a clear or a consistent psychological profile of the Chicana from empirical data.

Personality Characteristics

In 1969, Hishiki found Mexican-American sixth-grade girls to possess lower self-concepts than Anglo-American girls of the same grade level. In a multiethnic study three years later, Larkin (1972) found that girls from homes that gave boys higher status had lower self-esteem than their brothers. Thus, Chicanas had lower self-esteem than Chicanos.

A second dissimilarity between the sexes has been found in the area of field dependence and field independence, concepts proposed by Dyk and Witkin in 1965. Briefly, field dependence-independence refers to an individual's response to external versus internal cues in forming a perceptual judgment.

Ramirez and Price-Williams (1974) found girls to be more field dependent or field "sensitive" than boys in a study of black, Anglo-American, and Mexican-American school children. This study was a followup of earlier research in which Castañeda, Ramirez, and Herold (1972) found Mexican-American students to be more field dependent than Anglo-Americans.

In a study of settled and migrant Mexican-Americans, Gecas (1973) found that Mexican-American girls expressed greater awareness of their physical selves and their body images than Mexican-American boys. This awareness of their physical selves, however, may be accompanied by a tendency on the part of Chicanas to possess more diffuse and less defined psychic selves.

Brenneis, Brooks, and Roll (1975) conducted a study of ego modalities in the manifest dreams of male and female Chicanos in which they discovered striking dissimilarities. Males tended to organize their internal psychic world around a highly visible, well demarcated self which was seen as robust, randomly active, and engaged in contentious interactions with unfamiliar characters. Chicanas reported a less sharply defined, less active, and less contentious self that engaged in a greater range of interactions with more familiar characters. These dream selves also appeared to place less emphasis on boundaries, to possess greater predictability, and to engage in more goal-directed locomotion. It therefore seems that while Chicanas may have less well defined psychic selves, these psychic selves are more peaceful and aware of others in their lives.

Further indication of Chicanas' awareness of their physical selves is found in another dream study by Roll and Brenneis (1975). In this study, they found Mexican-American females to have a higher incidence of dreams of death than Mexican-American males, who did not differ from Anglo-American males and females. The researchers explain these findings as the results of a greater tendency of Chicano women to carry the influences of the traditional culture.

Besides experiencing more death dreams, Chicanas were also found to report a greater incidence of depression than Chicanos, who exhibit more aggression (Stoker & Meadow, 1974). These findings were the result of a study of Mexican-American and Anglo-American

Espiritu Indigena, mural detail, painted by Graciela Carrillo, Santa Fe, NM.

children brought for treatment to child guidance clinics, and this sample did not come from a normal population. Nevertheless, Stoker and Meadow explain their results as related to culturally determined aspects of family structure, role conflicts, and personality. It appears, then, that Mexican-American males suffering from psychological stress are more likely to direct it outward while females are more likely to turn it inward.

Although Mexican-American girls are not as likely to act out their psychological conflicts as are boys, a study by Littlefield (1974) showed them to be more self-disclosing. When black, Anglo, and Chicano ninth-graders were given Rivenbark's revision of Jourard's self-disclosure scale, females reported more self-disclosure than males, across ethnic groups. Mexican-American females indicated a preference for a same-sex friend as the target of self-disclosure. Mothers were ranked second, opposite-sex friends third, and fathers last as confidantes.

Social Dimensions

A 1968 study by Werner and Evans of perceptions of prejudice in Mexican-American four- and five-year-olds found that school accelerated children's ability to discriminate and evaluate color differences. While both girls and boys attributed goodness to white dolls and badness to dark dolls, the boys had a greater tendency to perceive the white adult male dolls as larger than dark ones of the same size. Also, girls did not reject the dark dolls with vehemence, as did boys.

While Chicanas did not reject the dark skinned dolls as much as Chicanos in the Werner and Evans study, another study indicated that they do not choose other Chicanos as frequently as boys. Padilla, Ruiz, and Rice (1973) asked a sample of black, Anglo, and Chicano school children to react to photographs of unknown children. Each subject was presented with photographs of six children of his or her own sex, representing the three ethnic groups studied. Among other directions they were given, they were asked to identify the photograph of the child they would "most like to be" and the child they would most like to have as a friend. Only the Chicano children displayed a strong preference for their own ethnic group which is interpreted to reflect pride in group, heritage, and self. However, 81 percent of the Chicano boys wanted to be like the photographed Chicanos, but only 58 percent of the Chicana girls chose other Chicanas. Again, in choosing a friend, 75 percent of the Chicano boys chose Chicanos, while only 53 percent of the Chicanas did so. As previously

*Although Chicanas have a responsibility to understand that Chicanos face
oppression and discrimination, this does not mean that the Chicana
should be a scapegoat for the man's frustrations.*

Mirta Vidal, "Chicanas Speak Out," 1971

stated, there is an apparent contradiction between these findings and those of the previous
study.

In terms of cooperative versus competitive
behavior, the available research again appears
to be somewhat contradictory. Madsen and
Shapira (1970) conducted three experiments
measuring cooperative and competitive behavior of black, Anglo, and Chicano seven- to
nine-year-olds. In the first experiment, Mexican-American boys were less competitive
than Mexican-American girls. In the two subsequent experiments, all groups were equally
competitive. Kagan and his colleagues (unpublished ms.) have found inconsistent results
when comparing the behavior of Chicano boys
and girls. Although they found Chicanos to be
consistently more cooperative than Anglos,
their comparisons of Chicano boys and girls
are inconclusive. However, in their most recent studies (unpublished ms.) they have discovered Chicana girls to be significantly less
competitive than Chicano boys. It should be
noted that a similar sex difference has
emerged between Anglos, girls being less competitive than boys.

Kagan thought (personal communication)
this difference may be caused by a shift in experimental methodology. Previously children
participated in the experiments in pairs, while

Pacos Tacos, mural detail, painted by Graciela Carrillo; assistant, Susan
Cervantes, San Francisco, CA. © 1974.

Both Chicanos and gabachos have been guilty of the merciless stereotyping of females as docile, helpless, emotional, irrational, and intellectually inferior creatures who are best suited to be sex objects, domestic servants, and typists.

Patricia Cruz, *Imagénes de la Chicana*

---

in the two most recent studies, they were tested individually. When two children are involved in a competitive endeavor, it appears that the pace is set by the more competitive member of the dyad. Therefore, the individual's behavior, without the influence of another individual, probably reflects more accurately his or her own base level of competitive drive. Under these circumstances, Mexican-American girls appear to be more "prosocial," as Kagan terms such behavior, than are boys.

Academic Achievement

The competitiveness required for success in American schools and the lack of cooperative learning methods in our public schools appear to place Chicanas at a serious disadvantage. This may be one of the reasons for the low academic achievement of Mexican-American females. In successive studies, Mason (1967, 1969) administered the California psychological inventory (C.P.I.) to American Indian, Chicano, and Anglo students. The C.P.I. measures attitudes toward self, so-called "social maturity," and achievement motivation. In the 1967 study, Mason found that Mexican-American females' responses across the eighteen subtests were the most consistently negative of all groups. This parallels the findings of Ramirez, Taylor, and Petersen (1971) who found that Mexican-American females differed from males in their responses to the school situations picture stories test which is scored for power, achievement, affiliation, and rejection. On power and affiliation, differences between the scores of males and females were slight; however, females scored lower on achievement and higher on rejection than males.

From these data, the emerging picture of the Chicana's academic performance appears to be negative; but other studies introduce a more positive note. Mason's second study (1969) of American Indian, Anglo, and Chicano students showed a change in the scores of Chicano males and females, females scoring higher than in the first study (Mason, 1967) and males relatively lower. A 1974 study by Fisher of nonintellectual attributes of children in first-grade bilingual-bicultural programs also showed gains on the part of Chicanas. In this study, the Anglo and Chicano children were tested on the Piers-Harris children's self-concept scale and the Howard maze test in order to assess self-concept, self-description, and stimulus-seeking activity. The results indicated that the bilingual-bicultural program significantly enhanced the self-concepts of Chicano girls, but not of Chicano boys. While boys remained unchanged, girls were found to be happier and more satisfied and expressed feelings that their behavior at school had improved. Mexican-American girls also increased their stimulus-seeking activity, that is, they became more open to environmental stimuli, while boys showed no significant change.

Summary of Research

A summary of the psychological differences between Mexican-American males and females appears to indicate that Mexican-American females are suffering more from oppression. With respect to personality characteristics, Chicanas show: (a) lower self-esteem, (b) more field dependence, (c) greater identity with families and homes that tend to give

When a family is involved in a human rights movement, as is the
Mexican-American family, there is little room for a woman's liberation
movement alone.

Enriqueta Longauex y Vasquez, in Robin
Morgan (ed.), *Sisterhood Is Powerful*, 1970

males more status, (d) more concern about their physical selves, (e) less well defined psychic selves, (f) more death dreams, and (g) more depression. With respect to social dimensions, Chicanas appear not to reject dark skin as much as Chicanos, yet choose Mexican-Americans socially less frequently than do boys. Chicanas also appear to be more prosocial and less competitive than Chicano males. In school, Chicano girls show less achievement and a more generalized negative reaction than boys.

Despite a fairly consistent picture of the effects of oppression, it appears that Chicanas are also more responsive to positive intervention. They appear to benefit more from supportive programs than do males. They also tend to be more self-disclosing, a characteristic that makes them better candidates for traditional therapeutic intervention.

The only conclusion to be drawn from this survey of psychological research on Mexican-Americans is that the data are insufficient. There is a pressing need for carefully conducted studies using Mexican-American females as subjects and for the wide dissemination of the information resulting from these studies. Most important, one must be very cautious in drawing conclusions about Chicanas on the basis of psychological tests and techniques that clearly suffer from Anglocentric bias and were not designed to assess the psychological state of the Chicana.

Androgyny

As was previously noted, the increasing contact of Mexican-Americans with the dominant culture and the resulting acculturation is rapidly modifying sex-role attitudes. Meanwhile, concepts regarding sex-role identification in the dominant culture are also being altered. In both the field of psychology and society at large, masculinity and femininity have traditionally been dichotomized, so that an individual was considered feminine or masculine, but not both. It has been proposed that individuals might be psychologically androgynous, therefore possessing masculine *and* feminine characteristics and that androgynous people may be more psychologically healthy than sex-typed individuals (Bem, 1974).

In a study of black, Asian-American, Mexican-American, and Anglo-American high school women, Hawley (1975) found a correlation between ethnicity and sex-role orientation. Anglo females were the most androgynous, while black females and Chicanas were more sex-typed in their responses. She found, however, that IQ scores were a better predictor of sex-role orientation than ethnic identity, with high IQ girls more likely to be androgynous in orientation than low IQ girls across all ethnic groups studied.

Senour and Warren (1976) used the Bem sex-role inventory (BSRI) to assess ethnic differences in masculinity, femininity, and androgyny among Anglos, blacks, and Chicanos. The inventory was administered to community college students: 60 black males, 64 black females, 83 Chicanos, 97 Chicanas, 106 Anglo males, and 144 Anglo females. A two-way analysis of variance (sex by race) was used to analyze the results separately for masculinity, femininity, social desirability, and androgyny.

As expected, significant sex differences

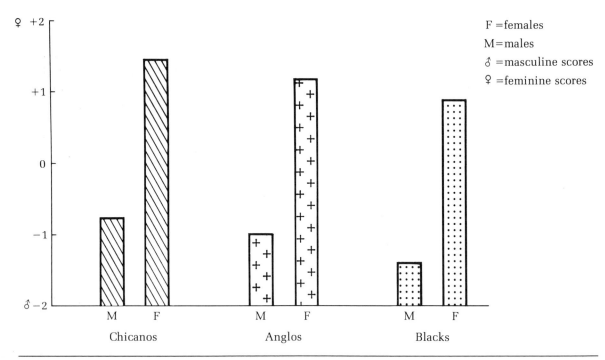

Figure 1.
The y axis represents the mean androgyny *t*-ratio for each ethnic group. This is a bipolar scale with a positive score indicating a higher endorsement of feminine items and a negative score indicating a higher endorsement of masculine items. Note the differences between ethnic groups with Chicanos as a group describing themselves in the most feminine sex-typed terms and blacks as a group describing themselves in the most masculine sex-typed terms.

were found, females scoring higher on femininity and lower on masculinity than males. Androgyny scores also differed, females scoring in the feminine direction and males in the masculine direction on androgyny.

An interesting finding was that, as a group, blacks scored in the masculine direction on androgyny, while both Anglos and Chicanos scored in the feminine direction, $F(2, 548) =$ 3.33, $p < .036$. The androgyny score is a reflection of the relative strength of a masculine and feminine orientation in a person's self-description. The greater the absolute value of a person's androgyny score, the more the person is sex typed or sex reversed. High positive scores indicate an endorsement of feminine items over masculine items, while high negative scores indicate an endorsement of masculine items over feminine items. The closer the score is to zero, the greater the extent of agreement between the individual's endorsement of masculine and feminine items.

Figure 1 illustrates the differences found among the groups on androgyny. As can be seen, Chicano males scored –.80 while Chicanos scored 1.29. Anglo males scored –1.00 while females scored 1.09. Black males scored –1.43 while females scored .88. Of the three ethnic groups, Chicanos, then, demonstrated the greatest tendency to endorse feminine items over masculine items and Chicano women did so more than did any other category of respondents.

There were, however, no significant sex by race interactions in any of the analyses. Chicanos did not emerge as super masculine in comparison to black or Anglo males, and Chicanas were found to be no more feminine than their black and Anglo counterparts, although there was a tendency in this direction.

It should be noted, however, that the BSRI is an Anglocentric measure and that the black and Chicano subjects used in this study were presumably moderately to highly acculturated. Perhaps future research on ethnicity and sex roles can control these factors and thereby clarify the role of ethnicity in sex-role development and orientation.

Summary

Prior to terminating this chapter, it seems appropriate to reiterate that it would be incautious to accept at face value the profile of the Chicana that has emerged from the work cited. The use of Freudian analysis in examining the Mexican family, the absence of empirical support for much of the work describ-

Queen of Ability by Consuelo Gonzalez Amezcua. Reprinted with permission of Ms. Zare Gonzalez.

ing Chicano sex roles, the lack of research by Mexican-American women on Mexican-American women, and the insufficiency of current research tools and methodologies should be kept in mind. In addition, this work does not give information on the numerous Chicanas that do not conform to the general norms. On the other hand, it would be equally incautious to simply dismiss the existing literature and research. Careful analysis of each study, article, and book should first be conducted.

It appears that traditionally, the Mexican-American woman has accepted the roles of mother, wife, and homemaker where she has functioned as the pillar of family life. Subservience to her father and later to her husband has long been accepted in silence. It is, however, becoming increasingly apparent that the Chicana is affected by a dominant culture which is in the midst of a sex-role revolution. Although at a different pace than her Anglo counterpart, the Chicana is also changing her traditional sex roles. Since culture is dynamic, this is inevitable.

It seems important that social science research be conducted on the emerging Chicana. Such studies would be useful not only for purposes of developing a psychology of the Chicana but also a means of feedback on the effects sex-role changes will have on Mexican-American culture. It is imperative that the Chicana achieve her full human potential, for she possesses a wealth of human resources that remains untapped by her *raza* (race) and her country. Both for the sake of her fulfillment and for her contribution to society, barriers to her full participation in whatever aspects of life she chooses to involve herself must be eliminated. It seems equally imperative, however, that this struggle be conducted in a manner that avoids polarization from the Chicano, for the Mexican-American woman is only half of a people in need of liberation.

Shirley Hill Witt

The Two Worlds of Native Women

Living in Two Worlds

There is no native person in North America untouched by the Anglo world, the White Man's World, the American Way. Nor are any immune to its infectiousness. Yet few self-identifying American Indians live exclusively in the non-Indian world. To be "Indian" carries for many a sense of homeland (reservation, tribe, community) and duty to one's people, no matter where one currently resides, or whether one ever returns, or whether those duties are ever discharged. This implies that native peoples are aware of and practice to varying degrees two, often widely contrasting, life styles. To move between these two worlds can be a feast of appreciation for human ingenuity, or it can be the bitterest trap.

Indian children typically learn two sets of ways—neither perfectly—whether they live in an apartment in Minneapolis or attend the Bureau of Indian Affairs School on the San Juan Pueblo in New Mexico. No one knows his or her own culture perfectly. But neither is a person limited to ingesting a set number of cultural traits or ways. It is sometimes thought that a person learns one set of lifeways—like a glass being filled with liquid—and that is all they can learn. Furthermore, in this line of thinking, to learn more (such as another culture) some of the liquid must be poured out in order to make way for the new liquid. This view sees the process of learning another culture as a *replacement* of traits, predicating a limit to human intelligence and plasticity. It is a kind of tunnel-visioned view often found among monocultured people.

The viewpoint guiding this essay, however, is that we are limited only by our intelligence and our ability to learn, and what one culture has created is learnable by members of another. Rather than pouring out one liquid to make way for another in the glass, this view recognizes that there can be *additional* glasses each with its varying amount of "cultural liquid" restricted only by our intellectual capability and thirst. No one learns any culture perfectly, thus additional cultural traits from divergent traditions may be that much harder to learn, or may be learned less accurately.

Native people, then, find themselves participating to a greater or lesser extent both in the Indian world as defined by their tribal affiliation, and in the White Man's World. This term, the White Man's World, is not to be taken as a quaint archaic phrase: the world of the white women is essentially invisible to Indians. Even if perceived, it is irrelevent since the white *man's* world is the one making an impact upon Indian life and Indian individuals. It is still the Great White Father [sic] who determines the quality of life for native as well as all other Americans.

Our Many Worlds

The "Indian World" that provides the cultural backdrop for the enculturating individual is by no means a monolithic entity. Native peoples may be members of one or more units such as clans, bands, rancherias, pueblos, communities, reservations, tribes, or nations. This list includes some of the possible social and demographic groups to which one may belong.

Pottery Sellers by Pablita Velard. Reprinted by permission of Philbrook Art Center, Tulsa, Oklahoma

There are 287 tribal governments within the United States, nearly another hundred that found themselves terminated from federal status during the 1950s, and 130 tribes that have never been recognized by the federal government.[1] Of some 600 different cultures believed to have existed in the continental United States,[2] some 500 appear to have survived in one shape or another. The 1970 census indicates that there are 792,730 Native Americans living in every state of the Union and the District of Columbia (an increase of 122 percent since 1950).[3] This number does not include some 34,538 Eskimos and Aleuts,[4] which would then bring the total to 827,268. Many knowledgeable people believe the true figure approaches the 1 million mark,[5] with as many as 10 million people believed to be carrying some degree of Indian blood.[6]

Among those numbers are thousands of detribalized Indians who became disenfranchised by accident of fate, for example, through adoption, or by design, such as through deliberate parental attempt to leave Indian ethnicity behind. Great numbers of these "lost" Indians are seeking reidentification with their past and people. The attempt to regain Alcatraz Island was staged in large part by such youth who constituted themselves into a conglomerate body entitled "Indians of All Tribes."

By now it should be clear to the reader that the Indian world is a vast diffuse concept that can mean many different things to many people, Indian or otherwise. For the purpose of this essay, we will examine the record of tribal women as they seek to achieve success in the Native and white worlds, two entities of great amorphousness yet highly compelling in their demands.

This report briefly draws a generalized picture of Pre-Columbian America's variety of cultures, particularly with respect to women's status and roles in their societies. Then a section is offered which discusses Native women in the world of work, followed by an exposition of the world of education as it affects them.

From Strength Before Columbus

As many as 280 distinct aboriginal societies existed in North America prior to the arrival of Columbus. In several, the roles of native women stand in stark contrast of those of Europeans. These societies were matriarchal, matrilineal, and matrilocal—which is to say that women largely controlled family matters, inheritance passed through the female lines, and upon marriage the bride usually brought her groom into her mother's household.

In a matrilocal household all the women were blood relatives and all the males were outsiders. This sort of residence pattern was frequently seen among agricultural societies in which women bore the responsibility for farming. It guaranteed a close-knit working force of women who had grown up with each other and the land.

Somewhat similar was the style of acquiring a spouse called "bride service" or "suitor service." In this case, the erstwhile husband went to live and work in his future bride's home for a period of time, proving his ability to manage a family of his own. This essentially resulted in temporary matrilocal residence. After the birth of the first child, the husband usually took his family with him to live among his own kin.

In matrilineal, matrilocal society, a woman forever remained part of her original household, her family of orientation. All the women she grew up with stayed nearby, although she "lost" her brothers to other households. All the husbands were outsiders brought into the family at the time of marriage.

In such societies, usually agricultural, the economy was maintained largely by females. The fields and harvests were the property of women. Daughters inherited rights to fields and the like through their mothers—fields in which they had worked all their lives in one capacity or another, from chasing away crows as a child to tilling the soil as an adult.

Women working together certainly characterized aboriginal economy. This life style was roughly similar in such widespread groups as the Iroquois, the Mandan, the Hopi and Zuni, and various Eastern Pueblos. Among the Hopi and the Zuni the husband joined the bride's household upon marriage. The fields were owned by the women, as were their products, the house, and related implements. However, the men labored in the gardens and were (with the unmarried brothers) responsible for much or most of the work.

The strong and influential position of women in Navajo society extended beyond social and economic life. Navajo women also controlled a large share of the political and religious life of the people, called the Diné. Hogans, herds, and equipment were passed down through the female line, from mother to daughters. Like the Iroquois, women were integral to the religious cycle. The Navajo female puberty ceremony ranked among the most important of Diné activities.

Although the lives of Native American women differed greatly from tribe to tribe, their life styles exhibited a great deal more independence and security than those of the European women who came to these shores. Indian women had individual freedom within tribal life that women in more "advanced" societies were not to experience for several generations. Furthermore—and in contrast—native women increased in value in the estimation of their society as they grew older.

Self Portrait #3, painting by Wendy Rose, Hopi, © 1975 Wendy Rose

Their cumulative wisdom was considered one of society's most valuable resources.

What then does the picture look like today?

Indian Women in the World of Work

There is no uniform, consistent, and accurate data base that measures employment, unemployment, and underemployment among American Indians. The BIA estimates speak to the reservation situation for the most part. Off-reservation statistics are entirely implausible.

What is clear is the fact that Native Americans find themselves at the bottom of any list ranking levels of employment and education. And when such a list is segregated into male and female classifications, Indian women are consistently the lowest paid, lowest ranked, most unemployed segment of the national workforce.

To the extent that Indian employment is federal employment, federal employment essentially means employment in the Department of Interior (mainly BIA) or in the Department of Health, Education and Welfare Health Service, Indian Health Branch.

Of all groups, 59.7 percent are males and 40.3 percent are females, and of those 13,229 employees, 32.7 percent are Indian females.[7] Underscoring these figures, a full one-third of all BIA employees are Indian women whose average GS grade is a dismal GS-5.[8] Even when the training is apparently adequate, it is no easy step for Native women to attain higher positions in the federal system.

Translating occupational levels into income levels brings home the greater message of the poverty of Indian women. A 1969 tally by DOL'S Women's Bureau showed that of 233,266 some 36.3 percent (84,700 individuals) had no incomes at all.[9] Their median income was $1,697—the lowest for any group in the country. Table 1 displays some interesting comparisons in median wages:

A nation is not conquered until the hearts of its women are on the ground. Then, it is done, no matter how brave its warriors nor how strong its weapons.

Cheyenne Proverb

TABLE 1

Group	Wage
White men	$7,391
White women	4,777
Pilipino women	3,513
Japanese women	3,236
Chinese women	2,686
Black women	2,041
Hispanic women	2,016
Native American women	1,697

SOURCE: U.S. Department of Commerce, *Statistical Abstract of the United States* (1971); *Negro Population* (1973); *Persons of Spanish Origin* (1973); *Japanese, Chinese, and Filipinos in the United States* (1973).

Median income for women family heads was $3,198 and only 6 percent of all Indian women heads of families received incomes of $10,000 or more. Of 4,087 individual Indians earning $15,000 or more, only 517 were women.[10]

Native Women in the World of Education

For generations the education of Indian children was channeled by the federal government into its Bureau of Indian Affairs schools or the schools set up by a myriad collection of church missions. The goal was assimilatory, its technique was regimentation, and its product was, among other things, sexist.

With constant pressure from native parents through the decades, change has occurred in the picture of Indian education in recent years. Also, in part for its own reasons—the government policy to reduce the educational responsibility of the BIA—more and more of the teaching duties have been turned over to public schools and schools run by native peoples. It is estimated that some 63 percent of Indian students are now in public schools operated by local district or county school boards, nearly 31 percent are in schools operated by the BIA, and about 6 percent are in mission schools.[11]

What are the current levels of achievement of Indian children as compared to other minority students and white students of non-metropolitan areas? Coleman's[12] data show that Indian pupils rank just below the national performance average during the first four school years, and then they drop substantially. This is generally due to the practice of running non-English speaking children through a beginner class at the age of six and then first grade at seven and to the fact that Indian children are frequently held back one or more times in their school career.[13]

The median educational attainment for Indian women as of 1970 was 10.5 years, as compared to their 1950 median of 7.4 years of schooling and 10.4 for Indian men in 1970.[14] It is also clear that the urban setting provides greater access to education when it is seen that urban native women completed 11.4 years of school as opposed to rural non-farm Indian women who reached only 9.7 years.[15]

The BIA boarding school is a specter that is only recently receding into the gloom of failed experiments perpetrated upon the Indian communities, and it is by no means invisible yet. While it continues to stalk, Indian children

Navajo Woman Praying by Sybil Yazzie, Collection of Red Cloud Indian School

of the Anglo world. Quoting from an earlier essay:[16]

> And so, generation after generation of native women have been processed through a system clearly goal-oriented. That is to say, the Government's master plan for women has been to generate an endless stream of domestics and, to a lesser extent, secretaries. The vocational choices for native children in boarding schools have always been exceedingly narrow and sexist. Boys do woodworking, car repair, house painting, or farmwork; while girls do domestic or secretarial work.

When we review the occupational distribution of Indian women today, it comes as no surprise to find nearly all of them among the female-work ghetto employees found the nation over. It was designed that way.

A recent and most definitive—and perhaps only—investigation of Native women in higher education is that of Dr. Clara Sue Kidwell, a Choctaw now at University of California-Berkeley.[17] Her study of 61 responses to questionnaires sent out to junior college and college women generated some very interesting results. For example, she observes that a general pattern appears which suggests that "Native American women are either graduating from high school at later ages than people who go through the educational system in 12 years, or that they are not entering college directly from high school," that is, they are older.[18]

still are being herded off to schools hundreds of miles away from home from the age of 6 on, to become indoctrinated into the BIA's version

American Indians from all of the countries of the Americas are rising up and demanding their rightful voice in the world—and the right to live according to our own visions. . . . We do not believe that our way of life is perfect or has ever been so. But as we look at what the whiteman is doing to us, to himself, and to the Earth our Mother, we see that we do have a way of life. The whiteman has a way of death. American Indian women have wisdoms and insights that are valuable, if not necessary, to the dialogue on women's rights—and the dialogue on human rights. . . . Today, as always, American Indian women well understand that there can be no liberation of Indian women as women until all Indian people are free of colonial oppression.

from *Native American Women,* 1975

Her sample ranged between 18 and 42 years of age. All but 16 attended public schools. Strong interest, motivation, and commitment to the pursuit of advanced degrees characterized the group, and their motivation stemmed primarily from their desire for a professional career and need for future employment.[19] Of least importance (perhaps because of its scarcity?) was the encouragement by teachers and counselors. She notes that under the category called "other," the respondents listed as motivating factors community encouragement, boredom with present job, self-fulfillment, ambition, and "nowhere else to go."

Kidwell's data indicate a strong encouragement on the part of parents and family members for their daughters to seek a college education. In fact, she reports that "It would seem that parents may be *more* [emphasis added] anxious for the female offspring to go to college than for their male offspring to do so."[20] Yet, once in the (non-Indian) academic world, 30 respondents reported that they had felt discrimination against them as a result of their being Indian, 10 described discrimination against them as women, and 9 responded to the question that they had suffered under the double bind of being both an Indian and a woman.[21] Kidwell tentatively concludes that "the major source of discrimination (and thus potentially a negative factor in the woman's college career) stemmed from racism rather than sexism."[22] Fifty-three of the 61 women polled denied that they felt they were going against Indian culture by going to college.

In conclusion, Kidwell described the motivation and aspirations of those native women surveyed who are professionally employed:

If the Native American faculty and professional women questioned and the women currently in graduate school who were interviewed are highly unusual in their accomplishments in relation to most Native American women, they are also strongly committed to their sense of Native American identity and they are committed to playing an active role in assisting other Indian women (and Indian students generally) to get through college. They are also strongly committed to playing some role that will benefit Native American communities in the country today.[23]

Conclusion

Native women have a diversified heritage, though one which holds a potential far greater than is currently realized. To the extent that the world of the Great White Father is willing to open itself to Native Americans, Indian women have a unique vision and contribution to bring. It may be that for Native women

It is time to ascend to the
Mountain tops
To begin to chant the
Music of our visions.

—Rain Parrish

Psychological Oppression

This section presents a theory of psychological oppression that may be viewed as a sociopolitical analysis of the psychology of women at the intrapsychic and interpersonal levels. By extension, the presentation of psychological oppression could apply to any subordinated group (for example, on a racial or socioeconomic basis) in relation to the dominant group, although the primary focus here remains on women as a subordinated group.

Although published in 1951, the analysis presented in the first article by Helen Mayer Hacker remains remarkably relevant with only minor, though important, changes due to historical developments. One such change is that in 1951, women did not fully qualify as a minority group since, although discriminated against, they were not aware of such discrimination and lacked feelings of group identification and minority group consciousness. As Hacker points out, though, there were a few sex-conscious women in the National Woman's Party who, since the passage of the constitutional amendment granting women the right to vote, continued to work toward passage of the Equal Rights Amendment (ERA). With the recent reemergence of the feminist movement, however, women now have such identification and an ever increasing consciousness of their oppression (Hacker, 1974), as evidenced by the comparatively vast number of women advocating the rights of women, including current efforts to ensure passage of the ERA.

Modifying slightly Hacker's analysis for lack of group membership, it could be said that for women to lack minority group consciousness, they must distort their reality by unconsciously denying either group membership, the disesteem with which the group is regarded, or the

existence of the group altogether. It is argued here that despite the resurgence of the women's movement, many women continue to unconsciously deny their minority group status and their experience as members of a subordinate group.

It is this distortion of experience, its behavioral effects and emotional consequences combined with the lack of awareness or only partial awareness, that is referred to as psychological oppression. The unconscious psychological processes of identification with the dominant group and internalization of the dominant group's norms by a subordinate group member are also implied by the term. This includes internalization of the negative stereotypes and beliefs of the subordinate group of which one is a member. Low self-esteem leading to self-hatred and hostility toward other subordinate group members are further results of psychological oppression, according to this theory.

Hacker's paper includes a chart comparing the minority group status of blacks and women, including the accommodation attitudes of the subordinated position. Psychological oppression in terms of this chart would be evidenced by acceptance on the part of subordinate group members as one's "nature" the ascribed attributes of women, the rationalization of women's status and the accommodation attitudes.

It would be interesting to include children as a third column in the chart as feminists are also concerned with the oppression of children. It has been argued that even the "childlike" behavior of children is in part due to the historical development of children as a subordinated class (Ariès, 1965). The addition of children in the chart may also provide further

The myth of childhood has an even greater parallel in the myth of femininity. Both women and children were considered asexual and thus "purer" than man. Their inferior status was ill-concealed under an elaborate "respect." One didn't discuss serious matters nor did one curse in front of women and children; one didn't openly degrade them, one did it behind their backs. (As for the double standard about cursing: A man is allowed to blaspheme the world because it belongs to him to damn—but the same curse out of the mouth of a woman or a minor, i.e., an incomplete "man" to whom the world does not belong, is considered presumptuous, and thus an impropriety or worse.)

Shulamith Firestone, *The Dialectic of Sex,*
1970

---

insight into the relationship of women and children, for example, the parallel between "feminine" and "childlike" qualities.

"Femininity," then may be essentially the behavioral and emotional manifestations of psychological oppression. Jo Freeman (1971) has also noted the similarity of "femininity" to "minority group character structure:

Let us further examine the effects on women of minority group status. Here, an interesting parallel emerges, but it is one fraught with much heresy. When we look at the *results* of female socialization we find a strong similarity between what our society labels, even extols, as the typical "feminine" character structure and that of oppressed peoples in this country and elsewhere.

In his classic study on *The Nature of Prejudice*, Allport devotes a chapter to "Traits Due to Victimization." Included are such personality characteristics as sensitivity, submission, fantasies of power, desire for protection, indirectness, ingratiation, petty revenge and sabotage, sympathy, extremes of both self- and group hatred and self- and group glorification, display of flashy status symbols, compassion for the underprivileged, identification with the dominant group's norms, and passivity (Allport, 1954). Allport was primarily concerned with Jews and Negroes, but compare his characterization with the very thorough review of the literature on sex differences among young children made by Terman and Tyler (1954). For girls, they listed such traits as sensitivity, conformity to social pressures, response to environment, ease of social control, ingratiation, sympathy, low levels of aspiration, compassion for the underprivileged, and anxiety. They found that girls compared to boys were more nervous, unstable, neurotic, socially dependent, submissive, had less self-confidence, lower opinions of themselves and of girls in general, and were more timid, emotional, ministrative, fearful, and passive. . . .

This combination of group self-hate and distortion of perceptions to justify that group self-hate are precisely the traits typical of a "minority group character structure" (Clark & Clark, 1947). . . . These traits, as well as the others typical of the "feminine" stereotype, have been found in the Indians under British rule (Fisher, 1954), in the Algerians under the French (Fanon, 1963), and in black Americans (Myrdal, 1944). There seems to be a correlation between being "feminine" and experiencing status deprivation (pp. 124–126).

If women are psychologically oppressed, they should have low self-esteem. It is interesting, then, that Maccoby and Jacklin (1974) report that females do not have lower self-esteem than males from childhood through adolescence (see the section on psychological sex differences). In a partial reanalysis of the data upon which their conclusions are based, Block (1976) does, however, find evidence for lower self-esteem in girls of some age groups.

It is hard to fight an enemy who has outposts in your head.

Sally Kempton, *Esquire*, 1970

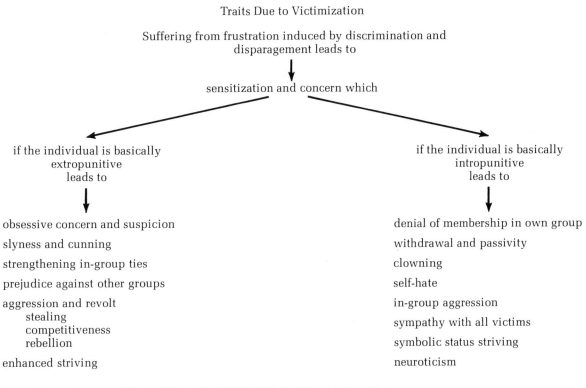

Traits Due to Victimization

Suffering from frustration induced by discrimination and disparagement leads to

sensitization and concern which

if the individual is basically extropunitive leads to

if the individual is basically intropunitive leads to

obsessive concern and suspicion

slyness and cunning

strengthening in-group ties

prejudice against other groups

aggression and revolt
    stealing
    competitiveness
    rebellion

enhanced striving

denial of membership in own group

withdrawal and passivity

clowning

self-hate

in-group aggression

sympathy with all victims

symbolic status striving

neuroticism

From Allport, Gordon, THE NATURE OF PREJUDICE © 1954, Addison-Wesley Publishing Company, Inc., p. 160, chart, "Traits Due to Victimization," in our book. Reprinted with permission.

Indirect evidence for low self-esteem in women has been found in the classic study by Broverman et al. (1972), in which a series of opposite adjectives were identified first as either male or female traits, and then as to whether they were socially desirable. There

IT'S LUCKY I'M
WHITE AND MIDDLE-CLASS —
OTHERWISE I'D HAVE A
PROBLEM.

© Ellen Levine, from *All She Needs . . .*, Quadrangle, 1973

was a high percentage of agreement about these traits among both male and female college students. The following were considered male traits and deemed desirable for any person to have:

> aggressive, independent, unemotional, hides emotions, objective, not easily influenced, dominant, likes math and science, not excitable in a minor crisis, active, competitive, logical, worldly, skilled in business, direct, knows the way of the world, feelings not easily hurt, adventurous, makes decisions easily, never cries, acts as a leader, self-confident, not comfortable about being aggressive, ambitious, able to separate feelings from ideas, not dependent, not conceited about appearance, thinks men are superior to women, talks freely about sex with men.

Traits considered female and deemed desirable for any person to have were the following:

> does not use harsh language, talkative, tactful, gentle, aware of the feelings of others, religious, interested in own appearance, neat in habits, quiet, strong need for security, appreciates art and literature, expresses tender feelings.

As Freeman (1971) has suggested, the female role does have positive aspects, but they are not those attributes for which society offers its highest rewards.

Returning to Hacker's comparison of women and Blacks, we also find differences between these two groups in terms of minority group status. First of all, the two groups differ in terms of their social distance from the dominant group, a conventional measure of degree of discrimination. Second, the magnitude of discrimination is greater for Blacks than for (white) women.

These factors may play a special role in women's failure to develop minority group consciousness in a number of ways. First of all, because of the lesser degree of social distance, women may be more likely to accept the dominant group's attitudes toward them. Second, white middle-class women especially by virtue of their association to white men through kinship and marital ties, have access to power and authority, and enjoy a materially comfortable life. These women may even establish a sense of personal worth based on the status of the men with whom they are associated. Because of these factors, based on white women's close proximity to white men, it can be seen that the cult of "femininity" may be especially required to maintain the subordinate status of white women. "Femininity," then, may spread through racial minority groups as these groups adopt the dominant (white) culture's values and norms. White women's social status and access to resources,

Psychological oppression is a pervasive aspect of modern capitalism. The choices of bourgeois existence are madness, total apathy, and conformity.

Jerome Agel, *Rough Times*, 1973

power, and authority through their relationships to white men and their materially comfortable lives would be deterrents to developing minority group consciousness and would at least partially explain why white women may prefer psychological oppression and "femininity" to consciousness and action.

Hacker draws further implications from the concept of social distance by suggesting a redefinition of it in emotional rather than physical terms. Since men and women marry each other, there is obviously a minimum of social distance, but, she points out, "the presence of love does not in itself argue for either equality of status or fullness of communication. We may love those who are either inferior or superior to us and we may love persons whom we do not understand." She thus implies that "love" can take place within the context of emotional distance. Furthermore, "since inequalities of status are preserved in marriage, a dominant group member may be willing to marry a member of a group which, in general, he would not wish admitted to his club," indicating that men may "love" women although they may not like them. Firestone (1970) has developed a more thorough analysis of love based on present inequalities, and the next section explores further the topic of relationships and intimacy.

Finally, in establishing women's minority-

group status, Hacker refers to two particularly noteworthy concepts regarding women's culture. First, women have a *subculture*—the beauty parlor or the kitchen, for example. Feminists (Burris, 1973) have also argued for the existence of women's subculture, a global phenomenon known as the "Fourth World," which remains submerged under worldwide patriarchy. Second, Hacker refers to the lack of a *culture* with which women can identify, though more recently (1974) she notes the present basis for creating a culture. Other feminists have also discussed the difficulties of a lack of a positive alternative culture based on female solidarity (Battle-Sister, 1971). Recently, however, as a result of the women's movement, a Female culture is being created (see Polk's paper on the women's movement).

Following Hacker's essay is a paper by Nancy Henley and Jo Freeman, which provides an analysis and documentation of the behavioral manifestations of psychological oppression. See Henley (1977) for a further elaboration of these. To refer to the chart in Hacker's paper, this would be an expansion of the "accommodation attitudes": rising inflections, smiles, laughs, downward glances, flattering manner, and so forth. As Henley and Freeman state, "by being continually reminded of their inferior status in their interactions with others, and continually compelled

*Any intelligent woman who reads the marriage contract, and then goes
into it, deserves all the consequences.*

Isadora Duncan, *My Life*, 1927

---

to acknowledge that status in their own patterns of behavior, women learn to internalize society's definition of them as inferior so thoroughly that they are often unaware of what their status is."

When women do *not* acknowledge their inferior status through verbal or nonverbal behavior, they receive negative social sanctions. Negative labeling of women as "unfeminine" or "mentally ill" are usually sufficient means of social control. It may be postulated that according to principles of psychological oppression as a group phenomenon, women even more than men perform the social control functions on behalf of the dominant group. Chesler (1972, p. 175) has mentioned the "policing" of women by women.

The next two articles continue the theme of psychological oppression by examining the psychological effects on women of male aggression toward women in the forms of physical and sexual violence. Some feminist anthropologists have theorized that male violence toward women is the basis for female subordination to men cross-culturally (Quinn, 1977; Webster, 1977). This would be consistent with the data and theory presented in the next article by Marjorie Whitaker Leidig. She finds that women of all races and economic classes in the U.S. are subject to and experience equivalent levels of violence from men of (approximately) corresponding races and economic classes. Leidig presents a conceptualization of various acts of violence including hassling, rape, physical and emotional abuse,

and incest along a continuum of severity. She provides evidence for numerous linkages among these and the myths surrounding their occurrence. She then provides a feminist analysis in that male violence toward women serves to maintain patriarchy by which all men benefit from some men's violence toward women. Virtually all women are threatened by the possibility of male violence and are therefore controlled through fear and kept in their place. This may indeed be a very important basis for psychological and real oppression of women.

The final paper in this section, by Judith Herman and Lisa Hirschman, focuses on incest by developing a theory of sexuality in a patriarchal context and by presenting and discussing data from incest victims. Through case reports of these victims, the relationships among various family members are described, particularly mother-daughter and father-daughter relationships. The emotional dynamics of these women and the psychological consequences of the incest are also described.

Similar to Leidig, these authors note the underreporting of the occurrence of incest. Herman and Hirschman further suggest the probable rate of occurrence of similar psychological dynamics to be even higher. "We suspect that many women have been aware of, and frightened by, seductive behavior on the part of their own fathers. For every family in which incest is consummated, there are undoubtedly hundreds with essentially similar, if less extreme, psychological dynamics." To the

It has been argued that, when killing is viewed as not only permissible but heroic behavior sanctioned by one's government or cause, the fine distinction between taking a human life and other forms of impermissible violence gets lost, and rape becomes an unfortunate but inevitable by-product of the necessary game called war.

Susan Brownmiller, *Against Our Will: Men, Women and Rape*, 1975

---

extent that these may be fairly common dynamics, there may be further implications for female psychology and female sexuality.

Similar to victims of male violence as discussed by Leidig, the mistreatment of incest victims has often been compounded by traditional (patriarchal) psychotherapists. In contrast, feminist therapists would emphasize the external, non-intrapsychic power dynamics involved within the context of the family and the larger society. Feminist therapeutic efforts would involve not only individual psychotherapy, but group and family therapy, as well as treatment for the society as a whole.

From a feminist perspective, power dynamics as they affect women intrapsychically, via psychological oppression, and interpersonally, as Henley and Freeman describe, or as they are carried out through various acts of aggression and violence, including incest, cannot be ended until the existence of patriarchy is ended.

For Further Reading

Brownmiller, S. 1976. *Against Our Will.* New York: Simon and Schuster.

Freeman, J. (Ed.). 1979. *Women: A Feminist Perspective.* (Second ed.) Palo Alto: Mayfield.

Gager, N., and Schurr, C. 1976. *Sexual Assault: Confronting Rape in America.* New York: Grosset & Dunlap.

Griffin, S. 1979. *Rape: The Power of Consciousness.* New York: Harper & Row.

Hacker, H. M. 1975. Class and Race Differences in Gender Roles. In *Gender and Sex in Society,* Lucile Duberman (Ed.). New York: Praeger.

Henley, N. 1977. *Body Politics: Power, Sex, and Nonverbal Communication.* Englewood Cliffs, N.J.: Prentice-Hall.

Herman, J. 1981. *Father-Daughter Incest.* Cambridge, Mass.: Harvard Univ. Press.

Komarovsky, M. 1962. *Blue Collar Marriage.* New York: Random House.

Moore, D. 1979. *Battered Women.* Beverly Hills, Calif.: Sage.

Rubin, L. B. 1976. *Worlds of Pain.* New York: Harper & Row.

Rush, F. 1980. *The Best-kept Secret: Sexual Abuse of Children.* Englewood Cliffs, N.J.: Prentice-Hall.

Russell, D. 1975. *Politics of Rape: The Victim's Perspective.* New York: Stein and Day.

Seifer, N. 1976. *Nobody Speaks For Me! Self-Portraits of American Working Class Women.* New York: Simon and Schuster.

Thorne, B., and Henley, N. (Eds.). 1975. *Language and Sex: Difference and Dominance.* Rowley, Mass.: Newbury House.

Walker, L. 1979. *The Battered Woman.* New York: Harper & Row.

Helen Mayer Hacker

Women as a Minority Group

Although sociological literature reveals scattered references to women as a minority group, comparable in certain respects to racial, ethnic, and national minorities, no systematic investigation has been undertaken as to what extent the term "minority group" is applicable to women. That there has been little serious consideration of women as a minority group among sociologists is manifested in the recently issued index to *The American Journal of Sociology* wherein under the heading of "Minority Groups" there appears: "See Jews; Morale; Negro; Races and Nationalities; Religious Groups; Sects." There is no cross-reference to women, but such reference is found under the heading "Family."

Yet it may well be that regarding women as a minority group may be productive of fresh insights and suggest leads for further research. The purpose of this paper is to apply to women some portion of that body of sociological theory and methodology customarily used for investigating such minority groups as Negroes, Jews, immigrants, etc. It may be anticipated that not only will principles already established in the field of intergroup relations contribute to our understanding of women, but that in the process of modifying traditional concepts and theories to fit the special case of women new viewpoints for the fruitful reexamination of other minority groups will emerge.

In defining the term "minority group," the presence of discrimination is the identifying factor. As Louis Wirth has pointed out, "minority group" is not a statistical concept, nor need it denote an alien group. Indeed for the present discussion I have adopted his definition: "A minority group is any group of people who because of their physical or cultural characteristics, are singled out from the others in the society in which they live for differential and unequal treatment, and who therefore regard themselves as objects of collective discrimination."[1] It is apparent that this definition includes both objective and subjective characteristics of a minority group: the fact of discrimination and the awareness of discrimination, with attendant reactions to that awareness. A person who on the basis of his group affiliation is denied full participation in those opportunities which the value system of his culture extends to all members of the society satisfies the objective criterion, but there are various circumstances which may prevent him from fulfilling the subjective criterion.

In the first place, a person may be unaware of the extent to which his group membership influences the way others treat him. He may have formally dissolved all ties with the group in question and fondly imagine his identity is different from what others hold it to be. Consequently, he interprets their behavior toward him solely in terms of his individual charac-

Foot-Stool by Romaine Brooks; Courtesy of National Collection of Fine Arts, Smithsonian Institution; Gift of the Artist

teristics. Or, less likely, he may be conscious of his membership in a certain group but not be aware of the general disesteem with which the group is regarded. A final possibility is that he may belong in a category which he does not realize has group significance. An example here might be a speech peculiarity which has come to have unpleasant connotations in the minds of others. Or a lower class child with no conception of "class as culture" may not understand how his manners act as cues in eliciting the dislike of his middle class teacher. The foregoing cases all assume that the person believes in equal opportunities for all in the sense that one's group affiliation should not affect his role in the larger society. We turn now to a consideration of situations in which this assumption is not made.

It is frequently the case that a person knows that because of his group affiliation he receives differential treatment, but feels that this treatment is warranted by the distinctive characteristics of his group. A Negro may believe that there are significant differences between whites and Negroes which justify a different role in life for the Negro. A child may accept the fact that physical differences between him and an adult require his going to bed earlier than they do. A Sudra knows that his lot in life has been cast by divine fiat, and he does not expect the perquisites of a Brahmin. A woman does not wish for the rights and duties of men.

In all these situations, clearly, the person does not regard himself as an "object of collective discrimination."

For the two types presented above: (1) those who do not know that they are being discriminated against on a group basis; and (2) those who acknowledge the propriety of differential treatment on a group basis, the subjective attributes of a minority group member are lacking. They feel no minority group consciousness, harbor no resentment, and, hence, cannot properly be said to belong in a minority group. Although the term "minority group" is inapplicable to both types, the term "minority group status" may be substituted. This term is used to categorize persons who are denied rights to which they are entitled according to the value system of the observer. An observer who is a firm adherent of the democratic ideology will often consider persons to occupy a minority group status who are well accommodated to their subordinate roles.

No empirical study of the frequency of minority group feelings among women has yet been made, but common observation would suggest that, consciously at least, few women believe themselves to be members of a minority group in the way in which some Negroes, Jews, Italians, etc., may so conceive themselves. There are, of course, many sex-conscious women, known to a past generation as feminists, who are filled with resentment at

Woman has to learn that exchanges—it is a fundamental law of political economy—are based on the value the merchandise offered has for the buyer, and not for the seller: she has been deceived in being persuaded that her worth is priceless.

Simone de Beauvoir, *The Second Sex*, 1953

---

the discriminations they fancy are directed against their sex. Today some of these may be found in the National Woman's Party which since 1923 has been carrying on a campaign for the passage of the Equal Rights Amendment.* This amendment, in contrast to the compromise bill recently passed by Congress, would at one stroke wipe out all existing legislation which differentiates in any way between men and women, even when such legislation is designed for the special protection of women. Equal Rights Amendment proponents hold the position that women will never achieve equal rights until they abjure all privileges based on what they consider to be only presumptive sex differences.

Then there are women enrolled in women's clubs, women's auxiliaries of men's organizations, women's professional and educational associations who seemingly believe that women have special interests to follow or unique contributions to make. These latter might reject the appellation of minority group, but their behavior testifies to their awareness of women as a distinct group in our society, either overriding differences of class, occupation, religion, or ethnic identification, or specialized within these categories. Yet the number of women who participate in "women's affairs" even in the United States, the classic land of associations, is so small that one cannot easily say that the majority of women display minority group consciousness. However, documentation, as well as a measuring instrument, is likewise lacking for minority consciousness in other groups.

Still women often manifest many of the psychological characteristics which have been imputed to self-conscious minority groups. Kurt Lewin[2] has pointed to group self-hatred as a frequent reaction of the minority group member to his group affiliation. This feeling is exhibited in the person's tendency to denigrate other members of the group, to accept the dominant group's stereotyped conception of them, and to indulge in "mea culpa" breast-beating. He may seek to exclude himself from the average of his group, or he may point the finger of scorn at himself. Since a person's conception of himself is based on the defining gestures of others, it is unlikely that members of a minority group can wholly escape personality distortion. Constant reiteration of one's inferiority must often lead to its acceptance as a fact.

Certainly women have not been immune to the formulations of the "female character" throughout the ages. From those, to us, deluded creatures who confessed to witchcraft to modern sophisticates who speak disparagingly of the cattiness and disloyalty of women, women reveal their introjection of prevailing attitudes toward them. Like those minority groups whose self-castigation outdoes dominant group derision of them, women frequently exceed men in the violence of their vituperations of their sex. They are more severe in moral judgments, especially in sexual matters. A line of self-criticism may be traced from Hannah More, a blue-stocking herself, to Dr. Marynia Farnham, who lays most of the world's ills at women's door. Women express themselves as disliking other women, as preferring to work under men, and as finding ex-

---

*Ed. note: See introduction to this section.

The glorification of the "woman's role," then, seems to be in proportion to society's reluctance to treat women as complete human beings; for the less real function that role has, the more it is decorated with meaningless details to conceal its emptiness.

Betty Friedan, *The Feminine Mystique*, 1963

clusively female gatherings repugnant. The *Fortune* polls conducted in 1946 show that women, more than men, have misgivings concerning women's participation in industry, the professions, and civic life. And more than one-fourth of women wish they had been born in the opposite sex.[3]

Militating against a feeling of group identification on the part of women is a differential factor in their socialization. Members of a minority group are frequently socialized within their own group. Personality development is more largely a resultant of intra- than inter-group interaction. The conception of his role formed by a Negro or a Jew or a second-generation immigrant is greatly dependent upon the definitions offered by members of his own group, on their attitudes and behavior toward him. Ignoring for the moment class differences within the group, the minority group person does not suffer discrimination from members of his own group. But only rarely does a woman experience this type of group belongingness. Her interactions with members of the opposite sex may be as frequent as her relationships with members of her own sex. Women's conceptions of themselves, therefore, spring as much from their intimate relationships with men as with women. Although this consideration might seem to limit the applicability to women of research findings on minority groups, conversely, it may suggest investigation to seek out useful parallels in the socialization of women, on the one hand, and the socialization of ethnics living in neighborhoods of hetereogeneous population, on the other.

Even though the sense of group identifica-

---

from **Snapshots of a Daughter-in-Law**

Sigh no more, ladies.
                                    Time is male
and in his cups drinks to the fair.
Bemused by gallantry, we hear
our mediocrities over-praised,
indolence read as abnegation,
slattern thought styled intuition,
every lapse forgiven, our crime
only to cast too bold a shadow
or smash the mould straight off.

For that, solitary confinement,
tear gas, attrition shelling.
Few applicants for that honor.

Adrienne Rich

---

tion is not so conspicuous in women as in racial and ethnic minorities, they, like these others, tend to develop a separate sub-culture. Women have their own language, comparable to the argot of the underworld and professional groups. It may not extend to a completely separate dialect as has been discovered in some preliterate groups, but there are words and idioms employed chiefly by women. Only the acculturated male can enter into the conversation of the beauty parlor, the exclusive shop, the bridge table, or the kitchen. In contrast to men's interest in physical health, safety, money, and sex, women attach greater importance to attractiveness, personality, home, family, and other people.[4] How much of the "woman's world" is predicated on their relationship to men is too difficult a question to discuss here. It is still a

*Let me state here and now that the black woman in America can justly
be described as a "slave of a slave."*

*Men may be cruelly exploited and subjected to all sorts of dehumanizing
tactics on the part of the ruling class, but they have someone who is
below them—at least they're not women.*

Frances Beal in Robin Morgan (ed.),
Sisterhood Is Powerful, 1970

---

controversial point whether the values and behavior patterns of other minority groups, such
as the Negroes, represent an immanent development, or are oriented chiefly toward the rejecting world. A content analysis contrasting
the speech of "housewives" and "career
women," for example, or a comparative analysis of the speech of men and women of similar
occupational status might be one test of this
hypothesis.

We must return now to the original question
of the aptness of the designation of minority
group for women. It has been indicated that
women fail to present in full force the subjective attributes commonly associated with minority groups. That is, they lack a sense of
group identification and do not harbor feelings
of being treated unfairly because of their sex
membership. Can it then be said that women
have a minority group status in our society?
The answer to this question depends upon the
values of the observer whether within or outside the group—just as is true in the case of
any group of persons who, on the basis of
putative differential characteristics are denied
access to some statuses in the social system of
their society. If we assume that there are no
differences attributable to sex membership as

such that would justify casting men and
women in different social roles, it can readily
be shown that women do occupy a minority
group status in our society.

Minority Group Status of Women

Formal discriminations against women are too
well known for any but the most summary description. In general they take the form of
being barred from certain activities or, if admitted, being treated unequally. Discriminations against women may be viewed as arising
from the generally ascribed status "female"
and from the specially ascribed statuses of
"wife," "mother," and "sister." (To meet the
possible objection that "wife" and "mother"
represent assumed, rather than ascribed, statuses, may I point out that what is important
here is that these statuses carry ascribed expectations which are only ancillary in the
minds of those who assume them.)

As female, in the economic sphere, women
are largely confined to sedentary, monotonous
work under the supervision of men, and are
treated unequally with regard to pay, promotion, and responsibility. With the exceptions of
teaching, nursing, social service, and library

MY BOSS MAY BE
A BIG MAN
BUT I'VE GOT
A LITTLE WOMAN

© Ellen Levine, from *All She Needs . . .*, Quadrangle, 1973

work, in which they do not hold a proportionate number of supervisory positions and are often occupationally segregated from men, they make a poor showing in the professions. Although they own 80 percent of the nation's wealth, they do not sit on the boards of directors of great corporations. Educational opportunities are likewise unequal. Professional schools, such as architecture and medicine, apply quotas. Women's colleges are frequently inferior to men's. In co-educational schools women's participation in campus activities is limited. As citizens, women are often barred from jury service and public office. Even when they are admitted to the apparatus of political parties, they are subordinated to men. Socially, women have less freedom of movement, and are permitted fewer deviations in the proprieties of dress, speech, manners. In social intercourse they are confined to a narrow range of personality expression.

In the specially ascribed status of wife, a woman—in several states—has no exclusive right to her earnings, is discriminated against in employment, must take the domicile of her husband, and in general must meet the social expectation of subordination to her husband's interests. As a mother, she may not have the guardianship of her children, bears the chief stigma in the case of an illegitimate child, is rarely given leave of absence for pregnancy. As a sister, she frequently suffers unequal distribution of domestic duties between herself and her brother, must yield preference to him in obtaining an education, and in such other psychic and material gratifications as cars, trips, and living away from home.

If it is conceded that women have a minority group status, what may be learned from applying to women various theoretical constructs in the field of intergroup relations?

Social Distance Between Men and Women

One instrument of diagnostic value is the measurement of social distance between dominant and minority group. But we have seen that one important difference between women and other minorities is that women's attitudes and self-conceptions are conditioned more largely by interaction with both minority and dominant group members. Before measuring social distance, therefore, a continuum might be constructed of the frequency and extent of women's interaction with men, with the poles conceptualized as ideal types. One extreme

Pig Boss by Karen Breschi. Permission given by the artist

would represent a complete "ghetto" status, the woman whose contacts with men were of the most secondary kind. At the other extreme shall we put the woman who has prolonged and repeated associations with men, but only in those situations in which sex-awareness plays a prominent role, or the woman who enters into a variety of relationships with men in which her sex identity is to a large extent irrelevant? The decision would depend on the type of scale used.

This question raises the problem of the criterion of social distance to be employed in such a scale. Is it more profitable to use we-feeling, felt interdependence, degree of com-

munication, or degrees of separation in status? Social distance tests as applied to relationships between other dominant and minority groups have for the most part adopted prestige criteria as their basis. The assumption is that the type of situation into which one is willing to enter with average members of another group reflects one's estimate of the status of the group relative to one's own. When the tested group is a sex-group rather than a racial, national, religious, or economic one, several important differences in the use and interpretation of the scale must be noted.

1. Only two groups are involved: men and women. Thus, the test indicates the amount of homogeneity or we-feeling only according to the attribute of sex. If men are a primary group, there are not many groups to be ranked secondary, tertiary, etc. with respect to them, but only one group, women, whose social distance cannot be calculated relative to other groups.

2. Lundberg[5] suggests the possibility of a group of Catholics registering a smaller social distance to Moslems than to Catholics. In such an event the group of Catholics, from any sociological viewpoint, would be classified as Moslems. If women expressed less social distance to men than to women, should they then be classified sociologically as men? Perhaps no more so than the legendary Negro who, when requested to move to the colored section of the train, replied, "Boss, I'se done resigned from the colored race," should be classified as white. It is likely, however, that the group identification of many women in our society is with men. The feminists were charged with wanting to be men, since they associated male physical characteristics with masculine social privileges. A similar statement can be made

about men who show greater social distance to other men than to women.

Social distance may be measured from the standpoint of the minority group or the dominant group with different results. In point of fact, tension often arises when one group feels less social distance than the other. A type case here is the persistent suitor who underestimates his desired sweetheart's feeling of social distance toward him.

3. In social distance tests the assumption is made of an orderly progression—although not necessarily by equal intervals—in the scale. That is, it is not likely that a person would express willingness to have members of a given group as his neighbors, while simultaneously voicing the desire to have them excluded from his country. On all scales marriage represents the minimum social distance, and implies willingness for associations on all levels of lesser intimacy. May the customary scale be applied to men and women? If we take the expressed attitude of many men and women not to marry, we may say that they have feelings of social distance toward the opposite sex, and in this situation the usual order of the scale may be preserved.

In our culture, however, men who wish to marry must perforce marry women, and even if they accept this relationship, they may still wish to limit their association with women in other situations. The male physician may not care for the addition of female physicians to his hospital staff. The male poker player may be thrown off his game if women participate. A damper may be put upon the hunting expedition if women come along. The average man may not wish to consult a woman lawyer. And so on. In these cases it seems apparent that the steps in the social distance scale must be re-versed. Men will accept women at the supposed level of greatest intimacy while rejecting them at lower levels.

But before concluding that a different scale must be constructed when the dominant group attitude toward a minority group which is being tested is that of men toward women, the question may be raised as to whether marriage in fact represents the point of minimum social distance. It may not imply anything but physical intimacy and work accommodation, as was frequently true in non-individuated societies, such as preliterate groups and the household economy of the Middle Ages, or marriages of convenience in the European upper class. Even in our own democratic society where marriage is supposedly based on romantic love there may be little communication between the partners in marriage. The Lynds[6] report the absence of real companionship between husband and wife in Middletown. Women have been known to say that although they have been married for twenty years, their husband is still a stranger to them. There is a quatrain of Thoreau's that goes:

> *Each moment as we drew nearer to each*
> *A stern respect withheld us farther yet*
> *So that we seemed beyond each other's reach*
> *And less acquainted than when first we met.*

Part of the explanation may be found in the subordination of wives to husbands in our culture, which is expressed in the separate spheres of activity for men and women. A recent advertisement in a magazine of national circulation depicts a pensive husband seated by his knitting wife, with the caption, "Sometimes a man has moods his wife cannot understand." In this case the husband is worried

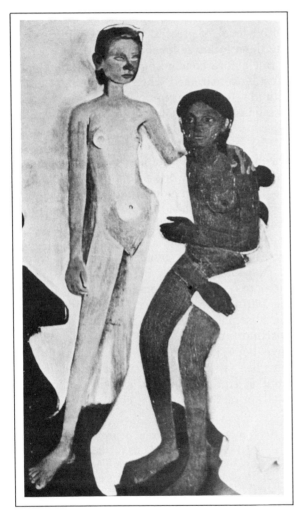

Two Girls by Amrita Sher-gil, 1939. Oil on canvas. Collection Vivan Sundaram, New Delhi.

about a pension plan for his employees. The assumption is that the wife, knowing nothing of the business world, cannot take the role of her husband in this matter.

The presence of love does not in itself argue for either equality of status nor fullness of communication. We may love those who are either inferior or superior to us, and we may love persons whom we do not understand. The supreme literary examples of passion without communication are found in Proust's portrayal of Swann's obsession with Odette, the narrator's infatuation with the elusive Albertine, and, of course, Dante's longing for Beatrice.

In the light of these considerations concerning the relationships between men and women, some doubt may be cast on the propriety of placing marriage on the positive extreme of the social distance scale with respect to ethnic and religious minority groups. Since inequalities of status are preserved in marriage, a dominant group member may be willing to marry a member of a group which, in general, he would not wish admitted to his club. The social distance scale which uses marriage as a sign of an extreme degree of acceptance is inadequate for appreciating the position of women, and perhaps for other minority groups as well. The relationships among similarity of status, communication as a measure of intimacy, and love must be clarified before social distance tests can be applied usefully to attitudes between men and women.

Caste-Class Conflict

Is the separation between males and females in our society a caste line? Folsom[7] suggests that it is, and Myrdal[8] in his well-known Appendix 5 considers the parallel between the position of and feelings toward women and Negroes in our society. The relation between women and Negroes is historical, as well as analogical. In the seventeenth century the legal status of Negro servants was borrowed from that of women and children, who were under the patria potestas, and until the Civil War there was considerable cooperation between the Abolitionist and woman suffrage movements. According to Myrdal, the problems of both groups are resultants of the transition from a pre-industrial, paternalistic scheme of life to individualistic, industrial capitalism. Obvious similarities in the status of women and Negroes are indicated in Chart 1.

While these similarities in the situation of women and Negroes may lead to increased understanding of their social roles, account must also be taken of differences which impose qualifications on the comparison of the two groups. Most importantly, the influence of marriage as a social elevator for women, but not for Negroes, must be considered. Obvious, too, is the greater importance of women to the dominant group, despite the economic, sexual, and prestige gains which Negroes afford the white South. Ambivalence is probably more marked in the attitude of white males toward women than toward Negroes. The "war of the sexes" is only an expression of men's and women's vital need of each other. Again, there is greater polarization in the relationship between men and women. Negroes, although they have borne the brunt of anti-minority group feeling in this country, do not constitute the only racial or ethnic minority, but there are only two sexes. And, although we have seen that social distance exists between men and women, it is not to be compared with the social segregation of Negroes.

At the present time, of course, Negroes suffer far greater discrimination than women, but since the latter's problems are rooted in a biological reality less susceptible to cultural manipulation, they prove more lasting. Women's

Untitled drawing by Melissa Mathis

privileges exceed those of Negroes. Protective attitudes toward Negroes have faded into abeyance, even in the South, but most boys are still taught to take care of girls, and many evidences of male chivalry remain. The factor of class introduces variations here. The middle class Negro endures frustrations largely without the rewards of his white class peer, but the lower class Negro is still absolved from many responsibilities. The reverse holds true for women. Notwithstanding these and other differences between the position of women and Negroes, the similarities are sufficient to render research on either group applicable in some fashion to the other.

Exemplary of the possible usefulness of applying the caste principle to women is viewing some of the confusion surrounding women's roles as reflecting a conflict between class and caste status. Such a conflict is present in the

Perhaps nothing is so depressing an index of the inhumanity of the male supremacist mentality as the fact that the more genial human traits are assigned to the underclass: affection, response to sympathy, kindness, cheerfulness.

Kate Millett, *Sexual Politics*, 1969

CHART 1
CASTELIKE STATUS OF WOMEN AND NEGROES

Negroes	Women
1. High Social Visibility	
a. Skin color, other "racial" characteristics	a. Secondary sex characteristics
b. (Sometimes) distinctive dress—bandana, flashy clothes	b. Distinctive dress, skirts, etc.
2. Ascribed Attributes	
a. Inferior intelligence, smaller brain, less convoluted, scarcity of geniuses	a. ditto
b. More free in instinctual gratifications. More emotional, "primitive," and childlike. Imagined sexual prowess envied	b. Irresponsible, inconsistent, emotionally unstable Lack strong super-ego Women as "temptresses"
c. Common stereotype "inferior"	c. "Weaker"
3. Rationalizations of Status	
a. Thought all right in his place	a. Woman's place is in the home
b. Myth of contented Negro	b. Myth of contented woman—"feminine" woman is happy in subordinate role
4. Accommodation Attitudes	
a. Supplicatory whining intonation of voice	a. Rising inflection, smiles, laughs, downward glances
b. Deferential manner	b. Flattering manner
c. Concealment of real feelings	c. "Feminine wiles"
d. Outwit "white folks"	d. Outwit "menfolk"
e. Careful study of points at which dominant group is susceptible to influence	e. ditto
f. Fake appeals for directives; show of ignorance	f. Appearance of helplessness
5. Discriminations	
a. Limitations on education—should fit "place" in society	a. ditto
b. Confined to traditional jobs—barred from supervisory positions Their competition feared No family precedents for new aspirations	b. ditto
c. Deprived of political importance	c. ditto
d. Social and professional segregation	d. ditto
e. More vulnerable to criticism	e. e.g., conduct in bars
6. Similar Problems	
a. Roles not clearly defined, but in flux as result of social change Conflict between achieved status and ascribed status	

... A typical minority-group stereotype—woman as nigger—if she knows her place (home), she is really a quite lovable, loving creature, happy and childlike.

Naomi Weisstein, *Psychology Today* (Oct. 1969)

thinking and feeling of both dominant and minority groups toward upper class Negroes and educated women. Should a woman judge be treated with the respect due a judge or the gallantry accorded a woman? The extent to which the rights and duties of one role permeate other roles so as to cause a role conflict has been treated elsewhere by the writer.[9] Lower class Negroes who have acquired dominant group attitudes toward the Negro resent upper class Negro pretensions to superiority. Similarly, domestic women may feel the career woman is neglecting the duties of her proper station.

Parallels in adjustment of women and Negroes to the class-caste conflict may also be noted. Point 4 "Accommodation Attitudes" of the foregoing chart indicates the kinds of behavior displayed by members of both groups who accept their caste status. Many "sophisticated" women are retreating from emancipation with the support of psychoanalytic derivations.[10] David Riesman has recently provided an interesting discussion of changes "in the denigration by American women of their own sex" in which he explains their new submissiveness as in part a reaction to the weakness of men in the contemporary world.[11] "Parallelism" and "Negroidism" which accept a racially restricted economy reflect allied tendencies in the Negro group.

Role segmentation as a mode of adjustment is illustrated by Negroes who indulge in occasional passing and women who vary their be-

> **The Process of Dissolution**
>
> *my husband held me*
> *responsible for his failures.*
> *when he scolded me*
> *he had my father*
> *written all over his face.*
> *our marriage ended*
> *as my childhood*
> *continued; the men in my life*
> *still try teaching me lessons,*
> *and i have not ceased entirely*
> *from kicking myself hard*
> *to please them: damn you*
> *daddy. damn your redundant*
> *face.*
>
> Susan Efros

havior according to their definition of the situation. An example of the latter is the case of the woman lawyer who, after losing a case before a judge who was also her husband, said she would appeal the case, and added, "The judge can lay down the law at home, but I'll argue with him in court."

A third type of reaction is to fight for recognition of class status. Negro race leaders seek greater prerogatives for Negroes. Feminist women, acting either through organizations or as individuals, push for public disavowal of any differential treatment of men and women.

Women have served all these centuries as looking-glasses possessing the magic and delicious power of reflecting the figure of man at twice its natural size.

Virginia Woolf, *A Room of One's Own*, 1929

Race Relations Cycle

The "race relations cycle," as defined by Robert E. Park,[12] describes the social processes of reduction in tension and increase of communication in the relations between two or more groups who are in a common territory under a single political or economic system. The sequence of competition, conflict, accommodation, and assimilation may also occur when social change introduces dissociative forces into an assimilated group or causes accommodated groups to seek new definitions of the situation.[13] The ethnic or nationality characteristics of the groups involved are not essential to the cycle. In a complex industrialized society groups are constantly forming and re-forming on the basis of new interests and new identities. Women, of course, have always possessed a sex-identification though perhaps not a group awareness. Today they represent a previously accommodated group which is endeavoring to modify the relationships between the sexes in the home, in work, and in the community.

The sex relations cycle bears important similarities to the race relations cycle. In the wake of the Industrial Revolution, as women acquired industrial, business, and professional skills, they increasingly sought employment in competition with men. Men were quick to perceive them as a rival group and made use of economic, legal, and ideological weapons to eliminate or reduce their competition. They excluded women from the trade unions, made contracts with employers to prevent their hiring women, passed laws restricting the employment of married women, caricatured the working woman, and carried on ceaseless propaganda to return women to the home or

keep them there. Since the days of the suffragettes there has been no overt conflict between men and women on a group basis. Rather than conflict, the dissociative process between the sexes is that of contravention,[14] a type of opposition intermediate between competition and conflict. According to Wiese and Becker, it includes rebuffing, repulsing, working against, hindering, protesting, obstructing, restraining, and upsetting another's plans.

The present contravention of the sexes, arising from women's competition with men, is manifested in the discriminations against women, as well as in the doubts and uncertainties expressed concerning women's character, abilities, motives. The processes of competition and contravention are continually giving way to accommodation in the relationships between men and women. Like other minority groups, women have sought a protected position, a niche in the economy which they could occupy, and, like other minority groups, they have found these positions in new occupations in which dominant group members had not yet established themselves and in old occupations which they no longer wanted. When women entered fields which represented an extension of services in the home (except medicine!), they encountered least opposition. Evidence is accumulating, however, that women are becoming dissatisfied with the employment conditions of the great women-employing occupations and present accommodations are threatened.

What would assimilation of men and women mean? Park and Burgess* in their clas-

---

*Ed. note: Robert E. Park and Ernest W. Burgess. *Introduction to the Science of Sociology.* Chicago: University of Chicago Press (2nd ed.), 1924.

sic text define assimilation as "a process of interpenetration and fusion in which persons and groups acquire the memories, sentiments, and attitudes of other persons or groups, and, by sharing their experiences and history, are incorporated with them in a cultural life." If accommodation is characterized by secondary contacts, assimilation holds the promise of primary contacts. If men and women were truly assimilated, we would find no cleavages of interest along sex lines. The special provinces of men and women would be abolished. Women's pages would disappear from the newspaper and women's magazines from the stands. All special women's organizations would pass into limbo. The sports page and racing news would be read indifferently by men and women. Interest in cookery and interior decoration would follow individual rather than sex lines. Women's talk would be no different from men's talk, and frank and full communication would obtain between the sexes.

The Marginal Woman

Group relationships are reflected in personal adjustments. Arising out of the present contravention of the sexes is the marginal woman, torn between rejection and acceptance of traditional roles and attributes. Uncertain of the ground on which she stands, subjected to conflicting cultural expectations, the marginal woman suffers the psychological ravages of instability, conflict, self-hate, anxiety, and resentment.

In applying the concept of marginality to women, the term "role" must be substituted for that of "group."[15] Many of the traditional devices for creating role differentiation among boys and girls, such as dress, manners, activities, have been de-emphasized in modern urban middle class homes. The small girl who wears a play suit, plays games with boys and girls together, attends a co-educational school, may have little awareness of sexual differentiation until the approach of adolescence. Parental expectations in the matters of scholarship, conduct toward others, duties in the home may have differed little for herself and her brother. But in high school or perhaps not until college she finds herself called upon to play a new role. Benedict[16] has called attention to discontinuities in the life cycle, and the fact that these continuities in cultural conditioning take a greater toll of girls than of boys is revealed in test scores showing neuroticism and introversion.[17] In adolescence girls find the frank, spontaneous behavior toward the neighboring sex no longer rewarding. High grades are more likely to elicit anxiety than praise from parents, especially mothers, who seem more pleased if male callers are frequent. There are subtle indications that to remain home with a good book on a Saturday night is a fate worse than death. But even if the die is successfully cast for popularity, all problems are not solved. Girls are encouraged to heighten their sexual attractiveness, but to abjure sexual expression.

Assuming new roles in adolescence does not mean the complete relinquishing of old ones. Scholarship, while not so vital as for the boy, is still important, but must be maintained discreetly and without obvious effort. Mirra Komarovsky[18] has supplied statements of Barnard College girls of the conflicting expectations of their elders. Even more than to the boy is the "all-around" ideal held up to girls, and it is not always possible to integrate the roles of good date, good daughter, good sorority sister, good student, good friend, and good citizen. The superior achievements of college men over college women bear witness to the crippling division of energies among women. Part of the explanation may lie in women's having interiorized cultural notions of feminine inferiority in certain fields, and even the most self-confident or most defensive woman may be filled with doubt as to whether she can do productive work.

It may be expected that as differences in privileges between men and women decrease, the frequency of marginal women will increase. Widening opportunities for women will call forth a growing number of women capable of performing roles formerly reserved for men, but whose acceptance in these new roles may well remain uncertain and problematic. This hypothesis is in accord with Arnold Green's[19] recent critical reexamination of the marginal man concept in which he points out that it is those Negroes and second-generation immigrants whose values and behavior most approximate those of the dominant majority who experience the most severe personal crises. He believes that the classical marginal man symptoms appear only when a person striving to leave the racial or ethnic group into which he was born is deeply identified with the family of orientation and is met with grudging, uncertain, and unpredictable acceptance, rather than with absolute rejection, by the group he is attempting to join, and also that he is committed to success-careerism. Analogically, one would expect to find that women who display marginal symptoms are psychologically bound to the family of orientation in which they experienced the imperatives of both the traditional and new feminine roles, and are seeking to expand the occupational (or other) areas open to women rather than those who content themselves with established fields. Concretely, one might suppose women engineers to have greater personality problems than women librarians.

Other avenues of investigation suggested by the minority group approach can only be mentioned. What social types arise as personal adjustments to sex status? What can be done in the way of experimental modification of the attitudes of men and women toward each other and themselves? What hypotheses of intergroup relations may be tested in regard to men and women? For example, is it true that as women approach the cultural standards of men, they are perceived as a threat and tensions increase? Of what significance are regional and community variations in the treatment of and degree of participation permitted women, mindful here that women share responsibility with men for the perpetuation of attitudes toward women? This paper is exploratory in suggesting the enhanced possibilities of fruitful analysis, if women are included in the minority group corpus, particularly with reference to such concepts and techniques as group belongingness, socialization of the minority group child, cultural differences, social distance tests, conflict between class and caste status, race relations cycle, and marginality. I believe that the concept of the marginal woman should be especially productive, and am now engaged in an empirical study of role conflicts in professional women.

Nancy Henley and Jo Freeman

The Sexual Politics of Interpersonal Behavior

Social interaction is the battlefield where the daily war between the sexes is fought. It is here that women are constantly reminded where their "place" is and here that they are put back in their place, should they venture out. Thus, social interaction serves as the most common means of social control employed against women. By being continually reminded of their inferior status in their interactions with others, and continually compelled to acknowledge that status in their own patterns of behavior, women learn to internalize society's definition of them as inferior so thoroughly that they are often unaware of what their status is. Inferiority becomes habitual, and the inferior place assumes the familiarity—and even desirability—of home.

Different sorts of cues in social interaction aid this enforcement of one's social definition, particularly the verbal message, the nonverbal message transmitted within a social relationship, and the nonverbal message transmitted by the environment. Our educational system emphasizes the verbal message and teaches us next to nothing about how we interpret and react to the nonverbal ones. Just how important nonverbal messages are, however, is shown by the finding of Argyle et al. (1970) that nonverbal cues have over four times the impact of verbal ones when both verbal and nonverbal cues are used. Even more important for women, Argyle found that female subjects were more responsive to nonverbal cues (compared with verbal ones) than male subjects. If women are to understand how the subtle

forces of social control work in their lives, they must learn as much as possible about how nonverbal cues affect people, and particularly about how they perpetuate the power and superior status enjoyed by men.

Even if a woman encounters no one else directly in her day, visual status reminders are a ubiquitous part of her environment. As she moves through the day, she absorbs many variations of the same status theme, whether or not she is aware of it: male bosses dictate while female secretaries bend over their steno pads; male doctors operate while female nurses assist; restaurants are populated with waitresses serving men; magazine and billboard ads remind the woman that home maintenance and child care are her foremost responsibilities and that being a sex object for male voyeurs is her greatest asset. If she is married, her mail reminds her that she is a mere "Mrs." appended to her husband's name. When she is introduced to others or fills out a form, the first thing she must do is divulge her marital status, acknowledging the social rule that the most important information anyone can know about her is her legal relationship to a man.

These environmental cues set the stage on which the power relationships of the sexes are acted out, and the assigned status of each sex is reinforced. Though studies have been made of the several means by which status inequalities are communicated in interpersonal behavior, they do not usually deal with power relationships between men and women.

And yet wherever there exists the display of power there is politics, and in women's relations with men there is a continual transfer of power, there is, continually, politics.

Sally Kempton, *Esquire*, 1970

Goffman (1956, pp. 64, 78–79) has pointed to many characteristics associated with status:

> Between status equals we may expect to find interaction guided by symmetrical familiarity. Between superordinate and subordinate we may expect to find asymmetrical relations, the superordinate having the right to exercise certain familiarities which the subordinate is not allowed to reciprocate. Thus, in the research hospital, doctors tended to call nurses by their first names, while nurses responded with "polite" or "formal" address. Similarly, in American business organizations the boss may thoughtfully ask the elevator man how his children are, but this entrance into another's life may be blocked to the elevator man, who can appreciate the concern but not return it. Perhaps the clearest form of this is found in the psychiatrist-patient relation, where the psychiatrist has a right to touch on aspects of the patient's life that the patient might not even allow himself to touch upon, while of course this privilege is not reciprocated.
>
> Rules of demeanor, like rules of deference, can be symmetrical or asymmetrical. Between social equals, symmetrical rules of demeanor seem often to be prescribed. Between unequals many variations can be found. For example, at staff meetings on the psychiatric units of the hospital, medical doctors had the privilege of swearing, changing the topic of conversation, and sitting in undignified positions; attendants, on the other hand, had the right to attend staff meetings and to ask questions during them ... but were implicitly expected to conduct themselves with greater circumspection than was required for doctors.... Similarly, doctors had the right to saunter into the nurses' station, lounge on the station's dispensing counter, and engage in joking with the nurses; other ranks participated in this informal interaction with doctors, but only after doctors had initiated it.

A status variable widely studied by Brown and others (1960, 1961, 1965) is the use of terms of address. In languages that have both familiar and polite forms of the second person singular ("you"), asymmetrical use of the two forms invariably indicates a status difference, and it always follows the same pattern. The person using the familiar form is always the superior to the person using the polite form. In English, the only major European language not to have dual forms of address, status differences are similarly indicated by the right of first-naming; the status superior can first-name the inferior in situations where the inferior must use the superior's title and last name. An inferior who breaks this rule by inappropriately using a superior's first name is considered insolent (see Brown, 1965, pp. 92–97).

According to Brown, the pattern evident in the use of forms of address applies to a very wide range of interpersonal behavior and invariably has two other components: (1) whatever form is used by a superior in situations of status inequality can be used reciprocally by intimates, and whatever form is used by an inferior is the socially prescribed usage for non-intimates; (2) initiation or increase of intimacy is the right of the superior. To use the example of naming again, friends use first names with each other while strangers use titles and last names, though "instant" intimacy is considered proper in some cultures, such as our own, among status equals in informal settings. Status superiors, such as professors, specifically tell status inferiors, such as students, when they can use the first name, and often rebuff them if they assume such a right unilaterally.

Although Brown did not apply these patterns to status differences between the sexes, their relevance is readily seen. The social

. . . The female is rendered innocuous by her socialization. Before assault she is almost universally defenseless both by her physical and emotional training.

Kate Millett, *Sexual Politics*, 1969

rules say that it is boys who are supposed to call girls for dates, men who are supposed to propose marriage to women, and males who are supposed to initiate sexual activity with females. Females who make "advances" are considered improper, forward, aggressive, brassy, or otherwise "unladylike." By initiating intimacy they have stepped out of their place and usurped a status prerogative. The value of such a prerogative is that it is a form of power. Between the sexes, as in other human interaction, the one who has the right to intitiate greater intimacy has more control over the relationship. Superior status brings with it not only greater prestige and greater privileges, but greater power.

These advantages are exemplified in many of the various means of communicating status. Like the doctors in Goffman's research hospital, men are allowed such privileges as swearing and sitting in undignified positions, but women are denied them. Though the male privilege of swearing is curtailed in mixed company, the body movement permitted to women is circumscribed even in all-woman groups. It is considered unladylike for a woman to use her body too forcefully, to sprawl, to stand with her legs widely spread, to sit with her feet up, or to cross the ankle of one leg over the knee of the other. Many of these positions are ones of strength or dominance. The more "feminine" a woman's clothes are, the more circumscribed the use of her body. Depending on her clothes, she may be expected to sit with her knees together, not to sit cross-legged, or not even to bend over. Though these taboos seem to have lessened in recent years, how much so is unknown, and there are recurring social pressures for a "return to femininity," while etiquette arbiters as-

sert that women must retain feminine posture no matter what their clothing.

Prior to the 1920s women's clothes were designed to be confining and cumbersome. The dress reform movement, which disposed of corsets and long skirts, was considered by many to have more significance for female emancipation than women's suffrage (O'Neill, 1969, p. 270). Today women's clothes are designed to be revealing, but women are expected to restrict their body movements to avoid revealing too much. Furthermore, because women's clothes are contrived to reveal women's physical features, rather than being loose like men's, women must resort to purses instead of pockets to carry their belongings. These "conveniences" have become, in a time of blurred sex distinctions, one of the surest signs of sex, and thus have developed the character of stigma, a sign of woman's shame, as when they are used by comics to ridicule both women and transvestites.

Women in our society are expected to reveal not only more of their bodies than men but also more of themselves. Female socialization encourages greater expression of emotion than that of the male. Whereas men are expected to be stolid and impassive, and not to disclose their feelings beyond certain limits, women are expected to express their *selves*. Such self-expression can disclose a lot of oneself, and, as Jourard and Lasakow (1958) found, females are more self-disclosing to others than males are. This puts them at an immediate disadvantage.

The inverse relationship between disclosure and power has been reported by other studies in addition to Goffman's earlier cited investigation into a research hospital. Slobin, Miller, and Porter (1968) stated that individuals in a

---

Women's Laughter

1.
When did I first become aware—
hearing myself on the radio?
listening to tapes of women in groups?—
of that diffident laugh that punctuates,
that giggle that apologizes,
that bows fixing parentheses before, after.
That little laugh sticking
in the throat like a chicken bone.

That perfunctory dry laugh
carries no mirth, no joy
but makes a low curtsy, a kowtow
imploring with praying hands:
forgive me, for I do not
take myself seriously.
Do not squash me.

2.
Phyllis, on the deck we sit
telling horror stories
from the Marvel Comics of our lives.
We exchange agonies, battles and after each
we laugh madly and embrace.

That raucous female laughter
is drummed from the belly.
It rackets about kitchens,
flapping crows
up from a carcass.
Hot in the mouth as horseradish,
it clears the sinuses
and the brain.

3.
Phyllis, I had a friend
who used to laugh with me
braying defiance, as we roar
with bared teeth.
After the locked ward
where they dimmed her with drugs
and exploded her synapses,
she has now that cough
fluttering in her throat
like a sick pigeon
as she says, but of course
I was sick, you know,
and laughs blood.

Marge Piercy

---

business organization are "more self-disclosing to their immediate superior than to their immediate subordinates." Self-disclosure is a means of enhancing another's power. When one has greater access to information about another person, one has a resource the other person does not have. Thus not only does power give status, but status gives power. And those possessing neither must contribute to the power and status of others continuously.

Another factor adding to women's vulnerability is that they are socialized to *care* more than men—especially about personal relationships. This puts them at a disadvantage, as Ross articulated in 1921 in what he called the "Law of Personal Exploitation": "In any sentimental relation the one who cares less can exploit the one who cares more" (p. 136). The same idea was put more broadly by Waller and Hill (1951) as the "Principle of Least Interest": "That person is able to dictate the conditions of association whose interest in the

> **Man:** *Do you know the Women's Movement has no sense of humor?*
> **Woman:** *No . . . but hum a few bars and I'll fake it!*

continuation of the affair is least" (p. 191). In other words, women's caring, like their openness, gives them less power in a relationship.

One way of indicating acceptance of one's place and deference to those of superior status is by following the rules of "personal space." Sommer (1969, Chap. 2) has observed that dominant animals and human beings have a larger envelope of inviolability surrounding them—i.e., are approached less closely—than those of a lower status. Willis (1966) made a study of the initial speaking distance set by an approaching person as a function of the speakers' relationship. His finding that women were approached more closely than men—i.e., their personal space was smaller or more likely to be breached—is consistent with their lower status.

Touching is one of the closer invasions of one's personal space, and in our low-contact culture it implies privileged access to another person. People who accidentally touch other people generally take great pains to apologize; people forced into close proximity, as in a crowded elevator, often go to extreme lengths to avoid touching. Even the figurative meanings of the word convey a notion of access to privileged areas—e.g., to one's emotions (one is "touched" by a sad story), or to one's purse (one is "touched" for ten dollars). In addition, the act of touching can be a subtle physical threat.

Remembering the patterns that Brown found in terms of address, consider the interactions between pairs of persons of different status, and picture who would be more likely to touch the other (put an arm around the shoulder or a hand on the back, tap the chest, hold the arm, or the like): teacher and student; master and servant; policeman and accused; doctor and patient; minister and parishioner; adviser and advisee; foreman and worker; businessman and secretary. As with first-naming, it is considered presumptuous for a person of low status to initiate touch with a person of higher status.

There has been little investigation of touching by social scientists, but the few studies made so far indicate that females are touched more than males are. Goldberg and Lewis (1969) and Lewis (1972) report that from six months on, girl babies are touched more than boy babies. The data reported in Jourard (1966) and Jourard and Rubin (1968) show that sons and fathers tend to refrain from touching each other and that "when it comes to physical contact within the family, it is the daughters who are the favored ones" (Jourard, 1966, p. 224). An examination of the number of different regions in which subjects were touched showed that mothers and fathers touch their daughters in more regions than they do their sons; that daughters touch their fathers in more regions than sons do; and that males touch their opposite-sex best friends in more regions than females do. Overall, women's mean total "being-touched" score was higher than men's.

Jourard and Rubin take the view that "touching is equated with sexual intent, either consciously, or at a less-conscious level" (p. 47), but it would seem that there is a sex difference in the interpretation of touch. Lewis reflects this when he writes, "In general, for men in our culture, proximity (touching) is restricted to the opposite sex and its function is primarily sexual in nature" (p. 237). Waitresses, secretaries, and women students are quite used to being touched by their male superordinates, but they are expected not to

Ask leading questions: *A subtle way of giving advice is to ask leading questions, such as "Have you ever thought of doing it this way?" . . . The key word is you. In this way you bring him into the picture so the ideas will seem like his own.*

Insight: *When expressing your viewpoint use words that indicate insight such as "I feel." Avoid the words "I think" or "I know."*

Don't appear to know more than he does: *Don't be the all-wise, all-knowing wife who has all the answers and surpasses her husband in intelligence.*

Don't talk man to man: *Don't "hash things over" as men do and thereby place yourself on an equal plane with him. . . . Keep him in the dominant position so that he will feel needed and adequate as the leader.*

Helen Andelin, *Fascinating Womanhood,*
1963

"misinterpret" such gestures. However, women who touch men are often interpreted as conveying sexual intent, as they have often found out when their intentions were quite otherwise. Such different interpretations are consistent with the status patterns found earlier. If touching indicates either power or intimacy, and women are deemed by men to be status inferiors, touching by women will be perceived as a gesture of intimacy, since it would be inconceivable for them to be exercising power.

A study by Henley (1970) puts forward this hypothesis. Observations of incidents of touch in public urban places by a white male research assistant, naive to the uses of his data, in which age, sex, and approximate socioeconomic status were recorded, indicated that higher-status persons do touch lower-status persons significantly more. In particular, men touched women more, even when all other variables were held constant. When the settings of the observations were differentially examined, the pattern showed up primarily in the outdoor setting, with indoor interaction being more evenly spread over sex combinations. Henley has also reported observations of greater touching by higher status persons (including males) in the popular culture media; and a questionnaire study in which both females and males indicated greater expectancies of being touched by higher status persons, and of touching lower status and female ones, than vice versa.

The other nonverbal cues by which status is indicated have likewise not been adequately researched—for humans. But O'Connor (1970) argues that many of the gestures of dominance and submission that have been noted in the primates are equally present in humans. They are used to maintain and reinforce the status hierarchy by reassuring those of higher status that those of lower status accept their place in the human pecking order.

The most studied nonverbal communication among humans is probably eye contact, and here too one finds a sex difference. It has repeatedly been found that women look more at another in a dyad than men do (Exline, 1963; Exline, Gray, & Schuette, 1965; Rubin, 1970). Exline, Gray, and Schuette suggest that "willingness to engage in mutual visual interaction is more characteristic of those who are oriented towards inclusive and affectionate inter-

To be submissive is to defer to masculine strength; is to lack muscular development or any interest in defending oneself; is to let doors be opened, to have one's arm held when crossing the street. To be feminine is to wear shoes which make it difficult to run; skirts which inhibit one's stride; underclothes which inhibit the circulation. Is it not an intriguing observation that those very clothes which are thought to be flattering to the female and attractive to the male are those which make it impossible for a woman to defend herself against aggression?

Susan Griffin, "Rape: The All-American Crime," 1971

---

personal relations" (p. 207), but Rubin concludes that while "gazing may serve as a vehicle of emotional expression for women, [it] in addition may allow women to obtain cues from their male partners concerning the appropriateness of their behavior" (p. 272). This interpretation is supported by Efran and Broughton's (1966) data showing that even male subjects "maintain more eye contact with individuals toward whom they have developed higher expectancies for social approval" (p. 103).

Another possible reason why women gaze more at men is that men talk more (Argyle, Lalljee, & Cook, 1968), and there is a tendency for the listener to look more at the speaker than vice versa (Exline et al., 1965).

It is especially illuminating to look at the power relationships established and maintained by the manipulation of eye contact. The mutual glance can be seen as a sign of union, but when intensified into a stare it may become a way of doing battle (Exline, 1963). Research reported by Ellsworth, Carlsmith, and Henson (1972) supports the notion that the stare can be interpreted as an aggressive gesture. These authors write, "Staring at humans

---

A Work of Artifice

The bonsai tree
in the attractive pot
could have grown eighty feet tall
on the side of a mountain
till split by lightning.
But a gardener
carefully pruned it.
It is nine inches high.
Every day as he
whittles back the branches
the gardener croons,
It is your nature
to be small and cozy,
domestic and weak;
how lucky, little tree,
to have a pot to grow in.
With living creatures
one must begin very early
to dwarf their growth:
the bound feet,
the crippled brain,
the hair in curlers,
the hands you
love to touch.

Marge Piercy

Their [men's] violence is amazing. Yet these men feel that the woman or the child is to blame for not being "friendly." Because it makes them uncomfortable to know that the woman or the child or the black or the workman is grumbling, the oppressed groups must also appear to like their oppression—smiling and simpering though they may feel like hell inside. The smile is the child/woman equivalent of the shuffle; it indicates acquiescence of the victim to his own oppression.... My "dream" action for the women's liberation movement: a smile boycott, at which declaration all women would instantly abandon their "pleasing" smiles, henceforth smiling only when something pleased them.

Shulamith Firestone, *The Dialectic of Sex,* 1970

From the Point of View of the Victim

Purpose: To get in touch with the hidden strength and subtle forms of power and control of the victim position.

Directions: Choose a partner and sit facing each other. Take turns doing the following (or, this exercise may be done alone by writing your responses to the following):

1. Think of an experience in which you were the victim and tell (or write) the story from that point of view.
2. Now, tell the story again, keeping the facts the same except that now tell it from the point of view of the other person being the victim.

What is your experience upon retelling the story? How have your attitudes or feelings changed about what happened as a result of seeing the situation in a different way? What are some of the advantages of the victim position? The disadvantages?

---

the gesture as well as men, but often in modified form. While looking directly at a man, a woman usually has her head slightly tilted, implying the beginning of a presenting gesture or enough submission to render the stare ambivalent if not actually submissive."*

The idea that the averted glance is a gesture of submission is supported by the research of Hutt and Ounsted (1966) into the characteristic gaze aversion of autistic children. They remark that "these children were never attacked [by peers] despite the fact that to a naive observer they appeared to be easy targets; this indicated that their gaze aversion had some signalling function similar to 'facing away' in the kittiwake or 'head-flagging' in the herring gull—behavior patterns which Tinbergen (1959) has termed 'appeasement postures.' In other words, gaze aversion inhibited any aggressive or threat behavior on the part of other conspecifics" (p. 354).

Gestures of dominance and submission can be verbal as well as nonverbal. In fact, the sheer use of verbalization is a form of dominance because it can quite literally render someone speechless by preventing one from "getting a word in edgewise." As noted earlier, contrary to popular myth, men do talk

can elicit the same sort of responses that are common in primates; that is, staring can act like a primate threat display" (p. 310).

Though women engage in mutual visual interaction in its intimate form to a high degree, they probably back down when looking becomes a gesture of dominance. O'Connor points out, "The direst stare or glare is a common human gesture of dominance. Women use

---

*"Presenting" is the term for the submissive gesture seen in primates, of presenting the rump to a dominant animal; O'Connor also points out that it is a human female submissive gesture as well, seen, for example, in the can-can.

---

from **Letter to a Sister Underground**

Our smiles and glances,
the ways we walk, sit, laugh, the games we
    must play
with men and even oh my Ancient Mother
    God the games
we must play among ourselves—these are the
    ways we pass
unnoticed, by the Conquerors.
They're always watching,
invisibly electroded in our brains,
to be certain we implode our rage against
    each other
and not explode it against them:
the times we rip and tear at the twin
for what we have intricately defended in our-
    selves;
the mimicry of male hierarchy, male ego,
male possessiveness, leader/follower,
    doer/thinker, butch/femme
yes also when we finally learn to love each
    other physically.

Roles to survive a death-in-life until
that kind of life becomes worthless enough
to risk losing even precious It.

Our subterranean grapevine, which men, like
    fools, call gossip,
has always been efficient.
Our sabotage has ranged from witches'
    research
into herbal poisons to secretaries' spilling
    coffee on the files
to housewives' passive resistance
in front of their soap-opera screens
to housemaids' accidentally breaking china
to mothers' teaching their children to love
    them
a little bit better than their fathers.
    And more.

Robin Morgan

---

more than women, both in single-sex and in mixed-sex groups. Within a group a major means of asserting dominance is to interrupt. Those who want to dominate others interrupt more; those speaking will not permit themselves to be interrupted by their inferiors, but they will give way to those they consider their superiors. Zimmerman and West [1975] found in a sample of 11 natural conversations between women and men that 46 of the 48 interruptions were by males.

Other characteristics of persons in inferior status positions are the tendencies to hesitate and apologize, often offered as submissive gestures in the face of threats or potential threats. If staring directly, pointing, and touching can be subtle nonverbal threats, the corresponding gestures of submission seem to be lowering the eyes from another's gaze, falling silent (or not speaking at all) when interrupted or pointed at, and cuddling to the touch. Many of these nonverbal gestures of submission are very fa-

He said we were both free. Yes, we're both free. He's free to find someone who will wash his socks, and I'm free to find another slave master.

Anne Battle-Sister, *Journal of Marriage and the Family*, 1971

---

miliar. They are the traits our society assigns as desirable secondary characteristics of the female role. Girls who have properly learned to be "feminine" have learned to lower their eyes, remain silent, back down, and cuddle at the appropriate times. There is even a word for this syndrome that is applied only to females: coy.

In verbal communication one finds a similar pattern of differences between the sexes. As mentioned earlier, men have the privilege of swearing, and hence access to a vocabulary not customarily available to women. On the surface this seems like an innocuous limitation, until one realizes the psychological function of swearing: it is one of the most harmless and effective ways of expressing anger. The alternatives are to express one's feelings with physical violence or to suppress them and by so doing turn one's anger in on oneself. The former is prohibited to both sexes (to different degrees) but the latter is decisively encouraged in women. The result is that women are "intropunitive"; they punish themselves for their own anger rather than somehow dissipate it. Since anger turned inward is commonly viewed as the basis for depression we should not be surprised that depression is considerably more common in women than in men, and in fact is the most prevalent form of "mental illness" among women. Obviously, the causes of female depression are complex (Bart, 1971; Chesler, 1972).

Swearing is only the most obvious sex difference in language. Key (1972) has noted that sex differences are to be found in phonological, semantic, and grammatical aspects of language as well as in word use (see also Lakoff, 1973). Austin (1965) has commented that "in our culture little boys tend to be nasal ... and little girls, oral" (p. 34), but that in the "final stages" of courtship the voices of both men and women are low and nasal (p. 37). The pattern cited by Brown (1965), in which the form appropriately used by status superiors is used between status equals in intimate situations, is again visible: in the intimate situation the female adopts the vocal style of the male.

In situations where intimacy is not a possible interpretation, it is not power but abnormality that is the usual interpretation. Female voices are expected to be soft and quiet—even when men are using loud voices. Yet it is only the "lady" whose speech is refined. Women who do not fit this stereotype are often called loud—a word commonly applied derogatorily to other minority groups or out groups (Austin, 1965, p. 38). One of the most popular derogatory terms for women is "shrill," which, after all, simply means loud (out of place) and high-pitched (female).

In language, as in touch and in most other aspects of interpersonal behavior, status differences between the sexes mean that the same traits are differently interpreted when displayed by each sex. A man's behavior toward a woman might be interpreted as an expression of either power or intimacy, depending on the situation. When the same behavior is engaged in by a woman and directed toward a man, it is interpreted only as a gesture of intimacy—and intimacy between the sexes is always seen as sexual in nature. Because our values say that women should not have power over men, women's nonverbal communication is rarely interpreted as an expression of

---

from **Doing It Differently**

We will be equal, we say, new man and new woman.
But what man am I equal to before the law of court
*   or custom?*
The state owns my womb and hangs a man's name
*   on me*
like the tags hung on dogs, my name is, property
*   of. . . .*
The language betrays us and rots in the mouth
with its aftertaste of monastic sewers on the palate.
Even the pronouns tear my tongue with their metal
*   plates.*

You could strangle me: my hands
can't even encircle your neck.
Because I open my mouth wide and stand up roaring
I am the outlawed enemy of men.
A party means what a bullfight does to the bull.
The street is a gauntlet.

I open my mail with tongs.
All the images of strength in you, fathers and
*   prophets and heroes,*
pull against me, till what feels right to you
wrongs me, and there is no rest from struggle.

We are equal if we make ourselves so, every day,
*   every night*
constantly renewing what the street
*   destroys.*
We are equal only if you open too on your heavy
*   hinges*
and let your love come freely, freely, where it will
*   never be safe,*
where you can never possess.

Marge Piercy

---

power. If the situation precludes a sexual interpretation, women's assumption of the male prerogative is dismissed as deviant (castrating, domineering, unfeminine, or the like).*

Of course, if women do not wish to be classified either as deviant or as perpetually sexy, then they must persist in playing the proper role by following the interpersonal behavior pattern prescribed for them. Followed repeatedly, these patterns function as a means of control. What is merely habitual is often seen as desirable. The more men and women interact in the way they have been trained to from birth without considering the meaning of what they do, the more they become dulled to the significance of their actions. Just as outsiders observing a new society are more aware of the status differences of that society than its members are, so those who play the sexual politics of interpersonal behavior are usually not conscious of what they do. Instead they continue to wonder that feminists make such a mountain out of such a "trivial" molehill.

---

*We are not suggesting that just because certain gestures associated with males are responded to as powerful, women should automatically adopt them. Rather than accepting male values without question, individual women will want to consider what they wish to express and how, and will determine whether to adopt particular gestures or to insist that their own be responded to appropriately meanwhile.

Marjorie Whittaker Leidig

Violence Against Women: A Feminist-Psychological Analysis

Acts of violence against women have recently been eliciting both lay and professional attention. Rape became a serious focus of the Women's Liberation Movement about ten years ago; in fact, it was one of the first major issues women rallied around (Connell & Wilson, 1974). Public speak-outs and workshops were held, rape was openly discussed in consciousness-raising groups, police training was organized by feminists in an effort to sensitize police to their handling of sexual assault victims, programs were directed toward state and national legislation regarding sexual assault as a crime, and medical personnel were educated toward better care of victims in the emergency room and/or hospital setting. Numerous professional books and articles have been published: scientific and empirical studies on rapist/victim variables, incidence reports of sexual assault and analyses of victims (Brodsky, 1976a,b; Chappel, 1976; Pacht, 1976; Russell, 1975), personal accounts from victims themselves (Medea & Thompson, 1974; Russell, 1975), and studies on the psychological handling of the victim herself (Burgess & Holmstrom, 1974). Several authors, including Russell (1975), Brownmiller (1976), and Gager and Schurr (1976) have written thought-provoking books providing feminist analyses of the crime of sexual assault.

A second major violence against women recently described by feminists has been that of the battered woman. First was an emotional description by battered women themselves from England (Pizzey, 1974), followed by Gelles (1974), Steinmetz and Straus (1974), Martin (1976), Roy (1977), Davidson (1978), and Walker (1979). Personalized accounts of woman-wife abuse intermingled with formal data collection, attempts at state and national legislation, sensitization of police to the ubiquitous "domestic disturbance" call, and public education have been aimed at medical, legal, and religious interventions. Safe houses, temporary shelters, and "hot lines" emerged similarly in response to the battered woman as to the sexual assault victim.

Currently, feminist concerns have shifted to include yet another act of violence against young female victims—that of incest. Within the family, the battering of wives and the sexual abuse of girl children have soberly illustrated that the family home is not necessarily the haven of tranquillity it was once assumed to be. Local mental health centers and child abuse teams are keenly aware of the heretofore unsuspected high incidence of girl-child incest (Butler, 1978). As public awareness of child abuse has increased, so has the rate of referrals to these systems or to the criminal justice system. Although the topic of incest has interested psychologists and social scientists for years, it was not until Florence Rush wrote her article on the "Sexual Abuse of Children" (Connell & Wilson, 1974) that it was seen as a particularly feminist issue. There is currently a spate of new books and articles on incest (Armstrong, 1978; Butler, 1978; Herman & Hirschman, 1977; MacFarlane, 1978; Meiselman, 1978), and some of these view girl-child incest from a feminist perspective.

Recently, other behaviors interpreted as victimizing women have been noted. Sexual harassment on the job has been described and documented by Farley (1978), Evans (1978), and by the Working Women's Institute in New York (1975). Pornography has also been focused upon, at women's conferences (e.g., San Francisco, 1978) and in books and professional articles (Brownmiller, 1976; Diamond, 1980; Russell, 1975). Sexual abuse of women clients by male psychotherapists has also been addressed by feminist psychologists (Belote, 1974; Chesler, 1972; Holroyd & Brodsky, 1977) as well as by the popular press (Freeman & Roy, 1976). Prostitution, a topic frequently publicized by the media, is now being examined from a feminist perspective in terms of the sex-role stereotyping of the prostitute as well as discriminatory law enforcement (James, 1978). An additional set of somewhat less noxious male behaviors viewed increasingly from a pro-woman stance are obscene telephone calls, indecent exposures, "Peeping Tom" behaviors, and probably the most commonly experienced set of behaviors for girls and women, sexual "street hassling."

This paper has several purposes. The first is to conceptualize various acts of violence against women along a continuum and to specify their sexual and physical dimensions. Second, linkages will be suggested among all of these acts of violence to provide a model for considering them together. Third, common myths further connecting them will be noted.

Finally, a feminist-psychological analysis of their occurrence will be undertaken.

A study of violence against women seems necessary to an understanding of the psychology of women since it would seem that virtually all women are affected by the *threat* of male violence if not its actual occurrence. Moreover, it would seem that all women are subjected to the actual occurrence of violence if in no other form than the ubiquitous media portrayals of women as victims. Even media portrayals of women in sex-role stereotyped ways could be seen as violence against women in the sense that they present inaccurate and limited versions of the female sex role to women, and are no doubt harmful to women's self-concepts. This paper will not deal with these aspects of the media though they have been documented and discussed elsewhere (McArthur & Resko, 1975; Miller, 1974; Mosher, 1976; Smith, 1974; Stemple & Tyler, 1974; and Sternglanz & Serbin, 1974).

It is assumed here that women are subjected to many more forms and incidents of violence than they allow themselves to experience consciously as such. This would indicate an area of the "female psyche" that is at least in some ways out of awareness although this has emotional and intellectual consequences nonetheless and is an important determinant in controlling and directing women's behavior.

Violence against women is also important to the psychology of women since it affects women's mental and emotional health. Psychologists and feminists have elaborated upon the theoretical aspects of violence against women and have contributed to the development of psychological treatment of victims. Furthermore, feminists have made valuable

efforts toward changing the system, which is a major source of male violence according to feminist analyses.

Continuum of Acts of Violence Against Women

What, then, specifically, are these acts of violence? It is difficult to place them on a continuum from "less noxious" to "most noxious" in terms of the degradation, hurtfulness, coerciveness, and/or injury involved. In a pilot study, a sample of 523 Denver women age sixteen and above, contacted through a county hospital system, were asked to rate acts of violence in terms of seriousness (Leidig & Evans, 1976). It was found that while there was high agreement that certain acts were less hurtful than others (e.g., "street hassling," obscene telephone calls) and that other acts were very noxious (e.g., rape with injury), agreements were difficult *within* the categories of "least hurtful," "moderate," and "most hurtful." There was also inconsistent agreement among the sample in scaling them along a continuum. With these provisos in mind, the following continuum of least hurtful to most hurtful acts of violence is tentatively suggested.

At the least hurtful end of the continuum would be "street hassling," which generally would include male verbal "compliments,"

rude stares, and noises accompanying women as they walk down the street. Moving along the continuum would be other public sexual "hassling"—grabbing or touching a woman's sexual anatomy without her permission, including "accidental" physical contact with a woman's sexual or genital body areas in subways, elevators, or other crowded areas when such contact is actually intentional.

Further down the continuum would be a grouping of three acts that are defined as against the law and prosecutable in most states, but rarely reported by girls and women: obscene telephone calls, exhibitionism or indecent exposures, and "Peeping Tomism." Somewhere in this area of the continuum would be sexual harassment on the job, which, as Farley (1978) has described, can range from simple coercive stares from male office workers to actual sexual assaults. Similarly found in this area of the continuum would be sexual abuses by male psychotherapists and male professionals (physicians, lawyers, dentists, etc.) of female clients/patients, again ranging from minimally noxious behaviors (e.g., patting the woman client on her knee or bottom) to outright sexual assaults or sexual intercourse (as described poignantly in Freeman & Roy, 1976).

Pornography and prostitution are also included in this area of the continuum of violence against women. Pornography can be

Nowhere is woman treated according to the merit of her work, but rather as a sex. It is therefore almost inevitable that she should pay for her right to exist, to keep a position in whatever line, with sex favors. Thus it is merely a question of degree whether she sells herself to one man, in or out of marriage, or to many men.

Emma Goldman, *Anarchism and Other Essays*, 1911

delineated further into pornography as a medium for expressing cultural norms about male power (Diamond, 1980), which is seen as affecting all women, or as outright violence against pornography models for coercive purposes (Russell, 1975). With prostitution there are, of course, very complicated arguments and feminists have sometimes been divided on the prostitution issue. If we separate discriminatory law enforcement with prostitutes from their victimization in terms of sex-role stereotyping and from the blatantly sexist theories which have been proposed by social scientists to explain causality, then the victimization/violence aspects of prostitution can be seen more clearly.

Continuing along the continuum is the area of sexual assault, which can be further divided into three major categories: "date rapes," marital rapes, and stranger-to-stranger assaults. (Incest, of course, could be included here, but since it is such an enormously complicated sexual assault, it will be categorized by itself.) "Date rapes" and marital rapes are rarely reported, while stranger-to-stranger rapes are. Rapes are clearly near the most hurtful end of the spectrum.

The battering of women can also be delineated into psychological and physical abuse, which will be explained later. This act of violence appears to deserve a place near the most hurtful end of the violent continuum because of its devastating medical, psychological, and coercive consequences on the women involved.

The most serious of all the acts of violence, it seems to the author, is girl-child incest. Incest is defined here as the occurrence of usually *protracted* sexual coerciveness, usually toward a girl-child, by a trusted family member, usually a male.

Acts of violence can also be specified by sexual and/or physical coercion. Most of the acts can be seen as *sexual* violence, for example, rape, incest, pornography, harassment on the job, abuses between therapist and client. On the other hand, battering fits most clearly the physically-abusive dimension, since it is chiefly accomplished through physical abuse to the body. However, as experts, clinicians, and researchers in the battered woman area can attest, many acts of violence against women combine a physical *and* sexual component. Marital rapes are often seen as a part of the physical violence husbands do to wives (studies by Walker, 1978–80, and by Frieze, in progress). Likewise, physical injuries are also seen as a part of sexual assaults. Pornography models, while most often posing for sexual themes, are now beginning to report their physical abuse (Russell, 1975).

For all of these examples of sexual and/or physical abuse, even when there is no actual abuse, there can often be the *threat* of its oc-

ARE FOURTEEN STITCHES ENOUGH TO FILE A COMPLAINT ON WIFE BATTERING?

from *Sugar Daddys a Sticky Myth*, copyright bülbül 1976, Arachne Publishing, Mountain View, CA. 94040

currence, which can be an effective means of social control. Gillespie (1976) offers a clear example of this:

> A husband and a wife are at a party. The wife says something that the husband does not want her to say. He quickly tightens the muscles around his jaw and gives her a rapid, but intense, direct stare. Outsiders don't notice the interaction, though they may have a vaguely uncomfortable feeling that they are intruding on something private. The wife, who is acutely sensitive to the gestures of the man on whom she is dependent, immediately stops the conversation, lowers or turns her head slightly, averts her eyes, or gives off some other gesture of submission which communicates acquiescence to her husband and reduces his aggression. The wife has been put in her place. (p. 203)

Walker (1979) specifically delineates between psychological and physical battering. While physical abuse is clear-cut (e.g., cutting, punching, slapping, hitting, shoving, etc.), the issue of psychological abuse appears more vague and is often less understood, probably because there are no physical residuals. Psychological abuse appears to be qualitatively different from normal marital or relational discord. It is the use of behaviors, though not physical, to undermine equality in a relationship which make the other person (usually the wife) feel invisible, terrified, discounted, or, even worse, non-human. Some have even called it "brain-washing." Walker (1979) quotes a poignant example of a battered woman who said that the worst abuses she incurred (even though she had been physically beaten many times) were those that were psychological—for example, being made to get down on "all fours" and walk like an animal around the house. Flick (1978) quotes another example of a woman being forced by her husband to play "Russian Roulette" with a gun loaded with one bullet aimed at her head, although there were never any physical injuries involved. Further examples of psychological abuse are those incidents of overpossessive jealousy and accusations, deprivation of mobility and freedom (e.g., locking a woman inside the house), and time restrictions such as timing her errands and then making accusations of marital infidelity if she fails to return within specified time limits.

Linkages Among Acts of Violence Against Women

Numerous linkages can be made among these various acts of violence against women. One similarity is that they are all "tip-of-the-iceberg" phenomena in that they are all underreported. Contrary to the popular myths, which assume that women report sexual assault at the "drop of a hat" scornfully to revenge a man, women actually grossly underreport this felonious crime (Brownmiller, 1976;

NO SENATOR, I DON'T WANT TO JOIN YOUR STAFF!

Clark & Lewis, 1977; Gager & Schurr, 1976; Medea & Thompson, 1974; Russell, 1975). Similar findings are noted with battered women (Martin, 1976; Roy, 1977; Walker, 1979) and the extreme underreporting of girl-child incest has also been documented (Rush, 1974; Russell, 1978; Schultz, 1976).

In the preliminary research mentioned previously (Leidig & Evans, 1976), a sample of 523 women aged sixteen and older were asked anonymously whether they had experienced the "less noxious" sexual behaviors. Seventy-six percent of our sample had received one or more obscene telephone calls, 86 percent had their bodies commented upon by strangers on the street, 43 percent had been the victim of an indecent exposure, 17 percent had been the victim of a "Peeping Tom," and 60 percent had been unwilling victims of "sexual grabbing of body parts." *Yet the majority of the sample had not reported any of these acts.*

Evans (1978) notes that in a survey completed in 1975 on 155 working women, 70 percent said they had experienced sexual harassment on the job. Carey (1977) interviewed 401 working women, *all* of whom had suffered sexual harassment at work. In Evans's 1975 survey, only 18 percent of the women who said they were harassed complained about it through established channels. The reasons stated by these women are the usual reasons given about nonreporting: fear that nothing would be done, feeling that their claims would be treated lightly or ridiculed, fearing that *they* would be blamed or would suffer some repercussions if they complained, and, finally, feelings of guilt.

There are other reasons for non- or underreporting of noxious male sexual or physical behaviors. One may be women's fear of "causing a scene," which can be seen as acting within feminine sex role boundaries or as "cultural shuffling," illustrating gestures of *submission* by remaining passive and silent (Henley, 1977). With the less noxious behaviors (i.e., "street hassling") there is still another reason for low reporting—women do not define the behavior as objectionable. The majority of women have been socialized to be complimented rather than angered by these aggressive behaviors from men.[1] Another reason for the nonreporting of violent or noxious male behaviors is a general resignation or feeling of inevitability about men's behavior—"after all, men will be men."

If the "softer" violences are nonreported, or minimally reported, so are the "harder" violences. Estimates of actual incidence vary among experts and depend upon the specific crime. For rape, estimates range from half of all occurring rapes being reported (Denver District Attorney, 1977) to a one-in-ten report

---

[1] I can remember my own mother reproaching me for being irritated when as a young girl truck drivers whistled at both my mother and me. Most women report a similar kind of socialization.

The male is the aggressor, the soldier laying siege to the castle; the woman is the guardian of the gate, and defender of the sacred treasure. If the male forces his way in with a battering ram and captures the treasure, he has succeeded in his purpose. There is no cause for guilt or remorse. The woman, on the other hand, has failed in her purpose. She has allowed the treasure to be taken and feels herself to be at fault. She suffers from feelings of guilt, besides the feelings of violation, humiliation and defeat.

Andrea Medea and Kathleen Thompson (eds.),
Against Rape, 1974

---

rate (Hursch, 1977). Walker (1979) suggests a one-in-ten report rate for the battered woman. Estimates of actual report rates of incest tend to be even lower (Butler, 1978).

Another linkage among all the various acts of violence against women is that it is largely unidirectional, a fact often ignored in analyses of "victimology." With few exceptions, males are the perpetrators and females the victims and not vice versa. Male victims are the rare exceptions and are usually the victims of other men. In an unpublished study (Leidig, 1977) of sexual assault cases seen in the emergency room of Denver General Hospital in an 11-month period between 1976 and 1977, 305 cases were admitted and treated. Five of these 305 cases were males (1.5 percent), ranging in age from 5 to 35 years old (the perpetrators in each of these 5 cases were adult males). "Battered husbands" are reported to comprise about the same percentage of the total battered population (Walker, 1979). Rush (1974) and others report that male children comprise about 10 percent or less of the incest population. Herman and Hirschman (1977) note that 92 percent of the victims are female and 97 percent of the offenders are male. In the case of the male incest or rape victim, then, the perpetrator is almost always a male. Mothers are the rare offenders when the incest victim is a boy child. Even in the "softer" violences,

such as pornography, there is the similarity of the female model and the male viewer, or what Millett (1969) has described as the centrality of "male domination and female subjugation."

A further similarity among these various victimizing behaviors is that until the advent of the Women's Movement in the late 1960s none of these acts was taken very seriously by the culture or its institutions. Worse yet, they were (and often still are) joked about. Women historically have listened to "wife battering jokes," jokes about rape, have heard incest described by men as "the game the whole family can play," and heard male employees and employers alike describe sexual harassment on the job as "just good fun" or even "complimentary" (Evans, 1978). Sexual and physical violences against women have been and continue to be trivialized, discounted, ignored, or made to seem invisible. Even the psychology profession whose responsibility is to take such claims seriously has been remiss.[2]

It is interesting to note, however, the seriousness that child abuse has been accorded

---

[2]For example, a male psychologist who, upon hearing recent concerns about sexual abuses between therapists and female clients, noted to me that "there just isn't that much of it"; "women clients who report it must be bragging," and that "it's all in the minds of those feminists who take everything so seriously."

Rape Poem

There is no difference between being raped
and being pushed down a flight of cement
  steps
except that the wounds also bleed inside.

There is no difference between being raped
and being run over by a truck
except that afterward men ask if you
  enjoyed it.

There is no difference between being raped
and being bit on the ankle by a rattlesnake
except that people ask if your skirt was
  short
and why you were out alone anyhow.

There is no difference between being raped
and going head first through a windshield
except that afterward you are afraid
not of cars
but half the human race.

The rapist is your boyfriend's brother.
He sits beside you in the movies eating
  popcorn.
Rape fattens on the fantasies of the normal
  male
like a maggot in garbage.

Fear of rape is a cold wind blowing
all of the time on a woman's hunched back.
Never to stroll alone on a sand road
  through pine woods,

never to climb a trail across a bald
without that aluminum in the mouth
when I see a man climbing toward me.

Never to open the door to a knock
without that razor just grazing the throat.
The fear of the dark side of hedges,
the back seat of the car, the empty house
rattling keys like a snake's warning.
The fear of the smiling man
in whose pocket is a knife.
The fear of the serious man
in whose fist is locked hatred.

All it takes to cast a rapist to be able to see
  your body
as jackhammer, as blowtorch, as
  adding-machine-gun.
All it takes is hating that body
your own, your self, your muscle that
  softens to flab.

All it takes is to push what you hate,
what you fear onto the soft alien flesh.
To bucket out invincible as a tank
armored with treads without senses
to possess and punish in one act,
to rip up pleasure, to murder those who
  dare
live in the leafy flesh open to love.

                                        Marge Piercy

in contrast to wife-woman abuse. Many years ago, books, research funding, and service-delivery programs were instituted for the detection and treatment of the battered child (Kempe & Helfer, 1968). Numerous sources have hypothesized that the incidence of the battered woman may actually be many times greater than that of the battered child (Roy, 1977; Steinmetz & Straus, 1974; Walker, 1979). It took the Women's Movement to force the issue of the battered woman onto an unaccepting and disbelieving public. Even today, after years of documentation of physical abuse against women, the general public, as well as the psychology profession, are still quibbling.[3]

A fourth linkage among all the acts of violence against women is "blaming the victim." Nowhere is it applied more clearly than in the case of violence against women. The pornography model elicits minimal sympathy because "she's a free agent" and "knows what she's doing." The woman complaining of sexual harassment on the job has "asked for it"; she must have been seductive or flirtatious. The psychotherapy client must have fabricated sexual abuse ("unconscious distortion" or "transference") or brought it on herself by her seductive behavior toward her therapist.[4]

The battered woman gets blamed for her own physical abuse with comments such as "she provoked it" and "she likes it, why else would she stay?" The young girl incest victim gets blamed for her "collusion" in the act (by being provocative for example). The rape victim gets blamed for her dress, manner of self-presentation, or location. If she was engaging in a high-risk behavior (such as hitch-hiking) this is seen as evidence of her own collusion. The prostitute or pornography model rarely if ever reports a sexual assault—who would believe her? Gates (1978) notes that "despite an apparent rise in the consciousness of the general public with respect to these crimes, the victims continue to be subjected to a second "victimization" by the criminal justice system, the community, and sometimes their families, who suggest that the women contributed to their criminal victimization or even "deserved it." This is true victim-blaming.

It appears that the more intimacy there is between the perpetrator and the victim, the more blaming-of-the-victim occurs. That is, marital and "date rapes" produce more victim blaming than "stranger-to-stranger" rapes. Adult-to-child sexual molestation focuses more blame on the child the closer the relationship. In addition, the closer the relationship, the less the *reporting* (Schultz, 1976). So, for example, if a stranger molests a female child it is less likely that she will be blamed and more likely that a report will be made, than if she were molested by a family member.

There is another linkage among these victimizing behaviors. They all serve to keep women in their prescribed place and they support cultural sex-role stereotypes. If all of these male behaviors place women in some sort of physical and/or psychological fear,

---

[3]I recently noted in a public display the public glorification of woman-battering. I was attending a regional psychological convention in Las Vegas and decided to attend a night-club show. In one of the acts, entitled "Vestal Virgins," young topless women were lashed to the masts of a galleon ship with leather straps. Amidst grand musical accompaniment, the ship was burned. The audience seemed to love it. The battering of women, whether by burning, slapping, or discounting continued in the twentieth century, unfortunately supported by strong positive public opinion.

[4]Should a psychotherapy client act in a sexually seductive manner, the psychotherapist is professionally, ethically, and legally required not to act on [his] sexual feelings and is required to deal with any behavior the client presents in a psychotherapeutic manner.

which several authors have now suggested (Brownmiller, 1976; Gates, 1978; Russell, 1975), women remain helpless, dependent upon male protection,[5] geographically limited, subservient, and frightened.[6]

The behaviors mentioned above—helplessness, dependence upon male protection, geographical and mobility limitations, subservience, and fright—fit with behaviors already described by psychologists as culturally-specific to psychologically healthy women (Broverman, Vogel, Broverman, Clarkson, & Rosenkrantz, 1972). Specifically, the behaviors psychologists have ascribed to normal women's personalities are less independence, more submissiveness, less aggression, and less adventurousness than men. It would seem that violence or fear of violence, whether physical or sexual, could be a powerful force in the maintenance of sex-role stereotyping, especially for women.

Common Myths About Acts of Violence Against Women

The final linkage among all of these acts of violence is the commonality of the numerous myths attached to them. Probably the most common myth underlying them is the "victim precipitation" myth. It has also been called "female provocation," which, of course, has as its most basic assumption "blaming the victim." In crimes against women, victim precipitation arguments are used more often than in other crimes. That is, when a man is robbed or murdered, the crime, in most cases, is duly recorded, investigated, and the offender prosecuted. The victim is rarely asked if he provoked it, encouraged it, dreamed about it ahead of time, or wished it would happen. When a woman's body is violated, either by sexual assault or by physical injury, or when unwanted passes are made at her by a trusted professional or an employer, she most decidedly *is* asked if she provoked it, encouraged it, dreamed about it ahead of time, or wished it would happen. These questions are asked of her by the police, her therapist, her minister, priest or rabbi, and her physician.

Another myth closely linked to the victim-precipitation myth is the "female masochism" myth. This is the basis of the "lie-back-and-enjoy-it" phrase so often utilized by men. It has as its most basic assumption that women enjoy sexual and physical violence against them by men. It again diverts the blame from the perpetrator and blames the victim. A police officer asking a rape victim during an investigation if she had an orgasm while being raped is an example of the use of the female masochism myth. Numerous psychological forefathers (and, unfortunately, fore*mothers* are as well) have contributed voluminously to this myth. According to them women do not mind pain, humiliation, and objectification as much as men.[7]

---

[5]Nancy Henley calls it a "protection racket" (1977).

[6]When I have interviewed battered women in conjunction with research, I have heard these women describe this process in some detail. The beatings and sexual abuse serve to keep them scared and submissive. The batterer reinforces this notion as well, for while the acute battering episode is occurring, he says "I'll teach you a lesson for nagging me, for talking back to me, for provoking me." The battered woman quickly learns her "lesson"—which is to remain submissive and frightened. She learns not to talk back.

[7]Although both theoretical and empirical work has supposedly supported this myth, I have never in my own experience of working with retrospective incest victims, sexual assault victims, battered women, women victims of sexual harassment on the job, or women victims of my own male professional colleagues heard a woman say she enjoyed her injuries, lacerations, degradation, or sexual attacks. What I *have* seen (e.g., in emergency rooms) have been unconscious, immobilized, fearful, pained, and, in one or two cases, dead women.

Though woman needs the protection of one man against his whole sex, in pioneer life, in threading her way through a lonely forest, on the highway, or in the streets of the metropolis on a dark night, she sometimes needs, too, the protection of all men against this one.

Elizabeth Cady Stanton, *History of Woman Suffrage*, Vol. 1, with Susan B. Anthony and Matilda Gage, 1881

In a brilliantly conceptualized book, Rush (1980) explains how the processes of woman-blaming, victim-precipitation, and/or female masochism are utilized to cover up the real issues involved in the high incidence of sexual abuse of girl children. Rush notes that

> children know when they have been humiliated and exploited. Freud knew that the sexual abuse of children existed, but he could not reconcile the implications of that abuse with either his self-image or his identification with other men of his class, and thus he *altered his telling of reality.* (p. 32, italics mine)

In Freud's 1897 letter to Wilhelm Fliess (Freud, 1954), he said,

> Then there was the astonishing thing that in every case blame was laid on perverse acts by the father ... it was hardly credible that perverted acts against children were so general. (p. 215)

The retrospective incest victim's telling of reality is disbelieved, victim-blaming utilized, and the presumption of fantasy or the girl-child's "desire" made to be the chief focus of psychological inquiry (Herman & Hirschman, 1977). If girls' and women's childhood sexual molestation stories were believed, if they and their mothers were not psychologically charged with "collusion," if girls were not accused of "precipitation," an unbelieving public might have to take women's stories seriously. Large groups of both high and low status males could be implicated for their misogynous behavior toward females. Rush explains that a great deal of cultural alteration of reality has to occur to obscure the facts (1978).

An additional myth often used to explain violence against women is the "psychopathic deviance" model. It has often been thought that if men batter, rape, molest, harass, or objectify women, it is because they are psychological deviants. No one who rapes, beats women, or sexually molests a child can be in (his) "right mind," therefore, he must be "sick" or abnormal.

Earlier research tended to show that indeed these men did have serious psychopathology (Bromberg, 1965; Gebhard et al., 1969; West, 1965). However, these studies did not compare them to other incarcerated individuals and, more importantly, it has been estimated recently that only 2 percent of actual committed rapists are charged, convicted, and incarcerated (Clark & Lewis, 1977; Schram, 1978). This research, then, has serious limitations in that only a select and probably biased sample is studied. These earlier results may also reflect the effect of this myth on scientific research.

More recent works (Amir, 1971; Brodsky, 1976a; Chapell, 1976; Pacht, 1976) have concluded on the basis of research that there are no general psychological characteristics of rapists and there do not seem to be higher rates of psychopathology among these individuals. What has been found instead is a heterogeneous population of males varying in intelligence, presence or absence of defined psychopathology, passivity vs. activity, ag-

> In the system of chivalry, men protect women against men. This is not unlike the protection relationship which the Mafia established with small businesses in the early part of this century. Indeed, chivalry is an age-old protection racket which depends for its existence on rape.
>
> Susan Griffin, "Rape: The All-American Crime," 1971

gressiveness vs. non-aggressiveness, and so forth. Brodsky (1976a) notes that:

> a search for a single psychological type of assailant is futile in view of the diversity of individuals and personal reactions. (p. 5)

Pacht (1976) also notes that it is a myth to think of the rapist as a member of a homogeneous group:

> some rapists do not show any indication of psychological pathology and others appear to have significant emotional or behavioral problems. (p. 93)

In the area of incest, Butler (1978) notes additionally that:

> men who are reported as incestuous aggressors seldom have prior criminal records. They have little or no psychiatric history, are not necessarily excessive drinkers, and appear to be of average intelligence and education. Their work histories are steady, and their marital histories primarily monogamous. (p. 79)

Another of the additional, consistent discussions found in the older rape or victimization literature has been a further victimization of women, for it is often the *mother* or the *wife* of the perpetrator who is blamed. The mother is blamed for her son's deviant upbringing, or the wife is blamed for either "collusion" or not providing enough sexual activity. Ironically, the mother and not the father of the batterer is sometimes seen as causal for her

son's battering of his wife because she was a battered wife herself!

Another myth regarding violence against women is the class and race myth. Only lower socioeconomic or nonwhite women, according to this myth, are raped, beaten, molested, or sexually exploited, or only lower socioeconomic or nonwhite men are the perpetrators of these acts. A myriad of research is now negating this myth (Chapman & Gates, 1978; Walker, 1979; Farley, 1978; Gelles, 1974; Walker & Brodsky, 1976). All evidence now suggests that rape, battering, incest, and other victimizations of women occur across all socioeconomic levels and racial categories at approximately the same rates. The most viable explanation for the higher report rate, at times, by the low-income or nonwhite rape or battered victim, is that these people are more often connected to any number of social services that record such cases.

Another myth utilized in the theorizing about women as victims of violence is the so-called "fantasy" myth. Women, according to this myth, have fantasies about being whistled at, molested, gang-raped, and even beaten. Pornography is based on this myth. A concern about women admitting the possible occurrence of some of these fantasies is that it may be seen as tantamount to support for their own victimization. Actually a more likely explanation of such fantasies may be that they simply reflect exposure to the content of a culture in which women are in reality victimized by men. It is hardly surprising that women and girls have many of these fantasies, since these

from *Sugar Daddys a Sticky Myth*, copyright bülbül 1976, Arachne
Publishing, Mountain View, CA. 94040

ideas abound in women's and men's popular magazines, movies, television programs, and books. This fantasy issue has also been used against women in psychotherapy. In the exploration surrounding an act of violence against the woman client, the possibility of a thought/fantasy/dream/nightmare about a similar event is explored. This is often used as evidence that the victim wished such an event would occur and that it was perhaps even unconsciously motivated.

A myth that may be unfair to *men* is the following: Men have higher sexual or aggressive drives, therefore they need to release sexual or aggressive tension more than women. This myth assumes that men cannot control their behavior. Recent research on human sexuality does not support men's greater sexual drive (Masters & Johnson, 1966; Sherfey, 1973). On the contrary, *women* may have greater sexual potential than men. On the other hand, sex differences research does support a greater aggressive drive in males (Maccoby & Jacklin, 1974), which appears to be related to higher levels of testosterone. To make the leap, however, from what may be a physiologically based behavior (i.e., male aggression) to justifying its occurrence when it victimizes another group of people (i.e., women) is questionable.

Running concurrent to the above myth is the "stress myth." This has been utilized as causal explanation for woman abuse, incest, and a host of crimes against women. The myth operates as follows: He was under stress from his job, family, wife's pregnancy, and he did not have the impulse control he normally has. While current research (Walker, 1979) is investigating the role of external stress in violence toward women, in the meantime it serves to justify male violence as well. "Excusing the behavior" on the basis of external stress can provide both the victim and the perpetrator with a convenient explanation. Particularly if the dyad is an intimate one (boss-employee sexual harassment, father-daughter incest, husband-wife battering), the stress explanation allows for rationalization, thus relieving the perpetrator of responsibility and allowing the dyad to return to their previous manner of relating to each other.

The (male) stress myth also obscures and fails to validate *women's* stress. There is a great deal of stress women experience in their careers, housework, and childcare (Bryson et al., 1976; Holmstrom, 1972; Bernard, 1972). It would appear that the culture allows, excuses, and even justifies outward, aggressive expression of stress for men and allows only inward, depressive expression of stress for women.

Feminist Analysis and Overview of Violence Against Women

Why does violence against women occur? If it is *not* because women precipitate it or like it; if it is *not* due to psychologically disturbed, stressed, lower-class men, or nonwhite men; if

Man's discovery that his genitalia could serve as a weapon to generate fear must rank as one of the most important discoveries of prehistoric times, along with the use of fire and the first crude stone axe. From prehistoric times to the present, I believe, rape has played a critical function. It is nothing more or less than a conscious process of intimidation by which all men keep all women in a state of fear.

Susan Brownmiller, *Against Our Will: Men, Women, and Rape*, 1975

it is of mammoth proportions, yet largely unreported, what explanations or analyses can we use to explain the occurrence of these victimizing behaviors?

From a feminist perspective, the reasons for violence toward women involve a male dominated culture in terms of power, economics, and control over women's bodies. A male-dominated culture needs and maintains anti-woman behaviors because it is to men's advantage in maintaining their position of power vis-à-vis women. Martin (1976) notes that the battering of women cannot occur in a marriage between true equals. This assumption could be extended to all violence against women: violence cannot occur where there is complete equality. From a feminist analysis *sexism*—not general "violence in America," external stress, alcohol, or psychological abnormality—is a major foundation if not *the* foundation for violence against women.

If psychopathic deviance, poor socialization, poor stress management, or poor impulse control can be found in the perpetrator, he can then be seen in need of psychological treatment. Therefore, he should avail himself of psychotherapy. The trouble is, he often does not go; or he may seek psychotherapy only when he fears losing his wife. In the case of other perpetrators (e.g., incestuous fathers, rapists, exhibitors, or obscene telephone callers), the seeking of psychotherapy is often a stipulation of the court.

Instead of seeing these male behaviors as

Disarm Rapists, Betsy Warrior, Anarchist Feminist 1970 ©

abnormal, deviant, or "sick," it seems far more parsimonious to theorize that these very behaviors on the part of men are to some extent socially accepted behaviors. Who would ever suggest psychotherapy to a man for visiting a prostitute? Who would ever think therapy appropriate for a man "cat-calling" on the street? Who would refer a male to a psychologist after a marital or date rape? To the extent that males are reinforced for dominance, taking

Once in a Cabinet we had to deal with the fact that there had been an outbreak of assaults on women at night. One minister suggested a curfew: women should stay home after dark. I said, "But it's the men who are attacking the women. If there's to be a curfew, let the men stay home, not the women."

Golda Meir, in Andrea Medea and Kathleen Thompson (eds.), *Against Rape*, 1974

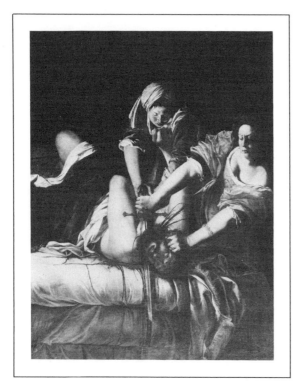

Judith by Artemesia Gentileschi, Galleria Palatina, Palazzo Pitti, Florence

control of women, and the overt expression of strong anger, the man who displays violence against women, whether by sexually objectifying her on the street, using her services as a pornography model, seducing her within the psychotherapeutic setting because she is "sexually dysfunctional," sexually harassing her on the job, or beating her up, may well be the perfectly socialized male.

Furthermore, it is hypothesized that *all* men benefit from violence against women, whether rape, woman-beating, sexual harassment, or the use of pornography. This does not imply that all men have committed these acts; they most obviously have not. Some have committed some acts (particularly the less serious ones) and not others (the more serious ones). For example, it could be hypothesized that almost all men have engaged in jokes at women's expense, engaged in small to moderate amounts of sexual coercion, used pornography in one form or another (from *Penthouse* to *Hustler*), made some unwanted remark or noise at women on the street, made a sexual liaison an implied part of a favor (e.g., job advancement), and possibly visited a prostitute and felt *she* was the "bad" one. These behaviors are minor violences against women on the continuum presented at the beginning of the paper. These are also examples of sexism and results of the cultural values that define women as secondary or as the "other" as de Beauvoir (1953) has pointed out. Women are *not* equal in most men's minds nor do they enjoy equal status in terms of having their needs taken seriously, receiving payment for their work, or gaining entry into certain occupational areas (e.g., engineering or dentistry). Greer (1970) radically suggests that men basically hate women: an analysis of violence against women would certainly lead one to consider the veracity of this idea seriously.

Because some or many men have committed

Anger or revolt that does not get into the muscles remains a figment of the imagination.

Simone de Beauvoir, *The Second Sex*, 1953

crimes against women, *all* men benefit from the consequences. These consequences are powerful and positive ones for men. They include women giving up control to men; putting men's needs ahead of their own through fear of annoying, bothering, or "provoking" a man, thereby remaining incongruous with one's own beliefs and perceptions; and remaining "shuffling," second-class citizens.

Just as blacks and other ethnic minorities have "learned their lessons well" with reference to the majority group, so have women. Just as blacks have learned traditionally that nonacquiescence to white men's rules could get them lynched, women have also learned that nonacquiescence to *any* man's rules can get them victimized as well. While all women may not be entirely conscious of incest, rape,

battering, or sexual harassment, it is believed here that all women's behavior is affected by the conscious or unconscious *fear* of the occurrence of these events.

Brownmiller (1975) points out that blacks were never able to get their own victimization stopped—that it took good, caring whites to stop this deadly action. So it will be with women's victimization. All the rape crisis lines, battered women's shelters, sexual-harassment-on-the-job suits or actions, incest programs, rape whistles, or malpractice suits against male practitioners will only be what is called in public health "secondary prevention." Real changes will only occur when "primary prevention" is instituted—the reduction or elimination of sexism and men's socially sanctioned hatred of women.

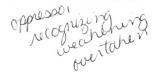

Judith Herman and Lisa Hirschman

Father-Daughter Incest

A Feminist Theoretical Perspective

The incest taboo is universal in human culture. Though it varies from one culture to another, it is generally considered by anthropologists to be the foundation of all kinship structures. Lévi-Strauss describes it as the basic social contract; Mead says its purpose is the preservation of the human social order.[1] All cultures, including our own, regard violations of the taboo with horror and dread. Death has not been considered too extreme a punishment in many societies. In our laws, some states punish incest by up to twenty years' imprisonment.[2]

In spite of the strength of the prohibition on incest, sexual relations between family members do occur. Because of the extreme secrecy which surrounds the violation of our most basic sexual taboo, we have little clinical literature and no accurate statistics on the prevalence of incest. This paper attempts to review what is known about the occurrence of incest between parents and children, to discuss common social attitudes which pervade the existing clinical literature, and to offer a theoretical perspective which locates the incest taboo and its violations within the structure of patriarchy.

The Occurrence of Incest

The Children's Division of the American Humane Association estimates that a minimum of 80,000–100,000 children are sexually molested each year.[3] In the majority of these cases the offender is well known to the child, and in about 25 percent of them, a relative. These estimates are based on New York City police records and the experience of social workers in a child protection agency. They are, therefore, projections based on observing poor and disorganized families who lack the resources to preserve secrecy. There is reason to believe, however, that most incest in fact occurs in intact families and entirely escapes the attention of social agencies. One in 16 of the 8,000 white, middle-class women surveyed by Kinsey et al. reported sexual contact with an adult relative during childhood.[4] In the vast majority of these cases, the incident remained a secret.

A constant finding in all existing surveys is the overwhelming predominance of father-daughter incest. Weinberg, in a study of 200 court cases in the Chicago area, found 164 cases of father-daughter incest compared with 2 cases of mother-son incest.[5] Maisch, in a study of court cases in the Federal Republic of Germany, reported that 90 percent of the cases involved fathers and daughters, stepfathers and stepdaughters, or (infrequently) grandfathers and granddaughters.[6] Fathers and sons accounted for another 5 percent. Incest between mothers and sons occurred in only 4 percent of the cases. Incest appears to follow the general pattern of sexual abuse of children, in which 92 percent of the victims are female, and 97 percent of the offenders are male.[7]

It may be objected that these data are all based on court records and perhaps reflect only a difference in complaints rather than a difference in incidence. The Kinsey reports, however, confirm the impression of a major discrepancy between the childhood sexual contacts of boys and girls. If, as noted above, more than 6 percent of the female sample reported sexual approaches by adult relatives, only a small number of the 12,000 men surveyed reported sexual contact with any adult, relative or stranger. (Exact figures were not reported.) Among these few, contact with adult males seemed to be more common than with adult females. As for mother-son incest, the authors concluded that "heterosexual incest occurs more frequently in the thinking of clinicians and social workers than it does in actual performance."[8] None of the existing literature, to our knowledge, makes any attempt to account for this striking discrepancy between the occurrence of father-daughter and mother-son incest.

Common Attitudes Toward Incest in the Professional Literature

Because the subject of incest inspires such strong emotional responses, few authors have even attempted a dispassionate examination of its actual occurrence and effects. Those who have approached the subject have often been unable to avoid defensive reactions such as denial, distancing, or blaming. We undertake this discussion with the full recognition that we ourselves are not immune to these reactions, which may be far more apparent to our readers than to ourselves.

Undoubtedly the most famous and consequential instance of denial of the reality of incest occurs in Freud's 1897 letter to Fliess. In it, Freud reveals the process by which he came to disbelieve the reports of his female patients and develop his concepts of infantile sexuality and the infantile neurosis: "Then there was the astonishing thing that in every case blame was laid on perverse acts by the father, and realization of the unexpected frequency of hysteria, in every case of which the same thing applied, though it was hardly credible that perverted acts against children were so general."[9]

Freud's conclusion that the sexual approaches did not occur in fact was based simply on his unwillingness to believe that incest was such a common event in respectable families. To experience a sexual approach by a parent probably *was* unlikely for a boy: Freud concluded incorrectly that the same was true for girls. Rather than investigate further into the question of fact, Freud's followers chose to continue the presumption of fantasy and made the child's desire and fantasy the focus of psychological inquiry. The adult's desire (and capacity for action) were forgotten. Psychoanalytic investigation, then, while it placed the incest taboo at the center of the child's psychological development, did little to dispel the secrecy surrounding the actual occurrence of incest. As one child psychiatrist commented: "Helene Deutsch and other followers of Freud have, in my opinion, gone too far in the direction of conceptualizing patients' reports of childhood sexual abuse in terms of fantasy. My own experience, both in private practice and with several hundred child victims brought to us ... [at the Center for Rape Concern] ... in Philadelphia, has convinced me that analysts too often dismissed as fantasy what was the real sexual molestation of a child.... As a result, the victim was isolated and her trauma compounded."[10]

Even those investigators who have paid attention to cases of actual incest have often shown a tendency to comment or make judgments concerning the guilt or innocence of the participants. An example:

These children undoubtedly do not deserve completely the cloak of innocence with which they have been endowed by moralists, social reformers, and legislators. The history of the relationship in our cases usually suggests at least some cooperation of the child in the activity, and in some cases the child assumed an active role in initiating the relationship.... It is true that the child often rationalized with excuses of fear of physical harm or the enticement of gifts, but there were obviously secondary reasons. Even in the cases where physical force may have been applied by the adult, this did not wholly account for the frequent repetition of the practice.

Finally, a most striking feature was that these children were distinguished as unusually charming and attractive in their outward personalities. Thus, it was not remarkable that frequently we considered the possibility that the child might have been the actual seducer, rather than the one innocently seduced.[11]

In addition to denial and blame, much of the existing literature on incest shows evidence of social and emotional distancing between the investigators and their subjects. This sometimes takes the form of an assertion that incestuous behavior is accepted or condoned in some culture other than the investigator's own. Thus, a British study of Irish working-class people reports that father-daughter incest, which occurred in 4 percent of an unselected outpatient clinic population, was a "cultural phenomenon" precipitated by social isolation or crowding, and had "no pathological effects."[12] The several investigators who have also reported instances where children, in their judgment, were not harmed by the incest experience do not usually state the criteria on which this judgment is based.[13] Still other investigators seem fearful to commit themselves to an opinion on the question of harm. Thus, for example, although 70 percent

of the victims in Maisch's survey showed evidence of disturbed personality development, the author is uncertain about ascribing this to the effects of incest per se.

A few investigators, however, have testified to the destructive effects of the incest experience on the development of the child. Sloane and Karpinski, who studied five incestuous families in rural Pennsylvania, conclude: "Indulgence in incest in the post-adolescent period leads to serious repercussions in the girl, even in an environment where the moral standards are relaxed."[14] Kaufman, Peck, and Tagiuri, in a thorough study of eleven victims and their families who were seen at a Boston clinic, report: "Depression and guilt were universal as clinical findings.... The underlying craving for an adequate parent ... dominated the lives of these girls."[15]

Several retrospective studies, including a recent report by Benward and Densen-Gerber, document a strong association between reported incest history and the later development of promiscuity or prostitution.[16] In fact, failure to marry or promiscuity seems to be the only criterion generally accepted in the literature as conclusive evidence that the victim has been harmed.[17] We believe that this finding in itself testifies to the traditional bias which pervades the incest literature.

Our survey of what has been written about incest, then, raises several questions. Why does incest between fathers and daughters occur so much more frequently than incest between mothers and sons? Why, though this finding has been consistently documented in all available sources, has no previous attempt been made to explain it? Why does the incest victim find so little attention or compassion in the literature, while she finds so many authorities who are willing to assert either that the incest did not happen, that it did not harm her, or that she was to blame for it? We believe that a feminist perspective must be invoked in order to address these questions.

Incest and Patriarchy

In a patriarchal culture, such as our own, the incest taboo must have a different meaning for the two sexes and may be observed by men and women for different reasons.

Major theorists in the disciplines of both psychology and anthropology explain the importance of the incest taboo by placing it at the center of an agreement to control warfare among men. It represents the first and most basic peace treaty. An essential element of the agreement is the concept that women are the possessions of men; the incest taboo represents an agreement as to how women shall be shared. Since virtually all known societies are dominated by men, all versions of the incest taboo are agreements among men regarding sexual access to women. As Mitchell points out, men create rules governing the exchange of women; women do not create rules governing the exchange of men.[18] Because the taboo is created and enforced by men, we argue that it may also be more easily and frequently violated by men.

The point at which the child learns the meaning of the incest taboo is the point of initiation into the social order. Boys and girls, however, learn different versions of the taboo. To paraphrase Freud once again, the boy learns that he may not consummate his sexual desires for his mother because his mother belongs to his father, and his father has the power to inflict the most terrible of punishments on him: to deprive him of his maleness.[19] In compensation, however, the boy learns that when he is a man he will one day possess women of his own.

When this little boy grows up, he will probably marry and may have a daughter. Although custom will eventually oblige him to give away his daughter in marriage to another man (note that mothers do not give away either daughters or sons), the taboo against sexual contact with his daughter will never carry the same force, either psychologically or socially, as the taboo which prohibited incest with his mother. *There is no punishing father to avenge father-daughter incest.*

What the little girl learns is not at all parallel. Her initiation into the patriarchal order begins with the realization that she is not only comparatively powerless as a child, but that she will remain so as a woman. She may acquire power only indirectly, as the favorite of a powerful man. As a child she may not possess her mother *or* her father; when she is an adult, her best hope is to *be* possessed by someone like her father. Thus, according to Freud she has less incentive than the boy to come to a full resolution of the Oedipus complex.[20] Since she has no hope of acquiring the privileges of an adult male, she can neither be rewarded for giving up her incestuous attachments, nor punished for refusing to do so. Chesler states the same conclusion more bluntly: "Women are encouraged to commit incest as a way of life. . . . As opposed to marrying our fathers, we marry men like our fathers . . . men who are older than us, have more money than us, more power than us, are taller than us, are stronger than us . . . our fathers."[21]

A patriarchal society, then, most abhors the idea of incest between mother and son, because this is an affront to the father's prerogatives. Though incest between father and daughter is also forbidden, the prohibition carries considerably less weight and is, therefore, more frequently violated. We believe this understanding of the asymmetrical nature of the incest taboo under patriarchy offers an explanation for the observed difference in the occurrence of mother-son and father-daughter incest.

If, as we propose, the taboo on father-daughter incest is relatively weak in a patriarchal family system, we might expect violations of the taboo to occur most frequently in families characterized by extreme paternal dominance. This is in fact the case. Incest offenders are frequently described as "family tyrants": "These fathers, who are often quite incapable of relating their despotic claim to leadership to their social efforts for the family, tend toward abuses of authority of every conceivable kind, and they not infrequently endeavor to secure their dominant position by socially isolating the members of the family from the world outside. Swedish, American, and French surveys have pointed time and again to the patriarchal position of such fathers, who set up a 'primitive family order.' "[22] Thus the seduction of daughters is an abuse which is inherent in a father-dominated family system; we believe that the greater the degree of male supremacy in any culture, the greater the likelihood of father-daughter incest.

A final speculative point: since, according to this formulation, women neither make nor enforce the incest taboo, why is it that women apparently observe the taboo so scrupulously? We do not know. We suspect that the answer may lie in the historic experience of women both as sexual property and as the primary caretakers of children. Having been frequently obliged to exchange sexual services

for protection and care, women are in a position to understand the harmful effects of introducing sex into a relationship where there is a vast inequality of power. And, having throughout history been assigned the primary responsibility for the care of children, women may be in a position to understand more fully the needs of children, the difference between affectionate and erotic contact, and the appropriate limits of parental love.

A Clinical Report

The following is a clinical case study of fifteen victims of father-daughter incest. All the women were clients in psychotherapy who reported their incest experiences to their therapists after the fact. Seven were women whom the authors had personally evaluated or seen in psychotherapy. The remaining eight were clients in treatment with other therapists. No systematic case-finding effort was made; the authors simply questioned those practitioners who were best known to us through an informal network of female professionals. Four out of the first ten therapists we questioned reported that at least one of her clients had an incest history. We concluded from this admittedly small sample that a history of incest is frequently encountered in clinical practice.

Our combined group of six therapists (the authors and our four informants) had interviewed close to 1,000 clients in the past five years. In this population, the incidence of reported father-daughter incest was 2–3 percent. We believe this to be a minimum estimate, since in most cases no particular effort was made to elicit the history. Our estimate accords with the data of the Kinsey report,[23] in which 1.5 percent of the women surveyed stated that they had been molested by their fathers.

For the purposes of this study, we defined incest as overt sexual contact such as fondling, petting, masturbation, or intercourse between parent and child. We included only those cases in which there was no doubt in the daughter's mind that explicit and intentionally sexual contact occurred and that secrecy was required. Thus we did not include in our study the many women who reported seductive behaviors such as verbal sharing of sexual secrets, flirting, extreme possessiveness or jealousy, or intense interest in their bodies or their sexual activities on the part of their fathers. We recognize that these cases represent the extreme of a continuum of father-daughter relationships which range from the affectionate through the seductive to the overtly sexual. Information about the incest history was initially gathered from the therapists. Those clients who were willing to discuss their experiences with us in person were then interviewed directly.

The fifteen women who reported that they had been molested during childhood were in other respects quite ordinary women. Nothing obvious distinguished them from the general population of women entering psychotherapy (see Table 1). They ranged in age from fifteen to fifty-five. Most were in their early twenties at the time they first requested psychotherapy. They were all white. Four were single, seven married, and four separated or divorced. Half had children. The majority had at least some college education. They worked at common women's jobs: housewife, waitress, factory worker, office worker, prostitute, teacher, nurse. They complained mostly of depression and social isolation. Those who were married or recently separated complained of marital

TABLE 1
CHARACTERISTICS OF INCEST VICTIMS ENTERING THERAPY

Characteristic	Victims (N)
Age (years):	
15–20	3
21–25	7
26–30	2
30+	3
Marital Status:	
Single	4
Married	7
Separated or divorced	4
Occupation:	
Blue collar	4
White collar	4
Professional	3
Houseworker	1
Student	3
Education:	
High school not completed	4
High school completed	2
1–2 years college	3
College completed	5
Advanced degree	1
Presenting complaints:	
Marital problems	5
Depression	3
Anxiety	3
Social isolation	4
Drug or alcohol abuse	4
Suicide attempt	2

problems. The severity of their complaints seemed to be related to the degree of family disorganization and deprivation in their histories rather than to the incest history per se. Five of the women had been hospitalized at some point in their lives; three were or had been actively suicidal, and two were addicted to drugs or alcohol. Seven women brought up the incest history among their initial complaints; the rest revealed it only after having established a relationship with the therapist. In some cases, the history was not disclosed for one, two, or even three years after therapy had begun.

The incest histories were remarkably similar (see Table 2). The majority of the victims were oldest or only daughters and were between the ages of six and nine when they were first approached sexually by their fathers or male guardians (nine fathers, three stepfathers, a grandfather, a brother-in-law, and an uncle). The youngest girl was four years old; the oldest fourteen. The sexual contact usually took place repeatedly. In most cases the incestuous relationship lasted three years or more. Physical force was not used, and intercourse was rarely attempted with girls who had not reached puberty; the sexual contact

TABLE 2

CHARACTERISTICS OF THE INCEST HISTORY

Characteristic	Incidence
Daughter's place in sibship:	
Oldest daughter	9
Only daughter	3
Middle or youngest daughter	1
Unknown	2
Daughter's age at onset of incestuous relationship (years):	
4	1
5	0
6	2
7	3
8	4
9	2
10	0
11	1
12	0
13	0
14	1
Unknown	1
Duration of incestuous relationship (years):	
Single incident	1
1–2	1
3–4	3
5–6	5
7–10	2
Unknown	3

was limited to masturbation and fondling. In three cases, the relationship was terminated when the father attempted intercourse.

> LENORE: I had already started to develop breasts at age nine and had my period when I was eleven. All this time he's still calling me into bed for "little chats" with him. I basically trusted him although I felt funny about it. Then one time I was twelve or thirteen, he called me into bed and started undressing me. He gave this rationale about preparing me to be with boys. He kept saying I was safe as long as I didn't let them take my pants down. Meantime he was doing the same thing. I split. I knew what he was trying to do, and that it was wrong. That was the end of the overt sexual stuff. Not long after that he found an excuse to beat me.

In all but two of these fifteen cases the sexual relationship between father and daughter remained a secret, and there was no intervention in the family by the courts or child-protection authorities. Previous studies are based on court referrals and therefore give the erroneous impression that incest occurs predominantly in families at the lower end of the socioeconomic scale. This was not the case in the families of our victims. Of these, four fathers were blue-collar workers, two were white-collar workers, six were professionals, and the occupations of three were not known. The fathers' occupations cut across class lines. Several held jobs that required considerable personal competence and commanded social respect: college administrator, policeman, army officer, engineer. Others were skilled workers, foremen, or managers in factories or offices. All the mothers were houseworkers. Five of the fifteen families could certainly be considered disorganized, with histories of poverty, unemployment, frequent moves, alcoholism, violence, abandonment, and foster care. Not surprisingly, the women who came from these families were those who complained of the most severe distress. The majority of the families, however, were apparently intact and maintained a façade of respectability.

The Incestuous Family Constellation

Both the apparently intact and the disorganized families shared certain common features in the pattern of family relationships. The most striking was the almost uniform estrangement of the mother and daughter, an estrangement that preceded the occurrence of overt incest. Over half the mothers were partially incapacitated by physical or mental illness or alcoholism and either assumed an invalid role within the home or were periodically absent because of hospitalization. Their oldest daughters were often obliged to take over the household duties. Anne-Marie remembered being hidden from the truant officer by her mother so that she could stay home and take care of the younger children. Her mother had tuberculosis. Claire's mother, who was not ill, went to work to support the family because her father, a severe alcoholic, brought home no money. In her absence, Claire did the housework and cooking and cared for her older brother.

At best, these mothers were seen by their daughters as helpless, frail, downtrodden victims, who were unable to take care of themselves, much less to protect their children.

ANNE-MARIE: She used to say, "give with one hand and you'll get with the other" but she gave with two hands and always went down. . . . She was nothing but a floor mat. She sold out herself and her self-respect. She was a love slave to my father.

CLAIRE: I always felt sorry for her. She spent her life suffering, suffering, suffering.

Some of the mothers habitually confided in their oldest daughters and unburdened their troubles to them. Theresa felt her mother was "more like a sister." Joan's mother frequently clung to her and told her, "You're the only one who understands me." By contrast, the daughters felt unable to confide in their mothers. In particular, the daughters felt unable to go to their mothers for support or protection once their fathers had begun to make sexual advances to them. Some feared that their mothers would take action to expel the father from the house, but more commonly these daughters expected that their mothers would do nothing; in many cases the mothers tolerated a great deal of abuse themselves, and the daughters had learned not to expect any protection. Five of the women said they suspected that their mothers knew about the incest and tacitly condoned it. Two made attempts to bring up the subject but were put off by their mothers' denial or indifference.

Only two of the fifteen women actually told their mothers. Both had reason to regret it. Paula's mother reacted by committing her to an institution: "She was afraid I would become a lesbian or a whore." Sandra's mother initially took her husband to court. When she realized that a conviction would lead to his imprisonment, she reversed her testimony and publicly called her twelve-year-old daughter a "notorious liar and slut."

The message that these mothers transmitted over and over to their daughters was: your father first, you second. It is dangerous to fight back, for if I lose him I lose everything. For my own survival I must leave you to your own devices. I cannot defend you, and if necessary I will sacrifice you to your father.

At worst, the mother-daughter relations were marked by frank and open hostility. Some of the daughters stated they could remember no tenderness or caring in the relationship.

MARTHA: She's always picking on me. She's so fuckin' cold.

PAULA: She's an asshole. I really don't like my mom. I guess I am bitter. She's very selfish. She did a lousy job of bringing me up.

The most severe disruption in the mother-daughter relationship occurred in Rita's case. She remembers receiving severe beatings from her mother, and her father intervening to rescue her. Though the physical attacks were infrequent, Rita recalls her mother as implacably hostile and critical, and her father as by far the more nurturant parent.

Previous studies of incestuous families document the disturbance in the mother-daughter relationship as a constant finding.[24] In a study of eleven girls who were referred by courts to a child guidance center, Kaufman et al. reported that the girls uniformly saw their mothers as cruel, unjust, and depriving, while the fathers were seen much more ambivalently: "These girls had long felt abandoned by the mother as a protective adult. This was their basic anxiety. . . . Though the original sexual experience with the father was at a genital level, the meaning of the sexual act was pregenital, and seemed to have the purpose of receiving some sort of parental interest."[25]

In contrast, almost all the victims expressed some warm feelings toward their fathers. Many described them in much more favorable terms than their mothers. Some examples:

ANNE-MARIE: A handsome devil.

THERESA: Good with kids. An honest, decent guy.

LENORE: He was my confidant.

RITA: My savior.

Although it may seem odd to have expressed such attitudes toward blatantly authoritarian fathers, there are explanations. These were men whose presentation to the outside world made them liked and often respected members of the community. The daughters responded to their fathers' social status and power and derived satisfaction from being their fathers' favorites. They were "daddy's special girls," and often they were special to no one else. Feelings of pity for the fathers were also common, especially where the fathers had lost social status. The daughters seemed much more willing to forgive their fathers' failings and weaknesses than to forgive their mothers, or themselves.

SANDRA: He was a sweet, decent man. My mother ruined him. I saw him lying in his bed in the hospital, and I kept thinking why don't they let him die. When he finally did, everyone cried at the funeral but me. I was glad he was dead. He had a miserable life. He had nothing. No one cared, not even me. I didn't help him much.

The daughters not only felt themselves abandoned by their mothers, but seemed to perceive their fathers as likewise deserted, and they felt the same pity for their fathers as they felt for themselves.

The victims rarely expressed anger toward their fathers, even about the incestuous act itself. Two of the three women who did express anger were women who had been repeatedly beaten as well as sexually abused by their fathers. Not surprisingly, they were angrier about the beatings than about the sexual act, which they viewed ambivalently. Most women expressed feelings of fear, disgust, and intense shame about the sexual contact and stated that they endured it because they felt they had no other choice. Several of the women stated that they learned to deal with the sexual approach by "tuning out" or pretending that it was not happening. Later, this response generalized to other relationships. Half of the women acknowledged, however, that they had felt some degree of pleasure in the sexual contact, a feeling which only increased their sense of guilt and confusion.

> KITTY: I was in love with my father. He called me his special girlfriend.
> LENORE: The whole issue is very complicated. I was very attracted to my father, and that just compounded the guilt.
> PAULA: I was scared of him, but basically I liked him.

Though these women sometimes expressed a sense of disappointment and even contempt for their fathers, they did not feel as keenly the sense of betrayal as they felt toward their mothers. Having abandoned the hope of pleasing their mothers, they seemed relieved to have found some way of pleasing their fathers and gaining their attention.

Susan Brownmiller, in her study of rape as a paradigm of relations between men and women, refers briefly to father-daughter incest. Stressing the coercive aspect of the situation, she calls it "father-rape."[26] To label it thus is to understate the complexity of the relationship. The father's sexual approach is clearly an abuse of power and authority, and the daughter almost always understands it as such. But, unlike rape, it occurs in the context of a caring relationship. The victim feels overwhelmed by her father's superior power and unable to resist him; she may feel disgust, loathing, and shame. But at the same time she often feels that this is the only kind of love she can get, and prefers it to no love at all. The daughter is not raped, but seduced.

In fact, to describe what occurs as a rape is to minimize the harm to the child, for what is involved here is not simply an assault, it is a betrayal. A woman who has been raped can cope with the experience in the same way that she would react to any other intentionally cruel and harmful attack. She is not socially or psychologically dependent upon the rapist. She is free to hate him. But the daughter who has been molested is dependent on her father for protection and care. Her mother is not an ally. She has no recourse. She does not dare express, or even feel, the depths of her anger at being used. She must comply with her father's demands or risk losing the parental love that she needs. She is not an adult. She cannot walk out of the situation (though she may try to run away). She must endure it, and find in it what compensations she can.

Although the victims reported that they felt helpless and powerless against their fathers, the incestuous relationship did give them some semblance of power within the family. Many of the daughters effectively replaced their mothers and became their fathers' surrogate wives. They were also deputy mothers to the younger children and were generally given some authority over them. While they resented being exploited and robbed of the freedom ordinarily granted to dependent children, they did gain some feeling of value and importance from the role they were given. Many girls felt an enormous sense of responsibility for holding the family together. They also knew that, as keepers of the incest secret, they had an extraordinary power which could be used to destroy the family. Their sexual contact with their fathers conferred on them a sense of possessing a dangerous, secret power over the lives of others, power which they derived from no other source. In this situation, keeping up appearances and doing whatever was necessary to maintain the integrity of the family became a necessary, expiating act at the same time that it increased the daughters' sense of isolation and shame.

> THERESA: I was mortified. My father and mother had fights so loud that you could hear them yelling all over the neighborhood. I used to think that my father was really yelling at my mother because she wouldn't give him sex. I felt I had to make it up to him.

What is most striking to us about this family constellation, in which the daughter replaces the mother in her traditional role, is the underlying assumption about that role shared apparently by all the family members. Customarily, a mother and wife in our society is one who nurtures and takes care of children and husband. If, for whatever reasons, the mother is unable to fulfill her ordinary functions, it is apparently assumed that some other female must be found to do it. The eldest daughter is a frequent choice. The father does not assume the wife's maternal role when she is incapacitated. He feels that his first right is to continue to receive the services which his wife formerly provided, sometimes including sexual services. He feels only secondarily responsible for giving care to his children. This view of the father's prerogative to be served not only is shared by the fathers and daughters in these families, but is often encouraged by societal attitudes. Fathers who feel abandoned by their wives are not generally expected or taught to assume primary parenting responsibilities. We

should not find it surprising, then, that fathers occasionally turn to their daughters for services (domestic and sexual) that they had formerly expected of their wives.

The Victims

The fifteen women who reported their incest experiences were all clients in psychotherapy. That is to say, all had admitted to themselves and at least one other person that they were suffering and needed help. Although we do not know whether they speak for the vast majority of victims, some of their complaints are so similar that we believe that they represent a pattern common to most women who have endured prolonged sexual abuse in childhood at the hands of parents.

One of the most frequent complaints of the victims entering therapy was a sense of being different, and distant, from ordinary people. The sense of isolation and inability to make contact was expressed in many different ways:

> KITTY: I'm dead inside.
> LENORE: I have a problem getting close to people. I back off.
> LOIS: I can't communicate with anyone.

Their therapists described difficulty in forming relationships with them, confirming their assessment of themselves. Therapists frequently made comments like "I don't really know whether I'm in touch with her," or "she's one of the people that's been the hardest for me to figure out." These women complained that most of their relationships were superficial and empty, or else extremely conflictual. They expressed fear that they were unable to love. The sense of an absence of feeling was most marked in sexual relationships, although most women were sexually responsive in the narrow sense of the word; that is, capable of having orgasms.

In some cases, the suppression of feeling was clearly a defense which had been employed in the incestuous relationship in childhood. The distance or isolation of affect seemed originally to be a device set up as protection against the feelings aroused by the molesting father. One woman reported that when she "shut down," did not move or speak, her father would leave her alone. Another remembered that she would tell herself over and over "this isn't really happening" during the sexual episode. Passive resistance and dissociation of feeling seemed to be among the few defenses available in an overwhelming situation. Later, this carried over into relations with others.

The sense of distance and isolation which these women experienced was uniformly painful, and they made repeated, often desperate efforts to overcome it. Frequently, the result was a pattern of many brief unsatisfactory sexual contacts. Those relationships which did become more intense and lasting were fraught with difficulty.

Five of the seven married women complained of marital conflict, either feeling abused by their husbands or indifferent toward them. Those who were single or divorced uniformly complained of problems in their relationships with men. Some expressed negative feelings toward men in general:

> STEPHANIE: When I ride the bus I look at all the men and think, "all they want to do is stick their pricks into little girls."

Most, however, overvalued men and kept searching for a relationship with an idealized protector and sexual teacher who would take care of them and tell them what to do. Half the women had affairs during adolescence with older or married men. In these relationships, the sense of specialness, power, and secrecy of the incestuous relationship was regained. The men were seen as heroes and saviors.

In many cases, these women became intensely involved with men who were cruel, abusive, or neglectful, and tolerated extremes of mistreatment. Anne-Marie remained married for twenty years to a psychotic husband who beat her, terrorized their children, and never supported the family. She felt she could not leave him because he would fall apart without her. "We were his kingdom," she said, "to bully and beat." She eventually sought police protection and separation only after it was clear that her life was in danger. Her masochistic behavior in this relationship was all the more striking, since other areas of her life were relatively intact. She was a warm and generous mother, a valued worker, and an active, respected member of her community. Lois was raped at age nineteen by a stranger whom she married a week later. After this marriage ended in divorce, she began to frequent bars where she would pick up men who beat her repeatedly. She expressed no anger toward these men. Three other women in this group of fifteen were also rape victims. Only one expressed anger toward her attackers; the others felt they "deserved it." Some of the women recognized and commented on their predilection for abusive men. As Sandra put it: "I'm better off with a bum. I can handle that situation."

Why did these women feel they deserved to be beaten, raped, neglected, and used? The answer lies in their image of themselves. It is only through understanding how they perceived themselves that we can make sense of their often highly destructive relations with others. Almost every one of these fifteen women described herself as a "witch," "bitch," or "whore." They saw themselves as socially "branded" or "marked," even when no social exposure of their sexual relations had occurred or was likely to occur. They experienced themselves as powerful and dangerous to men: their self-image had almost a magical quality. Kitty, for instance, called herself a "devil's child," while Sandra compared herself to the twelve-year-old villainess of a popular melodrama, *The Exorcist*, a girl who was possessed by the devil. Some felt they were invested with special seductive prowess and could captivate men simply by looking at them. These daughters seemed almost uniformly to believe that they had seduced their fathers and therefore could seduce any man.

At one level, this sense of malignant power can be understood to have arisen as a defense against the child's feelings of utter helplessness. In addition, however, this self-image had been reinforced by the long-standing conspiratorial relationship with the father, in which the child had been elevated to the mother's position and did indeed have the power to destroy the family by exposing the incestuous secret.

Moreover, most of the victims were aware that they had experienced some pleasure in the incestuous relationship and had joined with their fathers in a shared hatred of their mothers. This led to intense feelings of shame, degradation, and worthlessness. Because they had enjoyed their fathers' attention and their mothers' defeat, these women felt responsible for the incestuous situation. Almost uniformly, they distrusted their own desires and needs and did not feel entitled to care and respect. Any relationship that afforded some kind of

pleasure seemed to increase the sense of guilt and shame. These women constantly sought to expiate their guilt and relieve their shame by serving and giving to others and by observing the strictest and most rigorous codes of religion and morality. Any lapse from a rigid code of behavior was felt as confirming evidence of their innate evilness. Some of the women embraced their negative identity with a kind of defiance and pride. As Sandra boasted: "There's *nothing* I haven't done!"

Those women who were mothers themselves seemed to be preoccupied with the fear that they would be bad mothers to their children, as they felt their mothers had been to them. Several sought treatment when they began to be aware of feelings of rage and resentment toward their children, especially their daughters. Any indulgence in pleasure seeking or attention to personal needs reinforced their sense that they were "whores" and unfit mothers. In some, the fear of exposure took the form of a constant worry that the authorities would intervene to take the children away. Other mothers worried that they would not be able to protect their daughters from a repetition of the incest situation. As one victim testified:

I could a been the biggest bum. My father called me a "big whore" and my mother believed him. I could a got so disgusted that I could a run around with anyone I saw. I met my husband and told him about my father and my child. He stuck by me and we was married. I got to the church and I'm not so shy like I was. It always come back to me that this thing might get on the front pages and people might know about it. I'm getting over it since the time I joined the church.

Her husband testified:

The wife is nervous and she can't sleep. She gets up yesterday night about two o'clock in the morning and starts fixing the curtains. She works that way till five, then she sleeps like a rock. She's cold to me but she tells me she likes me. She gets cold once in a while and she don't know why herself. She watches me like a hawk with those kids. She don't want me to be loving with them and to be too open about sex. It makes her think of her old man. I got to take it easy with her or she blows up.[27]

In our opinion, the testimony of these victims, and the observations of their therapists, is convincing evidence that the incest experience was harmful to them and left long-lasting scars. Many victims had severely impaired object relations with both men and women. The overvaluation of men led them into conflictual and often intensely masochistic relationships with men. The victims' devaluation of themselves and their mothers impaired development of supportive friendships with women. Many of the victims also had a well-formed negative identity as witch, bitch, or whore. In adult life they continued to make repeated ineffective attempts to expiate their intense feelings of guilt and shame.

Therapy for the Incest Victim and Her Family

Very little is known about how to help the incest victim. If the incestuous secret is discovered while the victim is still living with her parents, the most common social intervention is the destruction of the family. This outcome is usually terrifying even to an exploited child, and most victims will cooperate with their fathers in maintaining secrecy rather than see their fathers jailed or risk being sent away from home.

We know of only one treatment program specifically designed for the rehabilitation of the incestuous family.[28] This program, which operates out of the probation department of the Santa Clara County Court in California, involves all members of the incestuous family in both individual and family therapy and benefits from a close working alliance with Daughters United, a self-help support group for victims. The program directors acknowledge that the coercive power of the court is essential for obtaining the cooperation of the fathers. An early therapeutic goal in this program is a confrontation between the daughter and her mother and father, in which they admit to her that she has been the victim of "poor parenting." This is necessary in order to relieve the daughter from her feeling of responsibility for the incest. Mothers appear to be more willing than fathers to admit this to their daughters.

Though this program offers a promising model for the treatment of the discovered incestuous family, it does not touch the problem of undetected incest. The vast majority of incest victims reach adulthood still bearing their secrets. Some will eventually enter psychotherapy. How can the therapist respond appropriately to their needs?

We believe that the male therapist may have great difficulty in validating the victim's experience and responding empathically to her suffering. Consciously or not, the male therapist will tend to identify with the father's position and therefore will tend to deny or excuse his behavior and project blame onto the victim. Here is an example of a male therapist's judgmental perception of an incest victim:

This woman had had a great love and respect for her father until puberty when he had made several sexual advances toward her. In analysis she talked at first only of her good feelings toward him because she had blocked out the sexual episodes. When they were finally brought back into consciousness, all the fury returned which she had experienced at the age of thirteen. She felt that her father was an impotent, dirty old man who had taken advantage of her trusting youthful innocence. From some of the details which she related of her relationship to her father, *it was obvious that she was not all that innocent.* [Our italics][29]

Not surprisingly, the client in this case became furious with her therapist, and therapy was unsuccessful.

If the male therapist identifies with the aggressor in the incest situation, it is also clear that the female therapist tends to identify with the victim and that this may limit her effectiveness. In a round-table discussion of experiences with incest victims, most of the contributing therapists acknowledged having shied away from a full and detailed exploration of the incestuous relationship. In some cases the therapist blatantly avoided the issue. In these cases, no trust was established in the relationship, and the client quickly discontinued therapy. In effect, the therapists had conveyed to these women that their secrets were indeed too terrible to share, thus reinforcing their already intense sense of isolation and shame.

Two possible explanations arise for the female therapist's flight. Traditional psychoanalytic theory might suggest that the therapist's own incestuous wishes and fantasies are too threatening for her to acknowledge. This might seem to be the most obvious reason for such a powerful countertransference phenomenon. The second reason, though less apparent, may be equally powerful: the female therapist confronting the incest victim reexperiences her own fear of her father and rec-

ognizes how easily she could have shared the victim's fate. We suspect that many women have been aware of, and frightened by, seductive behavior on the part of their own fathers. For every family in which incest is consummated there are undoubtedly hundreds with essentially similar, if less extreme, psychological dynamics. Thus the incest victim forces the female therapist to confront her own condition and to reexperience not only her infantile desires but also her (often realistic) childhood fears.

If the therapist overcomes this obstacle, and does not avoid addressing the issue with her client, another trap follows. As one therapist put it during the round-table discussion: "I get angry *for* her. How can she *not* be angry with her father?" Getting angry for a client is a notoriously unsuccessful intervention. Since the victim is more likely to feel rage toward the mother who abandoned her to her fate than toward her father, the therapeutic relationship must provide a place where the victim feels she can safely express her hostile feelings. Rage against the mother must be allowed to surface, for it is only when the client feels she can freely express her full range of feelings without driving the therapist away that she loses her sense of being malignantly "marked."

The feminist therapist may have particular difficulty facing the degree of estrangement between mother and daughter that occurs in these families. Committed as she is to building solidarity among women, she is bound to be distressed by the frequent histories of indifference, hostility, and cruelty in the mother-daughter relationship. She may find herself rushing to the defense of the mother, pointing out that the mother, herself, was a victim, and so on. This may be true, but not helpful.

Rather than denying the situation or making excuses for anyone, the therapist must face the challenge that the incestuous family presents to all of us: How can we overcome the deep estrangement between mothers and daughters that frequently exists in our society, and how can we better provide for the security of both?

Beyond Therapy

For both social and psychological reasons, therapy alone seems to be an insufficient response to the situation of the incest victim. Because of its confidential nature, the therapy relationship does not lend itself to a full resolution of the issue of secrecy. The woman who feels herself to be the guardian of a terrible, almost magical secret may find considerable relief from her shame after sharing the secret with another person. However, the shared secrecy then recreates a situation similar to the original incestuous relationship. Instead of the victim alone against the world, there is the special dyad of the victim and her confidant. This, in fact, was a difficult issue for all the participants in our study, since the victims once again were the subject of special interest because of their sexual history.

The women's liberation movement has demonstrated repeatedly to the mental health profession that consciousness raising has often been more beneficial and empowering to women than psychotherapy. In particular, the public revelation of the many and ancient sexual secrets of women (orgasm, rape, abortion) may have contributed far more toward the liberation of women than the attempt to heal individual wounds through a restorative therapeutic relationship.

The same should be true for incest. The victims who feel like bitches, whores, and witches might feel greatly relieved if they felt less lonely, if their identities as the special guardians of a dreadful secret could be shed. Incest will begin to lose its devastating magic power when women begin to speak out about it publicly and realize how common it is.

We know that most cases do not come to the attention of therapists. and those that do, come years after the fact. Thus, as a social problem incest is clearly not amenable to a purely psychotherapeutic approach. Prevention, rather than treatment, seems to be indicated. On the basis of our study and the testimony of these victims, we favor all measures which strengthen and support the mother's role within the family, for it is clear that these daughters feel prey to their fathers' abuse when their mothers are too ill, weak, or downtrodden to protect them. We favor the strengthening of protective services for women and children, including adequate and dignified financial support for mothers, irrespective of their marital status; free, public, round-the-clock child care, and refuge facilities for women in crisis. We favor the vigorous enforcement (by female officials) of laws prohibiting the sexual abuse of children. Offenders should be isolated and reeducated. We see efforts to reintegrate fathers into the world of children as a positive development, but only on the condition that they learn more appropriate parental behavior. A seductive father is not much of an improvement over an abandoning or distant one.

As both Shulamith Firestone and Florence Rush have pointed out, the liberation of children is inseparable from our own.[30] In particular, as long as daughters are subject to seduction in childhood, no adult woman is free. Like prostitution and rape, we believe father-daughter incest will disappear only when male supremacy is ended.

Relationships: Sexuality and Intimacy

This section on sexuality and intimacy draws upon articles in previous sections. Most notably, the article by Leonore Tiefer on contemporary sex research has direct relevance to female sexuality. According to Tiefer, sexual research has been based on "masculinity" and the male experience of sexuality so that our knowledge about human sexuality and specifically female sexuality is impoverished.

The conceptualization of this section derives from Tiefer's and other feminist analyses of women's experience. For women, sexuality is embedded in the context of emotional relationships. The corresponding stereotypic male reality of sexual experience is more narrowly confined to the physical aspects of genital sexuality. Furthermore, according to the male view of reality, women's emphasis on nongenital and emotional aspects of sexuality has been considered "immature."

The first paper in this section, by Nancy Chodorow, provides insight into these and other apparent gaps in women's and men's experiences of sexuality and the apparent gaps in intimacy in their emotional relationships with one another. Although Chodorow's article may seem difficult upon first reading it is well worth the reader's efforts and the explication that follows in this introduction may make it more readily understood.

According to Chodorow, the fact that women occupy the social role of mother has differential psychological effects on the two sexes. Because females share the same biological sex as the mother, less psychological and emotional differentiation from the mother is necessary in order to attain the gender identification of female. Based on dissimilar biologic sex, males must establish a greater degree of differentiation in order to achieve a male gen-der identification. Such differentiation is established and maintained by denial and repression of affectional and relational needs with an intolerance of these in others as well. As a result of these differences, the two sexes have different standards of emotional closeness or intimacy.

It is interesting to review the content of Table 1 (see "General Introduction," p. 10) in the context of Chodorow's thesis. The psychological characteristics of the "masculine" (obsessive) personality may be seen as avoiding emotional closeness and intimacy whereas the "feminine" (hysterical) personality may be seen as attempting to establish intimacy or reacting to the lack of it. Also, the patriarchal mode of consciousness is based on separateness, dualism, and dichotomy which are compatible with the greater emotional differentiation (and lesser capacity for intimacy) of the male, whereas the matriarchal mode is based on union among disparate elements, which is compatible with the lesser emotional differentiation (and greater capacity for intimacy) of the female.

According to Chodorow (1971), men also establish and maintain gender identity through denigration and devaluation of women in addition to denial and repression of emotional needs. Referring to Table 1 of the "General Introduction" again, it may be seen that valuing the other as inferior while identifying with the superior is characteristic of the patriarchal mode of consciousness. According to Chodorow's theory, the denigration and devaluation of women betrays the underlying fear of maternal omnipotence (see also Lederer, 1968, for elaboration of men's unconscious fear of women). This latter possibility could also correspond to the patriarchal mode of conscious-

All human life on the planet is born of woman. The one unifying, incontrovertible experience shared by all women and men is that months-long period we spent unfolding inside a woman's body ... most of us first know both love and disappointment, power and tenderness, in the person of a woman.

We carry the imprint of this experience for life, even into our dying. Yet there has been a strange lack of material to help us understand and use it. We know more about the air we breathe, the seas we travel, than about the nature and meaning of motherhood. In the division of labor according to gender, the makers and sayers of culture, the namers, have been the sons of the mothers. There is much to suggest that the male mind has always been haunted by the force of the idea of dependence on a woman for life itself, the son's constant effort to assimilate, compensate for, or deny the fact that he is "of woman born."

Adrienne Rich, *Of Woman Born*, 1976

---

ness when the valuations shift and the self is occasionally identified with inferior and the other as superior. Also to be noted from Table 1, the "masculine" (obsessive) need for control and perfectionism would be compatible with the need for identification with the superior and omnipotence. Patriarchal dynamics could be seen as the interplay of these with the fear of its opposite—omnipotence of the other (maternal omnipotence). These, however, are probably only some of the possible relationships between the intrapsychic and interpersonal levels of the "Feminine" and the "Masculine."

On a societal level, these intrapsychic and interpersonal patterns are exacerbated by the economic structure. Because of women's economic dependence on men, women actually may remain more sensible and rational in love relationships whereas men may be more romantic and idealizing according to Chodorow. This would be consistent with the earlier feminist theory (Millett, 1970) that since the sexes have had unequal economic and material power, women have had to barter their sexual availability in return for economic and material security in the sister institutions of prostitution and marriage. And that

> "falling in love" is no more than the process of alteration of male vision—through idealization, mystification, glorification—that renders void the woman's (sex) class inferiority. (Firestone, 1970 p. 132)

Another aspect of Chodorow's theory that deserves comment is that women are of primary emotional importance to both men and women. A recent overview of the social psychology of relationships confirms this (Safilios-Rothschild, 1981). The emotional well-being of women with respect to marital status (see the articles by Radloff and Cox and by Gove in the next section) would support the notion that while marriage (relationships with women) has a positive effect on men, marriage (relationships with men) is less healthy for women. Other recent research has found that women do the "emotion work" in their relationships with men (Fishman, 1978). Again, this is consistent with earlier feminist observations. Though stated on a cultural level, the following could be applied to the personal level as well:

> So, if women are a parasitical class living off, and at the margins of, the male economy, the reverse too is true: *(Male) culture was (and is) parasitical, feeding on the emotional strength of women without reciprocity.* (Firestone, 1970, p. 127)

While Chodorow's paper attempts to integrate feminist and psychoanalytic theories, the article by Mary Jane Sherfey attempts to integrate the results of sexuality research with psychoanalytic theory. This article is an excerpt from a much longer treatise dealing with

Cultural distortion of sexuality explains also how female sexuality gets twisted into narcissism: women make love to themselves vicariously through the man, rather than directly making love to him. At times this cultural barrage of man/subject, woman/object desensitizes women to male forms to such a degree that they are even orgasmically affected.

Shulamith Firestone, *The Dialectic of Sex,*
1970

women's multiple orgasmic potential and the possibility of a biologically based, inordinate sexual drive in women. Sherfey argues that historically the suppression of female sexuality occurred with the shift from matriarchy to patriarchy and was necessary for the development of civilization and the establishment of the family and private property.

This highly provocative thesis regarding the historical development of men's control of women's sexuality would seem to be corroborated by evidence as to the present universality of patriarchal restrictions of women's sexuality (Patai, 1967).

While Sherfey's thesis could be interpreted as providing the justification for patriarchy, another possibility for the universal control of women's sexuality is that the suppression of all aspects of women's lives, including sexuality, would be necessary for the establishment of patriarchy. Regardless, Sherfey's thesis suggests that the discrepancy between women's sexual potential and their present sexual lives is a measure of the toll patriarchy has taken on the lives of women.

Men control women's sexuality on an interpersonal level by splitting women's sexuality into the "madonna" role, in which maternal and nurturing qualities are revered, and the "whore" role, in which insatiable sexual urges are desired. By splitting women's sexual functions, men also obtain a greater degree of control over their fear of women. In Chodorow's

terms, men avoid intimacy and the threat of re-experiencing maternal omnipotence by splitting their relationship to a female into two or more part-relationships, so that no one female can become emotionally or sexually threatening. The male choice of younger female sexual objects, as presented in the paper on father-daughter incest by Herman and Hirschman may also be seen in terms of the male desire for omnipotence and his need to be in control.

At a societal level, men and (male) culture have controlled women's sexuality through their definitions of it. Psychoanalytic theory, for example, failed to discover and then ignored scientific evidence of women's multiple orgasmic capacity. In the meantime, it constructed a dual orgasm theory for women based on men's sexual needs (Koedt, 1970), a theory we now know to be erroneous. In addition, men control female biological functions through research and practices regarding abortion and birth control, pregnancy, and childbirth. Thus women have been prevented from having control over their own bodies and reproductive functioning. This is beginning to change, however, as women establish alternative health care practices and institutions and attempt to change existing health care structures.

In the next article, Kristiann Mannion surveys the psychological literature on the lesbian, from psychoanalytic theories, which

*The power of the mother has two aspects: the biological potential or
capacity to bear and nourish human life, and the magical power invested
in women by men, whether in the form of Goddess-worship or the fear
of being controlled and overwhelmed by women. We do not actually
know much about what power may have meant in the hands of strong,
prepatriarchal women. We do have guesses, longings, myths, fantasies,
analogues. We know far more about how, under patriarchy, female
possibility has been literally massacred on the site of motherhood. Most
women in history have become mothers without choice, and an even
greater number have lost their lives bringing life into the world.*

Adrienne Rich, *Of Woman Born*, 1976

---

assume psychopathology, to empirical studies
of the lesbian as a real person in the social
and personal roles of "working woman, lover,
mate, and, frequently, mother." In reviewing
the empirical evidence on psychopathology,
Mannion finds little if any support. Instead,
she finds various methodological problems in
the research and heterosexual biases in both
methodology and interpretation of results. On
the basis of the psychological literature on
personal and social roles, she concludes that
there are greater similarities than differences
between lesbians and heterosexual women.

It is interesting to note that one difference is
that lesbians tend to be more "masculine,"
less "feminine," and more androgynous than
heterosexuals. Perhaps this may indicate that
lesbians are in some ways psychologically
healthier than heterosexuals by not restricting
themselves to a "feminine" sex role. In addition, it may be that "femininity" is relevant
mainly to white middle-class heterosexual
women who are also, interestingly enough, the
most economically dependent on men.

On the basis of Chodorow's theory, it might
be assumed that just as women's friendships
with other women may be more emotionally
satisfying than their friendships with men, lesbian relationships may also be more emotionally satisfying the heterosexual ones.
Another possibility is that these relationships
may involve more complex ways of relating
not found in heterosexual relationships, or in
the psychological literature.

The remaining articles in this section deal
with the topic of motherhood. The first of
these by Nancy Felipe Russo is from a special
issue of *Psychology of Women Quarterly* on
"The Motherhood Mandate." Russo examines
the relationship of sex roles and fertility variables within the context of the social structure.
Motherhood has provided a justification for
discrimination against women in the past. Currently, three factors have altered the relationship of these variables—women's labor force
participation, reproductive freedom, and voluntary childlessness. Issues regarding these
three areas relevant to white and minority
women, middle- and working-class women,
and young and old women are presented and
discussed. Russo also raises the issue of population planning, a concern of many feminists.

The final paper in this section by Rosalind
C. Barnett and Grace K. Baruch continues two
themes introduced by Russo—the assumed
centrality of women's reproductive role and
the lack of emphasis on the importance of
work to women. Barnett and Baruch find that
theories of human development are based on
men's experiences and are therefore not particularly relevant or useful to understanding
the lives of women over the life cycle. The
psychological literature has an overabundance
of research relating the psychology of older
women to their reproductive functions of
menopause and the empty nest, and very little
research or apparent interest in women in relation to work, despite the great numbers of

Is it not really remarkable . . . that so little recognition and attention are paid to the fact of men's secret dread of women? . . . The man . . . has very obvious strategic reasons for keeping his dread quiet. But he also tries by every means to deny it even to himself. This is the purpose of the efforts . . . to "objectify" it in artistic and scientific creative work. We may conjecture that even his glorification of women has its source not only in his cravings for love, but also in his desire to conceal his dread. A similar relief, however, is also sought and found in his disparagement of women that men often display ostentatiously in their attitudes. The attitude of love and adoration signifies: "There is no need for me to dread a being so wonderful, so beautiful, nay, so saintly." That of disparagement implies: "It would be too ridiculous to dread a creature who, if you take her all round, is such a poor thing."

Karen Horney, "The Dread of Woman," 1932

---

employed women and mothers. Available evidence indicates that women who work may derive positive effects for their mental health. Due to women's longer life span, decreased fertility rates, increasing educational opportunities, and labor force participation, these authors suggest that future research be more relevant to women by focusing on locus of control and attributions and on social networks and support systems, and in general, the importance of work to women.

Again, the data reported by Barnett and Baruch are consistent with the data and theory presented thus far in this section on relationships—that women rely on their spouse emotionally less than do men. This would support the notion that intimacy and sexuality may have very different meanings for the two sexes. The possible relation of this to mental illness rates in women, particularly with regard to marital status, will be discussed more fully in the next section.

For Further Reading

Blaxall, M., and Reagan, B. B. (Eds.). 1976. Women and the workplace: The implication of occupational segregation (Special issue). *Signs: Journal of Women in Culture and Society*, 1, (3), pt. 2.

Bryson, J., and Bryson, R. 1978. Dual career couples (Special issue). *Psychology of Women Quarterly*, 3 (1).

Chodorow, N. 1978. *The Reproduction of Mothering: Psychoanalysis and the Sociology of Gender.* Berkeley: Univ. California Press.

Hite, S. 1976. *The Hite Report: A Nationwide Study of Female Sexuality.* New York: Dell.

Klaich, D. 1974. *Woman + Woman: Attitudes toward Lesbianism.* New York: William Morrow.

Long-Laws, J., and Schwartz, P. 1977. *Sexual Scripts: The Social Construction of Female Sexuality.* Hinsdale, Ill.: Dryden.

Oakley, A. 1975. *Woman's Work: The Housewife, Past and Present.* New York: Random House.

Russo, N. 1979. The motherhood mandate (Special issue). *Psychology of Women Quarterly*, 4 (1).

Safilios-Rothschild, C. 1981. Women and relationships (Special issue). *Psychology of Women Quarterly*, 5 (3).

Stimpson, C. (Ed.). The labor of women: Work and family (Special issue). *Signs: Journal of Women in Culture and Society*, 4 (4).

Stimpson, C., and Spector-Person, E. (Eds.). 1980. Sex and sexuality (Special issue). *Signs: Journal of Women in Culture and Society*, 5 (4).

Stimpson, C., Stanton, D. C., and Burstyn, J. N. (Eds.). 1980. Sex and sexuality (Special issue). *Signs: Journal of Women in Culture and Society*, 6 (1).

Wolff, C. 1971. *Love Between Women.* New York: Harper Colophon.

Wysor, B. 1974. *The Lesbian Myth, Insights and Conversations.* New York: Random House.

Nancy Chodorow

Oedipal Asymmetries and Heterosexual Knots

One of our most common everyday perceptions is that heterosexual couple relationships are difficult. This article argues that these difficulties are not accidental but systematically created as part of the reproduction of the family. The psychoanalytic account of feminine and masculine oedipal development shows that a family structure in which women mother produces women and men with asymmetrical relational needs and wants. These lead people to form heterosexual relationships containing contradictions, which tend to undermine them.

We are faced in our daily lives, in the novels we read and the movies we see, with a puzzling observation. People, for the most part, marry, and marry heterosexually. At the same time, male-female relationships seem to become strained in regularized ways that we recognize and come to expect. These facts are often taken to be socially accidental or due to the psychological peculiarities of particular women and men. In this article, I suggest that we can make better sense of these same facts if we understand them as part of the routine process of family reproduction. Beginning from Freud's early analysis of family structure and psychosexual development, and the methodology this points us to, I show how the psychological propensities, needs, and wants which lead people to form new family or fam-

ily-like relationships undermine those very relationships they serve to form.

Drawing on facts often still familiar to us, Freud (1908) tells the following story: Sexual repression is a cornerstone of socialization in the bourgeois family. For women, this is an absolute; for men, it is occasionally offset by the double standard permitting, or even requiring, premarital sexual experience. What is most likely to happen is that when a girl is finally "allowed" to fall in love, she isn't really ready, is uncertain of her feelings, and as a result of extensive training in suppression, is sexually unresponsive. Because sex gives her no pleasure, she is unlikely to care much about the potential outcome of sex: children. By the time she matures, separates herself psychologically from her parents, and starts to love and desire her husband, their relationship is beyond repair, and her husband is no longer interested in her or it. She is then liable to turn her interest to her child or children. But it is an inappropriately sexualized interest, which, circularly, awakens precociously in them a sexuality which must be suppressed. As Freud (1908:35) puts it, "the training that precedes marriage directly frustrates the very aim of marriage."

This general picture often is exacerbated by two further outcomes of training for marriage and relationship. One, suggests Freud (again pointing to a fact, at least until recently, still

---

Ed. note: A glossary follows this article.

with us), is that the *verbal* message of premarital abstention comes down most heavily on heterosexual coitus. This, he suggests, pushes both young men and women to seek substitute sexual gratification—masturbation, homosexual sexual activity, and what he calls "perversions." In men, he tells us later (1910), it may also lead to a splitting of the erotic heterosexual object into the good nonsexual woman and the sexual woman who can't be respected. Again, faced with their eventual push into heterosexual marriage, neither partner is particularly prepared for coital satisfaction. Secondly, a woman may resent her husband intensely because of her disappointing sexual and marital experience,[1] but deny this and try to act the loving wife because her socialization tells her that a wife loves and idealizes her husband. This suppression and turning inward of anger again leads to neurosis, undercutting her marriage, and revenging herself on her husband perhaps even more than straightforward expression of rage might have done.

Freud thus gives a sociological account of the intertwining of the bourgeois Victorian marriage and psyche, the way bourgeois marriage reproduces its dominant sexual modes (sexual repression and heterosexual coitus) while at the same time undermining these. This account gives us some insight into those concrete internal contradictions which must have aided and continue to aid the extrafamilial social and economic forces which then as now work to alter the family based on ideals of romantic love and heterosexual intimacy. At the same time, it points to a useful methodology, one capable of yielding a profound analysis of the structural fabric of family relationships, self, and psyche.

I

It is almost a truism to state that consideration of the woman-man relationship—as a sexual relationship, a core family relationship, a strongly enforced ideological goal and expectation—brings us near the heart of the sociology of gender. In an extremely interesting contribution to the development of feminist theory, Gayle Rubin (1975) pushes further Levi-Strauss's argument (1949; 1956) that all kinship systems rest at least partly on marriage and the sexual division of labor, by pointing out that the vast world variety of marriage rules, regulating whom one can and cannot marry, all presuppose heterosexual unions, and require that individuals come to be dis-

[1]"Marriage under the present cultural standard has long ceased to be a panacea for the nervous sufferings of women; even if we physicians in such cases still advise matrimony, we are nevertheless aware that a girl must be very healthy to 'stand' marriage" (Freud, 1908:32). Durkheim's claim (1897) that marriage raises the suicide rates of women must be seen as comment on the same institution, I think.

In our society, the husband is assigned a superior status. It helps if he actually is somewhat superior in ways—in height, for example, or age or education or occupation—for such superiority, however slight, makes it easier for both partners to conform to the structural imperatives. The girl wants to be able to "look up" to her husband, and he, of course, wants her to. The result is a situation known sociologically as the marriage gradient.

Jessie Bernard, *The Future of Marriage,* 1972

---

posed to mate heterosexually.[2] Once stated, this claim becomes obvious, yet it is precisely such a crucially important claim which Levi-Strauss, and all other family theorists, have assumed and passed over. Heterosexuality, then, is one fundamental organizational principle of the family, and of what Rubin calls the "sex/gender system" of any society.[3]

A second fundamental organizational principle of the family and the social organization of gender, a principle also assumed and not analyzed by theorists of kinship and the family, is the sexual and familial division of labor in which women mother (Chodorow, 1971, 1974). That is, almost universally, women take primary responsibility for infant care; spend more time with infants and children than men; have primary affectional ties with infants (are the infant's primary attachment figure); are substitute parents if a biological mother isn't parenting. The amount of time fathers or other men spend with infants and children (and with boys vs. with girls) certainly varies widely from society to society, but fathers are never routinely the child's primary parenting person.

Thus, two major organizational rules can describe for us possibly all hitherto extant family systems.[4] We can understand the rela-

[2]Her argument that marriage, based on the exchange of women and the rule of obligatory heterosexuality, is basic to male dominance, is of course of central concern to me, though not analytically relevant to my argument here, and at least in the case of the exchange of women, to my mind problematic for an understanding of male dominance in the current historical period.

[3]Analytically parallel to the Marxian view that a mode of production consists in the technology and social organization through which a society appropriates and transforms nature for purposes of human consumption, and transforms the experience of human needs to require further changes, Rubin suggests, as a preliminary formulation, that a society's sex/gender system is "a set of arrangements by which the biological raw material of human sex and procreation is shaped by human, social intervention and satisfied in a conventional manner.... The realm of human sex, gender, and procreation has been subjected to, and changed by, relentless social activity for millennia. Sex as we know it—gender identity, sexual desire and fantasy, concepts of childhood—is itself a social product" (1975:165–6). This formulation includes the way in which biological sex becomes cultural gender, the sexual division of labor, the social relations for the production of gender and of sexual worlds, and the rules and regulations of sexual object choice. Kinships systems, suggests Rubin, are "observable and empirical forms of sex/gender systems," and "are made up of, and reproduce, concrete forms of socially organized sexuality" (169). Though Rubin's ostensible focus is on the whole panoply of sex/

gender arrangements, in fact her focus is upon the domain of marriage and the creation of married and marriageable individuals. She does not raise for analytic scrutiny the organization of parenting, procreation, and babies. Though the substance of this paper was planned and written, and its argument formulated, before I read Rubin, I am certainly indebted to her for the force, and hopefully the persuasiveness, with which I am able to point to heterosexuality as a central feature of sex/gender systems.

[4]These organizational rules, appropriately, are reflected in feminine personality, which, Johnson (1975a) argues, consists in two components—the heterosexual and the maternal—created developmentally through different experiences and relationships.

Untitled drawing by Melissa Mathis

tions between these as a two-stage process. People enter into marriage, which then legitimates the production of children (this *doesn't* necessarily mean that the marriage partners produce these children, though this is usually the case), whom women then care for, and for whom men become important second, which, in turn, creates them gendered, heterosexual, and ready to marry.[5]

However, it is the case that the development of this heterosexual object choice, and the nature and meaning of adult heterosexual experience, differs for men and women, and this is *because* women mother. The traditional psychoanalytic account of masculinity and femininity begins from this perception. In our society, marriage has assumed a larger and larger emotional weight supposedly offsetting the strains of increasingly alienated and bureaucratized work in the paid economy.[6] It no longer has the economic and political basis Levi-Strauss described. As production, education, religion, and care for the sick and aged leave the home, the family in general has collapsed in upon its psychological and personal

functions. The contradictions between women's and men's heterosexuality which women's mothering produces now stand out with particular clarity and gain special significance. It is these contradictions that I would now like to discuss—contradictions growing out of the nuclear family of advanced industrial capitalist society, and out of asymmetries in feminine and masculine oedipal experience which result from women's performing those mothering functions which are expected of them.[7]

II

According to psychoanalytic theory, heterosexual erotic orientation is a primary outcome of the oedipus complex for both sexes.[8] Boys and girls differ in this, however. Boys retain one primary love object throughout their boyhood. For this reason, the development of masculine

[5]See Chodorow, 1971, 1974; Johnson, 1975a: Mitchell, 1974; G. Rubin, 1975. This process also creates women ready to mother, which is the subject of my forthcoming book, *The Reproduction of Mothering* (University of California Press, forthcoming). For the purposes of this paper, I am cutting into the cycle in a different place and starting from the social fact of women's mothering.
[6]See, e.g., Berger and Kellner, 1974; Parsons and Bales, 1955; Zaretsky, 1973.

[7]Though some implications of this account probably hold in many other societies and other family structures, the specifics of these implications must be worked out before I would claim its universality. I am not arguing here, then, that Freud solves the universal Levi-Straussian exchange problem (nor do I think it is universal in the first place) as do Rubin and Mitchell. As several critics of Mitchell have pointed out, there is a fundamental discontinuity between Freud and Levi-Strauss concerning the dyadic location of important incest taboos, the reasons for exogamy, and the question of which men exchange which women (see First, 1974, Johnson, 1975b, Long, 1974, Ortner, 1975).
[8]Superego formation is another primary outcome, but not relevant to my account here.

The original meaning of the word "Family" (familia) . . . is the total number of slaves belonging to one man. The term was invented by the Romans to denote a new social organism, whose head ruled over wife and children and a number of slaves and who was invested under Roman paternal power with rights of life and death over them all.

Friedrich Engels, *The Origin of the Family, Private Property and the State*, 1942

---

heterosexual object choice is relatively continuous. In theory, the boy resolves his oedipus complex by repressing his attachment to his mother. He is therefore ready in adulthood to find a primary relationship with someone *like* his mother. When he does, the relationship is given meaning from its psychological reactivation of what was from its inception and for a long time an intense and exclusive relationship—first an identity, then a "dual-unity," finally a two-person relationship.

Things are not so simple for the girl. Because her first love object is a woman,[9] a girl, in order to attain her proper heterosexual orientation, must transfer her primary object choice to her father and men.[10] Thus, as Johnson (1975a) argues, drawing upon social psychological studies for confirmation, the father's behavior and family role, and the girl's relationship to him, are crucial to the development

---

[9]I have reflected recently on the puzzling psychoanalytic claim concerning the child's original bisexuality. Though people may theoretically or potentially be "constitutionally bisexual" (whatever that means), it seems clear that empirically, in the situation where women mother, it is much more correct to speak of primary gynosexuality, or matrisexuality in children of both genders.

[10]According to the account, she must also transfer her erotism from clitoris to vagina, and her erotic mode from active to passive. Regarding the former, it has been shown (see Masters and Johnson, 1966) that there is no physiological basis for a hypothesis of two kinds of feminine orgasm. Regarding the latter, there are huge definitional and conceptual problems with the psychoanalytic notion of activity-passivity (see Weisskopf, 1972). Once we remove (legitimately, I think) the instinctual component of these distinctions, the way they are experienced psychologically becomes derivative from the secondary to the larger issue of heterosexual relationship itself.

of heterosexual orientation in her. But fathers, in contrast to mothers, are comparatively unavailable physically and emotionally (Mitscherlich, 1963, talks of the "invisible father" of the mid-century industrial capitalist society). A father's main familial function is being a breadwinner, and his own training for masculinity may have led him to deny emotionality.

This creates an asymmetry in the feminine and masculine oedipus complex, and, as the psychoanalytic account stresses, difficulties in the development of female sexuality (given, that is, heterosexuality as a developmental goal). Freud formulates this asymmetry: "It is only in male children that there occurs the fateful simultaneous conjunction of love for the one parent and hatred of the other as a rival" (1931:92). The girl, by contrast, does in all likelihood turn to her father as an object of primary interest from the exclusivity of the relationship to her mother, but the girl's libidinal turning to her father does not substitute for her attachment to her mother. Instead, the girl retains and builds upon her preoedipal tie to her mother (an intense tie characterized by primary identification—a sense of oneness; primary love—not differentiating between her own and her mother's interests; and extensive dependence) together with oedipal attachments to *both* her mother and her father. These latter are characterized by eroticized demands for exclusivity, feelings of competition, jealousy. She retains the (internalized) early relationship, including its implications

Marriage is the destiny traditionally offered to women by society. It is still true that most women are married, or have been, or plan to be, or suffer from not being. The celibate [single] woman is to be explained and defined with reference to marriage whether she is frustrated, rebellious, or even indifferent in regard to that institution.

Simone de Beauvoir, *The Second Sex*, 1953

---

for the nature of her unconscious but fundamental definition of self in relationship, and internalizes these other relationships in addition, and not as replacement.

Thus, for girls there is no absolute change of object nor exclusive attachment to the father. If there is an absolute component to the change of object, it is at most a concentration on her father of genital, or erotic, cathexis. Affective interest, however, remains dual: the clinical corollary to Freud's claim is that love for the father and rivalry with the mother (which would be the mirror image of the masculine oedipus complex) is always tempered by love for the mother. This happens regardless of the girl's intention, and is the result of the intensity (and ambivalence) of the relation which develops with her mother in a situation of relatively exclusive maternal parenting.

Both Helene Deutsch (1944) and Ruth Mack Brunswick (1940, in an article formulated in close collaboration with Freud, and considered to be his final word on the subject of women) speak to this outcome, stressing (we might say, bewailing) the lack of what they would consider to be the final success in the girl's turn to the father and, therefore, the consequent problems of heterosexual attachment. According to Brunswick, the girl, embittered and hostile toward her mother, does "seek to transfer her libido to the father," but "this transference is beset by difficulties arising from the tenacity of the active and passive preoedipal mother-attachment" (1940:238).

Deutsch adds that the girl does normally make a *tentative* choice in favor of her father, turning to him "with greater intensity, although still not exclusively" (1944:32), and Brunswick confirms this outcome, pointing to the number of adult women who come for analytic treatment incapable of contact with men, and suggesting that this may be no more than an exaggeration of the normal oedipal resolution (1940:250–251):

> Between the exclusive attachment to the mother on the one hand and the complete transfer of the libido to the father on the other hand, the innumerable gradation of normal and abnormal development are to be found. It might also be said that partial success is the rule rather than the exception, so great is the proportion of women whose libido has remained fixed to the mother.

What this account suggests is that the oedipal situation, and the genesis of heterosexual orientation, is for the girl at least as much a mother-daughter concern as it is that of a daughter and father. The turn to the father is embedded in a girl's external relationship to her mother and in her relation to her mother as an internal object.[11]

What stands out here is the external and internal relational complexity of the feminine oedipus complex as opposed to the masculine. The girl's internal oedipus situation (her oedipal " 'family,' " as Laing would call it in "The Family and 'the family,' " 1971) is multilayered. Her relationship of dependence and

---

[11]See Freedman, 1961, for an excellent clinical account of this.

Housewife

Some women marry houses.
It's another kind of skin; it has a heart,
a mouth, a liver and bowel movements.
The walls are permanent and pink.
See how she sits on her knees all day,
faithfully washing herself down.
Men enter by force, drawn back like Jonah
into their fleshy mothers.
A woman is her mother.
That's the main thing.

Anne Sexton

Myself and My Mother

Purpose: To explore our relationships with our mothers.

Directions:

1. Write a biography of your mother.* (You may need to interview her or another family member to gain the necessary information.)
2. Try to include the following kinds of information:

   When and where was your mother born? What were her parents like (such as ethnic and economic background)? What were the important influences on her as a child? What is/was her relationship like with your father? Did/does she work? What are her main interests? What are your earliest memories of her? What is your relationship like with her—in the past and now? What messages or advice did she give you about being a woman? In what ways are you like/unlike your mother?
3. What did you learn? What did you experience? Share your experiences with the class.

How do you feel about your mother? How do you feel toward her now that you have written her biography?

*(or stepmother, sister, or whatever woman was most important to you while you were growing up.)

attachment to her mother continues; her oedipal attachments to her mother, then her father, are simply added on. The implication here is that the relationship to the father is often secondary, and at most emotionally equal, to that of the mother—that the relationships which compose the oedipus situation are competing for primacy. As Deutsch puts it (1932, 1944), the girl oscillates in a bisexual relational triangle, in which her relation to her father is emotionally in reaction to, interwoven and competing for primacy with, her relation to her mother.

The implications of this are twofold. First, the nature of the heterosexual relationship differs for boy and girl. Most women emerge from their oedipus complex oriented to their father and men as primary *erotic* objects, but it is clear that men tend to remain more *emotionally* secondary, or at most emotionally equal, in contrast to the primacy and exclusivity of the oedipal boy's emotional tie to his mother and women. Secondly, because the father is a second important love object, who becomes important structurally in the context of a relational triangle, the feminine inner object world is more complex than the masculine.

The girls' relation to her father is not only not of the same exclusivity as that of the boy toward his mother, but because mother and father are not the same *kind* of parent, its nature and intensity differ as well. Children first experience the social and cognitive world as continuous with themselves; they do not differentiate objects. Their mother, as first caretaking figure, is not a separate person and has no separate interests, and one of their first developmental tasks is the establishment of a self with boundaries, requiring the experience of self and mother as separate. In addition, this lack of separateness is in the context of the infant's total dependence upon the mother for physical and psychological survival. As A. Balint (1939) suggests, it is the forced recognition of the mother's separateness and separate interests which constitutes the entrance of the reality principle into the infant's life. The experience of self in the original mother-relation remains both seductive and frightening: unity was bliss, yet means the loss of self and absolute dependence. The father, by contrast has always been differentiated and known as a separate person with separate interests, and the child has never been totally dependent upon him. He has not posed the original narcissistic threat (the threat to basic ego integrity and boundaries) nor provided the original narcissistic unity (the original experience of oneness) to the girl. Oedipal love for the mother, then, contains a threat to selfhood which love for the father never does. Love for the father, in fact, is not simply the natural emergence of heterosexuality. Rather, it is an attempt on the girls' part to break her primary unity and dependence.

The other side of this attempt also affects the nature of the girl's relation to her father and to men. Janine Chasseguet-Smirgel (1964)

Linen Closet by Sandra Orgel copyright 1972. Reprinted by permission of the artist.

Ghost of a Chance

You see a man
trying to think.

You want to say
to everything:
Keep off! Give him room!
But you only watch,
terrified
the old consolations
will get him at last
like a fish
half-dead from flopping
and almost crawling
across the shingle,
almost breathing
the raw, agonizing
air
till a wave
pulls it back blind into the triumphant
sea.

Adrienne Rich

and Bela Grunberger (1964) speak to this issue, and in particular to the peculiar duality of men's secondary yet at the same time primary importance to women. The father and men, while emotionally secondary and not exclusively loved, are also idealized. There are a number of reasons for this. First, the girl's father is a last ditch escape from maternal omnipotence so it is important that the girl not drive him away. Second, his distance and ideological position of authority in the family,

and often her mother's interpretation of his role to her children, make the development of a relationship based on his real strengths and weaknesses difficult. Finally, the girl herself does not receive the same kind of love from her mother as a boy does (i.e., a mother, rather than confirming her daughter's oppositeness and specialness, experiences her as one with herself: her relationship to her daughter is more "narcissistic," that to her son more "anaclitic"). Thus, a daughter turns to her father looking for this kind of confirmation and a sense of separateness from her mother, and cares especially about being loved. She (and the woman she becomes) is willing to deny her father's limitations (and those of her lovers or husband) as long as she feels loved, and she is more able to do this because his distance means that she does not really know him. The relationship, then because of the father's distance and importance to her, is to a large extent on a level of fantasy and idealization. It lacks the grounded reality which a boy's relation to his mother has.[12]

These differences in the kind of love, and the experience of self in relation to father and mother, are reinforced by temporal differences in entry into the oedipal situation, which also grow out of the asymmetry in the mother's and father's position in the family. The discovery of the length and intensity of the preoedipal mother-daughter relationship was a major step

[12]I have discussed elsewhere (1971; 1974) the way in which the fact that a mother is real and a father fantasied affects the nature of processes of masculine and feminine identification and role assumption, focusing especially on the difficulties of masculine identification in the context of a boy's fantasied and abstracted relationship to his father.

forward in psychoanalytic theory, and constituted the base for a fundamental reformulation of the psychology of women (Lampl-de Groot, 1927; Freud, 1931). Because of the father's relative distance and unavailability, coupled with the intensity of the mother-child relationship, girls tend to enter the oedipal situation later than boys.

On the other hand, the availability of the mother and invisibility of the father may mean early entry of the boy into the oedipal situation. Slater (1968) and J. Whiting (1958) have both suggested that in the absence of men, mothers, cross-culturally, may early sexualize their relation to sons. Bibring (1953) argues that this is indeed the case in many mid-twentieth century nuclear family households, where there is a strong, active mother who runs the household and exhibits other traits of superiority to her husband (e.g., in cultural or social spheres) and a father, who, for a variety of reasons (he is generally ineffectual; he is efficient and competent as a professional but considers the family to be his wife's sphere; he is so busy in his work that he is rarely at home) is uninvolved in and unavailable for family life.[13] In these situations, she suggests, there is too much of mother: "the little boy finds himself . . . faced by a mother who appears to be as much in need of a husband as the son is of a father" (p. 281). The mother,

Magritte, *Untitled* (two shrouded lovers kissing). © by ADAGP, Paris, 1981

then, sexualizes her relationship to her son early, so that "oedipal" issues of sexual attraction and connection, and jealousy, become fused with "preoedipal" issues of primary love and oneness. By contrast, since the girl's relationship to her father develops later, her sense of self is more firmly established. If oedipal and preoedipal issues are fused for her, it is also in relation to her mother, and not to her father.

Finally, a girl does not "resolve" her oedipus complex to the same extent as the boy. Freud suggests that a boy's oedipus complex is normally "abandoned, repressed, and . . . entirely destroyed," that in contrast, girls "remain in it for an indeterminate length of time; they demolish it late and, even so, incompletely" (1933:129). A girl represses neither her preoedipal and oedipal attachment to her mother nor her oedipal attachment to her father. This means that she grows up with more ongoing preoccupation with internalized ob-

---

[13]Bibring here seems to be talking about middle-class and professional households. It seems to me that the same would hold for working-class fathers away from home much of the time because of work, spending recreational time in the company of men, and where the emotional division of the sexes and the sexual division of spheres is ideologically more pronounced than in the supposedly egalitarian middle and upper-middle classes.

Distances

You travel across the room.
Two chairs and a table
are between us; the shapes
of your words are between us.
Straight and cold as railroad track

I lie in my old roadbed
measuring distances—
waiting for you to pass
over me once again,
on your way somewhere else.

Linda Pastan

---

ject relationships and with external relationships as well.[14] Clinical accounts suggest that Freud's characterization of the masculine resolution may be rather idealized, but that nonetheless, a boy's repression of his oedipal maternal attachment (and preoedipal dependence) does tend to be *more* absolute than the girl's.

The traditional explanation for this difference (proposed by Freud in 1924) is that because the girl is already "castrated," she has no motive for breaking up her infantile sexual world and organization, and can retain a less repressed desire for her father. My reading of the account, stressing the determining primacy of social relational experience and not genital difference, locates this difference in the nature of the oedipal attachments themselves. The

greater intensity and quality of threat in the boy's relationship to his mother requires its repression in the son, whereas the less intense, less reciprocated, non-exclusive relation of a girl to her father enables this relationship, and the whole triangular affective constellation, to remain an ongoing part of her psychic world.

Masculine personality, then, comes to be founded more on the repression of affect and the denial of relational needs and a sense of connection than feminine personality (preparing the boy, parenthetically, for participation in the alienated, affect-free public world of work, where relationships are contractual and universalistically constructed).

By contrast, the girl's situation, in which the father and men, if erotically primary, are most likely affectively secondary, continues into adulthood. Deutsch expresses well the complexity of the developmental layering in women's psyche, and non-exclusive position of men, and the effect of these on the adult woman's participation in relationships (1944:205):

Let us recall that we left the pubescent girl in a triangular situation and expressed the hope that later she would dissolve the sexually mixed triangle ... in favor of heterosexuality. This formulation was made for the sake of simplification. Actually, whether a constitutional bisexual factor contributes to the creation of such a triangle or not, this triangle can never be given up completely. The deepest and most ineradicable emotional relations with both parents share in its formation. It succeeds another relation, even older and more enduring—the relationship between mother and child, which every man or woman preserves from his birth to his death. It is erroneous to say that the little girl gives up her

---

[14]According to Deutsch (1944) and Blos (1957; 1962), the content and development of pubertal relationships confirms and reproduces this.

Trying to Talk with a Man

Out in this desert we are testing bombs,

that's why we came here.

Sometimes I feel an underground river
forcing its way between deformed cliffs
an acute angle of understanding
moving itself like a locus of the sun
into this condemned scenery.

What we've had to give up to get here—
whole LP collections, films we starred in
playing in the neighborhoods, bakery win-
*   dows*
full of dry, chocolate-filled Jewish cookies,
the language of love-letters, of suicide notes,
afternoons on the riverbank
pretending to be children

Coming out to this desert
we meant to change the face of
driving among dull green succulents
walking at noon in the ghost town
surrounded by a silence

that sounds like the silence of the place
except that it came with us
and is familiar
and everything we were saying until now
was an effort to blot it out—
Coming out here we are up against it

Out here I feel more helpless
with you than without you
You mention the danger

and list the equipment
we talk of people caring for each other
in emergencies—laceration, thirst—
but you look at me like an emergency

Your dry heat feels like power
your eyes are stars of a different magnitude
they reflect lights that spell out: EXIT
when you get up and pace the floor

talking of the danger
as if it were not ourselves
as if we were testing anything else.

Adrienne Rich

first mother relation in favor of the father. She only gradually draws him into the alliance, develops from the mother-child exclusiveness toward the triangular parent-child relation and continues the latter, just as she does the former, although in a weaker and less elemental form, all her life. Only the principal part changes; now the mother, now the father plays it. The ineradicability of affective constellations manifests itself in later repetitions.

The implication of this statement is confirmed by cross-cultural examination of family structure and relations between the sexes,

which suggests that conjugal closeness is probably the exception and not the rule.[15]

We can summarize, then, several differences in female and male oedipal experience, all of which make women important on a basic emotional level to men (and to women) in a way that men are not important to women. Girls enter adulthood with a complex layering of af-

---

[15]This claim comes from my reading extensively in the ethnographic literature and is confirmed by anthropologist Michelle Z. Rosaldo, personal communication.

Women tend to seek identification with the person whom they love. A woman likes to follow her man and will even change her political ideas or her religion in her attempt to achieve once more that sense of union with another that was hers in the beginning. Even the modern woman who consciously admits a man's right to live his life without accounting for every moment of his day and expects to do the same herself, still wants to share his inmost thoughts and feelings, for that to her is the essence of true relationship. Not so man. For him, separation is inevitable, and it is from his island of separateness that he tries to relate. For him the woman's attempts to probe the inmost recesses of his mind feels, consciously or unconsciously, like a threat to engulf him.

Irene de Castillejo, *Knowing Woman: A Feminine Psychology*, 1973

---

fective ties and a rich, ongoing inner object world. Boys, to begin with, have a simpler oedipal situation and more direct affective relationships, and this situation is repressed in a way that the girl's is not. Second, the mother remains a primary internal object to the girl: the heterosexual relationship is on the model of a non-exclusive, second relationship for her, whereas for the boy, it recreates an exclusive, primary relationship.

The complexities of this situation are illuminated by sociological and clinical findings. Conventional wisdom has it, and much of our everyday observation confirms, that women are the romantic ones in our society, the ones for whom love, marriage and relationships matter. However, several studies point to ways that men love and fall in love romantically, women sensibly and rationally.[16] Most of these studies, rightly, I think, argue that in the current situation, where women are economically dependent on men,[17] women must, in fact, make rational calculations for the provision of themselves and their children. This position suggests that women's apparent romanticism is an emotional and ideological mask for their very real economic dependence. On the societal level, given especially economic inequality, men are exceedingly important to women. The recent tendency for women to initiate divorce and separation more than men—as income becomes more available to them, as recession hits masculine jobs indiscriminately with feminine, as the feminist movement begins to remove the stigma of "divorcee"—further confirms this.

These capacities have their mirror in some of the psychological and developmental differences I have discussed. Just as women, in adulthood, are objectively dependent on men economically, so also in childhood they are objectively dependent on men (their fathers) as escape from maternal domination. Their developed ability on this level to romanticize rational decisions—to not see, or to ignore, the failings of father (and other men), because he is not around to be known well, and because of their dependence—stands women in good stead in this adult situation.

There is another side to this situation, however. On a more profound level, women have acquired developmentally a real capacity for rationality and distance, through the rationality, distance, and emotional secondariness of their earliest relationship to a man in conjunction with their close and emotional re-

[16]See, e.g., Baum, 1971; Hochschild, 1975; Kephart, 1967; Z. Rubin, 1975.

[17]Rhea Wilson recently pointed out to me that even in the nineteenth century (though this was certainly the period of transition) men of most classes were dependent on their wives for the production of many essentials of life which were still home produced rather than produced for and therefore purchasable in the market.

lation to a woman. More direct evidence for the psychological primacy and profundity of this latter stance comes from findings about the experience of loss itself. George Goethals reports the clinical finding that loss of at least the first adult relationship for males "throws them into a turmoil and a depression of the most extreme kind" (1973:96), a melancholic reaction to object-loss of the type Freud first describes clinically (1917), in which they withdraw and are unable to look elsewhere for new relationships. He implies, by contrast, that first adult loss may not result in as severe a depression for a woman, and claims that his women patients did not withdraw to the same extent and were, in fact, more able to look elsewhere for new relationships. Zick Rubin (1975) who studied couples breaking up, reports a similar finding, that the men he studied tended to be more depressed and lonely after a breakup than the women. Equally striking, he found that women more than men, were likely to initiate the breakup of a relationship in which they were more involved than their partner. Jessie Bernard (1972:20–21:354), discussing people at a later age, reports that the frequency of psychological distress, death and suicide is much higher among recently widowed men than women, and indicates that the same difference can be found in a comparison of divorced men and women.

The implication in all these cases is that

Woman

*she wanted to be a blade
of grass amid the fields
but he wouldn't agree
to be the dandelion*

*she wanted to be a robin singing
through the leaves
but he refused to be
her tree*

*she spun herself into a web
and   looking for a place to rest
turned to him
but he stood straight
declining to be her corner*

*she tried to be a book
but he wouldn't read*

*she turned herself into a bulb
but he wouldn't let her grow*

*she decided to become
a woman
and though he still refused
to be a man
she decided it was all
right*

Nikki Giovanni

women have other resources and a certain distance from the relationship. (In the marriage case, Bernard would argue that women gain from getting out of it.) Internally, my account

Imperfections—on the part of the spouse, to be sure—inevitably make their appearance during the long period of living closely together. They set in motion a minor avalanche, which automatically keeps growing, as it rolls down the mountain slope of time. If, perhaps, a husband clings to the illusion of his independence, he will react with secret bitterness to his feeling needed and tied down by his wife. She, in turn, senses his suppressed rebellion, reacts with hidden anxiety, lest she lose him, and out of this anxiety instinctively increases her demands on him. The husband reacts to this with heightened sensitivity and defensiveness— until finally the dam bursts, neither one having understood the underlying irritability.

Karen Horney, "Problems of Marriage," 1932

---

would argue, the women have a richer, ongoing inner world to fall back on, and the man in their life does not represent the intensity and exclusivity which the woman represents to the man; externally, they also retain and develop more relationships. It is likely then, that, developmentally, men cannot become emotionally important to women on the same fundamental level as women are to men.

This process is furthered by men themselves, who, it turns out, collude in maintaining this distance as a result of their own oedipal resolution, which has led to the repression of their affective relational needs. According to psychoanalysts Chasseguet-Smirgel (1964) and Grunberger (1964), men, in their attempt to deny their own needs for love, come often to be intolerant of those who can express the need for love. Women, by contrast, have not repressed these needs, and still want love and confirmation, and, as I have suggested, may be willing to put up with limitations in their masculine lover or husband in exchange for some evidence of caring and love.[18]

Men, however, must both defend themselves against the threat and, at the same time, because needs for love do not disappear through repression, do tend to find themselves in heterosexual relationships. This is reinforced by their training for masculinity and the sociological situation of their relationships in the public world, both of which make deep primary relationships with other men hard to come by and don't allow children to become important in a way that they are to women.[19] These relationships to women, deriving their meaning and dynamics partly from the man's relation to his mother, must be difficult. In particular, the kind of maternal treatment of sons described by Bibring (1953), Slater (1968) and Whiting, et al. (1958) creates relational problems in sons. As Chasseguet-Smirgel (1964) and Bibring (1953) suggest, and as Slater describes so well, when a boy's mother has treated him as an extension of herself, and, at the same time, as a sexual object, he tends to continue to use his masculinity and possession of a penis as a narcissistic defense. In adulthood, he will tend to look on relationships with women for narcissistic-phallic reassurance rather than for mutual affirmation and love. Chasseguet-Smirgel also suggests that what Brunswick calls the boy's "normal con-

---

[18]For clinical confirmation of this, see Chasseguet-Smirgel and Grunberger, for sociological confirmation, Kephart, 1967.

[19]Booth (1972) reports that women's friendships in our society are affectively richer than men's. Along the same lines, Komarovsky (1974) found that men students confide more in a special woman friend and that they had to maintain a certain front of strength with men. Moreover, these men felt at a disadvantage vis-à-vis their woman confidante, because she tended to have a number of other people whom she could and did confide in.

tempt" for women—a standard outcome of the oedipus complex—is a pathological and defensive reaction to the same sense of inescapable maternal omnipotence, rather than a direct outcome of genital differences.

This situation reinforces in daily life what the woman first experienced developmentally and intrapsychically in relation to men. While she is likely to become and remain erotically heterosexual, she is encouraged by this situation to look elsewhere to fulfill relational needs. One way that women fulfill these needs is through the creation and maintenance of important personal relations with other women. Cross-culturally, social sex segregation is the rule: women tend to have closer personal ties with each other than men have, and to spend more time in the company of women than they do with men. In our society, there is some sociological evidence that women's friendships are affectively richer (Booth, 1972)—a finding certainly confirmed by most writing from the men's liberation movement. In other societies, and in most subcultures of our own, women remain in adulthood involved with female relatives—their mothers, sisters, sisters-in-law (or even co-wives).[20] These relationships are one way of

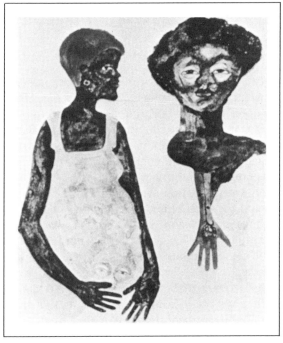

There's Something Between Us by Suzanne Jackson. Reprinted by permission of Bill Russell.

resolving and recreating the mother-daughter bond and are an expression of women's general relational capacities and definition of self in relationship. A second way is by having a child, turning her marriage into a family, and recreating for herself the primary intense unit which a heterosexual relationship tends to recreate for men (both because a relation to a woman is to someone like his mother, his first

---

[20]See for cross-cultural confirmation, most ethnographies, and also Rosaldo and Lamphere (1974). For our society, see Booth (1972), and for concrete illustration, Bott (1957), Gans (1967), Komarovsky (1962), Young and Willmott (1957).

Is it possible that the male is sexually dependent on the female to a higher degree than the woman is on him, because in women part of the sexual energy is linked to generative processes? Could it be that men, therefore, have a vital interest in keeping women dependent on them?

Karen Horney, "The Distrust Between the
Sexes," 1931

---

love object, and because women, for all the developmental reasons I have suggested, tend to be available to relational needs in a way that men are not).

III

Because women care for children, then, heterosexual symbiosis has a different "meaning" for men and women (just as does mother-infant symbiosis for mother and infant). Freud originally ("a man's love and a woman's are a phase apart psychologically," 1933:134), and psychoanalytic thinkers after him,[21] all point to a way in which women and men, though 'meant for each other,' and usually looking for intimacy with each other, are, because of the social organization of parenting, not meant for each other, and do not fulfill each other's needs.

As a result of being parented by a woman, both sexes are looking for a return to this emotional and physical union. A man achieves this directly through the heterosexual bond which replicates for him emotionally the early mother-infant exclusivity which he seeks to recreate. He is supported in this endeavor by women, who, through their own development, have remained open to relational needs, have retained an ongoing inner affective life, and have learned to deny the limitations of masculine lovers for both psychological and practical reasons.

Men, generally, though, both look for and fear exclusivity. Throughout their development, they have tended to repress their affective relational needs and sense of connection, and to develop and be more comfortable with ties based more on categorical and abstract role expectations, particularly in relation to other males. Even when they participate in an intimate heterosexual relationship, it is likely to be with the ambivalence created by an intense relationship which one both wants and fears, demanding from women, then, what they are at the same time afraid of receiving. The relationship to the mother thus builds itself directly into contradictions in masculine heterosexual commitment.

As a result of being parented by a woman and growing up heterosexual, women have different and a more complex set of relational needs, in which exclusive relationship to a man is not enough. This is because women experience themselves as part of a relational triangle in which their father and men are emotionally secondary, or at most equal, in importance to their mother and women. Women, therefore, need primary relationships to women as well as to men. In addition, the relation to the man itself has difficulties. Idealization, growing out of a girl's relation to her father, involves denial of real feelings and to a certain extent an unreal relationship to men.

The contradictions in women's heterosexual relationships, though, do not inhere only in

---

[21]See M. Balint (1936), Brunswick (1940), Deutsch (1944), Chasseguet-Smirgel (1964), Grunberger (1964).

Even a marriage is not made secure until the wife has succeeded in making her husband her child as well and in acting as a mother to him.

Sigmund Freud, "The Psychology of Women," 1933

the outcome of early childhood relationships. As I have suggested, men themselves, because of their own development and socialization, grow up rejecting their own and others' needs for love, and, therefore, find it difficult and threatening to meet women's emotional needs. Thus, given the masculine personality which women's mothering produces, the emotional secondariness of men to women, and the social organization of gender and gender roles, a woman's relationship to a man is unlikely to provide satisfaction for the particular relational needs which women's mothering and the concomitant social organization of gender have produced in women.

The two structural principles of the family, then, are in contradiction with each other. The family reproduces itself in form: for the most part people marry, and marry heterosexually; for the most part, people form couples heterosexually. At the same time, it undercuts itself in content: as a result of men and women growing up in families where women mother, these heterosexual relations, married or not, are liable to be strained in the regularized ways I have described.

In an earlier period, father absence was less absolute, production centered in the home, and economic interdependence of the sexes meant that family life and marriage was not and did not have to be a uniquely or fundamentally emotional project. The heterosexual asymmetry which I have been discussing was only one aspect of the total marital enterprise, and, therefore, did not overwhelm it. Woman

The Family by Su Negrin. Permission of Times Change Press

in this earlier period could seek relationships to other women in their daily work and community. With the development of industrial capitalism, however—and the increasingly physically isolated, mobile, and neolocal nuclear family it has produced—other primary relationships are not easy to come by on a routine, daily, ongoing basis. At the same time, the public world of work, consumption, and

I submit that love is essentially a much simpler phenomenon—it becomes complicated, corrupted, or obstructed by an unequal balance of power. We have seen that love demands a mutual vulnerability or it turns destructive: the destructive effects of love occur only in a context of inequality. But because sexual inequality has remained a constant—however its degree may have varied—the corruption "romantic" love became characteristic of love between the sexes. . . .

Shulamith Firestone, *The Dialectic of Sex*, 1970

---

leisure leaves people increasingly starved for affect, support, and a sense of unique self. The heterosexual relationship itself gains in emotional importance at the very moment when the heterosexual strains which mothering produces are themselves sharpened. In response to these emerging contradictions, divorce rates soar, people flock to multitudes of new therapies, politicians decry and sociologists document the end of the family. And there develops a new feminism.

Glossary*

Affect General term for feelings and emotions.

Anaclitic (lit.: leaning on) Freud (1914) distinguished two types of object-choice: narcissistic and anaclitic. *Narcissistic object-choice* . . . occurs when [one] chooses an object on the basis of some real or imagined similarity with [oneself], while *anaclitic object-choice* occurs when the choice is based on the pattern of childhood dependence on someone unlike [oneself]. . . .

Cathexis . . . Used to describe the quantity of energy attaching to any object-representation or mental structure.

Libidinal . . . The adjective corresponding to the technical term **Libido.**

Libidinal infantile development Classical theory postulates a series of phases of libidinal development through which the individual passes from infancy until [he or she] reaches the latency period,

these phases being synchronous with a parallel series of phases of ego-development. . . .

Libido Hypothetical form of mental energy, with which processes, structures, and object representations are invested. . . .

Narcissism . . . Classical theory distinguishes between *primary narcissism*, the love of self which precedes loving others, and *secondary narcissism*, love of self which results from introjecting and identifying with an object . . . is used as a technical term to categorize all forms of investment of energy (libido) in the self.

Object That towards which action or desire is directed; that which the subject requires in order to achieve instinctual satisfaction; that to which the subject relates himself. In psychoanalytical writings, objects are nearly always persons. . . . This terminology confuses readers who are more familiar with "object" in the sense of a "thing," i.e., that which is not a person. Hence:

> *Object-relations (hip)* The relation of the subject to [his or her] object, *not* the relation between the subject and the object, which is an *interpersonal* relationship. This is because psychoanalysis is a psychology of the individual and therefore discusses objects and relationships only from the point of view of a single subject. An object-relationship may be either an external or an internal object. . . .

Oedipus complex Group of largely unconscious ideas and feelings centering around the wish to possess the parent of the opposite sex and eliminate that of the same sex. The complex emerges, according to classical theory, during the *oedipal phase* of libidinal and ego development, i.e., between the

*Reprinted with permission from Charles Rycroft, *A Critical Dictionary of Psychoanalysis*. New York: Basic Books, 1968.

ages of three and five. . . . The complex is named after the mythical Oedipus, who killed his father and married his mother without knowing that they were his parents. . . . *Resolution of the Oedipus complex* is achieved typically by identification with the parent of the same sex and (partial) temporary renunciation of the parent of the opposite sex, who is "rediscovered" in [his or her] adult sexual object. . . . Its first published appearance was in the [Freud's] *Interpretation of Dreams* (1900). It re-mained a cornerstone of psychoanalytical theory up to, say, 1930, but since then psychoanalysis has become increasingly mother-oriented and concerned with the *pre-oedipal relationship to the mother.* . . .

Pre-oedipal [The adjective] referring to those stages of libidinal development which preceded the oedipal, and to the relationship to the mother during them.

Mary Jane Sherfey, M.D.

A Theory on Female Sexuality

No doubt the most far-reaching hypothesis extrapolated from biological data is the existence of the universal and physically normal condition of women's inability ever to reach complete sexual satiation in the presence of the most intense, repetitive orgasmic experiences, no matter how produced. Theoretically, a woman could go on having orgasms indefinitely if physical exhaustion did not intervene.

It is to be understood that repetitive orgasms leading to the satiation-in-insatiation state will be most apt to occur in parous[1] and experienced women during the luteal phase[2] of the menstrual cycle. It is one of the most important ways in which the sexuality of the primate and human female differs from the primate and human male at the physical level; and this difference exists only because of the female's capacity to produce the fulminating pelvic congestion and edema. This capacity is mediated by specific hormonal combinations with high fluid-imbibing action which are found only in certain primates and, probably, a very few other mammalian species.

I must stress that this condition does not mean a woman is always consciously unsatisfied. There is a great difference between satisfaction and satiation. A woman may be emotionally satisfied to the full in the absence of any orgasmic expression (although such a state would rarely persist through years of frequent arousal and coitus without some kind of physical or emotional reaction formation). Satiation-in-insatiation is well illustrated by Masters' statement, "A woman *will usually* be satisfied with three to five orgasms...." I believe it would rarely be said, "A man will usually be satisfied with three to five ejaculations." The man *is* satisfied. The woman *usually wills* herself to be satisfied because she is simply unaware of the extent of her orgasmic capacity. However, I predict that this hypothesis will come as no great shock to many women who consciously realize, or intuitively sense, their lack of satiation....

It seems that the vast majority of cases of coital frigidity are due simply to the absence of frequent, prolonged coitus. This statement is supported by unpublished data which Masters and Johnson are now accumulating. Following this logical conclusion of their previous research, they began treating a series of couples with severe, chronic frigidity or impotence. All had received prior medical and, often, psychiatric treatment to no avail. For the women, none of whom had ever experienced orgasms after five or more years of marriage, treatment consisted of careful training of the husband to use the proper techniques essential to all women and the specific ones required by his wife. In many cases this in itself was sufficient. In the others, daily sessions were instigated of marital coitus followed by prolonged use of the artificial phallus (three to four hours or more). Thus far, with about fifty women treated, every woman but one responded within three weeks at most and usually within

---

[1] "Parous" describes women who have had at least one child.

[2] The luteal phase is the post-ovulatory phase of the menstrual cycle.

a few days. They began at once to experience intense, multiple orgasms; and once this capacity was achieved after the exposure to daily prolonged coitus, they were able to respond with increasing ease and rapidity so that the protracted stimulation was no longer necessary. It is too early for thorough follow-ups, but initial impressions are most favorable.

Should these preliminary findings hold, an almost total biological etiology of coital frigidity will be proved. The inordinate sexual, orgasmic capacity of the human female will fall in line with that of the other higher primates—and the magnitude of the psychological and social problems facing modern mankind is difficult to contemplate.

Historical Perspective and Cultural Dilemma

The nature of female sexuality as here presented makes it clear that, just as the vagina did not evolve for the delivery of big-headed babies, so women's inordinate orgasmic capacity did not evolve for monogamous, sedentary cultures. It is unreasonable to expect that this inordinate sexual capacity could be, even in part, given expression within the confines of our culture: and it is particularly unreasonable to expect the delayed blooming of the sexuality of many women after the age of thirty or so to find adequate avenues of satisfaction. Less than one hundred years ago, and in many places today, women regularly had their third or fourth child by the time they were eighteen or nineteen, and the life span was no more than thirty-five to forty years. It could well be that the natural synchronization of the peak periods for sexual expression in men and women has been destroyed only in recent years.

These findings give ample proof of the conclusion that neither men nor women, but especially not women, are biologically built for the single-spouse, monogamous marital structure or for the prolonged adolescence which our society can now bestow upon both of them. Generally, men have never accepted strict monogamy except in princple. Women have been forced to accept it: but not, I submit, for the reasons usually given.

The human mating system, with its permanent family and kinship ties, was absolutely essential to man's becoming—and remaining—man. In every culture studied, the crucial transition from the nomadic, hunting, and food-gathering economy to a settled, agricultural existence was the beginning of family life, modern civilization, and civilized man. In the preagricultural societies, life was precarious, population growth slow, and infanticide often essential to group survival. With the domestication of animals and the agriculture revolution, for the first time in all time, the survival of a species lay in the extended family with its private property, kinship lineages, inheritance laws, social ordinances, and, most significantly, many surviving children. Only in that carefully delineated and rigidly maintained large-family complex could the individual find sufficient security to allow his uniquely human potentialities to be developed through the long years of increasingly helpless childhood—and could populations explode into the first little villages and towns.

Many factors have been advanced to explain the rise of the patriarchal, usually polygamous, system and its concomitant ruthless subjugation of female sexuality (which necessarily subjugated her entire emotional and intellectual life). However, if the conclusions

We are entitled to keep to our view that in the phallic phase of girls the clitoris is the leading erotogenic zone. But it is not, of course, going to remain so. With the change to femininity the clitoris should wholly or in part hand over its sensitivity, and at the same time its importance, to the vagina.

Sigmund Freud, "The Psychology of
Women," 1933

---

reached here are true, it is conceivable that the *forceful* suppression of women's inordinate sexual demands was a prerequisite to the dawn of every modern civilization and almost every living culture. Primitive woman's sexual drive was too strong, too susceptible to the fluctuating extremes of an impelling, aggressive erotism to withstand the disciplined requirements of a settled family life—where many living children were necessary to a family's well-being and where paternity had become as important as maternity in maintaining family and property cohesion. For about half the time, women's erotic needs would be insatiably pursued; paternity could never be certain; and with lactation erotism, constant infant care would be out of the question.

There are many indications from the prehistory studies in the Near East that it took perhaps five thousand years or longer for the subjugation of women to take place. All relevant data from the 12,000 to 8,000 B.C. period indicate that precivilized woman enjoyed full sexual freedom and was often totally incapable of controlling her sexual drive.[3] Therefore,

I propose that one of the reasons for the long delay between the earliest development of agriculture (c. 12,000 B.C.) and the rise of urban life and the beginning of recorded knowledge (c. 8,000–5,000 B.C.) was the ungovernable cyclic sexual drive of women. Not until these drives were gradually brought under control by rigidly enforced social codes could family life become the stabilizing and creative crucible from which modern civilized man could emerge.

Although then (and now) couched in superstitious, religious and rationalized terms, behind the subjugation of women's sexuality lay the inexorable economics of cultural evolution which finally forced men to impose it and women to endure it. If that suppression has

---

[3] "Today it is unfashionable to talk about former more matriarchal orders of society. Nevertheless, there is evidence from many parts of the world that the role of women has weakened since earlier times in several sections of social structure." The evidence given here lends further support to this statement by J. Hawkes and L. Woolley. See *History of Mankind, Vol. I: Prehistory and the Beginnings of Civilization* (New York: Harper & Row, 1963). However, I

must make it clear that the biological data presented support only the thesis on the intense, insatiable erotism in women. Such erotism could be contained within one or possibly several types of social structures which would have prevailed through most of the Pleistocene period.

I am indebted to Prof. Joseph Mazzeo of Columbia University for calling my attention to the fact that the first study on the existence of a pre-Neolithic matriarchal society was published in 1861: Bachofen's *Das Mutterecht* (Basel: B. Schwabe, 1897). Indeed, Bachofen's work remains an unsurpassed, scholarly analysis of the mythologies of the Near East, hypothesizing both a matriarchal society and the inordinate erotism of women. His entire thesis was summarily rejected by twentieth-century anthropologists for lack of objective evidence (and cultural bias). On several scores, the ancient myths have proved more accurate than the modern scientists' theories. I suspect this will be another instance in which the myths prove faithful reflections of former days.

> *The superiority of the vaginal orgasm seems almost a demoniac determination on Freud's part to complete the Victorians' repression of feminine eroticism, to stigmatize the remaining vestiges of pleasure felt by women and thus make them unacceptable to the women themselves. For there were still women whose sexuality hadn't been completely destroyed, as evidenced by one Dr. Isaac Brown Baker, a surgeon who performed numerous clitoridectomies on women to prevent the sexual excitement which, he was convinced, caused "insanities," "catalepsy," "hysteria," "epilepsy" and other diseases.*

> Susan Lydon, *Ramparts*, 1968

---

been, at times, unduly oppressive or cruel, I suggest the reason has been neither man's sadistic, selfish infliction of servitude upon helpless women nor women's weakness or inborn masochism. The strength of the drive determines the force required to suppress it.

The hypothesis that women possess a *biologically determined*, inordinately high, cyclic sexual drive is too significant to be accepted without confirmation from every field of science touching the subject. Assuming this analysis of the nature of women's sexuality is valid, we must ask ourselves if the basic intensity of women's sexual drive has abated appreciably as the result of the past seven thousand years of suppression (which has been, of course, only partial suppression for most of the time). Just within the very recent past, a decided lifting of the ancient social injunctions against the free expression of female sexuality has occurred. This unprecedented development is born of the scientific revolution, the product of both efficient contraceptives, and the new social equality and emotional honesty sweeping across the world (an equality and honesty which owe more to the genius of Sigmund Freud than to any other single individual). It is hard to predict what will happen should this trend continue—except one thing is certain: if women's sexual drive has not abated, and they prove incapable of controlling it, thereby jeopardizing family life and child care, a return to the rigid,

enforced suppression will be inevitable and mandatory. Otherwise the biological family will disappear and what other patterns of infant care and adult relationships could adequately substitute cannot now be imagined.[4]

Should the hypothesis be true that one of the requisite cornerstones upon which all modern civilizations were founded was *coercive* suppression of women's inordinate sexuality, one looks back over the long history of women and their relationships to men, children, and society since the Neolithic revolution with a deeper, almost awesome, sense of the ironic tragedy in the triumph of the human condition.

Summary

Recent embryological research has demonstrated conclusively that the concept of the initial anatomical bisexuality or equipotentiality of the embryo is erroneous. All mammalian embryos, male and female, are anatomically female during the early stages of fetal life. In humans, the differentiation of the male from the female form by the action of fetal androgen begins about the sixth week of embryonic life and is completed by the end of the third month. Female structures develop

---

[4]On the contrary, communal family structures, with men *and* women sharing child care, are not only imaginable, but already in experimental practice.

The sexual frigidity of women . . . is a phenomenon that is still insufficiently understood. Sometimes it is psychogenic and in that case accessible to influence; but in other cases it suggests the hypothesis of its being constitutionally determined and even of there being a contributory anatomical factor.

Sigmund Freud, "The Psychology of
Women," 1933

---

autonomously without the necessity of hormonal differentiation. If the fetal gonads are removed from a genetic female before the first six weeks, she will develop into a normal female, even undergoing normal pubertal changes if, in the absence of ovaries, exogenous hormones are supplied. If the fetal gonads are similarly removed from a genetic male, he will develop into a female, also undergoing normal female pubertal changes if exogenous hormones are supplied. The probable relationship of the antonomous female anatomy to the evolution of viviparity is described.

From this surprising discovery of modern embryology and other biological data, the hypothesis is suggested that the female's relative lack of differentiating hormones during embryonic life renders her more sensitive to hormonal conditioning in later life, expecially to androgens, since some embryonic and strong maternal estrogenic activity is present during embryonic life. This ready androgen responsivity provides the physiological means whereby androgen-sensitive structures could evolve to enhance the female's sexual capacity. In the primates, the marked development of the clitoral system, certain secondary sexual characteristics including skin erotism, and the extreme degree of perineal sexual edema (achieved in part by progesterone with its strong androgenic properties) are combined in various species to produce an intense aggressive sexual drive and an inordinate, insatiable

capacity for copulations during estrus.[5] The breeding advantage would thus go to the females with the most insatiable sexual capacity. The infrahuman female's insatiable sexual capacity could evolve only if it did not interfere with maternal care. Maternal care is insured by the existence of the extreme sexual drive only during estrus and its absence during the prolonged postpartum anestrus of these animals.

The validity of these considerations and their relevance to the human female are strongly supported by the demonstration of comparable sexual physiology and behavior in women. This has been accomplished by the research of Masters and Johnson, and a summary of their findings of the actual nature of the sexual response cycle in women is presented. Their most important observations are:

A. There is no such thing as a vaginal orgasm distinct from a clitoral orgasm. The nature of the orgasm is the same regardless of the erotogenic zone stimulated to produce it. The orgasm consists of the rhythmic contractions of the extravaginal musculature against the greatly distended circumvaginal venous plexi and vestibular bulbs surrounding the lower third of the vagina.

B. The nature of the labial-preputial-glandar mechanism which maintains continuous stim-

---

[5]Estrus is that time when a female animal, because of the hormonal milieu, is capable of conception and desirous of copulation. Strictly speaking, true estrus does not occur in the human female.

Human beings have taken a hostile attitude toward that in themselves which is living, and have alienated themselves from it. This alienation is not of biological, but of social and economic origin. It is not found in human history before the development of the patriarchal social order.

Wilhelm Reich, *The Function of the Orgasm,*
1942

ulation of the retracted clitoris during intra-vaginal coition has been described. By this action, clitoris, labia minora, and lower third of the vagina function as a single, smoothly integrated unit when traction is placed on the labia by the male organ during coitus. Stimulation of the clitoris is achieved by the rhythmical pulling on the edematous prepuce. Similar activation of the clitoris is achieved by preputial friction during direct clitoral area stimulation.

C. With full sexual arousal, women are normally capable of many orgasms. As many as six or more can be achieved with intravaginal coition. During clitoral area stimulation, when a woman can control her sexual tension and maintain prolonged stimulation, she may attain up to fifty or more orgasms in an hour's time.

From these observations and other biological data, especially from primatology, I have advanced four hypotheses:

1. The erotogenic potential of the clitoral glans is probably greater than that of the lower third of the vagina.... The evolution of primate sexuality has occurred primarily through selective adaptations of the perineal edema and the clitoral complex, not the vagina.

2. Under optimal arousal conditions, women's orgasmic potential may be similar to that of the primates described. In both, orgasms are best achieved only with the high degree of pelvic vasocongestion and edema associated with estrus in the primates and the

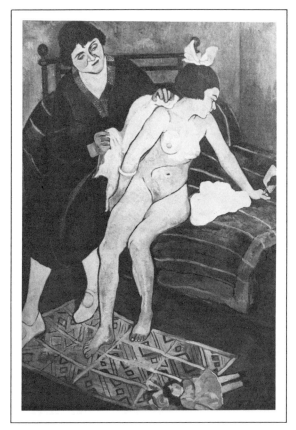

The Abandoned Doll by Suzanne Valadon. From the collection of Wallace and Wilhelmina Holladay

luteal phase of the menstrual cycle in women or with prolonged, effective stimulation. Under these conditions, each orgasm tends to increase pelvic vasocongestion; thus the more

Most clinicians have not thought deeply about the sociopolitcal—or the psychological—conditions that are necessary for female sexual self-definition. Women can never be sexually actualized as long as men control the means of production and reproduction. Women have had to barter their sexuality (or their capacity for sexual pleasure) for economic survival and maternity. Female frigidity as we know it will cease only when such bartering ceases. . . . From a psychological point of view female frigidity will cease when female children are surrounded by and can observe non-frigid female adults.

Phyllis Chesler, *Women and Madness*, 1972

The *Lock* by Leonor Fini; reprinted by permission of the artist

orgasms achieved, the more can be achieved. Orgasmic experiences may continue until physical exhaustion intervenes.

3. In these primates and in women, an inordinate cyclic sexual capacity has thus evolved leading to the paradoxical state of sexual insatiation in the presence of the utmost sexual satiation. The value of this state for evolution is clear: with the breeding premium going to the primate females with the greatest pelvic edema, the most effective clitoral erotism, and the most aggressive sexual behavior, the satiation-in-insatiation state may have been an important factor in the adaptive radiation of the primates leading to man—and a major barrier to the evolution of modern man.

4. The rise of modern civilization, while resulting from many causes, was contingent on the suppression of the inordinate cyclic sexual drive of women because *(a)* the hyperhormonalization of the early human females associated with the hypersexual drive and the prolonged pregnancies was an important force in the escape from the strict estrus sexuality and the much more important escape from lactation asexuality. Women's uncurtailed continuous hypersexuality would drastically interfere with maternal responsibilities; and *(b)* with the rise of the settled agriculture economies, man's territorialism became expressed in property rights and kinship laws. Large families of known parentage were mandatory and could not evolve until the inordinate sexual demands of women were curbed.

Finally, the data on the embryonic female primacy and the Masters and Johnson research on the sexual cycle in women will re-

SEVEN YEARS IN ANALYSIS
AND NOW THEY TELL ME
ABOUT THE MYTH OF THE
VAGINAL ORGASM

quire emendations of psychoanalytic theory. These will be less than one might think at first sight. Other than concepts based on innate bisexuality, the rigid dichotomy between masculine and feminine sexual behavior, and derivative concepts of the clitoral-vaginal transfer theory, psychoanalytic theory will remain. Much of the theory concerning the "masculine" components of female sexuality will also remain but will be based on a different biological conception. Certainly, much of present and past sexual symbolism will take on richer meanings.

It is my strong conviction that these fundamental biological findings will, in fact, strengthen psychoanalytic theory and practice in the area of female sexuality. Without the erroneous biological premises, the basic sexual constitution and its many manifestations will be seen as highly moldable by hormonal influences, which in turn are so very susceptible to all those uniquely human emotional, intellectual, imaginative, and cultural forces upon which psychoanalysis has cast so much light. The power of the psychic processes will stand the stronger. Therefore it may be safely predicted that these new biological findings will not "blow away" Freud's "artificial structure of hypotheses" but will transpose it to a less artificial and more effective level.

In any event, and regardless of the validity of my own conclusions, it is my hope that this presentation of recent major contributions from biology and gynecology bearing on female sexual differentiation and adult functioning will aid in the integration of psychological and biological knowledge and will provide a firm biological foundation upon which all future theories of female psychosexuality must rest.

Kristiann Mannion

Psychology and the Lesbian: A Critical Review of the Research

Introduction

The study of the psychology of female homosexuality is rooted in psychoanalytic theory. Early research, which consisted primarily of a few clinical studies, evolved from the prevailing theory that healthy female sexuality is a product of accepting one's biological destiny to become mother. Lesbianism, a failure to achieve heterosexuality, is, at best, a case of arrested development; at worst, a pathological deviance caused by a disruption in the process of achieving healthy female sexuality.

As a result of the social changes of the 1960s, the psychology of women became a credible topic for research. As a social group, lesbians became more visible and accessible to researchers. Concurrently, psychologists became aware that most of our understanding about lesbianism came from theory substantiated only by clinical experience or from studies of homosexual men. The need for an empirical basis upon which to shape theory led to an upsurge in research, which was, however, still biased by analytical thinking. Consequently the studies focus on psychopathology or deviant childhood history.

With the latter half of the 1970s there has been a new trend in the psychological literature. The concepts of masculinity and femininity, the emotional and behavioral correlates of sex roles, the impact of socialization on psychological development have all become topics for scientific inquiry. Likewise, the study of lesbianism has shifted from the emphasis on deviance to the study of the lesbian in the context of her social and personal functioning in her many roles as working woman, lover, mate, and, frequently, mother.

The purpose of this paper is to review the major sources of empirical research about the homosexual woman. The first area includes a review of the traditional theory of lesbian behaviors and the research, using projective techniques, which attempt to validate psychoanalytic theory. Although many professionals no longer accept these theories, they still shape the theoretical position from which many therapists approach the lesbian who seeks treatment, and linger as bias in other therapists who are naive in their understanding of the psychology of women and lesbians in particular.

The second area of research reviewed includes the extensive documentation of personality characteristics that can be identified on paper-and-pencil personality inventories or, in some cases, through structured diagnostic interviews by trained clinicians. These have become vastly important in defining some of the parameters of emotional functioning, identifying possible areas of difficulty and, as shall be seen, in helping erase the image of the lesbian as "sick." The third area comprises the studies that explore the early childhood history of lesbians in hopes of defining a set of family dynamics that might "cause" homosexual development.

For final consideration is the research that looks at the lesbian in the context of her social functioning. This includes the awareness and exploration of homosexuality; the lesbian's acceptance or rejection of traditional sex-role related behaviors; and the ways in which the lesbian, in'.uenced by feminism and the gay community, forms and maintains significant personal relationships. Not to be excluded is her ability to perform in the role of mother and the effect of her parenting on the development of her children.

Psychoanalytic Theory and the Lesbian

According to Freud (1925/1961) all children are motivated by an anaclitic identification, a primary asexual identification based on love for the mother and a fear of loss of her (oral) gratification, and a secondary identification, the identification with the aggressor, aimed at the avoidance of punishment and castration. The male child experiences the Oedipal attachment to his mother and perceives his father as a rival for the mother's love, fearing that his father will castrate him in retaliation for his sexual wishes for the mother. Identification with the father permits the boy to enjoy his mother vicariously and reduces the threat of castration. Through this identification the Oedipal problems are settled and the boy achieves a healthy male identification and an attraction for female figures like his mother.

It was in his essay "Female Sexuality" that Freud (1931/1961) recognized that the Oedipal paradigm does not work adequtely for the girl for two reasons. One is that since she has no penis, she has nothing in the way of castration to fear, thus no basis for the identification with the aggressor to ward off castration suggested

for the boy. Secondly, while the boy retains a female for his love object throughout the Oedipal trauma and its resolution, the girl begins life with a homosexual attachment to the mother, and must succeed in acquiring an opposite-sex love object. The following is Freud's final thinking on the nature of feminine sexual identification (1931/1961, 1933/1964).

The little girl who discovers the male sex organ goes through a decisive shock experience and grasps in an instant that she is a deprived, mutilated creature, and is thus seized by "penis envy." While at first believing that her condition is the result of punishment for some unknown crime, she realizes that the sexual characteristic is universal. She recognizes too that it is her mother, similarly deprived, who is responsible for her mutilated state. A consequence of this realization is a loosening of the relationship with the mother as the primary love object and the beginning of a hostile identification with her. This rushes the girl into an appropriate Oedipal attachment to the father who is desirable because he is the possessor of the prized organ. When the girl realizes that she cannot possess a penis herself, she gives up her wish for the penis and replaces it instead with a wish for a child. With that purpose in mind, she takes her father as a love object. Eventually realizing that her attachment to the father will have to be abandoned, she turns her affection toward other more appropriate males who can serve the same purpose.

Another element in this process is the role of masturbation in the preoedipal child. Children discover the pleasurable centers in the clitoris and penis. Freud equated the clitoris to the penis and described the female child as

The lesbian's yearning for her mother's love is always put in jeopardy through the existence of a male ... one wonders why lesbians] are so much resented by men and women. Because of the pride and vanity of the male, only few men would consider lesbians to be serious rivals. Men's dislike of them goes back to a fundamental psychological cause: The need for the mother in a woman. The male wants to be "fed" by the female. He needs ego support throughout his life. A lesbian who "feeds" (loves) another woman puts him and his world into chaos; she is a rival because she takes away maternal support which should be HIS not HERS.

Charlotte Wolff, *Love Between Women*, 1971

---

basically masculine, that is, fixated on clitoral stimulation. Upon discovery of the penis, however, the female child is embarrassed by the minuscule size of her penis-like apparatus, and rejects masturbation, thereby (symbolically) rejecting the masculine mode of sexuality. This event occurs at the same time as the Oedipal transference. Thus the development of an appropriate sexual identification is accompanied by a rejection of clitoral sexuality, from which emerges a passive-receptive state of vaginal responsiveness.

It is the failure of the girl to accept her sexuality and identify with the mother that may lead the girl into homosexuality. Upon discovery of the male penis, the girl may refuse to accept her deprived state and remain fixated at the level of clitoral excitement, and be compelled to behave as though she were a man. Or, later on, having made an attachment to her father, she may be unable to transfer that love to another man. Unable to give up her father, who of course cannot reciprocate any kind of romantic love, she may revert to her original masculine complex and remain fixated there. In either case the end result is a masculine identification and potential for homosexual development. Choice of a homosexual love object is a result of her fixation at the preoedipal attachment to the mother.

The first empirical approach to the study of lesbianism is the attempt to validate the psychoanalytic position. These studies employ projective techniques, derived from the same theories, which are expected to uncover signs of maternal hostility or hostility against women in general, primitive regressions and fixations, or signs of penis envy and castration anxieties. It is particularly important to note here that the Rorschach technique, typically used in this group of studies, has been criticized for its failure to produce cogent evidence of clinical validity. A subject's response to the cards can be influenced by numerous factors entirely unrelated to the unconscious content of the subject (Zubin, 1954, 1956; Dana, 1970). Insofar as the technique validates the presence of psychoanalytic features, the projective studies produced comparable results.

In their single case study, Fromm and Elonen (1951) found deprecation of all human figures. Similarly, Armon's (1960) sample produced unusual human-animal combinations, whereas Hopkins (1970) found that lesbians deprecated human figures. At the same time, heterosexuals and lesbians in Hopkins's study made an equal number of statements deprecating male figures. Armon and Hopkins both concluded that lesbians experience less gratification in human relationships and have limited emotional reactivity. These same conclusions were, however, drawn from two different response categories and are therefore open to questions of validity. Both authors claim to have found evidence of anxiety and hostility toward items generally considered to represent females or the mother, thus likely indicating a disturbed maternal relationship which may be a contributing factor to the etiology of female homosexuality.

In overall comparison, the lesbians showed no greater degree of psychopathology. There is some evidence to show that lesbian and heterosexual women share some common problems, such as perceiving men as powerful and threatening figures, but that in other areas their conflicts are different. Armon was forced to conclude:

> The failure to find clear-cut differences which are consistent for the majority of the group would suggest that homosexuality is not a clinical entity. On the basis of present indications it would seem unwise to make generalizations about female homosexuals as a group or to assume that homosexuality is associated with gross personality disorders. The absence of dramatic differences between homosexuals and heterosexuals on projective tests should influence the conception that homosexuality is necessarily associated with deep regression and concordant limitations in personality functioning. (p. 309)

It would seem that at least some of Freudian theory is in question since lesbians show no signs of serious oral regression or fixation as the theory would indicate. Apparently there are fewer differences than commonalities between homosexual and heterosexual women.

The Secret Feast by Leonor Fini; reprinted by permission of the artist

There is little from the projective data to suggest that female homosexuality is an identifiable clinical entity.

Psychological Functioning: Results of Personality Assessment Studies

The major premise upon which the belief that lesbian samples will perform differently from heterosexual controls (i.e., show neurotic trends) on paper-and-pencil personality inventories is rooted in the theory that lesbianism is a neurotic defense mechanism, a protection against the preoedipal anxieties reviewed earlier. Frequently used indices are the California Psychological Inventory, the Edwards Personal Preference Schedule, the Eysenck Personality Inventory, the Catell 16 PF, and the Minnesota Multiphasic Personality Inventory (MMPI). The anticipated differences for lesbians are higher mean scores on scales that have a high loading on neurotic symptomatology; or higher mean scores on those that measure a "masculine" orientation, such as dominance, aggression, need to achieve; or, finally, lower mean scores on scales measuring "feminine" qualities, such as nurturance, submission, or conformity. In addition to paper-and-pencil inventories, some studies have relied on clinical interviews and the diagnostic skills and objectivity of the examiners.

Freedman (1968, 1971, 1975a, 1975b) used the Eysenck Personality Inventory, a test specifically directed toward measuring neuroticism and emotional instability, and the Personal Orientation Inventory, a measure of self-actualization, to assess the psychological adjustment of eighty-two lesbian members of the Daughters of Bilitis in comparison with sixty-seven heterosexual controls from an international women's service organization. The majority of lesbians were single and employed, whereas the majority of controls were married

and unemployed outside the home. This selection of subjects is fairly representative of subsequent studies as well and exemplifies the early difficulty in appropriate selection of sample populations for comparison.

Freedman combined the resultant scores on the two inventories to give a rating of psychological adjustment for each subject and found no difference between the ratings of the two groups. On the Personal Orientation Inventory highly significant differences were found between the groups on several individual scales descriptive of qualities possessed by fully functioning or self-actualizing persons, lesbians scoring in a positive direction. They did seem, however, to be more masculinity identified with respect to motivational patterns of work satisfaction, a finding noted in the earliest group of research (Terman & Miles, 1936; Grygier, 1957) and validated in subsequent data (Ohlson & Wilson, 1974; Oberstone & Sukoneck, 1976; Adelman, 1977; Heilbrun & Thompson, 1977).

Freedman concludes that the results of this study suggest that women who engage in homosexual relations are, to a certain extent, different in their psychodynamics from women whose mode of adjustment is heterosexual, but points out that in most instances it is difficult to determine whether these differences are initially part of the core aspects of the lesbian personality, or whether the differences are the result of the lesbian's response to societal pressures that force her to become inner-directed, aware, and sensitive, as well as self-reliant in meeting her physical and economic needs. However, these differences do not detract from the ability of the lesbian to function effectively in society. Even if homosexual "acting out" is a defense mechanism, Freedman has suggested, this possible "acting out" may not be as maladaptive as previously thought. Freedman's finding of no psychopathology in lesbian women has been validated throughout most of the literature; instead, such labels as self-confident (Thompson, McCandless, & Strickland, 1971) and independent (Hopkins, 1969) are suggested. In fact, other researchers have found greater pathology in the heterosexual controls, particularly with regard to scores on scales used to measure neurosis (Wilson & Greene, 1971; Siegelman, 1972). In one comparison of lesbians with heterosexual controls using the MMPI, heterosexual women scored significantly higher on three scales classically indicative of symptoms relative to anxiety and neurosis—Hypochondriasis, Hysteria, and Psychasthenia (Ohlson & Wilson, 1974).

Oberstone and Sukoneck (1976) present a methodologically sound and comprehensive study comparing matched samples of single heterosexual women and single lesbian subjects, hoping to correct for problems noted earlier in selection of married women as controls. Women completed an MMPI and an interview questionnaire, which included questions pertaining to current living patterns, roles and relationships, behavior and friendship patterns, and drinking, drug, and suicidal behavior. MMPI profiles were rated by two independent clinical psychologists, eminent in the field and versed in theory and research on homosexuality.

The lesbian sample scored higher on the MF scale (Masculinity), consistent with previous findings in the literature. With the MF scale removed from the profiles, expert judges were unable to find any lesbian characteristics that would distinguish their profiles, thus suggesting that single women, regardless of sexual orientation, are very much alike.

In this sample, 68 percent of the lesbians reported living with a lover, as compared to 24 percent of the heterosexual women. The only effect this factor may have had on subsequent findings is with regard to reports of greater interpersonal satisfaction by the lesbian group. It does, however, elucidate the difficulties in selecting an appropriate comparison group for supposedly matched samples, and questions the assumption made by the authors that the legal status of marriage is the relevant variable.

Adelman (1977) controls for living status in her comparison using the MMPI on women who were either lesbians or heterosexual, living alone or cohabiting with a lover. She found that single women living alone, regardless of sexual orientation, were the most psychologically homogeneous, possessing the qualities of defensiveness and naivete. Lesbians again scored higher on the Masculinity scale. They also scored higher, within normal limits, on the Schizophrenia scale. With the Harris Lingoes scales applied the elevated scores were the result of subscale items pertaining to interpersonal estrangement. Adelman suggests that the rather secretive life style lived by most lesbians could easily be reflected in this subscale.

The slight support for the presence of pathology in lesbian samples comes from Kenyon (1968a), in his study of British lesbians, and from Saghir et al. (1970), who made psychiatric assessments of their subjects using clinical interviews. Aware of his questionable selection

I have no doubt that lesbianism makes a woman virile and open to any sexual stimulation, and that she is more often than not a more adequate and lively partner in bed than a "normal" woman.

Charlotte Wolff, *Love Between Women*, 1972

---

of many actively bisexual women in the lesbian sample, Kenyon (1968d) reinterpreted his data, using only exclusively hetero- and homosexual subjects as comparison groups, and found no pathology.

Contrary to later findings by Oberstone and Sukoneck (1976), Saghir et al. noted serious problems with excessive alcohol use in the homosexuals, and found also that homosexual women had a higher frequency of dropping out of college. Since entrance into college occurs at the same time as the late adolescent generally explores her homosexuality, it is a time of relatively high conflict and inner turmoil that makes academic success difficult. Although there was a trend toward more psychiatric disorders in the lesbians, the authors were forced to conclude that the majority of those studied were able to achieve, adapt, and be productive citizens. While being a homosexual seems to be compatible with functional and interpersonal productivity, Saghir and Robins suggest that the risk of having a psychiatric disorder or intrapersonal conflict seems to be greater for the lesbian than the single heterosexual.

The implication is that being a lesbian per se is not a problem, but that integration of one's lesbian identity into social and cultural functioning may lead to problems. Lee (1977) and Cass (1979) describe the cognitive maneuvers that are part of the "coming out" process of homosexuals. It entails the recognition of oneself as having a "deviant identity," followed by acts of self-disclosure to significant others, and ongoing resolution of cognitive dissonance that results from the feedback of oth-

ers regarding one's sexual behavior. As a result of the continuing homophobia that characterizes our cultural bias against homosexuality, the lesbian's ability or willingness to disclose her identity is restricted. Jourard (1971) points out that the greater the discrepancy between an aspect of the real behavioral self that is seen as salient to one's character and the representation of that aspect to others, the greater the likelihood of stress and anxiety. Greene (1977), in her unpublished doctoral dissertation, found that, in college women, conflict over one's homosexual feelings, suppression of those feelings, and lack of affirmation from the environment were factors present in those lesbians who displayed the greatest amount of depression in day-to-day recordings of mood changes.

Riddle and Sang (1978) identify the effects of stress overload in the lesbian's daily life. Most social intercourse is weighed with the ongoing decision to disclose or to remain discreet about her sexuality and her personal life. Her most valued relationships are not validated by society; frequently her lover is ignored or denied by family; she is threatened by loss of custody of her children should an angry ex-husband or relative press the issue of her sexuality in a custody hearing. In addition, as a woman who must generally be economically self-sufficient, career barriers that may be annoying to a married woman can become devastating to the lesbian.

Perhaps one of the most trying emotional stresses for lesbian lovers is the taboo against expressing all but the most innocent of affection in public. Women have been traditionally

*To learn to love one's woman-self
has been made to seem both
intolerable and difficult.
To learn to love another woman
in one's self is both, and also
worth it.*

Robin Morgan

conditioned to express sexuality and affection at the same time. Compartmentalizing one set of behaviors as only permissible at home from socially acceptable behaviors is a painful experience. This secretive existence is counterproductive to a healthy individual, let alone to interpersonal functioning. The end product is frequently guilt and anxiety about oneself and one's sexuality.

The degree to which overt expression of lesbianism is related to anxiety was examined by Ferguson and Finkler (1978). They found that the degree to which a woman is involved in lesbianism, as measured by her degree of participation in lesbian behaviors, is unrelated to anxiety. Overt lesbianism, measured by the number and kind of lesbian behaviors expressed publicly or socially, was found to be related to anxiety only with lesbians of lower socioeconomic status. Professionally employed lesbians with social status did not appear to be particularly anxious about themselves, without regard to degree of overt expression. The authors suggest that professional credibility may lend some protection from assault; the lower status lesbian is perhaps subject to greater stress from factors apart from her anxieties about her sexuality.

Although there is conflicting evidence that, as a group, lesbians drink more or frequent bars more often than heterosexuals, historically the gay bar has been a cultural institution and significant as the only meeting ground for developing companionship with other gay people. Some studies, as pointed out by Diamond and Wilsnack (1978), have rated the incidence of alcohol abuse and alcoholism

to 25 to 35 percent of the lesbian population. Alcohol abuse in women has received increasing scientific attention, yet there is only one study at this point that attempts to integrate our knowledge of alcoholism with empirical study of the alcoholic lesbian. Diamond and Wilsnack explore the four major theories of alcoholism as they might explain alcoholism in the lesbian female: The dependency theory predicts that lesbian drinkers will have strong dependency needs and will drink in response to the frustration of those needs, or that drinking will produce an enhanced sense of dependency gratification. The power theory predicts that lesbian drinkers will drink when their sense of personal power is threatened and will experience enhanced feelings of power after drinking. A third approach suggested by sex-role research is that drinking reduces stress related to sex-role conflict and causes self-perceptions and behavior to shift in the direction of the desired self-image. Finally, drinking is thought to occur in response to feelings of low self-esteem and lead to an enhanced self-perception and improved self-image. Results of this study substantiated each of these theories. The authors note that the women reported a high incidence of dependency behaviors, but an even more striking association was found between drinking and power-related behaviors. The changes brought about by drinking were predominantly in the traditional masculine direction, toward greater dominance, assertiveness, and activity. The authors suggest that, in consideration of the research findings that lesbians are independent and self-sufficient, as a group they may be less able to deal

You say I am mysterious

You say I am mysterious.
Let me explain myself:
In a land of oranges
I am faithful to apples

Elsa Gidlow

The Strangers by Leonor Fini; reprinted by permission of the artist

with (or have less opportunity to explore) dependency needs. Thus drinking may offer lesbians a way to overcome dependency needs, or perhaps facilitate aggressive demands for dependency gratification.

Biographical History of the Lesbian

Research that explores family background is guided by an assumption that some relevant element in the family history of the lesbian will distinguish her from nonlesbian control samples. This single set of etiological factors will thus account for the development of homosexuality. Most factors are thought to involve experiences with the parents, which are interpreted with reference to the psychoanalytic concept of the Oedipal conflict. More recently, learning theorists have emphasized the same experiences but interpreted them with an eye on the relative effects of adequate and inadequate heterosexual role models (Bell, 1973).

Interpretation of the data becomes a formidable task. First of all, causal statements cannot be drawn from data obtained in the manner of a post hoc study. Any exploration of biographical data is dependent upon clinical technique and subject to the interpretation, hence the bias, of the interviewer. The validity of the data is further dependent upon the subject's accurate recollection of childhood incidents and emotional responses. Accurate recollection of childhood features may be biased by whatever motivations the lesbian may have to recall only selectively those elements from her biography that will help her accept or reconcile her sexuality. No single dynamic within a family constellation is experienced by each family member in the same way, thus the child's capacity to perceive and cope with the perception may have a more significant impact on development than the actual fact. A further assumption is that the direction of effect is from the parent to child, whereas the child's awareness of her budding lesbianism may cause confusion and anxiety throughout the family structure. Biographical studies fail to acknowledge that the lesbian's attitudes about her upbringing and about her parental relationship may be formulated from the perspective of the adult who, as a lesbian, has had to make many personal inquiries into the meaning of heterosexuality and the nature of sex roles, and who, as an adult, may suffer

---

parental rejection because of her lesbian life style.

With these considerations in mind, some biographical similarities have been found. Bene (1965) concludes that the difference between the relations homosexual and heterosexual women had with their fathers is far greater than the difference between the group's relations with their mothers, and suggests that the unsatisfactory relation between the lesbian and her father is connected to the girl's lesbian development. Her findings are supported by Thompson (1971) who showed that significantly more lesbians than controls had hostile and distant fathers. Gundlach and Riess (1968) found that lesbians were ignored or rejected by their mothers, and fathers withheld warmth and affection. Kenyon (1968b, 1968c), Loney (1973), and Poole (1972) report greater overall family disruption, whereas Saghir and Robins (1973) and Wolff (1971) implicate disrupted mother-daughter bonds. The largest number of studies suggest that the father-daughter bond is more often characterized by a lack of closeness and a degree of hostility that has been generated by a father who has failed to meet the affectional needs of his child. Lynn's (1974) review of the role of the father in the development of the female child's sex-role orientation strongly suggests that if heterosexual role-taking is part of feminine sex-role orientation, the father of the lesbian has played a significant part in the failure of his daughter to adopt a heterosexual orientation.

More recent, however, is evidence indicating that many lesbians report happy childhoods (Hogan, Fox, & Kirchner, 1977). In this survey of 205 lesbians, it was found that these women were generally raised by both parents whose marriages were rated as being composed of a balance of good and bad features, of both happiness and periods of unhappiness. In 60 percent of the cases, the subjects were equally close to both parents; yet 45 percent of the mothers and 30 percent of the fathers were viewed as being rejecting. With statistics such as these, it becomes apparent that even though a considerable percentage report problems within the family, an equal or greater number report a more positive background.

At this juncture the cited studies have examined assumedly well-functioning lesbian samples without prior psychiatric history, or have noted psychiatric incidence without controlling for its effect on other factors considered. There are two additional studies comparing family background features in lesbians with known emotional problems. In the first (Kaye, Berl, Clare, Eleston, Gershwin, Gershwin, Kogan, Torda, & Wilbur, 1967) the lesbian's analyst completed a questionnaire regarding family background. The overall impression of the mother, regardless of the daughter's sexual orientation, is that she poses significant problems to the daughter. The composite of the lesbian's father is a possessive, puritanical individual who manifests inverted Oedipal strivings toward his daughter. The second study, based on comparisons of case records from an outpatient clinic, found excessive family disorganization in both control and lesbian samples (Swanson, Loomis, Lukesh,

Cronin, & Smith, 1972). Although both of these are retrospective clinical studies, the general point is well taken: family pathology is more predictive of psychopathology in general than future lesbianism. This evidence was further substantiated by an exhaustive study by Gundlach and Riess (Riess, 1974). The trend in these data suggests a progression of family disturbance: heterosexuals with no therapy have the least disruption or pathology in the family followed by controls with therapy. Homosexuals with no therapy have a greater number of background disturbances than heterosexuals in therapy, while homosexual women with therapy show the greatest amount of family pathology and disruption. Siegelman (1974) carries the analysis further and identifies lack of parental love, parental rejection, and excessive demands as being related to development of neurosis, while lack of closeness to parents, degree of family security, and parental friction are related to lesbianism, these factors being related to lack of appropriate heterosexual role modeling. In other words, there is no obvious conclusion to be drawn from the data available about the parental factors that may contribute to lesbian development without the issue being clouded with the related variables of the lesbian's psychological health.

Lesbian Sexuality, Sex-Roles, and Relationships

The lesbian's first homosexual arousal is experienced by a large number of women prior to adolescence. Consistent with earlier reports that as many as one-quarter of the women experienced homosexual contact as early as 6 to 10 years (Saghir & Robins, 1973; Hedblom, 1973), Hogan, Fox, and Kirchner (1977) report that 30 percent of their sample experienced lesbian contact before age 12 and another 60 percent between the ages of 13 and 17. Califia (1979) found that the range for the first sexual experience with another woman was from 7 to 40 years, with a mean age of 20. Frequently reported is a long lapse between the first awareness of homosexual arousal and first homosexual contact; and another lapse between the first sexual encounter and entry into the lesbian community (Hedblom, 1973; Schäfer, 1976; Riddle & Morin, 1977; deMonteflores & Schultz, 1978). The lesbian's first sexual encounter is typically an outgrowth of mutual attachment and affection for a close friend. Women avoid labeling themselves as lesbian by emphasizing the affectional component and seeing the first affair as "special." The lesbian must acknowledge that the relationship is indicative of her developing sexual orientation as she emerges with a lesbian identity and enters the lesbian community.

Here we are faced with the recognition that lesbians are socialized as women and that they typically participate in adolescent heterosexual activities. Unlike men who are taught to identify their sexual needs early, women are brought up to articulate their sexual needs at a later age. Most homosexual women can perform heterosexually, do become involved with men before or during their emergence as lesbians, and some marry (Saghir & Robins, 1973; Gundlach & Riess, 1968; Hedblom, 1973; Hogan et al., 1977; Peplau et al., 1978). Thus it is understandable that many lesbians do not emerge with a lesbian identity until early adulthood. As emphasized by Blumstein and Schwartz (1977), we need to be aware that early sexual experiences do not always predict adult sexuality. One's sexuality and choice of sex-object are changeable throughout life so long as one is aware of and receptive to this potential.

There is evidence from the research that the women's movement has had substantial effect on the development of lesbian sexuality. Many of the women studied by Blumstein and Schwartz (1977) felt encouraged by the tenets of the women's movement to examine their feelings toward other women and to learn to be close to them. They reported that their feeling of respect and liking for other women was similar to feelings they had for men for whom they also had erotic feelings. Although some sexual encounters were initiated for political reasons, erotic response to women became primary for some and homosexual attraction became a motivating factor in the development of subsequent relationships.

By and large the typical lesbian appears to be sexually active and satisfied with her sexuality. Three-fourths of the women in Peplau et al.'s (1978) group found sex extremely satisfying. Over 70 percent almost always had orgasm with their current partner; 80 percent reported never feeling guilty about sex. Califia's (1979) respondents mirrored those findings. Only 7 of 286 women had never had an orgasm. The majority of these women reported sexual fantasy, enjoy erotica, include masturbation in their sexual behavior, and feel positive about doing so as a sexual expression. In addition, they report positive feelings about the appearance of their genitals and indicate an overall positive attitude toward their own body and toward their sexuality in general. Within this group 67.5 percent enjoy oral sex and experience orgasm during this act. This is, as the authors point out, the most intimate contact with female genitals and indicates

again the generally positive attitude toward female sexuality.

Less clearly positive and more ambivalent attitudes toward sexuality were expressed by the women in the Hogan et al. (1977) study. They compare their findings to those of Gundlach and Riess (1968) who believe that although lesbians are orgasmic with women, sex is not a major factor in a lesbian relationship, interpersonal factors being more important.

Only recently has research shifted toward exploration of those factors that are relevant to functioning in a lesbian relationship. The available literature on lesbianism suggests two distinct value orientations that may influence lesbian relationships (Peplau, Cochran, Rook, & Padesky, 1978). The first, *dyadic attachment* concerns an emphasis on establishing emotionally close and secure love relationships. Most women are exposed to socialization pressures that encourage strong dyadic attachments. Young women have been taught to value close and permanent relationships based on love and romance, not sex.

The second value orientation, *personal autonomy,* concerns an emphasis on independence and self-actualization, which may lead to a questioning of traditional patterns of love relationships. As we have seen, the psychological research strongly indicates that lesbians develop qualities of independence, self-actualization, and strength. For lesbians, it is suggested that these values are closely tied to feminism which encourages the redefinition of romantic relationships away from traditional models.

How these seemingly dichotomous orientations affect the love relationships of 127 lesbians was studied by Peplau et al. They looked

*All women are lesbians except those who don't know it . . . until women
see in each the possibility of a primal commitment which includes sexual
love they will be denying themselves the love and value they readily
accord to men thus affirming their second class status.*

Jill Johnston, *Lesbian Nation*, 1973

---

at these value orientations within the context of social functioning, being particularly concerned with the impact of feminism on orientation toward love relationships.

How women behave within the relationship is directly related to the relative value placed on attachment or autonomy. Women who emphasize attachment spend more time with the partner, report greater closeness and satisfaction, see the relationship lasting, and are not concerned with needs for personal independence creating difficulties. Women who placed a strong emphasis on autonomy spend less time with the partner, are more likely to place career needs first, have a sexually open relationship, and express worry about having a dependent partner. Regardless of values expressed, most of the women reported a high degree of closeness and satisfaction in their current relationship. A majority reported that both they and their partner shared equally in power. In an unpublished source of information regarding the same group, the authors report that the women in equal-power relationships described their relationships as closer, reported greater satisfaction with both the overall relationship and with their sexual activity. The women in equal-power relationships reported greater liking, that is feelings of affection and respect for their partner, and have more positive predictions for the outcome of their relationship (Caldwell & Peplau, 1979).

Feminism was a significant factor in the lives of many of the women studied. Politically inactive or moderate women were similar in their expression of need for attachment. The most politically radical lesbians scored signif-

icantly higher on personal autonomy. The autonomous women were generally younger, had entered their relationship more recently, and gave less importance to long-term relationships.

The tendency of the bulk of the existing studies on lesbians has been to group all homosexual women without regard to distinctions within the group. An important research finding by Nyberg (1976) directly related to this concern was that homosexual females who do not participate in the gay community are substantially dissimilar from lesbians who are active in the gay community. This difference was shown in the fact that the gay community plays an important role in facilitating sexual gratification for women. Gay men are similar in their sexual aspirations and fulfillment regardless of community membership; gay women in the community are more like both groups of men; nonmember lesbians were markedly different from any of the three groups. One of the significant realizations to emerge from this reiterates the potential impact of social/political activism on subsequent attitudes and behaviors.

Further evidence for the interaction effects of the lesbian community on subsequent functioning comes from Furgeri (1977). She compared lesbian couples in which at least one partner was over forty or under thirty years. She found that younger couples had met in feminist activities; older couples in social activities. The younger women were more open and relaxed while the older lesbians expressed more tension and some jealousy over the greater freedom and comfort experienced by younger lesbians. The feminist movement

Because the Women's Movement is a plot of women who are lesbians— and a plot of women who are virgins, heterosexuals, celibates, and bisexuals. And we conspirators are all unlearning the absurd prefixes to the word "sexual" and beginning to discover, create, define ourselves as women.

Robin Morgan, Ms. (Sept. 1975)

played a significant role in the lives of these women. The directions characterized by the women was from an expression of lesbianism to feminist involvement, or for some from feminism to lesbian involvement.

Very little is known about the elements that contribute to a lasting and happy lesbian marriage. Existing research points toward the fact that the ordering of priorities that lead to marital satisfaction in general is likely to be found in lesbian relationships, the priorities being the importance of personal development, companionship, and affection (Ramsay, Latham, & Lindquist, 1978), as well as ability to communicate and similarity of interests (Cochran, 1978). Most couples meet in social settings rather than sexual ones, see monogamous relationships as desirable, and maintain fidelity in their relationships. Individuals carry on a social life that includes the partner and those who are involved in gay or feminist organizations tend to include the lover in these activities (Tuller, 1978; Cotton, 1975; Schäfer, 1977).

Basing her research on heterosexual studies that showed that whereas each sex tends to have the same priorities in selection of a permanent "ideal mate," each sex manifests considerable distortion of the perception of the priorities of both opposite and same-sex peers, Laner (1977) explored the permanent partner priorities of a group of heterosexual and homosexual men and women. She asked each group to rank six characteristics (honesty, affection, intelligence, looks, money, and sense of humor) as to their relative importance in selection of a mate, and to rate them in terms of priority for each other group. She found that

homosexuals, like heterosexuals, tend to respond to their potential partner according to what each thinks the other wants in a mate, thus facing the same set of adjustment problems as anyone else. Laner suggests further that value consensus and perceptual accuracy of one another's priorities are perhaps more important in homosexual relations because of the greater tendency of gay couples to function in a shared relationship. Heterosexuals who function in a very traditional manner, on the other hand, have a greater degree of parallel interaction, with each partner living predominantly in his or her own social structure, thus creating less difficulty when value consensus and personality fit are more discrepant. Within lesbian and male gay relationships as well, the greatest report of marital satisfaction appears to come from those couples who have flexible and low sex-role differentiated relationships (Pendergrass, 1975; Ramsay, Latham, & Lindquist, 1978; Cardell, Finn, & Marecek, 1979).

Psychological androgyny, low sex-role differentiation, in lesbians is a feature that appears with increasing frequency throughout the literature. On two popularly used indices of masculinity and femininity, the Adjective Check List and the Bem Sex Role Inventory (BSRI), lesbians tend to view themselves as androgynous (Clingman & Fowler, 1976; Van Cleave, 1978) or as either masculine or androgynous (Heilbrun & Thompson, 1977). There is recent evidence, however, to indicate that one's sex-role identity on the BSRI is not necessarily predictive of role-typed behavior in lesbian couples (Cardell, Finn, & Marecek, 1979). In other words, the partner with the most feminine sex-role identity as measured on the inventory may be just as likely to change the oil in the car or initiate sex, stereotypically male behaviors.

Among lesbian couples studied, continuing evidence arises to substantiate the growing trend toward reduction in role stereotyping in couple relationships (Oberstone & Sukoneck, 1976; Furgeri, 1977; Hogan et al., 1977; Sang, 1977; Tuller, 1978). Role playing among lesbians means that each partner assumes either a traditionally understood masculine or feminine role. Role dichotomization is one of the most popularly held characterizations of gay couples as well as being a salient feature in the identity formation and functioning of many lesbians. The importance of role playing, particularly prior to the women's movement, was that it provided some recognizable pattern of social interaction for the lesbian who otherwise had no role model. Role playing set rules for the couple relationship, organized the division of labor, and helped stabilize the relationship. For many women who rejected the limited roles of women, circa 1950, playing "butch" was an opportunity to express less traditional values and behaviors. Androgyny was not a recognizable option.

Basing her research on the growing belief in androgyny as a life style in the lesbian community, Laner (1978) studied the content of "personals" advertisements in a lesbian periodical to see whether there would be an underrepresentation of "butch/feminine" claims or desires in the lesbian ads. One of the most striking findings was that lesbians stressed occupational, educational, and intelligence characteristics, whereas heterosexuals advertising in a singles publication mentioned personal appearance characteristics. A tally of preferred sex-role statements found in the advertisements revealed that 91 percent of the lesbians made no mention of preferred sex role, and an additional 7 percent made specific mention that stereotyped roles were unwanted in the prospective relationship. At least among lesbians who advertise for a partner, those findings are overwhelmingly supportive of the notion that gay women are moving toward greater sex-role homogeneity.

The implications of androgyny as a sex-role position and the multiple influences of feminism and the gay community on the lesbian relationship are issues of overwhelming importance. Laner speculates that one result of the changes, should they continue in the present direction, will be to reduce the stability and permanence of lesbian relationships which, according to the almost classic work of Simon and Gagnon (1967), has characterized them in the past. The undercurrent in the literature implicates the movement toward radical feminism/lesbianism with a concurrent movement toward acceptance of the view that lesbian sexuality has an active and demanding nature, greater sexual expressiveness, greater emphasis on autonomy, and resultant lessening in the importance of permanent and stable relationships.

A final consideration with regard to sexuality and forming relationships is the effect of aging on the lesbian's sexuality and her pursuit of sexual and social relationships. Virtually nothing is known about lesbian aging. Since lesbians allegedly place greater importance on interpersonal qualities and less on physical characteristics, will they be less affected by the aging process? Some preliminary work (Laner, 1979) suggests that the aging lesbian appears to be less preoccupied with age than heterosexual peers, and likely to be very

A History of Lesbianism

How they came into the world,
the women-loving-women
came in three by three
and four by four
the women-loving-women
came in ten by ten
and ten by ten again
until there were more
than you could count

   they took care of each other
   the best they knew how
   and of each other's children,
   if they had any.

How they lived in the world,
the women-loving-women
learned as much as they were allowed
and walked and wore their clothes
the way they liked
whenever they could. They did whatever
they knew to be happy or free
and worked and worked and worked.
The women-loving-women
In America were called dykes
and some liked it
and some did not.

they made love to each other
the best they knew how
and for the best reasons.

How they went out of the world,
the women-loving-women
went out one by one
having withstood greater and lesser
trials, and much hatred
from other people, they went out
one by one, each having tried
in her own way to overthrow
the rule of men over women,
they tried it one by one
and hundred by hundred,
until each came in her own way
to the end of her life
and died.

   The subject of lesbianism
   is very ordinary; it's the question
   of male domination that makes everybody
   angry.

Judy Grahn

involved in social/political and service activities as a way to continue to shape meaning in her mature life (Minnigerode & Adelman, 1978).

Parenting: Lesbian Mothers and Their Children

Of the approximately 20 million homosexuals in the United States, it is estimated that there exist between 1.5 million (Hunter & Polikoff, 1976) and 3.3 million (Martin, 1978) lesbian mothers. When the lesbian mother "comes out" or is discovered, she faces the threat of losing custody of her children. During the past ten years many of these mothers have been fighting for the right to maintain custody of their children. A contested lesbian-mother-child custody case runs an average of two to three years and costs an estimated five to ten thousand dollars (Thetford, 1978). Although the mother's chance of being granted custody is increasing, custody is often made conditional upon a significant alteration of the

Two Women Gossiping. Reproduced by Courtesy of the Trustees of the British Museum

mother's life style. The mother is not allowed to live with her partner, to participate in the gay rights movement, or to associate with other known lesbians (Hunter & Polikoff, 1976). Apparently the court assumes that these restrictions will circumvent the supposed dangers to children being raised by a lesbian parent. The effect of these decisions on the psychological well-being of the lesbian mother is not known but is currently being explored (Rand, 1979).

Green (1978) has published some early findings on the sexual identity of children raised by homosexual or transsexual parents. The finding of appropriate gender identity in all but one of thirty-seven children defies psychoanalytic thinking and social learning theory, which predict that a transsexual or homosexual parent should have a marked effect on the development of a child's sexual identity. These theories, however, deny the impact of cultural expectations, the effect of peers, and the effect of the media on a child's development of sexual identity, sex role, and sex-object choice.

A very recent study by Lewin and Lyons (1979) concentrates on the lesbian mother, the organization of family life, and the social concomitants of sexual orientation, with the emphasis being upon the entire social system rather than on the psychological status of the mother. Forty-three lesbian and thirty-seven heterosexual mothers, formerly married, with children ranging from one to twenty years, were given lengthy interviews focusing primarily on the adaptive strategies pursued by the mother and the influence of either sexual orientation on the resources available to mothers and the choices they made with respect to the utilization of their resources. The researchers report a wide range of overall similarities between lesbian and heterosexual mothers' adaptations to single parenthood and family headship. Specific findings include both mothers' reliance upon family support in dealing with issues of child care, financial help with economic problems, and emotional support. Mothers are important sources of emotional support; kinship ties are expressed by the frequency of holidays spent together.

Both groups of mothers had an interest in facilitating the child's relationship with the former husband. Lesbian mothers are more likely to rely upon ex-husbands to provide a male role model, apparently because the lesbian has fewer male resources to draw upon. Although most of the women see themselves as having initiated the dissolution of their

Sappho's Reply

My voice rings down through thousands of
*   years*
To coil around your body and give you
*   strength,*
You who have wept in direct sunlight,
Who have hungered in invisible chains,
Tremble to the cadence of my legacy:
An army of lovers shall not fail.

Rita Mae Brown

marriage and most were generally positive about the subsequent effects of having done so, being a single mother is a less comfortable experience. Hetero- and homosexual mothers experience a sense of isolation and pressure in bearing full responsibility for their children and maintenance of a household. Sometimes these responsibilities are shared by a lover; some lovers refuse to take a full parental responsibility. Lesbian mothers, unlike heterosexuals, express greater feelings of vulnerability to the hostility of outsiders who might disapprove of the lesbianism, and are likely to be "discreet" in order to avoid unpleasant consequences for themselves or for their children.

Lewin and Lyons conclude that motherhood itself, single motherhood, is the basic structure within which lesbian and heterosexual mothers organize their lives, and determines the fundamental limits within which other areas of activity must be confined. Given the preponderance of evidence presented throughout this article that there are far more similarities than differences between lesbians and heterosexual women, these findings are of no surprise. At the same time, the important application of studies such as these is in the courts, where it must be emphasized that sexual ori-

entation is not predictive of parenting capability. Further studies are yet to be published on the development of children raised by lesbians.

Conclusion

The growth of serious research on this aspect of female sexuality is characterized by a highly identifiable progression from the individual case study, focusing on the internal forces that shape pathological deviance, to research that all but ignores the internal process of the individual, focusing on the social and cultural influences that shape the behavioral correlates of lesbian sexuality. This shift in the research is not accidental; it is highly reflective of the growing awareness that the lesbian is most typically a healthy individual who shapes and is shaped by her functioning in the heterosexual macrocosm and the homosexual microcosm.

The extensive comparisons of lesbian subjects with heterosexual women failed to identify any personality characteristics in the lesbian indicative of psychopathology. The type of research tool used, however, did produce some difference in results. The projective studies, though unable to substantiate much of psychoanalytic theory, identified some evidence of anxiety or hostility directed toward the mother, consistent with the theory's position on female homosexuality. Studies using inventories that measure current functioning painted a surprising picture of the lesbian as being fully functioning and, in some cases, less neurotic than her heterosexual counterpart. Hopkins's results using both projective data (1970) and inventory data (1969) elucidate this difference. Diagnostic interviews, biographical studies, and clinical studies also succeed in identifying potential problem areas and some consistent background features suggestive of etiology. This may mean that if one is determined to find problems, they can be found; or that the subtleties of pathology are evident only to the trained eye of the clinician.

If there is one characteristic that comes through from personality studies, it is the label "masculine." Many lesbians have developed personality traits that facilitate their ability to function independently, these characteristics being no different from those possessed by many self-actualizing individuals. The cultural norm defines these characteristics as masculine. At one time the "butch" role was the only viable alternative to suffocating femininity. The feminist movement has facilitated a new lesbian consciousness that presents sex-role androgyny as an alternative, giving new meaning to an old label, or better yet, changing it entirely.

In historical perspective, the lesbian has been credited for her ability to form lasting and meaningful sexual relationships. Like most women, she learned to value and work for stable monogamous relationships, at times mirroring the heterosexual role model for lack of anything different or better to try. Feminist and radical lesbian politics have had an impact on the lesbian relationship by presenting various life style alternatives, with the potential to change, for better or worse, this feature of lesbian bonding. Presently, however, "married" lesbians who have formed and maintained stable relationships are in many ways no different from other married couples, heterosexual or gay. Where difference occurs is in the fact that most lesbian couples function in relationships based on egalitarian values and nondifferentiated sex-role behaviors.

All the findings presented in this paper suggest that sexual orientation alone may have limited effects on almost every aspect of daily living. The data suggest that homosexual and heterosexual women are psychologically similar in spite of divergences in life style, and that the demands of the ordinary daily routine, within the current social and cultural framework, work to shape similarities in personality and social functioning.

Nancy Felipe Russo

Overview: Sex Roles, Fertility and the Motherhood Mandate

Abstract: The centrality of motherhood to woman's identity is characterized as a mandate that is built into our social institutions as well as our psyches. This mandate is reflected in the assumptions of the models and methods of research in the psychology of women. An examination of the impact of the motherhood mandate is encouraged and complexities that must be reflected in research models and methods are underscored. These complexities include the need for (1) appreciation of the context of the phenomena studied; (2) interactionist approaches, including multivariate models and methods; and (3) a multidisciplinary perspective, including biological, psychological, social and structural levels of analysis. Two facets of the changing context having profound implications for the meaning of motherhood are reproductive freedom and voluntary childlessness.

The implications of the centrality of motherhood to woman's identity are not sufficiently appreciated by researchers in the field of the psychology of women. Motherhood is on a qualitatively different plane than other sex roles for women in our society. It is a mandate that pervades our social institutions as well as our psyches (Bernard, 1974).

Put simply, the mandate of motherhood in its traditional form requires that a woman have at least two children (historically as many as possible, and preferably sons), and raise them "well." She can, however, become educated, work, and be active in public life, as long as she first fulfills this obligation. The kicker in this scheme is the definition of

"well." A "good" mother must be physically present to serve her infant's every need. As the child enters school, a mother may pursue other activities—but only those permitting her to be instantly available should her child "need" her (Russo, 1976).

Incompatibility with other roles is thus built into society's definition of good motherhood. No matter how well a woman manages multiple roles (for example, mother and worker), she is in violation of the motherhood mandate and may face personal feelings of guilt and ostracism by family members, peers, and others. Both sexes must deal with society's reproductive ethic. But fatherhood has demanded that men participate in multiple roles to provide for their families. Only recently has conflict between filling a provider role and serving the needs of one's children emerged as an issue for men (Fein, 1978).

As early as 1916, Leta Hollingworth analyzed "social devices for impelling women to bear children," and provided examples of how this pronatalist bias in research on women contributed to such devices (Hollingworth, 1916). This bias continues to be reflected in our research. My purpose here is to encourage an examination of the motherhood mandate in the United States, and to suggest some of the complexities that must be reflected in our theories and methods if understanding of the interrelationships among sex role and fertility variables is to advance. Appreciation of such complexities requires recognition of the im-

*. . . Biological possibility and desire are not the same as biological need.
Women have child-bearing equipment. For them to choose not to use the
equipment is no more blocking what is instinctive than it is for a man
who, muscles or no, chooses not to be a weightlifter.*

Betty Rollin, *Look* (May 1971)

Pregnant Woman by Alice Neel. Permission of artist

plications of the changing context for the
meaning of motherhood.

The Context

Kearney (1979) reminds us that childbearing
takes place in the context of a social structure
that influences sex roles as well as fertility.
The motherhood mandate continues to be
used to justify institutional discrimination that
denies females equal access to education, employment, insurance benefits, and credit
(Russo, 1976). Ironically, reform efforts on behalf of women can work to women's detriment
in the longer run if they increase institutionalized support for motherhood. To understand the processes involved we must examine
the context that subtly and not-so-subtly influences the nature and meaning of childbearing
in our society.

The women's movement has brought tremendous changes in the social structure, in

sex role relationships, and in woman's concept
of self. Three related facets of the changing
context of motherhood that have profound implications for interrelationships among sex
role and fertility variables and thus for our
theories and methods are: (1) workforce participation of mothers; (2) reproductive freedom
(that is, the ability to control one's reproduction without coercion); and (3) voluntary childlessness.

Workforce Participation of Mothers

In 1947, less than one-third of all women were
in the workforce; in 1978, nearly half of all
women were in the workforce. This dramatic
increase in labor force participation is due almost entirely to change in the behavior of
married women. In 1940, 15 percent of married women were employed outside the home;
in 1978, nearly half of all married women are
so employed. The relationship of women's labor force participation to childbearing and
childrearing is changing in complex ways.
Forty-one percent of all mothers with children
under the age of six are in the labor force.
Nearly half of all mothers with children under
eighteen are in the labor force (Odendahl &
Smith, 1978).

The papers of Beckman (1979) and of Thornton and Camburn (1979) take independent
looks at the multivariate relationships among
sex role and fertility variables for women who
seek to combine home and work roles. These
studies illustrate some of the conceptual and
methodological sophistication that will be
needed to investigate causality of such relationships. At the same time, they also illustrate
the limitations of multivariate techniques that

Motherhood affords an instant identity. First through wifehood, you are somebody's wife; then you are somebody's mother. Both give not only identity and activity, but status and stardom of a kind.

Betty Rollin, *Look* (May 1971)

rely on assumptions of linearity and unidirectional relationships.

Beckman makes an important conceptual distinction between attitudes and behavior in her study and underscores the need to separate analyses by ethnic group. The motherhood mandate reflects the norms of the majority group in our society, but the context of motherhood is very different for minority women.

Beckman reports a number of significant complex relationships between sex role behaviors within and outside of the family, but the low correlations lead her to conclude that the interrelationships are subtle. Such subtlety demands refinement in our definitions of sex role. As Hare-Mustin (1979) notes, changing role requirements of motherhood per se are only recently receiving systematic study. The development of procedures to study motherhood rather than mothers is an important direction for research.

Thornton and Camburn point to the power of perceived role definitions on childbearing variables. They report that what they describe as "home orientation" plays a "central and vital role in defining women's status and place." A closer look at the nature of home orientation reveals that it basically involves beliefs about the impact of a mother's working on her children's development, her relationship with her children, her happiness if she devotes herself to her children, and her guilt if she does not. An explicit conceptual distinction between motherhood role expectations and other family-related responsibilities is needed in further research. The quantification of the direct, indirect, and reciprocal mechanisms by which be-

liefs about motherhood relate to women's exercise of options are a major challenge to our methods.

Allison's study of role conflict of women in infertile couples provides yet another dimension to this challenge (1979). Her work is a cogent reminder that understanding interrelationships among sex role and fertility variables will require more than complex multivariate statistical approaches. Conceptual models that integrate biological, psychological, social, and structural levels of analyses must be developed.

Future research can build on the work of Beckman, Thornton and Camburn, and Allison by making conceptual distinctions between perceived prescriptions and proscriptions of the motherhood role, and the perceived incompatibility of these prescriptions and proscriptions with those of other sex roles (for example, that of wife) for women of different ethnic groups. Such distinctions might explain some of the unexpected correlations between traditional attitudes and behaviors and fertility variables found in these studies. Correlations between sex role and fertility variables will continue to be problematical, however, as long as women are not able to attain reproductive freedom.

Reproductive Freedom

Kearney (1979) describes how changes in laws, policies, and education that enable women to control their reproduction continue to meet intense resistance and controversy. Nonetheless, in 1976, 1 in 12 marital births was unwanted by the parents at the time of conception, compared with 1 in 5 just a decade ago (Planned

Notes from the Delivery Room

Strapped down,
victim in an old comic book,
I have been here before,
this place where pain winces
off the walls
like too bright light.
Bear down a doctor says,
foreman to sweating laborer,
but this work, this forcing
of one life from another
is something that I signed for
at a moment when I would have signed
  anything.
Babies should grow in fields;
common as beets or turnips
they should be picked and held
root end up, soil spilling
from between their toes—
and how much easier it would be later,
returning them to earth.
Bear up . . . bear down . . . the audience
grows restive, and I'm a new magician
who can't produce the rabbit
from my swollen hat.
She's crowning, someone says,
but there is no one royal here,
just me, quite barefoot,
greeting my barefoot child.

Linda Pastan

Parenthood, 1977). Despite such progress, 250,-000 to 300,000 married women in the U.S. each year still have unwanted births. A disproportionate number are low and marginal income women (Munson, 1977). The subsequent physical, psychological, social, and economic consequences continue to provide major barriers to the improvement of women's status, impeding women's ability to take advantage of other reforms.

Kearney points out that abortion's role in controlling reproduction is greater for vulnerable groups. In 1975, three-quarters of the one million women having abortions were unmarried; one-third of them were teenagers. The abortion rate for nonwhite women is at least double that for whites in every age category (Tietze, 1977).

Denying public funds for abortion has its most direct impact on the reproductive freedom of poor mothers, since they are least able to afford abortions otherwise. The average abortion cost is $280—an expensive item considering the average monthly welfare payment for a family is $238 (Lincoln, Doring-Bradley, Lindheim, & Cotterill, 1977).

Unwanted childbearing has been linked with poverty, child abuse and filicide, juvenile delinquency, marital disruption, and a variety of other psychological, social, and economic ills (Terhune, 1974). Evidence suggests that individuals may overestimate their ability to adapt to a new infant (especially the first-born), but the reverse does not appear to be true. Data from the methodologically sophisticated Hawaii Pregnancy, Birth Control, and Abortion Study suggest that women decide to terminate their pregnancies based on an evaluation of objective factors related to each woman's capacity to care for the child (Steinhoff, Smith, & Diamond, 1972).

The methodological problems of studies of unwanted pregnancy and childbearing are a major source of frustration to researchers. However, it does appear that if a woman requests an abortion, to deny her the service means to force her to bear an offspring that is at higher risk for a variety of physical, psychological, social, and economic problems (Forss-man & Thuwe, 1966; Dytrych, Matejcek, Schuller, David, & Friedman, 1975). In contrast, the few methodologically sound studies of legalized abortion "on request" suggest that the psychological implications of such abortions are mostly benign (Shusterman, 1976).

Research on controversies surrounding abortion and unwanted childbearing reflects the current context of imperfect contraception. Advances in reproductive technology might eliminate these controversies. However, Fidell, Hoffman, and Keith-Spiegel's study (1979) of the implications of the ability to select the sex of one's offspring reminds us that such advances have other social implications. It also underscores the need for feminist evaluation of technological advances in reproductive control.

Those authors conclude that the use of sex-choice techniques given current preferences for male first-borns may, on balance, be detrimental to the status of women by strengthening the sex-typing of both sexes. They also report that respondents who approve of the goals of the women's movement are more likely than those who disapprove of those goals to desire a female first-born child. Since women in that group were also more likely to say they did not want any children, the authors suggest that one strategy for minimizing the detrimental impact of sex-choice techniques might be to foster pronatalism among feminists.

This suggestion raises a number of issues, the most obvious being the potential conflict between feminist and population concerns. More important here is the illustration of the potential of the motherhood mandate to influence feminist thought. Women have tradi-

Elsie by Karen Breschi. Permission given by the artist

tionally been encouraged to overlook their personal needs and circumstances and have children for the good of a variety of people, including "only" children, grandparents, and husbands. Adding "other women" to this list does not recognize the pervasive and devastating consequences of the motherhood mandate for women. It also does not recognize the im-

... I try to distinguish between two meanings of motherhood, one superimposed on the other: the potential relationship of any woman to her powers of reproduction and to children; and the institution, which aims at ensuring that that potential—and all women—shall remain under male control. This institution has been a keystone of the most diverse social and political systems. It has withheld over one-half the human species from the decisions affecting their lives; it exonerates men from fatherhood in any authentic sense; it creates the dangerous schism between "private" and "public" life; it calcifies human choices and potentialities. In the most fundamental and bewildering of contradictions, it has alienated women from our bodies by incarcerating us in them.

Adrienne Rich, *Of Woman Born*, 1976

---

plications of the ability to opt for voluntary childlessness for the definition of motherhood.

Voluntary Childlessness

Houseknecht's research (1979) documents the need to look at the interactions between personality characteristics and environmental supports for the childless decision over the life cycle. The voluntary childless decision is a phenomenon deserving of study in its own right. But, as Kearney (1979) notes, the apparent increase in voluntary childlessness since 1960 and the organization of an advocacy group for child-free couples, the National Organization for Non-Parents (NON), signal profound changes for the meaning of motherhood that deserve attention as well.

There is overwhelming scientific evidence that we value what we perceive ourselves to have freely chosen (Worchel & Cooper, 1976). Insofar as voluntary childlessness is considered a valued option for women in our society, motherhood itself becomes an option rather than a mandate. Perceiving oneself to have chosen a motherhood *option* should result in an increased commitment to that choice. Investigating the impact of that commitment must be included in priorities for research on parenting and other family relationships, particularly research on the mother-child relationship.

The implications of a context having voluntary childlessness as a legitimate option go beyond an impact on the family unit. Since the motherhood mandate pervades our institutions (for example, insurance and tax systems), the widespread assumption that women can and will legitimately opt for voluntary childlessness would force a reexamination and restructuring of those institutions. Some of this examination is beginning to occur (Peck & Senderowitz, 1974). For example, NON has a project that is aimed toward sensitizing publishers, educators, and teachers to pronatalist bias in textbooks.

In discussing the impact of the ability to choose to remain childless, the actuality of that ability for women must be considered. We have seen that the ability to control reproduction is not equally accessible to all women in our society. Advances in contraceptive technology have made it all too easy to assume reproductive freedom as a given, with research on voluntary childlessness proceeding from that premise. The issues of voluntary childlessness thus become those of mature middle class women who have sufficient experience and resources to control their fertility. The choice is denied to other segments of our society, particularly the poor and the young. This not only limits the ability of women in those groups to choose the option of childlessness—

Despite the numerous ways in which men have attempted to mimic or colonize the "gloriousness" of biological maternity (and consequently, to devalue or punish it in women), men, particularly in Christian culture, are not very "maternal" to their children, their wives, their mistressess, their prostitutes, their secretaries, their housekeepers—or to each other.

Phyllis Chesler, *Women and Madness*, 1972

it means that they are denied the potential benefit of *choosing* to have children. Motherhood in this context has a very different meaning for those groups.

Houseknecht's research on voluntary childlessness points to the importance of autonomy and achievement orientation in women exercising that option. Whether or not some women arrived at the decision to remain childless through a series of postponements after marriage or via an early decision before marriage, they were equally characterized by these attributes. Thornton and Camburn (1979) report an association between a women's orientation toward planning and her unwanted childbearing. These very different studies illustrate how the ability to control one's reproduction is not derived solely from technological means.

Freeman's (1977) research on abortion dramatically illustrates the effects of not teaching women to plan and value their lives for their ability to control their reproduction. Most women in her sample were faced with unwanted pregnancies because they had not seen themselves as instrumental in planning pregnancy. As Freeman describes it "pregnancy happened to them.... Their experiences had trained them to be receptive, to value themselves in terms of other's responses more than through their own contributions.

Tod und Frau by Kathe Kollwitz; by permission of Prof. Dr. Arne A. Kollwitz, Berlin, and Kornfeld und Klipstein, Bern

They had no history of feeling what they did made any difference, that their own actions and decisions had value to themselves and others" (Freeman, p. 510).

Unwanted pregnancy can be considered a direct reflection of women's disadvantaged status. Little girls are socialized to have low self-esteem, high need for approval, and aspirations limited to motherhood. We have taught little boys to denigrate little girls, to separate sex from affection and to exploit the opposite sex through "conquest" (Russo & Brackbill, 1973; Scales, 1977). These are not characteristics that provide a foundation for responsible sexual behavior on the part of either sex, young or old.

Reproductive freedom also comes from the ability to say "no" to males who would ask that a woman engage in unprotected intercourse counter to her self-interest; it involves having goals and aspirations that make planning one's life (and avoiding unwanted pregnancy) meaningful; it involves developing a sense of competence and independence in women so that if they do develop an intimate relationship they will have the knowledge and ability to minimize the risk of unwanted pregnancy.

Relationships between sex roles and fertility variables are thus indeed complex, even when one limits the analyses to the U.S. The articles discussed here only highlight some of the dimensions of this complexity. They document the importance of developing models that integrate biological, psychological, social, and structural variables. They demonstrate the importance of context, the changing character of which demands special attention to ethnic group differences as well as cohort and time-of-measurement effects. They show the need to take an interactionist perspective that recognizes continuous socialization throughout the life cycle.

Toward An Interactionist Perspective

The development of an interactionist perspective in our research requires more than the computer technology and the statistical techniques to analyze multivariate interaction effects. It requires the development of theoretical formulations that explicate mechanisms of interaction and the research designs to test them. Such formulations will require going beyond the question of how *much* variance in behavior our studies can explain to the question of *how* the variance is produced. To advance our knowledge we thus must seek to study *metavariance* of behavior, that is, to study the variance of the variance (Russo, 1972, 1979). Switching the perspective of our models from means to variances will hopefully lay the foundation for a focus on process. Achieving such a focus is perhaps the greatest challenge facing researchers who seek to understand the psychology of women.

Rosalind C. Barnett and Grace K. Baruch

Women in the Middle Years: A Critique of Research and Theory

Research and theory on women in the middle years reflect assumptions and biases that limit our understanding and impair our ability to resolve conflicting findings about women's well-being. Such theorists as Erikson and Levinson focus on chronological age and assume an inappropriate sequence of stages and events. In most research, the centrality of women's reproductive role is assumed and the importance of their work role pattern is ignored. Thus menopause and the "empty nest" receive disproportionate attention. Too little attention is given to stages of the family life cycle and the conditions and status of work. Two active research areas that appear promising for understanding adult women are also discussed: locus of control and attributions; and social networks and support systems.

Although it is now widely acknowledged that the middle years, for both men and women, are a time of development and change rather than of stability and decline, relatively little is known about these years. Bernice Neugarten (1968) commented on the state of knowledge about human adulthood: "Not only is there a paucity of data, but more important, we are without a useful theory." Brim and Abeles (1975) described the middle years as a "largely unexplored phase of the human life cycle." Particularly with respect to women, theoretical work is in its infancy and empirical findings tend to be scattered and noncumulative.

Yet, the need for knowledge about the middle years in women is increasingly urgent. A longer life span and overpopulation, combined with women's increasing educational attainments and labor force participation, have made obsolete much of previous research and theory. Moreover, there is evidence, although not completely consistent, that women are especially vulnerable to distress and dissatisfaction.

In this paper we review selected theories and research in order to examine such impediments to understanding as assumptions and biases, limitations and stereotypes. We then briefly point to conceptual areas that promise to be fruitful for the study of adult women.

An illustration of certain weaknesses of current theory and research can be found in the literature concerning the mental health and well-being of women in the middle years.

A Case of Conflicting Evidence: The Well-Being of Adult Women

In their study of the perceived quality of life, Campbell, Converse, and Rodgers (1976) find no evidence that women's lives are any less rewarding or satisfying than are men's. Yet findings from a variety of research studies indicate a significantly higher level of distress among women. Lowenthal, Thurnher, and Chiriboga (1975), in their study of four groups of men and women facing life transitions (high school seniors, newlyweds, "empty nest" (middle-aged), and preretirement couples) found

With what a price we pay for the glory of motherhood. . . .

Isadora Duncan, *My Life*, 1927

The Family by Marisol Escobar (1962). Painted wood and other materials, in three sections, 6'10⅝" × 65½". Collection, The Museum of Modern Art, New York, Advisory Committee Fund

that the middle-aged women were the most distressed group. They had poorer self-concepts, were the lowest in life satisfaction, most pessimistic, highest in existential despair, and most negative toward their spouses. Other studies, for example, that of Gurin, Veroff, and Feld (1960), indicate that women have poorer self-concepts, feel more inadequate as parents

and more dissatisfied with their marriages, and report more problems and psychiatric symptomatology than do men, although they do not differ from men in global ratings of general happiness.

Recent careful reanalyses of mental health data suggest that if one considers all forms of mental illness, including, for example, such often ignored categories as alcoholic disorders, women are no more disturbed than men. However, compared to men they do suffer more from such specific disabilities as depression, neurotic disorders, and functional psychoses. Several researchers report that this finding is not due to artifacts of reporting nor to women's greater willingness to admit symptoms, nor to biases of mental health professionals (Radloff, 1975; Guttentag, Salasin, Legge, & Bray; Weissman & Klerman).

We shall now analyze theoretical and empirical approaches that may have impeded efforts to resolve these conflicting findings.

Theoretical Considerations

In two major theories of adult development, those of Erikson (1959) and Levinson et al. (1976), adult development is seen as proceeding linearly through a series of stages, each of which poses certain tasks for resolution. For Erikson, for example, the task of identity formation is associated with late adolescence and early adulthood. However, for women, especially those who have children, issues of personal identity often do not become critical until child-rearing responsibilities diminish in the late thirties and forties. Recognizing problems of fit between his theory and the experiences of many women, Erikson suggests that the resolution of their identity crises occurs after choice of a mate. The implications of Erikson's theoretical position are ominous. Women, but not men, require a spouse before they can complete as crucial a task as identity formation; not marrying implies never establishing one's identity.

Similar problems of fit occur with respect to Levinson's theory, which was developed through intensive interviewing of a small sample of men. He views one's twenties as a time for entering marriage and the world of work; and one's thirties as a time for establishing oneself in these arenas. Toward forty there is reconsideration of one's commitments and often attempts to free oneself from a previously central mentor, the famous BOOM phenomenon—becoming one's own man. It is hard to know how to think of women within this theory—a woman may not enter the world of work until her late thirties, she seldom has had a mentor, and even women with life-long career commitments rarely are in a position to reassess their commitment pattern by age forty.

Both Erikson's and Levinson's models reflect male experience. Perhaps for this reason, they focus on chronological age as a key variable and they assume a continuous, uninterrupted

---

**She Doesn't Want to Bring
the Tides in Any More**

*Every time she tugs the sun across the sky
some old wound
comes apart at the seams.
But housekeeping by the clock means keeping
every star prompt. She puffs along,
blowing a strand of graying hair out of her
   eyes,
but she gets each planet to its place
on time. She bruises a hip
moving all this furniture around.*

*She steers clouds, fans winds, and slices
or mends the moon, according to the day.
Worst of all is bringing in the tides.
One hand brings them in on one side,
the other pushes them away;*
                              *while her knee
keeps the tipped earth spinning on its axis
precariously.*

*No wonder she went away and sat down on a
   sand dune,
wishing she were grass.
If she sits still long enough,
rain will come to her.*

                              Ruth Whitman

---

series of events such as marriage and occupational commitment. (Loevinger's stage theory of ego development [1966] is not based on chronological age. However, this theory has not yet had a major impact on the mainstream of research and theory on the middle years.)

It is true that men and women share certain universal experiences linked to age. Near forty, both may have a sense of time running out and may have to deal with stresses associated with adolescent children and aging parents. Yet if one begins with a consideration not of the male experience but of the reality and variations of women's lives, it is unlikely that chronological age would be seen as the central variable. Furthermore, the concept of stage, which is also central to these theories, is not used with sufficient rigor: the processes and mechanisms underlying the sequence of stages and accompanying crises remain to be worked out (Brim, 1976).

For women, then, the approach of these theorists seems inappropriate, particularly because they fail to take into account varying role patterns a woman may occupy. Numerous combinations of career, marriage, and children may occur with respect to both the timing and the degree of commitment, and each has different ramifications. Independent of role pattern, the stage of a woman's family life cycle—whether she has no children, young children, or grown children—also has a powerful impact upon her life experience.

Empirical Studies: Limitations and Biases

The link between theoretical and empirical work concerning women in the middle years is weak. For example, in attempting to explain the high level of distress in the middle-aged women they studied, Lowenthal et al. (1975) suggest that the findings may be evidence for Freud's view of adult women. He saw women in the menopausal years as frequently suffering from unresolved, recurrent Oedipal conflicts and perceived most women as rigid and worn out developmentally, because of their early, difficult psychosexual development. Such theoretical formulations at best reflect the social realities and mores of earlier times and thus seem outmoded and inadequate explanations. When such formulations guide the design and interpretation of empirical studies, their value is greatly diminished.

Underlying many studies of women in the middle years is a belief in the biological determinism of feminine behavior. Certain subtle assumptions about women are widely shared and reflected in research, although not always stated: that the mind-body relationship is somehow closer for women than for men; that biological influences are thus stronger for women (Parlee, 1975). Because of this view, a woman's life is too often seen only in terms of her reproductive role; menopause and the "empty nest" become the major events of the middle years. Furthermore, marriage and children are conceptualized as crucial to a woman's well-being. Evidence to the contrary is greeted with surprise (Maas & Kuypers, 1974) or its significance not understood. For example, the middle-aged women studied by Lowenthal et al. (1975) reported that they were looking forward to the empty nest. Given the assumption of centrality of the child-rearing function to women's well-being, the researchers doubted these self-reports, which have since been supported by follow-up studies (Lowenthal, 1975). The researchers suggested that the women's anxiety and despair about their children leaving home must be too deep to be tapped, even in lengthy interviews.

Indeed, the very use of the term "menopausal" women or "empty nest" women to describe certain groups of subjects reflects fixed assumptions about the centrality of these events. The work of Neugarten, Wood, Kraines, and Loomis (1968) and McKinlay and Jefferys (1974) has shown that menopause is not seen as a central or distressing event by women in or past that stage. And Campbell (1976), reflecting on the results of his recent survey, has stated that "the empty nest has a reputation that is not deserved." Findings from several studies (Campbell et al., 1976; Lowenthal, 1975; Radloff, 1975) confirm that the well-being of women whose children have left home is higher, and the incidence of depression lower, than in women living with young children. Yet, despite contradictory evidence, the assumption persists that certain life styles are necessary for happiness among women.

Perhaps the best illustration of the impact of outmoded assumptions, stereotypes, and biases is the way researchers deal with the variable of work. Although 90 percent of all women work for pay at some point in their lives, paid employment has not been conceptualized as central to the lives of women, who are not expected to function as economic providers or to derive self-esteem and identity from this role. Since industrialization separated work and family life, women have been seen as primarily committed to the family and as thus out of place and unreliable at places of employment (Coser & Rokoff, 1970).

This view is reflected even in the selection of subjects for study. In one major study of the impact of menopause, women who worked were simply excluded from the sample, apparently because they were too deviant (Van Keep & Kellerhals, 1975). In a major ongoing longitudinal study of retirement, married women are excluded on the grounds that it is their husband's retirement that has the important impact on their lives (Sherman, 1974). Whatever validity such decisions once had, their function today is to limit the usefulness of the findings.

When women who work *are* included in studies, and even when work is treated as an important variable, as in comparisons of working versus non-working women, relevant differentiations among workers are rarely made. Physicians and sales clerks, the career-committed and those who would prefer to be at home, are too often treated as one group. In studies based upon probability samples, the numbers of women working in high-prestige professions are too small to be useful in data analysis (Campbell et al., 1976).

Yet aspects of work status, such as level of occupation and of commitment, appear to have a profound effect upon women's experiences, particularly in the second half of the life span. Judith Birnbaum (1975) studied satisfaction and self-esteem at mid-life in comparable groups of married professionals with children, single professionals, and "homemakers," that is, women who had not worked since the birth of their first child. Both groups of professional women were more satisfied and had higher self-esteem than did the women who had lived out the traditional role pattern. In Sears and Barbee's (1977) analysis of Terman's sample of gifted women, married women were less satisfied with their life patterns than were women who were single, divorced, or widowed. Satisfaction was highest

from *Sugar Daddys a Sticky Myth,* copyright bülbül 1976, Arachne Publishing, Mountain View, CA. 94040

among women who were both single and income producers.

These studies do not address the problem of cohort effects. Furthermore, there may be an interaction of age and work status. In Birnbaum's (1975) study, the women were from about thirty-five to fifty; in Sears and Barbee's they were in their sixties. During the early adult years, commitment to work might not have been a more satisfying pattern than a solely domestic pattern. Moreover, working women in these studies were in relatively high-prestige occupations. Most women who work hold routine, low-level jobs. Thus assessment of occupational level is crucial for understanding the impact of work on women's lives.

Kanter's (1975) recent analysis of the impact of structural conditions of employment suggests other specific components of the work situation which may affect satisfaction, self-esteem, and well-being, as well as women's work-related behavior and attitudes. She points out that the conditions under which many women work—namely, low level of occupation, the absence of opportunity for advancement, lack of power, and tokenism—are related to low career aspirations and commitment, and to low self-esteem (in men as well

as women). Because most studies fail to take into account these qualitative aspects of work, the studies conclude that for women, in contrast to men, work satisfaction has little effect on well-being (Bradburn & Caplovitz, 1965; Campbell et al., 1976).

The failure to deal adequately with the variable of work reflects assumptions about the centrality of marriage and children, menopause and empty nest, over work-related issues. One cannot understand the impact of marriage and children upon women in a vacuum; without careful consideration of work status, the heated debate about whether marriage and children are a "health hazard" for women (Bernard, 1972; Campbell et al., 1976; Glenn, 1975) may not be resolvable.

Another limiting assumption concerning women and work is that for women who are married and have children, the work role has been seen almost exclusively as a source of conflict, ambivalence, and overload (Hall & Gordon, 1973); beneficial, invigorating, health-maintaining aspects of combining roles have been overlooked. Yet Gove and Tudor (1973) have argued that, for men, access to sources of satisfaction in both work and family accounts for their lesser tendency to psychiatric symptomatology. Moreover, in a study of stressful

It is possible, of course, that the only effect of . . . sheltering is to create in women a generalized dependency which will then be transferred to the husband and which will enable her all the more readily to accept the role of wife in a family which still has many patriarchal features.

Mirra Komarovsky, *American Sociological Review* (Aug. 1950)

events and mitigators of stress among women living in London, Brown, Bhrolchain, and Harris (1975) found that for women who were both under stress and unable to turn to a confidante, work served to prevent the development of psychiatric symptomatology; only 14 percent of such women who worked developed symptoms, compared with 79 percent of those who did not work. Thus, the traditional role pattern, as Bailyn (1976) points out, although perhaps still adaptive in early adult years, soon beings to "exact a toll." Perhaps it is this toll that has led researchers to focus so much on problems and dysfunctions—on losses such as the menopause and the empty nest—rather than on positive influences on women's mental health.

Future Theory and Research

How can a theory of women in the middle years be developed? We have already suggested the necessity of including certain variables as elements in such a theory—work status and conditions, role pattern, and stage of the family life cycle. At present, no theoretical framework links these variables. Indeed, it is premature to expect to formulate a comprehensive theory. As Lowenthal (1975) points out, given the present state of knowledge, researchers should "systematically explore concepts of a number of disciplines in order to locate potentially useful building blocks toward the eventual development of an interdisciplinary science of adult development and aging."

In the spirit of Lowenthal's suggestion, we suggest two additional "potentially useful" conceptual areas: (a) locus of control and attributions; and (b) support systems and social networks. The task of integrating these into other areas of research remains.

Locus of Control and Attributions

Locus of control (Rotter, 1966) refers to whether one believes that what happens to one is mainly contingent on one's own behavior (internal locus) versus is independent of one's behavior or outside one's own control (external locus). Attribution research deals with how people understand and explain the causes of their successes and failures, for example, luck, effort. The causes tend to fall on two dimensions—stable/unstable and internal/external (Weiner, Frieze, Kukla, Reed, Rest, & Rosenbaum, 1971).

Although there is conflicting evidence on this point it appears that women are more likely to see what happens to them as independent of their own behavior than are men, and they also more often attribute their successes to external and/or unstable factors. However, one's confidence, self-esteem, and sense of competence are best served by attributing success to internal stable factors and failure to external unstable ones (Frieze, 1975). Furthermore, the sense of being in charge of one's life fosters self-esteem while feelings that one is not in charge are associated with depression and a sense of helplessness (Seligman, 1974). Thus research on locus of control and attributions is highly relevant to understanding women's experiences and attitudes.

Social Networks and Support Systems

Campbell (1976) has stated that progress in understanding well-being requires exploration of social networks and supports. Empirical evidence is consistent with this view. Support systems and social networks can be conceptualized as buffers against stress, as "protective social processes" (Caplan, 1974). Social networks usually refer to the number, frequency, proximity, and quality of social contacts; support systems are most typically studied in relation to patterns of help utilization—what persons or institutions are turned to for help with problems.

Bradburn and Caplovitz (1965) found that positive components of happiness correlated highly with participation in social networks and social interactions. Brown et al. (1975) found that, for women under stress, the most powerful mitigator was a confidante, a person who is rated highest on a scale of practical and emotional support.

In a study of the differential use of helping systems by men and women, Warren (1975) found that women relied on help from a spouse less than did men; sex differences were more pronounced in blue-collar, compared with white-collar subjects. She also found social class differences in the helping sources available to women. White-collar women had a greater variety of resources (coworkers, physicians) than did blue-collar women, who typically experience more stress. Research on patterns of networks and supports thus bears directly upon understanding women's lives.

Conclusion

Our concern that research and theory on women in the middle years go beyond a focus on problems and dysfunctions ought not to be taken to mean that we are complacent or sanguine about women's well-being. Recent studies document the increasing incidence of depression in women, which is occurring at earlier ages, particularly in women with young children. Those who are single parents and who work at low-paying jobs are particularly at risk, and it is fortunate that intervention attempts are not awaiting the final word from academe (Guttentag et al.).

The situation of older women, particularly those living out the traditional role pattern, also requires thoughtful intervention. In an interview study of a sample of U.S. women, Weiss and Samuelson (1958) asked, "What are the things you do that make you feel useful or important?" They report, "A rather substantial proportion of women in the older age groups said that nothing made them feel useful and important." Judith Bardwick (1975) has commented that only the sense of challenge and commitment and the possibility of new undertakings can make the middle years rewarding. Yet Marjorie Lowenthal (1975) has pointed out the painful situation of middle-aged women whose deepest desire is for a way to grow and develop, but who see no way to do so. We are hopeful that sound theoretical and empirical work on women in the middle years will point to ways of preventing and mitigating such distress and will thus promote well-being.

Mental Illness or Social Problem?

In the previous sections, the intrapsychic, interpersonal, and societal effects of patriarchy on the psychology of women have been analyzed. In this section we assess their emotional consequences. Henley and Freeman (see their article) have postulated that when women's behavior deviates from "femininity," it is labelled "mentally ill," and that this acts as a means of controlling women's behavior. Chesler's theoretical proposal (1972) is that "what we consider 'madness,' whether it appears in women or men, is the acting out of the devalued female role or the total or partial rejection of one's sex-role stereotype."

In Phyllis Chesler's paper here (portions of which also appear in her book *Women and Madness* [1972]), the topics of why women are labelled "mentally ill" more often than men, why their "mental illness" is self-destructive, and how marriage and psychotherapy can be seen as similar institutions for women are presented.

According to Chesler, women have higher rates of "mental illness." Recently, Walter Gove (1980) has updated these psychiatric illness rates and has obtained similar results. In his article (also included here), he gives a detailed account of how mental illness is defined and provides justification and explanation for such definitions. His article originally appeared in a special issue of *Psychology of Women Quarterly*, "Woman as Patient," and in this same issue is a reply to Gove in which problems with such definitions are pointed out (Johnson, 1980). According to Johnson, since alcoholism and drug abuse, as well as violent, antisocial, and destructive behavior, are not defined as mental illness, then much of men's mental illness is not recognized as such. Johnson gives an example:

"A battered woman and her husband come for therapy; they report that the battering has occurred over a five-year period. The woman expresses great distress, is depressed, feels worthless, is not functioning well, and so forth. The man has a severe problem with alcohol and periodically explodes violently at his wife. He rarely experiences discomfort over the battering. He has come to therapy with his wife only because she has threatened to leave him unless they enter therapy."

According to Gove's definition, it is the wife who suffers from mental illness, but the husband does not. She would be diagnosed as neurotic depressive, whereas the husband would be considered alcoholic and personality disordered, thus not mentally ill in Gove's view. (Johnson, 1980, p. 365)

The issue of definition is a valid one, and remains unresolved. According to Gove, when an eclectic definition of mental illness is used, the sex differential in mental illness rates becomes less clear and perhaps equivalent. Johnson (1980), on the other hand, suggests that we shift the research question from sex differential rates of mental illness to studying the relationship between sex roles and various emotional problems. (One possible starting point may be that in terms of personality disorders, those affecting men more than women are obsessive, paranoid, and antisocial; those affecting women more than men are hysterical, dependent, and borderline (DSM III, 1980).)

Chesler's analysis of the quality of mental illness for women is in accordance with their "feminine" sex role. Similar to the theory of psychological oppression presented earlier in this book, Chesler's theory sees women's mental illness as the product of a "slave psychol-

Women are impaled on the cross of self-sacrifice. Unlike men, they are categorically denied the experience of cultural supremacy, humanity, and renewal based on their sexual identity—and on the blood sacrifice, in some way, of a member of the opposite sex. In different ways, some women are driven mad by this fact. Such madness is essentially an intense experience of female biological, sexual, and cultural castration, and a doomed search for potency.

Phyllis Chesler, *Women and Madness*, 1972

---

ogy" in which women are "unconsciously 'on strike' against persons (actual or internal) to whom they relate with subservience and against whom they wage an unending and unsuccessful covert rebellion" (Szasz, as quoted in Chesler).

Betsy Belote in the next article sees "normal femininity" in similar terms. Belote reviews the literature on masochism and hysteria, and compares descriptions of these with a description of a healthy female as judged by clinicians. Based on the congruity among these, she concludes that masochism, hysteria, and "femininity" in women may be similarly derived from acceptance of a subordinated position relative to men in society. Also to be considered is that these traits in women may be preferred by men as suggested by Karen Horney in Belote's paper.

Another important topic in women's mental illness is the double bind, discussed by both Chesler and Belote. Both cite the Broverman et al. (1970) study, in which clinicians described what they considered a mentally healthy female, male, and person (sex unspecified). What was considered healthy for a person and for a male was similar, but what was healthy for a female differed from what was healthy for a person. Gove offers evidence that this is no longer the case, while Johnson (1980) argues that there are some suggestions in the literature that clinicians may now be aware of the purposes of such investigations and may know how to give the "correct" (non-sexist) response, though their basic attitudes and practices may not have changed substantially. If the original findings hold, this would be an example of a double bind for women. A woman cannot be a mentally healthy person and a mentally healthy adult female at the same time; by choosing either one, she loses. Double binds and mental illness in women have also been discussed elsewhere (Chesler, 1972; Kaschak, 1976).

Chesler compares marriage and psychotherapy and finds them similar institutions for women. In both, women seek personal salvation through relationships to men to whom they take a subordinate status, and whom they allow to define the situation and control the conversation through rewards. From Chodorow's theory, it can be assumed that in both marriage and psychotherapy, women relate to men who cannot provide the emotional contact they search for in intimate relationships, due to men's apparent need for emotional distance from women. Similarly, according to Belote, women become "hysterical" in response to men's emotional incapabilities. These implications support Chesler's analysis that if psychotherapy does not "incorporate a feminist awareness, female patients cannot, by definition, get better."

Depression is a common denominator for the various kinds of mental illnesses affecting women. Chesler (1972) has related depression in women to women's loss of power and the fact that women are losers in a patriarchy. Depression has also been associated with the emotional results of psychological oppression

The problem that has no name—which is simply the fact that American women are kept from growing to their full human capacities—is taking a far greater toll on the physical and mental health of our country than any known disease.

Betty Friedan, *The Feminine Mystique*, 1963

and the unexpressed rage at the cultural double binds confronting women. If the choice is either rage or depression, women may choose the latter since it is sex-role compatible and in choosing the former they risk rejection as "unfeminine" or "mentally ill," or even worse, emotional or physical abuse. (See Leidig's paper on male violence.)

Lenore Radloff and Sue Cox present the topic of depression as related to a learned susceptibility or learned helplessness in women. Various theories of depression are briefly described including a model of depression proposed by the first author. Evidence supporting learned helplessness in women is presented and the results of a community survey are discussed in terms of the model. Controlling for a number of factors, sex differences in depression do not disappear, leading to the conclusion that women are in fact more depressed than men.

The finding that married women are more depressed than unmarried women, while the reverse is true for men, is interesting. Radloff and Cox relate this finding to learned helplessness differential selectivity in marriage, in that women who are more "helpless" or more "feminine" are also more likely to get married. Perhaps they are also preferred as marriage partners by men. Conversely, the more helpless men would be less likely to marry. It would follow then, that married women would be more helpless and therefore more susceptible to depression than women in other marital status categories, while the reverse would be

true for men. In contrast, Gove dismisses the possibility of learned helplessness and attempts to explain the differential effects of marital status in terms of aspects of the marital role itself for women.

A comparison of treatment implications is also interesting and instructive. If Radloff's model is correct, and depression in women is based on a learned susceptibility, then perhaps it can be unlearned. This model is also discussed in terms of other groups—the young, the poor, the disadvantaged—for whom learned helplessness may also be a relevant explanatory concept. In addition to a learned susceptibility, depression may have external sources as well. People may be confronted with too many stresses or precipitating events over which they have had no control (for example, poverty). In these cases, more than unlearning susceptibility may be required, such as restructuring the environment to reduce the probability of the occurrence of precipitating factors, or stresses. This public health model of treatment could be considered a feminist one in that interventions would occur at both the individual and societal levels.

Gove's discussion of treatment approaches is very much in contrast in that he primarily focuses on the level of individual treatment. Although he correctly identifies the treatment issue as one of social control or societal change, his discussion contains many misunderstandings of feminism and feminist psychotherapy. For example, Gove assumes that feminist therapists would be involved in societal change only. On the contrary, most feminist psychotherapists would see *both* individual and societal factors in *both* the etiology and treatment of emotional disorders. (There are differences, however, among feminist therapists and these will be presented more fully in Kaschak's paper in the section on change and liberation.)

Feminist psychotherapists would argue with many of Gove's other assumptions. For example, he assumes that the traditional therapist is not a political agent. Feminists would argue that both feminist and traditional therapists are political agents. Gove assumes that psychotherapy and feminism are separate realms of discourse. Feminists would disagree strongly, and they are involved in developing theories integrating the two. Contrary to Gove's statements based on 1971 data, women are increasingly seeking female and feminist therapists as they begin to consider their problems in feminist terms. Gove assumes that changing the environment is relatively easy. Feminists would assert that it is not always so, although when a woman's consciousness is raised, changes usually occur.

Gove's discussion of the possibility of women jeopardizing their relationships with men and the potential danger to these women in emotional terms seems somewhat contradictory. It seems that the danger would be more to the men involved. Earlier in his article Gove states "higher rates of mental illness appear to be limited to married women, with never-married, widowed, and divorced women having comparable, if not lower, rates than their male counterparts." While divorce is a serious issue for women, men seem to suffer more from divorce and emotional breakups of relationships than do women (see Chodorow's paper), just as men seem to benefit more emotionally from marriage than do women.

Women have been in culturally produced double binds, and so now are psychotherapists—whether to change the individual, or the society, or both,—and, whether to promote change in feminist or traditional directions. According to feminist analysis, unless there are societal, interpersonal, and individual changes in feminist directions, women (and men) cannot "get better." In the meantime, it is quite possible that traditional therapeutic efforts may be neutral at best, and, more likely, destructive to women.

For Further Reading

Blum, H. P. (Ed.). 1977. *Female Psychology: Contemporary Psychoanalytic Views.* New York: International Universities Press.

Brodsky, A. M., and Hare-Mustin, R. (Eds.). 1980. *Women and Psychotherapy.* New York: Guilford.

Chesler, P. 1972. *Women and Madness.* New York: Doubleday.

Collett, E. R. (Ed.). 1981. *Women & Therapy, I* (1) (in press).

Davidson, C. V., and Abramowitz, S. I. (Eds.). 1980. Woman as patient (Special issue). *Psychology of Women Quarterly, 4* (3).

Franks, V. and Burtle, V. (Eds.) 1974. *Women in Therapy: New Psychotherapies for a Changing Society.* New York: Brunner/Mazel.

Gomberg, E., and Franks, V. (Eds.) 1979. *Gender and Disordered Behavior: Sex Differences in Psychopathology.* New York: Brunner/Mazel.

Miller, J. B. (Ed.). 1973. *Psychoanalysis and Women.* New York: Penguin.

Mitchell, J. 1974. *Psychoanalysis and Feminism.* New York: Pantheon.

Schaffer, K. F. 1980. *Sex-role Issue in Mental Health.* Reading, Mass.: Addison-Wesley.

Strouse, J. (Ed.). 1974. *Women and Analysis: Dialogues on Psychoanalytic Views of Femininity.* New York: Dell.

Tennov, D. 1975. *Psychotherapy: The Hazardous Cure.* New York: Abelard-Schuman.

Weissman, M. M. and Paykel, E. S. 1974. *The Depressed Woman.* Chicago: Univ. of Chicago Press.

Phyllis Chesler

Women as Psychiatric and Psychotherapeutic Patients

This paper presents a feminist interpretation of mental illness based on national statistics, mental health surveys, psychological and sociological experiments, psychological analytic theories and practices, and on an original study. An analysis of NIMH statistics revealed that 125,351 more women than men have been psychiatrically hospitalized from 1964-1968. From 1950-1968, 223,268 more women than men were hospitalized in state mental asylums. Female patients generally outnumber males in private treatment, and both significantly prefer a male rather than a female therapist. These facts are discussed as one of the effects of sex-role stereotyping and the oppression of women.

Like all sciences and valuations, the psychology of women has hitherto been considered only from the point of view of men. It is inevitable that the man's position of advantage should cause objective validity to be attributed to his subjective, affective relations to women ... the question then is how far analytical psychology also, when its researches have women for their object, is under the spell of this way of thinking (Horney, 1926/1967).

Although Karen Horney wrote this in 1926, very few psychiatrists and psychologists seem to have agreed with and been guided by her words. Female psychology is still being viewed from a masculine point of view. Contemporary psychiatric and psychological theories and practices both reflect and influence our culture's politically naive understanding and emotionally brutal treatment of women.

Female unhappiness is viewed and "treated" as a problem of individual pathology, no matter how many other female patients (or nonpatients) are similarly unhappy—and this by men who have studiously bypassed the objective fact of female oppression. Woman's inability to adjust to or to be contented by feminine roles has been considered as a deviation from "natural" female psychology rather than as a criticism of such roles.

I do not wish to imply that female unhappiness is a myth conjured up by men; it is very real. One of the ways white, middle-class women in America attempt to handle this unhappiness is through psychotherapy. They enter private therapy just as they enter marriage—with a sense of urgency and desperation. Also, black and white women of all classes, particularly unmarried women, comprise the largest group of psychiatrically hospitalized and "treated" Americans. This paper will present the following analysis:

1. that for a number of reasons, women behave in the manner labeled "mentally ill" more often and more easily than men do; that their "mental illness" is mainly self-destructive; and that they are punished for their self-destructive behavior, either by the brutal and impersonal custodial care given them in mental asylums, or by the relationships they have with most (but not all) clinicians, who implicitly encourage them to blame themselves or to take responsibility for their unhappiness in order to be "cured."

2. that both psychotherapy and marriage, the two major socially approved institutions for white, middle-class women, function similarly, i.e., as vehicles for personal "salvation" through the presence of an understanding and benevolent (male) authority. In female culture, not being married, or being unhappily married, is experienced as an "illness" which psychotherapy can, hopefully, cure.

This paper will discuss the following questions: What are some of the facts about women as psychiatric or psychotherapy patients in America. What "symptoms" do they present? Why are more women involved, either voluntarily or involuntarily with mental health professionals than are men? Who are the psychotherapists in America and what are their views about women? What practical implications does this discussion have for women who are in a psychotherapeutic relationship?

General Statistics

A study published in 1970 by the U.S. Department of Health, Education, and Welfare (Table 1) indicated that in both the black and white populations significantly more women than men reported having suffered nervous breakdowns, having felt impending nervous breakdowns,[1] psychological inertia and dizziness. Both black and white women also reported higher rates than men for the following symptoms: nervousness, insomnia, trembling hands, nightmares, fainting and headaches. White women who were never married reported fewer symptoms than white married or separated women. These findings are essentially in agreement with an earlier study published in

1960, by the Joint Commission on Mental Health and Illness. The Commission reported the following information for nonhospitalized American adults: (1) Greater distress and symptoms are reported by women than by men in all adjustment areas. They report more disturbances in general adjustment, in their self-perception, and in their marital and parental functioning. This sex difference is most marked at the younger age intervals. (2) A feeling of impending breakdown is reported more frequently by divorced and separated females than by any other group of either sex. (3) The unmarried (whether single, separated, divorced or widowed) have a greater potential for psychological distress than do the married. (4) While the sexes did not differ in the *frequency* with which they reported "unhappiness," the women reported more worry, fear of breakdown, and need for help (Gurin, Veroff and Feld, 1960).

What such studies do not make clear is how many of these "psychologically distressed" women are involved in any form of psychiatric or psychological treatment. Other studies have attempted to do this. William Schofield (1963) found that the average psychiatrist sees significantly more female than male patients. A study published in 1965 reported that female patients outnumbered male patients three to two in private psychiatric treatment (Buhn, Conwell and Hurley, 1965). Statistics for public and private psychiatric hospitalization in America do exist and of course, are controversial. However, statistical studies have indicated certain trends. According to NIMH statistics 125,351 more women than men were psychiatrically hospitalized and/or treated on an outpatient basis from 1964 through 1968. These facilities include general hospitals, pri-

---

[1]At all age levels.

TABLE 1

SYMPTOM RATES BY SEX, SEX AND AGE, AND SEX AND RACE (PER 100)

Symptom and sex	Total	Age							Race	
	18–79 years	18–24 years	25–34 years	35–44 years	45–54 years	55–64 years	65–74 years	75–79 years	White	Negro
Nervous breakdown										
Male	3.2	1.3	1.8	3.5	3.0	5.4	5.4	1.5	3.2	2.8
Female	6.4	1.0	3.6	5.0	7.3	12.7	10.7	13.1	6.0	10.4
Felt impending nervous breakdown										
Male	7.7	6.9	7.4	8.6	11.7	6.4	3.1	2.2	7.7	8.2
Female	17.5	14.6	21.6	19.3	18.8	14.5	13.8	10.2	17.8	16.1
Nervousness										
Male	45.1	43.5	47.5	51.9	48.1	37.7	36.6	30.2	47.2	31.3
Female	70.6	61.4	74.4	75.0	72.5	72.6	62.9	65.6	73.2	55.2
Inertia										
Male	16.8	17.2	16.1	17.6	16.3	16.9	18.2	12.1	16.9	17.1
Female	32.5	31.0	34.0	35.2	31.1	29.7	31.9	35.6	33.1	29.5
Insomnia										
Male	23.5	20.4	16.7	20.8	26.8	27.0	35.9	26.5	24.1	20.4
Female	40.4	28.0	33.5	33.7	42.8	53.8	59.0	51.0	40.9	38.9
Trembling Hands										
Male	7.0	7.6	6.5	5.4	5.7	8.8	10.0	8.5	6.9	7.1
Female	10.9	10.4	12.2	12.1	10.6	9.3	9.2	13.0	10.6	12.3
Nightmares										
Male	7.6	5.7	9.4	7.7	7.7	8.2	5.8	6.5	6.9	13.0
Female	12.4	12.8	15.8	14.7	9.9	7.5	11.6	11.8	12.3	14.3

vate hospitals, state and county hospitals, outpatient clinics, Veterans' Administration hospitals and outpatient clinics, and excludes all private psychotherapeutic treatment. Between 1950 and 1968, 223,268 more women than men were hospitalized in state and county mental hospitals. Earlier studies have reported that admission rates to both public and private psychiatric hospitals are significantly higher for women than men (Maltzberg, 1959). Unmarried people (single, divorced or widowed) of both sexes are disproportionately represented among the psychiatrically hospitalized (Dayton, 1940; Zigler and Phillips, 1960). Thus, while according to the 1970 HEW report, single, white women in the general population

TABLE 1 (CONTINUED)
SYMPTOM RATES BY SEX, SEX AND AGE, AND SEX AND RACE (PER 100)

Symptom and sex	Total	Age							Race	
	18–79 years	18–24 years	25–34 years	35–44 years	45–54 years	55–64 years	65–74 years	75–79 years	White	Negro
Perspiring hands										
Male	17.0	23.2	24.9	17.7	14.7	11.0	7.9	3.0	17.0	16.8
Female	21.4	28.6	27.7	24.2	19.6	15.0	9.2	5.9	22.2	16.0
Fainting										
Male	16.9	17.6	15.7	15.7	18.1	17.3	17.8	17.2	17.5	13.8
Female	29.1	28.5	33.2	29.9	27.0	26.2	29.7	24.8	30.4	20.5
Headaches										
Male	13.7	13.0	12.8	13.8	15.2	15.6	11.3	10.0	13.8	11.9
Female	27.8	24.0	31.6	29.6	29.5	25.9	24.2	19.3	27.5	30.9
Dizziness										
Male	7.1	6.3	3.0	5.0	7.6	10.7	12.8	14.3	6.9	9.2
Female	10.9	8.4	9.5	8.5	10.1	14.3	16.9	16.6	10.3	15.7
Heart palpitations										
Male	3.7	3.3	2.0	2.1	3.9	7.2	6.4	1.5	3.6	4.8
Female	5.8	1.7	3.1	4.7	6.2	9.7	10.4	14.8	5.7	6.4
SCALE MEAN VALUE Male										
White	1.70	1.72	1.70	1.72	1.78	1.69	1.66	1.19	1.70	....
Negro	1.55	1.25	1.03	1.37	1.79	1.87	2.23	2.99	....	1.55
Female										
White	2.88	2.61	3.07	2.93	2.89	2.86	2.82	2.80	2.88	....
Negro	2.65	1.91	2.61	2.60	2.52	3.27	3.79	2.62	....	2.65

report less psychological distress than married or separated white women (Srole et al., 1962), women (as well as men) who are psychiatrically *hospitalized* tend to be unmarried.

Private psychotherapy, like marriage, is an integral part of middle class female culture. Patients entering private therapy betray significantly different attitudes towards men and women therapists. A number of them indicate that they feel sex is important in the therapeutic relationship by voluntarily requesting a therapist of a particular sex.

I have recently completed a study of 1,001 middle-income clinic outpatients (538 women and 463 men) who sought therapeutic treatment in New York City from 1965 to 1969. Pa-

TABLE 2

PERCENTAGE DISTRIBUTION OF PATIENT THERAPIST PREFERENCE, MARITAL STATUS, AGE, AND RELIGION

	Women (N=159)	Men (N=99)	Total (N=258)
Therapist preference	%	%	%
Male	49	40	45
Female	31	25	29
None	20	35	26
Marital Status			
Single	69	63	
Married/living with someone	17	24	
Divorced/separated	14	13	
Age			
Under 30	75	69	
Over 30	25	31	

	Women (N=59)				Men (N=99)			
Religion:	Jewish %	Catholic %	Protestant %	None %	Jewish %	Catholic %	Protestant %	None %
	40	19	16	25	41	22	14	23

tient variables, such as sex, marital status, age, religion, occupation, and so forth, were related to patient requests for a male or a female therapist at the time of the initial interview (Tables 2 and 3). These findings are based on a sample of 258 people (159 women and 99 men) who voluntarily requested either a male or a female therapist or who voluntarily stated that they had no sex-of-therapist preference. Twenty-four percent of the 538 women and 14 percent of the 463 men requested a therapist specifically by sex. The findings were as follows:

1. Sixty-six percent of the patients were single and 72 percent were under 30. Whether male or female, they significantly requested a male rather than a female therapist. ($x^2 = 17.2$ p < .001). This preference was significantly re-

lated to marital status in women ($x^2 = 12.6$ p < .02) but not in men ($x^2 = 4.4$ n.s.). Specifically, single women prefer a male therapist significantly more than a female therapist and significantly more than having no sex-preference at all ($x^2 = 21.7$ p < .001). This suggests that a woman may be seeking psychotherapy for very different reasons than a man; and that these reasons are probably related to or strictly determined by her relationship (or lack of one) to a man. The number of requests for female therapists was approximately equal to the number of "no preference" requests for both men and women. Age, rather than marital status, was a significant determinant of sex-of-therapist preference for men ($x^2 = 39.7$ p < .001) but not for women ($x^2 = 2.5$). Specifically, men under 30 prefer male therapists.

TABLE 3
THE RELATIONSHIP BETWEEN THERAPIST PREFERENCE AND PATIENT MARITAL STATUS

Marital Status: Therapist Preference	Female Preference			Male Preference		
	Male %	*Female* %	*None* %	*Male* %	*Female* %	*None* %
Single	54	30	16	44	28	29
Married/living with someone	41	37	22	25	25	50
Divorced	35	26	39	53	23	23

Single women, under or over 30, of any religion, requested male therapists more often than married or divorced women did. Legally married women (N = 21) requested female therapists more often than any of the other sample groups. Age and marital status were independent for men (x^2 = 23.4) and for women (x^2 = 16.5).

2. While all of the male patients regardless of their marital status requested male therapists rather than female therapists, some differential trends did exist. A higher percentage of divorced men (53 percent) requested male therapists, as compared with either divorced women (53 percent vs. 35 percent), married women (53 percent vs. 41 percent), married men (53 percent vs. 25 percent), or single men (53 percent vs. 44 percent). There was a significant relation between a male patient's request for a male therapist and his age (under thirty) and his religion: Specifically, 63 percent of the Jewish male patients (who composed 40 percent of the entire male sample and 73 percent of whom were under thirty) requested male therapists—a higher percentage than in any other group.

3. Some of the most frequent reasons given by male patients for requesting male therapists were: greater respect for a man's mind; general discomfort with and mistrust of women; and specific embarrassment about "cursing" or discussing sexual matters, such as impotence, with a woman.[2] Some of the most common reasons given by female patients for requesting male therapists were: greater respect for and confidence in a man's competence and authority; feeling generally more comfortable with and relating better to men than to women; and specific fear and mistrust of women as authorities and as people, a reason sometimes combined with statements about dislike of the patients' own mothers.[3] In general, both men and women stated that they trusted and respected men—as people and as authorities—more than they did women, whom they generally mistrusted or feared.

Patients who requested a female therapist generally gave fewer reasons for their preference; one over-thirty woman stated that "only a female would understand another female's problems"; another woman stated that she

[2]One wonders why women are not equally "embarrassed" about discussing their impotence (frigidity) with male therapists.

[3]This, as well as the significantly greater female preference for a male therapist, supports Goldberg's 1968 findings of female antifemale prejudice. See P. Goldberg, "Are women prejudiced against women," *Trans-action*, April 1968, pp. 28–30.

Mermaid Overwhelmed by Octopus by Ernestine Mills. Collection H. W. and Dora Jane Janson

sees "all males as someone to conquer" and is "less open to being honest with them." Almost all of the male patients who *gave reasons* for requesting a female therapist were homosexual. Their main reasons involved expectations of being "sexually attracted" to a male therapist, which they thought would distract or upset them. One nonhomosexual patient felt he would be too "competitive" with a male therapist.

4. Thirty-six percent of the male and 37 percent of the female patients reported generally unclassifiable symptoms during the initial clinic interview. Thirty-one percent of the female and 15 percent of the male patients reported depression as their reason for seeking therapy; 25 percent of the male and seven percent of the female patients reported active homosexuality; 15 percent of the female and 14 percent of the male patients reported anxiety; eight percent of the female and seven percent of the male patients reported sexual impotence; four percent of the male and three percent of the female patients reported drug or alcoholic addicion. The fact that at least twice as many female as male patients report depression, and almost four times as many male as female patients report homosexuality accords with previous findings and with national statistics.

5. Male and female patients remained in therapy for approximately equal lengths of time (an average of 31 weeks for males and 28 weeks for females). However, those men who requested male therapists remained in therapy longer than any other patient group (an average of 42 weeks compared to an average of 30 weeks for females requesting a male therapist; an average of 34 weeks for male and 31 weeks for female patients requesting a female therapist; an average of 12 weeks for male and 17 weeks for female patients with a stated "no preference").

In other words, male patients who requested (and who generally received) a male therapist remained in treatment longer than their female counterparts. Perhaps one of the reasons for this is that women often get married and then turn to their husbands (or boy friends) as authorities or protectors, whereas men generally do not turn to their wives or girl friends as authorities, but rather as nurturing mother-surrogates, domestics, sex objects, and perhaps, as friends. They usually do not turn to women for expert advice; hence, when they decide they need this kind of help, they tend to remain in therapy with a male therapist. Female patients, on the other hand, can transfer their needs for protection or salvation from one man to another. Ultimately, a female patient or wife will be disappointed in her husband's or therapist's mothering or saving capacities and will continue the search for salvation *through a man* elsewhere.

Presenting Symptoms

Studies of childhood behavior problems have indicated that boys are most often referred to child guidance clinics for aggressive, destructive (antisocial), and competitive behavior; girls are referred for personality problems, such as excessive fears and worries, shyness, timidity, lack of self-confidence, and feelings of inferiority (MacFarlane et al., 1954; Phillips, 1956; Gilbert, 1957; Petersen, 1961; Terman and Tyler, 1954). This should be compared with adult male and female psychiatric symptomatology: "the symptoms of men are also much more likely to reflect a destructive hostility toward others, as well as a pathological self-indulgence ... Women's symptoms, on the other hand, express a harsh, self-critical, self-depriving and often self-destructive set of attitudes" (Phillips, 1969). A study comparing the symptoms of male and female mental hospital patients, found male patients significantly more assaultive than females and more prone to indulge their impulses in socially deviant ways like robbery, rape, drinking, and homosexuality (Zigler and Phillips, 1960). Female patients were more often found to be self-deprecatory, depressed, perplexed, suffering from suicidal thoughts, or making actual suicidal attempts (U.S. Department Justice, 1969).

According to T. Szasz (1961), symptoms such as these are "indirect forms of communication" and usually indicate a "slave psychology":

Dorothea Greenbaum. *Drowned Girl.* 1950. Tennessee marble. 9 × 10½ × 11″. Collection of Whitney Museum of American Art.

Social oppression in any form, and its manifestations are varied, among them being ... poverty ... racial, religious, or sexual discrimination ... must therefore be regarded as prime determinants of indirect communication of all kinds (e.g., hysteria).

At one point in *The Myth of Mental Illness* Szasz refers to the "dread of happiness" that seems to afflict all people involved in the "Judaeo-Christian ethic." Although he is not talking about women particularly, his analysis seems especially relevant to our discussion of female psychiatric symptomatology:

In general, the open acknowledgment of satisfaction is feared only in situations of relative oppression (e.g., all-suffering wife vis-à-vis domineering husband). The experiences of satisfaction (joy, contentment) are inhibited lest they lead to

---

The Invisible Woman

The invisible woman in the asylum corridor
sees others quite clearly,
including the doctor who patiently tells her
she isn't invisible,
and pities the doctor, who must be mad
to stand there in the asylum corridor,
talking and gesturing
to nothing at all.

The invisible woman has great compassion.
So, after a while, she pulls on her body
like a rumpled glove, and switches on her
  voice
to comfort the elated doctor with words.
Better to suffer this prominence
than for the poor young doctor to learn
he himself is insane.
Only the strong can know that.

Robin Morgan

an augmentation of one's burden ... *the fear of* *acknowledging satisfaction is a characteristic* *feature of slave psychology.* (emphasis added)

The "properly exploited" slave is forced to labor until he shows signs of fatigue or exhaustion. Completion of his task does not signify that his work is finished and that he may rest. At the same time, even though his task is unfinished, he may be able to influence his master to stop driving him—and to let him rest—if he exhibits signs of imminent collapse. Such signs may be genuine or contrived. Exhibiting signs of fatigue or exhaustion—irrespective of whether they are genuine or contrived (e.g., "being on strike" against one's boss)—is likely to induce a feeling of fatigue or exhaustion in the actor. I believe that this is the mechanism responsible for the great majority of so-called chronic fatigue states. Most

of these were formerly called "neurasthenia," a term rarely nowadays used. Chronic fatigue or a feeling of lifelessness and exhaustion are still frequently encountered in clinical practice.

Psychoanalytically, they are considered "character symptoms." Many of these patients are unconsciously "on strike" against persons (actual or internal) to whom they relate with subservience and against whom they wage an unending and unsuccessful covert rebellion (Szasz, 1961).*

The analogy between "slave" and "woman" is by no means a perfect one. Women have been conceptualized (Engels, 1942) as the first group to be enslaved by another group, and therefore, in some sense, as the prototypes for all subsequent forms of enslavement (along class or racial lines). Women are still conditioned to exhibit the signs and "symptoms" of slavery (in Szasz' sense), and *this* is what our culture, and our clinicians, recognize as "mental illness." When men exhibit "female" behavior they too are viewed, or view themselves, as "mentally ill." When women exhibit "male" behavior they too are often viewed as "mentally ill" (lesbians, "aggressive" career-women, "promiscuous" women, etc.). In general, men are conditioned to behave aggressively or "criminally." If they are poor or black men, they will often commit acts that will lead to jail, or to institutions for the "criminally insane." If they are white or wealthy men they will usually proceed with business and war as usual. They are not apt to receive or bestow upon themselves the "mental illness" label.

---

*The Myth of Mental Illness, Thomas S. Szasz, excerpts from pp. 213, 194–195, 263–264. Copyright © 1961 by Hoeber Medical Division of Harper & Row, Publishers, Inc. Reprinted by permission of the publishers.

"What does a woman see in a woman that she can't see in a man?"
Doctor Nolan paused. Then she said, "Tenderness."

Sylvia Plath, *The Bell Jar*, 1963

Why Are There More Female Patients?

Psychiatrists and psychologists have traditionally described the signs and symptoms of various kinds of real and felt oppression as mental illness. Women often manifest these signs, not only because they are oppressed in an objective sense, but also because the sex role (stereotype) to which they are conditioned is composed of just such signs. For example, Phillips and Segal (1969) report that when the number of physical and psychiatric illnesses were held constant for a group of New England women and men, the women were more likely to seek medical and psychiatric care. They suggest that women seek psychiatric help because the social role of women allows them to display emotional and physical distress more easily than men. "Sensitive or emotional behavior is more tolerated in women, to the point of aberration, while self-assertive, aggressive, vigorous physical demonstrations are more tolerated among men."

Women who are hospitalized, either voluntarily or involuntarily, remain within the "female culture" which encourages and enforces a sense of worthlessness and dependency. Male mental patients are "punished" more than male convicts in that *all* mental patients are treated as women (as infantile, untrustworthy, "emotional," etc.).

It may be that more women than men are involved in psychotherapy because it—along with marriage—is one of the only two socially approved institutions for middle-class women. That these two institutions bear a strong similarity to each other is highly significant. For most women the psychotherapeutic encounter is just one more instance of an unequal rela-

> **Gesture**
>
> *It is a gesture I do*
> *that grew*
> *out of my mother*
> *in me.*
>
> *I am trying to remember*
> *what she*
> *was afraid to say*
> *all those*
>
> *years, fingers folded*
> *against her mouth,*
> *head turned away.*
>
> Beverly Dahlen

tionship, just one more opportunity to be rewarded for expressing distress and to be "helped" by being (expertly) dominated. Both psychotherapy and marriage isolate women from each other; both emphasize individual rather than collective solutions to woman's unhappiness; both are based on a woman's helplessness and dependence on a stronger male authority figure; both may, in fact, be viewed as reenactments of a little girl's relation to her father in a patriarchal society (Foucault, 1967); both control and oppress women similarly— yet, at the same time, are the two safest havens for women in a society that offers them no others.

Both psychotherapy and marriage enable women to safely express and defuse their anger by experiencing it as a form of emotional illness, by translating it into hysterical symptoms: frigidity, chronic depression, phobias, and the like. Each woman as patient thinks

What we call "normal" is a product of repression, denial, splitting, projection, introjection and other forms of destructive action on experience. . . . If our experience is destroyed, our behavior will be destructive. Jack may act upon Jill in many ways. He may make her feel guilty for keeping on "bringing it up." He may invalidate her experience. This can be done more or less radically. He can indicate merely that it is unimportant or trivial, whereas it is important and significant to her. Going further, he can shift the modality of her experience from memory to imagination: "It's all in your imagination." Further still, he can invalidate the content: "It never happened that way." Finally, he can invalidate not only the significance, modality and content, but her very capacity to remember at all, and make her feel guilty for doing so into the bargain.

Ronald D. Laing, *The Politics of Experience,*
1967

---

these symptoms are unique and are her own fault. She is neurotic, rather than oppressed. She wants from a psychotherapist what she wants—and often cannot get—from a husband: attention, understanding, merciful relief, a *personal solution*—in the arms of the right husband, on the couch of the right therapist (Steinem, 1970). The institutions of therapy and marriage not only mirror each other, they support each other. This is probably not a coincidence, but is rather an expression of the American economic system's need for geographic and psychological mobility, i.e., for young, upwardly mobile "couples" to "survive," to remain more or less intact in a succession of alien and anonymous urban locations, while they carry out the function of socializing children.

The institution of psychotherapy may be used by many women as a way of keeping a bad marriage together, or as a way of terminating it in order to form a good marriage. Some women, especially young and single women, may use psychotherapy as a way of learning how to catch a husband by practicing with a male therapist. Women probably spend more time during a therapy session talking about their husbands or boy friends—or lack of them—than they do talking about their lack of an independent identity or their relations to other women.

The institutions of psychotherapy and marriage both encourage women to talk—often endlessly—rather than to act (except in their socially prearranged roles as passive women or patient). In marriage the talking is usually of an indirect and rather inarticulate nature. Open expressions of rage are too dangerous, and too ineffective for the isolated and economically dependent women. Most often, such "kitchen" declarations end in tears, self-blame, and in the husband's graciously agreeing with his wife that she was "not herself." Even control of a simple—but serious—conversation is usually impossible for most wives when several men, including their husbands, are present. The wife-women talk to each other, or they listen silently to a group of women talking; even if there are a number of women talking and only one man present, the man will question the women, perhaps patiently, perhaps not, but always in order to ultimately control the conversation from a superior position.

In psychotherapy the patient-woman is encouraged—in fact directed—to talk, by a therapist who is expected or perceived to be as superior or objective. The traditional thera-

Woman—Which Includes Man, of Course: An Experience in Awareness

Purpose: To increase awareness of how culture, psychology, and psychotherapy, as well as our thoughts and feelings, come from a Male point of view.

Directions: Close your eyes, find a comfortable position, and relax while someone reads to you the following:

1. Consider reversing the generic term Man. Think of the future of Woman, which, of course, includes both women and men. Feel into that, sense its meaning to you—as a woman—as a man.
2. Think of it always being that way, every day of your life. Feel the everpresence of woman and feel the nonpresence of man. Absorb what it tells you about the importance and value of being woman—of being man.
3. Recall that everything you have ever read all your life uses only female pronouns— she, her—meaning both girls and boys, both women and men. Recall that most of the voices on radio and most of the faces on TV are women's—when important events are covered—on commercials, and on the late talk shows. Recall that you have no male senator representing you in Washington.
4. Feel into the fact that women are the leaders, the power-centers, the prime-movers. Man, whose natural role is husband and father, fulfills himself through nurturing children and making the home a refuge for woman. This is only natural to balance the biological role of woman who devotes her entire body to the race during pregnancy.
5. Then feel further into the obvious biological explanation for woman as the ideal— her genital construction. By design, female genitals are compact and internal, protected by her body. Male genitals are so exposed that he must be protected from outside attack to assure the perpetuation of the race. His vulnerability clearly requires sheltering.
6. Thus, by nature, males are more passive than females and have a desire in sexual relations to be symbolically engulfed by the protective body of the woman. Males psychologically yearn for this protection, fully realizing their masculinity at this time—feeling exposed and vulnerable at other times. The male is not fully adult until he has overcome his infantile tendency to penis orgasm and has achieved the mature surrender of the testicle orgasm. He then feels himself a "whole man" when engulfed by the woman.
7. If the male denies these feelings, he is unconsciously rejecting his masculinity. Therapy is thus indicated to help him adjust to his own nature. Of course, therapy is administered by a woman, who has the education and wisdom to facilitate openness leading to the male's growth and self-actualization.
8. To help him feel into his defensive emotionality he is invited to get in touch with the "child" in him. He remembers his sister's jeering at his primitive genitals that "flop around foolishly." She can run, climb and ride horseback unencumbered. Obviously, since she is free to move, she is encouraged to develop her body and mind in preparation for her active responsibilities of adult womanhood. The male vulnerability needs female protection, so he is taught the less active, caring virtues of homemaking.
9. Because of his clitoris-envy, he learns to strap up his genitals, and learns to feel ashamed and unclean because of his nocturnal emissions. Instead he is encouraged to dream of getting married, waiting for the time of his fulfillment—when "his woman" gives him a girl-child to care for and carry on the family name. He knows that if it is a boy-child he has failed somehow—but they can try again.

Open your eyes. What did you experience? Record this and share it with the class.

"Woman—Which Includes Man, of Course," original and revision copyright © 1970 and 1972 respectively by Theodora Wells.

We must ask ourselves why there should have to be any power struggle at all between the sexes. At any given time, the more powerful side will create an ideology suitable to help maintain its position and to make this position acceptable to the weaker one. . . . It is the function of such an ideology to deny or conceal the existence of a struggle. Here is one of the answers to the question . . . as to why we have so little awareness of the fact that there is a struggle between the sexes. It is in the interest of men to obscure this fact; and the emphasis they place on their ideologies has caused women, also, to adopt these theories.

Karen Horney, "The Distrust Between the Sexes," 1931

---

pist may be viewed as ultimately controlling what the patient says through a subtle system of rewards (attention, interpretations, and so forth) or rewards withheld—but, most ultimately, controlling in the sense that he is attempting to bring his patient to terms with the female role, i.e., to an admission and acceptance of dependency. Traditionally, the psychotherapist has ignored the objective facts of female oppression. Thus, in every sense, the female patient is still not having a "real" conversation—either with her husband or her therapist. But how is it possible to have a "real" conversation with those who directly profit from her oppression? She would be laughed at, viewed as silly or crazy, and if she persisted, removed from her job—as secretary or wife, perhaps even as patient.

Psychotherapeutic talking is indirect in the sense that it does not immediately or even ultimately involve the woman in any reality-based confrontations with the self. It is also indirect in that words—*any* words—are permitted, so long as certain actions of consequence are totally avoided (such as not paying one's bills).

Who Are the Psychotherapists and What Are Their Views About Women?

Contemporary psychotherapists, like ghetto schoolteachers, do not study themselves or question their own motives or values as easily or as frequently as they do those of their "neurotic" patients or their "culturally deprived" pupils. However, in a 1960 study Schofield (1963) found that 90 percent of psychiatrists were male; that psychologists were predominantly males, in a ratio of two to one; and that social workers (the least prestigious and least well-paying of the three professional categories) were predominantly females, in a ratio of two to one. The psychologists and psychiatrists were about the same age, an average of forty-four years; the social workers' average age was thirty-eight. Less than five percent of the psychiatrists were single; 10 percent of the psychologists, six percent of the social workers, and one percent of the psychiatrists were divorced. In other words, the majority of psychiatrists and psychologists are middle-aged married men, probably white, whose personal backgrounds were seen by Schofield as containing "pressure toward upward social mobility." In 1960 the American Psychiatric Association totaled 10,000 male and 983 female members.

What must further be realized is that these predominantly male clinicians are involved in a political institution that has taken a certain traditional view of women. A great deal has been written about the covertly or overtly patriarchal, autocratic, and coercive values and techniques of psychotherapy (e.g., Goffman,

But it is equally true that our knowledge of women in another society, or another period of history, or women in contemporary societies, will always be incomplete unless women themselves are involved as full partners, with their experience taken into account, in any research effort. It was Freud's refusal to listen to what Karen Horney was trying to tell him about women and about his biased male perception that kept his theories about women at the level of projections of his early-childhood perceptions of sex differences. If Horney's perceptions of Freud's distortions and her experience of the way in which women experienced womanhood in the culture he and she shared had been couched in terms that Freud could have accepted, the history of psychoanalysis would have been different.

Margaret Mead, 1976

1961; Szasz, 1961; Bart, 1971; Scheff, 1966). Freud believed that the psychoanalyst-patient relationship must be that of "a superior and a subordinate." The psychotherapist has been seen—by his critics as well as by his patients—as a surrogate parent (father or mother), saviour, lover, expert, and teacher—all roles that foster "submission, dependency, and infantilism" in the patient: roles that imply the therapist's omniscient and benevolent superiority and the patient's inferiority (Freud, 1914/1957). (Szasz has remarked on the dubious value of such a role for the patient and the "undeniable" value of such a role for the "helper.") Practicing psychotherapists have been criticized for treating unhappiness as a disease (whenever it is accompanied by an appropriately high verbal and financial output); for behaving as if the psychotherapeutic philosophy or method can cure ethical and political problems; for teaching people that their unhappiness (or neurosis) can be alleviated through individual rather than collective efforts; for encouraging and legitimizing the urban middle-class tendency toward moral irresponsibility and passivity; for discouraging emotionally deprived persons from seeking "acceptance, dependence and security in the more normal and accessible channels of friendship" (Schofield, 1963). Finally, the institution of psychotherapy has been viewed as a form of social and political control that of-

fers those who can pay for it temporary relief, the illusion of control, and a self-indulgent sense of self-knowledge; and that punishes those who cannot pay by labeling their unhappiness as psychotic or dangerous, thereby helping society consign them to asylums where custodial care (rather than therapeutic illusions) is provided.

These criticisms, of course, apply to both male and female therapy patients. However, the institution of psychotherapy differentially and adversely affects women to the extent to which it is similar to marriage, and insofar as it takes its powerfully socialized cues from Freud and his male and female disciples (Helene Deutsch, Marie Bonaparte, Marynia Farnham, Bruno Bettelheim, Erik Erikson, Joseph Rheingold), viewing woman as essentially "breeders and bearers," as potentially warm-hearted creatures, but more often as simply cranky children with uteri, forever mourning the loss of male organs and male identity. Woman's fulfillment has been couched—inevitably and eternally—in terms of marriage, children, and the vaginal orgasm.[4]

In her 1926 essay entitled "The Flight from Womanhood," Karen Horney says:

[4]The traditional psychoanalytic theories about women, especially Freud's, have been well and fully criticized by Karen Horney, Simone de Beauvoir, Clara Thompson, Natalie Shainess, Betty Friedan, Albert Adler, Thomas Szasz, and Harry Stack Sullivan.

There is one further consideration. Owing to the hitherto purely masculine character of our civilization, it has been much harder for women to achieve any sublimation that would really satisfy their nature, for all the ordinary professions have been filled by men. This again, must have exercised an influence upon women's feelings of inferiority, for naturally they could not accomplish the same as men in these masculine professions and so it appeared that there was a basis in fact for their inferiority. It seems to me impossible to judge to how great a degree the unconscious motives for the flight from womanhood are reinforced by the actual social subordination of women.

Karen Horney, "The Flight from
Womanhood," 1926

The present, analytical picture of feminine development (whether that picture be correct or not) differs in no case by a hair's breadth from the typical ideas that the boy has of the girl.

We are familiar with the ideas that the boy entertains. I will therefore only sketch them in a few succinct phrases, and for the sake of comparison will place in a parallel column our ideas of the development of women.

The Boy's Ideas	Our Psychoanalytic Ideas of Feminine Development
Naive assumption that girls as well as boys possess a penis	For both sexes it is only the male genital which plays any part
Realization of the absence of the penis	Sad discovery of the absence of the penis
Idea that the girl is a castrated, mutilated boy	Belief of the girl that she once possessed a penis and lost it by castration
Belief that the girl has suffered punishment that also threatens him	Castration is conceived of as the infliction of punishment
The girl is regarded as inferior	The girl regards herself as inferior. Penis envy
The boy is unable to imagine how the girl can ever get over this loss or envy	The girl never gets over the sense of deficiency and inferiority and has constantly to master afresh her desire to be a man
The boy dreads her envy	The girl desires throughout life to avenge herself on the man for possessing something which she lacks[5]

The subject of women seems to elicit the most extraordinary and yet authoritative pro-

---

[5]Freud's indirect rejoinder, made in his 1931 essay entitled "Female Sexuality," is as follows:

It is to be anticipated that male analysts with feminist sympathies, and our women analysts also, will disagree with what I have said here. They will hardly fail to object that such notions have their origin in the man's "masculinity complex," and are meant to justify theoretically his innate propensity to disparage and suppress women. But this sort of psychoanalytic argument reminds us here, as it so often does, of Dostoevsky's famous 'knife that cuts both ways.' The opponents of those who reason thus will for their part think it quite comprehensible that members of the female sex should refuse to accept a notion that appears to gainsay their eagerly coveted equality with men. The use of analysis as a weapon of controversy obviously leads to no decision.

At the turn of the century, then, in social and political thinking, in literary and artistic culture, there was a tremendous ferment of ideas regarding sexuality, marriage and family, and women's role. Freudianism was only one cultural product of this ferment. Both Freudianism and Feminism came as reactions to one of the smuggest periods in Western civilization, the Victorian Era, characterized by its familycenteredness, and thus its exaggerated sexual oppression and repression. Both movements signified awakening: but Freud was merely a diagnostician for what Feminism purports to cure. . . . Freudianism was the perfect foil for feminism, because, though it struck the same nerve, it had a safety catch that feminism didn't—it never questioned the given reality.

Shulamith Firestone, *The Dialectic of Sex*, 1970

---

nouncements from many "sensitive" psychoanalysts:

Sigmund Freud:

(Women) refuse to accept the fact of being castrated and have the hope of someday obtaining a penis in spite of everything . . . I cannot escape the notion (though I hesitate to give it expression) that for woman the level of what is ethically normal is different from what it is in man. We must not allow ourselves to be deflected from such conclusions by the denials of the feminists who are anxious to force us to regard the two sexes as completely equal in position and worth (1925/1961).

We say also of women that their social interests are weaker than those of men and that their capacity for the sublimation of their interests is less . . . the difficult development which leads to femininity [seems to] exhaust all the possibilities of the individual (1933/1964).

Erik Erikson:

. . . young women often ask whether they can 'have an identity' before they know whom they will marry and for whom they will make a home. Granted that something in the young woman's identity must keep itself open for the peculiarities of the man to be joined and of the chil-

dren to be brought up, I think that much of a young woman's identity is already defined in her kind of attractiveness and in the selectivity of her search for the man (or men) by whom she wishes to be sought (1964).

Bruno Bettelheim:

. . . as much as women want to be good scientists and engineers, they want first and foremost, to be womanly companions of men and to be mothers (1965).

Joseph Rheingold:

. . . woman is nurturance . . . anatomy decrees the life of a woman . . . When women grow up without dread of their biological functions and without subversion by feminist doctrines and therefore enter upon motherhood with a sense of fulfillment and altruistic sentiment we shall attain the goal of a good life and a secure world in which to live (1964).

These are all familiar views of women. But their affirmation by experts indirectly strengthened such views among men and *directly* tyrannized women, particularly American middle-class women, through the institution of psychotherapy and the tyranny of published "expert" opinion, stressing the importance of

The castration complex of girls is also started by the sight of the genitals of the other sex. They at once notice the difference and, it must be admitted, its significance too. They feel seriously wronged, often declare that they want to "have something like it too," and fall a victim to "envy for the penis," which will leave ineradicable traces on their development and the formation of their character and which will not be surmounted in even the most favourable cases without a severe expenditure of psychical energy.

Sigmund Freud, "The Psychology of
Women," 1933

---

the mother for healthy child development. In their view, lack of—or superabundance of—mother love causes neurotic, criminal, psychiatric, and psychopathic children!

Most child development research, like most birth control research, has centered around women, not men: for this is "women's work," for which she is totally responsible, which is "never done," and for which, in a wage-labor economy, she is never directly paid. She does it for love and is amply rewarded—in the writings of Freud et al.

The headaches, fatigue, chronic depression, frigidity, "paranoia," and overwhelming sense of inferiority that therapists have recorded about their female patients have not been analyzed in any remotely accurate terms. The real oppression (and sexual repression) of women remains unknown to the analysts, for the most part. Such symptoms have not been viewed by most therapists as "indirect communications" that reflect a "slave psychology." Instead, such symptoms have been viewed as hysterical and neurotic productions, as underhanded domestic tyrannies manufactured by spiteful, self-pitying, and generally unpleasant women whose *inability to be happy as women* probably stems from unresolved penis envy, an unresolved Electra (or female Oedipal) complex, or from general, intractable female stubbornness.

In a rereading of some of Freud's early case histories of female "hysterics," particularly his case of Dora (1905/1953), what is remarkable is not his brilliance or his relative sympathy for the female "hysterics," rather, it is his tone: cold, intellectual detective-like, controlling, sexually Victorian. He really does not like his "intelligent" eighteen-year-old patient. For example, he says:

> For several days on end she identified herself with her mother by means of slight symptoms and peculiarities of manner, which gave her an opportunity for some really remarkable achievements in the direction of intolerable behavior.

The mother has been diagnosed, unseen, by Freud, as having "housewife's psychosis."

L. Simon reviews the plight of Dora:

> . . . she (Dora) had been brought to Freud by her father for treatment of . . . 'tussis nervosa, aphonia, depression, and taedium vitae.' Despite the ominous sound of these Latinisms it should be noted that Dora was not in the midst of symptom crisis at the time she was brought to Freud, and there is at least room for argument as to whether these could be legitimately described as symptoms at all. If there was a crisis, it was clearly the father's. Nevertheless, Freud related the development of these 'symptoms' to two traumatic sexual experiences Dora had had with Mr. K., a friend of the family. Freud eventually came to explain the symptoms as expressions of her disguised sexual desire for Mr. K., which he saw, in turn, as derived from feelings she held toward

In [Freud's] paper "Analysis Terminable and Interminable," published in English in 1937, he says the following: "The feminine wish for a penis . . . is the source of acute attacks of depression . . . because . . . they (women) feel analysis will avail them nothing. We can only agree when we discover that their strongest motive in coming for treatment was the hope that they might somehow still obtain a male organ." Such pessimism would only be warranted if it were assumed that it is the actual physical male organ which women are demanding from analysis, whereas it seems to me that when such a wish is expressed the woman is but demanding in this symbolic way some form of equality with men.

Clara Thompson, "Cultural Pressures in the Psychology of Women," 1942

---

her father. Freud attempted, via his interpretations, to put Dora in closer touch with her own unconscious impulses.

. . . Indeed, the case study could still stand as an exemplary effort were it not for a single, but major, problem having to do with the realities of Dora's life. For throughout his therapeutic examination of Dora's unconscious Freud also knew that she was the bait in a monstrous sexual bargain her father had concocted. This man, who during an earlier period in his life had contracted syphilis and apparently infected his wife . . . was now involved in an affair with the wife of Mr. K. There is clear evidence that her father was using Dora to appease Mr. K., and that Freud was fully aware of this . . . At one point Freud states: 'Her father was himself partly responsible for her present danger for he had handed her over to this strange man in the interests of his own love-affair.' But despite this reality, despite his full knowledge of her father's predilections, Freud insisted on examining Dora's difficulties from a strictly intrapsychic point of view, ignoring the manner in which her father was using her, and denying that her accurate perception of the situation was germane.

. . . Freud appears to accept fully the willingness of these men to sexually exploit the women around them. One even finds the imagery of capitalism creeping into his metapsychology. Freud's work with Dora may be viewed as an attempt to deal with the exploitation of women that characterized that historical period without even an admission of the fact of its existence. We may conclude that Freud's failure with Dora was a function of his inappropriate level of conceptual-

ization and intervention. He saw that she was suffering, but instead of attempting to deal with the conditions of her life he chose—because he shared in her exploitation—to work within the confines of her ego (1970).

Although Freud eventually conceded (but not to Dora) that her insights into her family situation were correct, he still concluded that these insights could not make her "happy," Freud's own insights—based on self-reproach, rather than on Dora's reproaching of those around her—would hopefully help her discover her own penis envy and Electra complex; somehow this would magically help her to adjust to, or at least to accept, her only alternative in life: housewife's psychosis. If Dora had not left treatment (which Freud views as an act of revenge), her cure, presumably would have involved her regaining (through desperation and self-hypnosis) a grateful respect for her patriarch-father; loving and perhaps serving him for years to come; or getting married and performing these service functions for a husband or surrogate-patriarch.[6]

---

[6]Freud was not the only one who disliked Dora. Twenty-four years later, as a forty-two-year-old married woman, Dora was referred to another psychiatrist, Felix Deutsch, for "hysterical" symptoms. Let me quote his description of her:

The patient then started a tirade about her husband's indifference toward her offerings and how unfortunate her marital life had been . . . this led her

Szasz (1961) comments on the "hysterical" symptoms of another of Freud's female patients, Anna O., who fell "ill" while nursing her father.

> Anna O. thus started to play the hysterical game from a position of distasteful submission: she functioned as an oppressed, unpaid, sick-nurse, who was coerced to be helpful by the very helplessness of a (bodily) sick patient. The women in Anna O.'s position were—as are their counterparts today, who feel similarly entrapped by their small children—insufficiently aware of

what they valued in life and of how their own ideas of what they valued affected their conduct. For example, young middle-class women in Freud's day considered it their duty to take care of their sick fathers. They treasured the value that it was their role to take care of father when he was sick. Hiring a professional servant or nurse for this job would have created a conflict for them, because it would have symbolized to them as well as to others that they did not love ('care for') their fathers. Notice how similar this is to the dilemma in which many contemporary women find themselves, not, however, in relation to their fathers, but rather in relation to their young children. Today, married women are generally expected to take care of their children; they are not supposed to delegate this task to others. The 'old folks' can be placed in a home: it is all right to delegate their care to hired help. This is an exact reversal of the social situation which prevailed in upper middle-class European circles until the First World War and even after it. Then, children were often cared for by hired help, while parents were taken care of by their children, now fully grown.*

To Freud, it was to Anna's "great sorrow" that she was no longer "allowed to continue nursing the patient."

We may wonder to what extent contemporary psychotherapists still view women as Freud did, either because they believe his theories, or because they are men first and so-called objective professionals second: it may still be in their personal and class interest to (quite unmaliciously) remain "Freudian" in their treatment of women. Two studies relate to this question.

As part of Schofield's 1960 study, each of the

---

to talk about her own frustrated love life and her frigidity ... resentfully she expressed her conviction that her husband had been unfaithful to her ... tearfully she denounced men in general as selfish, demanding, and ungiving ... (she recalled that) her father has been unfaithful even to her mother ... she talked mainly about her relationship to her mother, of her unhappy childhood because of her mother's exaggerated cleanliness ... and her lack of affection for her ... she finally spoke with pride about her *brother's* career, but she had little hope that her *son* would follow in his footsteps ... more than 30 years have elapsed since my visit at Dora's sickbed ... from (an) informant I learned the additional pertinent facts about the fate of Dora ... she clung to (her son) with the same reproachful demands she made on her husband, who had died of a coronary disease—*slighted and tortured by her almost paranoid behavior, strangely enough, he had preferred to die ... rather than divorce her. Without question only a man of this type could have been chosen by Dora for a husband. At the time of her analytic treatment she had stated unequivocally* 'men are all so detestable that I would rather not marry. This is my revenge.' *Thus, her marriage had served only to cover up her distaste of men ... (Dora's) death from a cancer of the colon, which was diagnosed too late for a successful operation, seemed a blessing to those who were close to her. She had been, as my informant phrased it, 'one of the most repulsive hysterics' he had ever met.*
My italics. Felix Deutsch, A footnote to Freud's 'Fragment of an analysis of a case of hysteria,' *The Psychoanalytic Quarterly*, 1957, 26.

The Myth of Mental Illness, excerpts from pp. 213, 194–195, 263–264.

psychotherapists were asked to indicate the characteristics of his "ideal" patient, "that is, the kind of patient with whom you feel you are efficient and effective in your therapy." Schofield reports that "for those psychotherapists who did express a sex preference, a preference for females was predominant in all three professional groups." The margin of preference for female patients was largest in the sample of psychiatrists, nearly two-thirds of this group claiming the female patients as "ideal".[7] From 60 to 70 percent of each of the therapist groups place the ideal patient's age in the twenty to forty year range. Very rarely do representatives of any of the three disciplines express a preference for a patient with a graduate degree (M.A., M.D., Ph.D.).

Summarizing his findings, Schofield suggests that the efforts of most clinical practitioners are "restricted" to those clients who present the Yavis syndrome—youthful, attractive, verbal, intelligent, and successful. And, we may add, hopefully female.

A recent study by Broverman et al. (1970) supports the hypothesis that most clinicians still view their female patients as Freud viewed his. Seventy-nine clinicians (forty-six male and thirty-three female psychiatrists, psychologists, and social workers) completed a sex-role stereotype questionnaire. The questionnaire consists of 122 bipolar items, each of which describe a particular behavior or trait. For example:

very subjective . . . very objective
not at all aggressive . . . very aggressive

The clinicians were instructed to check off those traits that represent healthy male, healthy female, or healthy adult (sex unspecified) behavior. Both male and female clinicians had different standards of mental health for men and women. Their concepts of healthy mature men do not differ significantly from their concepts of healthy mature adults, but their concepts of healthy mature women do differ significantly from those for men or for healthy adults. Finally, what is judged healthy for adults, sex unspecified, and for adult males, is in general highly correlated with previous studies of social desirability as perceived by nonprofessional subjects.

It is clear that for a woman to be healthy she must "adjust" to and accept the behavioral norms for her sex even though these kinds of behavior are generally regarded as less socially desirable. As the authors themselves remark, "This constellation seems a most unusual way of describing any mature, healthy individual."

Obviously, the ethic of mental health is masculine in our culture. Women are perceived as childlike or childish, as *alien* to most male therapists. It is therefore especially interesting that some clinicians, especially psychiatrists, prefer female patients. Perhaps their preference makes good sense; a male therapist may receive a real psychological "service" from his female patient: namely, the experience of controlling and feeling superior to a female being upon whom he has projected many of his own forbidden longings for dependency, emotionality, and subjectivity and from whom, as a superior expert, as a doctor, he is protected as he cannot be from his mother, wife, or girl friend. And he earns money to boot!

---

[7]Less than one-third of the psychiatrists and one-fourth of the psychologists expressed a preferred sex in their ideal patient.

Some Polemical Conclusions and Suggestions

Private psychoanaysis or psychotherapy is a commodity available to those women who can buy it, that is, to women whose fathers, husbands, or boy friends can help them pay for it.[8] Like the Calvinist elect, those women who can *afford* treatment are already "saved." Even if they are never happy, never free, they will be slow to rebel against their psychological and economic dependence on men. One look at their less-privileged (poor, black, and/or unmarried) sisters' position is enough to keep them silent and more or less gratefully in line. The less-privileged women have no real or psychological silks to smooth down over, to disguise, their unhappiness; they have no class to be "better than." As they sit facing the walls, in factories, offices, whorehouses, ghetto apartments, and mental asylums, at least *one* thing they must conclude is that "happiness" is on sale in America—but not at a price they can afford. They are poor. They do not have to be bought off with illusions; they only have to be controlled.

Lower-class and unmarried middle-class women do have access to free or sliding-scale clinics, where, as a rule, they will meet once a week with minimally experienced psychotherapists. I am not suggesting that *maximally* experienced psychotherapists have acquired any expertise in salvation that will benefit the poor and/or unmarried woman. I am merely pointing out that the poor woman receives what is generally considered to be "lesser" treatment.

Given these facts—that psychotherapy is a commodity purchasable, by the rich and most indirectly (in the form of psychiatric incarceration) inflicted on the poor; that as an institution, it socially controls the minds and bodies of middle-class women via the adjustment-to-marriage ideal and the minds and bodies of poor and single women via psychiatric incarceration; and that most clinicians, like most people in a patriarchal society, have deeply antifemale biases—it is difficult for me to make practical suggestions about "improving" therapeutic treatment. If marriage in a patriarchal society is analyzed as the major institution of female oppression, it is logically bizarre to present husbands with helpful hints on how to make their wives "happier." Nevertheless, wives, private patients, and the inmates of mental asylums already exist in large numbers. Therefore, I will make several helpful suggestions regarding woman, "mental illness," and psychotherapy.

Male psychologists, psychiatrists, and social workers must realize that as scientists they know nothing about women; their expertise, their diagnoses, even their sympathy is damaging and oppressive to women. Male clinicians should stop treating women altogether, however much this may hurt their wallets and/or sense of benevolent authority. For most women the psychotherapeutic encounter is just one more power relationship in which they submit to a dominant authority figure. I wonder how well such a structure can encourage independence—or healthy dependence—in a woman. I wonder what a woman can

---

[8]There are many women who spend most of their salary on their "shrink," and who live with men or with their parents, usually under infantilizing conditions, in order to do so. One wonders who exactly, and how many at that, can pay for private psychoanalytic or psychotherapeutic treatment—treatment that costs anywhere from fifteen to fifty dollars per session, two to five times a week, for anywhere from two to five years. None but a small urban minority can afford such treatment at its supposed "best."

learn from a male therapist (however well-intentioned) whose own values are sexist? How free from the dictates of a sexist society can a female as patient be with a male therapist? How much can a male therapist empathize with a female patient? In *Human Sexual Inadequacy* (1970) Masters and Johnson state that their research supported unequivocally the "premise that no man will ever fully understand a woman's sexual function or dysfunction . . . (and the same is true for women) . . . it helps immeasurably for a distressed, relatively inarticulate or emotionally unstable wife to have available a female co-therapist to interpret what she is saying and even what she is attempting unsuccessfully to express to the uncomprehending husband and often to the male co-therapist as well." I would go one step further here and ask: what if the female cotherapist is male-oriented, as much of a sexist as her male counterpart? What if the female therapist has never realized that she is oppressed as a woman? What if the female therapist views marriage and children as sufficient fulfillment for women—except herself?

What "therapeutic" suggestions can I make? Obviously, if "mental illness" does exist, it is not effectively or humanely cured or even isolated in the psychiatric hospital. If it doesn't exist, psychiatric hospitals function as political prisons—for the aged, the young, the unmarried, the poor, the black, and the female. Private treatment for those who can afford it probably serves as a substitute family or friendship institution, and very occasionally, as a legitimate form of religion (that of self-knowledge). However, at its best, if such private treatment does not incorporate a feminist awareness, female patients cannot, by definition, get "better."

Betsy Belote

Masochistic Syndrome, Hysterical Personality, and the Illusion of a Healthy Woman

Keep me rather in this cage, and feed me sparingly, if you dare. Anything that brings me closer to illness and the edge of death makes me more faithful. It is only when you make me suffer that I feel safe and secure. You should never have agreed to be a god for me if you were afraid to assume the duties of a god, and we all know that they are not as tender as all that.

—Pauline Reage*

The dynamics of masochism are crucial to an understanding of woman's psychological, social, and sexual relationship to man in this culture. From a feminist point of view, it is clear that woman's role is subservient to that of a man's, and it is mainly in relation to a man that she achieves a worthwhile, respected identity, i.e., as wife and mother. Unless she is outstandingly productive or brilliant in a professional field, an unmarried woman is usually considered a failure, or someone to be pitied. Thus, the great majority of women view heterosexual relationships as the most valuable part of life, and throw the greatest part of their mental and emotional selves into developing and maintaining a relationship with a man. Upon entering this relationship, the woman's status and value is increased in the eyes of society, but the price she pays for this kind of acceptance is dear: it comprises her selfhood, her independence, her autonomy, her freedom to master her life and to find purpose and

meaning beyond that of biological reproduction or supporting her husband in his life's work.

This paper presents a review of the concept of masochism as defined in the psychological literature, and compares its characteristics with those of the hysterical personality and the "healthy" woman. Various approaches to the origin of the phenomenon will be considered: (a) theories which emphasize an instinctual origin of masochism, as first formulated by Freud; (b) theories which stress biological influences; (c) theories which integrate the above-mentioned models with sociocultural concepts; and (d) theories which stress an adaptational or socially learned basis of masochism.

The term "masochism" was first conceptualized by Krafft-Ebing in 1882, based on the writings of Sacher-Masoch, the romantic French novelist, on the relationship between sex and cruelty. Krafft-Ebing (1937) described the symptoms, but not the origins of masochism. These include: (1) extreme dependence on the love object; (2) extreme submission to, and lust for the object who is cruel (which over time, changes to lust and desire for the cruelty itself); and (3) an "oversexed" condition in certain individuals who require painful stimulation in order to feel excited. Such individuals were described as being sexually inhibited, and compulsively striving to overcome this inhibition through various adaptive maneuvers.

---

*Reage, Pauline. *Story of O.* New York; Grove Press, Inc.

Freud's formulation takes for granted a sadomasochistic relationship which was inherent in the authoritarian society toward which he lacked insight. The woman clearly has to be dominant or submissive, "masculine" or "feminine". . . . Freud's ideal of femininity clearly wavers between the sadomasochistic poles—the narcissistic, vain, self-contained creature demanding a man's adoration and the weak, submissive, clinging woman seeking a big, strong man to adore.

Maurice Green (ed.), *Interpersonal Psychoanalysis: The Selected Papers of Clara M. Thompson*, 1964

Instinctual Theory

Krafft-Ebing's (1937) sexual definition of masochism was accepted and elaborated upon by Freud (1905/1953, 1915/1957, 1919/1955, 1931/1961a). He defined it as a primary instinctual drive, and outlined three types: moral, erotogenic, and feminine. Moral masochism is that type which is found in all people as a certain attitude towards life, and is an especially significant factor in the life of social, national, and religious bodies. It shares with other types of masochism the unconscious tendency to seek pain and enjoy suffering. Moral masochism is supposedly based on unconscious processes, and guilt related to Oedipal wishes; thus, it is basically sexual in character. Moral masochists receive punishment from their superegos, e.g., by being failures in a career, having unhappy marriages, or misfortunes and disappointments of every kind relating to life and love. Feelings of guilt and corresponding wishes to be punished, which are unconsciously working through the inner authority of the superego, destroy all their plans. A typical example of Freud's moral masochism occurring in everyday life is that of the woman who loses sexual interest in her husband, and due to feeling guilty about her lack of interest, punishes herself by missing a pleasureful opportunity, losing her prized wedding ring, or forcing herself to have sex with him.

Erotogenic masochism was explained by Freud (1931/1961a) in the following way: Physical pain, or emotional fright and horror, produces sexual excitement independent of the attitude towards the inflicting object. Freud did not explain or discuss the relationship between sexual synergism with pain and discomfort and the psychological components of masochism. Neither did his concept of erotogenic masochism explain its psychic genesis, except to say it was instinctual. However, he did indicate that moral and feminine masochism were ultimately grounded in actual erotogenic masochism.

Feminine masochism, according to Freud (1919/1955, 1931/1961b), is an expression of "feminine nature," and therefore not considered aberrant in women. Interestingly, he was concerned with the *men* who suffered this disorder, rather than the women. Freud identified passivity with femininity, and masochism with passivity. Thus, masochism in the male was a primary feminine wish, and therefore a serious violation of sex-role standards. Men who are afflicted with feminine masochism enjoy the fantasy of being sexually abused and impregnated against their wish, which to Freud is a frequent unconscious desire of many women. He stated that men who are masochistic in a feminine style experience feeling loved through punishment. The beating woman represents a composite figure: the loving and loved woman (mother), plus the punishing attitude of the father. The male masochist wants to adopt a passive feminine attitude towards the father, in order to be loved like mother, who was both used and loved by father. Since the male masochist takes the position of a woman with the father, he experiences hostility against the woman (self), who was both preferred by the father and who herself preferred the father to the little boy.

The origin of all three types of masochism, in Freud's (1931/1961a) view, is in the instincts of Eros and Thanatos, or, the sexual urge and the death wish (aggression). Eros is seen as a constructive, productive urge; Thanatos as destructive, dissolving, and annihilating. The two instincts fight each other throughout life. The sadistic person uses destructive aggression in order to achieve sexual gratification, and thus quell the destructive urge. For example, a man wooing a woman and asserting power over her demonstrates sadism, yet his ultimate goal is Eros, or union with the woman. The origin of masochism is explained by Freud as the death instinct being nurtured by the sadist. According to later psychoanalysts, Freud's hypothesis of the origin of masochism provides a rough framework, but it is grossly reductionistic. The death instinct hypothesis skims over the question of the psychological derivation of masochism and does not acknowledge the existence of social and cultural factors.

Biologically Based Theories

Helene Deutsch (1930), a psychoanalyst, relates masochism in women to sexual anatomy, stating that to be feminine is to be masochistic. To her, masochism in women is characterological, originating in the realization by a little girl that she has no penis. The young girl gives up her active-sadistic orientation at-

tached to the clitoris when see sees that she lacks the anatomical organ that gives meaning to such an orientation. The shock of this realization leaves a lasting influence and her clitoral sadism is turned inwards to become masochism. The supporting evidence Deutsch used in formulating her theory was weak and biased, consisting primarily of other psychoanalysts' observations of sadistic fantasies in neurotic children, and reconstructions out of the analysis of neurotic adults.

Deutsch wanted to understand the significance of femininity, which to her meant "the passive-masochistic disposition of the mental life of women" (1930, p. 48). She states (1944, p. 278) that masochism is an "elemental power in female mental life," and that it is psychobiologically necessary in all women in order to serve towards the preservation of the species. More specifically, it is necessary for all women, according to Deutsch, to enjoy the "pain" of menstruation and childbirth in order to preserve human life. To Deutsch, one of woman's main tasks in life is to govern this masochism, steer it in the right directions, and thereby protect herself and the future of mankind.

Sandor Rado (1933), in his early writings, agreed with Deutsch that the biological and genital endowment of women forces their sexual development into masochistic channels. He explains that little girls become narcissistically shocked following their discovery of the penis; but, he postulated, the effect of the shock varies depending on the little girl's emotional condition. If the shock occurs in the period of early sexual experimentation, it is a particularly painful experience, in addition to a narcissistic blow. It is so because it arouses in the young girl the belief that males can derive more pleasure out of masturbation than females. This awareness of the possibility of superior pleasure destroys the enjoyment of attainable, but inferior, pleasure. Since, according to Rado, individuals always want what is superior, and lose interest in things that do not match up to their idea of the best, the young girl decathects her own sexuality. However, the extreme mental pain resulting from the discovery of her inferior organ excites her sexually and provides her with a substitute gratification. Thus, the only way she can attain satisfaction is through suffering. She then becomes masochistic in her sexual strivings. The masculinity wish, or a woman's wish to be a man is, to Rado, merely a defense against her basic underlying masochism.

Deutsch's (1930, 1944) and Rado's (1933) views of masochism hold that at root masochism is the result of a woman's genital and reproductive organs in contrast to an instinctual drive (Freud). The problem with the biological view is that it assumes "penis envy" as a phenomenon of *all* women resulting from their awareness of the organ itself, rather than their awareness of the superior position males have in the culture. Young girls likely view the penis as a symbol of power which grants preferential treatment in the society, which may lead them to believe that it gives superior pleasure and consequently to devalue their own genitals. The distinction here, however, is that social and cultural values determine the young girl's attitudes about herself, rather than some arbitrary idea regarding the intrinsic superiority of the penis. The genetic theory also stresses that it is natural and healthy for women to seek pain and to enjoy it (intercourse, menstruation, childbirth) in order to maintain the species, rather than learning to

adapt to it because they have no choice. Recent authors (Bardwick, 1971) have pointed out that the great majority of women today choose to avoid the pain of childbirth through use of pain-relieving anesthesias. It therefore seems clear that biological theories of masochism are based on conjectured evidence, and thus are seriously deficient as explanations.

Theories Integrating Biological and Socio-cultural Influences

Theodore Reik (1941) intensively studied Freud's concept of masochism as it applies to both sexes, and followed it with a definition which includes both biological and social-cultural components. He criticized Freud's instinctual formulation of masochism as a primary instinct, on the basis that erotogenic masochism which Freud claimed had a biological, constitutional basis proves to be "nothing but an infantile physiological precondition for the possible development of masochistic sensations later on, if certain psychic elaborations lead up to it" (1941, p. 30). Since no traces of this destructive, self-annihilating instinct have been found in the infant, according to Reik, Freud's explanation is no more than conjecture.

Reik (1941, p. 141) described masochism as a means to an end, rather than an end in itself:

> The masochist is a person of strongly sadistic disposition, who has been diverted from his instinctual aim by the vision of punishment. This anxiety prevents his achieving satisfaction, and in his conflict between anxiety and urge for pleasure, he finally decides to get rid of his anxiety by that flight forward. He consequently does not strive for discomfort and punishment as such. He

asks for them because they mark the only possible way to untroubled pleasure.

Thus, according to Reik, the masochist does not strive for pain, but for sadistic lust and pleasure, which must be paid for through punishment. He distinguishes the masochism of men from the masochism of women. Biological circumstances such as menstruation, defloration, and childbirth, to Reik, foster an inclination to masochism in women. Cultural factors, such as passive roles women are educated and reinforced to accept, and the suppression of aggressive and violent impulses, favor a vague, mild masochism and a more than mild sadism in women in this culture. He continues by saying that although biological circumstances favor an inclination towards masochism in women, they need not necessarily lead to it. Reik, however, draws a line between the masochism women suffer as a result of cultural roles and their biological state and "masochism as a crude instinctual perversion" in which discomfort, shame, or disgrace are desired. The latter, Reik (1941, p. 212) feels occurs much more often among men.

Masochism as an instinctual aberration and as character seems to disagree with the idea of masculinity and be more in harmony with the idea of the woman. Freud expressed this same opinion by saying masochism sustained an intimate relation to femininity.

The masochistic fantasy in women, to Reik, is supposedly composed of yielding and surrendering themes. In contrast, masochism in men is characterized by ferocity, aggressiveness, vigor, and resoluteness. According to Reik, the difference between male and female experiences of masochism is based on the male's penis, which, he posits, is the carrier of aggression. In another vein, Reik, like Freud, viewed the female superego as weaker and more yielding than the male's. The female conscience therefore experiences guilt less intensely and does not promote self-punishment to the same degree as the male conscience. Female masochism, then, takes the form of enjoyment of passivity, submission, and suffering. The woman also enjoys her partner's strength and power, as well as humiliation as a sexual object, and sexual self-humiliation.

Although Reik (1941), as noted above, recognizes the influence of cultural factors and biological circumstances in encouraging the development of "mild masochism" in women, he distinguishes between that and a more perverted masochism which involves suffering pain, being beaten and tied up, and disgraced and humiliated in an extreme way. While he agreed with Freud that to be feminine was to be passive, he did not feel that being passive included being masochistically perverted.

Edmund Bergler (1949) integrated the instinctual and the adaptational views of masochism. He defined two different types: perversion masochism and psychic masochism. Perversion masochism is that type in which the individual experiences bodily pain as pleasurable, while psychic masochism is based on displaced aggression which results in self-punishment and produces unconscious pleasure. The psychic masochist counteracts her own aggression with feelings of guilt and receives libidinal pleasure by being humiliated and defeated. Thus, according to Bergler, the psychic masochist enjoys pain and seeks it out in order to gratify her libido. Bieber (1966) clarifies that there is a difference between

Alcestis on the Poetry Circuit

(In Memoriam *Marina Tsvetaeva, Anna Wickham, Sylvia Plath, Shakespeare's sister, etc. etc.*)

The best slave
does not need to be beaten.
She beats herself.

Not with a leather whip,
or with sticks or twigs,
not with a blackjack
or a billyclub,
but with the fine whip
of her own tongue
& the subtle beating
of her mind
against her mind.

For who can hate her half so well
as she hates herself?
& who can match the finesse
of her self-abuse?

Years of training
are required for this.
Twenty years
of subtle self-indulgence.
self-denial;
until the subject
thinks herself a queen
& yet a beggar—
both at the same time.

She should mistrust herself
in everything but love.
She should choose passionately
& badly.

She should feel lost as a dog
without her master.
She should refer all moral questions
to her mirror.
She should fall in love with a cossack
or a poet.

She must never go out of the house
unless veiled in paint.
She must wear tight shoes
so she always remembers her bondage.
She must never forget
she is rooted in the ground.

Though she is quick to learn
& admittedly clever,
her natural doubt of herself
should make her so weak
that she dabbles brilliantly
in half a dozen talents
& thus embellishes
but does not change
our life.

If she's an artist
& comes close to genius,
the very fact of her gift
should cause her such pain
that she will take her own life
rather than best us.

& after she dies, we will cry
& make her a saint.

Erica Jong

self-injury, which is intrinsic to masochism, and submission to a stronger opponent, as in "normal" male-female relationships, which he does not see as masochistic, in contrast to some feminist positions.

Biological and instinctual theories are not

Daddy's Girl, always tense and fearful, uncool, unanalytical, lacking objectivity, appraises Daddy, and thereafter, other men, against a background of fear ("respect") and is not only unable to see the empty shell behind the aloof façade, but accepts the male definition of himself as superior. . . .

Valerie Solanis, *Scum Manifesto*, 1967–1968

---

acceptable for reasons stated earlier. However, the sociocultural aspect which integrationists consider may be useful as explanatory concepts for masochism.

Adaptational Theory

Adaptational theories of masochism present the view that masochism is a socially conditioned defense against deep feelings of fear. This view differs from the instinctual and biological models in that it posits that masochism is *exclusively* learned, socially conditioned behavior.

Karen Horney (1923–1937/1967) was one of the first psychoanalysts to discuss the influence of social and cultural factors in the development of masochism. In her early writings on masochism, she criticized Rado's (1933) biological formulation and provided a major clarification. Horney asserted that Rado's theory implied that the sex life of the majority of women was pathologic, and was in contradiction to Freud's pleasure principle concept (which states that individuals seek satisfaction in every situation). Horney noted that even assuming that little girls do suffer shock from the realization of an unattainable source of pleasure, it does not logically follow that the pain should affect her sexually. She stated that if Rado's formulation was correct it should follow that little boys would perceive their fathers' larger penises as the source of greater pleasure. Horney's final point was that it makes no sense that the little girl's shock reaction to penis awareness should have a lasting, permanent effect driving her to seek suffering throughout her life.

Horney's first hypothesis regarding masochism was that all masochistic strivings are ultimately directed towards getting rid of the self, experienced as conflicted and limited. Furthermore, to her, not all suffering was masochistic, but rather, often merely an accidental by-product of neurotic conflict. Horney (1939/1966) modified this first hypothesis when she attempted to answer the question of whether striving for the relinquishment of self ultimately determines the masochistic process. This modification pointed out two major characteristics of the masochist: first, there is a tendency towards self-minimizing, the result of which is to feel unattractive, insignificant, inefficient, stupid, and worthless. The masochist thus tends to be inconspicuous, and to cringe into a corner. Second, the masochist demonstrates a tendency towards personal dependency as a life condition. This type of individual feels as incapable of living without the presence, benevolence, love, or friendship of another person as she is of living without oxygen.

> The masochistic [woman] feels [she] cannot do anything on [her] own, and expects to receive everything from the partner: love, success, care, protection. Without ever realizing it, and mostly in contrast to [her] conscious modesty and humility, [her] expectations are parasitic in character. [Her] reasons for clinging to another person are so stringent that [she] may exclude from awareness the fact that the partner is not and never will be the appropriate person to fulfill [her] expectations; . . . (Horney, 1939/1966 pp. 251–252)

Masochistic trends, in Horney's view, arise out of the same circumstances which promote

The innately logical mind of woman, her unique sense of balance, orderliness, and reason, rebels at the terrible realization that justice has been an empty word, that she has been forced for nearly two millennia to worship false gods and to prostrate herself at their empty shrines.

Elizabeth Gould Davis, *The First Sex*, 1971

perfectionistic and narcissistic trends. All are simply psychological defenses originating from a combination of adverse environmental influences upon the child. These early experiences make her view the world as potentially hostile. The narcissist copes with these negative feelings through self-inflation, the perfectionist by overconformity to standards, while the masochist looks for safety through becoming attached to a person perceived as more powerful and ultimately becoming dependent upon this person.

> By submerging [her] own individuality entirely and by merging with the partner the masochistic [woman] gains a certain reassurance ... to be compared with that achieved by a small endangered nation which surrenders its rights and its independence to a powerful and aggressive nation and thereby wins protection. One of the differences is that the small nation knows it does not take this step because of its love for the bigger nation, while in the neurotic's mind the process often takes on the appearance of loyalty, devotion or great love. But actually the masochistic [woman] is incapable of love, nor does [she] believe the partner or anyone else can love [her] (Horney, 1939/1966 p. 253)

To Horney, masochistic dependency is replete with hostility (at the inevitable imperfections of the partner). This hostility is expressed in a passive-aggressive manner, i.e., through excessive dependency and moral indignation. She distinguishes between masochistic character structure and masochistic sexual perversions. In short, the masochistic character structure explains the perversion, but the perversion does not explain the character. The

perversion is simply the result of the masochistic dependency and unobtrusiveness carried to the extreme.

Horney stated that the cultural reality of male supremacy makes it difficult for any woman to escape some degree of masochism. She points out that male doctrines which define the feminine as innately weak, overly emotional, dependent, and limited in their ability to work well alone, influence women to act in those ways. Horney also states that the fact that women who display these characteristics are preferred by men as marital partners and lovers is profound reinforcement for women to act in those ways. Since most people want to be approved of and accepted, it follows that most women will adopt the kind of social behavior for which they will be rewarded. As a consequence, a great majority of women internalize these feminine characteristics and it is assumed by some theoreticians that this behavior is actually the "nature" of women. Horney (1935/1967, p. 231) explains:

> It therefore seems no exaggeration to say that in such social organizations, masochistic attitudes (or rather milder expressions of masochism) are favored in women while they are discouraged in men. Qualities like emotional dependence on the other sex (clinging vine), absorption in "love," inhibition of the expansive, autonomous development, etc., are regarded as quite desirable in women but are treated with opprobrium and ridicule when found in men.

Wilhelm Reich (1949) also discarded Freud's instinctual concept and replaced it with an adaptive interpretation. He viewed masochism as a defense involving: (1) the choosing of a

---

The Friend

We sat across the table.
he said, cut off your hands.
they are always poking at things.
they might touch me.
I said yes.

Food grew cold on the table.
he said, burn your body.
it is not clean and smells like sex.
it rubs my mind sore.
I said yes.

I love you, I said.
that's very nice, he said
I like to be loved,
that makes me happy.
Have you cut off your hands yet?

Marge Piercy

lesser injury, and (2) a means of punishing significant figures whom the masochist perceived as denying him love in childhood. Reich's argument revolves around the fact that Freud's instinctual hypothesis is in direct contradiction to Freud's pleasure principle theory, a point which had also been made by Horney (1939/-1966). Furthermore, Reich proposed that masochism is associated with an excessive need for love based on great fear of being left alone. The masochist also fears success, which symbolizes genital exposure. In regard to the fear of genital exposure, Reich was speaking exclusively of masochism in males.

Clara Thompson (1931–1961/1964) emphasized the manipulative aspects of masochism as it occurs in interpersonal relationships. To her, the masochistic person is attempting to gain the love, security, and dependency which was lacking in childhood. The masochist's behavior demonstrates passive dependency and hostile aggression, suffering, martyrdom. In her view, the masochist provokes guilt in others, who feel compelled to assume burdens of care and responsibility; this mechanism then becomes a transactional device for personal gain. To Thompson, masochism is an adaptive mechanism, or a defense. She described its origins as follows:

> The thumbnail sketch is this—no affection from either parent, parents at war with each other. One of them can be seduced into a show of concern for the child if the child can demonstrate that he has suffered at the hands of the other, or if he can create some other situation of suffering. This is the nearest to love that the child can ever achieve. Through suffering, he either plays on the sense of guilt of the parent or parents, and thus gets some compensatory attention, or he succeeds in getting them to battle with each other. Again, if you can't be loved you can at least get attention, and maybe if you suffer enough you will be forgiven.
>
> This pattern becomes a way of life. There are two possible lines of development. One is an exaggerated taking of the blame to oneself. There is usually a quality of insincerity in this attitude. The patient says "I deserve to suffer because I am so bad or so worthless." . . . The other attitude is that of the martyr: "I have given you the best years of my life, and this is my reward." Both are devices to get attention through suffering. (1931–1961/1964:186)

According to Thompson, intimacy is the ultimate goal of the masochistic person. There is

*Just as a bird that flies about
and beats itself against the cage,
finding at last no passage out
it sits and sings, and so overcomes its rage.*

Abraham Cowley (1618-1667)

never open hostility, rather anger is expressed by means of making another person feel guilty, or getting another person to fight for her own life or actions.

Irving Bieber (1966) sees sadism and masochism as maladaptive, pathological responses to a threat or a perception of a threat in every context of experience. He distinguished self-destructive impulses and acts from those that are defensive and aiming towards preserving life, love, etc. He considers only the latter to be masochistic and states that while sexual masochism is relatively uncommon, non-sexual masochism is demonstrated in most psychiatric patients (most of whom, he fails to mention, are women).

Masochistic defenses appearing in non-sexual behaviors are particularly evident in attitudes and acts felt to be competitive. Fears, whether real or fancied of antagonizing competitors by successful performance and fear of evoking competitive or hostile feelings among rivals tend to induce self-sabotaging tactics (Bieber, 1966, p. 266).

Bieber states further that masochism in general is a defensive reaction to a threat, just as submission is a defensive, self-protective posture. He sees passivity, however, as pathological, and not a characteristic which is basic to the nature of women:

Passivity is not a feminine characteristic; it is the manifestation of a chronic inhibition of protective resources and it is pathological for females as for males. Submission is one of the basic social responses of the species to a threat. In Western culture, however, passivity, sub-

missiveness, dependency are more acceptable for females; but such culture themes do not establish these attitudes and behaviors as non-pathological. Rather, they indicate that women are not yet fully emancipated (Bieber, 1966, p. 267).

Rado (1956) revised his earlier (1933) explanation of masochism and began stressing adaptational theory. In his new formulation, both sadist and masochist develop "pain-dependence" early in life in response to disciplinary stress. The individual later pursues punishment as the only means by which he can obtain "license to gratify forbidden desires." The disorder is thus one of the conscience rather than of sexual function.

Simone de Beauvoir (1970) clarifies that masochism exists in a woman only when she chooses to abdicate her will to that of another person and thus becomes the possession of that person. She disagrees with Deutsch (1930, 1944) that through being penetrated by a man in the act of intercourse, a woman is masochistic, and states that this act may represent transcendence of self or the unity of self with the lover, rather than abdication. To de Beauvoir, an individual is masochistic when her own ego is viewed as separate from the self and is regarded as being totally dependent upon the will of another.

De Beauvoir holds that masochism is a way of escaping from the conflicts created by woman's "sexual destiny" by wallowing in it, rather than a solution to it. The true solution to de Beauvoir, is to overcome her passivity and establish an equal relationship with her male partner.

Adaptational theories, unlike instinctual and biological theories of masochism, hold that

Reverse Paranoia *(as defined by Leonard Roy Frank): Affected persons imagine they are safe when, in fact, they are in danger.*
Paranoia: Affected persons imagine they are in danger when, in fact, they are not.

Madness Network News, 1975

---

masochism is socially conditioned, learned behavior. Out of all the theoreticians who hold this view however, only Horney (1939/1966, 1923-1937/1967) actually makes the connection between culturally influenced sex roles and masochism in women. In the view of this researcher, Horney's analysis of masochism is a feminist one, because she has gone to the very root of it by making the connection between the sociopolitical structure, sex roles, and the psychological syndrome itself.

The Hysterical Personality

Almost all of the writers who have discussed the "hysterical personality" agree that it is found almost exclusively in women. In fact it is often described as a caricature of femininity. *The Diagnostic and Statistical Manual of Mental Disorders* (1968) defines it as follows:

> These behavior patterns are characterized by excitability, overreactivity, and self-dramatization. This self-dramatization is always attention seeking and often seductive, whether or not the patient is aware of its purpose. These personalities are also immature, self-centered, often vain, and usually dependent on others.

Freud did not discuss the "hysterical personality," but rather "hysterical conversion." Although the two are different in symptomatology, they are similar in dynamics, according to classical psychoanalytic theory, as both disorders entail unresolved Oedipal conflicts, penis envy, and oral fixation which lead to ambivalent, repressed sexuality. In his paper on female sexuality (1931/1961b), Freud discussed the "normal" female. In that paper he asserts that the well-adjusted female is one who accepts the fact that she has no penis, and thus substitutes for this lack by turning her attention to the wish for a baby. In his paper on libidinal types, Freud (1931/1961a) describes the "erotic type" as a person whose main interest in life is focused on love and loving, but above all on being loved. The dread of losing love makes her particularly dependent. Freud's description of the "erotic type" is similar to descriptions of the "hysterical personality," the masochistic woman, and the "normal" female in this society.

Wilhelm Reich (1949) pointed out that the "hysterical personality" was very seductive and sexually provocative, yet usually "frigid" in sexual relationships. Reich felt that the "hysterical personality's" actual needs were for affection and nurturance, not sex. Furthermore, to Reich, the hysterical personality is characterized by sharp disappointment reaction, imaginativeness, lack of conviction, compliance, readily giving way to depreciation and disparagement, the compulsive need to be loved, overdependency on others for approval, and powerful capacity for dramatization and somatic compulsion. Reich's major concern however, was with the underlying "oral fixation" of the "hysterical personality," rather than the symptomatology.

Marmor (1953) agreed with Reich that the underlying oral character is the most important variable in determining the "hysterical personality" rather than the symptomatology. The "hysterical personality," to Marmor, is resistant to change, immature, has an unstable, weak ego, is very suggestible and can cease symptomatology quickly, but the underlying character structure does not change: i.e., "If you (therapist) will love and protect me, I will be whatever you want." In this way symptoms may disappear, but the underlying oral dependency remains.

Easser and Lesser (1965) noted that the "hysterical personality" is an expression of heightened femininity, and they observed that therapists are often "duped" by it.

> The rubric [of hysteria] connotes the hysterical woman, hysterical attacks, in short, "a caricature of femininity." Hysterics are wont to live up to, in fact, to exaggerate their role. They apply themselves to whatever name one may call them. The psychoanalyst in his countertransference can be aroused by the contagion of the exaggerated effect. He finds himself "holding the bag" emotionally, provoked into overplaying his role as a therapist, while his patient changes a course and heads down a new emotional alley, perhaps a blind one. (p. 391)

Martin (1971) described the extreme dependency needs of the "hysterical personality" and maintained that these needs were illustrative of a symbiotic character structure involving unresolved separation anxiety. In intimate relationships, the love object is depended upon to supplement the "hysterical personality's" deficient ego. The hysterical woman can put up with tremendous hostility emanating from an intimate involvement, but not the loss of the object. It is interesting that this same description is given by Horney (1939, 1973) for the masochistic woman.

Howard Wolowitz (1972) considered the issue of cultural factors contributing to the development of the "hysterical personality." He noted, as did Parsons (1955), that sex-role socialization of men emphasizes mastery-achievement responsibilities. As a consequence, women usually feel strongly inclined to elicit strong positive emotional responses from others, and by so doing, measure their own value and worth. The major contribution of Wolowitz's paper is its development and discussion of the fact that *every* American woman is conditioned to develop an hysterical character in nonpathological, or acceptable form. The cultural factor which creates this "hysterical" response in women is the oppression of being stereotyped as inferior, and the resulting lack of skills, power, and equal opportunity.

Wolowitz also says that the "hysterical personality" has difficulty making friends with same-sexed individuals. These individuals feel more at ease with men than women, as they are less competitive with men. As children, they often have been competitive with their mothers, sisters, female cousins, and peers, all for the attention of a male figure. "Hysterical personalities" attempt to find in men the nurturance they missed in their own mothers, and cannot receive from other women due to disappointment in women. However, since most men cannot provide the emotional expressiveness the "hysterical personality" needs, she continues to have an unconscious longing for a maternal figure. "Hysterical personalities" seek responsivity and self-validation from others; therefore, they are high in "other-directedness," and in their frantic effort to gain love and attention, "hysterical personalities," according to Wolowitz, sacrifice feelings of realness and genuineness, losing themselves in the roles that they play. Feelings of falseness, emptiness, and loneliness result. Furthermore, they often utilize sex to buy companionship or a sense of immediate worth and power. Traits such as charm, flirtatiousness, provocativeness, exhibitionism, and suggestibility, void of genuineness, are the chief instruments utilized in their struggle to get love and attention.

The Female Masochist, the Hysterical Personality, and the Illusion of the "Healthy" Female

While many authors have noted the similarity between the "hysterical personality" and femininity, and masochism and femininity, none have pointed out the relationship among all three of these syndromes.

One of the most striking features of masochism and hysteria as expressed by women is its subtlety and invisibility to the acculturated American. This is so because masochistic and hysterical behavior is so similar to the concept of "femininity" that the three are not clearly distinguishable. That women are accepted and rewarded for exhibiting passivity and dependence in their behavior, affect, and cognitive styles has been repeatedly validated (Beller and Neubauer, 1963; Bieri, Bradburn, & Galinsky, 1958; Brim, Glass, Lavin, & Goodman, 1962; Kagan and Moss, 1962; Maccoby, 1966; McGuire, 1961; Sears, Whiting, Nowlis, & Sears, 1953; Spangler & Thomas, 1962; Vaught, 1965; Witkin, Dyk, Fatterson, Goodenough, & Karp, 1962).

While the female sex role is viewed as an inferior one by dominant (male) societal standards, the role is also viewed as "healthy" for women by these same standards. Table 1 demonstrates that the characteristics of a "healthy" female closely parallel the characteristics of the masochistic and hysterical personalities.

The characteristics of the healthy female were derived from a recent study by Broverman, Broverman, Clarkman, Rosencrantz, and Vogel (1970). Their findings indicated that both male and female psychotherapists adhere to societal stereotypes of women as inferior beings. A questionnaire containing 122 bipolar items describing particular behaviors or traits was sent to a random sample of clinicians of both sexes. They were instructed to check those items which best described a healthy male, healthy female, and healthy adult (sex unspecified). The results clearly pointed out the strong sexist bias of both male and female psychotherapists. The typical clinician's concept of the healthy mature man was similar to that of a healthy mature adult in general, while the picture of the healthy mature female differed strongly from both. According to the study, healthy women differ from healthy men in being:

> . . . more submissive, less independent, less adventurous, more easily influenced, less aggressive, less competitive, more easily excitable in minor crises, more easily hurt, more emotional, more conceited about their appearance, less objective, and less interested in math and science (p. 6).

Thus, one can be a healthy male and a healthy adult at the same time but not a healthy woman and a healthy adult. Furthermore, the results indicated that healthy male characteristics are viewed as more socially desirable than healthy female characteristics.

Because the accepted model of the "healthy" female is childlike, inferior, and non-expansive; and the model for the healthy adult is a masculine one, it becomes impossible for any woman to be mature or healthy according to the dominant standards. This puts woman in a most frustrating double-bind: she is damned if she accepts the traditional feminine role, and damned if she does not. The

I became a feminist as an alternative to becoming a masochist.

Sally Kempton, *Esquire*, 1970

TABLE 1

A COMPARISON OF THE CHARACTERISTICS OF
MASOCHISM, THE HYSTERICAL PERSONALITY
AND THE HEALTHY FEMALE

Female Masochism*	Hysterical Personality**	Healthy Female***
	Overreactivity	More emotional
	Excitability	More easily excitable in a minor crisis
Emotional dependence	Dependency	Less independent
Low self-esteem	Low self-esteem	
Accepts pain		More easily hurt
Fears success		Less competitive
Self-sabotage		More easily influenced
Self-denial		More submissive
Perceives world as hostile		Less aggressive
Inhibition of expansive, autonomous development	Lack of orgasmic sexual response	Less adventurous
Use of weakness and helplessness to woo the other sex	Seductiveness	More conceited about appearance
Absorption in love		Less objective
		Dislikes math and science

*Horney (1939/1966, p. 229)
**Diagnostic and Statistical Manual of Mental Disorders (1968), Reich (1949)
***Broverman, et al. (1970)

most she can hope for is to find security through adjusting to being inferior, thus becoming masochistic and hysterical as well.

Conclusion

The preceding discussion has attempted to demonstrate the pathology inherent in "normal" femininity through illustrating its similarity to both masochism and the hysterical personality. Moreover, this pathology is invisible, because it is accepted as "normal" by the mainstream of American culture.

The woman who accepts the feminine role is placed in an impossible emotional bind since the role itself is pathological. Furthermore, the woman who rejects the feminine role is considered deviant and therefore unacceptable. This "damned if she does, damned if she does not" proposition ultimately leads many women to their own madness. A feminist analysis is suggested here as one alternative to this bind. Through such analysis women may better prepare themselves to break away from femininity and develop their own personal standards and styles of behavior.

Lenore Sawyer Radloff and Sue Cox

Sex Differences in Depression in Relation to Learned Susceptibility

There is a considerable body of research showing that women have higher rates of certain mental illnesses than men. Gove and Tudor (1973) reviewed community surveys, first admissions to psychiatric hospitals, psychiatric care in general hospitals, and psychiatric outpatient care in private and public clinics in North America and Western Europe between World War II and 1970. After evaluating their findings, they suggested that the likeliest explanation lay in the social roles of women, particularly married women, in modern industrial society.

More recently, strong evidence that depression in particular is more common among women than among men has been found not only in studies of psychiatric patients but also in household surveys of random samples of the general population using self-report measures of depressive symptoms. In their review of this evidence, Weissman and Klerman (1977) conclude that patterns of sex differences cannot be explained entirely by sex biases in symptom reporting and help-seeking or by genetic and endocrine factors alone. They suggest that the effects of social roles and social stresses are also important in relation to sex differences in depression, and that this is a promising area of research.

The focus of this paper will be on the psychosocial aspects of depression and certain selected theories of depression. For a review of the biological basis of depression and other psychological theories see Williams, Katz, and

Shield (1972), Akiskal and McKinney (1975), and Friedman and Katz (1974). Theories of depression that could be relevant to sex differences and in particular to depression in women are first presented, followed by a model of depression that has been proposed by the first author as an attempt to integrate several cognitive and behavioral models. Data on depression that have been presented elsewhere (Radloff, 1975; Radloff, 1980; Radloff & Rae, 1979; Radloff & Rae, in press) are discussed here in terms of the model and in terms of other related work.

Definitions of Depression

There are a variety of definitions of depression and its symptoms; a diagnosis of clinical depression depends on the pattern of symptoms as well as their severity and duration. One way of classifying the symptoms of depression (e.g., see Beck, 1967) is into a syndrome of four dimensions. The *cognitive dimension* includes hopeless, helpless beliefs and the conviction that nothing will ever get better. The *motivational/behavioral dimension* includes reduced activity and feeling apathetic and lacking in energy. Depression often interferes with normal activities and especially disrupts interpersonal relationships. The *affective dimension* includes feeling sad, blue, depressed, and unable to enjoy. The depressed person may also feel irritable and anxious, even quite openly angry and hostile,

---

An Expression

anger
is killing
my face.
it squints all day
despite cool remarks
it thinks the sun
is after it.
it thinks the whole world
is after it!
building armies
above the brow

anger
is killing
my face.
it squints all day
despite cool remarks
it thinks the sun
is after it.

it thinks the whole world
is after it!
building armies
above the brow
just in case.

meanwhile, no one
notices; even suspects
go about private
maneuvers.
one day,
wrinkles will tell
stories like old soldiers
when my lips have nothing
left to say,
pain will lean forward
and speak
for itself.

                                    Susan Efros

---

especially with the people closest to her or him (Weissman and Paykel, 1974). This anger is apparently not used to communicate and solve problems but rather simply to express distress. The so-called *"vegetative"* dimension includes disturbances of appetite and sleep. Most commonly, depressives have insomnia and a loss of appetite, but some sleep much more than usual, and/or overeat. These symptoms usually appear only in fairly severe depression (McLean, 1976).

Theories of Depression

Object Loss

In psychoanalytic theory, object loss refers to the loss of a cathected object. Here, an object refers to the internal psychological representation of an external person or thing. Internal objects are invested with a lesser or greater amount of intrapsychic emotional energy (cathexis). Since external object loss usually elicits secondary intrapsychic object loss, the term object loss has been used somewhat loosely to apply to both the social event and the psychological process involved. (Intrapsychic loss or decrease in investment of emotional energy in an internal object may occur, however, even when the external person or thing still exists.) Some examples of object loss might be the loss of an important relationship, a job, a social role, or an activity.

Depressive reactions to a traumatic separation from their mothers has been studied in

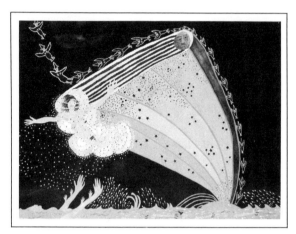

Jumping Off the Golden Gate Bridge by Ann Leda Shapiro. Reprinted by permission.

human infants and children (Bowlby, 1969, 1973; Spitz, 1965) and in other primates as well (Scott & Senay, 1973).

Aggression Turned Inward

The aggression turned inward hypothesis was originally proposed by Abraham (1911/1948) and Freud (1917/1957) and was elaborated upon by other psychoanalytic theorists. (See Mendelsohn [1960] for a summary and review of these theories.) For Abraham, aggressive impulses toward a love object became redirected toward the self upon the loss of the object. Freud, however, assumed that the aggression toward another became directed against the self by means of object identification, a more primitive process occurring before relationship to an object is established. Most psychoanalytic theories include in their formulations of depression extreme oral dependency, intense narcissistic needs, low self-esteem, a severe and punishing superego, and feelings of guilt in relation to aggression turned inward.

Critique of Psychoanalytic Theories

Psychoanalytic theories have been presented because of their historical importance and to provide a context for the theories which follow. Unfortunately, psychodynamic formulations are seldom stated in ways amenable to empirical testing, and are therefore beyond the usual empirical research methods which would allow these theories to be confirmed or disconfirmed.

It is interesting, however, that there are parallels between psychoanalytic descriptions of depressives and those of the "feminine personality." This similarity has also been noted by Weissman and Klerman (1977), and in fact they credit recent feminist critique with the linking together of these two aspects of psychoanalytic theories, which had existed and remained unconnected for fifty years.

According to psychoanalytic theory, the "*normal* feminine personality" is characterized by narcissism, masochism, low self-esteem, excessive dependency, and inhibited hostility as a result of the female resolution of the oedipal situation. This could be seen as indirect validation of these psychoanalytic theories, since the higher rates of depression in women may be related to female psychological development within psychoanalytic terms. According to psychoanalytic theory, however, the etiology of depression lies within the oral and anal stages of psychosexual development, whereas the origins of the "female personality" are presumed to occur in the phallic stage, so the connection is questionable. Furthermore, there is empirical support for only very limited aspects of the psychoanalytic descriptions of both the depressed and the female personality (e.g., see Chodoff, 1972).

One possible explanation for the similarities between depression and "femininity" (particularly low self-esteem, which has been empirically validated) may be that they are both the result of relative powerlessness and helplessness.

Learned Helplessness

In an interpretive review of research studies on depression, Weissman and Klerman (1977) suggest that "elements of the traditional female role *either through learned or real helplessness,* may contribute to depression" (italics added). In discussing depression in the context of powerlessness, Bart (1975) also suggests that the learned helplessness model of depression (Seligman, 1975) is useful in understanding the "depressenogenic" features of the traditional female role.

The experimental paradigm for learned helplessness is a dog strapped in a harness who receives traumatic and uncontrollable electrical shocks. When the animal is no longer harnessed and receives electrical shocks, it will typically sit or lie, quietly whining, until the shock terminates, making no attempt to cross a barrier and thus escape the shock. An animal not previously subjected to inescapable and uncontrollable shocks will typically run and howl, quickly learning to cross the barrier to escape the pain. The first animal by contrast seems to give up and passively accept the pain.

What is crucial about learned helplessness is the extent to which having no control over traumatic events in the past leads a person to believe that nothing that she or he does matters, and further leads to failure to act or try to respond in adaptive ways to *current* trauma. By passive acceptance of current trauma, the person continues to feel that she or he has no control over the pain, which leads to further development of negative expectations and a sense of helplessness, hopelessness, and powerlessness.

Reinforcement

Behavioristic theory of human behavior and behavior modification as a psychotherapeutic method had their beginnings in controlling the behavior of animals by means of reinforcement. Behavioral approaches to depression (e.g., Lewinsohn, 1975) suggest that depression is related to a loss of major sources of positive reinforcement, and to low rates of reward or rewarded behavior. In addition, the "sick role" or certain depressive behaviors may be positively reinforced.

According to reinforcement theory, depression can be seen as a "vicious cycle," similar to learned helplessness. A lack of rewards can lead to fewer initiated responses and more passivity, which results in even fewer rewards.

Cognition

Cognitive theories of depression focus on the thoughts of the depressed person, which begin with a sense of loss. Low self-esteem, self-reproaches and self-criticisms, pessimism and hopelessness also pervade the cognitive processes of the depressed person. The "cognitive triad" (Beck, 1967) refers to a negative view of the self, the outside world, and the future. The negative attitudes described by this theory predispose a person to depression and maintain it, although the actual occurrence of depression also depends on precipitating events. The cognitive view is that cognitions determine affect, so that events interpreted pessimistically will lead to depressed affect.

Stress and Life Events

The relationship of life events (often interpreted as stressors) to the onset of illness has been established (Holmes & Masuda, 1973; Paykel, 1973). Such stressors may increase susceptibility to depression as well as to other forms of illness. More recent work by Brown and Harris (1978) on life stresses and depression present an analysis of depression in terms of life events and conditions as provoking agents, which interact with individual vulnerability factors such as those related to socioeconomic status and mastery.

A Sequential Model of Learned Susceptibility and Precipitating Factors

Previous work of the first author (Radloff & Rae, 1979; Radloff & Rae, in press) presents a sequential model of susceptibility and precipitating factors in depression which combines features of several other theories of depression: the reinforcement model (Lewinsohn, 1975), the learned helplessness model (Seligman, 1975), the attribution model (Abramson, Seligman, & Teasdale, 1978), the cognitive model (Beck, 1976), and the sequential model (McLean, 1976). This model suggests that the four types of symptoms in the syndrome of depression (cognitive, behavioral, affective, and somatic) are logically linked together in a causal sequence. Furthermore, the symptoms are of such a nature that they reinforce each other so that the sequence can become a vicious cycle.

The epidemiologic (or "disease") model assumes that the probability that an individual will develop a given disease depends on that individual's susceptibility to the disease and the exposure to the precipitating factors that initiate the disease. In the case of depression, both susceptibility and precipitating factors may include social and biological factors. It is here suggested that there is a component of susceptibility that is a learned habit, which could be called a "helpless style of coping" and that the precipitating factors that would activate this kind of susceptibility would be problems or stresses that need to be coped with.

General learning theory has shown that in the presence of a goal (to achieve a reward or avoid a punishment), the response that leads to success in reaching the goal (i.e., is reinforced) will be "learned" (i.e., will be more likely to occur again in similar circumstances). Learning will not occur if any part of the sequence is absent, that is, if there is no goal, no response, no reinforcement, or no contingency between response and reinforcement. A person may fail to learn to cope if one or more of these factors is consistently missing. For example, extremely overprotected or "spoiled" children may learn as little as children in an extremely deprived environment. People cannot learn to obtain rewards by their own responses if rewards are either always or never available regardless of their actions (lack of contingency). They may also fail to develop goals if they never lack anything or if they never have anything. Learning will also fail if the person cannot or does not make the responses that would lead to success in reaching a goal (lack of appropriate skills). When rewards or punishments are completely independent of a person's responses, the result is what Seligman (1975) has called an "uncontrollable situation." It has been found that experiences in such situations may lead the person to generalize this helplessness to new situations, and that this generalized "learned helplessness" is related to depression.

It is possible that a person can also learn to *not cope* (as well as fail to learn to cope). If successful responses that are rewarded are also consistently punished, the person will be in conflict and may try to solve it by avoiding the situation entirely (e.g., giving up the goal). It is also possible that people can be directly taught not to cope by instruction or example (e.g., discouragement or disparagement by significant others). Whatever its origin, failure to cope may become a generalized habit of not responding even when there is a goal that could be reached by some possible response. It may also be verbalized in helpless cognitions ("nothing I do matters," "I can't cope," "I can't do anything right") which are characteristic of depression.

It is suggested here that the cognitive dimension of depression (the expectation that goals cannot be reached by any responses available to the person) is a basic factor in learned *susceptibility* to depression. Depression itself will not occur unless a goal situation occurs. In other words, the precipitating factors that activate this type of susceptibility are goals (rewards desired or punishments to be escaped or avoided). Given a goal situation and the expectation that nothing the person can do will influence the outcome, then the person is unlikely to try to do anything. This lack of activity is like the motivational/behavioral dimension of depression. Depending on the environment and the generality of the helpless cognitions, such a person would be faced with more and more inescapable punishments and fewer and fewer rewards.

This would result in pain, anxiety, sadness, and lack of enjoyment (the affective dimension of depression). There is speculation and some evidence (e.g., Brenner, 1979) that the vegetative dimension of depression may follow from severe and prolonged affective disturbance.

Theoretically, then, depression develops sequentially, but in real life it is no doubt a vicious cycle. The lack of coping would strengthen the helpless cognitions (and also contribute to low self-esteem). The sleep and appetite disturbances would reduce energy level and aggravate the motivational/behavioral deficit. The sadness and apathy would interfere with social relationships, thereby reducing reinforcements still further. The depression would continue to deepen unless the cycle were interrupted. For treatment, intervention at any point in the cycle might be effective. Reduction in precipitating factors may also be necessary in cases where they are abnormally numerous or stressful.

Learned Susceptibility to Depression in Women

It is helpful to distinguish susceptibility from precipitating factors in interpreting the sex difference in depression. There could be a sex difference in susceptibility, in exposure to precipitating factors, or both. Precipitating factors are generally assumed to be outside environmental "insults." If men and women differ in the degree of *exposure* to these factors, and if these factors affect men and women in the same way, then this might contribute to the sex difference in depression. There may also be a sex difference in various *susceptibility* factors both innate and learned. Sex linked biological factors have not yet been identified,

Le Trajet by Romaine Brooks; Courtesy of National Collection of Fine Arts, Smithsonian Institution; Gift of the Artist

although there is fairly strong evidence that the learning history of women is more likely to lead to the type of learned susceptibility to depression described above (i.e., lack of instrumental coping). This has been reviewed elsewhere (Radloff & Monroe, 1978), so only a brief summary and a few examples will be given here.

The most plentiful evidence comes from studies of sex role stereotypes. Stereotypes reflect what we expect from people. Studies have consistently found that people expect females (even healthy newborn babies) to be weaker, less able to get what they want by their own actions, and therefore more in need of help and protection than males (Block, 1975; Rubin et al., 1974). There is evidence that people are more likely to do things for girls, while boys are shown how to do things for themselves (Latane & Dabbs, 1975; Unger, 1976).

In the studies of childrearing practices reviewed by Maccoby and Jacklin (1974), only one consistent sex difference was found: the actions of boys more frequently *have consequences* than do the actions of girls. Granted, boys are often punished (especially for aggres-

sion), but both rewards and punishments depend on the boys' behavior. Boys can therefore learn to control rewards and punishments by their own actions. In contrast, an observational study of nursery schools (Serbin et al., 1973) found that girls got fewer reactions than did boys from adults for all behaviors, including aggression. The authors describe, for example, a small girl who struck out aggressively in anger and was totally ignored. Even her best temper tantrum had no effect on her environment. That is the ultimate in helplessness, and is reminiscent of the clinical descriptions of the impotent rage of the angry depressive.

For males in our culture, achievement and competence are clearly rewarded. For females, they have mixed results. Some studies have found that females who displayed competence were simply ignored (Wolman & Frank, 1975). For example, studies of small group problem-solving found that females were less listened to, were more often interrupted, and had less influence on the group decisions. An extreme example is the study where females were given the right answer ahead of time, but still could not get the group to accept it (Altemeyer & Jones, 1974). Other studies found that competent females sometimes got rewards, but were often also punished, especially by social rejection. The "fear of success" studies (Horner, 1968; Winchel et al., 1974; Feather & Raphelson, 1974) illustrate this: when a female was portrayed as successful, especially in achievement-oriented ways, people predicted many bad consequences of her success. In another study, male and female actors portrayed assertive and nonassertive roles. The assertive females were rated by observers as less likeable and more in need of psychotherapy than nonassertive females; the reverse was true for the male actors (Costrich et al., 1975). In reviewing such studies, Unger (1976) pointed out the parallel between the treatment of women and of low status individuals.

Other studies found that females who succeeded on a task were more likely than males to attribute their success to luck or other factors that would not allow them to take credit for their success. This could produce a cognitive barrier to learning, by blocking the effectiveness of positive reinforcement. It was also found that females were less likely than males to expect to succeed in the future, and were less likely to *attempt* to succeed in the future (Feather & Simon, 1975; Frieze et al., 1975). Recently, it has been found that depressed people were likely to have similar attribution style: when they did well at something they attributed it to luck, but when they failed they took all the blame (Rizley, 1978). This attribution could be described as a generalized expectancy of failure to cope.

Many studies have found that work produced by females was rated as less significant (Goldberg, 1968; Lavach & Lanier, 1975) and was less rewarded by pay, promotions, and status than comparable work produced by men. "Women's work" is sometimes defined as "pleasing other people." Success at this would be unpredictable, and the rewards very intangible.

In summary, for "competent behavior," which in our culture is highly praised, females (compared with males) have been found to get fewer rewards, to have less control over their rewards, and to have more of their rewards accompanied by punishment. Women have also been instructed by the stereotypes that competent instrumental behavior is not ex-

Spring, the Resurrection, II, by Mary Barnes. From *Mary Barnes: Two Accounts of a Journey Through Madness,* copyright © 1971 by Mary Barnes and Joseph Berke. Reproduced by permission of Harcourt Brace Jovanovich, Inc.

pected of them. That this "training in helplessness" has been effective is shown by their attribution style (taking less personal credit for success), and their low expectations of success. The behavioral effect is seen in their reduced rates of attempting to solve problems.

In conclusion, it is suggested that depression is a special problem for women not because they are biologically female, nor because they may be exposed to more current stressors, but also because they have learned to be more susceptible to depression. While there may be many sources of learned susceptibility that would affect both sexes equally, stereotyped sex role socialization is an added source of susceptibility to depression for women.

Some Data on Sex Differences in Depression

The data presented here came from a mental health interview survey sponsored by the Center for Epidemiologic Studies at the National Institute of Mental Health, conducted in Kansas City, Missouri, in 1971–1972 and in Washington County, Maryland in 1971–1973. Individuals aged eighteen years and over were randomly selected for interview from a representative sample of households. Response rates were 74.8 percent in Kansas City and 80.1 percent in Washington County.

The racial compositions of the samples reflected those of the populations: there were about 24 percent nonwhite in Kansas City, and only 2 percent in Washington County. Preliminary analyses suggested that the whites and nonwhites should not be combined because

TABLE 1

CENTER FOR EPIDEMIOLOGIC STUDIES DEPRESSION SCALE (CES-D)

INSTRUCTIONS FOR QUESTIONS: Below is a list of the ways you might have felt or behaved. Please tell me how often you have felt this way during the past week. HAND CARD A.
Rarely or none of the time (less than 1 day)
Some or a little of the time (1–2 days)
Occasionally or a moderate amount of time (3–4 days)
Most or all of the time (5–7 days)

During the Past Week:	Rarely	A Little	Moderate	Most
I was bothered by things that usually don't bother me.	0	1	2	3
I did not feel like eating; my appetite was poor.	0	1	2	3
I felt that I could not shake off the blues even with help from my family or friends.	0	1	2	3
I felt that I was just as good as other people.	3	2	1	0
I had trouble keeping my mind on what I was doing.	0	1	2	3
I felt depressed.	0	1	2	3
I felt that everything I did was an effort.	0	1	2	3
I felt hopeful about the future.	3	2	1	0
I thought my life had been a failure.	0	1	2	3
I felt fearful.	0	1	2	3
My sleep was restless.	0	1	2	3
I was happy.	3	2	1	0
I talked less than usual.	0	1	2	3
I felt lonely.	0	1	2	3
People were unfriendly.	0	1	2	3
I enjoyed life.	3	2	1	0
I had crying spells.	0	1	2	3
I felt sad.	0	1	2	3
I felt that people disliked me.	0	1	2	3
I could not get "going."	0	1	2	3

TABLE 2
AVERAGE DEPRESSION SCORES (CES-D)a:
SEX BY MARITAL STATUS

Marital Status	Male		Female		Total	
	N	$\overline{X}$	N	$\overline{X}$	N	$\overline{X}$
Married	778	7.33	930	9.53	1708	8.53
Divorced/separated	66	7.89	145	13.71	211	11.89
Never married Not-head	71	10.27	61	12.79	132	11.43
Never married Head	51	9.84	87	7.93	138	8.64
Widowed	45	12.78	267	10.26	312	10.62
Total	1011	7.94	1490	10.10	2501	9.23

Analysis of Variance
 Interaction sex x marital status p = .0001b
 Sex p = .03
 MS p = .0001
aHigher score indicates more depressive symptomatology
bp values rounded

they may differ in relationships among some variables. The numbers of nonwhites were too small to analyze separately in detail, so the present findings cover analyses of whites only, with a sample size of 2,515 whites (876 in Kansas City, 1639 in Washington County).

There are many ways of measuring depression. In the data reported here, degree of depression is operationally defined as the score on a depression scale called the CES-D scale (see Table 1). The score consists of the number of symptoms of depression experienced during the past week, weighted by frequency/duration of each symptom. A higher score indicates a higher level of depression. (For more information about this scale, see Radloff, 1977.)

The questionnaire used in this survey asked over 300 separate questions, including the CES-D scale. The present analyses cover only the CES-D scale and some of the more objec-

tive sociodemographic factors that have previously been found to relate to depression (Silverman, 1968; see also Radloff, 1975; Radloff & Rae, 1979; Radloff, 1980; and Radloff & Rae, in press, for further details).

Overall, the average scores on the depression scale were higher for women than for men, but this was true only among the married, the divorced/separated, and the never-married who were not living in their own households (mostly young people living with parents). Among the widowed and the never-married living in their own households, the men's scores were as high as or higher than the women's (see Table 2).

Other social factors associated with more depression for both sexes included youth (those age 18–24 were more depressed than all other age groups), low education, low income, low status employment, and physical illness (current or recent). Among males, but not females, currently employed workers were less depressed than others. For both males and females, those who have had children but were not living with them ("empty nest" parents) were less depressed than others (see Table 3). Note that the average depression scores for females were higher than those for comparable males throughout Table 3, except in the high level professionals. In some cases, however, the sex difference was quite small.

Returning to the sex/marital status interaction, the social factors were analyzed by sex separately for each marital status, to determine whether the interaction might be due to differences in these other factors. None of them seemed to account for the sex/marital status pattern. Even when matched on several of these factors at a time, the married and divorced/separated women were more depressed than comparable men, but the widowed and never-married (living in their own

TABLE 3
AVERAGE DEPRESSION SCORES (CES-D) BY SEX AND OTHER SOCIAL FACTORS

	Male		Female		Total	
	N	$\overline{X}$	N	$\overline{X}$	N	$\overline{X}$
Age*						
18–24	146	10.51	189	13.48	335	12.19
25 up	866	7.51	1296	9.62	2162	8.78
Education*						
Less than h.s.	375	8.27	608	11.22	983	10.09
High school	331	8.52	507	10.00	838	9.41
Greater than h.s.	304	6.94	369	8.44	673	7.76
Income*						
Less than $4000	121	10.06	311	11.58	432	11.16
$4000 or more	827	7.70	1034	9.47	1861	8.68
Occupational Status*						
1. High level prof.	45	5.76	5	2.80	50	5.46
2. Mid level prof.	100	6.11	69	8.14	169	6.94
3. Low level prof.	98	7.39	33	8.24	131	7.60
4. Sales & clerical	88	7.50	181	8.73	269	8.33
5. Skilled manual	207	7.25	22	11.77	229	7.69
6. Semi-skilled manual	108	8.99	100	10.91	208	9.91
7. Unskilled man.	42	8.74	41	9.73	83	9.23
8. Housewife, retired, other	259	8.64	912	10.31	1171	9.94
9. Unemployed or student	64	10.98	127	11.64	191	11.42

*Analysis of variance overall p<.02 for both sexes.

TABLE 3 (CONTINUED)
AVERAGE DEPRESSION SCORES (CES-D) BY SEX AND OTHER SOCIAL FACTORS

	Male		Female		Total	
	N	X̄	N	X̄	N	X̄
Illness*						
No	307	6.61	382	8.35	689	7.58
Yes	705	8.52	1108	10.71	1813	9.86
Occupational Role**						
Worker	798	7.59	636	9.61	1434	8.49
Housewife	—	—	510	10.53	510	10.53
Retired	148	8.53	212	9.67	360	9.20
Unemployed	46	10.35	115	11.44	161	11.13
Student	20	12.00	17	12.41	37	12.19
Parental Status*						
Not live with children (NLW)	288	6.81	477	9.15	765	8.27
Live with (LW)						
children	468	8.35	691	10.81	1159	9.82
No children	256	8.46	322	9.99	578	9.31

*Analysis of variance overall p<.02 for both sexes.
**p<.01 for males; not significant for females.

households) were not (Radloff, 1975; Radloff, 1980).

It has been suggested that having a job outside the home might help the mental health of married women. In these data, however, among the married, the working wives were not significantly different from the housewives. Both were significantly more depressed than the working husbands. This held true even when controlled for total family income, amount of time spent doing housework, and presence and ages of children (Radloff, 1975; Radloff, in press). This finding should be interpreted with caution, however. The measure of housework may not have been adequate to reflect the strain of double-duty for employed wives. It also fails to take the quality of the wife's employment into account. The married women were working at much lower level jobs than the men. Those few who were working at professional or managerial jobs had very low depression scores (even lower than comparable husbands). Interestingly, the unemployed husbands were more depressed than unemployed wives, while in the *non*-married groups (including never-married, widowed, and divorced/separated) the unemployed women were much more depressed than the unemployed men.

Regarding the effects of children, three groups have been compared: those who never had children; those who had children living with them at the time of the interview; and those who had children but were not living

with them (the "empty nest" group). Among the married, this last group ("empty nest") was significantly *less* depressed than the other groups (Radloff, 1975). This held true even when controlled for age, income, and age of youngest child (Radloff, in press). The presence of children and the absence of money helps to explain the very high depression scores of divorced/separated women. The divorced/separated women were more likely to be living with children and to have incomes of less than $4,000 compared with divorced/separated men. Controlling for these factors reduced but did not completely eliminate the sex difference in this group. The women were still more depressed (Radloff, 1980).

Aside from marital status, a large variety of social and demographic risk factors have been examined and found to relate to CES-D scores in the same direction for men and women. Simply matching on these factors, however, did not eliminate the sex differences in depression. There was some indication that the relationship of depression to the risk factors was somewhat stronger for women than for men. Matching men and women on these variables resulted in quite similar levels of depression at low (more favorable) levels of the variables; as factors associated with depression increased, the discrepancy between men's and women's depression scores increased (Radloff & Rae, in press).

Discussion

The model of learned susceptibility to depression that we have described above is helpful in hypothesizing reasons for the empirical patterns of relationships of depression to other social variables. The most consistent of these are: higher levels of depression associated with youth, low education, low income, physical illness, life events, and losses; and the sex/marital status interaction. Some of the variables seem related to learned susceptibility, some to presence of precipitating factors, and some to both. Some may also be related to innate susceptibility or to selective factors.

The kind of learning history that would lead to learned susceptibility to depression (the helpless-hopeless cognitive component) has already been shown to be more common for women than for men. Seligman (1975) has analyzed a variety of other risk factors for depression, especially poverty and school failure, in terms of learned helplessness. "A child reared in ... poverty will be exposed to a vast amount of uncontrollability" (p. 159). A background of poverty and/or poor education would reduce a person's chances of learning effective coping habits and leave the person more vulnerable to depression. Since past poverty and poor education are often correlated with current poverty and low status occupations (including unemployment), the high

bül bül © 73

levels of depression in these groups may be at least partly due to learned susceptibility. If the high level of depression in the young is a fairly recent development, it might be partly due to a misguided application of permissive or "child centered" philosophies. If parents are afraid to deprive a child of any pleasures, regardless of the child's own behavior, the child may never learn to cope. It may also simply be that increased competence and therefore decreased susceptibility may come with age from experience and maturity.

The variables may also be associated with higher levels of precipitating factors. Poverty, low education, unemployment, youth, life changes (especially marital separation and bereavement), and physical illness are all likely to present a person with many and difficult problems to be solved. They may also often be accompanied by a lack of or reduction in the supportive resources that normally help people solve their problems. If such conditions persist, or if the problems they create are actually unsolvable, learned susceptibility may be increased as well. An excess of such stressful conditions may contribute to the high depression in the young, who have higher rates of life changes as well as high unemployment rates and low income. Women, on the average, also have lower income and education than men, and are more likely to be responsible for young children.

The present findings on the effects of children are in contrast to Bart's (1971) study of middle-aged women in psychiatric hospitals. She found depression to be associated with "the empty nest" particularly in women who had been overinvolved in the mother role and who were not employed outside the home. The present results are consistent with other studies, however, where it has been found that the presence of children in the home is associated with more symptoms of distress (Bernard, 1975), and lower life satisfaction (Campbell, Converse, & Rodgers, 1976). Pearlin and Lieberman (1977) found that married people who reported that their last child had left home and/or married within the past four years were (nonsignificantly) lower on a measure of psychological distress (anxiety and depression symptoms) than parents who did not report these events.

Explanations of the sex/marital status interaction are more complex, and involve social roles and selectivity in marriage patterns as well as learned susceptibility and precipitating factors. Gove (1972) reviewed studies of mental illness that reported marital status as well as sex. All studies agreed in finding higher rates among women than men among the married. In other marital status categories, however, the results were less consistent, with a majority showing higher rates for men than women among the never-married, the di-

347

Marriage is the woman's proper sphere, her divinely ordered place, her natural end. It is what she is born for, what she is trained for, what she is exhibited for. It is, moreover, her means of honorable livelihood and advancement. But—she must not even look as if she wanted it!

Charlotte Perkins Gilman, *Women and Economics*, 1898

---

vorced, and the widowed. The studies with age adjustment supported this result. The results of the present study agree with these findings, except with respect to the divorced.

Speculations about the effects of marriage on women by Gove and by Bernard (1973) emphasized the role of housewife. The assumption was that the married man has two major sources of satisfaction (job and family) but that the married woman has only one (family). Further, the role the housewife plays in the family may be a source more of frustration than of satisfaction. The effects of small children on the mother's control over her own life were pointed out by Bernard. If the married woman has a job outside the home, she is still likely to be mainly responsible for household duties and therefore to be under the stress of overwork. Finally, her job is likely to be of lower income and status, and less a source of satisfaction than is her husband's.

Another possible explanation for the sex difference in depression could be that men (or married men) might experience the same distress but manifest it in different ways, including alcoholism, physical illness, and denial of symptoms. Studies (Gove, 1973; Clancy & Gove, 1974) have shown that although nonmarried men are high on these problems, married men are not. Research has consistently confirmed the good health (mental and physical) of *married* men. Additional evidence is available from the present study for the many scales used in the interview, including use of medications, disability days, a short "aggression scale," alcohol problems (slightly modi-fied Mulford Scale), and the Crowne-Marlowe Scale for Social Desirability. The married men were low on all items, compared with married women and nonmarried men.

Another alternative explanation discussed by Gove (1972), Bernard (1973), and others is differential selectivity in marriage. Psychological problems may be cause or effect of marital status. The selective pattern suggested is that mental illness may prevent men from marrying but may not prevent women from marrying. It takes a certain degree of mental health for a man to live up to the tradition that he must initiate the decision to marry and be prepared to support himself, a wife, and possibly children. Bernard (1973) also points out that the tradition for a woman to "marry a man she can look up to" means that women who remain single may be the "cream of the crop" while men who remain single may be the "bottom of the barrel." Specific to depression, it is very likely that the learned susceptibility factor described above (helpless, hopeless, unable to cope) would make a man less likely to marry. Such a style is compatible with traditional views of "femininity" however, and might make a woman *more* likely to marry. The data presented here are consistent with the notion that the less helpless women and the more helpless men may be most likely to stay unmarried long enough to be heads of their own households. There is some indirect evidence that the more passive/dependent women do not consider any life style except marriage, while more active women can tolerate the single life (Bernard, 1974, pp. 35–39).

When, finally, we vary both marital status and sex, by comparing married men and unmarried women, we find relatively little overall difference so far as mental health is concerned, superiorities and inferiorities tending to cancel out. But the women are spectacularly better off so far as psychological distress symptoms are concerned, suggesting that women start out with an initial advantage which marriage reverses.

Jessie Bernard, *The Future of Marriage*, 1972

The sex/marital status interaction can be better understood by combining this notion of selectivity (more susceptible men and less susceptible women are likely to stay unmarried) with the learned susceptibility and precipitating factors model of depression. The overall sex difference in learned susceptibility would predict that women would be more depressed than men in all groups. Precipitating factors, however, would vary by marital and parental status, with the divorced/separated living with children under most stress and the married whose children have become independent under least stress. The multiplicative relationship of susceptibility and precipitating factors suggests that the sex difference would be greater in groups under greater stress.

First consider the "ever-married." On the average, due to differential selectivity in marriage, the women would have higher susceptibility to depression. In the currently married, with relatively low levels of stress, both sexes should have relatively low levels of depression, with the women somewhat higher than the men. This is what has been empirically found. Assuming that the divorced/separated are exposed to more precipitating factors, both men and women should have higher levels of depression than the married, with the increase larger for women. The women do follow this pattern, but the divorced/separated men have very low depression scores. This can be partly explained by income and responsibility for children. The few men who are like the women on these factors have higher depression scores than married men. There may also

---

Wild Women Blues

*I've got a different system
And a way of my own,
When my man starts kicking
I let him find another home.
I get full of good liquor
And walk the street all night,
Go home and put my man out
If he don't treat me right,
Wild women don't worry,
Wild women don't have the blues.*

*You never get nothing
By being an angel child,
You better change your ways
And get real wild.
I want to tell you something
I wouldn't tell you no lie,
Wild women are the only kind
That really get by,
'Cause wild women don't worry,
Wild women don't have blues.*

Ida Cox

---

be some bias in the sample of divorced/separated men; the less mentally healthy may be living in transient situations, group quarters, or with families-of-origin so that they would be less likely to be interviewed. Some may also be in the armed services, jails, or mental institutions. This bias would be counterbalanced by any tendency for the healthier men to remarry.

The widowed should be similar to the married in susceptibility, but should have higher depression and a larger sex difference because of increased precipitating factors. The fact that widowed men are *more* depressed than the women may be partly because widowhood is less common for men and therefore less expected and more stressful for men than for women. It may also be that many men are literally "helpless around the house." Selective factors may also be involved: more men than women remarry after being widowed. If we assume the less depressed men are the more likely to remarry, then those men who remain widowed would be the more depressed.

To explain the pattern of findings in the never-married, we may consider those who were *not* living in their own households as "not-yet-married," and assume that their susceptibility to depression was similar to the married. Their relative youth and lack of independence would predict overall higher depression than in the married for both sexes, with the women higher than the men, as was observed.

The never-married who *were* heads of their own households would be the only group where susceptibility to depression is predicted (by selectivity in marriage) to be higher in the men than the women. Assuming a level of precipitating factors similar to the married would predict the pattern of depression scores which were observed.

In conclusion, it should first be emphasized that the learned factors in depression discussed here are only part of the picture: the part that is most relevant to associations of de-

pression with sex and social factors. There are genetic and biochemical factors in depression, which may also be correlated with some of these factors and therefore contribute to the findings. It must also be noted that the data reported here are based on self-reported symptoms *not* on a clinical diagnosis. These symptoms are associated with a variety of types of depression as well as other mental health problems and also occur to some extent in healthy people. Therefore, the results as well as the theoretical speculations should be interpreted with caution.

With these cautions in mind, it can be suggested that the learned susceptibility-precipitating factors model of depression deserves further study. It does provide a plausible explanation of empirical findings that cannot comfortably be explained by genetic and biochemical factors alone. Particularly for women, this is an encouraging note, since if susceptibility to depression is partly learned then it can perhaps be unlearned. Research can be designed to test the efficacy of methods predicted by the model to reduce susceptibility to depression (e.g., Beck, 1976). The model also calls attention to the role of life stresses and could guide service providers toward more effective outreach and early intervention programs. The integration of experimental research, epidemiologic studies, and treatment outcome evaluation with theoretical models can improve our understanding of the nature of depression and eventually lead to more effective prevention and control.

Walter R. Gove

Mental Illness and Psychiatric Treatment Among Women

When mental illness is precisely defined as a functional disorder involving acute distress or disorganization (or both), women are consistently found to have higher rates of mental illness than men. This sex difference appears to be real and not an artifact of response bias, patient behavior, or clinician bias. The higher rates of mental illness among women can be linked to aspects of their societal role and particularly to aspects of the marital role. Therapists who treat women whose mental illness is in part a response to the characteristics of conventional sex roles have no treatment alternatives that are not in some way problematic. The treatment alternative chosen has, in the broadest sense, political implications for the society at large.

In the feminist (e.g., Bernard, 1971a, 1971b; Chesler, 1971a, 1971b, 1972) as well as the more academic literature (e.g., Bagley, 1977; Gove, 1978, 1979a; Gove & Tudor, 1973, 1977; Pearlin, 1975), it is commonly asserted that women have higher rates of mental illness than men. This is a controversial position that can be challenged on many grounds. The first part of this paper examines issues that lead to the conclusion that women have higher rates of mental illness. How mental illness should be defined and possible biases that may be involved in determining its incidence are discussed. The second part of the paper looks at two possible explanations of the sex differential in rates of mental illness: (a) sex and marital roles of men and women; and (b) learned helplessness among women. The third part of the paper briefly explores some societal implications of the psychiatric treatment of women. Particular attention is paid to the therapist's role as an agent of social control or change.

Do Women Have Higher Rates of Mental Illness?

To a substantial extent, Chesler (1971a, 1972) drew her conclusion that women have higher rates of mental illness than men from NIMH reports concerning psychiatric treatment in mental hospitals, general hospitals, and outpatient psychiatric clinics. Earlier studies, most of which were based exclusively on data from mental hospitals, had consistently indicated that from at least 1910 to the early sixties men had higher rates of psychiatric treatment (Bohn, Gardner, Alltop, Knatterval, & Solomon, 1966; Dorn, 1938; Dunham, 1959; Kramer, Pollack & Redick, 1961). Furthermore, if one were to limit oneself to data from mental hospitals, one would necessarily conclude that in recent years men were increasingly more likely than women to receive psychiatric treatment. For example, for state and county mental hospitals the ratio of male to female patients was 1.14 in 1946, 1.32 in 1955, and 2.27 in 1972 (Kramer, 1977).

Chesler (1972) contends that both absolute and relative increases in rates of psychiatric treatment for women began around 1964. This period was a time of expansion in the scope and availability of psychiatric services, and there was a substantial increase in the number of persons who received these services. For example, the number of persons seen in mental health facilities excluding private outpatient care was 1,673,352 in 1955, 2,636,525 in 1965, and 6,409,477 in 1975 (Taube & Redick, 1977). The increase in the rate of persons receiving inpatient psychiatric care was comparatively slight, however, and occurred solely in general hospitals, federally assisted community mental health centers, and VA hospitals. At the same time there was a very sharp decline in the rate of inpatient treatment in state and county mental hospitals and no change in private psychiatric hospitals (Taube & Redick, 1977). The vast increase in psychiatric treatment occurred in nonprivate outpatient psychiatric services (233 patients per 100,000 population in 1955, 2,185 per 100,000 in 1975; Taube & Redick, 1977).

Following Chesler (1972), this would imply that in recent years women had much higher rates of treatment in settings other than mental hospitals and particularly in outpatient facilities. The most recent data for all treatment settings to provide a breakdown by gender of the patient are for 1971 (Kramer, 1977). They show that women have slightly higher rates of inpatient treatment in private mental hospitals and general hospitals and slightly higher rates of outpatient psychiatric treatment. Men, in contrast, have much higher rates of treatment in state and mental hospitals and particularly in VA hospitals. Overall, men have higher rates of psychiatric treatment when all facilities are combined (2049.2 per 100,000 for men versus 1863.5 per 100,000 for women). In short, the data on psychiatric treatment, excluding private outpatient care, show that men have higher rates of psychiatric treatment. Thus if we equate psychiatric treatment with mental illness, these data indicate that women do not have higher rates of mental illness than men.

Very serious questions can be raised about the appropriateness of equating being in psychiatric treatment with being mentally ill. Elsewhere I (Clancy & Gove, 1974; Gove, 1978, 1979a; Gove & Tudor, 1973, 1977) have strongly argued that many persons in psychiatric treatment are not mentally ill, at least when mental illness is narrowly and precisely defined. Many disorders, such as alcoholism and drug abuse, appear to have fallen into the domain of psychiatry due to historical accident and the successful entrepreneurship of the psychiatric profession (Gove, 1976) and do not fit a precise definition of mental illness.

A Precise Definition of Mental Illness

The position taken in this paper is that mental illness is most appropriately treated as a specific phenomenon involving personal discomfort (as indicated by distress, anxiety, depression, etc.), or mental disorganization (as indicated by confusion, thought blockage, motor retardation, and, in the more extreme cases, hallucinations and delusions), or a combination of both conditions, that is not caused by an organic or toxic condition. The two major categories of psychiatric dysfunction that fit this definition are the neurotic disorders and the functional psychoses. The chief characteristic of the neurotic disorders is either anxiety or depression, or both, in the absence of psychotic disorganization. The functional psychoses are psychotic disorders with no established organic cause (APA, 1968).

The two other categories that fit this definition are not often used. Transient situational disorders are acute symptomatic responses to overwhelming situations in which there is no underlying personal disturbance. When the situational stress diminishes, so do the symptoms. This diagnosis is assigned mainly to children and adolescents and only occasionally to adults. The other category is comprised of the psychological disorders. These are characterized by somatic symptoms that appear to be the consequence of emotional tension, although the person may sometimes be unaware of the tension. The psychophysiologic disorders do not fit within the definition of mental illness being used here as clearly as the other disorders. They are included, however, because they are functional disorders and they reflect a fair amount of distress, albeit in a somewhat masked form.

There are a number of reasons for treating these disorders as a distinct set which corresponds to a relatively narrow definition of mental illness. First, there is a similarity in symptomatology—persons in all these diagnostic categories are typically severely distressed. Second, these disorders respond to the same general forms of therapy, namely, drug therapy and psychotherapy (Gove, 1978; Gove & Tudor, 1973: Kazdin & Wilson, 1978; Kellner, 1975; Klein & Davis, 1969; Malan, 1973; Smith & Glass, 1977). Third, cross-cultural and historical evidence suggests that the concept of mental illness does not typically include the types of disorders we are excluding (Gove, 1978; Gove & Tudor, 1977; Murphy, 1976).

Two frequently used diagnostic categories do not fit this precise definition of mental illness—the acute and chronic brain syndromes and the personality disorders. The brain syndromes are caused by a physical condition, either brain damage or toxins, and are not functional disorders (APA, 1968). Most investigators clearly believe it is important to distinguish between the brain syndromes and the disorders we are classifying as mental illness. The fact that the brain syndromes make up

approximately 25 percent of the first admissions to public mental hospitals emphasizes the need to distinguish between the incidence of psychiatric treatment and the incidence of mental illness as defined in this paper.

Persons with a personality disorder do not experience personal discomfort, being neither anxious nor distressed, nor do they suffer from any form of psychotic disorganization. They are viewed as mentally ill because they do not conform to social norms and are usually forced into treatment because their behavior is disruptive to others. These persons are characterized by aggressive, impulsive, goal-directed behavior which is either antisocial or asocial in nature and creates serious problems with and for others (APA, 1968; Dohrenwend, 1975; Klein & Davis, 1969; Kolb, 1973). Not only are the symptoms associated with the personality disorders different from those associated with mental illness as we have defined it, but the forms of therapy effective in the treatment of mental illness are not effective in the treatment of the personality disorders (Gove, 1978; Gove & Tudor, 1977; Klein & Davis, 1969; Malan, 1973). Moreover, data from non-western societies are consistent with the distinction between the personality disorder and what we are labeling mental illness. Persons in these societies who manifest the behavior that would lead to a diagnosis of a personality disorder in our society are viewed as deviants, but not as ill, and shamans and healers do not believe that such behavior can be cured or changed (Murphy, 1976). In fact, the personality disorders have only recently come to be considered within the domain of psychiatry (e.g., Robbins, 1966).

It is worth noting that labeling theory, which provides the most comprehensive alternative theoretical explanation of mental illness to the one provided by the psychiatric perspective, would also exclude these disorders from the definition of mental illness. For example, Scheff (1966), who presents by far the clearest and most elaborate labeling explanation of mental illness, treats mental illness as residual deviance—namely, deviance for which we have no name and for which there is no societal role. As alcoholism, drug addiction, mental retardation, and senility are socially recognized categories with relatively clearly defined expectations for behavior, Scheff does not see them as residual rule breaking (i.e., mental illness). Thus I, a proponent of the psychiatric perspective (Scheff, 1975), and Scheff, one of its leading critics, are in agreement that these four forms of behavior should not be treated as mental illness.

Sex Differences Using a Precise Definition of Mental Illness

Applying this precise definition of mental illness to national data for 1966, Gove and Tudor (1973) found that women uniformly had higher rates of psychiatric treatment in mental hospitals, inpatient psychiatric treatment in general hospitals, and outpatient care in psychiatric clinics. Similarly, comprehensive reviews of studies conducted in Western industrial nations after World War II of the practices of private psychiatrists, the psychiatric care provided by general physicians, and the results of the community surveys of mental illness showed, without exception, that women had higher rates of mental illness (Gove & Tudor, 1973). The studies themselves did not use a consistent definition of mental illness, although the vast majority of the cases considered would fit under the definition of mental illness used in this paper.

An updating of these reviews (Gove, 1979a) showed that in all the studies of practices of general physicians and private psychiatrists, women had higher rates of psychiatric treatment. Of the 35 community studies covered in the second review, 34 showed women to have higher rates of mental illness. The one exception, a small study ($n = 683$) by Brunetti (1973), indicated that the rates of mental illness between the sexes are so similar that if one more woman had been mentally ill, women would have had higher rates. In short, the work using a precise definition of mental illness consistently shows women to have higher rates than men.

Data on patients in institutional settings have not been updated. As noted above, the most recent complete statistics on treatment in institutional settings are those for 1971 presented in Kramer (1977). Kramer uses diagnostic categories consistent with recent NIMH practices. Previously, persons with alcohol and drug abuse problems were categorized under the brain syndrome diagnoses if they entered treatment in a toxic state and usually categorized as having a personality disorder if they entered in a nontoxic state. Kramer, however, treats alcoholic and drug disorders as two separate diagnostic categories. This means that persons diagnosed in his study as having an organic brain syndrome almost all had some form of senile disorder. He also combined the neurotic and psychotic depressive disorders. Kramer's data show men to have higher rates of psychiatric treatment than women. If, however, consistent with our precise definition of mental illness, we eliminate from consideration alcoholics, drug addicts, persons with an organic brain syndrome, and the mentally retarded, then women emerge as having higher rates of treatment for mental illness in state and county mental hospitals, general hospitals, community mental health centers (inpatient and outpatient), and other outpatient psychiatric services, as well as for all settings combined. Thus the most recent data on treatment in institutional settings are consistent with the earlier data presented in Gove and Tudor (1973).

In summary, if one uses a precise and narrow definition of mental illness, then the data uniformly indicate that women have higher rates of mental illness. In contrast, if one uses an eclectic definition, which includes a much wider range of deviant behavior, then the evidence is mixed. With an eclectic definition, women have higher rates in community surveys, private practices of psychiatrists, and among persons receiving psychiatric treatment from general physicians, whereas men have slightly higher rates in institutionalized settings as a combined category, although this is not true of some specific institutional settings. It is critical to recognize that the eclectic definition of mental illness encompasses a variety of very different phenomena. Regardless of the reader's preference for the precise or eclectic definition, he or she should keep in mind that in the remainder of this paper the term "mental illness" will be used to refer to a functional disorder involving the overt manifestation of distress, or mental disorganization, or a combination of both.

Are the Higher Rates for Women an Artifact of Response Bias?

Phillips and Segal (1969) have argued that in our society women are expected to be more emotional than men and as a consequence it is less stigmatizing for women to verbalize emotional problems. Women are presumed to be aware of this fact and are thus more willing than men to discuss their emotional difficulties. Thus it is the position of Phillips and Segal that the apparent higher rates of mental illness among women that are found in community surveys are an artifact of societal norms which make women more willing than men to articulate their emotional problems. Unfortunately, they present no evidence bearing directly on their argument. Phillips and Segal limit their discussion to respondent behavior in community surveys. Their argument, however, has frequently been expanded by others who see the processes they describe as reflecting a generalized response set that would lead women to seek psychiatric treatment.

In a series of three studies (Clancy & Gove, 1974; Gove & Geerken, 1977a; Gove, McCorkel, Fain, & Hughes, 1976), my associates and I examined the possibility that the reports of more psychiatric symptoms by women in community surveys are an artifact of response bias. We employed the same general techniques as Phillips (Phillips & Clancy, 1970, 1972) and measured three types of response bias: perceived desirability or undesirability of psychiatric symptoms, need for approval, and tendency to yeasay or naysay. In all, we have used seven mental health scales, slightly varied our indices of response bias, and used different interviewing techniques (telephone interviews once, direct interviews twice).

Perception that psychiatric symptoms were not particularly undesirable, a tendency to yeasay, and a lack of need for approval were all fairly consistently related to the reporting of high rates of psychiatric symptoms. In all of the studies, however, there were no sex differences in the perceived desirability of psychiatric symptoms or in the respondents' need for approval, and in two studies there were no sex differences in the tendency to yeasay or naysay. In Clancy and Gove (1974), however, women were more likely than men to naysay. As a consequence, in all but one case we found that controlling for response bias had no effect on the reports of either men or women, and in the one exception (Clancy & Gove, 1974) the controls resulted in an increase in the rates of women. As this is the only evidence bearing on Phillips and Segal's position, and it is all negative, it is reasonable to conclude that the higher rates of reports of psychiatric symptoms among women are not an artifact of sex differences in response bias. These studies, of course, bear most directly on community surveys which consistently find women more likely to report that they experience psychiatric symptoms.

Are the Higher Mental Illness Rates for Women an Artifact of Clinician or Patient Behavior?

A frequently cited study of Broverman, Broverman, Clarkson, Rosenkrantz, and Vogel (1970) indicates that clinicians tend to see the average man as more emotionally healthy than the average woman. This finding, which is consistent with data on sex-role stereotypes among the general population (McKee & Sherriffs, 1957, 1959; Sherriffs & McKee, 1957), has often been interpreted as suggesting that clinicians are more likely to perceive women as mentally ill, regardless of actual level of disorder. This presumed bias on the part of clinicians might account for the higher rates of treated mental illness among women (e.g., Ab-

ernathy, 1976: Abramowitz & Dokecki, 1977; Chesler, 1971b, 1972).

By now there is a fairly extensive body of clinical judgment analogue studies in which the evidence of such sex bias has been examined. This literature clearly suggests that for comparable levels of psychiatric disorder clinicians are not more likely to perceive mental illness in women than in men. For example, Abramowitz, Roback, Schwartz, Yasuna, Abramowitz, and Gomes (1976) found that "the impact [on clinical judgments] of varying the patient's gender was surprisingly slight. The patient received a better prognosis (p <.05) and elicited slightly more empathy (p <.10) when identified as a woman" (p. 708). Similarly, Gomes and Abramowitz (1976) concluded that "the main outcome of this investigation was the absence of consistent effects due to any of the four variables—patient sex and role-appropriateness and therapist sex and sex-role traditionalism—implied in the polemic literature as likely sources of clinical bias.... To the extent that any sex bias was exposed, it tended to favor the female-identified rather than the male-identified stimulus-person" (pp. 10–11). In fact, they found that the sex-role deviant female was perceived as especially mature, even by clinicians whose personal reaction to her was largely negative. Systematic reviews of these experimental studies are presented in Abramowitz and Dokecki (1977) and Zeldow (1978). These studies clearly suggest that the higher rates of treatment among women are not due to discrimination against women by clinicians.

It might appear that the Broverman et al. (1970) finding that clinicians tend to perceive men as being in better mental health than women contradicts the results of the clinical judgment analogue studies, which would suggest that clinicians do not discriminate against women. This is the position taken by Davidson and Abramowitz (1980), who caution that the analogue studies are suspect because clinicians may have discerned the issue being investigated and carefully tempered their response. It can easily be argued, however, that the results of the two types of studies are entirely consistent and there is no contradiction to be explained away. If the average woman is in poorer mental health, as the community studies indicate, then results like those of Broverman et al. (1970) would not reflect a bias on the part of clinicians but, rather, an accurate perception of reality. In short, given the other data available, it is quite reasonable to assume that the perceptions by clinicians that women tend to be in poorer mental health and the finding that most clinicians are not biased against women "patients" in analogue studies are both valid and in no way contradictory.

The data reported by Broverman et al. (1970), Abramowitz et al. (1976), Gomes and Abramowitz (1976), McKee and Sherriffs (1957, 1959), and Sherriffs and McKee (1957) in fact suggest that expectations regarding appropriate behavior are probably more stringent for males than for females. It appears that both clinicians and members of the general community expect women to manifest poorer mental health. If this is true, males may be more likely than females to experience a negative societal reaction for comparable levels of mental illness. Tudor, Tudor, and Gove (1977) found that both the literature and the national data on the treatment for mental illness support such an interpretation. Furthermore,

males are much more likely than females to be institutionalized for other forms of mental impairment (Tudor, Tudor, & Gove, 1979).

To my knowledge, there are only three community studies that allow one to look at the help-seeking behavior of men and women controlling for level of impairment or perceived need for help. Two national studies (Gove, 1978; Gurin, Veroff, & Feld, 1960) demonstrate, controlling for level of self-defined impairment, that women are no more likely than men to seek professional help. In fact the very slight differences suggest men are more likely to seek help. Using a strategically drawn sample and controlling for level of self-defined disorder, Blumenthal (1967) found that men were more likely to seek help than women ($p < .01$). In summary, the existing data indicate that women are no more likely than men to seek professional help for comparable levels of mental illness.

Some of the best data on the path into psychiatric treatment are those provided by Fink, Shapiro, Goldensohn, and Daily (1969), who studied an insured group of 30,000 persons in New York City. In terms of visits to family physicians, "men were slightly below the medical group average with an index of 0.93 while women were slightly above with an index of 1.07" (a value of 1.0 indicates a rate equivalent to the medical group average). However, the index of psychiatric diagnosis by general physicians was 0.63 for men and 1.37 for women, indicating women were much more likely to receive a psychiatric diagnosis. Furthermore, the data showed that among persons receiving a psychiatric diagnosis, men and women were equally likely to receive a screening interview by a psychiatrist and were also equally likely to subsequently enter psychiatric treatment.

In conclusion, the evidence strongly suggests that the higher rates of mental illness among women in our society reflect real differences and are not artifactual.

Explanations of the Higher Rate of Mental Illness Among Women

Sex and Marital Roles of Men and Women

Given that women do have higher rates of mental illness, this could plausibly be due to characteristics of their societal roles and life experiences or to biological factors. Elsewhere (Gove, 1978; Gove & Tudor, 1977) I have discussed in detail the evidence which suggests that the differences are not due to innate biological differences. My major reason for believing that the higher rates of mental illness among women are largely due to societal and not to biological factors is that they generally appear to be specific to particular societies at particular times (although the evidence is not conclusive) and, more important, women have higher rates only within specific roles. In particular, higher rates of mental illness appear to be limited to married women, with never-married, widowed, and divorced women having comparable, if not lower, rates than their male counterparts (e.g., Gove, 1972a, 1972b, 1973, 1979c).

In a recent overview of the literature on depression, Weissman and Klerman (1977) concluded that women had higher rates of depression than men and that these differences were not artifactual. They reviewed evidence bearing on the possibility that the higher rates of depression among women could be due to genetic factors, their social status, the experience of more severe life events, or various endocrinological factors including premenstrual tension, oral contraceptives, and postpartum depression. They concluded that the higher rate of depression among women was primarily due to their disadvantaged social status and emphasized the link between marriage and depression.

There are a number of reasons for assuming that married women find their roles to be more frustrating and less rewarding than married men. In recent times the role of housewife has lost many of its societal functions; consequently, the wife contributes relatively less instrumentally to the household than in the past. The majority of wives still do not hold jobs and are restricted to one major societal role, that of housewife, whereas men occupy two such roles, that of household head and worker. A man typically has two sources of gratification, his family and his work, whereas a woman has only one, her family. Children, particularly when they are very young, channel women into situations in which the women are isolated from adult interaction yet confront seemingly incessant demands (Gove & Geerken, 1977b).

Even when a woman works, she typically occupies a less satisfying position than the married male. Women are discriminated

In 1970, Margaret Mead was quoted by Robert Williams as warning women in the Women's Liberation Movement that they might literally be driving men insane. The reverse seems more likely. It is wives who are driven mad, not by men but by the anachronistic way in which marriage is structured today—or, rather, the life style which accompanies marriage today and which demands that all wives be housewives. In truth, being a housewife makes women sick.

Jessie Bernard, *The Future of Marriage*, 1972

against in the job market, and they frequently hold positions that are not commensurate with their education. Furthermore, women are much less likely to have a career orientation. Perhaps more important, working wives are under a greater strain than their husbands. In addition to their jobs, they almost invariably perform most of the household chores, which means that they work considerably more hours per day than their husbands (Geerken & Gove, 1978; Gove & Tudor, 1973; Szalai, 1972, 1975). The literature also suggests that they find many of their instrumental activities frustrating, for these are of low status, routine, boring, and require little skill. These factors suggest that the higher rates of mental illness among women can largely be attributed to the societal roles women occupy and particularly to the constraints associated with their marital roles.

Learned Helplessness Among Women

It has been widely noted that the role expectations that confront women are more diffuse than those that confront men and, perhaps more important, that the feminine role is characterized by preparing for and adjusting to contingencies (e.g., Angrist, 1969; Gove & Tudor, 1973; Rose, 1951). It certainly seems to be the case that, because of interaction of marriage, children, and work, women experience a much less structured career path than men. Gove and Tudor (1973) have suggested that this characteristic of the feminine role probably creates problems for some women and may increase the likelihood that they will experi-

NO YOU'RE NOT CRAZY! IT'S THE "NO PAY, NO SICK LEAVE, NO PENSION, NO APPRECIATION" HOUSEWIFE BLUES.

Ms Meg series, copyright bülbül 1980, Arachne Publishing, Mountain View, CA. 94040

ence emotional difficulties; however, they see the nature of this interaction as very complex.

It has become popular to assume that the contingent nature and subordinate status of the feminine role result in many women having very little control over their life and that this, in turn, may explain the higher rate of mental illness among women, particularly depression (e.g., Bagley, 1977; Radloff, 1975; Weissman & Klerman, 1977). This formulation has become known as the "learned helplessness hypothesis." To support this hypothesis, investigators have drawn almost exclusively

on an article by Seligman (1974), which reviews evidence that animals in laboratory experiments who have absolutely no control over frequently occurring physical trauma appear to become depressed. The Seligman article is intriguing; however, no evidence has been presented that the total lack of control and the severity of trauma experienced by animals in these experiments have much in common with the role of women in our society. Furthermore, one should be very cautious in extrapolating behavior data from animals in laboratory experiments to the everyday life situation of humans.

Although further research is certainly required, the available evidence suggests that the learned helplessness hypothesis, at least in the rather simplistic form in which it has been presented, does not explain the higher rates of mental illness among women. A key component of the hypothesis is that girls learn in childhood to be helpless (Weissman & Klerman, 1977). However, girls outperform boys academically (e.g., Northby, 1958), and young boys have higher rates of mental illness than young girls, apparently because they are less capable than girls of meeting the expectations that confront them (Gove & Herb, 1974). An-

other core premise of the learned helplessness hypothesis is that women are more likely than men to feel that they lack control over their lives and are trapped by their life circumstances. Data from a national probability sample, however, indicate there is no difference between men and women in the extent to which they (a) experience powerlessness or normlessness; (b) feel they have control over and experience satisfaction with their daily activities; and (c) feel trapped by their life circumstances (Gove, 1979b).

In conclusion, the evidence that exists runs counter to the learned helplessness hypothesis. This indirectly lends credence to the premise that the higher rates of mental illness among women largely reflect aspects of their marital role.

The Therapist as an Agent of Social Control or Societal Change

Now let us turn to some of the implicit political issues that follow from the premise that the higher rates of mental illness among women are primarily a product of their sex and marital roles. When an individual is so distressed or disorganized that his or her functioning is

impaired, both society and the people directly involved with that individual have an interest in seeing that he or she is restored to a state in which he or she can function effectively. If the individual's emotional disturbance is in part a reaction to aspects of the social system, then society has a particular concern with the way in which the therapist goes about alleviating the person's disturbance. The therapist who uses procedures that alleviate the disturbance by helping the person to adjust to characteristics of the social structure as it exists is correctly seen as an agent who helps maintain the status quo. In contrast, the therapist who uses procedures that lead to a change in aspects of the person's environment that are reflective of the basic social structure is correctly seen as an agent of social change.

Obviously the emotional disturbances of many persons reflect idiosyncratic life experiences and personality traits that have very little to do with general characteristics of the social structure. In such cases, the therapist is concerned with dealing with those idiosyncratic conditions and, presumably, the goals of the patient, therapist, and society are in concordance. In those cases, however, in which the mental illness of a woman reflects societal

conditions, the way the woman is treated inevitably has consequences for the maintenance or change of the societal structure, and her therapist is then, in the broadest sense of the word, a political agent.

Feminists are very aware that therapists may be viewed as political agents. Levin, Kamin, and Levine (1974) refer to therapists as the "medio-psychological correlates to the gendarme" (p. 327). Moss and Sachs (1975) state that "what distinguishes feminist therapy from other therapies is that we make our values explicit, and incorporate them into the therapy process to promote changes in women that we believe will lead to changes in the world and its ways" (p. 1.) These authors indicate that feminist therapy encourages women to locate the source of their problem in society and that feminist therapists seek an entirely different world, and their therapy and life style reflect this vision. Chesler (1971a) claims that it is impossible for a man to treat a woman effectively. "Male psychologists, psychiatrists, and social workers must realize that as scientists they know nothing about women; their diagnosis, even their sympathy, is damaging and oppressive to women. Male clinicians should stop treating women altogether, however much this may hurt their wallets and/or sense of benevolent authority" (p. 384). Radical feminists view feminism itself as therapy (Mander & Rush, 1974).

Most clinicians do not construe feminism, by itself, as a form of therapy. There are numerous reasons for this, and here we will touch on only the most obvious. First, most therapists are not feminists, particularly in the pure sense of the term. Among other things, the vast majority of therapists are male. Second, therapists are concerned with treating the emotional problems of the individual, and these problems almost invariably reflect a number of factors that are idiosyncratic to that individual. It is almost invariably the case that even when some of the factors reflect problems associated with the societal conditions of women, numerous other factors will also be involved. The therapist who focused only on feminist issues would be ignoring the array of other factors that are components of the individual's problem. Third, feminism is essentially a political ideology and social movement aimed at changing pervasive social conditions; therapy is aimed at getting the individual to function effectively and happily in a niche carved out of the existing world. Thus, although it is possible for feminism and therapy to interact, they largely involve separate realms of social discourse. Fourth, a substantial number of women do not see their problems in feminist terms and thus will not be receptive to feminist therapy as such. With regard to this latter point, not only do both men and women tend to prefer a male therapist, but the proportion preferring a male therapist is higher among women than men (Chesler, 1971a, 1971b).

Most therapists who treat women whose problems in part reflect the societal role of women are essentially faced with a choice between two strategies, neither of which is particularly satisfactory. The therapist can work to change the individual's perspective and reactions so that she can accept and function in the world as it exists. In this case, the therapist is essentially reinforcing the status quo and should be very sensitive to the fact that this is so. This approach has the advantage that the therapist has direct contact with and thus presumably some control over the person whose behavior and perspective is to be dealt with. This approach is particularly compatible with a heavy reliance on drug therapy. It has the clear disadvantage, however, of attempting to get the individual to accept and adjust to what probably is most appropriately perceived as an unfair and unjust, but perhaps unchangeable, situation and many patients may be unwilling or unable to make such an adjustment.

The other alternative is for the therapist to work to change the woman's microenvironment so that she no longer confronts inequalities in her daily life. This will almost always involve changing the behavior and attitudes of others, typically the husband and often children, as well as changing some of the life goals and activities of the woman. One of the consequences of this approach is that the woman's "consciousness" will probably be raised. The clear advantage to such an approach is that an effort is made to change the particular situation that is at least partially responsible for the woman's emotional difficulties. The disadvantage is that the therapist often will not have contact with all persons whose behavior and attitudes need to change and, regardless of contact, some of these persons may not desire to change. As the woman's "consciousness" will often be raised by such an approach and existing inequities brought out into the open, unless accompanying environmental change occurs, the person's immediate situation may deteriorate. This, of course, may lead to fairly drastic action, such as divorce. Since the divorced are by far in the poorest mental health of any marital category (Gove, 1972a, 1973, 1979c), there are obviously risks and limitations involved in this strategy. The therapist who elects this type of approach may take comfort from the belief that drastic changes in one's life situation *may* lead to long-term improvement. Furthermore, they may also take comfort from the fact that the very unhappily married are in even poorer mental health than the divorced (Gove & Style, 1977).

Toward Change and Liberation

A basic theme of this book of readings is that for change to occur on any level—intrapsychic, interpersonal, societal—it must take place on all levels. For any one group of people to be "liberated" all groups must be. This is indeed an enormous task, and one that may have only a small probability of being accomplished. In the meantime, some look toward the future with hope for an ideal, egalitarian society (if not world) where all social, economic, and personal ills have been removed and peace and harmony are restored. Others imagine the worst of what the present path of self-destruction might bring—the extremes of technological living devoid of any form of real human contact, the eventual annihilation of all natural and environmental life, the desolation and depravity of nuclear holocaust.

According to feminist analysis, the second of these possibilities would be the result of the extremes of the "masculine," obsessive, paranoid, antisocial personality. Some would say that solving the problem requires that men change. Men need to relinquish their sex role, to take responsibility for changing themselves and their relationships with women and men, and to work with others to change society. There are many aspects of the male sex role that make such change difficult, however. Men derive benefits from "masculinity," from the personal satisfaction of self-importance to the rewards society bestows upon them. The effects of their destructiveness are not experienced directly by them but are borne by others around them (interestingly, antisocial personalities have the worst prognosis in psychotherapy and are the most resistant to change, primarily because of this). Because men have been emotionally maintained by women, they have had little opportunity or motivation to develop the internal resources necessary to make required changes.

Despite these difficulties, some men see the benefit of de- and resocializing themselves and are trying to change. A recent review article (Harrison, 1978) summarizes their efforts, and the interested reader is encouraged to pursue this topic further.

The problem, however, may be an even larger one than men changing. The problem may require that "masculinity" change on all levels, including intrapsychic, interpersonal, and cultural—and for the patriarchal mode of consciousness and the cultural mode to lessen and for the matriarchal modes to expand. The problem and possible solutions extend to race and class as well. For both men and women, changing one's "masculinity" (as metaphor) in relation to race or class would be difficult in the terms outlined above in relation to sex class. (Appropriate substitutions could be made for race, class, and other minority groups.)

To return to changing the relations between the sex groups, many feminists have suggested alterations in the domestic and public spheres. From an anthropological perspective, we have seen the potential importance of the domestic relative to the public sphere (in "Biological and Cultural Perspectives"). Hacker's analysis of women as a minority group gives as a basis for lack of minority group awareness the fact that women live with men and are therefore more susceptible to the influence of the dominant group. This can be transformed to women's advantage, however, in that once minority group consciousness is attained, men will be more susceptible to changes from women. By now it should be clear that for women to continue to support the male sex

*For him she is sex—absolute sex, no less. She is defined and
differentiated with reference to man and not he with reference to her;
she is the incidental, the inessential as opposed to the essential. He is the
Subject, he is the Absolute—she is the Other.*

Simone de Beauvoir, *The Second Sex*, 1953

World's End by Leonor Fini; reprinted by permission of the artist

role and "masculinity" and to accept an inferi-
or status and "femininity" are contraindicated.
Of great importance is bringing men into the
domestic sphere and having men occupy the
social role of mother (Chodorow, 1976, 1978;
Rosaldo, 1974; Rich, 1976; Dinnerstein, 1976).
Alternatively, bringing women into the public

sphere may be equally important; economic
independence for women seems to be a key
factor in change. We have also seen the importance of female solidarity, which we hope can
be established across race and class groups
and can be developed across cultural and national groups as well.

Aside from these suggestions, articles in this
section focus on practical modes of change
that some women have found useful. These
represent approaches to psychological change
within the context of an overall analysis of
change, as suggested by the final article by
Barbara Bovee Polk.

Consciousness-raising (CR) groups are the
topic of the first article by Alberta J. Nassi and
Stephen I. Abramowitz. While some may argue that CR groups are phenomena of the
past, it may also be argued that CR groups do
still exist and that some women's studies
courses, for example, perform some CR group
functions. "Rap groups" and "support groups"
are similar to CR groups and all of these are
now more likely to be organized on a particular topic relevant to women's concerns as the
women's movement continues to grow and differentiate. CR groups continue to be an
organic process and, as Polk analyzes in the
final article, as women struggle to organize the
women's movement, the means are at least as
important as the ends. CR, "rap," and "support" groups function to build female solidarity, another important basis for change.

Nassi and Abramowitz describe the origins and nature of CR groups, and summarize the research on the process and outcome of these groups. In evaluating outcome research they find that although both empirical and nonempirical studies show some positive results, these findings are more apparent in the nonempirical studies. The authors discuss the implications of these findings in terms of whether the effects of CR groups are too subtle to be detected by measuring devices, or whether experimenter effects and the desire to please the experimenter may differentially affect the two kinds of studies. The authors suggest further research on CR groups compared with group psychotherapy in terms of mental health outcomes using both empirical and nonempirical methodologies.

The Nassi and Abramowitz article and the next one by Ellyn Kaschak on feminist psychotherapy provide a contrast to the difficulty Gove had in integrating psychotherapy and feminism. While Gove failed to see a connection between these two, Nassi and Abramowitz feel that the CR group defies categorization as either therapy or social movement since it is both. Both seek to make the unconscious conscious as a basis for change. Some feminists however do not want to view CR groups as therapy since this might imply that there are individual solutions, an idea which is antithetical to the basis of CR groups and to some kinds of feminist therapies. Kaschak includes in her paper the various types of feminist psychotherapies based on differing feminist theoretical orientations. These are compared in an extensive table and represent a first major attempt to clarify such differentiations, although other feminist therapists might propose different distinctions.

Themes found in the previous section on mental illness are reintroduced in these two articles. Again, the notion of contradictory standards of mental health are supplied as basic evidence of, and only one example of, double binds confronting women. These authors present CR groups and feminist psychotherapy as possible antidotes. Another issue raised in the previous section had to do with the failure of traditional therapists to understand women in the societal context, making their "sins of omission" as harmful as their "sins of commission." Both authors see CR groups and feminist psychotherapy as providing an understanding of the societal context. They differ, however, in that feminist psychotherapy may include individual psychopathology along with societal pathology, whereas CR groups tend to place more, if not exclusive, emphasis on societal pathology. There is diversity among feminist therapists, however, in the degree to which individual and societal pathologies are emphasized and, again, these are outlined in Kaschak's paper.

Assertiveness training (AT) is another process of change that could be considered an antidote to "femininity" and learned helplessness. Chesler has remarked that "The institutions of . . . psychotherapy and marriage both encourage women to talk—often endlessly—rather than to act" (1972, p. 109). Donna Moore provides an understanding of AT and its origins. She discusses its relevance to women with regard to sex role socialization and to various ethnic groups and social classes. She surveys the research findings on AT as well as the more practical aspects of actually taking such a course. She emphasizes that assertive techniques are learned as behavioral options rather than as directives to follow. In fact, a strong current throughout feminist therapies and CR groups is that their purpose is to increase awareness and choices, *not* to define and control women's behavior.

In contrast to the first three articles, which have a practical orientation, the next article by Linda Garnets and Joseph Pleck provides a theoretical understanding of the factors that may be involved in sex role change. Originally appearing in a special issue of *Psychology of Women Quarterly* on androgyny, the authors briefly summarize previous work on sex role identity, androgyny, and sex role transcendence. As the authors state, all of these have been implicated in mental health or degree of adjustment. Sex role transcendence is an interesting concept in that it is purported not to depend on prior concepts of "femininity" and "masculinity," unlike the concept of androgyny. To the extent that "femininity" may be more strongly associated with white, middle-class, heterosexuals (as indicated throughout this book), issues of sex role identity, androgyny, and sex-role transcendence may have somewhat less relevance to other groups,

which may already have transcended sex roles.

This is speculative, however, and the analysis provided by Garnets and Pleck is a complex and thorough one. They analyze sex role strain in terms of the discrepancy between ideal self-concept and same-sex ideal in relation to sex role salience. In their schema, degrees of sex role strain are related to degree of mental health. They suggest that their analyses have implications for individual and societal changes in sex roles and advocate a reduction in sex role salience.

The final article, by Barbara Bovee Polk, provides an analysis of change within the broader societal context. Although this article was written some time ago, the fundamental analysis for change has not altered. Polk assumes that regardless of origins, there are several nonmutually exclusive approaches to understanding female subordination. Of these relationships, value differences in male and female cultures, and differential power in male and female relationships have formed the basis of the psychology of women as presented in this book of readings. The economic approach, while also important, has remained in the background.

Polk further analyzes the ways in which men maintain power. Their normative power has particular relevance to psychology in that it labels what is mental illness and what is social problem (see the section on that topic), and may be used as a means of social control interpersonally (see Henley and Freeman on psychological oppression, and Moore on AT). Men's greater institutional, reward, expertise, and psychological power, as described by Polk, are documented and discussed by nearly all of the authors whose work appears in this collection. Finally, brute force as a form of male power has been elaborated in this volume (see Leidig on violence and Herman and Hirschman on incest).

The approaches to change Polk suggests are de- and resocialization of the self, to which all of the other articles in this section are also addressed. Henley and Freeman have provided a background and analysis for personal interactions and micro-role systems and, in combination with other articles in this section, provide further means for conducting this task. Polk suggests action directed toward changing individuals and institutions (also advocated by many of the other articles in this book) as well as building alternative institutions, all of which have continued since the writing of her article as has the growth of female solidarity. Finally, problems of power and authority within the women's movement are viewed not as extraneous but as part of the process of change. For women, the process of change is as important as its content, and this ultimately transforms the definition of power itself.

Guardian of the Phoenixes by Leonor Fini; reprinted by permission of the artist

For Further Reading

Assertiveness Training (see list at end of Moore's article).

Boston Women's Health Book Collective. 1971. *Our Bodies Ourselves.* New York: Simon and Schuster.

Daly, M. 1978. *Gyn/ecology: The Metaethics of Radical Feminism.* Boston: Beacon.

David, D., and Brannon, R. (Eds.). 1976. *The Forty-Nine Percent Majority: The Male Sex Role.* Reading, Mass.: Addison-Wesley.

Dinnerstein, D. 1976. *The Mermaid and the Minotaur: Sexual Arrangement and Human Malaise.* New York: Harper & Row.

Griffin, S. 1978. *Woman and Nature: The Roaring Inside Her.* New York: Harper & Row.

Harrison, J. B. 1978. Men's roles and men's lives.

Signs: Journal of Women in Culture and Society, 4, 324–336.

Kaplan, A. (Ed.). 1979. Psychological androgyny: Further considerations (Special issue). *Psychology of Women Quarterly, 3* (3).

Kaplan, A. G., and Bean, J. P. (Eds.). 1976. *Beyond Sex-Role Stereotypes: Readings Toward a Psychology of Androgyny.* Boston: Little, Brown.

Mander, A. V. and Rush, A. K. 1974. *Feminism As Therapy.* New York: Random House.

Rawlings, E. I., and Carter, D. K. (Eds.). 1977. *Psychotherapy for Women: Treatment Toward Equality.* Springfield, Ill.: Charles C Thomas.

Rich, A. 1976. *Of Woman Born: Motherhood as Experience and Institution.* New York: W. W. Norton.

Sargent, A. 1977. *Beyond Sex Roles.* New York: West.

Wellesley Editorial Committee. (Ed.). 1977. Women and national development: Complexities of change (Special issue). *Signs: Journal of Women in Culture and Society, 3* (1).

Alberta J. Nassi and Stephen I. Abramowitz

Raising Consciousness About Women's Groups: Process and Outcome Research

Although therapy is a misnomer for consciousness-raising (CR) groups, some criterion for "therapeutic" or desirable outcome is necessary for evaluating clinical and social psychological change in the CR format. Quantitative and non-quantitative process and outcome findings are reviewed, and implications for theory, research, and practice are discussed. Women in CR groups give testimony to their global effectiveness in fostering personal development as well as political awareness. Empirical findings likewise support the notion of the CR group as a potentiator of pro-feminist attitudes. However, those data are equivocal with regard to the formulation that any such liberalization of sociopolitical beliefs promotes personal growth and self-esteem.

The women's consciousness-raising (CR) group has constituted the basic unit of the Women's Liberation Movement. As Brodsky (1973) observed: "The technique of heightening self-awareness by comparing personal experiences was as basic to the continuance and solidarity of the movement as any other tactic" (p. 25). Although these groups are purported to promote personal self-awareness in the psychotherapeutic sense, their ultimate goal is group consciousness or class consciousness in the political sense (Mitchell, 1973). The CR group is unique in that it defies singular classification as either psychotherapy or a social movement. In fact, it derives much of its strength and impact from the ability to deal effectively with the confluence of personal and political variables.

There has been considerable controversy within the women's movement about the labeling of CR groups as therapy (Allen 1970; Hanisch, 1971). Feminists have maintained a distinctive antitherapy orientation:

Consciousness-raising is not "therapy," which implies the existence of individual solutions and falsely assumes that the male-female relationship is purely personal, but the only method by which we can ensure that our program for liberation is based on the concrete realities of our lives. (San Francisco Redstockings, 1969, p. 200)

The issue of regarding CR groups as therapeutic may be seen in the same spirit as Mitchell's (1974) admonition to feminists not to reject Freudian formulations on the basis of penis envy alone. That is, CR groups may have a profoundly therapeutic effect without being contaminated by the limitations of traditional psychotherapy. Hanisch (1971) acknowledges:

Perhaps certain groups may well be attempting to do therapy. Maybe the answer is not to put down the method of analyzing from personal experiences in favor of immediate action, but to figure out what can be done to make it work (pp. 156–157).

In this respect, feminist-oriented professionals have advocated the adoption of CR groups as an alternative to traditional psychotherapy for women (Barrett, Berg, Eaton & Pomeroy, 1974; Kirsh, 1974; Kravetz, 1977; Rice & Rice, 1973). Indeed, while these groups should remain distinct from traditional psychotherapy, they may, in fact, contribute to the evolution of a new form of therapy (Mander & Rush, 1974; Warren, 1976). Of relevance here are data gathered from a large sample of former participants indicating that purely political motivations for joining a CR group were significantly less important in 1973–74 than prior to 1973 (Lieberman & Bond, 1976).

Although therapy is a misnomer for CR groups, "some notion of 'therapeutic' or beneficial change is necessary to formulate sociological and clinical comparisons of individual change in the psychotherapeutic situation and the consciousness-raising group" (Kirsh, 1974, p. 336). As a step in this direction, CR groups will be considered here in terms of their nature and purpose, their distinction from traditional psychotherapy, empirical and nonempirical process and outcome findings and the implications for theory, research, and practice.

Nature and Purpose of Consciousness-Raising Groups

> The process of transforming the hidden, individual fears of women into a shared awareness of the meaning of them as social problems, the release of anger, anxiety, the struggle of proclaiming the painful and transforming it into the political—this process is consciousness raising. (Mitchell, 1973, p. 61)

Consciousness-raising is a translation of the Chinese revolutionary practice of "speaking bitterness" (Mitchell, 1973). Chinese peasants, subdued by violent coercion and abject poverty, transcended the notion that their fate was natural by articulating it. "Speaking bitterness" is the process of bringing to consciousness virtually unconscious oppression, which has an analogue in psychoanalytic work. Inasmuch as women's oppression is hidden far from consciousness, there is a tendency for women to interpret their situation as natural or their misery as personal. Speaking the unspoken is the initial step in challenging these assumptions. The individual's own realization of injustice catalyzes this process for the entire group.

The reinterpretation of CR groups for women was first instituted in 1965 by Redstockings, a New York-based group of radical feminists. The groups proliferated on urban college campuses and eventually spread throughout the United States. It was estimated that major cities contain between fifty and two hundred such groups (Eastman, 1973).

The feminist version of CR denotes the process whereby women congregate in a supportive atmosphere to examine their personal experiences as women with particular emphasis on social conditioning and sexism (Warren, 1976). The small group optimally involves six to ten women, who meet regularly for two to four hours a week. The average life span of a group ranges from six months to two years (Woman's Body, Woman's Mind, 1972).

While CR is not regarded as a mechanical exercise, a certain protocol has evolved which lends a striking consistency to the way groups are defined. Common group requirements include: (1) a serious desire for life changes and a willingness to share personal experiences in a climate of trust and confidentiality; (2) regular attendance at weekly meetings; (3) personal, subjective, and specific communications only; (4) acceptance of testimonials offered by other group members; and (5) nonauthoritarian structure with no designated leaders or monopolizing members (Warren, 1976; Woman's Body, Woman's Mind, 1972).

Allen (1970) has outlined four group processes that characterize the development of the CR group. The first stage, opening up, is the revelation of inner feelings and personal experiences, which usually fosters an atmosphere of intimacy and trust. Individualized expression expands to the second phase, sharing, which is the recognition of shared commonalities and the construction of a collage of similar experiences among women. The next stage is to analyze and synthesize the data from the previous stages. More general questions are posed about the devalued position of women, how this is maintained, and how to alter this status. The final stage is characterized by abstracting, which entails the development and discussion of theory, the recognition of the oppressive nature of social institutions, and the assessment of the role of the group in forming ideology and serving as an impetus for social change.

Whereas opening up and sharing are common to both therapy and CR groups, analyzing and abstracting represent a clear divergence. It is essential to emphasize that these analytically distinct stages are not discrete time periods. Although the order may be stable, the processes themselves are ongoing, so that analyzing and abstracting are not valid unless rooted in the present feelings and experiences of the participants.

Unlearning to Not Speak

Blizzards of paper
in slow motion
sift through her.
In nightmares she suddenly recalls
a class she signed up for
but forgot to attend.
Now it is too late.
Now it is time for finals:
losers will be shot.
Phrases of men who lectured her
drift and rustle in the piles:
Why don't you speak up?
Why are you shouting?
You have the wrong answer,
wrong line, wrong face.
They tell her she is womb-man,
babymachine, mirror image, toy,
earth mother and penis-poor,
a dish of synthetic strawberry icecream
rapidly melting.
She grunts to a halt.
She must learn again to speak
starting with I
starting with We
starting as the infant does
with her own true hunger
and pleasure
and rage.

Marge Piercy

Consciousness-Raising and Traditional Psychotherapy

Feminists have been careful to distinguish CR groups from therapy groups (Allen, 1970; Hanisch, 1971). The crux of the antitherapy

You can be up to your boobies in white satin, with gardenias in your hair and no sugar cane for miles, but you can still be working on a plantation.

Billie Holiday, *Lady Sings The Blues*, 1956

---

platform can be identified across the dimensions of ideology, structure, criteria, and content (cf. Kirsh, 1974; Warren, 1976).

Ideology

Psychotherapy assumes that personal problems are primarily psychogenic and thus amenable to resolution through personal adjustment. By contrast, CR groups are predicated on the notion that "the personal is political," which is to acknowledge the sociocultural context of personal conflicts and to emphasize the salience of social change (Hanisch, 1971). In a discussion of psychotherapy as a form of social control, Hurvitz (1973) underscored this point:

> Psychodynamic psychology, with concepts such as "Electra complex," "penis envy," "vaginal orgasm," etc., has fostered a view of women as appendages to men, as less developed human beings, and as "natural" or "instinctive" mothers and homemakers, fostering conditions and attitudes that create problems for many women. Psychotherapy thus presumes to help these women overcome their problems by inducing them to accept the very conditions that give rise to their complaints. (p. 235)

This point draws on a second ideological distinction. The various schools of therapy, almost without exception, profess political and ethical neutrality, so that value systems are usually denied or are implicit rather than explicit. Value change is an overt goal of CR, and these groups are expressly political in nature.

Structure

The patient-therapist relationship, as portrayed in the traditional medical model, is inherently unequal and hierarchical insofar as the therapist, usually a man, is in the position of authority over the woman patient (Chesler, 1971). Although part of this inequality may arise from clients' countertransference projections, it still seems reasonable to propose that the domination of traditional psychotherapy by men and medicine only aggravates feelings of infantilization. CR groups attempt to counteract traditional female dependence on male authority by promoting peer equality and a leaderless framework, so as to draw on the knowledge and skills of each individual. Inasmuch as leadership is assumed without formal designation, it has been suggested that it may be more accurate to identify the leadership as "group centered" to the extent that it is shared or transmitted to different members (Eastman, 1973).

Criteria

Concomitant with male domination in the therapeutic relationship is the employment of masculine criteria of mental health in the

LOOK CINDERELLA...MAYBE YOU SHOULD SKIP THE BALL,
AND JOIN A CONSCIOUSNESS RAISING GROUP INSTEAD.

from *I'm Not for Women's Lib ... But*, copyright bülbül 1976, Arachne Publishing, Mountain View, CA. 94040

treatment of women. Underlying these criteria is the implicit acceptance of the culturally prescribed feminine sex role and an account of personality in which masculine sex-role ideals are viewed as more socially desirable than feminine ones (Barrett et al., 1974; Whiteley, 1973). Indeed, psychotherapists have interpreted dissatisfaction with the feminine sex role as diagnostic of psychopathology, so that women who conform to the traditionally circumscribed role are seen as more healthy than those who do not adjust accordingly (Rice & Rice, 1973).

Clinicians have been shown to propagate a double standard of mental health that constitutes "a powerful negative assessment of women," (Broverman, Broverman, Clarkson, Rosenkrantz, & Vogel, 1970). That is, mental health professionals use different norms to define healthy women and healthy men. As compared with the latter, healthy women are viewed as more submissive, less independent, less adventurous, less objective, more easily influenced, less aggressive, less competitive, more excitable in crises, more emotional, more conceited about their appearance, and more susceptible to having their feelings hurt. Not only is the healthy woman defined by the negation of the standards for the healthy man, but these male standards also constitute the criteria for the healthy adult. Thus, women are trapped in a double bind in which they cannot

manifest traits considered healthy for *both* women and adults.

As a sociological phenomenon, the CR group has been identified by Kirsh (1974) as serving to usurp the power of standard maker from the out-group's possession. All women's groups, whether therapy or liberation groups, can help break the isolation of women from each other and provide new role models and avenues for self-definition. One result of taking the power of definition away from male therapists is to change the source of approval. Thus, women's CR groups institute their own set of values, judgments, and goals, and attempt to transcend the traditional emotional dependence on male approval.

Content

Barrett et al. (1974) have astutely pointed out that therapists are not only guilty of "sins of commission," but also "sins of omission." That is, therapists tend to underestimate and/or undermine so-called women's issues such as marriage-career conflict, division of labor in the family, sex-role socialization, female sexuality, abortion, and rape. Conflicts about such issues create role strain for women to the extent that they are dissonant with the traditional roles of wife and mother for which women in this culture have been trained. A woman seeking sex-role emancipation and experiencing the conflicts associated with this

In education, in marriage, in religion, in everything disappointment is the lot of women. It shall be the business of my life to deepen this disappointment in every woman's heart until she bows down to it no longer.

Lucy Stone, Speech (Oct. 17–18, 1855) in
Elizabeth Cady Stanton, Susan B. Anthony,
and Matilda Gage, *History of Woman
Suffrage*, Vol. 1, 1881

---

new aspiration may jar the therapist accustomed to traditional male and female roles. Insofar as the demand of women for equality poses a distinct threat to the therapist's sense of social power, CR groups provide a more viable outlet for the exploration of these issues. Moreover, from the standpoint of the women, all-female groups have been shown to facilitate more self-disclosure about personal feelings and significant relationships than mixed sex groups, where women direct most of their interaction toward men (Ariès, 1973).

Overview of the Research

CR Group Process

Information concerning CR group process is limited to two published (Eastman, 1973; Lieberman & Bond, 1976) and two unpublished (Krug, 1972; Striegel, 1975) reports. One of each pair (Lieberman & Bond, 1976; Striegel, 1975) is based on quantitative data. Although any information drawn from such a thin data base must be considered very tentative, some surprisingly convergent results were yielded by these divergent studies.

Lieberman and Bond (1976) and Striegel (1975) mailed survey questionnaires to large samples of former CR group participants on the East Coast. The response rate was approximately 40 percent in both studies, and both samples were comprised primarily of upper-middle-class Caucasian women. Lieberman and Bond reported former CR group members' recollections of the most significant group process to be: sharing commonalities, involvement, risk taking, insight, and role analysis. Striegel's respondents most frequently noted

open talking, new alternatives, new information, and emotional support in that regard. In addition, pressure to conform behaviorally or attitudinally to CR group norms was recalled by only a small proportion of women.

Eastman (1973) observed 25 CR group meetings of 11 married middle-class women, aged 23–42, whom she also interviewed. Consensus was found about the absence of an identifiable leader and about continuity in a shifting leadership focus as participants became differentially active in discussions. Agreement was reported on the primacy of personal and emotional expression over cognitive and political issues and on a shift from early support to later confrontation. A descriptive participant-observation and interview study of CR groups turned up two main content areas (Krug, 1972). One focus was on relationships among women, including competitiveness, need for honesty, and exploration of prejudices, and another focus was on differences that occur when women interact with other women as opposed to men. A gradual shift in emphasis occurred from personal concerns to political activity.

CR Group Outcome

Quantitative Studies. Reports of CR group outcome based on quantitative data are described in Table 1. Three of these studies are published, and the rest are unpublished doctoral dissertations.

The overriding questions of whether and what kind of changes are forged by women's groups have been addressed in only four investigations, all theses. Two studies (Burr, 1974; Kincaid, 1973) utilized as outcome criteria both the Personal Orientation Inventory

The emancipation or liberation of women involves more than political participation and the change of any number of laws. Liberation is equally important in areas other than politics; economics, reproduction, household, sexual and cultural emancipation are relevant.

Alice Rossi, The Feminist Papers, 1973

TABLE 1
QUANTITATIVE OUTCOME STUDIES OF WOMEN IN GROUPS

Author	Groups	Participants	Data Sources	Outcome
Abernathy, Abramowitz, Roback, Weitz, Abramowitz, and Tittler (1977)	Primarily didactic CR class 50-minute periods over 20 consecutive school days, and control group	25 female volunteers, juniors or seniors in advanced psychology and sociology classes at Southeastern public high school, 13 given CR treatment	Attitudes Toward Women Scale, Personal Orientation Inventory, Tennessee Self-Concept Scale	For CR group, shift in liberalism in attitudes toward women from 50th to 85th percentile, and increase in Inner Directedness. Acceptance of Aggression, Capacity for Intimate Contact, Existentiality, and Feeling Reactivity on the Personal Orientation Inventory; for control group, modest pro-feminist change in attitudes toward women and incidental decrements on POI; no self-concept changes in either condition
Burr (1974)	All female growth group and mixed sex growth groups	6 males, 15 females (6 in a mixed sex group, 9 in all female group), randomly selected from students who responded to counseling center announcement for personal growth group	Personal Orientation Inventory, Inventory of Feminine Values, researcher's scales for verbally expressed self-disclosure and inner directedness	Women in all-female group showed more positive change on ratings of self-disclosure, but not on other three measures
Dorn (1975)	Sex role awareness group and comparison group	34 college upperclassmen for treatment group and 41 for comparison group	Horner's Motivational Scoring System for fear of success from TAT, Scrambled Word Test, Generation Anagram Task, Attitudes Toward Women Scale	Degree of liberalization in attitudes toward women greater in sex role awareness group; no differential change in fear of success and verbal task performance

TABLE 1 (CONTINUED)
QUANTITATIVE OUTCOME STUDIES OF WOMEN IN GROUPS

Author	Groups	Participants	Data Sources	Outcome
Kincaid (1973)	CR group, 16 structured one-hour sessions, and no-treatment control group	48 community college women, aged 28 or over, randomly assigned to either of two experimental groups consisting of 12 members and a leader or to control group	Inventory of Feminine Values, Personal Orientation Inventory, Philosophy of Human Nature Scale	Relative to control condition, treatment failed to reduce discrepancy between view of real self and ideal woman, to increase expression of positive attitudes toward other women or to increase time competence; it did produce movement from "other" to "self" orientation in view of real self and ideal woman and greater inner directedness
Lieberman and Bond (1976)	CR groups	1,669 predominantly white, upper-middle-class, Northeastern women who represented about 40% of those sampled primarily from large women's organizations	26-page survey questionnaire that tapped respondents' personal stresses and social circumstances, nature of their CR groups, demographic information	CR experience rated positive by 80% of respondents, neutral by 14%, and negative by 6%
Sargent (1974)	CR group, 45½ hours	12 women and 9 men in a mixed group	TAT	Only changes in men, whose affiliation scores indicated concern for interpersonal relationships and friendships

(POI) and the Inventory of Feminine Values (IFV). The former is a personal growth and adjustment scale that indicates relative standing along two major dimensions of self-actualization, inner directedness (independent thinking over reliance on others' views), and time competence (present over past or future orientation). The latter scale assesses real self and ideal woman images. Kincaid (1973), the only investigator who employed a control group of treatment-seekers, found mixed results. Participants relative to controls moved toward self from other orientation in view of real self and ideal woman on the IFV and toward greater

TABLE 1 (CONTINUED)
QUANTITATIVE OUTCOME STUDIES OF WOMEN IN GROUPS

Author	Groups	Participants	Data Sources	Outcome
Sprinthall and Erickson (1974)	One semester "Psychology Growth for Women" class in practicum-seminar format, and regular class comparison group	High school sophomore females who did and who did not choose experimental curriculum	Personal journal, Attitudes Toward Women Scale, Loevinger Ego Development scales, Kohlberg Moral Maturity Test	Changes occurred in growth class only: increased sensitivity to feelings, empathy, psychological-mindedness and awareness of alternatives, more liberal attitudes toward women; shifts in ego development from Stage 3 (conformist) toward Stage 4 (conscientious) or from Stage 4 to Stage 5 (autonomous); average shift in moral maturity of one-third stage, from 3 (other-directed conformity) partway to 4 (general rules, rights, duties)
Striegel (1975)	CR groups	215 predominantly white, upper-middle-class Eastern women who represented 43% of those randomly sampled from list of 1,000 names compiled from large women's organizations	Researcher's Inventory of Raised Consciousness	Impact maximal on feelings about self and other women; moderate on relationship with men, division of household labor, financial responsibility and vocational choice; minimal on marriage, personal appearance, children and family, and location of residence

inner directedness on the POI, but no differential change occurred for self-ideal woman discrepancy or for time competence. Burr (1974) reported null results for both measures.

Dorn (1975) obtained mixed results with the Thematic Apperception Test (TAT) as a projective index of fear of success and the Attitudes Toward Women Scale (ATW) as a measure of

What is necessary is the ability to call the shots exactly as they are being played; to see our life in all its complexity; to recognize that sometimes we are the victims and sometimes men are the victims, but neither of us is always the victim. . . . What has made men our oppressors is their inability to face the contradictions, but what will allow us to become strong is our increased ability to face the contradictions. That, to me, is feminism carried to its magnificent conclusion.

Vivian Gornick, *Ms.* (July 1972)

---

beliefs about the rights and roles of women in society. Although members of a sex-role awareness group did not manifest a reduction in fear of success relative to their counterparts in a comparison group, they registered a greater shift toward pro-feminist sentiments. In a study that did not include a comparison baseline, Sargent (1974) failed to find changes in female CR participants' TAT-derived affectional, achievement, or power motives. Changes in male members' affectional scores indicated a concern for interpersonal relationships and friendships.

Two reports bear on the impact of introducing a didactic CR component into a formal educational curriculum. Abernathy, Abramowitz, Roback, Weitz, Abramowitz, and Tittler (1977) presented sex-role awareness materials and related CR information to high school upperclasswomen in 50-minute class periods held over 20 consecutive school days. CR volunteers who could not be accommodated were controls. Students exposed to the CR curriculum showed a relatively greater pro-feminist shift on the ATW, an increment in inner directedness but not in time competence on the POI, and no changes on the dimensions of the Tennessee Self-Concept Scale. Sprinthall and Erickson (1974) evaluated the effectiveness of a one-semester "Psychology Growth for Women" class for high school sophomore women using the ATW, Loevinger's Ego Development Scale, the Kohlberg Moral Maturity Test, and a personal journal as criteria.

Women in a regular class provided a rough comparison baseline. Changes occurred in the Growth class only. These women demonstrated increased affective sensitivity, more pro-feminist attitudes toward women and positive shifts in ego development and moral maturity.

Two findings based on large samples of former CR group participants deserve mention. Eighty percent of Lieberman and Bond's (1976) respondents rated their CR experiences as having been positive, 14 percent rated them as neutral, and 6 percent rated them as negative. Striegel (1975) found that former participants evaluated their CR experience as having maximal influence on feelings about themselves and other women and minimal influence on marriage, personal appearance, children and family, and location of residence.

In sum, quantitative studies of CR group outcome are limited in terms of both quantity and quality. However, the fact that the same criterion instruments have been employed in several investigations has produced a more convergent data base than would ordinarily be the case. What evidence can be marshalled to date appears to confirm the success of CR groups at contemporizing women's sentiments about their roles and privileges. A constraint on the otherwise impressive reproducibility of this finding across studies, however, is the possibility that the enhanced level of pro-feminist belief at posttesting reflects social desirability responses on the part of CR participants. An-

> *Only beginning and end are, so to speak, pure or unmodulated; and the fundamental chord therefore never strikes its listeners more forcefully and more beautifully than when it first sends its harmonizing sound into the world and never more irritatingly and jarringly than when it still continues to be heard in a world whose sounds—and thought—it can no longer bring into harmony.*
>
> Hannah Arendt, *Between Past and Future*, 1961

other possibility is that the pro-feminist shift, while genuine, is largely a short-term adaptation to group pressure, and thus not enduring. Such reservations tend to be countered by certain aspects of Striegel's (1975) previously reported follow-up findings.

By contrast, quantitative findings are equivocal with regard to the notion that any increased sociopolitical awareness resulting from participation in CR groups, including liberalization of attitudes toward women, enhances personal development and self-esteem. As has been pointed out elsewhere (Abernathy et al., 1977), change in self-concept or other personality realms should perhaps not be expected to occur until the woman has had sufficient time to explore her new attitudes and behaviors in real life, elicit reactions to them, and integrate a new social self-conception. To resolve this issue more adequately, follow-up investigations are needed in which post-post-testing is done at least six months after the last CR session.

Nonquantitative Studies. Research on CR group outcome based on testimonial evidence is summarized in Table 2. Four of the seven pertinent papers are published. Subjects generally have been pro-feminist, college-educated women, ranging in age from 19 to 42. Recruitment was facilitated by personal contacts and intermediaries. Cherniss (1972) was the only investigator who included a comparison group, matched for age, occupation, and marital status. Data were gathered by intensive interview and/or participant observation, often executed by the researcher.

Keeping in mind that the unquantified observations which provide the data for this category of studies are considered suspect insofar as they are highly susceptible to social desirability and investigator effects, the benefits of women's groups are nonetheless reported with striking consistency (Warren, 1976). Perusal of the right-hand column of Table 2 reveals that the research has yielded uniformly positive findings. Negative results, if found, have not been reported.

The following findings are among the favorable outcomes attributed to the CR experience: (1) more positive feelings about self, including more self-acceptance, improved self-image, higher self-esteem, and greater sense of competence (Acker & Howard, 1972; Eastman, 1973; Micossi, 1970; Newton & Walton, 1971; White, 1971; Whitely, 1973); (2) more positive attitudes toward other women (Cherniss, 1972; Eastman, 1973; Micossi, 1970; White, 1971; Whitely, 1973); (3) development of a sociopolitical perspective that recognizes the influence of sex-role conditioning and sex-role expectations (Acker & Howard, 1972; Eastman, 1973; Micossi, 1970; Newton & Walton, 1971); (4) revelation of traditional sex-role patterns (Acker & Howard, 1972; Newton & Walton, 1971; White 1971); (5) awareness and expression of anger (Acker & Howard, 1972; Cherniss, 1972; Whitely, 1973); and (6) redefi-

TABLE 2

NON-QUANTITATIVE OUTCOME STUDIES OF WOMEN IN GROUPS

Author	Groups	Participants	Data Sources	Outcome
Acker and Howard (Note 1)	CR group	Feminists	Interviews	Development of feminist identity and world view; definition of each member as more competent; establishment of new self-images and identities, and renovation of pattern resulting from acting without reference to male-defined statuses; ventilation of anger, frustration, and fear
Cherniss (1972)	CR group and comparison group matched for age, occupation, and marital status	12 women's liberationists and 8 comparison women aged 21–28, recruited through intermediaries and personal contacts	Unstructured, non-directive, 4–6 hour interviews that probed women's background and present experiences	CR groups led to adopting of social-political perspective, which reshaped and redefined perception of self and key figures; redefinition of mother resulted in more sympathetic view of role constraints and allayed maternal guilt, anger and depression; sense of trust, intimacy and community toward women developed, facilitating ventilation of anger

nition of significant others (Cherniss, 1972; Micossi, 1970; Newton & Walton, 1971). Thus, in contrast to the pattern of findings yielded by the empirical studies, the qualitative data suggest that women's groups promote self-development as well as sociopolitical awareness.

Conclusions and Implications

Although women in CR groups give personal testimony to their global benefits, the only favorable outcome consistently yielded by empirical studies has been a pro-feminist shift in attitudes toward women. The reason for the

TABLE 2 (CONTINUED)
NON-QUANTITATIVE OUTCOME STUDIES OF WOMEN IN GROUPS

Author	Groups	Participants	Data Sources	Outcome
Eastman (1973)	CR group	11 women, aged 23–42, married; education ranged from 1 year of college to master's level	Observation of 25 CR group sessions, interviews	All interviewees cited personally important benefits; 8 reported greater autonomy, confidence, self-knowledge, personal enrichment, changes in negotiation of interpersonal relationships; several made reference to overcoming passivity as a result of group support; more than half experienced growing sense of identity with other women and developed caring and trusting relationships with other group members; when invited to contrast CR to other groups, 8 mentioned quasi-therapeutic effect akin to sensitivity, encounter, and therapy groups
Micossi (1970)	CR group	Caucasian women, aged 19–41, some college educated, from upper-, middle-, and working-class backgrounds	Participant-observation, interviews	Increased self-awareness and higher self-esteem; redefinition of significant others; striking change in attitudes toward other women, formerly competitors, now sisters in a common effort; reappraisal of social institutions according to support of traditional sex roles and manifest discrimination

TABLE 2 (CONTINUED)
NON-QUANTITATIVE OUTCOME STUDIES OF WOMEN IN GROUPS

Author	Groups	Participants	Data Sources	Outcome
Newton and Walton (Note 3)	CR group	Women	Interviews	Altered world view; women perceived as group with definitive characteristics, society divided into major groups, men and women; identity changes occurred including different feelings about body image, sense of greater acceptance and of greater physical and sexual competence; feminists became primary reference group, and relationships with men turned more egalitarian; change in career orientation; more ambivalence toward professionalism and male-dominated institutions and more work effort for movement-oriented activities
White (Note 4)	CR group	Feminists	Interviews	Improved self-image, more self-respect, higher ambitions, more independence and more confidence; decreased prejudice toward other women; relationship with men became more equal and involved less stereotyped "feminine" role-playing, and tended to be more platonic than romantic
Whitely (1973)	CR group	Women, most with higher degrees, in counseling profession, employed by university or secondary school	Participant-observation	More positive feelings about self and other women; greater awareness and self-acceptance of anger

discrepancy in findings concerning CR groups as a potentiator of personal growth between the empirical and nonempirical studies is open to several explanations. The argument often made in the face of negative psychotherapy outcome data could be advanced here: The psychometric criteria employed in the quantitative studies may have been too crude to detect many of the subtle personality changes induced by CR groups. Group duration, which tended to be shorter in the quantitative studies, might also be invoked in this regard. Another possibility is predicated on two notorious shortcomings of testimonial data—social desirability artifacts and investigator preconception concerning the value of CR groups. Efforts to "please" the (presumably pro-feminist) investigator and/or the failure of the latter to monitor her own biases could have distorted results in a positive direction.

The question of whether the attitudinal changes effected by CR experiences radiate to the realm of personality has important theoretical and practical implications. More definitive research clearly is needed at a time when growing numbers of women are seeking out CR groups as an alternative to traditional psychotherapy rather than as a blueprint for political awakening (Lieberman & Bond, 1976). Investigations in which the richness of qualitative data is combined with the rigor of empirical procedures are recommended.

It has been suggested that certain standards for group psychotherapy outcome be adopted for assessing the efficacy of CR groups (Kravetz, 1977; Warren, 1976). Kravetz (1977) has recommended that comparative outcome studies of CR versus traditional psychotherapy groups be conducted. In these and related respects, research on the effectiveness of CR

Giving Birth to Myself by Ann Leda Shapiro. Reprinted by permission.

groups is bound by the same limitations as all research efforts on psychotherapy outcome (cf. Bergin & Strupp, 1972). As Kravetz (1977) has cautioned, however, the different and in certain instances antagonistic objectives of traditional therapies and CR experiences necessitate the selection of criterion measures of sufficient breadth to ensure an adequate test of both modalities.

Future researchers would also do well to avoid the weaknesses of previous research on CR groups. Investigators have not adequately identified the populations under investigation (i.e., demographic data) or the population to which findings can be generalized, nor indicated how the total sample is drawn from that population. Rarely has random assignment of subjects to treatments been carried out. The absence of adequate controls or comparison groups places severe limitations on the inferences and potential knowledge to be gained about CR effects. Especially in the empirical studies, there have been no independent checks to verify that the CR format was implemented as intended. The nonempirical studies can be cited in this regard for failure to report more extensively the nature of the CR experience.

A restricted range of outcome measures has been employed. Inasmuch as CR is designed to be a political as well as a personal process, the absence of political ideology and activity measures is striking. Furthermore, in the quantitative studies, groups were of such short duration that measures of change may have been deployed too early in what is considered the normal life span of the group. The growth and change that researchers attempted to gauge may have been in increments too small to produce statistically significant results.

The long-term effects of CR groups have not been considered, so that there is no documentation as to the resiliency of attitudinal or personal change. This is a critical oversight because short-term effects may be due to group pressure to adopt feminist ideology as opposed to enduring value changes. No deteri-

oration from participation in CR groups has been reported in the empirical or the nonempirical literature. Although inclusion of such findings might be regarded as inimical to the women's cause, such knowledge could be used to refine future CR efforts.

The relative paucity of research in this controversial area does not appear to be merely the result of a normal time lag between social phenomenon and scholarly notice. Many professionals have not taken the CR effort seriously, so that it has been considered unworthy of concentrated scientific attention. Inasmuch as social science research is a social institution unto itself, it is not insulated from the "masculine bias" that is embedded in all such institutions (Carlson, 1972). Moreover, the deficiencies of empirical work in particular may be due in part to the cultural association of quantification with masculinity, which acts as a deterrent to female investigators. Nor can the responsibility for the limitations of the research base be placed on the shoulders of the practitioners and investigators alone. Kravetz (1977) has discussed the kinds of resistances that should be expected by the traditional academic researcher who approaches the profeminist atmosphere of a CR group. To the extent that women have colluded in the suppression of research efforts in general and have avoided empirical research in particular, it is necessary to keep in mind that analysis and abstraction are central to the CR process (Allen, 1970).

Ellyn Kaschak

Feminist Psychotherapy: The First Decade

The late 1960s and early 1970s evidenced the rise of the second feminist movement in the United States. The lives of innumerable women in this country, as well as in many others, were dramatically and irrevocably altered as they participated in consciousness-raising (CR) groups and began to become aware that the problems of each woman were indeed the problems of every woman, that *the personal is political.* For each woman who learned that her deepest and most hidden feelings were not hers alone, but those of women in general, that there was not something wrong with her as a woman, but with all women in our society, there was an awakening. For the first time, women began to know and define who they were and to free themselves from the arbitrary and constricting roles by which they had been defined by society. They slowly and painstakingly began discovering themselves.

Sex Bias in Traditional Psychotherapy

Prior to these years, during the prefeminist era, psychology, in general, and psychotherapy, in particular, were almost exclusively the province of men. Chesler (1972) has estimated that, during the decade of the 1960s, 88 percent of all psychiatrists and clinical psychologists were men and the overwhelming majority of clients, women. As Weisstein (1971) so cogently stated, "Psychology has nothing to say about what women are really like, what they need and what they want, essentially because psychology does not know" (p. 209).

In the now well-known study of psychia-

trists, psychologists, and social workers by Broverman et al., (1970), therapists were asked to choose the qualities which they felt characterized the healthy adult, the adult male, and the adult female. Both male and female clinicians described male behavior as highly correlated with that of the healthy adult. Females, on the other hand, were considered to be less aggressive, more emotional, less independent, and so forth. In these terms, it is impossible to choose to be both a healthy adult human being and a healthy adult woman. In fact, according to such a definition, there can be no such thing as a healthy adult female person. This study and others (Fabrikant, 1974; Nowacki & Poe, 1973) began to reveal the sex bias in traditional therapists' conceptions of mental health, as did the report of the Task Force on Sex Bias and Sex Role Stereotyping in Psychotherapeutic Practice sponsored by the American Psychological Association (1975).

It was becoming increasingly obvious to feminists that traditional psychotherapy had served as an agent of social control, reflecting traditional values and enforcing traditional sex roles. As women and feminists, many psychologists and psychotherapists were becoming increasingly aware not only of the antifemale and intrapsychic bias of psychotherapy, but also of the discrepancy between their own experience as women and the psychology of MANkind which they had been taught during their academic and professional training.

In particular, psychoanalytic theory and practice had been highly visible and influential in developing a phallocentric world

Prospective Immigrants Please Note

*Either you will
go through this door
or you will not go through.*

*If you go through
there is always the risk
of remembering your name.*

*Things look at you doubly
and you must look back
and let them happen.*

*If you do not go through
it is possible
to live worthily*

*to maintain your attitudes
to hold your position
to die bravely*

*but much will blind you,
much will evade you,
at what cost who knows?*

*The door itself
makes no promises.
It is only a door.*

Adrienne Rich

view, which resulted in Freud's introduction of the notion of the dual orgasm in women, among other abuses. Although not based on any empirical data, the belief that the mature, healthy woman experiences a vaginal (phallocentric) orgasm was adopted by psychoanalysts and their followers. Unfortunately many women were influenced by this school of thought to believe that, since they did not have this dichotomous experience, they were immature or pathological. The results of the research of Masters and Johnson (1966), al-

though not motivated by any feminist or political interest, shattered the long-standing myth of the vaginal orgasm, establishing in the laboratory that women physiologically experience only one kind of orgasm. These results were to have a profound effect upon feminist practice, as well as on feminist psychologists' criticism of psychoanalysis (Koedt, 1970).

In addition, its belief in women's innate dependency and passivity and in motherhood as the only totally fulfilling role in life for women led feminists to indict psychoanalysis as harmful to women and in need of replacement by a truly therapeutic approach.

Chesler (1972), in *Women and Madness*, presented what was undoubtedly, in terms of consciousness raising, the most significant critique of the treatment of women by the psychiatric and psychological establishment to emerge during this period. Thus, just as feminist women were beginning to discover themselves, feminist psychologists and psychotherapists were faced with the task of creating a psychology of women and, along with it, a feminist therapy, whose goal would be change rather than adjustment. The development of feminist therapy as an antithesis to traditional therapy would be the task of the 1970s.

Such a therapeutic approach would necessarily have to address itself initially to the many misconceptions about and mistreatment of women by traditional psychoanalytic therapy as well as by traditional sexist approaches in general. As a result, feminist therapy's roots would be grounded in refuting and correcting the destructive and oppressive treatment of women. Feminist therapy would begin as an antithesis to the well-established thesis of psychoanalytic and other traditional therapies. In a sense, this phase in the development of feminist therapy would become the second step in a dialectical process, which has yet to reach a synthesis.

Feminist Therapy: Commonalities

Several threads would be interwoven throughout the 1970s to form the fabric of feminist therapy. The first of these involved the discovery that *feminism itself is therapeutic. Feminism as Therapy* by Mander and Rush (1974) provided a personal and experiential guide to the therapeutic aspects of feminism, as well as presenting one possible combination of feminism with psychotherapy. This particular combination included the use of Gestalt techniques, body awareness, and other experiential exercises.

An adjunct to this principle was reflected in an early article by Annette Brodsky (1973) which discussed the CR group as a model for psychotherapy with women. Having learned from the CR group experience that participation in small groups helped women to overcome their isolation and alienation from themselves and each other, many feminist therapists have selected groups as the preferred mode of treatment. These therapists believe that the group experience provides both support and validation of a nature that cannot be offered by the therapist alone, while mitigating the powerful role of the individual therapist.

The group experience allows women to identify broader social problems that have been mistakenly identified as individual ones. In this way, they have been able to begin to escape from society's double binds (Kaschak, 1976) and to facilitate change, both internal and external, individual and societal. The

The Encounter by Remedios Varo; reprinted by permission of Walter Gruen

group frequently offers the first opportunity "to leave the field," which, in a double bind, is the first entry into a world in which women can escape their excessive dependency on men. It is that excessive dependency on men to fulfill financial, psychological, and social needs which prevents women from being able to experience the absurdity of some of the choices they are asked to make (e.g., the results of the study by Broverman et al.). In such a situation, women depend on men for their very survival and, so, must deny part of their real and valid experiences, part of themselves, in order to survive. They may not comment on or even become aware of the paradoxical nature of double binding communication. Only when the recipient of double binding communications can safely allow herself to become aware that there is no correct response, no real choice involved, can she begin to change. "Leaving the field" in this way is made possible by the existence of women's groups, which can validate the individual woman's isolated experience and a women's community to which women can escape partially or totally.

Although there are similarities between CR groups and feminist therapy, there are also crucial differences. Leidig (1977) has provided a useful list of the differences between CR groups and feminist therapy, which is reproduced in Table 1.

Thus while participation in CR groups has proved therapeutic for women, the CR group becomes a feminist therapy group only when

TABLE 1
DIFFERENCES BETWEEN CR GROUPS AND FEMINIST THERAPY

CR	Feminist Therapy
1. Group	1. Individual, sometimes a group
2. Untrained women	2. Trained therapist
3. No payment or fees	3. Payment, usually on a negotiated basis
4. Purpose is *not* to solve personal problems, but rather to share collective, universal experiences	4. Purpose *is* to solve personal problems
5. Focus on external factors	5. Focus on internal *and* external factors
6. Group decides topic for sessions, or it may be a prearranged topic, e.g., housework	6. Client decides topic
7. Group shares experiences mutually	7. Client primarily shares experiences

feminist consciousness and principles are combined with an appropriate psychotherapeutic process.

Feminist therapy is also done individually by all but a few grassroots radical therapists (distinctions among feminist therapists will be outlined later in this paper). In fact, most feminist therapists utilize individual therapy as a major modality.

Feminist therapy has been identified with one specific technique. That technique, the major innovative and characteristic tool of feminist therapy, is the feminist analysis of the societal forms of oppression that affect all women, individually and collectively. This analysis allows the individual woman client to understand the ways in which her problems are the problems of all women and to become aware of forces of which she was previously unaware. Other than this feminist analysis, feminist therapy is not identified with any particular technique or school of psychotherapy, but instead uses many techniques in combination with a feminist analysis. In fact, Thomas (1977), in a survey of approximately 200 practicing feminist therapists, found that they subscribed to 33 different theoretical orientations, 24 of which were newly developing and nontraditional in nature.

As feminist therapists describe feminist therapy, it seems to be based on three components that are intertwined; first, a belief system comprised of feminist humanism and feminist consciousness, the two complementary parts of the feminist value system; second, a therapist-client relationship that renders the therapeutic process compatible with the feminist value system; and third, two processes—consciousness raising and placing emphasis on the commonality shared by all women. . . . (Thomas, 1977, p. 452)

Although the literature contains many discussions concerning the nature of feminist therapy, it is perhaps most clearly and concisely articulated by Leidig (1977), who has expanded Lerman's presentation (1974) to describe the ten defining aspects of feminist therapy:

1. The therapist is a *woman* and a feminist.
2. Feminist therapy assumes that all therapy is value laden and consequently makes its own value orientation explicit.
3. Feminist therapy is not identified with any specific technique.
4. The feminist therapist views the client as essentially competent.
5. Women are encouraged to assume personal power.
6. The personal is political.
7. Feminist therapy explores women's issues.
8. The feminist therapist encourages self-nurturance in women.
9. Feminist therapy deals with female sexuality.
10. Anger is a central issue.

As has been mentioned previously, this author considers the feminist analysis of women's status in society and its concomitant intrapsychic and interpersonal effects to be the hallmark technique of feminist therapy, much as the analysis of the unconscious is associated with psychoanalysis, and would, thus, modify point number 3 accordingly. Certain of Leidig's other points would be modified by feminist therapists who adhere to a less radical approach than hers. These distinctions will be dealt with in Table 2. Additionally, most feminist therapists agree that the feminist therapist has herself participated in a feminist analysis of her own life, such as CR group, strives to live in a manner congruent with feminist principles, and is familiar with current psychology of women and feminist therapy literature.

In our patriarchal society, there exists a clear power differential between men and women. That differential within societally defined relationships, including that of psychotherapist and client, has been a central focus of feminism and feminist therapy. Chesler (1971) has criticized traditional psychotherapy as an exploitative, patriarchal institution.

> Freud believed that the psychoanalyst-patient relationship must be that of a "superior and subordinate." The psychotherapist has been seen, by his critics as well as by his patients, as a surrogate parent, ... savior, lover, expert, and teacher.... (Chesler, 1972)

Tennov (1976) has also criticized the potentially negative influence on women of psychodynamic therapy and the powerful role of the psychotherapist, calling instead for social change.

Polk (1974) has identified six sources of male power: (1) *normative power*, acquired through control of traditional sex-role definitions; (2) *institutional power*, acquired through control of the institutions of social control and socialization; (3) *reward power*, based on the first two forms of power: men are able to reward women who conform to traditional sex roles and withhold reward from those who don't; (4) *expertise power*, men are the experts; (5) *psychological power*, men's social conditioning is more congruent with the value structures of social institutions than is women's; (6) *brute force*, for example, beating and rape as forms

TABLE 2

DISTINCTIONS AMONG FEMINIST AND NON-FEMINIST THERAPIES

Issues	Radical Grassroots Feminist Therapy	Radical Professional Feminist Therapy	Liberal Professional Feminist Therapy	Non-Sexist Therapy	Traditional Psychoanalytic Therapy
Feminism	The personal is political. Oppression of women must be eliminated by altering society at its very roots.	The personal is political. Oppression of women must be eliminated by altering society at its very roots.	The personal is political. Society's institutions must be changed so that they allow equal treatment and opportunity for both women and men.	Irrelevant to psychotherapy.	May be considered irrelevant or a result of unresolved psychodynamic conflicts from an earlier developmental level.
Feminist political awareness and application in psychotherapy	Sine qua non of effective therapy.	Sine qua non of effective therapy.	Sine qua non of effective therapy.	Irrelevant to psychotherapy, which is an apolitical act.	Irrelevant to psychotherapy, which is an apolitical act.
Own analysis of therapist	Participation in prior and current feminist analysis through CR groups, feminist therapy collectives, etc., is imperative.	Participation in prior and current feminist analysis through CR groups, feminist consultation, own feminist therapy is imperative.	Feminist consciousness is necessary but need not be acquired in any particular manner, although prior participation in CR groups is common.	Feminist analysis irrelevant. Own psychotherapy useful but not mandatory.	Must undergo a training psychoanalysis.
Values	Therapy is considered to be value based. Therapist's values must be made explicit.	Therapy is considered to be value based. Therapist's values must be made explicit.	Certain aspects of therapy based on values, which may be made explicit when relevant.	Certain aspects of therapy based on values, which may be made explicit when relevant, or therapy may be considered value free.	Irrelevant to psychotherapy, which is not based on values.
Sources of psychopathology	Environmentally determined. For women in this society, the result of oppression.	Result of individual development, as well as societal oppression of women. Can't eliminate possibility of biological sex differences, but reject innate differences based on anatomy.	Result of individual development, as well as societal oppression of women. Some biological sex differences exist, but reject innate differences based on anatomy.	Differ depending on particular model of functioning, but not based on innate anatomical differences.	Anatomy, biological differences, and early intrapsychic development.

TABLE 2 (CONTINUED)

DISTINCTIONS AMONG FEMINIST AND NON-FEMINIST THERAPIES

Issues	Radical Grassroots Feminist Therapy	Radical Professional Feminist Therapy	Liberal Professional Feminist Therapy	Non-Sexist Therapy	Traditional Psychoanalytic Therapy
Sex roles	Traditional sex roles should be completely abolished. Subscribe to androgynous model of mental health.	Traditional sex roles should be completely abolished. Subscribe to androgynous model of mental health.	Traditional sex roles should be abolished when possible or desired. Sex-specific differences in behavior that people choose to retain should be equally valued.	Traditional sex roles may be abolished when desired by client. Sex-specific differences in behavior that people choose to retain should be equally valued.	Reinforces traditional sex roles as normal. When not present, encourages their development.
Anger	Appropriate response to oppression and double binds for women in this society. The major affective issue for women.	Appropriate response to oppression and double binds for women in this society. May also be a reaction to unresolved individual conflicts. The major affective issue for women.	Appropriate response to oppression and double binds for women in this society. May also be a reaction to unresolved individual conflicts.	Not an issue unless it is one for the individual client.	A reflection of unresolved infantile and childhood conflicts.
Sexuality (mode of expression)	A question of choice. All non-exploitative forms are equally valid. Given present society, lesbianism less exploitative than heterosexuality.	A question of choice. All non-exploitative forms are equally valid.	A question of choice. All non-exploitative forms are equally valid. May consider alternatives to heterosexuality more difficult to maintain in current society.	A question of choice. May consider alternatives to heterosexuality more difficult to maintain in current society.	Mature heterosexuality is normal. Any other forms of sexual expression are immature, at best, pathological, at worst.
Therapeutic technique	Feminist analysis. Otherwise not identified with a particular technique, although tend to use Transactional Analysis or other techniques that client can understand as well as therapist.	Feminist analysis. Otherwise not identified with a particular technique.	Feminist analysis. Otherwise not identified with a particular technique.	Depends on particular school of psychotherapy.	Psychoanalysis.

TABLE 2 (CONTINUED)
DISTINCTIONS AMONG FEMINIST AND NON-FEMINIST THERAPIES

Issues	Radical Grassroots Feminist Therapy	Radical Professional Feminist Therapy	Liberal Professional Feminist Therapy	Non-Sexist Therapy	Traditional Psychoanalytic Therapy
Goals of psychotherapy	Enough individual change to be able to participate in social change. Both clients and therapists must be involved in social change.	Individual and social change. Therapists should become involved in social change; preferable but not mandatory for client.	Individual and social change although neither must directly participate in the latter.	Individual change, which may contribute to limited social change as a secondary effect, e.g., choices not made on the basis of sexist assumptions.	Adjustment to societal norms and traditional sex roles.
Power differential	Any difference considered inappropriate and a reflection of exploitative patriarchal relationships.	If non-exploitative, may be useful for development of therapeutic relationship and corrective emotional experience. Interpreted in feminist analysis.	If non-exploitative, may be useful for development of therapeutic relationship and corrective emotional experience. Interpreted in feminist analysis.	Part of the therapeutic relationship. Not used exploitatively.	Sine qua non of psychotherapy.
Transference	Exploitative. Interferes with therapy.	Exploitative. Interferes with therapy.	May be useful. Can't eliminate entirely.	Depends on school of therapy.	Basis of therapeutic relationship.
Expertise	Therapist is not an expert. Client is best expert on own process.	Client is best expert on own process, but therapist has certain skills and expertise.	Therapist's skills and psychological insights may outweigh client's self-awareness.	Therapist is the expert.	Therapist is the only expert, particularly on client's unconscious motivation.
Therapist self-disclosure	Necessary for equal relationship.	Necessary for elimination of exploitative aspects of power.	May be useful when appropriate or relevant to client's problem.	May be useful when relevant to client's problem.	Inappropriate. Interferes with transference.
Resistance	Unwillingness to define individual problems as societal results of oppression. Lack of feminist consciousness.	Lack of feminist consciousness as well as resistance to individual interpretations.	Resistance to individual interpretations. Need not see societal aspect of every problem.	Depends on school of therapy.	Entirely individual and subject of analysis.

TABLE 2 (CONTINUED)

DISTINCTIONS AMONG FEMINIST AND NON-FEMINIST THERAPIES

Issues	Radical Grassroots Feminist Therapy	Radical Professional Feminist Therapy	Liberal Professional Feminist Therapy	Non-Sexist Therapy	Traditional Psychoanalytic Therapy
Level of intervention	Societal. Group in service of societal.	Societal, group and individual.	Individual, group and societal.	Individual and group.	Predominantly individual.
Professional issues, e.g., fees	Negotiated by therapist and client.	Negotiated within certain parameters set by therapist.	May be negotiated within parameters set by therapist or may be set by therapist.	Set by therapist.	Set by therapist. Any attempt by client to negotiate seen as resistance to be dealt with as a therapeutic issue.
Locale	Therapist's home, client's home, or other mutually negotiated territory.	Therapist's office or home.	Therapist's office or home.	Therapist's office.	Therapist's office.
Therapist's training	Most frequently trained in alternative women's setting rather than academic or professional institutions.	Trained in academic and professional institutions.	Trained in academic and professional institutions.	Trained in academic and professional institutions.	Trained in academic and professional institutions, including a psychoanalytic institute.
Contact outside therapy sessions	Entirely appropriate and desirable, since all members of women's community.	Acceptable in social or political situations.	Acceptable in social or political situations.	Varies with school of therapy and practitioner.	Completely inappropriate and undesirable.
Gender of therapist	All feminist therapists are women. Men can't serve as role models or validate women's experience in this society.	All feminist therapists are women. Men can't serve as role models or validate women's experience in this society.	Majority are women, but some highly conscious men may be feminist therapists.	Both women and men may be equally effective.	Minority of therapists are women, particularly among psychiatrists.
Gender of client	All women.	Priority given to women.	Both women and men.	Both women and men.	Both women and men.

of coercive social control. All of these kinds of power have been operative within the traditional "therapeutic" relationship, the latter most frequently as an implied or explicit threat.

Feminist therapists take the position that power between therapist and client should either be equal or continually approach equality. While the client may attribute to the therapist a certain amount of power based on her expertise, the therapist does not exploit or exaggerate this difference, for example, by presenting omnipotent interpretations either subtly or overtly, verbally or nonverbally, or by using obscure clinical terms. The client is considered to be the best expert on her own behavior and competent to understand both the impressions and techniques of the therapist. Any power differential that mirrors the inferior position of women in our society can only maintain and reinforce the status quo. To go a step further, several investigators have taken the position that powerlessness or learned helplessness (femininity) is directly *responsible* for women's psychological disorders, such as depression (Bart, 1970; Radloff & Monroe 1978; Marecek, J., 1976) and interpersonal situations, for example, battering relationships (Walker, 1979). Thus, feminists have attempted to eliminate exploitative power differentials in the therapeutic relationship. Any power differences are part of the material of therapy and the focus of feminist analysis. While distinctions among feminist therapists exist with regard to the degree of power differential which they consider appropriate or therapeutic (these will be compared in Table 2), let us first continue to trace the common threads.

The perspective of feminist therapy is a cul-turally deterministic one, putting forth an environmental model of psychopathology and an androgynous model of mental health (Rawlings & Carter, 1977). The environmental model traces the sources of psychopathology to the social environment, not to the anatomy or biology of the individual. Furthermore, this model views the very act of psychotherapy as a social and political one.

One way to describe what is meant by androgyny is perhaps a maximal flexibility, an ability to respond in terms of the demands of a situation and one's own needs and abilities rather than in response to prescription and proscription. The androgynous person is, for example, able to be both active and passive, both independent and dependent, both emotional and intellectual. The androgynous individual is absolutely not a caricature of a member of her own or the "opposite" sex, but a new synthesis, an individual free to transcend traditional sex roles, an individual not confined by arbitrary, sexist restraints.

According to feminist theory, this is only one half of the change needed. An androgynous person can only function in an environment that affords an equal opportunity to all people, one that does not assign tasks, roles, and life styles on the basis of kind of genitals, color of skin, and so forth. Thus feminist therapists also actively facilitate and are involved in working toward the elimination of societal constraints. Only with the abolition of the arbitrary sex roles imposed by society, so that each person can choose the roles she or he will play on the basis of his or her own needs and abilities, along with the needs of a receptive social environment, will androgyny be possible, will feminist therapy have provided "a 'cure' for the most pervasive psychological disabilities of our time: impotence in women and frigidity in men" (Kaschak, 1976).

In feminist therapy, each woman seems to progress through several similar stages. Entering therapy with the belief that "there is something wrong with me," that "my unhappiness represents a personal failure" (Stage 1), she soon becomes aware, through the feminist analysis offered by the therapist or therapists, and the validation of her experience by other group members (Stage 2), that her problems are *both* individual and social in nature. With this awareness (Stage 3), in virtually every case, comes a tremendous amount of anger at others, at society, and sometimes at herself for having "been blind" for so long (Stage 4).

Exploring and working through this fourth stage to some constructive resolution really represents the heart of feminist therapy and the point at which it most clearly diverges from consciousness-raising. All anger does not necessarily disappear, but rather is channeled constructively into action and change (Stage 5). In addition, the client learns to give up culturally determined self-deprecatory and helpless behavior in favor of personal power and self-esteem. She learns to nurture herself and other women rather than only nurturing men and children. In this process, the client learns to value herself and other women as people. However, it is important to note that while the source of pathology is traced to the social environment, the feminist therapist does not permit such an analysis to preclude or replace individual responsibility or the existence of individual differences. Both levels of analysis and change are essential, according to all but the most radical grassroots feminist therapists, who trace all pathology to the social environment (see Table 2).

For Witches

today
i lost my temper.

temper, when one talks of metal
means strong,
perfect.

temper, for humans,
means angry
irrational
bad.

today i found my temper.
i said,
you step on my head
for 27 years you step on my head
and though I have been trained
to excuse you for your inevitable
clumsiness
today i think
i prefer my head to your clumsiness.

today i began
to find
myself.

tomorrow
perhaps
i will begin
to find
you.

Susan Sutheim

A major aspect of the five-stage process involves helping each client first to identify and then to reclaim and reintegrate lost parts of herself as a woman. Various parts are actually lost to all members of our society, regardless of gender, as a result of the rigid and artificial division of human characteristics known as sex roles. Traditionally each individual in our society has been able to function as only half a human being. He could deal with the outside world, she functioned within the home. Together they made up one fully functioning human being—named the Couple. No one could stand on her or his own two feet. People could only lean on each other as a way to survive. Individual development was seriously thwarted. In feminist therapy, clients learn to become whole human beings, to develop to their fullest potential.

Feminist therapists actively consider the needs and daily realities of women of various life styles and equally value all these life styles. Being "conscious" females in a patriarchy demands a certain sensitivity to nondominant life styles. In addition, they actively confront their own values and biases in order to be able to respond sensitively and knowledgeably to women of all ethnic groups, classes, and sexual orientations. They also take responsibility for their own limitations, however, in dealing with situations that they may not fully understand, as well as with the limits of even a feminist *psychotherapy* to bring about *social* change.

In keeping with feminist principles, feminist therapists are concerned with the availability of therapy to women of all classes and life styles, and typically set fees either with a degree of flexibility or with a willingness to negotiate. In feminist psychotherapy, the consumer or potential consumer is encouraged to shop around, to interview several therapists until she finds one whose personal approach, therapeutic styles, and values are congruent with her own. Making such information available to prospective and current clients requires a willingness on the part of the therapist to make herself more transparent,

more "known" than the traditional therapist. In other words, the protective garb of so-called "professional neutrality" is shed. Once again, the degree to which each group of feminist therapists is willing to relinquish this professional neutrality varies along the continuum presented in Table 2. The general process of psychotherapy, as well as more specific techniques and personal values of the therapist, may be discussed and explained to the client.

Consumer guidelines for choosing a therapist have been developed by the Association for Women in Psychology (1979). Their useful guide addresses such issues as: therapy vs. alternatives; limitations of therapy; how to find a therapist; how to choose a therapist; interest in feminist therapy; how to find a feminist therapist; using contracts in the therapy relationship; a bill of rights for the consumer of psychotherapy; how to tell if your therapist's sexism is interfering with your therapy; guidelines for consumer use of psychotherapeutic drugs; and dealing with grievances.

Ancillary resources, such as *A Woman's Guide to Therapy* (Friedman et al., 1979) also present a comprehensive guide to therapy for women, including such issues as what therapy can accomplish, how to avoid potentially destructive (sexist) practitioners, and what to expect as a function of the school of psychological thought or theory to which the therapist adheres. In addition, the *Feminist Therapist Roster* (Brodsky, 1972), coordinated by the Association for Women in Psychology, is available to potential consumers of feminist therapy in all regions of the United States.

Feminist therapy has replaced the traditional personal and intrapsychic focus of psychotherapy with a combined social and psychological perspective, one that recognizes oppression as a reality and involves women psychologists in action on both levels leading to its change. Thus, feminist involvement in psychology and psychotherapy has led to an increased concern with specific issues related to women: mother-daughter relationships (Chodorow, 1978; *Feminist Studies*, 1978; Confal, 1976), rape (Brownmiller, 1975; Griffin, 1971; Russell, 1974), father-daughter incest (Armstrong, 1978; Herman & Hirschman, 1977); battered women (Leidig, 1980), violence against women (Davidson, 1978; Martin, 1976; Walker, 1979), sexual dysfunction (Barbach, 1975), lesbianism (Mondanaro, 1977; Martin & Lyon, 1972), Third World women (Murray, 1981; True, 1981; Senour, 1978; Witt, 1981), and professional women (Steinberg, 1978). Particularly innovative modes of intervention include assertiveness training (Moore, 1981) and pre-orgasmic women's groups (Barbach, 1975), both of which depend heavily on behavioral techniques, rape hot lines, shelters for battered women, women's switchboards, and various forms of peer counseling. In addition, feminist involvement in psychotherapy has led to the introduction and promotion of groups for women designed to counter helplessness by teaching self-help in such traditionally mystifying areas as carpentry, auto mechanics, the legal system, and medical/gynecological care, to name a few. Women themselves have begun to define women's own experience and to develop their own culture.

The influence of feminist therapy during the decade of the 1970s has been a profound and pervasive one (see also Brodsky, 1980). During this time, an alternative, both viable and effective, to traditional psychotherapy has been developed, not by a single theoretician or group of theoreticians, but by literally hundreds of grassroots and professional women contributing to a process that has been as feminist in nature as has its still evolving therapeutic system.

Feminist Therapy: Distinctions

The development of feminist therapy has been atypical and, indeed, revolutionary not only in the manners already described, but in that it represents and reflects the political, psychological, and personal viewpoints of an entire spectrum of women. Just as feminism itself is not a homogeneous movement, but one responsive to the concerns of women of various backgrounds and life styles, so is feminist therapy. In an attempt to introduce a conceptual and practical framework by which the reader may be assisted in understanding this heterogeneous and still-evolving therapeutic approach, this author will offer several distinctions among practitioners.

Feminist therapists may be considered in three general categories. The first includes those who are politically radical feminists, have not been trained in traditional professional or academic programs, and do not practice in professional settings, but instead in collectives identified with the alternative women's culture. The second major group of feminist therapists can also be identified by their radical feminist ideology, but differ from the first by virtue of the fact that their training, and often their practices, are in academic and professional settings. These women are social workers, counselors, psychologists or psychiatrists, many of whom were originally grassroots feminist therapists who have, during the decade of the 1970s, completed formal

I met one remarkable case of this seeming loss of identity in a mediumistic woman who realized that in the absence of her husband or her son she felt completely vague, unfocused, and at a loss. She went to an analyst in the hope that he might help, but was shattered by the following dream: She visited her analyst and looked into the mirror he held up for her, but to her horror there was no reflection. This dream convinced her, as nothing else could have done, of her paramount need to learn to exist in her own right and not merely as a mediator for other people. That she had not understood how to achieve this was evidenced by another dream two years later: A voice said to her: "Don't try to have a reflection. Break the mirror."

Irene de Castillejo, *Knowing Woman:
A Feminine Psychology*, 1973

---

training. The third group of feminist therapists might be called liberal professional feminist therapists. As feminists, they subscribe to a liberal, rather than a radical, political ideology emphasizing revisions in current roles and institutions rather than the complete reorganization of our social structure. As therapists, they also present a traditional academic and professional background. These three groups of feminist therapists may, for the sake of clarity, be contrasted with traditional analytically-oriented practitioners, as well as with the increasing number of practitioners of nonsexist therapy. The latter model is, according to Rawlings and Carter (1977), based upon an egalitarian approach, but does not incorporate either the political values or the philosophy of feminism in its therapeutic values or strategies. The existence of a growing number of nonsexist therapists is a direct function of the profound influence of feminist therapy on the entire field. Many nonfeminist therapists, both male and female, have found the egalitarian aspects of the feminist approach to be congruent with their own developing value systems, while others have found it economically, if not ethically, unfeasible to continue blatantly sexist practices as women/consumers of psychotherapy learn their rights.

Table 2 has been designed to reflect what this author considers to be the current state of development and differentiation within the field of feminist therapy and is subject to change as the field evolves. The distinctions drawn are an attempt to introduce some clarity in what is no longer a unidimensional or monolithic therapeutic approach. The differences are often subtle, the categories not always discrete.

Feminist Therapy: The Next Decade

Having been created and developed in the decade of the 1970s, initially as a grassroots and underground movement, feminist therapy enters the 1980s, its second decade, as a legitimate, above-ground school of thought. Its main challenge, no doubt, will involve the continued integration and reintegration of feminism with the useful aspects of already extant forms of psychotherapy, as well as with the more nontraditional forms. A true Psychology of Women, along with a conceptually consistent feminist model of psychotherapy or taxonomy of mental health, remain to be developed. Thus, having developed as an antithesis, as a response to a traditional, sexist, and phallocentric school of thought, feminist therapy has evolved into a complex and differentiated approach to societal and psychological change for women, and, ultimately perhaps,

Now hysterical personality disorders are being understood as exaggerations of the traditional feminine sex role, an over-conditioned reaction in vulnerable women to their dependency on males for their self-esteem. This "disorder" turns out to be something they acquired in the normal process of being rewarded for cute dressing and acting coyly toward their fathers and of being fawned on by adults for performing and catering to their superficial needs. . . . As adults, these women have continued to manifest these traits past their usefulness and have leaned on approval of others, particularly males, as their sole source of self-esteem. Traditional therapies deal with insight into the inability of the manipulations to work and the substituting of less dramatic means to gain approval. The feminist perspective emphasizes the development of an independent self-identity and self-determination, so that the need for approval diminishes.

Annette Brodsky, *Psychology of Women Quarterly,* 1980

---

with women leading the way, for all people. In addition, the profound influence of feminist psychotherapy on other forms of therapy has increased, and will surely continue to increase, extending the practice of nonsexist therapy by those who do not practice feminist therapy. That is, feminist psychotherapy, now approximately ten years old, will continue to exercise a profound and revolutionary impact upon the institution of psychotherapy in general, as well as to develop into a cohesive and conceptually sophisticated school of thought. The decade to come, then, will be one of synthesis, of a recombination of feminism with the truly therapeutic aspects of other forms of psychotherapy. Feminist therapy will continue to grow both in depth and in breadth of applicability.

Donna M. Moore

Assertiveness Training: A Review

I. Introduction

The 1970s saw an explosion of classes, films, research, books and articles, training programs, and discussions regarding assertiveness. Assertiveness was the "miracle cure" for a variety of problems, including depression, anxiety, low self-esteem, alcoholism, aging, weight problems, job interviews, sexuality, drug abuse, crying spells, and family relations (Moore, 1978). Assertiveness has indeed been effective in improving self-esteem and interpersonal communications and overcoming anxiety, depression, shyness, and hostility (Jakubowski, 1977a, 1977b) which explains the popularity of assertion training (AT).

The notion that AT might be a cure-all has led to three major concerns among persons working in this field. First, while assertion is an important skill, it is not the only effective type of communication. Likewise, AT can be part of a broader strategy to change behaviors and feelings that are detrimental to self-esteem and the ability to cope effectively with one's environment and interpersonal relationships (Alberti & Emmons, 1978; Jakubowski & Lange, 1978). Second, the popularity of AT has created a large number of AT trainers; some of these persons are untrained and/or unethical. This concern has led to the development of training programs for trainers (Flowers & Booraem, 1975; Flowers & Goldman, 1976) and an ethical guide for trainers (Alberti et al.,

1976). The third concern stems from the other two. Persons enrolled in AT classes must be informed that assertion is not always the most adaptive behavior (Flowers, Cooper, & Whiteley, 1975). Major problems can occur if one attempts such behavior too soon, with the wrong person, or in the wrong setting. Such attempts can result in retaliation from others, which often ensures that the person will make no further attempts and will experience yet another "failure" (Lange & Jakubowski, 1976).

This paper examines assertiveness and AT, where they came from, when AT is needed and who needs it, and what research findings exist. It also treats AT goals, possible problems, and the rights and responsibilities of clients and trainers. Although both women and men can benefit from AT, this article focuses on women's needs and therefore uses feminine pronouns.

II. What Are Assertiveness and Assertiveness Training?

Definitions

Communication behaviors can be placed on a continuum from passive or nonassertive to aggressive. *Passive behavior* is not getting what you want or need unless someone else chooses to give it to you. This behavior negates active participation in need/goal achievement. *Aggressive behavior* is getting what you want or need without regard for the rights of others.

The aggressive person often finds that her relationships suffer as a result of her behavior. *Assertive behavior* is getting what you want or need without violating the rights of others. The assertive person is active, concerned for both herself and others, and willing to accept responsibility for herself while allowing others responsibility for themselves.

While virtually every book on AT points out that assertiveness includes the ability to express both positive and negative feelings (Moore, 1978), Butler (1976) describes two additional types of assertion: self-initiation (developing personal goals and plans for reaching them), and limit setting (not allowing others to violate one's rights).

Assertion, then, is a set of learned communication behaviors that allows one to overcome deficits in interpersonal functioning by expressing both positive and negative feelings. AT is a process that helps people reduce anxiety and fear; changes beliefs and attitudes; and motivates people to learn behaviors that allow them their own rights without violating those of others.

Advantages and Disadvantages

The advantages of assertiveness have been mentioned. However, there are also potential disadvantages. First, the woman who becomes assertive is often mislabeled, both by herself and by those around her. Labels like "bitchy," "masculine," "pushy," and "aggressive" are used to stifle assertiveness. The goal of such labeling is to resocialize assertive women into "feminine" behaviors. Women should be prepared to reject such labels and to redefine themselves using labels like "assertive," "positive," "open," "honest," and "leveling" (Phelps & Austin, 1977).

Second, newly assertive women make mistakes. Assertion is a new form of behavior, and errors are part of the learning process. It is important that women allow for errors and set goals for themselves, trying the least risky things first. Then a failure will not stifle further attempts; that is, assertion will not be extinguished before it becomes strongly internalized.

Third, assertion can negatively affect relationships if the other person does not know what is happening or is threatened by the new behavior. Since assertiveness is an open, honest way of communicating, it is usually beneficial to relationships. However, like all forms of change, it can produce stress. Women should be encouraged to share their AT with significant others in order to decrease or avoid such stress. If a relationship requires a woman to be dependent or passive, assertion can be damaging to it. Women have the choice between exhibiting assertiveness within such relationships or risking termination.

Finally, assertiveness does not guarantee that one will always get what one wants or needs. Because assertion involves recognizing one's own rights and responsibilities as well as those of others, it often involves compromise.

Jakubowski & Lange (1978) summarize these disadvantages thus:

> The major disadvantage of assertion is that it involves risk. However, our fears about risk taking are often unfounded. Much of the time other people accept, understand, and in some cases appreciate our assertiveness, especially when they are approached in a way that shows we have as high a regard for their rights, feelings, and preferences as our own. (p. 14)

III. Where Did Assertiveness Come From?

The term *assertive*, as used here, was first used by Wolpe (1958) in a book on reciprocal inhibition, a method of training wherein one behavior (e.g., anxiety) is inhibited when a second (e.g., assertiveness) is learned and becomes strong enough to replace the first. The concept had been used by Salter (1949) as a method for reducing anxiety and producing more appropriate behavior in a schizophrenic population. It was used as a behavior change technique in psychiatric hospital settings for a decade before clinicians used it with other populations and the public became aware of it (Cotler, 1975).

The term *assertive* arose as part of behavior therapy, a radical technique begun in the late 1940s that stated that "what you do influences who you are and how you feel about yourself. By changing the symptoms of neurotic behavior, you change you" (Fensterheim & Baer, 1975, p. 19). Before that time psychoanalytic therapy, which focuses on unconscious causes of behavior rather than behavior itself, had been a major mode of therapy (Schultz, 1969).

Behavior therapy replaced the question, "Why are you this way?" with "What can we do to change your behavior?" Although it was considered radical in the 1950s, behavior therapy is not part of the radical therapy movement.

The 1960s were a time of turmoil in the United States. Civil rights movements were growing, as was the protest over U.S. involvement in the Vietnam War. A multitude of demands and conflicts led to personal and public evaluation of ethical systems. Psychologists and therapists also examined what they were doing. This era saw the rise of both consciousness raising (CR) groups and radical therapy.

Two important publications stemmed from the activism of the 1960s. Agel and the Radical Therapist Collective produced *The Radical Therapist* (1971). The goal of radical therapy is to discontinue therapy processes that perpetuate oppression. It seeks to develop a therapy that helps people change, not adjust. Radical therapists believe that traditional therapists have not helped anyone but themselves, have pretended to be magicians, and have survived under false pretenses.

> Therapy is change, not adjustment. This *means* change—social, personal, and political.... A struggle for mental health is ... unless it involves changing this society which turns us into machines, alienates us from one another and our work, and binds us into racist, sexist, and imperialist practices.... (Agel, 1971, p. xi)

The "second wave of feminism" also stemmed from the 1960s. CR groups, which were formed to help women understand why they were depressed and who or what was oppressing them, also motivated women to demand personal, social, and political changes.

Both the radical therapists and the CR groups acted on the same premise: that the problem was not within individuals but within the society. Individuals were urged to help change society rather than adjust to it.

In 1974 Mander and Rush published a book, *Feminism as Therapy,* in which they claimed that therapy can be synonymous with socialization.

> Feminism means to me the freeing of all people from the restrictions of their culturally defined sexual roles and the focus on balancing out the centuries of negation of female energy by the positive assertion and development of it in the world today. It's not simply the idea that women can benefit from rediscovering themselves but also that our whole culture can benefit from correcting its psychic/sexual imbalance through each person becoming whole again. (p. 39)

Like radical therapy, "feminism is interested in change rather than adjustment" (Mander & Rush, 1974, p. 47).

Thus, therapeutic intervention has moved from behavior therapy in the 1950s to radical therapy and CR in the 1960s to feminist therapy in the 1970s. A major problem remains, however. Although the new forms of therapy encouraged people to change society rather than adjust to it and called for healthier ways of structuring (or unstructuring) sex roles, they often focused on attitude change and motivation. They rarely provided behaviors with which to enact the new thought processes. AT was a natural extension of CR (Jakubowski-Spector, 1973): It could teach specific skills. Not that all women who had been involved in CR, radical therapy, or feminist therapy took an AT class, or vice versa. The point is that the popularization of AT brought recognition of the need to couple attitude changes with behavioral training (Linehan, Goldfried, & Goldfried, 1975).

Jakubowski states three major reasons for AT's popularity in the 1970s:

> The first trend is the widespread acceptance of the new cultural imperative for self-actualization as a birthright for all people rather than as a privilege for a selected few. This imperative has had an especially powerful impact on women and consequently has led them to carefully examine their own potentials for growth.... The second converging trend is the growing flexibility of sex roles and the gradual opening of previously closed areas of employment to women. These changes have encouraged many women to enter new job and social situations outside of the home where they almost invariably need new assertive skills.... The third converging trend is the growth of the women's movement which has stimulated increasing numbers of women to aspire to be effective as well as sensitive and feminine. (1973, p. 1)

She warns that although the interest in assertiveness is recent, it is not a fad. It is a response to needs that have always existed but have only recently been recognized.

IV. When Is Assertiveness Training Needed?

Early assertiveness workers theorized that maladaptive levels of anxiety, unfounded fears, or nonadaptive expectations inhibit assertive behavior (Wolpe, 1958; Wolpe & Lazarus, 1966). This assumes that the person knows what to do but is so anxious about either the situation or the consequences of assertiveness that she is blocked from acting.

Training programs based on this theory focus largely on anxiety reduction and modification of beliefs.

A second reason for nonassertion is skill deficit—the relevant verbal and nonverbal skills have never been learned (Lazarus, 1971). Training programs aimed at this problem focus on learning new behaviors.

Fiedler and Beach (1976) suggest a third reason for nonassertion: The person has made a conscious decision that assertion may not be safe or appropriate:

> Prior to acting either assertively or nonassertively, people weigh the consequences that could be expected to result from either behavior and elect the behavior that appears most favorable. That is, the decision to act assertively in any situation varies according to the expected consequences. Differences between persons who tend in general to be assertive and those who tend in general to be less so lie in differences in their expectations about these consequences. (p. 2)

Adler (1977) summarizes the reasons for nonassertion by stating that people act unassertively because they (1) have never been exposed to better alternatives, (2) have been rewarded for nonassertion, (3) have been punished for assertiveness, or (4) believe irrational myths about assertiveness. Ideally, AT reduces anxiety caused by inexperience in expressing wants or needs directly; teaches new behaviors where needed; rewards the new behaviors while extinguishing older, nonadaptive behaviors; and teaches assessment skills so that one can select when and where to be assertive based on realistic judgments regarding appropriateness and risk.

V. Who Needs Assertiveness Training?

To determine who needs AT one must examine socialization processes that create either passive or aggressive (rather than assertive) behaviors. Although a number of populations can use AT (e.g., offenders, alcoholics, children, elderly; see Moore, 1978), this review is limited to the effects of sex role and cultural socialization.

Effects of Sex Role Socialization

Given the many advantages of assertiveness, both men and women could be interested in becoming more assertive. Why, then, has AT gained popularity largely with women? Women's early sex role messages stress passivity, nurturance, quietness, dependency, self-deprecation, and other "feminine" qualities (Broverman et al., 1970). These messages are contained in storybooks, toys, and television, and are reiterated implicitly and explicitly by parents, teachers, caretakers, and peers (Bloom, Coburn, & Pearlman, 1975). The price of such socialization is high. Women suffer greater depression (Weissman & Klerman, 1978) and other forms of mental illness (Chesler, 1972) and enjoy less life satisfaction. They also have trouble identifying their legitimate rights (Bem & Bem, 1970). Passivity takes a heavy toll on women in the form of lack of confidence, fear of success, lowered self-esteem, and impaired personal and professional relationships. Women are seen by both themselves and society as less competent than men (Deaux, 1976). The result is learned helplessness (Radloff & Monroe, 1978), in which women do not feel that they have control over their lives and therefore either do not attempt to be assertive or experience great anxiety when they do (Wolfe and Fodor, 1975).

Hartsook and colleagues (1976) compared women who enrolled in AT with two control groups and found that the former were highly concerned with the approval of others and moderately inhibited in expressing their needs. Following AT, subjects demonstrated reduced anxiety and increased assertiveness.

Men are socialized in the opposite manner: Masculinity means independence, competence, success, aggression, and dominance (Broverman et al., 1970). Male communication is usually either assertive or aggressive. Exhibition of these qualities and behaviors brings personal, political, and professional power (Deaux, 1976).

Wolfe and Fodor (1975) summarize the effects of sex role socialization as follows:

> . . . for males, socialization "tends to enhance experimental options . . . the male socialization experience involves learning to be assertive, competitive, independent, aggressive"; for females "the socialization process tends to reinforce the nurturant, docile, submissive and conservative aspects of the traditionally defined female role and discourages personality qualities conventionally defined as masculine: self-assertiveness, achievement orientation, and independence." It is largely through following out the nurturant, docile "programming"* of the female role—denying their own needs and devoting themselves to winning others' love and approval—that women in particular seem to wind

_____
*Ed. note: In this extract, Wolfe & Fodor are quoting J. H. Block, "Conceptions of Sex-role: Some Cross-cultural and Longitudinal Perspectives," *American Psychologist* (1973) 28, 512–526.

up with such severe deficits in assertive behavior. (p. 45)

The Cost of Ethnicity

Ethnic minorities are often socialized to avoid assertiveness. This may create a double bind for minority women. Three behaviors sometimes exhibited by minorities that indicate a need for AT are: (1) assertion within their own group but passivity within the dominant culture; (2) aggressive behaviors out of anger over oppression; (3) passivity within their own culture and within other cultures. These alternatives are not the only ones, of course, but they are the ones most often described in the literature and seen by the dominant culture.

There has been little research regarding the effects of socialization on the need for or effectiveness of AT for minority populations (Moore, 1978). However, some recent material (Alberti, 1977; Cheek, 1976) provides assistance in understanding AT from minority perspectives.

Grodner (1975) points out that AT might be appropriate for minority groups in view of their oppression by the larger culture, which leads to nonassertion being seen as adaptive by many minorities. For such training to be effective, however, it must deal with actual, rather than stereotypical, needs. Grodner points out that before such training is developed, the effects of culture, socioeconomic status, beliefs, and personality must be understood. He states that "a low level of assertiveness is not necessarily associated with a high level of anxiety or discomfort" in the Chicano lower class, although he found working- and middle-class Chicanos exhibiting such behaviors. This poses the question of whether differences in assertiveness are due to social class or culture: Grodner's work indicates that the two interact. He also cautions that one must not assume that people are uncomfortable with nonassertion.

In a review of AT for blacks, Cheek (1976) states that if AT is to be effective with black clients it must deal directly with interracial realities. He indicates that what is called nonassertion by trainers may be adaptive behavior for blacks:

> For purposes of survival, blacks learned early *not* to be assertive—*not* to be honest, *not* to exercise their own rights, or stand up for themselves. Under the debilitating color-conscious system of this society, blacks were (and still are) rewarded for telling whites what they wanted to hear ... with these different standards in mind the concept of assertiveness as applied to whites has been translated and modified to the realities of the black experience before we can say the term has equal meaning to both. (pp. 16–17)

Thus, until we know more about what cultural differences exist and how these affect the need for AT, trainers must recognize that differences may be adaptive, that not all subgroups can be characterized in the same manner, and that some differences may require different types of training or no training at all. In Grodner's words:

> A low level of assertiveness due to cultural inhibitions may have generalized to produce a low level of assertiveness with no cultural component. If this occurs, assertive training of selective behaviors and situations may be accomplished without bringing about cultural conflict. As always, the practitioner's ethical responsibility is to offer alternatives and allow the client to make the choice. Finally, it should be noted by the practitioner that the behavior of *individuals* does not conform to the average behavior ascertained for their *group*. The assertive behavior trainer should be aware of the wide range of behaviors exhibited and attainable for all people. (p. 147)

VI: Research Findings

Research in assertiveness has focused on three areas: definition and components of assertion; measurement of both assertion and AT effectiveness; and AT effectiveness (including optimal number of hours or sessions, techniques, etc.). In addition, we will examine studies of sex differences in assertion.

Definition and Components

Assertion is difficult to define because it is a complex construct with many components. Researchers agree that the four major components of assertion are (1) verbal behavior and communication style, (2) nonverbal behavior, (3) cognitive and attitudinal variables, and (4) autonomic or physiological variables (Butler, 1976; Eisler, Miller, & Hansen, 1973; Schwartz & Gottman, 1976). Alberti's (1977) CRIB chart defines assertion, aggression, and nonassertion in terms of four other components: the Context of the interaction, the internal or emotional Response to the situation, the actor's Intent, and the Behavior that results.

Measurement

A major problem with assertiveness tests is that most attempt to measure a single trait (Bodner, 1975). Rock (1977) found low convergent validity among assertiveness tests, thus supporting Wolpe and Lazarus' (1966) finding that assertiveness is not a unitary trait but is specific to differential stimuli and therefore requires subscales to assess various components.

Jakubowski and Lacks (1978) point out that there are two major reasons for assessing assertion: to determine whether a client can benefit from AT and to determine whether AT has changed a client's assertiveness.

Bodner (1975) outlines five types of measures for assertion: clinical measures, self-reports, observation, communication analysis, and physiological measures.

Clinical observations are descriptive and are not very useful for comparison with other types of research or therapy. Their advantage is that they stimulate interest in the field.

Self-report measures are abundant (Moore, 1978), although few have been tested for reliability or validity. They can be divided into existing standardized tests and measures developed specifically to evaluate assertion skills. With regard to the existing instruments, Bodner (1975) states:

> On the standardized assessment devices, attitude change has been demonstrated on the MMPI and Leary Interpersonal Checklist ... Spielberger Self Evaluation Questionnaire ... General Hostility Score ... Social Anxiety and Distress Scale and S-R Inventory of Anxiousness ... Social Behavior Inventory ... and the Taylor Manifest Anxiety Scale and Gough Adjective Checklist. ... Of particular note is that the Willoughby Personality Inventory does not discriminate between high and low assertive subjects ... and in one study was used only as a pretest diagnostic tool. ...
> The absence of reference to clinically accepted psychometric instruments such as the California Personality Inventory, Sixteen Personality Factors Questionnaire, and the single reference to the MMPI raises some questions as to their perceived usefulness by assertion researchers. While clinical researchers often use these instruments, their global approach to personality and psychopathology fails to focus on the behavioral components of assertion skills necessary in assertion training research. (pp. 91–92)

The first instrument developed to measure assertiveness was the Wolpe-Lazarus Assertiveness Questionnaire (1966). The test-retest reliability and validity of this instrument have not been established, and therefore it must be used with caution. The Rathus Assertiveness Scale (1972, 1973) was developed from a number of other tests and situations reported by college students. Both reliability and validity data are available for this scale, which reflects changes in assertion skills as a function of AT. Both of these tests are short and are easily administered and scored.

The Conflict Resolution Inventory (CRI), developed by McFall and Lillesand (1971), has undergone extensive validity and reliability testing and is a good measure of one subclass of assertion: ability to refuse unreasonable requests.

The College Self Expression Scale and the Adult Self Expression Scale were developed by Galassi and associates (Galassi et al., 1974; Gay, Hollandsworth, & Galassi, 1975). Both look at positive and negative assertion as well as self-denial in relation to significant others. They have undergone extensive reliability and validity testing, making them valuable in AT research.

Other paper-and-pencil tests are available and most AT books contain brief measures, although they tend to be global and unstandardized, and hence less valuable than those discussed above.

Observation sheets have been developed to rate specific assertive behaviors. The advantage of this method is that paraprofessionals can be trained to use it. The disadvantage is that only one such sheet has been validated to date (Bodner, 1975), making comparisons difficult.

Although a number of physiological measures, such as pulse rate, galvanic skin response, and blood alcohol level, have been used (Moore, 1978), Bodner (1975) notes a reluctance to employ such measures because of the difficulty of attaining such data and the need for additional expertise and equipment.

Communication analyses, both verbal and nonverbal, have been conducted on a wide range of behaviors, and standardized role playing has allowed for comparisons. Bodner (1975) states that while both measurement and inter-rater reliability are problems in judging nonverbal behaviors, Mehrabian (1972) has developed a scoring system for nonverbal communication analysis that may yield more consistent findings. Bodner points out that the development of standardized role playing and scoring criteria and the availability of videotape equipment should combine to yield valuable information.

In summary, researchers are beginning to develop reliable, validated tests that measure both global assertion and components of assertion. The result should be more specific information about assertion, its components, and the effectiveness of training techniques.

AT Effectiveness

The number of hours and sessions in AT varies (Moore, 1978). While it has been assumed that training spread over several weeks and conducted in a group setting would be most effective, the single study examining these factors (El-Shamy, 1977) found no significant differences between subjects who experienced one six-hour session and those who experienced six one-hour sessions. Further research is needed in this area.

Most research on AT effectiveness has focused on the best ways to change behavior (see Table 1). Role playing (or practice or behavior rehearsal) has been found to increase clients' learning of assertiveness as measured by both self-report measures and in vivo behavioral measures (Galassi et al., 1974; Kazdin, 1976a, 1976b; McFall & Lillesand, 1971; McFall & Marston, 1970). Both McFall and Twentyman (1973) and Rimm and colleagues (1976) found that rehearsal alone produced significant changes. McFall and Twentyman examined the additive effects of rehearsal, coaching, and modeling on self-report and behavioral indices; the results indicate that both rehearsal and coaching contributed significantly to behavior changes but that the largest effects occurred when these techniques were used together.

Wolfe and Fodor (1977) compared four groups: modeling-plus-behavior rehearsal (BT), modeling-plus-behavior rehearsal-plus-rational therapy (RBT), a consciousness raising group (CR), and a no-treatment waiting list (WL). Both BT and RBT showed significant improvement on paralinguistic scales and behavior measures, both of which generalized to nontreated situations. Only RBT showed reduction in situational anxiety, while CR proved ineffective.

Several studies have attempted to determine if rehearsal is most effective when conducted covertly or overtly. Although McFall and Twentyman (1973) found no significant dif-

TABLE 1

RELATIONSHIPS BETWEEN ASSERTIVENESS COMPONENTS, CAUSES FOR NONASSERTION, AND AT GOALS AND TECHNIQUES

Components of Assertiveness	Physiological	Behavioral (Verbal and Nonverbal)	Cognitive (Attitudes and Values)
Reasons for nonassertion	Maladaptive anxiety	Behavioral deficit	Irrational beliefs or conscious decisions regarding risk and appropriateness
AT Goals	Reduce anxiety and fears	Train effective behaviors	Change beliefs and attitudes, thus motivate to change behaviors
AT Techniques	Relaxation exercises, systematic desensitization, guided fantasies, lecture, bibliotherapy	Role play (practice, behavior rehearsal), modeling (covert and overt), coaching, feedback/reinforcement (live or video), homework	Lecture, bibliotherapy values clarification

ference between the two, other findings indicate that covert rehearsal produces behavior changes equal to or greater than those produced by overt rehearsal, probably because the client has internalized a reward system (Kazdin, 1976a, 1976b; McFall & Lillesand, 1971; Rosenthal & Reese, 1976).

Models and reinforcement also increase the effectiveness of AT, with multiple models more effective than single models (Kazdin, 1976a). Hersen and associates (1973) found that modeling plus instructions produced more changes than modeling alone.

Rehearsal is a major component of AT, usually with the therapist as coach. Flowers and Guerra (1974) found nonprofessional coaching superior to professional coaching for two reasons: (1) a person coached by a peer is superior in later measures of assertion to one coached by a professional; (2) a client who has been a coach learns AT better than one who has not been a coach. Flowers and Guerra be-

lieve this means employing nonprofessional client-coaches may most effectively utilize both professional and client time.

Finally, the effectiveness of videotaping for presenting models and providing feedback has been widely explored. Videotaping appears to have few additive effects when used with other methods, such as rehearsal, live modeling, and feedback from the trainer and other clients (Gormally et al., 1975; McFall & Twentyman, 1973).

In summary, any technique must be viewed in context. While rehearsal is effective in changing behavior, rational therapy should be used to change attitudes or anxiety levels (see Table 1). Further, the findings reported above have occurred largely in laboratories. Extensions to counseling or AT are difficult owing to the lack of common training packages or testing devices. Treatment time has varied, as have models, the questions explored, and test measures. Most studies have not specified the

Women whose psychological identities are forged out of concern for their own survival and self-definition, and who withdraw from or avoid any interactions which do not support this formidable endeavor, need not "give up" their capacity for warmth, emotionality, and nurturance. They do not have to forsake the "wisdom of the heart" and become "men." They need only transfer the primary force of their "supportiveness" to themselves and to each other—and never to the point of self-sacrifice. Women need not stop being tender, compassionate, or concerned with the feelings of others. They must start being tender and compassionate with themselves and with other women. Women must begin to "save" themselves and their daughters before they "save" their husbands and their sons, . . . (and) the whole world.

Phyllis Chesler, *Women and Madness*, 1972

---

role of trainer reinforcement and relationship variables. Again, further research is needed.

Generalization of behaviors learned in AT to other situations has been an important question in AT research. Although earlier researchers found little evidence of generalization (McFall & Twentyman, 1973), more recent researchers have found both generalization and retention several weeks following AT. As predicted by learning theory, generalization is strongest on tasks approximating the training situation, while unrelated situations exhibit much weaker generalization (Hersen et al., 1974; Kazdin, 1976a, 1976b).

Tests for retention of effects of AT are most often conducted through self-report tests and/ or in vivo behavioral measures. Retention has been found for up to a year on both types of measures, but again the retention appears directly related to the training itself; that is, behaviors utilized frequently are more likely to be retained than infrequently used behaviors or those that might be extinguished through negative reinforcement (Galassi et al., 1975; Kazdin, 1976a, 1976b).

Sex Differences: Do They Make a Difference?

While there has been little research on sex differences in assertion or AT effectiveness, the following studies have been conducted recently.

Orenstein and colleagues (1975) found males significantly more assertive than females on the Rathus Assertiveness Schedule. Another significant finding was that assertiveness varies inversely with neuroticism, trait anxiety, and interpersonal anxiety in both women and men.

A study of the relationship among birth order, family size, and assertiveness found no significant differences for males on either variable, while female firstborns and females from families with three or fewer sibs were significantly more assertive than later-born females and those from larger families (Hall & Beil-Warner, 1977).

In a review of the literature, Hollandsworth and Wall (1977) found data from self-report measures of assertion indicating that, without exception, males report higher frequencies of assertive behaviors than females. However, the means were significantly different for only 29 percent of the samples reviewed; further, there were sex differences in the areas in which assertiveness is exhibited. Males are more assertive on items related to bosses and supervisors, being outspoken when stating opinions, and taking the initiative in social contacts with members of the opposite sex. Females are more assertive in expressing love, affection, and compliments as well as expressing anger with parents.

What We Don't Know: Research Needs

Clearly, there are more questions than answers in the AT literature. Rich and Schroeder

If we women are ever to pull ourselves out of the morass of self-pity, self-destruction and impotence which has been our heritage for so long as we can remember, then it is perhaps even more important that we be supportive of each other's achievements and successes and strengths, than it is for us to be compassionate and understanding of each other's failures and weaknesses.

Anselma dell'Olio

(1976) state that AT research needs include developing a standardized procedure as well as standardized measuring instruments. Further, we need more information regarding optimal hours/sessions, generalization and retention effects, and sex differences.

VII: Assertiveness Training Classes

Goals and Techniques

There is no agreed-upon optimal set of AT techniques. Generally, however, AT is based on the premises that people can change their behaviors fairly quickly and that change comes through doing (Adler, 1977). Most AT classes include assessment of each client's assertiveness; definition of assertion; attempts to change the way people think about assertion; identification of trainees' rights and responsibilities and those of other people; and acquisition and development of specific behaviors through practice and feedback (see Suggested Further Readings). Each part of the definition given earlier implies a specific training goal for which there are specific techniques (see Table 1). (For exercises and formats, refer to the Suggested Further Readings.)

Goal 1: *Reducing Anxiety and Fear.* Techniques include relaxation exercises, systematic desensitization, guided fantasies, examination of irrational beliefs, and examination of fears. Relaxation exercises can be

The Tender Stone by Lenore Thomas Straus. Reprinted by permission.

found in several books (Bower & Bower, 1976; Fensterheim & Baer, 1975; Jakubowski & Lange, 1978; Lange & Jakubowski, 1976). They are most effective when trainees understand sex role socialization; the distinctions among assertion, aggression, and passivity; and their own problems and fears. Such exercises should not be introduced until trainees have

---

Feeling Righteous

The whole thing
came clear to me today
just the way it really is,
man on the top,
woman fighting from the bottom,
and I feel righteous.
I am hearing Nina Simone
sing out her song
you can't keep this woman down
and I feel
righteous.
the sound goes right through
my spine
and down to my toes
and I am
laughing
deep down inside myself because
I feel righteous.
there's nothing
hazy about it now.
the whole thing is
perfectly clear.
there's no way
to keep a righteous woman down.
we will be free; my heart
is free today
and you can hear it sing
the way we're all going to sing
because
we're all going to sing everyday
we're going to sing
every righteous,
goddamn day.

Susan Griffin

lectures, group discussions, modeling and reinforcement, value clarification exercises, and examination of how sex role socialization has led to current beliefs and how new roles may require new systems. Trainees examine their own rights and those of others. These include the right to

1. act in ways that promote one's own dignity and self-respect
2. be treated with respect
3. say no without feeling guilty
4. experience and express feelings
5. take time to think before answering or acting
6. make mistakes
7. feel good about oneself
8. ask for information and/or help
9. change one's mind
10. ask for what one wants or needs
11. decide how to spend one's time, energy, and money (Bloom, Coburn, & Pearlman, 1975; Jakubowski & Lange, 1978)

Jakubowski & Lange (1978) caution, however, that these rights do not give one license to disregard other people and that they bring with them responsibility for one's own actions and mistakes. This combination often proves problematic for women. Rather than seek compromises when rights are in conflict, women usually assume that they should concede their rights. This attitude seems to be generated by the notion that every interaction is based on a "win-lose" model. Women need to learn how to structure "win-win" interactions.

Goal 3: Motivation. Techniques include value clarification exercises and outlining the specific behaviors that each person wishes to

reached an appropriate level of trust in the group leader and other members.

Goal 2: Changing Beliefs and Attitudes. Techniques include reading assignments and

change. While most women in AT are already motivated to change, further motivation is created as they receive reinforcement through class interaction and success with assertive actions.

Goal 4: *Learning Behaviors.* Techniques include role playing, modeling, coaching, videotaped feedback, and behavioral assignments. This goal usually consumes most of the time in AT and requires careful attention if the new behaviors are to be retained.

Potential Problems for the Learner

Like other behaviors, assertion is learned faster when it is successful, that is, if it is rewarded. Rewards can come from either the learner or someone else, but must be meaningful to the learner. This may be why most AT is conducted in groups, where other clients can reinforce assertive behaviors. Further, most AT helps clients progress from the least to the most threatening behaviors to ensure early success and avoid extinction (Rimm & Masters, 1974).

During any learning process the learner will make some errors. Mistakes in assertiveness usually occur in the form of aggressive actions and should be tolerated as part of the learning process (Alberti & Emmons, 1978; Phelps & Austin, 1975).

Since assertiveness is only one communication behavior, one can choose when to exhibit it. That is, there are situations in which nonassertive or aggressive behaviors are more effective than assertive ones (Eisler et al., 1975). Indeed, part of being assertive is understanding that assertion is optional—it can be used when the person feels that it is the best option and is willing to take responsibility for her own behavior without feeling anxious or guilty

(Alberti & Emmons, 1978; Jakubowski-Spector, 1973).

An analogy to learning assertiveness is learning to ride a bicycle. One learns to ride a bicycle much faster if one does not fall down frequently and become discouraged or afraid of being injured. One makes some mistakes, of course, but if these do not cause major injuries one perseveres. One can choose when and where to ride the bicycle, knowing that some places are safer than others. And some people learn more easily and quickly than others.

Client and Trainer Rights and Responsibilities

What are the trainee's rights and responsibilities? Basically, they include knowing the trainer's qualifications and attitudes about women and assertiveness; what she can expect to get from training and what she will be expected to do during training; and the potential dangers in learning assertiveness. Clients should discuss these things with the trainer beforehand (Shelton, 1977).

Trainers are responsible for being well qualified. General qualifications for AT trainers (Alberti et al., 1976) include an understanding of the principles of learning; an understanding of anxiety and its effects on behavior; knowledge of the limitations of assertion and the potential dangers of AT; familiarity with AT theory and research; and evidence of competent performance under observation by a qualified trainer. Further, the trainer must be assertive herself, must understand the processes of sex role socialization and oppression of women, and must believe that these processes can be overcome through attitude and behavior changes.

Because women have long viewed men as experts and refused to make their own decisions and control their own lives, AT should help them regain their power and see themselves and other women as competent. Regarding the sex of trainers, Jakubowski (1977b) has stated:

> While a male therapist can provide male permission for a woman to act assertively, a female therapist may have several advantages: (1) a female therapist can be a model of a woman who is both feminine and assertive; (2) female members may more easily confide in a female therapist than in a male; and (3) female members may be less likely to enter into game playing to please a female therapist. On the other hand, Friedman's (1971) research suggests that a critical variable in assertion training is supplying information on how one can act assertively; therefore, it is possible that the therapist's ability to provide this information is more important than the therapist's sex. (pp. 168–169)

Suggested Further Reading

Adler, Ronald B. 1977. *Confidence in communication: A guide to assertive and social skills.* New York: Holt, Rinehart & Winston.

Alberti, Robert. 1977. *Assertiveness: Innovations, applications, issues.* San Luis Obispo: Impact Publishers.

Alberti, Robert, & Emmons, Michael. 1978. *Your perfect right.* Third Edition. San Luis Obispo: Impact Publishers.

Bloom, Lynn A., Coburn, Karen, & Pearlman, Joan. 1975. *The new assertive woman.* New York: Delacorte Press.

Bower, Sharon Anthony, & Bower, Gordon H. 1976. *Asserting yourself: A practical guide for positive change.* Reading, Mass.: Addison-Wesley Publishing Co.

Cotler, S. B., & Guerra, J. J. 1976. *Assertiveness training: A humanistic behavioral guide to self dignity.* Champaign, Ill.: Research Press.

Fensterheim, Herbert, & Baer, Jean. 1975. *Don't say yes when you want to say no.* New York: Dell Publishing.

Jakubowski, Patricia, & Lange, Arthur J. 1978. *The assertive option: Your rights and responsibilities.* Champaign, Ill.: Research Press.

Lange, Arthur J., & Jakubowski, Patricia. 1976. *Responsible assertive behavior: Cognitive/behavioral procedures for trainers.* Champaign Ill.: Research Press.

Phelps, Stanlee, & Austin, Nancy. 1975. *The assertive woman.* San Luis Obispo: Impact Publishers.

Linda Garnets and Joseph H. Pleck

Sex Role Identity, Androgyny, and Sex Role Transcendence: A Sex Role Strain Analysis

This paper first reviews three different theoretical constructs concerning the psychological significance of sex role related characteristics in personality functioning: sex role identity, androgyny, and sex role transcendence. A new conceptual analysis concerning sex-typing, sex role strain analysis, is presented. According to this analysis, the relationship between sex role related personality characteristics and psychological adjustment, especially self-esteem, is moderated by two variables: perception of the ideal member of the same sex, and sex role salience. These two variables, taken in conjunction with real self-concept, generate five sex role strain outcomes. The constructs of sex role identity, androgyny, and sex role transcendence are interpreted in terms of this sex role strain analysis. The implications of this analysis for current research and for understanding the dynamics of both individual and social change in sex roles are briefly described.

The goal of this paper is to present a new analysis of the relationship between personality characteristics traditionally associated with one sex or the other and psychological adjustment, especially self-esteem. This analysis, termed here sex role strain analysis, integrates disparate elements in previous theory and research in this area and suggests new directions for future research. To set the stage for this analysis, we first briefly review three major psychological constructs concerning the significance of sex role related personality characteristics: sex role identity, androgyny, and sex role transcendence.

We then introduce a new analysis which holds that the relationship between sex role related personality characteristics and adjustment is moderated by two variables not usually considered in previous approaches. The first variable is the individual's perception of the ideal member of his or her own sex. The second, sex role salience, is implied by Rebecca et al.'s (1976) discussion of sex role transcendence, but has not heretofore been explicitly operationalized or integrated with other variables in an analysis of patterns of sex-typing. Contradictory hypotheses concerning the relationship between sex role related characteristics and psychological adjustment in previous research using the constructs of sex role identity and androgyny are then shown to be interpretable and reconcilable in sex role strain analysis. A variety of other implications of sex role strain analysis for current research in this area, and for understanding the dynamics of individual and social change in sex roles, are also developed.

Three Constructs Analyzing Sex Role Related Traits

In the last three decades a large body of psychological research and theory has analyzed the psychological significance of the presence or absence of sex-typed characteristics in personality functioning. Three constructs have been especially significant: sex role identity, androgyny, and sex role transcendence. Each will be briefly discussed.

Androgyny suggests a spirit of reconciliation between the sexes; it suggests, further, a full range of experience open to individuals who may as women be aggressive, as men, tender; it suggests a spectrum upon which human beings choose their places without regard to propriety or custom.

Carolyn Heilbrun, *Toward a Recognition of Androgyny*, 1973

Sex Role Identity

Sex role identity (or sex identity), as exemplified in the work of Brown (1957, 1958), Miller and Swanson (1960), Lynn (1969), and Biller (1971), refers to an individual's configuration of sex-typed traits, attitudes, and interests, a configuration which ideally is congruent with, and thus affirms or validates, his or her biological sex. If the individual's traits, attitudes, and interests are not congruent with his or her biological sex, the individual's sex role identity is said to be inadequate, disturbed, or insecure. The traditional conception of psychological masculinity-femininity as a single bipolar trait dimension is an important component of the construct of sex role identity. However, as the terms are used here, though the construct of sex role identity incorporates a bipolar conception of masculinity-femininity, it goes theoretically beyond it. The construct of bipolar masculinity-femininity concerns only the psychometric organization of sex-typed traits, attitudes, and interests, but the construct of sex role identity goes further to postulate a relationship between being at the sex-appropriate end of this bipolar continuum and good psychological adjustment.

In some usages of the construct, sex role identity has been conceptualized as being multi-leveled. For example, Miller and Swanson (1960) distinguish "conscious" and "unconscious" levels of sex role identity assessed by different masculinity-femininity scales; Biller (1971) differentiates the "orientation," "preference," and "adoption" levels of sex role identity tapped by different sex-typing measures.

(It is sometimes erroneously thought that the concept of masculinity-femininity as a single bipolar trait dimension had never been challenged before Bem and others proposed viewing masculinity and femininity as two unipolar traits. Actually, the multi-leveled concept of sex role identity in effect views masculinity-femininity not as a *single* bipolar trait, but as composed of several, relatively independent bipolar traits.) These multi-leveled conceptions of sex role identity require somewhat more complex analyses of the relationship between masculinity-femininity scores and adjustment. In particular, theorists like Miller and Swanson hold that the combination of sex-appropriate identity at more surface levels of personality combined with sex-inappropriate identity at deeper levels is associated with certain distinctive, though less severe, forms of maladjustment than sex-inappropriate identity at both levels. Nonetheless, theorists using the construct of sex role identity can be generally described as postulating that being at the sex-appropriate end of a bipolarly-conceived masculinity-femininity dimension both reflects and leads to good adjustment.

Theorists using this construct have developed and tested many different hypotheses concerning the acquisition of sex role identity, especially variant versions of identification hypotheses. These hypotheses, however, are logically independent of the core assumption in the sex role identity construct that having sex-appropriate characteristics, viewed as organized in a single bipolar trait, is associated with good adjustment. These etiological hypotheses will not be developed further here.

\

> *Today the survival of some . . . stereotypes is a psychological straitjacket*
> *for both sexes.*
>
> Mirra Komarovsky, *Women in The Modern*
> *World,* 1953

Androgyny

Androgyny was first introduced and operationalized in academic psychology by Bem (1972, 1974), and has been further developed or operationalized by Block (1973), Heilbrun (1976), Spence and Helmreich (1978), and Berzins and Welling (1974). In contrast to the bipolar view of masculinity-femininity assumed by sex role identity theorists, the construct of androgyny presupposes that psychological masculinity and femininity are two orthogonal, unipolar dimensions. However, central to the construct, as it is currently used, is the view that androgyny is associated with better psychological adjustment than the other three possible combinations generated by classifying individuals as high or low on masculinity and femininity (often referred to as sex-typed, sex-reversed, and undifferentiated). That is, the construct of androgyny can be seen as incorporating but going theoretically beyond the unipolar, orthogonal view of masculinity and femininity by postulating a relationship between a particular pattern of scores on these dimensions and psychological adjustment—just as sex role identity incorporates but goes beyond the bipolar construct of masculinity-femininity.

Research is just beginning to explore the antecedents of unipolar masculinity and femininity, and specifically androgyny (Kelly & Worell, 1976; Woods, 1975; Spence & Helmreich, 1978). As was the case with bipolar masculinity-femininity and sex role identity, the processes by which androgyny is acquired are not theoretically central to its conception

as presently formulated, and need not be developed here.

Sex Role Transcendence

Sex role transcendence is just beginning to emerge as a theoretical construct and has been introduced and most explicitly formulated by Hefner, Rebecca, and Oleshansky (1975). They note that while the concept of androgyny represents a significant improvement over the earlier concept of sex role identity, androgyny still postulates the organization of personality into masculine and feminine components, even if it holds that these components are not mutually exclusive.

As Secor (1974) expresses it: "Androgyny, as a word structurally and as a concept culturally, tends to assume femininity and masculinity as set personality structures, which can be modulated, but which are set as conceptions as given" (p. 166).

Sex role transcendence theorists suggest that the ideal state in sex role development is not the combination or integration of masculine and feminine traits in the personality, but a stage in which masculinity and femininity are "transcended" as ways of organizing and experiencing psychological traits.

Further, sex role transcendence is embedded in a stage theory of sex role development. In individual development, transcendence is seen as superseding the androgynous stage in which the individual blends masculinity and femininity, which in turn supersedes the sex role identity stage of polarized sex roles. For sex role transcendent individuals, there is no relationship between having or not having sex

Great periods of civilization, however much they may have owed their beginnings to the aggressive dominance of the male principle, have always been marked by some sort of rise in the status of women. This in its turn is a manifestation of something more profound: the recognition of the importance of the "feminine" principle, not as other, but as necessary to wholeness.

Carolyn Heilbrun, *Toward a Recognition of Androgyny*, 1973

---

role related traits and psychological adjustment. At present, no way of operationalizing this "transcendence" of masculinity and femininity, or of differentiating androgynous and transcendent individuals, has been proposed or tested.

Sex Role Strain Analysis

We now introduce a sex role strain analysis of the relationship between sex role related personality characteristics and adjustment. In this analysis, the relationship between sex-typing and adjustment is moderated by two variables: the individual's ideal for his or her own sex, and the degree of the individual's sex role salience (a concept derived from the construct of sex role transcendence). Before introducing the analysis in detail, a brief statement of the goals of this analysis would be helpful.

First, in the wave of new research in the last decade concerning the various ways in which traditional sex role norms have had negative effects on individuals, it is curious that one of the most obvious negative impacts of traditional sex roles on individuals has hardly received any attention: traditional sex role norms set standards which, for a variety of reasons, many individuals of both sexes do not conform to, and as a result many of these individuals come to devalue themselves. The sociological theorists Turner (1970) and, more recently, Komarovsky (1976) have analyzed this process as one sub-type of a more general construct of sex role strain, referring to ways in which sex roles impact negatively on indi-

viduals. (Specifically, Komarovsky (1976) refers to this sub-type of sex role strain as, "lack of congruity or 'malfit' between idiosyncratic personality and social role," the second of her six modes of sex role strain. Turner (1970) describes this sub-type of sex role strain as occurring when "a relatively uniform role is ascribed arbitrarily to a set of people with highly varied potentialities" (p. 292).) There does not, however, appear to be any large-scale research which systematically analyzes the negative consequences of discrepancies between individuals' characteristics and individuals' standards or ideals for themselves deriving from larger social sex role norms. Though the term *sex role strain* has a somewhat more general meaning in the sociological analyses just cited, we will appropriate it here to refer specifically to discrepancies between an individual's perceptions of her or his personal characteristics and her or his standards for herself or himself deriving from sex role norms. This construct is currently being investigated in our research, and the analysis presented here will hopefully stimulate research on this important, but overlooked, process.

Second, we believe it is critical for the sex role field to develop the concept of sex role transcendence, specifically by operationalizing and developing measures of the degree to which individuals organize and experience personal characteristics as components of larger constructs of "masculinity" and "femininity" (whether bipolar or unipolar) which are significant and salient to them. We offer here a procedure for operationalizing this ad-

> *What is important now is that we free ourselves from the prison of gender and, before it is too late, deliver the world from the almost exclusive control of the masculine impulse.*
>
> Carolyn Heilbrun, *Toward a Recognition of Androgyny*, 1973

---

mittedly elusive concept, termed here *sex role salience*, which is currently being tested in our research. We hope that others will develop alternative methods.

Sex role strain analysis involves three primary variables, and two other variables derived from them. The primary variables are real self-concept, same-sex ideal, and sex role salience. The derived variables are discrepancy between real self and same-sex ideal, and sex role strain outcome.

Real Self-concept

This concept refers to the qualities and characteristics which individuals think they actually possess. It may be operationalized with any self-rating measure which yields separate scores for masculinity and femininity, either in the form of adjective self-ratings, such as the Bem (1974) Sex Role Inventory (BSRI), the Spence and Helmreich (1978) Personal Attributes Questionnaire (PAQ), and the Heilbrun (1976) Adjective checklist (ACL), as well as endorsements of self-descriptive statements, such as Berzins and Welling's (1974) PRF ANDRO scale. In our analysis, major attention is given to those individuals whose real self-concept is classified as either sex-typed (i.e., in the sex-appropriate direction) or androgynous. Sex-reversed and undifferentiated individuals are omitted from consideration in order to simplify our presentation and because for our purposes the sex-typed and androgynous groups are the most theoretically significant.

It should be emphasized that the classifi-

cation of the self-concept as sex-typed or androgynous refers only to whether individuals report having only those characteristics traditionally viewed as appropriate for their sex, or having characteristics traditionally considered appropriate for both sexes. This classification does not imply whether the individual either does or does not experience these characteristics as organized according to larger constructs of masculinity or femininity, a distinction addressed later by the construct of sex role salience. We should also note that implicit in the use of self-ratings to assess the self-concept is the notion that the self-concept is characterized by the qualities individuals think they have as well as the qualities they think they do not have (the latter especially for sex-typed individuals). Also, this analysis does not assume that all or even the majority of characteristics individuals think they have or do not have are relevant to classifying the self-concept as sex-typed or androgynous. While the self-concept is composed of both sex role related and non-sex role related aspects, we are concerned here only with the former. In addition, our analysis does not assume that self-concept includes only psychological characteristics and excludes other kinds of qualities, such as physical characteristics, age, and attitudes, which may or may not be sex-typed.

Same-Sex Ideal

This variable refers to the qualities and characteristics which individuals think members of their sex ought to possess. In this analysis, it is classified as either sex-typed (i.e., in the sex-appropriate direction) or androgynous. All the observations made above concerning the real self-concept apply here as well.

Discrepancy Between Real Self and Same-Sex Ideal

Given our classification of both real self and same-sex ideal as either sex-typed or androgynous, this discrepancy is low if real and ideal are classified the same way, and high if real and ideal are classified differently (i.e., one is sex-typed and the other androgynous). This discrepancy concept is indebted to the concept of discrepancy between real and ideal self, a concept with a long and venerable history in personality psychology. In particular, Rogers (1951) and other researchers (Rogers & Dymond, 1954) have interpreted changes in real-ideal self discrepancy as an outcome measure in "client-centered" psychotherapy research. Sex role strain analysis modifies this concept to refer specifically to discrepancies between the real self and that aspect of the ideal self-concept rooted in sex role norms. Hereafter, we refer to it simply as real-ideal discrepancy.

Sex Role Salience

Sex role salience can be viewed as the intrapsychic characteristic on which Rebecca et al.'s (1976) sex role "transcendent" individuals differ from non-transcendent individuals. It refers to the extent to which individuals do or do not experience and organize personality characteristics as parts of larger constructs of masculinity and femininity which they psychologically orient themselves to. The concept is intended to describe the difference, for example, between a woman who performs nurturant behaviors and who as a result perceives

herself simply as *nurturant,* and a woman who performs nurturant behaviors and who as a result experiences herself as *feminine.*

There are many possible ways to formulate and operationalize this concept. It probably can be assessed only indirectly, i.e., by observing phenomena interpreted as resulting from its presence. While many approaches are possible, we describe here several alternate methods currently being investigated in our research.

In one method, sex role salience is inferred to be present when there is high consistency in the individual's ratings of the same-sex ideal among the traits that are culturally understood as comprising masculinity, and high consistency among the traits that are culturally understood to comprise femininity. For example, if an individual's same-sex ideal includes aggressiveness, then it also includes other traits which are culturally perceived as comprising masculinity such as analyticalness, competitiveness, individualisticness, and dominance. High consistency is operationalized as low variance (computed within subjects) in the individual's scores on the adjectives classified as masculine, and low variance in the individual's scores on the adjectives classified as feminine. Low consistency is operationalized as high variance (computed within subjects) in the individual's scores on the adjectives classified as masculine with high variance in the individual's scores on the adjectives classified as feminine. That is, the higher the average of these two variances, the lower the sex role salience.

The second method involves comparing individuals' ratings of their ideal for their own sex with a measure not introduced earlier, ratings of their own ideal self. Differentiation be-

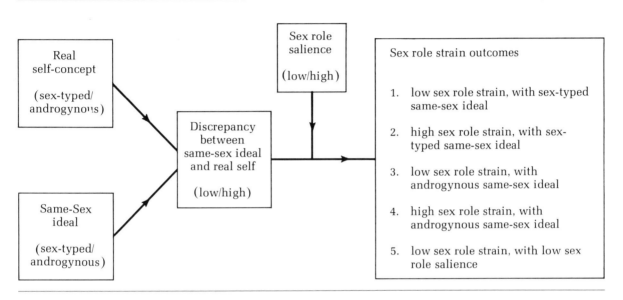

Figure 1. Antecedent conditions leading to sex role strain outcomes.

tween the two is interpreted as indicating low sex role salience. In the third method, respondents are asked to rate the extent to which they think various activities and behaviors are related to sex roles. High ratings on these items are interpreted as a direct measure of sex role salience.

For purposes of discussion, this analysis classifies individuals simply as being either high or low on sex role salience. An analysis of the sources of sex role salience is outside the scope of this paper. However, we assume there are numerous pathways by which individuals acquire sex role salience, including socialization practices in which people are taught to label their own qualities as masculine or feminine, societal structures and institutions that emphasize a causal link be-

tween sex-specific personality traits and social roles, and situations that generate a conscious awareness of discrimination based on sex.

Sex Role Strain Outcomes

Figure 1 schematically depicts our analysis of how real self-concept, same-sex ideal, real-ideal discrepancy, and sex role salience lead to sex role strain outcomes. Table 1 presents in more detail the exact combinations of these four variables leading to the five different sex role strain outcomes postulated in this analysis. (Table 1 also specifies the constructs in earlier analyses which the five sex role strain outcomes correspond to, to be discussed in the next section.)

The basic idea in the analysis is a simple one: discrepancy between the real self and

they do experience their personality characteristics as part of the lger constructs of masculinity & femininity, acclaimed by society, behaves in labeled

6 psych adjust   5

high self esteem

Low self esteem

high self esteem

Low self esteem

high self esteem

TABLE 1

SEX ROLE STRAIN OUTCOMES

other people read this way

do not experience norm characteristics

Sex role strain outcomes	Same-sex ideal (sex-typed/ androgynous)	Real self-concept (sex-typed/ androgynous)	Discrepancy between same-sex ideal and real self (low/high)	Sex role salience (low/high)	Corresponding constructs in previous analyses
1. Low sex role strain (with sex-typed ideal self)	Sex-typed[a]	Sex-typed	Low discrepancy	High salience	"Adequate" sex role identity
2. High sex role strain (with sex-typed ideal self)	Sex-typed	Androgynous	High discrepancy	High salience	"Inadequate" sex role identity
3. Low sex role strain (with androgynous ideal self)	Androgynous	Androgynous	Low discrepancy	High salience	Androgynous personality
4. High sex role strain (with androgynous ideal self)	Androgynous	Sex-typed	High discrepancy	High salience	Sex-typed personality
5. Low sex role strain (with low sex role salience)	Sex-typed or androgynous	Sex-typed[b] or androgynous	Low or high discrepancy	Low salience	Sex role transcendence

to be feminine (annotation by row 2)

as society (annotation by row 3)

culture perceives them as this: but they do no themselves as such. (annotation by row 5)

Point of article

a. "Sex-typed" means sex-typed in the sex-appropriate direction.
b. As Rebecca et al. (1976) use these concepts, it would be a contradiction in terms to describe a transcendent individual as having either an androgynous or a sex-typed real self, since transcendent individuals, by definition, do not experience their psychological characteristics as being linked to masculinity or to femininity. However, we use the terms androgynous and sex-typed in describing the individual's real self to classify the individual only according to how the culture perceives his or her objective characteristics, without implying how the individual experiences them. In our terminology, low sex role salience is the distinctive feature of transcendent individuals.

that part of the ideal self-concept that is culturally associated with gender leads to high sex role strain, except when sex role salience is low. In this latter case, sex role strain is always low. Sex role strain is viewed as an intrapsychic process associated with poor psychological adjustment, specifically, low self-esteem. We define sex role strain as resulting from real-ideal discrepancies in sex role related characteristics with high salience. We acknowledge that discrepancies between the real self, and the ideal self (as distinct from the same-sex ideal) may also be associated with low self-esteem. Our current research is empirically testing the relative impact of these two kinds of real-ideal discrepancies on adjustment. There are five distinct sex role strain outcomes in all:

1. low sex role strain (with sex-typed same-sex ideal)
2. high sex role strain (with sex-typed same-sex ideal)
3. low sex role strain (with androgynous same-sex ideal)
4. high sex role strain (with androgynous same-sex ideal)
5. low sex role strain (with low sex role salience).

The predictions derivable from this analysis are currently being tested.

Sex Role Strain Analysis of Earlier Constructs

This analysis makes possible some speculative alternative interpretations of relationships between sex-typing and psychological adjustment, specifically self-esteem, postulated by theorists using the constructs of sex role identity and androgyny. These alternative interpretations rely on a different causal mechanism whereby variations in the pattern of sex-typed traits lead to varying levels of self-esteem than sex role identity and androgyny

theorists assume, but nonetheless account for the same relationships. The relationship between having only sex-appropriate traits and good adjustment, predicted by sex role identity theorists, can be understood as holding true when individuals' same-sex ideals are sex-typed and sex role salience is high. Under these circumstances, having a sex-typed real self leads to low discrepancy and low strain, and therefore high self-esteem (outcome 1); while having an androgynous real self (i.e., including cross-sex characteristics) produces high discrepancy and high strain, and therefore low self-esteem (outcome 2).

Conversely, androgyny theorists' prediction that androgyny is associated with good adjustment, while having only sex-typed traits leads to poor adjustment can be understood as holding true when the same-sex ideal is androgynous. That is, in this case, having an androgynous real self leads to low discrepancy and low strain, and therefore high self-esteem (outcome 3). Having a sex-typed real self-concept is associated with high discrepancy, high strain, and therefore low self-esteem (outcome 4).

Individual and Social Change in Sex Roles

The sex role strain analysis presented above has several implications for individual and social change in sex roles which will be developed briefly. There are a variety of possible relationships between individuals' perceptions of the ideal members of their own sex and individuals' own personal ideal self-concepts. We earlier proposed low differentiation between ideal self and same-sex ideal as one operationalization of high sex role salience. For

---

some individuals who are high in sex role salience, the view of the ideal member of one's own sex that the individual holds, or that the individual perceives to be held by the culture in general or by his or her particular reference group, has a strong determinative effect on the individual's own ideal self-concept. Among others high in salience, the individual may actively choose to orient specifically to those particular reference groups whose perceptions of the ideal person of his or her sex correspond to the individual's own ideal self-concept. For individuals low in sex role salience, there should be no relationship between the ideal self-concept and perceptions of same-sex ideal held either by the larger culture or by the individual's particular reference groups.

It is useful to anticipate these several different kinds of relationships between individuals' sex role norms and their ideal self-concepts holding true in different subgroups, in order to understand the impact of cultural changes in sex role norms on the individual. Among those high in salience, shifts toward androgynous ideal images of men and women held by the culture as a whole, and the emergence of new reference groups with androgynous ideals for the sexes (e.g., the women's and men's movements), will exert pressure for change in individuals with traditional ideal self-concepts. It will also permit others with androgynous ideal self-concepts to find social validation for them. Our analysis suggests that these shifts in norms will therefore reduce sex role strain and its consequent low self-esteem in many individuals, specifically those with androgynous real self-concepts and high sex role salience. However, it also follows that for individuals with sex-typed real self-concepts and high salience, sex role strain and low self-esteem will be exacerbated if they are not able to find or maintain reference groups that retain traditional sex-typed perceptions of the ideal personality for their sex, or to successfully revive sex-typed norms in the larger culture.

This analysis suggests the critical importance of distinguishing between two components of sex role change: change in the social ideals or norms for men and women toward androgyny (or alternatively, an increase in the proportion of social reference groups with androgynous ideals); and reduction in sex role salience. The first kind of change is illustrated by the emergence or wider acceptance of a norm for the sexes that it is alright for men to be emotionally expressive and for women to achieve. The second kind of change is illustrated by individuals no longer psychologically linking—even positively linking—emotional expressiveness and achievement (or *any* psychological characteristics) with males and females by virtue of their sex. It is the difference between saying "it is alright and even desirable for men to be able to cry," and saying "crying (and all other behaviors as well) have nothing to do with whether or not a male is a 'man.'"

Challenging and broadening sex role norms, contributing to changes in individuals' same-sex ideals toward androgyny, is a useful and important first step in sex role change. However, it may simply change the distribution of sex role strain in society without reducing its overall incidence. That is, it may simply shift the burden of sex role strain and consequent low self-esteem from one subgroup of society to another, without reducing the total proportion of individuals who experience these negative states. While it is beyond the scope of this paper to suggest strategies for reducing sex role salience, it should be clear that this should be our long-run goal.

The Phenomenon by Remedios Varo; reprinted by permission of Walter Gruen

Barbara Bovee Polk

Male Power and the Women's Movement: Analysis for Change

The relationship between females and males in this and virtually every society has been a power relationship—of males over females. The current women's movement, a revitalization of earlier feminist movements, seeks to end or reverse this power relationship. As such, feminists are concerned with analyzing the nature of male power and the condition of women and developing organizations and vehicles for change that are consistent with feminist principles.

In this paper I shall consider four conceptualizations of women's oppression, their assessment of the various modes of male power, and their preferred strategies for changing the status of women in contemporary society. Throughout this paper, it is important to remember that the women's movement is not an organization with officers and a unified theory and set of activities. Instead, it consists of the ideas and activities of women responding to the conditions of their oppression whether as individuals, informal small groups, or large structured organizations. Although I see women who do not consider themselves to be "women's libbers" as part of the movement to the extent that they attempt to restructure their lives in nontraditional ways, here I am concerned with the theory and activities of those women who identify with the movement.

The Contemporary Condition of Women

Many individuals have attempted to account for the historical origins of the near universal oppression of women, grounding their theories in biological differences, evolutionary genetics, economic relationships, and so on. Although these are of interest to most feminists, we are aware that whatever its origins, oppression of women exists in the present and must be combatted now. For that reason most contemporary analyses do not deal in depth, if at all, with why and when questions, but rather attempt to understand the current relationship between the sexes as a basis for action.

Modal Analyses

I see four major approaches to understanding the contemporary condition of women: analyses in terms of sex roles, differences between feminine and masculine culture, male-female power relationships, and economic relationships.* Because the purpose of this paper is not to discuss the conflict and factions within the movement, I present a "modal" analysis of each viewpoint rather than ideal types. Ex-

---

*A basic tenet of the women's movement is that no one woman can speak for it. This paper expresses my own perspective on the movement, and it is limited by my own experiences, understanding, and biases. It must be read as such. The dozen women who reviewed an earlier draft suggested that I confront that problem directly. Perhaps it is useful to say, then, that by training and because I believe it is most politically effective at this time, I prefer the sex-role approach, heavily modified by acceptance of much of the cultural and power analyses. Although I believe that sexism is deeply embedded in capitalism and that its eradication will require a fundamental change in economic structure, I disagree with the socialist view outlined in this paper.

treme positions within each viewpoint are largely omitted and perspectives overlap to some degree, for in practice, most feminists subscribe to some combination of two or more perspectives. Although I refer to groups or writings which seem to me to fit a particular approach, it should be kept in mind that in no case is it possible to provide a "pure" example.

Sex-role Socialization. Drawing on social-psychological analysis, this approach views the contemporary oppression of women as the result of the inculcation of socially defined sex roles. This approach is the basic one adopted by most academic social scientists, including Alice Rossi, Cynthia Epstein, and Jessie Bernard, as well as other well-known feminists such as Gloria Steinem, Betty Friedan, Caroline Bird, and Germaine Greer. It is also the basic orientation of such national groups as the National Organization for Women, Women's Equity Action League, and the Women's Political Caucus.

The main components of this analysis are:

1. Each society *arbitrarily* views a wide variety of personality characteristics, interests, and behaviors as the virtually exclusive domain of one sex or the other. The fact that societies vary in their definition of feminine and masculine roles is proof that sex roles are based on social rather than on biological factors.

2. The parceling up of human characteristics into "feminine" and "masculine" deprives all of full humanness.

3. Sex roles are systematically inculcated in individuals, beginning at birth, by parents, the educational system, peers, the media, and religious institutions, and are supported by the social sciences and the economic, political, and legal structures of society. Individuals learn appropriate roles through role models and differential reinforcement.

4. Sex roles form the core of an individual's identity. Because self-evaluation is closely linked to sex ("That's a good girl/boy") and to adequacy of sex-role performance, the propriety of the role to which one was socialized becomes difficult to dislodge in adulthood, even when it is seen as dysfunctional. In addition, individuals often link concepts of their adequacy in sex *roles* to their adequacy in *sexual* interactions and vice versa. Thus, a threat to one's role definition is perceived as a threat to one's sexual identity. Such threats are a major mechanism for psychologically locking people into traditional roles.

5. Sex roles are basic roles and thus modify expectations in virtually all other roles. Differential expectations by sex in other roles leads to differential perception of the same behavior in a woman and a man (a businessman is strong-willed; a business woman, rigid). Differential expectations and selective perception limit the extent to which individuals can step outside their sex roles and are major mechanisms for the maintenance of sex roles.

6. Female and male roles form a role system in which the expectations for and behaviors of each sex have implications for the definitions of and behaviors of the other sex. (A man can't be a "gentleman" if a woman will not let him hold the door for her.)

7. The male role has higher status. This status is directly rewarding and provides access to other highly valued statuses and rewards; however, male status also places heavy pressures on men to maintain that status.

8. Males have power over females because of role definitions. "Being powerful" is itself a part of the masculine role definition. In addi-

The "control of nature" is a phrase conceived in arrogance, born of the Neanderthal age of biology and the convenience of man.

Rachel Carson, *The Silent Spring*, 1962

---

tion, the "rationality" assigned to the male role gives men access to positions of expertise as well as credibility, even when they are not experts.

Conflicting Cultures Approach. This approach focuses on value differences rather than role differences between the sexes. It points out that women who talk only in terms of role differences may seek a solution to their oppression by emulating male roles. The cultural approach is therefore a more overtly feminist analysis, focusing on the positive aspects of feminine culture. Examples of this approach include Firestone (1970), Burris (1971), and Solanas (1968), although the latter is quite different from the view presented here. The main ideas behind this approach follow.

1. Just as roles are dichotomized by sex, so are values. "Masculine" values include competitiveness, aggressiveness, independence, and rationality; "feminine" values include their counterparts: cooperativeness, passivity, dependence, and emotionality. These values are not inherent as male or female (according to most versions of this analysis) but are socially assigned and derived from sex-role definitions. *All* are important qualities of humanness.

2. Masculine values have higher status and constitute the dominant and visible culture of the society. They inform the structure of personal, political, and economic relationships and provide the standard for adulthood and normality (cf. de Beauvoir's [1953] discussion of woman as "the Other").

3. Women are oppressed and devalued be-

cause they embody an alternative culture. (In one version of this analysis [Burris, 1971], men are seen as colonizing women's bodies in order to subordinate an alien value system, much as men colonized the land and peoples of other civilizations.)

4. Men are socialized almost exclusively to the masculine value system, but women receive dual socialization because of the dominance of male institutions and because they must comprehend masculine values in order to survive (the slave syndrome). Dual socialization tempts women to try assimilation into the masculine culture, but it also gives women insight into the artificiality of the value dichotomization.

5. Masculine values are largely responsible for the crisis in our society. Competitiveness pits human against human and results in racism, sexism, and colonialism, as well as the rape of the natural environment in the pursuit of economic power: Aggressiveness leads to war. Exaggerated independence inhibits society's ability to solve common problems by failing to recognize the fundamental interdependence among humans and between humans and the physical environment. Excessive rationality is linked to the building of a runaway technological and scientific system incapable of recognizing and granting legitimacy to human needs and feelings.

Power Analysis. This perspective does not deny the importance of sex roles and cultural differences in bringing about and maintaining the oppression of women, but it views them as symptomatic of the primary problem, which is

In an age when man has forgotten his origins and is blind even to his most essential needs for survival, water along with other resources has become the victim of his indifference.

Rachel Carson, _The Silent Spring_, 1962

the domination of females by males. Thus, it is more concerned with focusing on the mechanisms of male power than on its origins; e.g., Millett (1970) and Chesler (1972). Its major tenents may be summarized as follows:

1. Men have power and privilege by virtue of their sex. They may and do oppress women in personal relationships, in groups, and on the job.

2. It is in men's interest to maintain that power and privilege. There is status in the ability to oppress someone else, regardless of the oppression one suffers oneself. In addition, power over women in personal relationships gives men what they want, whether that be sex, smiles, chores, admiration, increased leisure, or control itself.

3. Men occupy and actively exclude women from positions of economic and political power in society. Those positions give men a heavily disproportionate share of the rewards of society, especially economic rewards.

4. Marriage is an institution of personal and sexual slavery for women, who are duped into marrying by the love ethic or economic necessity.

5. Although most males are also oppressed by the system under which we live, they are not oppressed, as females are, _because of_ their sex.

6. Feminine roles and cultural values are the product of oppression. Idealization of them is dysfunctional to change.

7. Males have greater behavioral and economic options, including the option of oppressing women. Where individuals have wider options, they are responsible for their

> from **Merced**
>
> _For weeks now a rage_
> _has possessed my body, driving_
> _now out upon men and women_
> _now inward upon myself_
> _Walking Amsterdam Avenue_
> _I find myself in tears_
> _without knowing which thought_
> _forced water to my eyes_
> _To speak to another human_
> _becomes a risk_
> _I think of Norman Morrison_
> _the Buddhists of Saigon_
> _the black teacher last week_
> _who put himself to death_
> _to waken guilt in hearts_
> _too numb to get the message_
> _in a world masculinity made_
> _unfit for women or men_
>
> Adrienne Rich

choices. In this way, men are responsible, individually and collectively, for their oppression of women.

8. Men oppress women through the use of brute force, by restricting options and selectively reinforcing women within these options, through control of resources and major institutions, and through expertise and access to the media.

Socialist Perspective. This approach holds that the oppression of women is only one aspect of the destructiveness of a generally oppressive economic system and therefore contends that socialism is a prerequisite to feminism. As the

*Where a system of oppression has become institutionalized it is
unnecessary for individuals to be oppressive.*

Florynce Kennedy, "Institutionalized
Oppression vs. the Female," 1970

Big Daddy Draped by May Stevens. Reprinted by permission.

basis for outlining this viewpoint, I am using
the general orientation of The Socialist
Worker's Party and the International Social-
ists, as discussed with me in conversation, and
the writings of Reed (1969). Although I have
chosen to use the viewpoint of socialist organizations heavily dominated by males (thus they
are not feminist organizations), women in
these groups often form formal or informal
caucuses on feminist issues. Closely related
are the analyses of the unaffiliated, all-female

socialist groups, although these groups generally disagree with the following analysis by affirming the need for an independent women's
movement. Their approach is represented by
Mitchell (1971). Simone de Beauvoir's work,
The Second Sex, fits primarily into this category, although the work is so broad that it incorporates the main ideas from all analyses
presented here. That de Beauvoir identifies
with the socialist perspective on the women's
movement as presented here is clear in her
autobiography, *Force of Circumstances* (1965).

1. The oppression of women originated in
the concept of private property. Women were
defined as property largely because of their
ability to reproduce, thereby providing new
workers as well as heirs for the elite. Because
private property is the institution on which
capitalism is founded, the oppression of
women is fundamentally linked to capitalist
structures and is necessary to their continuation.

2. Sexism is functional to capitalism because
it enables capitalists to buy two workers for
the price of one. A man is paid a wage; his
wife, who is unpaid, provides the necessary
services for him to perform his job (even if
she, too, has a job).

3. Women provide a cheap reserve labor
force for capitalists, thereby holding down
wages and increasing profits.

4. Although the rebellion of women against
their roles is contrary to the interests of capitalism, an independent women's movement is
not, for it separates one oppressed group from
others and forestalls a coalition which could
overthrow the system.

. . . we as womenfolk can't as i see it be all that smug and satisfied about where we're at anyhow until the ascending female principle is better established at large.

Jill Johnston, *Gullible's Travels*, 1974

5. Equality for women is impossible until capitalism is replaced by socialism.

Male Power

These four perspectives on the contemporary condition of women differentially weigh and interpret the current sources of male power but are in general agreement as to what they are. For purposes of this discussion, I shall draw primarily upon the language of the power analysts because they have given the most systematic attention to this issue.

Normative Power. By virtue of their sex and their control of traditional sex-role definitions, men are able to manipulate women's behavior by ignoring, misrepresenting, devaluing, and discrediting women or their accomplishments, especially when women deviate from traditional roles. Some examples are the omission of women's contributions from history texts and the attribution of women's scientific discoveries and artistic achievements to men. In the extreme, the institutionalization of traditional sex-role definitions in the theories of the mental health professions allows males on a day-to-day basis to label female role deviants as "crazy" or to punish their deviations through incarceration (see Chesler, 1972).

Institutional Power. Not only do males have differential amounts of and access to money, education, and positions of influence, they use this control to limit life options for women and extend life options for men. For example, male control of the media, religion, and the educational system is used to influence public opin-

The Generals by Marisol Escobar, 1961-2, wood and mixed media, 87 × 28½"; Albright-Knox Art Gallery, Buffalo, N.Y., Gift of Seymour H. Knox, 1962.

ion and practice. Combined with normative power, males use these public socialization institutions to inculcate traditional role and value systems in both females and males, thereby reducing the probability that females will aspire to or succeed in moving beyond traditional roles.

When women do attempt to change or broaden their roles, they are blocked by male control of the economic institutions. Women lack skills and access to skills through formal

Power and violence are opposites; where the one rules absolutely, the other is absent. Violence appears where power is in jeopardy, but left to its own course it ends in power's disappearance.

Hannah Arendt, *Crises of The Republic*, 1972

Power

Living   in the earth-deposits   of our history

Today a backhoe divulged   out of a crum-
*   bling flank of earth*
one   bottle   amber   perfect   a   hundred-
*   year-old*
cure for fever   or melancholy   a tonic
for living on this earth   in the winters of this
*   climate*

Today I was reading about Marie Curie:
she must have known she suffered   from ra-
*   diation sickness*
her body bombarded for years   by the ele-
*   ment*
she had purified
It seems she denied to the end
the source of the cataracts on her eyes
the cracked and suppurating skin   of her
*   finger-ends*
till she could no longer hold   a test-tube or a
*   pencil*

She died   a famous woman   denying
her wounds
denying
her wounds   came   from the same source as
*   her power*

Adrienne Rich

dominance of economic institutions by males locks women into traditional roles.

Male dominance of law and politics supports their control through other institutional means. Thus laws are made, interpreted, and enforced with male self-interest in mind. For example, the Supreme Court, with one exception, has refused to apply the Fourteenth and Fifth Amendment guarantees of "equal protection under law" to women, making necessary a *special* constitutional amendment even to establish the legal basis for female equality in society.

The two areas women are said to control, domestic life and education of the young, are delegated to them by men, who retain final authority and monitor the way in which women carry out these roles.

Control of Options Through Reward Power. Men use their institutional and normative power to control women's life choices not only through restricting their options but also through reinforcing choices within them. This is a subtle form of control, as Skinner makes clear; since women do receive some rewards for "appropriate" behavior, those who rebel risk losing real rewards. The recent slight broadening of options is primarily a matter of reinforcing new forms of behavior and does not change the basic control of females by males, i.e., does not change who metes out reinforcement.

The Power of Expertise. In all areas—from international affairs, space technology, and

education as well as through recognized apprenticeship and trainee programs. Denied access to well-paid jobs, women lack money or access to money through loans which would enable them to change their condition. Thus,

> *Life in this society being, at best, an utter bore and no aspect of society*
> *being at all relevant to women, there remains to civic-minded,*
> *responsible, thrill-seeking females only to overthrow the government,*
> *eliminate the money system, institute complete automation and destroy*
> *the male sex.*

Valerie Solanis, *SCUM Manifesto*, 1967–1968

group dynamics to education, child rearing, and female sexuality—the experts are male. This is largely because male dominance of the educational institutions and the media allows males to select which individuals will become experts and which experts shall receive public exposure. For a woman, this means that when she wants information or advice in any field, she must rely for the most part on males whose expertise may serve the interests of male supremacy or male values rather than her own interests.

Psychological Power. Males, having suppressed feminine culture, have access to institutional power partly because they "fit" the value structures of the institutions better than do women (for example, see Epstein's [1971, Chap. 3] discussion of status-set typing, and Chafetz' [1974] illustration of the interaction between sex roles and professional roles, pp. 60–62). The confidence of being "right," of fitting, gives even incompetent men an important source of psychological power over women, who have not been so wholly socialized into the masculine value structure.

Brute Force. Not only are most men stronger than most women but they are trained to have or show confidence in their physical strength. Men physically dominate women by beating wives and girl friends or by rape and threat of rape. Rape is a form of social control (as pointed out by Reynolds, 1971) which serves to restrict women's autonomy and mobility. The threat of rape is reinforced by whistling and

> **from From the Prison House**
>
> *Underneath my lids another eye has opened*
> *it looks nakedly*
> *at the light*
>
> *that soaks in from the world of pain*
> *even when I sleep*
>
> *Steadily it regards*
> *everything I am going through*
>
> *and more . . .*
>
> *it sees*
> *the violence*
> *embedded in silence*
>
> *This eye*
> *is not for weeping*
> *its vision*
> *must be unblurred*
> *though tears are on my face*
>
> *its intent is clarity*
> *it must forget*
> *nothing*
>
> Adrienne Rich

other street hassles, which to women, implicitly carry the possibility of physical attack.

Approaches to Change—A New Society

Surrounded by male power, from sources which overlap and reinforce one another, women find that they must totally transform society to achieve their goal of freedom from oppression. As a result, strategies for change

Dropping out gives control to those few who don't drop out; dropping out is exactly what the establishment leaders want; it plays into the hands of the enemy; it strengthens the system instead of undermining it, since it is based entirely on non-participation, passivity, apathy and non-involvement. . . .

Valerie Solanis, *SCUM Manifesto*, 1967–1968

---

are many and diverse, giving the women's movement the appearance of a lack of direction. However, no one tactic is intended to accomplish the entire task. Groups choose targets and activities partly on the basis of their analyses of women's oppression, partly on the basis of available opportunities for action, and partly according to the personal dispositions of any particular group or collective of women. There is, then, no easy one-to-one match between the perspectives of the participants and the activities of the movement, which I briefly review in the following section.

De- or Resocialization of Oneself

Self-change is important for all perspectives, though in the socialist approach, it is seen as effected through social action. To the extent that sex-role definitions, value systems, and the power which is based on them are socialized characteristics, each of us to some extent participates in those definitions. The most prevalent activity in the women's movement, therefore, has been the small consciousness-raising or rap group in which women piece together an understanding of their oppression and challenge their assumptions about themselves, other women, and men. Within these groups, women find that their experiences, private fears, and self-doubts are not unique but common to many other women and related to their social conditioning. Personal experience thus becomes a basis for political analysis and action.

Most groups focus on building solidarity and support among members, replacing the distrust and dislike of other women with which many enter these groups. In addition, most groups raise questions about appropriate routes to liberation, challenge the notion that liberation means imitating male roles and values, and debate the extent to which individual freedom is possible in the absence of general structural change in the society. In this way, women begin to redefine and change themselves and build a basis for initiating larger changes.

Changing Personal Interactions and Micro-Role Systems

New definitions are useless if not put into action. All perspectives encourage actions to redefine personal relationships and micro-role systems, although they vary to some extent in the kinds of actions they favor. The sex-role analysis focuses heavily on individual change of personal relationships and the broadening of individual life options. The cultural perspective emphasizes decreasing dependence on emotional support from males and substituting strong alliances among women. The power perspective favors direct confrontation with males in all interactions—on the job, in the street, and in personal relationships.

Since, in a sex-role system, definitions are upheld and reinforced by both role actors, when a woman moves outside of traditional definitions, she forces a change in complementary roles. For example, the rap group is often important in providing support for married women seeking more egalitarian sharing of housework and child care, or attempting to return to school, take a job, or resume a ca-

When man substituted God for the Great Goddess he at the same time substituted authoritarian for humanistic values.

Elizabeth Gould Davis, *The First Sex*, 1971

reer; and for single women attempting to deal with the restrictiveness of a father or boyfriend. Through an analysis of the costs and rewards to both parties in a relationship, the group helps its members find ways of decreasing the rewards (increasing the costs) for male resistance to such changes, while increasing their rewards for more egalitarian behavior.

The support function of women's groups is a step toward substituting women for men as a basic reference group. This process reduces women's reliance on the kinds of rewards they receive from men. Approval and emotional support is instead sought within the group. In this way, a new set of sisterly relationships is formed, which, for some groups, involves mutual economic support in living communes and sexual gratification in lesbian relationships, making women largely self-sufficient and males almost irrelevant.

Still, almost all women must relate to men in less personal interactions. The power analysts, in particular, help each other develop strategies for confronting rather than ignoring street hassles, for confronting and changing condescending comments and gestures in work and other settings, and for challenging the "servant chores" (making coffee, buying presents, dusting the office, providing a sympathetic ear to the boss) which are a part of many female occupations.

Learning karate and other forms of self-defense as well as engaging in sports activities is one popular feminist strategy for combatting the physical power men have over women. Many women believe that if they develop their strength and learn to understand, use,

Great Goddess Tribe, 1974, Mary Beth Edelson. Reprinted by permission of the artist

and have confidence in their bodies, they will be less likely to be attacked physically and more able to defend themselves in the event of an attack. As men are aware that women are able to fight back, the attacker-victim role relationship should become less frequent.

In the attempt to change others through personal interaction and micro-role system change, women undermine several sources of male power. Normative power is further reduced by destroying traditional male roles through withholding cooperation, making them irrelevant, or challenging them directly. To the extent that women provide a support group for one another, they reduce the power of males to define women's options and control their behavior through rewards. Self-defense techniques reduce the threat of brute force. These small-scale attempts at change gradually produce new bases for more egalitarian interaction than traditional practices.

We are involved in a struggle for liberation: liberation from the exploitive and dehumanizing system of racism, from the manipulative control of a corporate society; liberation from the constrictive norms of "mainstream" culture, from the synthetic myths that encourage us to fashion ourselves rashly from without (reaction) rather than from within (creation).

Toni Cade, *The Black Woman*, 1970

Resocialization of Others

The second most prevalent activity of the women's movement has been use of or attacks on the media in order to extend the resocialization process beyond the boundaries of the movement. These activities have been engaged in primarily by women who use the sex-role perspective, which emphasizes socialization. The cultural approach and the power analysis both caution against dependence on media and media change as main tools of the movement, since the media are dominated by men. As a result, they warn, attempts by women to convey their ideas through the media will tend to distort the message in a way that ridicules or discredits the movement.

Those who use the media view it as a way of reaching and changing women who have not been exposed to rap groups. By publishing books, magazines, and articles, by speaking, producing radio and TV programs, by being interviewed or holding demonstrations covered by the media, women in the movement extend their insights to those outside it. In this way, countless women who do not identify with the movement begin to reevaluate and change their lives.

Women's access to the media also helps reshape men's understanding of the female condition. For those who believe that change can come about through convincing men of the disadvantages of their roles or of masculine values, the media provide major vehicles for reaching and changing men. Communicating with men in this way provides the beginnings of social legitimation for legal changes and lays the groundwork for a new value system in society.

Much attention is also focused on the socialization of children. A number of groups are publishing feminist books for children and compiling lists of children's literature offering a positive image of women. *Ms.* magazine has even published a children's record, containing liberated songs. In addition, several women's groups throughout the country have formed feminist child care centers or cooperatives.

Some academic women are concerned with building a social science that defines females as full participants in society and creates and supports new definitions of women. This attempt, however, has little support among many active feminists, who point out that the social sciences are male-dominated in membership, substance, and style, thus forcing academic women to work under non- or antifeminist constraints. I myself believe that the most exciting social-psychological analyses in the past five years have taken place in feminist groups. To the extent that this thinking has filtered into academic meetings and writing, it has been a grossly watered down and devitalized version of feminist thought (my own work not ex-

The women's struggle is the liberation of MEN. As women shed their roles, so goes the "masculine image," the "masculine ego," the "masculine hang-up." A man won't have to be tall, dark, strong, aggressive, competitive, rugged, or independent, any more than a woman has to be small, delicate, passive, artistic, or dependent. The old order will be destroyed for the creation of a new, emancipated order. Men will be free to create humanistic relationships from natural interactions. New relationships and new roles. New frontiers, new freedoms, new directions. Power to the sisters.

Yamamoto, *Gidra* (Jan. 1971)

---

cepted). Thus the movement puts little faith in the social sciences' provision of a basis for new images of women and society.

Changing Male Dominance of Institutions

So far, the approaches to change with which I have dealt focus heavily on undermining male normative and cultural power and substituting female group support for male approval. However, these approaches are limited by male control of social institutions, against which women have few resources. The main tactics we employ are legal action, direct action and moral pressure, and skill building.

Growing out of the civil rights movement, several legal changes in the past decade open new options to women. Under law, public accommodations must be available to women, and discrimination in hiring or pay on the basis of sex is illegal in any business or educational institution. These changes formally open the possibilities for women to travel freely, gain skills, and obtain economic and positional resources. However, none of these laws are adequately enforced. It has been incumbent upon women to identify discrimination and file suits or complaints with federal, state, or local agencies. This technique is currently in wide use by university women, who are filing complaints against institutions with HEW. In addition, local movement groups give support

and advice to individuals seeking redress of employment or pay discrimination cases and rent and loan discrimination.

Another attempt at law enforcement is a current project, coordinated through NOW, to challenge the renewal of TV and radio station FCC licenses on grounds of sexism (discrimination in employment and failure to provide fair and adequate service to a segment of the public).

Women seek to change as well as enforce laws. Campaigns, rallies, and marches in support of legalized abortion, welfare rights, and child care attempt to influence public opinion and bring public pressure to bear on legislators. This tactic is especially favored by socialist groups. In addition, ad hoc groups of women have pressured politicians for new laws—the Equal Rights Amendment, laws on the treatment of female criminals, changes in marriage and divorce laws, laws and procedures governing rape cases, etc.

Direct action includes sit-ins, economic boycotts, moral pressure, and attempts to form women's unions. Sit-ins and boycotts are used to draw attention to illegal and unjust institutional practices as well as to affect the economic position of those against whom they are directed. Groups employing these tactics often negotiate directly over their demands. In addition, these approaches sometimes speed up investigatory or legal action by providing

from **The Common Woman Poems**

VII. *Vera, from my childhood*

the common woman is as common as the best of bread
and will rise
and will become strong—I swear it to you
I swear it to you on my own head
I swear it to you on my common
woman's
head

Judy Grahn

adverse publicity and forcing a business or organization to defend itself publicly.

An example of successful moral pressure is the project of two Wayne State University women who analyzed the Detroit public school system's textbooks, using the latter's own guidelines on treatment of minority groups. As a result of their efforts, Detroit school guidelines now explicitly include females with other groups that must be portrayed fairly in school texts—an incentive for authors and publishers to produce such books.

Attempts to form women's unions in order to collectivize and institutionalize women's power to bargain for better working conditions, equitable pay, and job definitions which allow for promotion are under way in many parts of the country. They are also necessary because unions have been notoriously insensitive to the needs of women. (In Detroit, some UAW leaders crossed picket lines for the first time in their lives when their female staff went on strike.) Some women are organizing unions that cut across occupational types or place of employment and are attempting to pull employed women and housewives into one union, with demands that include pay for housework. Women's unions are most strongly promoted by groups using a power analysis.

A final, and less direct, way of changing institutions is through skill building. Women's lack of power in institutions stems partly from a lack of knowledge, skills, and confidence. Many feminist projects are devoted to building women's resources to enable them to challenge institutional power. Some groups, convinced that all individuals are capable of any activity, given the opportunity to learn and practice, build speaking and writing skills by seeking opportunities for all members to engage in those activities and by assigning members to fill speaking engagements by lot rather than by degree of competence.

Some professional women are actively recruiting women into their ranks. At Wayne State University and elsewhere, women law students accompany recruiters to college campuses, talking to women about careers in law and providing information about the field, entrance requirements, and preparation for Law Board exams. Women from other professions speak at high schools and on college campuses to encourage young women to consider new career opportunities. Within professions, women are beginning to form support groups or caucuses or to change the focus of existing women's professional organizations to consider the roles of women and ways in which they can implement feminine values within their occupations. The entrance of women into prestigious fields such as law, medicine, business, and education not only gives females a basis for power within those institutions but also begins the process of building female ex-

Witchcraft Was Hung, in History

Witchcraft was hung, in History,
But History and I
Find all the Witchcraft that we need
Around us, every Day—

Emily Dickinson

---

pertise as a counter to male expertise, and in some cases begins the systematic introduction of feminine values into institutional structures.

Building Alternative Institutions

Partly as a result of the cultural analysis, which argues that the institutions of society are corrupted by their weddedness to masculine values, and partly for reasons of sheer survival, many women are engaged in building alternative institutions that incorporate feminist values and can thereby serve as models for institutions in a new society.

The numerous women's self-help medical clinics primarily aim to break down male monopoly of basic medical information. They provide women with information about their bodies that enables them to stay healthy, know when something is wrong, know how to communicate with—and if necessary how to challenge—their doctors or seek alternative care. These clinics operate on the assumption that women lose control of their bodies partly through ignorance. They strive to reduce the distinctions between patients, aides, nurses, technicians, and doctors by teaching each other how to do breast and vaginal self-examinations and basic laboratory tests, and by sharing information on such topics as menopause and nutrition. Self-help groups also collect lists of doctors who are nonchauvinist and those whom women should avoid. Gradually

She is Light. Clitartists Collective—Shannon O'Brien, copyright 1973

these groups are beginning to negotiate with doctors, hospitals, and clinics for changes in the treatment of female patients, and, more radically, in the structure of the medical professions.

In the field of law, a group of female lawyers in San Francisco is using its expertise to train women in law. If a client wishes, she may work in the office, including the preparation of her own legal brief in lieu of some or all of her legal fees. The approach incorporates feminist values into the practice of law by reducing mystification of the law and monopolization of expertise. Status relationships are also equalized as lawyers frequently answer phones and type letters while clients prepare legal briefs.

Another alternative institution is the commune. Although the communal movement is not feminist, many women have seen its potential for providing an alternative to the nuclear family, which power analysts in particular view as a primary oppressive institution. Communes offer women who are already married an opportunity to reduce the sex-role pressures of the nuclear family by sharing work and home roles among several adults; single women find mixed or all-female communes a way of meeting social and economic needs and reducing the pressure on them to marry; single mothers have found that collective living with others in the same position eases child care and economic problems. An important component of all these communal styles is that they increase support among women, who live together rather than in isolated homes, and reduce their dependence on males. Hence they are alternatives especially favored by women using a cultural or power approach.

In the process of working for a feminist revolution, the women's movement has attempted to structure itself around its values for a new society. Since women have been placed in a largely powerless role in society, they are especially sensitive to the degradations associated with powerlessness. Therefore, in seeking change, the movement has sought organizational techniques which do not subject women to oppression within or without the movement. Most groups have been reluctant to recruit actively, depending instead on women coming to the movement when they become aware of their own oppression as women. As mentioned earlier, the media provide indirect recruitment, but most women avoid pressuring or coercing individuals with their views.

Problems with Power and Authority Within the Movement Itself

Because feminist values emphasize the right of each women to her own view and choice of activities, a major problem has been the coordination of activities without authoritarian leadership. Granting power to a leader puts other women in a position of subordination similar to the subordination of females to males. Groups have therefore avoided formally or informally institutionalized leadership in a variety of ways. Leadership tasks are often rotated. Steering committees are selected in representative ways to serve for short time periods. A typical practice is to send two women rather than one to speak before a group or explain a position or action to the press, on the assumption that differences in their perspective, experience, and style will reflect the diversity of the movement.

In many cities, feminist groups have organized as coalitions of smaller rap or action groups. Ideally, the coalition form assumes that differences do and will exist and leaves individuals free to support or not support the activities proposed by component groups. It provides a forum for debating ideological differences and coordinating action among those of different persuasions. There are serious criticisms within the movement of each of these organizational forms—but there is also widespread commitment to finding feminist solutions.

In this paper I have attempted to summarize the general perspectives and strategies of the women's movement. In doing so, I have omitted its many controversies—proponents of each approach often differ sharply and sometimes destructively. Each strategy has its detractors, who view it as ineffective, utopian, unnecessarily hostile, retreatist, or trivial. To males—who tend to evaluate a movement by the tightness of its organization, agreement on perspectives, goals, and tactics, and allegiance to a leader or leadership group—the women's movement looks directionless, unorganized, and ineffective. To feminists struggling with new selves and new forms of organization, the means are as important as the goals, and the struggles to coordinate efforts to obtain power for women is itself a small-scale model of a new society, one that accepts and works creatively with and for differences in viewpoint and life experience.

Star Hunter by Remedios Varo; reprinted by permission of Walter Gruen

APPENDIX A: References for Articles

Introductions

Allen, D. W. 1977. Basic treatment issues. In *Hysterical Personality*, Mardi Horowitz (Ed.). New York: Jason Aronson.

Allport, G. 1954. *The Nature of Prejudice*. Reading, Mass.: Addison-Wesley, pp. 142–161.

Ariès, P. 1965. *Centuries of Childhood: A Social History of Family Life*. New York: Random House.

Battle-Sister, A. 1971. Conjectures on the female culture question. *Journal of Marriage and the Family*, 33:411–420.

Bleier, R. 1979. Social and political bias in science: An examination of animal studies and their generalizations to human behavior and evolution. In *Genes and Gender: II*, E. Tobach and B. Rosoff (Eds.). New York: Gordian Press.

Block, J. H. 1976. Assessing sex differences: Issues, problems, and pitfalls. *Merrill-Palmer Quarterly*, 22 (4):283–308.

Bogen, J. E. 1969. The other side of the brain, II: An appositional mind. *Bulletin of the Los Angeles Neurological Society*, 34 (3):135–162.

Brodsky, A. M. 1980. A decade of feminist influence on psychotherapy. *Psychology of Women Quarterly*, 4 (3):331–344.

Broverman, I. K., Broverman, D. M., Clarkson, F. E., Rosenkrantz, P. S., and Vogel, S. R. 1970. Sex role stereotypes and clinical judgments of mental health. *Journal of Consulting and Clinical Psychology*, 34 (1):1–7.

Broverman, I. K., Vogel, S. R., Broverman, D. M., Clarkson, F. E., and Rosenkrantz, P. S. 1972. Sex-role stereotypes: A current appraisal. *Journal of Social Issues*, 28: 59–78.

Brush, L. R., Gold, A. R., and White, M. G. 1978. The paradox of intention and effect: A women's studies course. *Signs: Journal of Women in Culture and Society*, 3 (4):870–883.

Burris, B. 1973. Fourth world manifesto. In *Radical Feminism*, A. Koedt, E. Levine, and A. Rapone (Eds.). New York: Quadrangle/The New York Times, pp. 322–357.

Chesler, P. 1972. *Women and Madness*. Garden City, N.Y.: Doubleday.

Christ, C. P. 1976. Margaret Atwood: The surfacing of women's spiritual quest and vision. *Signs: Journal of Women in Culture and Society*, 2 (2):316–330.

Chodorow, N. 1971. Being and doing: A cross-cultural examination of the socialization of males and females. In *Woman in Sexist Society: Studies in Power and Powerlessness*, Vivian Gornick and B. K. Moran (Eds.). New York: Basic Books.

Chodorow, N. 1974. Family structure and feminine personality. In *Woman, Culture and Society*, M. Z. Rosaldo and L. Lamphere (Eds.). Stanford: Stanford Univ. Press.

Chodorow, N. 1976. Oedipal asymmetries and heterosexual knots. *Social Problems*, 23 (4):454–468.

Chodorow, N. 1978. *The Reproduction of Mothering: Psychoanalysis and the Sociology of Gender*. Berkeley: Univ. California Press.

Clark, K., and Clark, M. 1947. Racial identification and preference in Negro children. In *Readings in Social Psychology*, T. M. Newcomb and E. L. Hartley (Eds.). New York: Holt, Rinehart & Winston.

Corballis, M. C. 1980. Laterality and myth. *American Psychologist*, 35 (3):284–295.

Diagnostic and Statistical Manual of Mental Disorders (third ed.). 1980. (Referred to as DSM III.) Washington, D.C.: American Psychiatric Association.

Dinnerstein, D. 1976. *The Mermaid and the Minotaur: Sexual Arrangements and Human Malaise*. New York: Harper & Row.

Domhoff, W. 1973. But why did they sit on the

king's right in the first place? In *The Nature of Human Consciousness*, R. Ornstein (Ed.). San Francisco: W. H. Freeman.

Fanon, F. 1963. *The Wretched of the Earth*. New York: Grove Press.

Firestone, S. 1970. *The Dialectic of Sex: The Case for Feminist Revolution*. New York: William Morrow.

Fisher, L. 1954. *Gandhi*. New York: Signet Key.

Fishman, P. M. 1978. Interaction: The work women do. *Social Problems*, 25:397–406.

Freeman, J. 1971. Social construction of the second sex. In *Roles Women Play: Readings toward Women's Liberation*, M. H. Garskof (Ed.). Belmont, Calif.: Wadsworth, pp. 123–141.

Frodi, A., Macaulay, J., and Thome, P. R. 1977. Are women always less aggressive than men? A review of the experimental literature. *Psychological Bulletin*, 84 (4):634–660.

Galin, D. 1974. Implications for psychiatry of left and right cerebral specialization: A neurophysiological context for unconscious processes. *Archives of General Psychiatry*, 31:572–583.

Giovacchini, P. L. 1975. *Psychoanalysis of Character Disorders*. New York: Jason Aronson.

Goldenberg, N. R. 1976. A feminist critique of Jung. *Signs: Journal of Women in Culture and Society*, 2 (2):443–449.

Gordon, L. 1975. A socialist view of women's studies: A reply to the editorial, volumn 1, number 1. *Signs: Journal of Women in Culture and Society*, 1 (2):559–566.

Gove, W. 1980. Mental illness and psychiatric treatment among women. *Psychology of Women Quarterly*, 4 (3):345–362.

Hacker, H. M. 1974. Women as a minority group: Twenty years later. *International Journal of Group Tensions*, 4:122–141.

Harrison, J. B. 1978. Men's roles and men's lives. *Signs: Journal of Women in Culture and Society*, 4 (2):324–336.

Henley, N. M. 1977. *Body Politics, Power, Sex, and Nonverbal Communication*. Englewood Cliffs, N.J.: Prentice-Hall.

Jaynes, J. 1976. *The Origin of Consciousness in the Breakdown of the Bicameral Mind*. Boston: Houghton Mifflin.

Johnson, M. 1980. Mental illness and psychiatric treatment among women: A response. *Psychology of Women Quarterly*, 4 (3):363–371.

Kaschak, E. 1976. Sociotherapy: An ecological model for therapy with women. *Psychotherapy: Theory, Research and Practice*, 13 (1):61–63.

Koedt, A. 1970. The myth of the vaginal orgasm. In *Radical Feminism*, A. Koedt, E. Levine, and A. Rapone (Eds.). New York: Quadrangle/The New York Times, pp. 198–207.

Lederer, W. 1968. *The Fear of Women*. New York: Harcourt Brace Jovanovich.

Maccoby, E. E. (Ed.). 1966. *The Development of Sex Differences*. Stanford: Stanford Univ. Press.

Maccoby, E. E., and Jacklin, C. N. 1974. *The Psychology of Sex Differences*. Stanford: Stanford Univ. Press.

Mead, M. 1935. *Sex and Temperament in Three Primitive Societies*. New York: William Morrow.

Millett, K. 1970. *Sexual Politics*. New York: Doubleday.

Myrdal, G. 1944. *An American Dilemma*. New York: Harper.

Newton, E., and Webster, P. 1973. Matriarchy: As women see it. *Aphra*, 4 (3).

Ornstein, R. 1972. *The Psychology of Consciousness*. San Francisco: W. H. Freeman.

Ortner, S. B. 1974. Is female to male as nature is to culture? In *Woman, Culture, and Society*, M. Z. Rosaldo and L. Lamphere (Eds.). Stanford: Stanford Univ. Press.

Patai, R. 1967. *Women in the Modern World*. New York: Free Press.

Quinn, N. 1977. Anthropological studies on women's status. *Annual Review of Anthropology*, 6:181–225.

Rogers, S. C. 1978. Woman's place: A critical review of anthropological theory. *Comparative Studies in Society and History*, 20:123–173.

Rosaldo, M. Z. 1974. Woman, culture, and society: A theoretical overview. In *Woman, Culture, and Society*, M. Z. Rosaldo and L. Lamphere (Eds.). Stanford: Stanford Univ. Press.

Safilios-Rothschild, C. 1981. Toward a social psychology of relationships. *Psychology of Women Quarterly*, 5 (3) (in press).

Salzman, F. 1979. Aggression and gender: A critique of the nature-nurture question for humans. In *Genes and Gender: II*, E. Tobach and B. Rosoff (Eds.). New York: Gordian Press.

Shapiro, D. 1965. *Neurotic Styles*. New York: Basic Books.

Star, S. L. 1979. (a) The politics of right and left: Sex differences in hemispheric brain asymmetry. In *Women Look at Biology Looking at Women*, R. Hubbard, M. S. Henifin, and B. Fried (Eds.). Cambridge, Mass.: Schenkman.

Star, S. L. 1979. (b) Sex differences and the dichotomization of the brain: Methods, limits and problems in research on consciousness. In *Genes and Gender: II: Pitfalls in Research on Sex and Gender*, R. Hubbard and M. Lowe (Eds.). New York: Gordian Press.

Terman, L. M., and Tyler, L. 1954. Psychological sex differences. In *Manual of Child Psychology*, L. Carmichael (Ed.). New York: Wiley.

Webster, P. 1975. Matriarchy: A vision of power. In *Toward an Anthropology of Women*, R. R. Reiter (Ed.). New York: Monthly Review, pp. 141–156.

Webster, P. 1977. The politics of rape in primitive societies. *Michigan Discussions in Anthropology*, 3:99–106.

Wolowitz, H. M. 1972. Hysterical character and feminine identity. In *Readings on the Psychology of Women*, J. Bardwick (Ed.). New York: Harper & Row.

Biological and Cultural Perspectives

The Context and Consequences of Contemporary Sex Research: A Feminist Perspective

Leonore Tiefer

ACKNOWLEDGMENTS

The author gratefully acknowledges the assistance of Charles Tiefer, a former biochemist now at Harvard Law School, during the writing of this chapter.

Adams, H. B. "Mental illness" or interpersonal behavior? *American Psychologist*, 1964, *19*, 191–197.

Bakan, D. *The duality of human existence.* Chicago: Rand McNally, 1966.

Barber, B. *Science and the social order.* New York: Free Press, 1952.

Bardwick, J. M. Psychological correlates of the menstrual cycle and oral contraceptive medication. In E. J. Sachar (Ed.), *Hormones, behavior, and psychopathology.* New York: Raven Press, 1976.

Beach, F. A. Sexual attractivity, proceptivity and receptivity in female mammals. *Hormones and Behavior*, 1976, *7*, 105–138.

Bell, A. P. Research in homosexuality. Back to the drawing board. *Archives of Sexual Behavior*, 1975, *4*, 421–431.

Bem, S. L. Beyond androgyny: Some prescriptions for a liberated sexual identity. Keynote address for APA-NIMH conference on the Research Needs of Women. Madison, Wisconsin, 1975.

Bernard, J. Can science transcend culture? *Scientific Monthly*, 1950, *71*, 268–273.

Bing, E., and Rudikoff, E. Divergent ways of parental coping with hermaphroditic children. *Medical Aspects of Human Sexuality*, 1970, *4*, 73, 77, 80, 83, 88.

Block, J. H. Issues, problems, and pitfalls in assessing sex differences. A critical review of *The Psychology of Sex Differences. Merrill Palmer Quarterly*, 1976, *22*, 283–308.

Blume, S. S. *Toward a political sociology of science.* New York: Free Press, 1974.

Blumstein, P. W., and Schwartz, P. Lesbianism and bisexuality. In E. Goode and R. Troiden (Eds.), *Sexual deviance and sexual deviants.* New York: William Morrow and Co., 1974.

Brown, B. *New body, new mind.* New York: Harper and Row, 1974.

Bruner, J. S. Reason, prejudice, and intuition. In A. Tiselius & S. Nilsson (Eds.), *The place of values in a world of facts.* New York: Wiley, 1970.

Buss, A. R. The emerging field of the sociology of psychological knowledge. *American Psychologist*, 1975, *30*, 988–1002.

Buss, A. R. Galton and sex differences. An historical note. *Journal of the History of the Behavioral Sciences*, 1976, *12*, 283–285.

Carlson, R. Where is the person in personality research? *Psychological Bulletin*, 1971, *75*, 203–219.

Carlson, R. Understanding women: Implications for personality theory and research. *Journal of Social Issues*, 1972, *28*, 17–32.

Cronback, L. J. Beyond the two disciplines of scientific psychology. *American Psychologist*, 1975, *30*, 116–127.

Ehrhardt, A. A., and Baker, S. W. Fetal androgens, human central nervous system differentiation, and behavior sex differences. In R. C. Friedman, R. M. Richart, and R. L. Vande Wiele (Eds.), *Sex differences in behavior.* New York: Wiley, 1974a.

Ehrhardt, A. A., and Baker, S. W. Prenatal androgens, intelligence, and cognitive sex differences. In R. C. Friedman, R. M. Richart, and

R. L. Vande Wiele (Eds.), *Sex differences in behavior.* New York: Wiley, 1974b.

Eisenberg, L. The human nature of human nature. *Science,* 1972, *176,* 123–128.

Farson, R. E. Can science solve human dilemmas? In R. E. Farson (Ed.), *Science and human affairs.* Palo Alto, California: Science and Behavior Books, 1965.

Feldman, J. The savant and the midwife. *Impact of Science on Society,* 1975, *25,* 125–136.

Francoeur, A. K., and Francoeur, R. T. Hot and cool sex—closed and open marriage. In R. T. Francoeur and A. K. Francoeur (Eds.), *The future of sexual relations.* Englewood Cliffs, New Jersey: Prentice-Hall, 1974.

Frankel, C. The nature and sources of irrationalism. *Science,* 1973, *180,* 927–931.

Friedhoff, A. J. (Ed.) *Catecholamines and behavior. Vol. 2. Neuropsychopharmacology.* New York: Plenum Press, 1976.

Friedman, R. C., Richart, R. M., and Vande Wiele, R. L. *Sex differences in behavior.* New York: Wiley, 1974.

Gagnon, J. H. Sex research and social change. *Archives of Sexual Behavior,* 1975, *4,* 111–141.

Gastonguay, P. R. A sociobiology of man. *American Biology Teacher,* 1975, *37,* 481–486.

Hebb, D. O. What psychology is about. *American Psychologist,* 1974, *29,* 71–79.

Hellige, J. B. Hemispheric processing differences revealed by differential conditioning and reaction time performance. *Journal of Experimental Psychology: General,* 1975, *104,* 309–326.

Hessellund, H. Masturbation and sexual fantasies in married couples. *Archives of Sexual Behavior,* 1976, *5,* 133–148.

Hochschild, A. R. The sociology of feeling and emotion: Selected possibilities. In M. Millman and R. M. Kanter (Eds.), *Another voice: Feminist perspectives on social life and social science.* New York: Doubleday, 1975.

Jensen, G. D., Bobbitt, R. A., and Gordon, B. N. Sex differences in social interaction between infant monkeys and their mothers. In J. Wortis (Ed.), *Recent advances in biological psychiatry.* New York: Plenum Press, 1967.

Kanter, R. M. Women and the structure of organizations: Explorations in theory and behavior. In M. Millman and R. M. Kanter (Eds.), *Another voice: Feminist perspectives on social life and social science.* New York: Doubleday, 1975.

Kanter, R. M., Jaffe, D., and Weisberg, D. K. Coupling, parenting, and the presence of others: Intimate relationships in communal households. *The Family Coordinator,* 1975, *24,* 433–452.

Kinsey, A. C., Pomeroy, W. B., and Martin, C. E. *Sexual behavior in the human male.* Philadelphia: Saunders, 1948.

Kinsey, A. C., Pomeroy, W. B., Martin, C. E., and Gebhard, P. H. *Sexual behavior in the human female.* Philadelphia: Saunders, 1953.

Koch, S. The allures of ameaning in modern psychology. In R. E. Farson (Ed.), *Science and human affairs.* Palo Alto, California: Science and Behavior Books, 1965.

Larsson, K. Sexual behavior: The result of an interaction. In J. Zubin and J. Money (Eds.), *Contemporary sexual behavior: Critical issues for the 1970s.* Baltimore: Johns Hopkins University Press, 1973.

Levine, M. Scientific method and the adversary model. *American Psychologist,* 1974, *29,* 661–677.

Lewis, M. Early sex differences in the human. Studies of socioemotional development. *Archives of Sexual Behavior,* 1975, *4,* 329–335.

Lorber, J. Women and medical sociology: Invisible professionals and ubiquitous patients. In M. Millman and R. M. Kanter (Eds.), *Another voice: Feminist perspectives on social life and social science.* New York: Doubleday, 1975.

Maccoby, E. E., and Jacklin, C. N. *The psychology of sex differences.* Stanford: Stanford University Press, 1974.

Maslow, A. H. *The psychology of science: A reconnaissance.* New York: Harper and Row, 1966.

Masters. W. H., and Johnson, V. E. *Human sexual response.* Boston: Little, Brown and Co., 1966.

McCormack, T. Toward a nonexist perspective on social and political change. In M. Millman and R. M. Kanter (Eds.), *Another voice: Feminist perspectives on social life and social change.* New York: Doubleday, 1975.

Merton, R. K. *The sociology of science.* Chicago: The University of Chicago Press, 1963.

Mitchell, G. D. Attachment differences in male and female infant monkeys. *Child Development,* 1968, *39,* 611–620.

Moyle, R. M. Sexuality in Samoan art forms. *Archives of Sexual Behavior,* 1975, *4,* 227–247.

Myrdal, G. Biases in social research. In A. Tiselius and S. Nilsson (Eds.), *The place of values in a world of facts.* New York: Wiley, 1970.

Nash, J. A critique of social science models of contemporary society: A feminist perspective. *Annals of the New York Academy of Science,* 1975, *260,* 84–100.

Ovenden, M. W. Intimations of unity. In N. H. Stenek (Ed.), *Science and society: Past, present and future.* Ann Arbor: University of Michigan Press, 1975.

Owen, D. The 47, XXY male: A review. *Psychological Bulletin.* 1972, *78,* 209–233.

Parlee, M. B. The premenstrual syndrome. *Psychological Bulletin.* 1973, *80,* 454–465.

Pastore, N. *The nature-nurture controversy.* New York: King's Crown Press. Columbia University, 1949.

Petras, J. *Sexuality in society.* New York: Allyn-Bacon, 1973.

Phoenix, C. H. Prenatal testosterone in the nonhuman primate and its consequences for behavior. In R. C. Friedman, R. M. Richart, and R. L. Vande Wiele (Eds.), *Sex differences in behavior.* New York: Wiley, 1974.

Pirages, D. The unfinished revolution. In N. H. Stenek (Ed.), *Science and society: Past, present and future.* Ann Arbor: University of Michigan Press, 1975.

Radford, J. Reflections on introspection. *American Psychologist.* 1974, *29,* 245–250.

Reinisch, J. M. Effects of prenatal hormone exposure on physical and psychological development in humans and animals: With a note on the state of the field. In E. J. Sachar (Ed.), *Hormones, behavior, and psychopathology.* New York: Raven Press, 1976.

Roberts, M. On the nature and condition of social science. *Daedalus,* 1974, *103,* (3), 47–64.

Rosenblum, L. A. Sex differences, environmental complexity and mother-infant relations. *Archives of Sexual Behavior,* 1974, *3,* 117–128.

Rossi, A. S. Maternalism, sexuality, and the new feminism. In J. Zubin and J. Money (Eds.), *Contemporary sexual behavior: Critical issues for the 1970s.* Baltimore: Johns Hopkins University Press, 1973.

Sanford, N. Will psychology study human problems? *American Psychologist,* 1965, *20,* 192–202.

Schachter, S. Some extraordinary facts about obese humans and rats. *American Psychologist,* 1971, *26,* 129–144.

Schmidt, G., and Sigusch, V. Women's sexual arousal. In J. Zubin and J. Money (Eds.), *Contemporary sexual behavior: Critical issues for the 1970s.* Baltimore: Johns Hopkins University Press, 1973.

Schumpeter, J. A. Science and ideology. *American Economic Review,* 1949, *39,* 345–359.

Snow, C. P. The two cultures. *New Statesman,* 1956, *52,* 413–414.

Sociobiology Study Group. *Sociobiology—A new biological determinism.* Cambridge, Boston: SESPA/Science for the People, 1975.

Tyler, L. Design for a hopeful psychology. *American Psychologist,* 1973, *28,* 1021–1029.

Vance, E. B., and Wagner, N. N. Written descriptions of orgasm: A study of sex differences. *Archives of Sexual Behavior,* 1976, *5,* 87–98.

Wade, N. Sociobiology: Troubled birth for new discipline. *Science,* 1976, *191,* 1151–1155.

Wilson, E. O. *Sociobiology: The new synthesis.* Cambridge, Mass.: Harvard University Press, 1975.

Woman's Place: A Critical Review of Anthropological Theory

Susan Carol Rogers

1. Caroline Ifeka, "The female factor in anthropology," paper read at London Women's Anthropology Workshop (1973), p. 2.

2. Ellen Lewin, J. Collier, M. Rosaldo, and J. Fjellman, "Power strategies and sex roles," unpublished paper read at the 70th Annual Meeting, American Anthropological Association (New York, 1971), p. 12.

3. Many of the ideas in this section were expressed at the Conference on the Role of Women in the Preindustrial Family in Europe (Ann Arbor, 1974). A number of participants represented this point of view and, during the conference, made explicit many of the underlying assumptions in their work. Rayna Reiter, Harriet Rosenberg, and Miriam Cohen were most helpful in elucidating their ideas, and constructively criticizing mine. It is impossible, however, to attribute these ideas to any one individual, and I take responsibility for any distortions I may have inadvertently introduced in my interpretation of their point of view.

4. Rae Blumberg, "Toward a cross-society theory of factors determining female status," paper

read at Northwestern University Department of Sociology Colloquium (1974).

5. Dorothy Remy, "Towards an economic anthropology for women," paper read at London Women's Anthropology Workshop (1973), pp. 1, 3.

6. *Ibid.*, 1–2.

7. *Ibid.*, 3.

8. *Ibid.*, 4.

9. *Ibid.*, 5.

10. Peggy Sanday, "Toward a theory of the status of women." *American Anthropologist* 75 (1973), 1682.

11. *Ibid.*, 1694.

12. See for example, Michelle Rosaldo, "Women, culture and society: a theoretical overview," in Rosaldo and Lamphere (eds.) *Woman, Culture and Society* (Stanford, 1974), 17–18; Susan Harding, "Women and words in a Spanish village," in Rayna Reiter (ed.) *Toward an Anthropology of Women* (New York, 1975), 306–8.

13. William Stephens, *The Family in Cross-Cultural Perspective* (New York, 1963), p. 289 is one example.

14. Rosaldo, *op. cit.*, 21.

15. *Ibid.*, 23. See also Louise Lamphere, "Strategies, cooperation, and conflict among women in domestic groups," in Rosaldo and Lamphere, *op. cit.*, 97; Ortner, *op. cit.*, 17–18.

16. Lamphere, *op. cit.*, *passim*.

17. Rosaldo, *op. cit.*, 39.

18. *Ibid.*, 41.

19. *Ibid.*, 42. See also Ortner, *op. cit.*, 28.

20. See Michaelson and Goldschmidt, *op. cit.*, 332–3 for a more general view of sexual segregation as a cause or indication of low female status.

21. *Ibid.*, 335–7.

22. Blomberg, *op. cit.*

23. Rosaldo, *op. cit.*, 19.

24. Ortner, *op. cit.*, 10.

25. Michaelson and Goldschmidt, *op. cit.*, 330–1.

26. Leavitt *et al.*, *op. cit.*, 110–12, 123–4.

27. Kaberry, *op. cit.* (1952), 150, 152.

28. For instance, Green, *op. cit.*, 176; Marie-Paule de Thé, "Evolution féminine et évolution villageoise chez les Beti du Sud-Cameroun," *Bulletin IFAN* 30b (1968), 1537; Denise Paulme, "The social condition of women in two West African societies," *Man* 48 (1948), 44; Rogers, *op. cit.* (1975), 738.

29. Some of the examples found in the literature include: Green, *op. cit.*, 176; Sylvia Leith-Ross, *African Women: A Study of the Ibo of Nigeria* (London, 1939), p. 46; Robert Netting, "Marital relations in the Jos Plateau of Nigeria," *American Anthropologist* 71 (1969), *passim*.

30. Specific examples in various West African societies are described in Janheinz Jahn, "A Yoruba market woman's life," in Dundes, ed., *Every Man his Way* (Englewood Cliffs, 1968), p. 234; Judith Van Allen, " 'Sitting on a man': colonialism and the lost political institutions of Igbo women," *Canadian Journal of African Studies* 6 (1972); Carol Hoffer, *op. cit.*, (1972); R. Delarozière, "Les institutions politiques et sociales des populations dites Bamiléké," *Etudes Camerounaises* 25–6 (1949), 50; Robert Ritzenthaler, "*Anlu*: a women's uprising in the British Cameroons," *African Studies* 19 (1960), 1591–2.

31. For example, see Kaberry, *op. cit.* (1952), 49 on separate prestige systems; Leith-Ross, *op. cit.*, 164 on differentiated valuation of resources; Rogers, *op. cit.* (1975), 740 on differentiated attitudes toward male and female work.

32. Netting, *op. cit.*, 1044.

33. Kaberry, *op. cit.* (1939), 230.

34. *Ibid.*

35. See Nelson, *op. cit.*, for a discussion of the persistence of this assumption in anthropological literature.

36. R. S. Rattray, *Ashanti* (London, 1955), 84 (original publication, 1923). Rattray spent years in Ashanti and wrote voluminously on the precolonial and colonial periods of this monarchy during the first third of the twentieth century. His work is still considered to be the most complete and accurate ethnographic account of traditional Ashanti, and is frequently cited in more recent analyses of the culture. His observations about the status of women, particularly their considerable formal political roles, however, have gone largely ignored. For example, despite the fact that the head of state was a female position, having an elaborate female, as well as male, hierarchy under it, even analyses of the traditional political system sometimes fail altogether to mention women (e.g. H. Basehart, "Ashanti," in Gough and Schneider (eds.), *Matrilineal Kinship* (Berkeley, 1962), p. 270–97). More often, the female monarch is mentioned in passing, designated by the misnomer "queen mother," although she was never the king's

wife, and was not necessarily his mother. She did not hold her position by virtue of her relationship with him; indeed it was she who appointed him, and was above him in the state hierarchy.

37. Louise Tilly and Joan Scott, "Women's Work and the Family in Nineteenth Century Europe," *Comparative Studies in Society and History* 17 (1975).

38. Recent events in our society make particularly clear the point that even where power is believed to lie in positions of formal authority, most effective decision-making may actually be done through informal, covert channels. The facts remain, however, that *in our society* (1) formal authority is generally highly valued by both men and women, and (2) one does not gain access to high-level decision-making, either covert or overt, if one is largely restricted to household activities.

39. Leavitt *et al., op. cit.,* 124, 111; cf. Nelson, *op. cit.,* 560.

40. Jill Dubisch, "Dowry and the domestic power of women in a Greek island village," paper read at 70th Annual Meeting, American Anthropological Association (New York, 1971), p. 1.

41. Cf. Harding *op. cit.,* 306–7. I would argue in any case that class is a more important factor than sex in this type of domination. In the example given, *both* peasant men and women are dominated *as peasants.*

42. For example, see Conrad Arensberg and Solon Kimball, *Family and Community in Ireland* (Cambridge, Mass., 1968), p. 49; Henri Mendras, *La Fin des Paysans* (Paris, 1970), pp. 96–7; Robert Redfield, *Peasant Society and Culture* (Chicago, 1967), p. 60; original publication, 1956.

43. Ernestine Friedl, "The position of women: appearance and reality," *Anthropological Quarterly* 40 (1967), 98–105.

44. *Ibid.,* 106–7.

45. Dubisch, *op. cit.,* 3–4.

46. *Ibid.,* 6.

47. Friedl, *op. cit.* (1967), 107.

48. Nelson, *op. cit.,* 553.

49. *Ibid.,* 559.

50. Joyce Riegelhaupt, "Saloio women: an analysis of infomal and formal political and economic roles of Portuguese peasant women," *Anthropological Quarterly* 40 (1967), 122.

51. *Ibid.,* 119–21.

52. *Ibid.,* 125.

53. *Ibid.,* 123–4.

54. *Ibid.,* 120.

55. *Ibid.,* 124.

56. Beverly Chinas, *Isthmus Zapotecs: Women's Roles in Cultural Context* (New York, 1973), p. 1.

57. *Ibid.,* 2.

58. *Ibid.,* 93–5.

59. *Ibid.,* 100–1.

60. *Ibid., 108.*

61. *Ibid.,* 109.

62. *Ibid.,* 96–7.

63. *Ibid.,* 97.

64. Paulme, *op. cit.* (1963), 5.

65. *Ibid.,* 4.

66. Cf. Hoffer *op. cit.,* in which the formal political roles of Mende women in Sierra Leone are described and analyzed. Hoffer's work is fairly conventional in its approach to formal political structure but, in this context, this does not result in automatic exclusion of women.

67. Paulme, *op. cit.* (1963), 7.

68. *Ibid.,* 14.

69. For example, see Marc Swartz, "Introduction," in Swartz and Turner (eds.), *Political Anthropology* (Chicago, 1966), p. 14; Ronald Cohen, "The political system," in Cohen and Narroll (eds.), *Handbook of Method in Cultural Anthropology* (Garden City, 1971), pp. 487–8, 492.

70. See Julian Pitt-Rivers, *The People of the Sierra* (Chicago, 1961), pp. 200–1; Eric Wolf, "Kinship, friendship, and patron-client relations in complex societies," in Banton (ed.), *The Social Anthropology of Complex Societies* (London, 1966), p. 2, on the importance of informal behavior patterns in other research domains.

Psychological Sex Differences
Summary and Commentary

Eleanor Emmons Maccoby and Carol Nagy Jacklin

Bem, D. J., and Allen, A. 1974. On predicting some of the people some of the time: the search for cross-situational consistencies in behavior. *Psychological Review,* 81, 506–520.

Kohlberg, L. A cognitive-developmental analysis of children's sex-role concepts and attitudes. In E. E. Maccoby (ed.), *The development of sex differences.* Stanford, Calif.: Stanford University Press, 1966.

Raush, H. R. 1965. Interaction sequences. *Journal of Personality and Social Psychology, 2,* 487–99.

Serbin, L. A., O'Leary, K. D., Kent, R. N., and Tonick, I. J. 1973. A comparison of teacher response to the pre-academic and problem behavior of boys and girls. *Child Development,* 44, 796–804.

Slaby, R. G. University of Washington, personal communication, 1974.

Debatable Conclusions About Sex Differences: A Review of Maccoby and Jacklin

Jeanne H. Block

Mischel, W., & Moore, B. S. 1973. Effects of attention to symbolically-presented rewards upon self-control. *Journal of Personality and Social Psychology, 28,* 172–179.

Mischel, W., and Underwood, B. 1973. Instrumental ideation in delay of gratification. Unpublished manuscript, Stanford University.

Terman, L. M. & Tyler, L. E. 1954. Psychological sex differences. In L. Carmichael (ed.), *Manual of child psychology* (2nd ed.). New York: John Wiley & Sons, 1064–1114.

Tyler, L. E. 1965. *The psychology of human differences.* New York: Appleton-Century-Crofts.

Psychology of Women: Research Issues and Trends

Martha T. Shuch Mednick

I wish to thank Sandra Bayne, Mary Pasquella, and Anita Borodin and Saundra Murray for their assistance. This work was partly supported by a Howard University Faculty Research grant.

1. Millman, M. & R. M. Kanter. 1975. *Another Voice.* Anchor/Doubleday. New York, N.Y.
2. Gould, C. C. & M. W. Wartofsky. 1976. *Women and Philosophy.* G. P. Putnam's Sons. New York, N.Y.
3. Rosaldo, M. Z. & L. Lamphere. 1974. *Woman, Culture and Society.* Stanford University Press. Stanford, Calif.
4. *Signs, Journal of Women in Culture and Society.* University of Chicago. Chicago, Ill.
5. Lipman-Blumen, J. & A. R. Tickamyer. 1975. Sex roles in transition: a ten-year perspective. *Ann. Rev. Soc.* 1: 297–337.
6. Sicherman, B. 1975. Review essay: American history. *Signs* 1: 401–484.
7. Howe, I. 1976. *World of Our Fathers.* Harcourt Brace Jovanovich. New York, N.Y.
8. Pierce, C. 1975. Review essay: Philosophy. *Signs* 1: 487–503.
9. Reeves, N. 1971. *Womankind: Beyond the Stereotypes.* Aldine. Chicago, Ill.
10. Parlee, M. 1975. Review essay: Psychology. *Signs* 1: 119–138.
11. Mednick, M. T. S. 1976. Some thoughts on the psychology of women. *Signs* 1: 763–770.
12. Vaughter, R. M. 1976. Making connections: psychology of women. *Signs* 2:(1) 120–142.
13. Sherman, J. A. 1971. *On the Psychology of Women.* C. C Thomas. Springfield, Ill.
14. Russo, N. F. 1976. Beyond adolescence: some suggested new directions for studying female development in the middle and later years. In *Psychology of Women: Future Directions for Research.* J. A. Sherman & F. L. Denmark, Eds. Psychological Dimensions, New York, N.Y.
15. Hyde, J. S. & B. G. Rosenberg. 1976. *Half the Human Experience: The Psychology of Women.* D. C. Heath. Lexington, Mass.
16. Unger, R. K. & F. L. Denmark. 1975. *Woman, Dependent or Independent Variable?* Psychological Dimensions. New York, N.Y.
17. Shields, S. A. 1975. Functionalism, Darwinism and the psychology of women: a study in social myth. *Am. Psychol.* 30: 739–754.
18. Tangri, S. S. 1976. Using sex role research to guide public policy. Paper presented at Russell Sage College Conference on Sex Roles in American Society.
19. Sherman, J. A. 1975. Review of E. E. Maccoby & C. N. Jacklin, 1974, *The Psychology of Sex Differences. Sex Roles* 1: 297–301.
20. Block, J. H. 1976. Review of E. E. Maccoby and C. N. Jacklin, 1974, *The Psychology of Sex Differences.* Stanford University Press. Palo Alto, Calif. In *Contemp. Psychol.* 21: 517–522.
21. Maccoby, E. E. & C. N. Jacklin. 1974. *The Psychology of Sex Differences.* Stanford University Press. Palo Alto, Calif.
22. Birdsall, N. 1976. Review essay: women and population studies. *Signs* 1: 699–712.
23. Boehm, V. R. 1975. The competent woman manager: will success spoil women's lib? Paper presented at Am. Psychol. Assoc. Chicago, Ill.
24. Schein, V. E. 1973. The relationship between

sex-role stereotypes and requisite management characteristics. *J. Appl. Psychol.* 57: 95–100.

25. Weisstein, N. 1971. Psychology constructs the female: on the fantasy life of the male psychologist. In *Roles Women Play: Readings Towards Women's Liberation.* M. H. Garskof, Ed. Brooks-Cole. Belmont, Calif.

26. Kieffer, M. 1972. Psychology is not part of the solution. Unpublished manuscript.

27. Helson, R. 1972. The changing image of the career woman. *J. Soc. Issues* 28: 33–46.

28. Helson, R. 1976. Creativity in women. In *Psychology of Women: Future Directions of Research.* J. A. Sherman & F. L. Denmark, Eds. Psychological Dimensions. New York, N.Y.

29. McClelland, D. C. 1975. *Power: The Inner Experience.* Halstead Press, New York, N.Y.

30. Lewis, E. C. 1968. *Developing Woman's Potential.* Iowa State University Press. Ames, Iowa.

31. McKenna, W. & S. J. Kessler. 1974. Experimental design as a source of sex bias in social psychology. Paper presented at Am. Psychol. Assoc. New Orleans, La.

32. Prescott, S. & K. Foster. 1974. Why researchers don't study women. Paper presented at Am. Psychol. Assoc. New Orleans, La.

33. Sherman, J. A. & F. L. Denmark, Eds. 1976. *Psychology of Women: Future Directions of Research.* Psychological Dimensions. New York, N.Y.

34. Denmark, F. L., S. S. Tangri & S. McCandless. 1976. Affiliation: achievement and power: a new look. In *Psychology of Women: Future Directions of Research.* J. A. Sherman & F. L. Denmark, Eds. Psychological Dimensions. New York, N.Y.

35. Frieze, I. H., J. Fishers, M. C. McHugh & V. A. Valle. 1976. Attributing the causes of success and failure: internal and external barriers to achievement in women. In *Psychology of Women: Future Directions of Research.* J. A. Sherman & F. L. Denmark, Eds. Psychological Dimensions. New York, N.Y.

36. Astin, H. S. 1976. Women and work. In *Psychology of Women: Future Directions of Research.* J. A. Sherman & F. L. Denmark, Eds. Psychological Dimensions. New York, N.Y.

37. Laws, J. L. 1976. Work motivation and work behavior of women: new perspectives. In *Psychology of Women: Future Directions of Research.* J. A. Sherman & F. L. Denmark, Eds.

Psychological Dimensions. New York, N.Y.

38. Bem, S. 1976. Beyond androgyny: some presumptive prescriptions for a liberated sexual identity. In *Psychology of Women: Future Directions of Research.* J. A. Sherman & F. L. Denmark, Eds. Psychological Dimensions. New York, N.Y.

39. Schwartz, P. 1976. The social psychology of female sexuality. In *Psychology of Women: Future Directions of Research.* J. A. Sherman & F. L. Denmark, Eds. Psychological Dimensions. New York, N.Y.

40. Parlee, M. B. 1976. Psychological aspects of menstruation, childbirth, and menopause: an overview with suggestions for further research. In *Psychology of Women: Future Directions of Research.* J. A. Sherman & F. L. Denmark, Eds. Psychological Dimensions. New York, N.Y.

41. Unger, R. K. 1976. Status, power and gender: an examination of parallelisms. In *Psychology of Women: Future Directions of Research.* J. A. Sherman & F. L. Denmark, Eds. Psychological Dimensions. New York, N.Y.

42. Constantinople, A. 1973. Masculinity-femininity: an exception to a famous dictum? *Psychol. Bull.* 80(5): 389–407.

43. Rossi, A. 1964. The equality of women: an immodest proposal. *Daedalus* 93: 607–652.

44. Carlson, R. 1972. Understanding women: implications for personality theory and research. *J. Soc. Issues* 28(2): 17–32.

45. Helson, R. 1973. Heroic and tender modes in women authors of fantasy. *J. Pers.* 41: 493–512.

46. Bem, S. L. 1974. The measurement of psychological androgyny. *J. Consult. Clin. Psychol.* 42: 165–172.

47. Block, J. J. 1973. Conceptions of sex roles. *Amer. Psychol.* 28: 512–526.

48. Block, J., A. von der Lippe & J. H. Block, 1973. Sex role and socialization patterns: some personality concomitants and enviromental antecedents. *J. Consult. Clin. Psychol.* 41(3): 321–341.

49. Spence, J. T., R. Helmreich & J. Stapp. 1975. Ratings of self and peers on sex-role attributes and their relation to self-esteem. *J. Pers. Soc. Psychol.* 32: 29–39.

50. Berzins, J. I. 1975. New perspectives and sex roles and personality dimensions. Paper presented at Am. Psychol. Assoc. Chicago, Ill.

51. Spence, J. T. 1976. Personal communication.

52. Rebecca, M., R. Hefner & B. Oleshansky. 1976.

A model of sex-role transcendence. In *Beyond Sex Role Stereotypes: Readings towards a Psychology of Androgyny*. A. G. Kaplan & J. P. Bean. Little, Brown & Co. Boston, Mass.

53. Mednick, M. T. S. & H. J. Weissman. 1975. The psychology of women: selected topics. *Ann. Rev. Psychol.* 26: 1–18.

54. Mednick, M. T. S., S. S. Tangri & L. W. Hoffman. 1975. *Women and Achievement: Social and Motivational Analyses*. Halstead-Wiley. New York, N.Y.

55. Roby, P. A. 1976. Toward full equality: more job education for women. *School Rev.*

56. Current Population Reports, Bureau of the Census. 1976. *Women in the United States: A Statistical Portrait*. Special Studies Series P-23, No. 58. Washington, D.C.

57. Citizens Advisory Council on the Status of Women. 1975. *Women in 1975*. Washington, D.C.

58. Atkinson, J. W., Ed. 1958. *Motives in Fantasy, Action and Society*. Van Nostrand. New York, N.Y.

59. Stein, A. H. & M. M. Bailey. 1973. The socialization of achievement orientation in females. *Psychol. Bull.* 80(5): 345–366.

60. Zuerkman, M. & L. Wheeler. 1975. To dispel fantasies about fantasy based measures of fear of success. *Psychol. Bull.* 82: 932–946.

61. Condry, J. & S. Dyer. 1976. Fear of success: attributions of cause to the victim. *J. Soc. Issues.* 32(3): 63–84.

62. Hoffman, L. W. 1974. Fear of success in males and females: 1965 and 1972. *J. Cons. Clin. Psychol.* 42: 353–358.

63. O'Leary, V. & B. Hammack. 1975. Sex role orientation and achievement context as determinants of the motive to avoid success. *Sex Roles* 1: 225–234.

64. Caballero, C. M., P. Giles & P. Shaver. 1975. Sex role traditionalism and fear of success. *Sex Roles* 1: 319–326.

65. Weston, P. & M. T. Mednick. 1970. Race, social class and the motive to avoid success in women. *J. Cross-Cult. Psychol.* 1: 284–291.

66. Mednick, M. T. S. & G. R. Puryear. 1976. Race and fear of success in college women: 1968 and 1972. *J. Cons. Clin. Psychol.* 44(5): 787–789.

67. Mednick, M. T. S. & G. R. Puryear. 1975. Motivational and personality factors related to career goals of black college women. *J. Soc.*

Behav. Sci. 21: 1–30.

68. Frieze, I. 1975. Women's expectations for and causal attributions of success and failure. In *Women and Achievement: Social and Motivational Analyses*. M. T. S. Mednick, S. S. Tangri & L. W. Hoffman, Eds. Halstead-Wiley. New York, N.Y.

69. Gurin, P. B. & A. Pruitt. 1976. Counseling implications of black women's market position, aspirations, and expectations. Paper presented at Conference on Black Women, Nat. Inst. Education. Washington, D.C.

70. Winer, B. 1972. Attribution theory, achievement motivation and the educational process. *Rev. Educ. Res.* 42: 203–215.

71. Pasquella, M. 1976. Effects of sex-role orientation on causal attribution about achievement outcomes. Unpublished Master's thesis. Howard University. Washington, D.C.

72. Murray, S. R. & M. T. S. Mednick. 1975. Perceiving the causes of success and failure in achievement: sex, race and motivational comparisons. *J. Cons. Clin. Psychol.* 44: 881–885.

73. Tangri, S. S. 1976. A Feminist perspective on the ethical issues in population programs. *Signs.* 1(4): 895–904.

74. Boston Women's Health Collective. 1976. *Our Bodies, Ourselves*. 2nd ed. Simon & Schuster, New York, N.Y.

75. Task Force on Sex Bias and Sex-Role Stereotyping in Psychotherapeutic Practice. 1975. Report. *Am. Psychol.* 30: 1169–1175.

76. Tennov, D. 1973. Feminism, psychotherapy and professionalism. *Journal of Contemporary Psychotherapy*, 5: 107–111.

77. Buss, A. 1975. The emerging field of the sociology of psychological knowledge. *Am. Psychol.* 30: 988–1002.

78. Gergen, K. J. 1973. Social psychology as history. *J. Pers. Soc. Psychol.* 26: 309–320.

79. Cronbach, L. J. 1975. Beyond the two disciplines of scientific psychology. *Am. Psychol.* 30: 116–127.

80. Bart, P. B. & M. Grossman. 1976. Menopause. In *The Woman as a Patient*. M. T. Notman & C. Nadelman. Plenum Press. New York, N.Y.

81. Bart, P. 1970. Mother Portnoy's complaint. *Transaction 8*.

82. Neugarten, B. L. & N. Datan, 1974. The middle years. In *American Handbook of Psychiatry*. S. Arieta, Ed. 1. Basic Books. New York, N.Y.

83. Harding, E. 1975. *The Way of Women.* Harper & Row: New York, N.Y. (Originally published in 1933.)
84. Murray, S. R. & M. T. S. Mednick. 1976. Black women's achievement operation: motivational and cognitive factors. *Psychol. Women Qtrly.* 3: 247–259.
85. Oakley, A. 1974. *Woman's Work.* Pantheon. New York, N.Y.
86. Boserup, E. 1970. *Woman's Role in Economic Development.* George Allen & Unwin, Ltd. London, England.
87. Mednick, M. T. S. 1975. Social change and sex role inertia: the case of the kibbutz. In *Women and Achievement: Social and Motivational Analyses.* M. T. S. Mednick, S. S. Tangri & L. W. Hoffman, Eds. Halstead-Wiley. New York, N.Y.
88. Haavio-Mannila, E. 1971. Convergences between East and West: tradition and modernity in sex roles in Sweden, Finland and the Soviet Union. *Acta Sociologica* 14(1–2).
89. Lipman-Blumen, J. 1973. Role de-differentiation as a system response to crisis: occupational and political roles of women. *Soc. Inquiry* 43: 105–129.
90. Trey, J. E. 1972. Women in the war economy—World War II. *Rev. Radical Pol. Econo.* 4(3): 1–17.
91. Chesler, P. & E. J. Goodman. 1976. *Women, Money and Power.* Wm. Morrow & Co., Inc. New York, N.Y.
92. Crowley, J. E., T. E. Levitin & R. P. Quinn. 1972. Facts and fictions about the American working woman. Paper presented at Am. Psychol. Assoc. Honolulu, Hawaii.
93. Johnson, P. 1976. Women and power: toward a theory of effectiveness. *J. Soc. Issues* 32: 99–109.

Ethnic Diversity of Female Experience

Who Is That Person? Images and Roles of Black Women

Saundra Rice Murray

Abrahams, R. D. Negotiating respect: Patterns of presentation among black women. *Journal of American Folklore,* 1975, *88,* 58–80.

Allen, W. R. Family roles, occupational statuses, and achievement orientation among black women in the United States. *Signs,* 1979, *4,* 670–686.

Axelson, L. The working wife: Differences in perception among Negro and white males. *Journal of Marriage and the Family,* 1970, *32,* 457–464.

Beale, F. Double jeopardy: To be black and female. In T. Cade (Ed.), *The black woman: An anthology.* New York: New American Library, 1970.

Bell, R. The related importance of mother and wife roles among lower class women. In R. Staples (Ed.), *The black family: Essays and studies.* Belmont, Calif.: Wadsworth, 1971.

Blood, R. O., & Wolfe, D. M. Negro-white differences in blue-collar marriages in a northern metropolis. *Social Forces,* 1969, *48,* 59–63.

Bond, J. C., & Peery, P. Is the black male castrated? In T. Cade (Ed.), *The black woman: An anthology.* New York: New American Library, 1970.

Bonner, F. Black women and white women: A comparative analysis of perceptions of sex roles for self, ideal-self and the ideal male. In W. D. Johnson & T. L. Green (Eds.), *Perspectives on Afro-American women.* Washington, D.C.: ECCA Publications, 1975.

Bright, M. D. Fear of success and traditionality of occupational choice. Unpublished master's thesis, Howard University, 1970.

Bronfenbrenner, U. *The ecology of human development: Experiments by nature and design.* Cambridge, Mass.: Harvard University Press, 1979.

Brown, P., Perry, L., & Harburg, E. Sex role attitudes and psychological outcomes for black and white women experiencing marital dissolution. *Journal of Marriage and the Family,* 1977, *39,* 549–561.

Dance, D. Black eve or madonna? A study of the antithetical views of the mother in black American literature. In W. D. Johnson & T. L. Green (Eds.), *Perspectives on Afro-American women,* Washington, D.C.: ECCA Publications, 1975.

Darden, B. J., & Bayton, J. A. Self-concept and blacks' assessment of black leading roles in motion pictures and television. *Journal of Applied Psychology,* 1977, *62,* 620–623.

Dill, B. T. The dialectics of black womanhood. *Signs,* 1979, *4,* 543–555.

Donagher, P. C., Poulos, R. W., Liebert, R. M., & Davidson, E. S. Race, sex, and social example: An analysis of character portrayals on interracial television entertainment. *Psychological Reports,* 1975, *37,* 1023–1034.

Dumas, R. G. Dilemmas of black females in leadership. *Journal of Personality and Social Systems,* 1978, *2,* 3–19.

Entwisle, D., & Greenberger, E. Adolescents' views of women's work role. *American Journal of Orthopsychiatry*, 1972, *42*, 648–656.

Epstein, C. F. Positive effects of the multiple negative: Explaining the success of black professional women. *American Journal of Sociology*, 1972, *78*, 912–935.

Fichter, J. S. Career expectations of Negro college graduates. *Monthly Labor Review*, 1967, *90*, 36–42.

Fleming, J. Fear of success, achievement-related motives and behavior in black college women. *Journal of Personality*, 1978, *46*, 694–716.

Frazier, E. F. *The Negro family in the United States*. Chicago: University of Chicago Press, 1966.

Fugita, S., Wexley, K. N., & Hillery, J. M. Black-white differences in nonverbal behavior in an interview setting. *Journal of Applied Social Psychology*, 1974, *4*, 343–350.

Gump, J. P. Comparative analysis of black women's and white women's sex-role attitudes. *Journal of Consulting and Clinical Psychology*, 1975, *43*, 858–863.

Gump, J. P. Reality and myth: Employment and sex role ideology in black women. In J. A. Sherman & F. L. Denmark (Eds.), *The psychology of women: Future directions of research*. New York: Psychological Dimensions, 1978.

Gump, J. P., & Rivers, L. W. A consideration of race in efforts to end sex bias. In E. E. Diamond (Ed.), *Issues of sex bias and sex fairness in career interest measurement*. Washington, D.C.: U.S. Department of Health, Education and Welfare, National Institute of Education, Spring, 1975.

Gurin, P., & Epps, E. *Black consciousness, identity and achievement*. New York: Wiley, 1975.

Gurin, P., & Katz, D. *Motivation and aspiration in the Negro college*. Final report, U.S. Department of Health, Education and Welfare, 1966.

Gurin, P., & Pruitt, A. Counseling implications of black women's market position, aspirations and expectations. *Conference on the Educational and Occupational Needs of Black Women: Compendium*. Washington, D.C., National Institute of Education, 1977.

Haefner, J. E. Race, age, sex, and competence as factors in employer selection of the disadvantaged. *Journal of Applied Psychology*, 1977, *62*, 199–202.

Hamner, W. C., Kim, J. S., Baird, L., & Bigoness, W. J. Race and sex as determinants of ratings by potential employers in a simulated work-sampling task. *Journal of Applied Psychology*, 1974 *59*, 705–711.

Harley, S., & Terborg-Penn, R. (Eds.) *The Afro-American woman: Struggles and images*. Port Washington, N.Y.: Kennikat Press, 1978.

Harrison, A. O. Black women. In V. E. O'Leary, *Toward understanding women*. Monterey, Calif.: Brooks/Cole, 1977.

Harrison, A. O., & Minor, J. H. Interrole conflict, coping strategies, and satisfaction among black working wives. *Journal of Marriage and the Family*, 1978, *40*, 799–805.

Hess, R. S., & Shipman, V. C. Early experiences and the socialization of cognitive modes in children. *Child Development*, 1965, *36*, 869–886.

Horner, M. S. Sex differences in achievement motivation and performance in competitive and non-competitive situations. Unpublished doctoral dissertation, University of Michigan, 1968.

Horner, M. S. Toward an understanding of achievement-related conflicts in women. *Journal of Social Issues*, 1972, *28*, 157–175.

Hyman, H. H., & Reed, J. S. "Black matriarchy" reconsidered: Evidence from secondary analysis of sample surveys. *Public Opinion Quarterly*, 1969, *33*, 346–354.

Institute for Educational Policy. *Equal educational opportunity for blacks in U. S. higher education: An assessment*. Washington, D.C.: Howard University Press, 1976.

Jackson, J. Black women in a racist society. In C. V. Willie, B. M. Kramer, & B. S. Brown (Eds.), *Racism and mental health*. Pittsburgh: University of Pittsburgh Press, 1973.

Kamii, C. K., & Radin, N. L. Class differences in the socialization practices of Negro mothers. *Journal of Marriage and the Family*, 1967, *29*, 302–310.

Kane, F. J., Lachenbruch, P. A., Lokey, L., Chafetz, N., Auman, R., Pocuis, L., & Lipton, M. A. Motivational factors affecting contraceptive use. *American Journal of Obstetrics and Gynecology*, 1971, *110*, 1050–1054.

King, K., Abernathy, T. J., & Chapman, A. H. *Journal of Marriage and the Family*, 1978, *40*, 733–737.

King, M. C. The politics of sexual stereotypes. *The Black Scholar*, 1973, *3*, 12–23.

Ladner, J. *Tomorrow's tomorrow: The black*

woman. Garden City, N.Y.: Anchor Books, 1971.

Landry, B., & Jendrek, M. P. The employment of wives in middle-class black families. *Journal of Marriage and the Family,* 1978, *40,* 787–797.

LaRue, L. The black movement and women's liberation. In S. Cox (Ed.), *Female psychology: The emerging self.* Chicago: Science Research Associates, 1976.

Lee, E. C. Educational and occupational statistics of black women. *Conference on the Educational and Occupational Needs of Black Women: Compendium.* Washington, D.C., National Institute of Education, 1977.

Lewis, D. K. A response to inequality: Black women, racism, and sexism. *Signs,* 1977, *3,* 339–361.

Lewis, K. K. The black family: Socialization and sex roles. *Phylon,* 1975, *35,* 221–237.

Mack, D. E. The power relationship in black families and white families. *Journal of Personality and Social Psychology,* 1974, *30,* 409–413.

Mednick, M. T. S. *Factors influencing role-innovative career striving in black and white college women; The effect of expectancies, causal attribution, sex-role self-concept and achievement related motives.* Springfield, Va.: National Technical Information Service, 1979.

Mednick, M., & Puryear, G. R. Motivational and personality factors related to career goals of black college women. *Journal of Social and Behavioral Sciences,* 1975, *21,* 1–30.

Mednick, M. T. S., & Puryear, G. R. Race and fear of success in college women: 1968 and 1972. *Journal of Consulting and Clinical Psychology,* 1976, *44,* 787–789.

Melton, W., & Thomas, D. L. Instrumental and expressive values in mate selection of black and white college students. *Journal of Marriage and the Family,* 1976, *38,* 509–517.

Middleton, R., & Putney, S. Dominance in decisions in the family: Race and class differences. In C. V. Willie (Ed.), *The family life of black people.* Columbus, Ohio: Charles E. Merrill, 1960.

Minority women workers: A statistical overview. Washington, D.C.: U.S. Government Printing Office, 1977.

Mott, F. L. *Women, work and family.* Lexington, Mass: Lexington Books, 1978.

Murray, S. R., & Mednick, M. T. S. Black women's achievement orientation: Motivational and cognitive factors. *Psychology of Women Quarterly,* 1977, *1,* 247–259.

Murray, S. R., & Mednick, M. T. Perceiving the causes of success and failure in achievement: Sex, race, and motivational comparisons. *Journal of Consulting and Clinical Psychology,* 1975, *43,* 881–885.

Okediji, P. A. The occupational aspirations of black and white college females and their personality correlates. Unpublished master's thesis, Howard University, 1971.

O'Leary, V. C., & Harrison, A. O. Sex role stereotypes as a function of race and sex. Paper presented at the Annual Meeting of the American Psychological Association, Chicago, Illinois, September, 1975.

Owens, S. Self-esteem of black women in a comparative perspective. In W. D. Johnson and T. L. Green (Eds.), *Perspective on Afro-American women.* Washington, D.C.: ECCA Publications, 1975.

Petty, R. M. Effects of simultaneous and non-simultaneous arousal of motives. Unpublished master's thesis, Howard University, 1968.

Puryear, G. R., & Mednick, M. S. Black militancy, affective attachment and fear of success. *Journal of Consulting and Clinical Psychology,* 1974, *42,* 263–266.

Rainwater, L. *Behind ghetto walls,* Chicago: Aldine, 1970.

Rawles, B. The media and their effect on black images. *Conference on the Educational and Occupational Needs of Black Women: Compendium.* Washington, D.C., National Institute of Education, 1977.

Reid, P. T. Black matriarchy: Young and old. Paper presented at the Annual Meeting of the American Psychological Association, Toronto, August, 1978.

Reid, P. T. Racial stereotyping on television: A comparison of the behavior of both black and white television characters. *Journal of Applied Psychology,* 1979, *64,* 465–471.

Rushing, A. B. Images of black women in Afro-American poetry. In S. Harley and R. Terborg-Penn (Eds.), *The Afro-American woman: Struggles and images.* Port Washington, N.Y.: Kennikat Press, 1978.

Savage, J. E., Stearns, A. D., & Friedman, P. Relationship of internal-external locus of control, self-concept, and masculinity-femininity to fear of success in black freshmen and senior college women. *Sex Roles*, 1979, *5*, 373–383.

Scanzoni, J. *The black family in modern society*. Boston: Allyn-Bacon, 1971.

Scanzoni, J. Sex roles, economic factors, and marital solidarity in black and white marriages. *Journal of Marriage and the Family*, 1975(a), *37*, 130–144.

Scanzoni, J. *Sex roles, life styles, and childbearing*. New York: Free Press, 1975(b).

Schroth, M. L. Sex and grade-level differences in need achievement among black college students. *Perceptual and Motor Skills*, 1976, *43*, 135–140.

Scott, P. B. Preparing black women for nontraditional professions: Some considerations for career counseling. *Journal of the National Association for Women Deans, Administrators and Counselors*, 1977, Summer, 135–139.

Staples, R. *The black woman in America: Sex, marriage and the family*. Chicago: Nelson-Hall, 1973.

Staples, R. The myth of the black matriarchy. *The Black Scholar*, 1970, *1*, 8–16.

Steinmann, A., & Fox, D. J. Attitudes toward women's family role among black and white undergraduates. *The Family Coordinator*, 1970, 353–368.

TenHouten, W. D. The black family: Myth and reality. *Psychiatry*, 1970, *23*, 145–173.

Turner, B. F., & McCaffrey, J. H. Socialization and career orientation among black and white college women. *Journal of Vocational Behavior*, 1974, *5*, 307–319.

United States Commission on Civil Rights. *Window dressing on the set: Women and minorities on television*. Washington, D.C.: U.S. Government Printing Office, 1977.

United States Department of Labor. *The Negro family: The case for national action*. Washington, D.C.: U.S. Government Printing Office, 1965.

Vetter, L., & Stockburger, D. W. *Career patterns of a national sample of women*. (Research and Development Series No. 95). Columbus, Ohio: The Center for Vocational and Technical Education, 1974.

Weston, P., & Mednick, M. Race, social class, and the motive to avoid success in women. *Journal of Cross-Cultural Psychology*, 1970, *1*, 284–291.

Willie, C. V., & Greenblatt, S. L. Four "classic" stud-

ies of power relationships in black families: A review and look to the future. *Journal of Marriage and the Family*, 1978, *40*, 691–694.

Young, V. H. Family and childhood in a southern Negro community. *American Anthropologist*, 1970, *72*, 269–288.

Zegiob, L. E., & Forehand, R. Maternal interactive behavior as a function of race, socioeconomic status, and sex of the child. *Child Development*, 1975, *46*, 564–568.

The Profile of Asian American Women

Reiko Homma True

Arkoff, A., Meredith, G., and Dong, J. Attitudes of Japanese-American and Caucasian-American students toward marriage roles. *Journal of Social Psychology*, 1963, *59*, 11–15.

Asian American Women. Palo Alto: Stanford University, 1976.

Asian Women. Berkeley: University of California, 1971.

Benedict, R. *The chrysanthemum and the sword: Patterns of Japanese culture*. Boston: Houghton Mifflin, 1946.

Braun, J. and Chao, H. Attitudes toward women: A comparison of Asian born Chinese and American Caucasians. *Psychology of Women Quarterly*, 1978, *2*, 195–201.

Bulletin of concerned Asian scholars: Asian women, 1975, *7*.

Caudill, W. and DeVos, G. Achievement, culture and personality: The case of the Japanese Americans. *American Anthropologist*, 1956, *58*, 1102–1126.

Conference Discussions. Center for Japanese American Studies, San Francisco, 1979.

DHEW. *A study of selected socio-economic characteristics of ethnic minorities based on the 1970 census: II-Asian Americans*. HEW Publication, 1974, (OS) 75–121.

DHEW. Asian American field survey: Consumer survey data file. Office of Special Concerns, Office for Asian American Affairs, 1976.

Fillmore, L. W. and Cheong, J. L. The early socialization of Asian American female children. A paper presented at the Conference on Asian-Pacific American Women. August, 1976, San Francisco.

Fong, S. M. Identity conflicts of Chinese adolescents in San Francisco. In E. Brody (Ed.), *Mi-*

nority Group Adolescents in the United States. Baltimore: Williams and Wilkins, 1968.

Fong, P. and Cabezas, A. Economic and employment status of Asian-Pacific women. A paper presented at the Conference on Asian-Pacific American Women. Aug., 1976, San Francisco.

Fong, S. and Peskin, H. Sex role strain and personality adjustment of China born students in America: A pilot study. *Journal of Abnormal Psychology,* 1969, *74,* 563–567.

Fujitomi, I. and Wong, D. The new Asian-American woman. In Sue, S. and Wagner, N. (Eds.), *Asian Americans: Psychological Perspectives.* Palo Alto: Science and Behavior Books, 1973.

Gee, E. Issei: The first women. In *Asian women.* Berkeley: University of California, 1971.

Japanese American Citizen's League. *Report on Nisei retirement conference.* San Francisco, 1977.

Jen, L. Oppression and survival. In *Asian women.* Berkeley: University of California, 1971.

Kim, B. L. Asian wives of U.S. Servicemen: Women in shadows. *Amerasia Journal,* 1977, *1,* 91–116.

Kim, S. D. *An analysis of problems of Asian wives of U.S. servicemen.* Seattle: Demonstration Project for Asian Americans, 1975.

Kingston, M. H. *Woman warrior: Memoirs of a girlhood among ghosts.* New York: A. Knopf, 1976.

Lebra, J., Paulson, J. and Powers, E. *Women in changing Japan.* Boulder: Westview Press, 1976.

Lee, R. H. *The Chinese in the United States of America.* Hong Kong: Hong Kong U. Press, 1960.

Lott, J. T. and Pian, C. *Beyond stereotypes and statistics: Emergence of Asian and Pacific American women.* Washington, D.C.: Organization of Pan-Asian American Women, 1979.

Louie, G. Forgotten women. In *Asian Women.* Berkeley: University of California, 1971.

Maykovich, M. K. *Japanese American identity dilemma.* Tokyo: Waseda University, 1972.

Navarro, J. Immigration of Pilipino women to America. *Asian American women.* Palo Alto: Stanford University, 1976.

Nee, V. G. and Nee, B. *Longtime Californ: a documentary story of an American Chinatown.* New York: Random House, 1972.

Pian, C. Immigration of Asian women and the status of recent Asian women immigrants. A paper presented at the Conference on Asian-

Pacific American Women. San Francisco, Aug. 1976.

Sone, M. *Nisei daughter.* Boston: Little Brown, 1953.

Sunoo, H. H. and Sunoo, S. The heritage of the first Korean women immigrants in the U.S.: 1903–1924. *Korean Christian Scholars Journal,* Spring, 1977.

Takamure, I. *Josei no rekishi (History of Women).* Tokyo: Kobunsha, 1972.

U.S. Department of Labor. Orientals in American labor market, minorities in the labor market, Vol. II: *Manpower Administration,* 1975.

U.S. Immigration and Naturalization Services. *Annual Reports,* 1950–1975.

Wong, J. S. *Fifth Chinese daughter.* New York: Harper Bros., 1950.

Yamamoto, J. Japanese American identity crisis. In E. Brody (Ed.), *Minority group adolescents in the U.S.* Baltimore: Williams and Wilkins, 1968.

Yanagida, E. H. Cross-cultural considerations in the application of assertion training: A brief note. *Psychology of Women Quarterly,* 1979, *3,* 400–402.

Yanagisako, S. Women-centered kin networks in the Seattle Japanese American community. *Asian American women.* Palo Alto: Stanford University, 1976.

Yang, C. K. A Chinese village in early communist transition. Cambridge, Mass.: MIT Press, 1959.

Psychology of the Chicana

Maria Nieto Senour

Aramoni, A. *Psicoanalisis de la dinamica de un pueblo.* Mexico, D.F.: Universidad Nacional Autonoma de Mexico, 1961.

Bardwick, J. M. *Psychology of women: A study of biocultural conflicts.* New York: Harper & Row, 1971.

Bem, S. L. The measurement of psychological androgyny. *Journal of Consulting and Clinical Psychology,* 1974, *42,* 155–162.

Brenneis, C., Brooks, & Roll, Samuel. Ego modalities in the manifest dreams of male and female Chicanos. *Psychiatry,* 1975, *38,* 172–185.

Castañeda, A., Ramirez, M., & Herold, L. *Culturally democratic learning environments: A cognitive styles approach.* Prepared for the Multi-Lingual Assessment Project. Riverside Component, 1972.

Cotera, M. *Profile on the Mexican American woman.* Austin, Tex.: National Educational Laboratory, 1976.

Derbyshire, R. L. Adolescent identity crisis in urban Mexican-Americans in East Los Angeles. In E. B. Brody (Ed.), *Minority group adolescents in the United States.* Baltimore: The Williams and Wilkins Co., 1968.

Diaz-Guerrero, R. Neurosis and the Mexican family structure. *American Journal of Psychiatry,* 1955, *112,* 411–417.

Diaz-Guerrero, R. *Psychology of the Mexican: Culture and personality.* Austin, Tex.: University of Texas Press, 1975.

Dyk, R. B., & Witkin, H. A. Family experiences related to the development of differentiation in children. *Child Development,* 1965, *36,* 21–55.

Fabrega, H. J., Rubel, A., & Wallace, C. A. Working class Mexican psychiatric outpatients: Some social and cultural features. *Archives of General Psychiatry,* 1967, *16,* 704–711.

Fabrega, H., Swartz, J. D., & Wallace, C. A. Ethnic differences in psychopathology. I. Clinical correlates under varying conditions. *Archives of General Psychiatry,* 1968, *19,* 218–266. (a)

Fabrega, H., Swartz, J. D., & Wallace, C. A. Ethnic differences in psychopathology. II Specific differences with emphasis on the Mexican American group. *Psychiatric Research,* 1968, *6,* 221–235. (b)

Fabrega, H., & Wallace, C. A. Value identification and psychiatric disability: An analysis involving Americans of Mexican descent. *Behavioral Science,* 1968, *13,* 362–371.

Fisher, R. I. A study of non-intellectual attributes of children in first grade bilingual-bicultural programs. *Journal of Educational Research,* 1974, *67,* 323–328.

Gecas, V. Self-conceptions of migrant settled Mexican-Americans. *Social Science Quarterly,* 1973, *54,* 579–595.

Go, O. *Mexican American acculturation: Its relation to self-report anxiety and attitudes toward counseling and psychotherapy.* Unpublished master's thesis. California State College San Bernardino, 1975.

Gonzalez, F. *El Mexicano, psicologia de su destructividad.* Mexico, D.F.: Editorial Pax-Mexico, S.A., 1959.

Hawley, P. *The state of the art of counseling high school girls.* (Project Report No. 0675 P). The Ford Foundation Faculty Fellowship for Research on Women's Roles in Society, June 1975.

Hernandez, C. A., Haug, M. J., & Wagner, N. N. (Eds.), *Chicanos: Social and psychological perspectives.* St. Louis, Mo.: C. V. Mosby, 1971.

Hishiki, P. C. Self-concepts of sixth grade girls of Mexican-American descent. *California Journal of Educational Research,* 1969, *20,* 56–62.

Kagan, S., Zahn, G. L., & Gealy, J. *Competition and school achievement among Anglo-American and Mexican-American children.* Unpublished manuscript. University of California at Riverside.

Knight, B., & Kagan, S. *Development of altruism, equality, relative gains and rivalry in Anglo-American and Mexican-American children.* Unpublished manuscript. University of California at Riverside.

Jaco, E. G. Social factors in mental disorders in Texas. *Social Problems,* 1957, *4,* 322–328.

Kiev, A. *Transcultural psychiatry.* New York: The Free Press, 1972.

Larkin, R. W. Class, race, sex and preadolescent attitudes. *California Journal of Educational Research,* 1972, *23,* 213–223.

Littlefield, R. P. Self-disclosure among some Negro, White, Mexican American adolescents. *Journal of Counseling Psychology,* 1974, *2,* 133–136.

Madsen, W. Mexican-Americans and Anglo-Americans: A comparative study of mental health in Texas. In S. C. Plog and R. B. Edgerton (Eds.), *Changing perspectives in mental health.* New York: Holt, Rinehart, & Winston, 1969.

Madsen, M. C., & Shapira, A. Cooperative and competitive behavior of urban Afro-Americans, Anglo-Americans, Mexican-Americans, and Mexican village children. *Developmental Psychology,* 1970, *3,* 16–20.

Martinez, J. L., Jr., Martinez, S. R., Olmedo, E. L., & Golman, R. D. The Semantic Differential Technique: A comparison of Chicano and Anglo high school students. *Journal of Cross-Cultural Psychology,* 1976, *7,* 325–333.

Mason, E. P. Comparison of personality characteristics of junior high students from American Indian, Mexican and Caucasian ethnic backgrounds. *Journal of Social Psychology,* 1967, *73,* 145–155.

Mason, E. P. Cross-validation study of personality

characteristics of junior high students from American Indian, Mexican, and Caucasian ethnic backgrounds. *Journal of Social Psychology,* 1969, *77,* 15–24.

Murillo, N. The Mexican American family. In C. A. Hernandez, M. J. Haug, and N. N. Wagner (Eds.), *Chicanos: Social and psychological perspectives.* St. Louis: C. V. Mosby, 1971.

Padilla, A. M., & Ruiz, R. A. *Latino mental health: A review of literature.* National Institute of Mental Health, Washington, D.C.: U.S. Government Printing Office, 1973.

Padilla, A. M., Ruiz, R. A., & Rice, A. *Perception of self and future achievement among children of different ethnic backgrounds.* Unpublished manuscript, 1973.

Ramirez, M., & Price-Williams, D. R. Cognitive styles of children of three ethnic groups in the U.S. *Journal of Cross-Cultural Psychology,* June 1974, *5,* 212–219.

Ramirez, M., Taylor, C., & Petersen, B. Mexican-American cultural membership and adjustment to school. In C. A. Hernandez, M. J. Haug, and N. N. Wagner (Eds.), *Chicanos: Social and Psychological Perspectives.* St. Louis: C. V. Mosby, 1971.

Ramirez, S. *El Mexicano, psicologia de sus motivaciones.* Mexico, D.F.: Editorial Pax-Mexico, S. A., 1959.

Roll, S., & Brenneis, C. Chicano and Anglo dreams of death: A replication. *Journal of Cross-Cultural Psychology,* September 1975, *6,* 377–383.

San Martin, H. Machismo: Latin America's myth-cult of male supremacy. *il por UNESCO Courier,* 1975, *28,* 28–32.

Senour, M. N., & Warren, L. W. Sex and ethnic difference in masculinity, femininity, and androgyny. Paper presented at the meeting of the Western Psychological Association, Los Angeles, April 1976.

Stoker, D. H., & Meadow, A. Cultural differences in child guidance clinic patients. *International Journal of Social Psychiatry,* 1974, *20,* 186–202.

U.S. Bureau of the Census. *1970 Census of population: Subject reports ... Persons of Spanish surname.* Washington, D.C.: U.S. Government Printing Office, 1973.

Werner, N., & Evans, I. M. Perception of prejudice in Mexican-American preschool children. *Perceptual and Motor Skills,* 1968, *27,* 1039–1046.

The Two Worlds of Native Women

Shirley Hill Witt

1. U.S. Department of Health, Education and Welfare (DHEW), *A Study of Selected Socio-Economic Characteristics of Ethnic Minorities Based on the 1970 Census;* Vol. III, *American Indians,* July 1974, pp. 8, 18.

2. American Indian Policy Review Commission (AIRPRC), *Final Report.* Washington: USGPO, 1977, pp. iv, x.

3. William T. Hagan, *American Indians.* Chicago: University of Chicago Press, 1960, p. 3.

4. U.S. DHEW.

5. AIRPRC, pp. 2–6.

6. Hagan, p. 2.

7. Letter to Shirley Hill Witt from James C. Gabbard, Equal Opportunity Officer, U.S. Bureau of Indian Affairs, May 16, 1977.

8. See Table 1.

9. U.S. Department of Labor, Women's Bureau, *Handbook on Women Workers.* Washington: USGPO, 1975, pp. 47–48.

10. Ibid., pp. 47–48.

11. Estelle Fuchs and Robert J. Havighurst, *To Live on This Earth.* New York: Doubleday, 1972, p. 328.

12. James G. Coleman et al., *Equality of Educational Opportunity.* Washington: USGPO, 1966.

13. Fuchs and Havighurst, pp. 125–126.

14. U.S. Department of Labor, Women's Bureau, *Employment Standards Administration Bulletin.* Washington: USGPO, May 1977, p. 3.

15. Ibid.

16. Shirley Hill Witt, "Native Women Today," *Civil Rights Digest,* 6 (Spring 1974), 31.

17. Clara Sue Kidwell, *The Status of Native American Women in Higher Education.* Berkeley, Calif.: University of California, 1976.

18. Ibid., p. 11.

19. Ibid., pp. 12–13.

20. Ibid., p. 13.

21. Ibid.

22. Ibid., p. 14.

23. Ibid., p. 19.

Psychological Oppression

Women as a Minority Group

Helen Mayer Hacker

1. Louis Wirth, "The Problem of Minority

Groups," *The Science of Man in the World Crisis*, ed. by Ralph Linton (1945), p. 347.

2. Kurt Lewin, "Self-Hatred Among Jews," *Contemporary Jewish Record*, IV (1941), 219–232.

3. *Fortune*, September, 1946, p. 5.

4. P. M. Symonds, "Changes in Sex Differences in Problems and Interests of Adolescents with Increasing Age," *Journal of Genetic Psychology*, 50 (1937), pp. 83–89, as referred to by Georgene H. Seward, *Sex and the Social Order* (1946), pp. 237–238.

5. George A. Lundberg, *Foundations of Sociology* (1939), p. 319.

6. Robert S. and Helen Merrell Lynd, *Middletown* (1929), p. 120, and *Middletown in Transition* (1937), p. 176.

7. Joseph Kirk Folsom, *The Family and Democratic Society* (1943), pp. 623–624.

8. Gunnar Myrdal, *An American Dilemma* (1944), pp. 1073–1078.

9. Helen M. Hacker, Toward a Definition of Role Conflict in Modern Women (unpublished manuscript).

10. As furnished by such books as Helene Deutsch, *The Psychology of Women* (1944–1945) and Ferdinand Lundberg and Marynia F. Farnham, *Modern Woman: The Lost Sex* (1947).

11. David Riesman, "The Saving Remnant: An Examination of Character Structure," *Years of the Modern: An American Appraisal*, ed. by John W. Chase (1949), pp. 139–40.

12. Robert E. Park, "Our Racial Frontier on the Pacific," *The Survey Graphic*, 56 (May 1, 1926), pp. 192–196.

13. William Ogburn and Meyer Nimkoff, *Sociology* (2d ed., 1950), p. 187.

14. Howard Becker, *Systematic Sociology on the Basis of The "Beziehungslehre" and "Gebildelehre" of Leopold von Wiese* (1932), pp. 263–268.

15. Kurt Lewin, *Resolving Social Conflicts* (1948), p. 181.

16. Ruth Benedict, "Continuities and Discontinuities in Cultural Conditioning," *Psychiatry*, 1 (1938), pp. 161–167.

17. Georgene H. Seward, *op. cit.*, pp. 239–240.

18. Mirra Komarovsky, "Cultural Contradictions and Sex Roles," *The American Journal of Sociology*, LII (November 1946), 184–189.

19. Arnold Green, "A Re-Examination of the Marginal Man Concept," *Social Forces*, 26 (December 1947), pp. 167–171.

The Sexual Politics of Interpersonal Behavior

Nancy Henley and Jo Freeman

Argyle, M., Lalljee, M., & Cook, M. The effects of visibility on interaction in a dyad. *Human Relations*, 1968, 21:3–17.

Argyle, M., Salter, V., Nicholson, H., Williams, M., & Burgess, P. The communication of inferior and superior attitudes by verbal and non-verbal signals. *British Journal of Social and Clinical Psychology*, 1970, 9:222–31.

Austin, W. M. Some social aspects of paralanguage. *Canadian Journal of Linguistics*, 1965, 11:31–39.

Bart, P. B. Depression in middle-aged women. In V. Gornick and B. K. Moran, eds., *Woman in Sexist Society*. New York: Basic Books, 1971.

Brown, R. *Social psychology*. Glencoe, Ill.: Free Press, 1965.

Brown, R., & Ford, M. Address in American English. *Journal of Abnormal and Social Psychology*, 1961, 62:375–85.

Brown, R., & Gilman, A. The pronouns of power and solidarity. In T. A. Sebeak, ed., *Style in language*. Cambridge, Mass.: M.I.T. Press, 1960.

Chesler, P. *Women and Madness*. New York: Doubleday, 1972.

Efran, J. S., & Broughton, A. Effect of expectancies for social approval on visual behavior. *Journal of Personality and Social Psychology*, 1966, 4:103–7.

Ellsworth, P. C., Carlsmith, J. M., & Henson, A. The stare as a stimulus to flight in human subjects: A series of field experiments. *Journal of Personality and Social Psychology*, 1972, 21:302–11.

Exline, R. Explorations in the process of person perception: Visual interaction in relation to competition, sex, and need for affiliation. *Journal of Personality*, 1963, 31:1–20.

Exline, R., Gray, D., & Schuette, D. Visual behavior in a dyad as affected by interview content and sex of respondent. *Journal of Personality and Social Psychology*, 1965, 1:201–9.

Goffman, E. The nature of deference and demeanor. *American Anthropologist*, 1956, 58:473–502. Reprinted in E. Goffman, *Interaction ritual*. New York: Anchor, 1967, pp. 47–95.

Goldberg, S., & Lewis, M. Play behavior in the

year-old infant: Early sex differences. *Child Development*, 1969, 40:21–31.

Henley, N. The politics of touch. American Psychological Association, 1970. In P. Brown, ed., *Radical psychology*. New York: Harper & Row, 1973.

Hutt, C., & Ounsted, C. The biological significance of gaze aversion with particular reference to the syndrome of infantile autism. *Behavioral Science*, 1966, 11:346–56.

Jourard, S. M. An exploratory study of body accessibility. *British Journal of Social and Clinical Psychology*, 1966, 5:221–31.

Jourard, S. M., & Lasakow, P. Some factors in self-disclosure. *Journal of Abnormal and Social Psychology*, 1958, 56:91–98.

Jourard, S. M., & Rubin, J. E. Self-disclosure and touching: A study of two modes of interpersonal encounter and their interrelation. *Journal of Humanistic Psychology*, 1968, 8:39–48.

Key, M. R. Linguistic behavior of male and female. *Linguistics*, 1972, 88:15–31.

Lakoff, R. Language and woman's place. *Language in Society*, 1973, 2, 1:45–79.

Lewis, M. Parents and children: Sex-Role development. *School Review*, 1972, 80:229–40.

O'Connor, L. Male dominance: The nitty gritty of oppression. *It Ain't Me Babe*, 1970, 1:9.

O'Neill, W. L. *Everyone was brave: The rise and fall of feminism*. Chicago: Quadrangle, 1969.

Ross, E. A. *Principles of sociology*. New York: Century, 1921.

Rubin, Z. Measurement of romantic love. *Journal of Personality and Social Psychology*, 1970, 16:265–73.

Slobin, D. I., Miller, S. H., & Porter, L. W. Forms of address and social relations in a business organization. *Journal of Personality and Social Psychology*, 1968, 8:289–93.

Sommer, R. *Personal space*. Englewood Cliffs, N.J.: Prentice-Hall, 1969.

Tinbergen, N. Comparative study of the behavior of gulls: A progress report. *Behavior*, 1959, 15:1–70.

Waller, W. W., & Hill, R. *The family: A dynamic interpretation*. New York: Dryden, 1951.

Willis, F. N., Jr. Initial speaking distance as a function of the speakers' relationship. *Psychonomic Science*, 1966, 5:221–22.

Zimmerman, D., and West, C. Sex roles, interruptions and silences in conversation. In B. Thorne and N. Henley, eds., *Language and Sex*. Rowley, Mass.: Newburg House, 1975.

Violence Against Women: A Feminist-Psychological Analysis

Marjorie Whittaker Leidig

Amir, M. *Forcible Patterns of Rape*. Chicago: University of Chicago Press, 1971.

Armstrong, L. *Kiss Daddy Goodnight: A Speak-out On Incest*. New York: Hawthorne Publishers, 1978.

Belote, B. *Sexual Intimacy between Female Clients and Male Psychotherapists: Masochistic Sabotage*. Unpublished doctoral dissertation. California School of Professional Psychology, 1974.

Bernard, J. *The Future of Marriage*. New York: World Publishing Co., 1972.

Brodsky, S. Sexual Assault: Perspectives on Prevention and Assailants. In M. Walker & S. Brodsky (Eds.) *Sexual Assault*. Lexington, Mass.: D.C. Heath & Co., 1976, pp. 1–8. (a)

Brodsky, S. Prevention of Rape: Deterrence by the Potential Victim. In M. Walker & S. Brodsky (Eds.) *Sexual Assault*. Lexington, Mass.: D.C. Heath & Co., 1976, pp. 91–98. (b)

Bromberg, W. *Crime and the Mind*. Philadelphia: Lippincott Press, 1965.

Broverman, I., Vogel S., Broverman, D., Clarkson, F., Rosenkrantz, P. Sex role stereotypes: A current appraisal. *Journal of Social Issues*, 1972, *28*, pp. 59–78.

Brownmiller, S. *Against our Will*. New York: Simon & Schuster, 1976.

Bryson, R., Bryson, J., Licht, M. & Licht, B. The professional pair: husband and wife psychologists. *American Psychologist*, 1976, *31*, pp. 10–16.

Burgess, A. & Holstrom, L. *Rape: Victims of Crisis*. Bowie, Md.: Robert J. Brady Co., 1974.

Butler, S. *Conspiracy of Silence: The Trauma of Incest*. San Francisco: New Glide Publications, 1978.

Carey, S. Sexual Politics in Business. Unpublished paper, distributed by Working Women's Institute, New York, 1977.

Chapman, J. & Gates, M. *The Victimization of Women*. Beverly Hills: Sage Publications, 1978.

Chappell, D. Forcible Rape and the Criminal Justice System: Surveying Present Practices and Projecting Future Trends. In M. Walker & S. Brodsky (Eds.) *Sexual Assault*. Lexington,

Mass.: D.C. Heath & Co., 1976, pp. 9–22.

Chesler, P. *Women and Madness.* New York: Doubleday & Co., 1972.

Clark, L. & Lewis, D. *Rape: The Price of Coercive Sexuality.* Toronto, Canada: The Women's Press, 1977.

Connell, N. & Wilson, C. *Rape: The First Sourcebook for Women.* New York: New American Library, 1974.

Davidson, T. *Conjugal Crime.* New York: Hawthorne Books Inc., 1978.

de Beauvoir, S. *The Second Sex.* New York: Knopf Books, 1953.

Denver District Attorney, Personal communication, 1977.

Diamond, I. Pornography and Repression: A Reconsideration. *Signs,* 1980, *5,* 686–701.

Evans, H. & Leidig, M. *Noxious Sexual Experiences for Women.* Unpublished, 1977.

Evans, L. Sexual Harassment: Women's Hidden Occupational Hazard. In J. Chapman & M. Gates (Eds.) *The Victimization of Women.* Beverly Hills: Sage Publications, 1978.

Farley, L. *Sexual Shakedown: The Sexual Harassment of Women on the Job.* New York: McGraw-Hill Book Co., 1978.

Flick, D. *Historical Precedents for Current Attitudes Regarding Violence Against Women.* Panel presentation chaired by M. Leidig: Violence Against Women, American Psychological Association, Toronto, 1978.

Freeman, L. & Roy, J. *Betrayal.* New York: Stein & Day, 1976.

Freud, S. *The Origins of Psychoanalysis: Letters to Wilhelm Fliess, Drafts & Notes: 1887–1902.* New York: Basic Books, 1954, p. 215.

Frieze, I. "Causes and Consequences of Marital Rape." Paper presented at Division 35, Open Symposium, APA meeting, Montreal, 1980.

Frieze, I. Parsons, J., Johnson, P., Ruble, D., Zellman, G. *Women and Sex Roles.* New York: W. W. Norton & Co., 1978.

Gager, N. & Schurr, C. *Sexual Assault: Confronting Rape in America.* New York: Grosset & Dunlap, 1976.

Gates, M. Introduction. In J. Chapman & M. Gates (Eds.) *The Victimization of Women.* Beverly Hills: Sage Publications, 1978.

Gebhard, P. H., Gagnon, J. H., Pomeroy, W. B., Christienson, C. V. Sexual Aggression against Adult Females. In D. R. Cressy & D. A. Ward (Eds.) *Delinquent Crime and Social Process.* New York: Harper & Row, 1969, pp. 1049–1073.

Gelles, R. *The Violent Home.* Beverly Hills: Sage Publications, 1974.

Gillespie, D. Who has the power? The Marital Struggle. *Journal of Marriage and the Family,* 1971, *33,* 445–458.

Greer, G. *The Female Eunuch.* New York: McGraw-Hill, 1970.

Henley, N. *Body Politics.* Englewood Cliffs, New Jersey: Prentice-Hall Inc., 1977.

Herman, J. & Hirschman, L. Father-Daughter Incest. *Signs,* 1977, *3,* pp. 735–756.

Holmstrom, L. *The Two-Career Family.* Cambridge, Mass.: Schenckman, 1972.

Holroyd, J. & Brodsky, A. Psychologists' attitudes and practices regarding erotic and non-erotic physical contact with patients. *American Psychologist,* 1977, *32,* pp. 843–849.

Hursch, C. *The Trouble with Rape.* Chicago: Nelson-Hall, Inc., 1977.

James, J. The Prostitute as Victim. In J. Chapman & M. Gates (Eds.) *The Victimization of Women.* Beverly Hills: Sage Publications, 1978.

Kempe, H. & Helfer, R. *The Battered Child.* Chicago: University of Chicago Press, 1968.

Leidig, M. *Characteristics of Rape Victims at Denver General Hospital.* Unpublished manuscript, 1977.

Leidig, M. & Evans, H. "Noxious Sexual Experience." Questionnaire. Unpublished research, 1976.

Maccoby, E. & Jacklin, C. *The Psychology of Sex Differences.* Stanford: Stanford University Press, 1974.

MacFarlane, K. Sexual Abuse of Children. In J. Chapman & M. Gates (Eds.) *The Victimization of Women.* Beverly Hills: Sage Publications, 1978.

Martin, D. *Battered Wives.* San Francisco: Glide Publications, 1976.

Masters, W. & Johnson, V. *Human Sexual Response.* Boston: Little Brown & Co., 1966.

McArthur, L. Z. & Resko, B. G. The portrayal of men and women in American T. V. commercials. *Journal of Social Psychology,* 1975, *97,* 209–220.

Medea, A. & Thompson, K. *Against Rape.* New York: Farrar, Straus, & Giroux, 1974.

Meiselman, K. *Incest.* San Francisco: Jossey-Bass Publishers, 1978.

Miller, J. Sex roles in T.V. cartoons. *School Health Review*, 1974, *5*, 35–37.

Millett, K. *Sexual Politics*. New York: Doubleday, 1969.

Mosher, E. H. Portrayal of women in drug advertising: A medical betrayal. *Journal of Drug Issues*, 1976, *6*, 72–78.

Pacht, A. The Rapist in Treatment: Professional Myths and Psychological Realities. In M. Walker & S. Brodsky (Eds.) *Sexual Assault*. Lexington, Mass.: D. C. Heath & Co., 1976.

Pizzey, E. *Scream Quietly or the Neighbors will Hear*. Short Hills, New Jersey: Ridley Enslow Publishers, 1977. American Edition. English Edition, 1974.

Roy, M. *Battered Women*. New York: Van Nostrand Reinhold Co., 1977.

Rush, F. The Sexual Abuse of Children: A Feminist Point of View. In N. Connell & C. Wilson (Eds.) *Rape: The First Sourcebook for Women*. New York: New American Library, 1974.

Rush, F. *The Best-Kept Secret: Sexual Abuse of Children*. Englewood Cliffs: Prentice-Hall, 1980.

Russell, D. *Politics of Rape: The Victim's Perspective*. New York: Stein & Day, 1975.

Russell, D. Keynote speech, Sexual Violence Conference, Denver, Col., May 17, 1978.

Ryan, W. *Blaming the Victim*. New York: Vintage Books, 1972.

San Francisco Conference on Pornography. Sponsored by Women Against Violence in Pornography & Media, 1978.

Schultz, L. *Rape Victimology*. Springfield, Ill.: Charles C. Thomas, 1976.

Schram, D. Rape. In J. Chapman & M. Gates (Eds.) *The Victimization of Women*. Beverly Hills: Sage Publications, 1978.

Sherfey, M. *The Nature and Evolution of Female Sexuality*. New York: Vintage Books, 1973.

Smith, L. C. *Women: Target of the mood-altering drug industry*. Sociological Research Symposium IV, 1974, 901–911.

Steinmetz, S. & Straus, M. *Violence in the Family*. New York: Harper & Row, 1974.

Stemple, D. and Tyler, J. E. Sexism in advertising. *The American Journal of Psychoanalysis*, 1974, *34*, 271–273.

Sternglanz, S. H. & Serbin, L. A. Sex role stereotyping in children's television programs. *Developmental Psychology*, 1974, *10*, 710–715.

Walker, L. *The Battered Woman*. New York: Harper & Row, 1979.

Walker, L. Principal Investigator, Battered Women Syndrome Study, Funded by National Institute of Mental Health, 1978–1980.

Walker, M. & Brodsky, S. *Sexual Assault*. Lexington, Mass.: D. C. Heath & Co., 1976.

West, D. J. Clinical Types Among Sexual Offenders. In R. Slovenko (Ed.) *Sexual Behavior and the Law*. Springfield, Ill.: Charles C. Thomas, 1965, p. 250.

Working Women's Institute, Preliminary Survey, New York, 1975.

Father-Daughter Incest

Judith Herman and Lisa Hirschman

The authors gratefully acknowledge the contributions of the incest victims themselves and of the therapists who shared their experience with us. For reasons of confidentiality, we cannot thank them by name.

1. Claude Levi-Strauss, *The Elementary Structures of Kinship* (Boston: Beacon Press, 1969), p. 481; Margaret Mead, "Incest," in *International Encyclopedia of the Social Sciences*, ed. David L. Sills (New York: Crowell, Collier & Macmillan, 1968).
2. Herbert Maisch. *Incest* (London: Andre Deutsch, 1973), p. 69.
3. Vincent De Francis, ed., *Sexual Abuse of Children* (Denver: Children's Division of the American Humane Association, 1967).
4. Alfred Kinsey, W. B. Pomeroy, C. E. Martin, and P. Gebhard, *Sexual Behavior in the Human Female* (Philadelphia: Saunders & Co., 1953), pp. 116–22.
5. S. Kirson Weinberg, *Incest Behavior* (New York: Citadel Press, 1955).
6. See n. 2 above.
7. De Francis.
8. Alfred C. Kinsey, W. B. Pomeroy, and Clyde Martin, *Sexual Behavior in the Human Male* (Philadelphia: Saunders & Co., 1948), pp. 167, 558.
9. Freud, *The Origins of Psychoanalysis: Letters to Wilhelm Fliess, Drafts and Notes: 1887–1902* (New York: Basic Books, 1954), p. 215.
10. Joseph Peters, "Letter to the Editor," *New York Times Book Review* (November 16, 1975).

11. L. Bender and A. Blau, "The Reaction of Children to Sexual Relations with Adults," *American Journal of Orthopsychiatry* 7 (1937): 500–518.

12. N. Lukianowitz, "Incest," *British Journal of Psychiatry* 120 (1972): 301–13.

13. Yokoguchi, "Children Not Severely Damaged by Incest with a Parent," *Journal of the American Academy of Child Psychiatry* 5 (1966): 111–24; J. B. Weiner, "Father-Daughter Incest," *Psychiatric Quarterly* 36 (1962): 1132–38.

14. P. Sloane and E. Karpinski, "Effects of Incest on the Participants," *American Journal of Orthopsychiatry* 12 (1942): 666–73.

15. I. Kaufman, A. Peck, and L. Tagiuri, "The Family Constellation and Overt Incestuous Relations between Father and Daughter," *American Journal of Orthopsychiatry* 24 (1954): 266–79.

16. J. Benward and J. Densen-Gerber, *Incest as a Causative Factor in Anti-social Behavior: An Exploratory Study* (New York: Odyssey Institute, 1975).

17. Weinberg.

18. Juliet Mitchell, *Psychoanalysis and Feminism* (New York: Pantheon Books, 1974).

19. Freud, *Three Essays on the Theory of Sexuality* (New York: Avon Books, 1962).

20. Freud, "Some Psychical Consequences of the Anatomical Distinction between the Sexes" (1925), "Female Sexuality" (1931), and "Femininity" (1933), all reprinted in *Women and Analysis,* ed. Jean Strouse (New York: Viking Press, 1974).

21. Phyllis Chesler, "Rape and Psychotherapy," in *Rape: The First Sourcebook for Women,* ed. Noreen Connell and Cassandra Wilson (New York: New American Library, 1974), p. 76.

22. Maisch, p. 140.

23. Kinsey et al. (n. 4 above), p. 121.

24. Maisch.

25. Kaufman et al., p. 270.

26. S. Brownmiller, *Against Our Will: Men, Women and Rape* (New York: Simon & Schuster, 1975), p. 281.

27. Weinberg, pp. 151–52.

28. H. Giarretto, "Humanistic Treatment of Father-Daughter Incest," in *Child Abuse and Neglect—the Family and the Community,* ed. R. E. Helfer and C. H. Kemp (Cambridge, Mass.: Ballinger Publishing Co., 1976).

29. R. Stein, *Incest and Human Love: The Betrayal of the Soul in Psychotherapy* (New York: Third Press, 1973), pp. 45–46.

30. Shulamith Firestone, *The Dialectic of Sex: The Case for Feminist Revolution* (New York: Bantam Books, 1970); Florence Rush, "The Sexual Abuse of Children: A Feminist Point of View," in Connell and Wilson.

Relationships: Sexuality and Intimacy

Oedipal Asymmetries and Heterosexual Knots

Nancy Chodorow

I am grateful for the exceedingly helpful comments of Barbara Easton and Lillian Rubin on an earlier draft of this paper. Thanks also to Arlie Hochschild and Zick Rubin for allowing me to cite their unpublished papers.

Balint, Alice. 1939. "Love for the mother and mother-love." Pp. 91–108 in Michael Balint, Primary Love and Psychoanalytic Technique. [1965] New York: Liveright.

Balint, Michael. 1936. "Eros and Aphrodite." Pp. 59–73 in Primary Love and Psychoanalytic Technique. [1965] New York: Liveright.

Baum, Martha. 1971. "Love, marriage and the division of labor." Sociological Inquiry 41(1): 107–117.

Berger, Peter L. and Hansfried Kellner. 1974. "Marriage and the construction of reality." Pp. 157–174 in Rose L. Coser (ed.), The Family (Second Edition). New York: St. Martin's Press.

Bernard, Jessie. 1972. The Future of Marriage. New York: Bantam Books.

Bibring, Grete. 1953. "On the 'passing of the Oedipus complex' in a matriarchal family setting." Pp. 278–284 in Rudolph M. Loewenstein (ed.), Drives, Affects and Behavior. New York: International Universities Press.

Blos, Peter. 1957. "Preoedipal factors in the etiology of female delinquency." Psychoanalytic Study of the Child, XIV: 113–121.

———. 1962. On Adolescence. N. Y.: Free Press.

Booth, Alan. 1972. "Sex and social participation." American Sociological Review 37:183–193.

Bott, Elizabeth. 1957. Family and Social Network. London: Tavistock Publications.

Brunswick, Ruth Mack. 1940. "The preoedipal phase of the libido development." Pp. 231–253 in Robert Fliess (ed.), The Psychoanalytic Reader. [1969] New York: International Universities Press.

Chasseguet-Smirgel, Janine. 1964. "Feminine guilt and the Oedipus complex." Pp. 94–134 in Female Sexuality. [1971] Ann Arbor: The University of Michigan Press.

Chodorow, Nancy. 1971. "Being and doing: a cross-cultural examination of the socialization of males and females." Pp. 173–197 in Vivian Gornick and Barbara K. Moran (eds.), Woman in Sexist Society. New York: Basic Books.

———. 1974. "Family structure and feminine personality." Pp. 43–66 in Michelle Z. Rosaldo and Louise Lamphere (eds.), Woman, Culture and Society. Stanford: Stanford University Press.

———. 1978. The Reproduction of Mothering. Berkeley: University of California Press.

Deutsch, Helene. 1932. "On female homosexuality." Pp. 208–230 in Robert Fliess (ed.), The Psychoanalytic Reader. [1969] New York: International Universities Press.

———. 1944. Psychology of Women. Vol. 1. New York: Grune and Stratton.

Durkheim, Emile. 1897. Suicide. [1951] New York: The Free Press.

First, Elsa. 1974. "Review of Juliet Mitchell, Psychoanalysis and Feminism." New York Times May 19.

Freedman, David. 1961. "On women who hate their husbands." Pp. 221–237 in Hendrik Ruitenbeek (ed.), Psychoanalysis and Female Sexuality. [1966] New Haven: College and University Press Services.

Freud, Sigmund. 1908. " 'Civilized' sexual morality and modern nervousness." P. 179 in The Standard Edition of the Complete Psychological Works, Vol. IX.

———. 1910. "A special choice of object made by men." P. 164 in The Standard Edition of the Complete Psychological Works, Vol. XI.

———. 1917. "Mourning and melancholia." P. 239 in the Standard Edition, Vol. XIV.

———. 1924. "The passing of the Oedipus complex." P. 172 in the Standard Edition, Vol. XIX.

———. 1931. "Female sexuality." P. 223 in the Standard Edition, Vol. XXI.

———. 1933. "Femininity." Pp. 112–135 in New Introductory Lectures on Psychoanalysis. Standard Edition, Vol. XXII.

Gans, Herbert. 1967. The Levittowners. New York: Vintage Books.

Goethals, George W. 1973. "Symbiosis and the life cycle." British Journal of Medical Psychology, 46:91–96.

Grunberger, Bela. 1964. "Outline for a study of narcissism in female sexuality." Pp. 68–83 in Janine Chasseguet-Smirgel (ed.), Female Sexuality [1971] Ann Arbor: The University of Michigan Press.

Hochschild, Arlie Russell. 1975. "Attending to, codifying and managing feelings: sex differences in love." Paper presented to the American Sociological Association Meetings, San Francisco, August 29.

Johnson, Miriam M. 1975a. "Fathers, mothers and sex-typing." Sociological Inquiry 45(1):15–26.

———. 1975b. "Review of Juliet Mitchell, Psychoanalysis and Feminism." Contemporary Sociology, 4(5):489–491.

Kephart, William M. 1967. "Some correlates of romantic love." Journal of Marriage and the Family, 29:470–474.

Komarovsky, Mirra. 1962. Blue-Collar Marriage. New York: Vintage Books, 1967.

———. 1974. "Patterns of self-disclosure of male undergraduates." Journal of Marriage and the Family, 36(4):677–686.

Laing, R. D. 1971. "The family and the 'family.' " Pp. 3–19 in The Politics of the Family. New York: Vintage Books.

Lampl-de Groot, Jeanne. 1927. "The evolution of the Oedipus complex in women." Pp. 180–194 in Robert Fliess (ed.), The Psychoanalytic Reader. [1969] New York: International Universities Press.

Levi-Strauss, Claude. 1949. The Elementary Structures of Kinship. [1969] Boston: Beacon Press.

———. 1956. "The family." Pp. 261–285 in Harry Shapiro (ed.), Man, Culture and Society. London: Oxford University Press.

Long, Elizabeth. 1974. "Review of Juliet Mitchell, Psychoanalysis and Feminism." Telos 20:183–189.

Masters, William H. and Virginia E. Johnson. 1966. Human Sexual Response. Boston: Little, Brown.

Mitchell, Juliet. 1974. Psychoanalysis and Feminism. New York: Pantheon Books.

Mitscherlich, Alexander. 1963. Society without the Father. [1970] New York: Schocken Books.

Ortner, Sherry. 1975. "Oedipal Father, Mother's Brother, and the Penis: Review of Juliet Mitchell's Psychoanalysis and Feminism." Feminist Studies II: (2–3):167–182.

Parsons, Talcott and Robert F. Bales. 1955. Family, Socialization and Interaction Process. New York: The Free Press.

Rosaldo, Michelle Z. and Louise Lamphere (eds.). 1974. Woman, Culture and Society. Stanford: Stanford University Press.

Rubin, Gayle. 1975. "The traffic in women: notes on the 'political economy' of sex." Pp. 157–210 in Rayna R. Reiter (ed.), Toward an Anthropology of Women. New York: Monthly Review Press.

Rubin, Zick. 1975. "Loving and leaving." Unpublished paper.

Slater, Philip. 1968. The Glory of Hera. Boston: Beacon Press.

Weisskopf, Susan Contratto. 1972. "The psychoanalytic theory of female development." Unpublished Ed.D Dissertation, Harvard University.

Whiting, John W. M., Richard Kluckhohn, and Albert Anthony. 1958. "The function of male initiation rites at puberty." Pp. 359–370 in Eleanor E. Maccoby, T. M. Newcomb, and E. L. Hartley (eds.), Readings in Social Psychology. New York: Holt, Rinehart and Winston.

Young, Michael and Peter Willmott. 1957. Family and Kinship in East London. [1966] London: Penguin Books.

Zaretsky, Eli. 1973. "Capitalism, the family and personal life." Socialist Revolution 13–14:69–125 and 15:19–70.

Psychology and the Lesbian

Kristiann Mannion

Adelman, M. R. A comparison of professionally employed lesbians and heterosexual women on the MMPI. Archives of Sexual Behavior, 1977, 6, 193–201.

Armon, V. Some personality variables in overt female homosexuality. Journal of Projective Techniques, 1960, 24, 292–309.

Bell, A. Homosexualities: Their range and character. In J. K. Cole & R. Dienstbier (Eds.), Nebraska Symposium on Motivation (Vol. 21). Lincoln: University of Nebraska Press, 1973.

Bene, E. On the genesis of female homosexuality. British Journal of Psychiatry, 1965, III, 815–821.

Blumstein, P. W. & Schwartz, P. Bisexuality: some social psychological issues. Journal of Social Issues, 1977, 33, 30–45.

Caldwell, M. A. and Peplau, L. A. The Balance of Power in Lesbian Relationships. Preliminary draft, University California, Los Angeles, February, 1979.

Califia, P. Lesbian sexuality. Journal of Homosexuality, 1979, 4, 255–267.

Cardell, M., Finn, S., Marecek, J. Sex-role identity, sex-role behavior, and satisfaction in heterosexual, lesbian, and gay male couples, 1979, in press.

Cass, V. C. Homosexual identity formation: a theoretical model. Journal of Homosexuality, 1979, 4, 219–235.

Clingman, J. & Fowler, M. G. Gender roles and human sexuality. Journal of Personality Assessment, 1976, 40, 276–284.

Cochran, S. D. Romantic relationships: for better or for worse. Meeting of the Western Psychological Association, San Francisco, 1978.

Cotton, W. L. Social and sexual relationships of lesbians. The Journal of Sex Research, 1975, 11, 139–148.

Dana, R. (Review of Rorschach test, No. 6:237). In O. K. Buros (Ed.), Personality tests and reviews. Highland Park, New Jersey: The Gryphon Press, 1970, 1297–1300.

deMonteflores, C. & Schultz, S. Coming out: similarities and differences for lesbians and gay men. Journal of Social Issues, 1978, 34, 59–72.

Diamond, D. L. & Wilsnack, S. C. Alcohol abuse among lesbians: a descriptive study. Journal of Homosexuality, 1978, 4, 123–142.

Ferguson, K. D. & Finkler, D. An involvement and overtness measure for lesbians: its development and relation to anxiety and social Zeitgeist. Archives of Sexual Behavior, 1978, 7, 211–227.

Freedman, M. Homosexuality among women and psychological adjustment. Dissertation Abstracts, 1968, 28, 4294E–4295B. (University Microfilms No. 86–3308).

Freedman M. Homosexuality and psychological functioning. Belmont, California: Brooks/Cole, 1971.

Freedman, M. Far from illness: Homosexuals may be healthier than straights. Psychology Today, 1975, 8, 28–32. (a)

Freedman, M. Personal communication, April 14, 1975. (b)

Freud, S. [Some psychical consequences of the anatomical distinction between the sexes.] In J. Strachey (Ed. and trans.), The standard edition of the complete psychological works of Sigmund Freud (Vol. XIX). London: The Hogarth Press, 1961. (Originally published, 1925.)

Freud, S. [Female sexuality.] In J. Strachey (Ed. and trans.), The standard edition of the complete works of Sigmund Freud (Vol. XXI). London:

The Hogarth Press, 1961. (Originally published, 1931.)

Freud, S. [Femininity.] In J. Strachey (Ed. and trans.), *The standard edition of the complete works of Sigmund Freud* (Vol. XXII). London: The Hogarth Press, 1964. (Originally published, 1933.)

Fromm, E. O., & Elonen, A. S. Projective techniques in a case of female homosexuality. *Journal of Projective Techniques*, 1951, *15*, 185–230.

Furgeri, L. M. The lesbian/feminist movement and social change: female homosexuality, a new consciousness. *Dissertation Abstracts International*, 1977, *37*, 7999.

Green, Richard. Sexual identity of 37 children raised by homosexual or transsexual parents. *American Journal of Psychiatry*, 1978, *135*, 692–697.

Greene, D. M. Women loving women: an exploration into feelings and life experiences. *Dissertation Abstracts International*, 1977, *37*, 3608.

Grygier, T. Psychometric aspects of homosexuality. *Journal of Mental Science*, 1957, *103*, 514–526.

Gundlach, R., & Riess, B. F. Self and sexual identity in the female: A study of female homosexuals. In B. F. Riess (Ed.), *New Directions in Mental Health.* New York: Grune and Stratton, 1968.

Hedblom, J. Dimensions of lesbian sexual experiences. *Archives of Sexual Behavior*, 1973, *2*, 329–341.

Heilbrun, A. B. & Thompson, N. L. Sex-role identity and male and female homosexuality. *Sex-Roles*, 1977, *3*, 65–79.

Hogan, R. A., Fox. A. N., & Kirchner, J. H. Attitudes, opinions, and sexual development of 205 homosexual women. *Journal of Homosexuality*, 1977, *3*, 123–136.

Hopkins, J. Lesbian signs on the Rorschach. *British Journal of Projective Psychology and Personality Study*, 1970, *15*, 7–14.

Hopkins, J. The lesbian personality. *British Journal of Psychiatry*, 1969, *115*, 1433–1436.

Hunter, N. & Polikoff, N. Custody rights of lesbian mothers: legal theory and litigation strategy. *Buffalo Law Review*, 1976, *25*, 691–733.

Jourard, S. *Self disclosure.* New York: Wiley, 1971.

Kaye, H., Berl, S., Clare, J., Eleston, M., Gershwin, B., Gershwin, P., Kogan, L., Torda, C., & Wilbur, B. Homosexuality in women. *Archives of General Psychiatry*, 1967, *17*, 626–634.

Kenyon, F. E. Studies in female homosexuality: Psychological test results. *Journal of Consulting and Clinical Psychology*, 1968, *32*, 510–513. (a)

Kenyon, F. E. Studies in female homosexuality. IV: Social and psychiatric aspects. *British Journal of Psychiatry*, 1968, *114*, 1337–1343. (b)

Kenyon, F. E. Studies in Female homosexuality. V: Sexual development, attitudes and experience. *British Journal of Psychiatry*, 1968, *114*, 1343–1350. (c)

Kenyon, F. E. Studies in female homosexuality. VI: The exclusively homosexual group. *Acta Psychiatrica Scandinavica*, 1968, *44*, 224–37. (d)

Laner, M. R. Permanent partner priorities: gay and straight. *Journal of Homosexuality*, 1977, *3*, 21–39.

Laner, M. R. Media mating II: "personals" advertisements of lesbian women. *Journal of Homosexuality*, 1978, *4*, 41–61.

Laner, M. R. Growing older female: heterosexual and homosexual. *Journal of Homosexuality*, 1979, *4*, 267–275.

Lee, J. A. Going public: a study in the sociology of homosexual liberation. *Journal of Homosexuality*, 1977, *3*, 49–78.

Lewin, E. & Lyons, T. A. Lesbian and heterosexual mothers: continuity and difference in family organization. American Psychological Association Convention, New York, 1979.

Loney, J. Family dynamics in homosexual women. *Archives of Sexual Behavior*, 1973, *2*, 343–350.

Lynn, D. *The father: His role in child development*, Monterey, California: Brooks/Cole, 1974.

Martin, D. Concerns of the lesbian parent. Meeting of the Southeastern Psychological Association, Atlanta, Georgia, 1978.

Minnigerode, F. A. & Adelman, M. R. Elderly homosexual women and men: report on a pilot study. *The Family Coordinator*, 1978, October, 451–456.

Nyberg, K. L. Sexual aspirations and sexual behaviors among homosexually behaving males and females: the impact of the gay community. *Journal of Homosexuality*, 1976, *2*, 29–38.

Oberstone, A. K. & Sukoneck, H. Psychological adjustment and lifestyle of single lesbians and single heterosexual women. *Psychology of Women Quarterly*, 1976, *1*, 172–188.

Ohlson, E. L. & Wilson, M. Differentiating female homosexuals by use of the MMPI. *Journal of Sex Research*, 1974, *10*, 308–315.

Pendergrass, V. E. Marriage counseling with lesbian couples. *Psychotherapy: Theory, Research and Practice*, 1975, *12*, 93–96.

Peplau, L. A., Cochran, S., Rook, K., & Padesky, C. Loving women: attachment and autonomy in lesbian relationships. *Journal of Social Issues*, 1978, *34*, 7–27.

Poole, K. A. The etiology of gender identity and the lesbian. *Journal of Social Psychology*, 1972, *87*, 51–57.

Ramsey, J., Latham, J. D., & Lindquist, C. U. Long term same-sex relationships: correlates of adjustment. American Psychological Association Convention, Toronto: Canada, 1978.

Rand, Catherine. Personal communication. University of Cincinnati, Ohio, June, 1979.

Riddle, D. I. & Morin, S. F. Removing the stigma: Data from individuals. *APA Monitor*, November 1977, pp. 16, 28.

Riddle, D. I. & Sang, B. Psychotherapy with lesbians. *Journal of Social Issues*, 1978, *34*, 84–100.

Riess, B. New viewpoints on the female homosexual. In V. Franks & V. Burtle (Eds.), *Women in therapy: New therapies for a changing society*. New York: Brunner/Mazel Publishers, 1974.

Riess, B. F., Safer, J., & Yotive, W. Psychological test data on female homosexuality: A review of the literature. *Journal of Homosexuality*, 1974, *1*, 71–85.

Saghir, M., Robins, E., Walbran, B., & Gentry, K. Homosexuality: IV. Psychiatric disorders and disability in the female homosexual. *American Journal of Psychiatry*, 1970, *127*, 147–154.

Saghir, M., & Robins, E. *Male and female homosexuality: A comprehensive investigation*. Baltimore: Williams and Wilkins, 1973.

Sang, B. E. Lesbian relationships: A struggle towards couple equality. Meeting of the American Psychological Association, San Francisco, 1977.

Schäfer, S. Sexual and social problems of lesbians. *The Journal of Sex Research*, 1976, *12*, 50–69.

Schäfer, S. Sociosexual behavior in male and female homosexuals: a study in sex differences. *Archives of Sexual Behavior*, 1977, *6*, 355–364.

Siegelman, M. Adjustment of homosexual and heterosexual women. *British Journal of Psychiatry*, 1972, *120*, 477–481.

Siegelman, M. Parental background on homosexual and heterosexual women. *British Journal of Psychiatry*, 1974, *124*, 14–21.

Simon, W., & Gagnon, J. H. Femininity in the lesbian community. *Social Problems*, 1967, *15*, 212–221.

Swanson, D., Loomis, S., Lukesh, R., Cronin, R., &

Smith, J. Clinical features of the female homosexual patient: a comparison with the heterosexual patient. *Journal of Nervous and Mental Disease*, 1972, *155*, 119–124.

Thompson, N., McCandless, R., & Strickland, B. Personal adjustment of male and female homosexuals and heterosexuals. *Journal of Abnormal Psychology*, 1971, *78*, 237–240.

Terman, L., & Miles, C. *Sex and personality: studies in masculinity and femininity*. New York: McGraw-Hill, 1936.

Thetford, L. Existing support groups for lesbian mothers. Meeting of the Southeastern Psychological Association, Atlanta, Georgia, 1978.

Tuller, N. R. Couples: the hidden segment of the gay world. *Journal of Homosexuality*, 1978, *3*, 331–343.

Van Cleave, C. Self identification, self identification discrepancy and environmental perspectives of women with a same-sex sexual preference. *Dissertation Abstracts International*, 1978, *38*, 5932–5933.

Wilson, M., & Greene, R. Personality characteristics of female homosexuals. *Psychological Reports*, 1971, *28*, 407–412.

Wolff, C. *Love between women*. New York: Harper and Row, Publishers, 1971.

Zubin, J. Failures of the Rorschach technique. *Journal of Projective Techniques and Personality Assessment*, 1954, *18*, 303–315.

Zubin, J. The non-projective aspects of the Rorschach experiment: I. Introduction. *Journal of Social Psychology*, 1956, *44*, 179–192.

Overview: Sex Roles, Fertility, and the Motherhood Mandate

Nancy Felipe Russo

I would like to thank Georgia Babladelis, Susan Bram, Sharon Dyer, Murray Gendell, Alan Gross, Elaine Hilberman, Gloria Kamenseke, Allen Meyer, Howard Moss, Virginia E. O'Leary, Karen Paige, Joy Stapp, Sandra Tangri, Cheryl Travis, and Barbara Wallston for their assistance in the development of this issue of the *Psychology of Women Quarterly* devoted to sex roles and fertility. A special expression of appreciation goes to Sharon Dyer and Allen Meyer. Without their assistance the issue would have not been possible. Thanks also go to the authors, whose cooperation and patience through the long process that a special issue involves is deeply appreciated.

Allison, J. R. Roles and role conflict of women in infertile couples. *Psychology of Women Quarterly*, 1979, *4*, 97–113.

Beckman, L. J. The relationship between sex roles, fertility, and family size preferences. *Psychology of Women Quarterly*, 1979, *4*, 43–60.

Bernard, J. *The future of motherhood.* New York: Dial Press, 1974.

Dytrych, Z., Matejcek, Z., Schuller, V., David, H. P., & Friedman, H. Children born to women denied abortion. *Family Planning Perspectives*, 1975, *7*, 165–171.

Fein, R. Research on fathering: Social policy and an emergent perspective. *Journal of Social Issues*, 1978, *34*, 122–135.

Fidell, L., Hoffman, D. & Keith-Spiegel, P. Some social implications of sex-choice technology. *Psychology of Women Quarterly*, 1979, *4*, 32–42.

Forssman, H., & Thuwe, I. One-hundred and twenty children born after application for therapeutic abortion refused. *Acta Psychiatrica Scandinavica*, 1966, *42*, 71–88.

Freeman, E. Influence of personality attributes on abortion experiences. *American Journal of Orthopsychiatry*, 1977, *47*, 503–513.

Hare-Mustin, R. T. & Broderick, P. C. The myth of motherhood: a study of attitudes towards motherhood. *Psychology of Women Quarterly*, 1979, *4*, 114–128.

Hollingworth, L. Social devices for compelling women to bear and rear children. *American Journal of Sociology*, 1916, *22*, 19–29.

Houseknecht, S. K. Timing of the decision to remain voluntarily childless: evidence for continuous socialization. *Psychology of Women Quarterly*, 1979, *4*, 81–96.

Kearney, H. R. Feminist challenges to the social structure and sex roles. *Psychology of Women Quarterly*, 1979, *4*, 16–31.

Lincoln, R., Doring-Bradley, B., Lindheim, B. L., & Cotterill, M. A. The court, the congress and the president: Turning back the clock on the pregnant poor. *Family Planning Perspectives*, 1977, *9*, 207–214.

Munson, M. Wanted and unwanted births reported by mothers 15–44 years of age: United States, 1973, *Advance data from vital & health statistics of the National Center for Health Statistics*, August 10, 1977, No. 9.

Odendahl, T., & Smith, L. Women's employment.

Comment, 1978, *11*, 1–2.

Peck, E., & Senderowitz, J. (Eds.). *Pronatalism: The myth of mom and apple pie.* New York: Thomas Y. Crowell Co., 1974.

Planned Parenthood. *Planned births, the future of the family and the quality of American life.* New York: The Alan Guttmacher Institute, 1977.

Russo, N. F. Some observations on the role of personality variables in fertility research. *Conference proceedings: Psychological measurement in the study of population problems.* Institute for Personality Assessment and Research, University of California, Berkeley, 1972, 62–68.

Russo, N. F. Beyond adolescence: Suggested directions for studying female development in the middle and later years. In F. Denmark & J. Sherman (Eds.), *New Directions in research on the psychology of women.* New York: Psychological Dimensions, 1979.

Russo, N. F. The motherhood mandate. *Journal of Social Issues*, 1976, *32*, 143–154.

Russo, N. F., & Brackbill, Y. Population and youth. In J. Fawcett (Ed.), *Psychological perspectives on population.* New York: Basic Books, 1973.

Scales, P. Males and morals: Teenage contraceptive behavior amid the double standard. *The Family Coordinator*, July 1977, 211–222.

Shusterman, L. The psychosocial factors of the abortion experience: A critical review. *Psychology of Women Quarterly*, 1976, *1*, 79–106.

Steinhoff, P., Smith, R., & Diamond, M. The Hawaii pregnancy, birth control, and abortion study: Social psychological aspects. *Conference proceedings: Psychological measurement in the study of population problems.* Institute of Personality Assessment and Research, University of California, Berkeley, 1972, 33–40.

Terhune, K. *A review of the actual and expected consequences of family size.* Calspan report no. DP-5333-6-1, July 31, 1974.

Thornton, A. and Camburn, D. Fertility, sex role attitudes, and labor force participation. *Psychology of Women Quarterly*, 1979, *4*, 61–80.

Tietze, C. Induced Abortion: 1977 Supplement, *Reports of population/family planning*, 1977, *14*, 1–20.

Worchel, S., & Cooper, J. *Understanding social psychology.* Homewood, Ill.: Dorsey Press, 1976.

Women in the Middle Years: A Critique of Research and Theory

Rosalind C. Barnett and Grace K. Baruch

Bailyn, L. Discussant's comments at symposium, *Will the real middle-aged woman please stand up: Toward an understanding of adult development in women.* Presented at the meeting of the Eastern Psychological Association, New York, April, 1976.

Bardwick, J. M. *Middle age and a sense of the future.* Paper presented at the meeting of the American Sociological Association, San Francisco, 1975.

Bernard, J. *The future of marriage.* New York: World-Times, 1972.

Birnbaum, J. A. Life patterns and self-esteem in gifted family-oriented and career-committed women. In M. Mednick, S. Tangri, & L. Hoffman (Eds.), *Women and achievement: Social and motivational analyses.* New York: Wiley, 1975.

Bradburn, N. M. & Caplovitz, D. *Reports on happiness.* Chicago: Aldine, 1965.

Brim, O. G., Jr. Theories of the male mid-life crisis. *The Counseling Psychologist*, 1976, *6*, 2-9.

Brim, O. G., Jr., & Abeles, R. P. Work and personality in the middle years. *Items*, Social Science Research Council, 1975, *29*.

Brown, G. W., Bhrolchain, M. N., & Harris, T. Social class and psychiatric disturbance among women in an urban population. *Sociology*, 1975, *9*, 225-254.

Campbell, A. Subjective measures of well-being. *American Psychologist*, 1976, *31*, 117-124.

Campbell, A., Converse, P. E., & Rodgers, W. L. *The quality of American life.* New York: Russell Sage Foundation, 1976.

Caplan, G. Support systems. In G. Caplan (Ed.), *Support systems and community mental health.* New York: Behavioral Publications, 1974, 1-40.

Coser, R. L., & Rokoff, G. Women in the occupational world: Social disruption and conflict. *Social Problems*, 1970, *18*, 534-541.

Erikson, E. H. Identity and life-cycle. *Psychological Issues*, 1959, No. 1.

Frieze, I. H. Women's expectations for and causal attributions of success and failure. In M. Mednick, S. Tangri, & L. Hoffman (Eds.), *Women and achievement: Social and motivational*
analyses. New York: Wiley, 1975.

Glenn, N. D. The contribution of marriage to the psychological well-being of males and females. *Journal of Marriage and the Family*, 1975, *37*, 594-601.

Gove, W. R., & Tudor, J. F. Adult sex roles and mental illness. *American Journal of Sociology*, 1973, *78*, 812-835.

Gurin, G., Veroff, J., & Feld, S. *Americans view their mental health.* New York: Basic Books, 1960.

Guttentag, M., Salasin, S., Legge, W. W., & Bray, H. *Sex differences in the utilization of publicly supported mental health facilities.* Unpublished manuscript, Harvard University.

Hall, D. T., & Gordon, F. E. Career choices of married women: Effects on conflict, role behavior, and satisfaction. *Journal of Applied Psychology*, 1973, *59*, 47-58.

Kanter, R. M. Women and hierarchies. Paper presented at the meeting of the American Sociological Association, San Francisco, 1975.

Levinson, D. J., Darrow, C. M., Klein, E. B., Levinson, M. H., & McKee, B. Periods in the adult development of men: Ages 18-45. *The Counseling Psychologist*, 1976, *6*, 21-25.

Loevinger, J. The meaning and measurement of ego development. *American Psychologist*, 1966, *21*, 195-206.

Lowenthal, M. F. Psychosocial variations across the adult life course: Frontiers for research and policy. *The Gerontologist*, 1975, *15*, 6-12.

Lowenthal, M. F., Thurnher, M., & Chiriboga, D. *Four stages of life.* San Francisco: Jossey-Bass, 1975.

Maas, H. S., & Kuypers, J. A. *From thirty to seventy.* San Francisco: Jossey-Bass, 1974.

McKinlay, S. M., & Jefferys, M. The menopausal syndrome. *British Journal of Preventive and Social Medicine*, 1974, *28*, 108-115.

Neugarten, B. L. Adult personality: Toward a psychology of the life cycle. In B. L. Neugarten (Ed.), *Middle age and aging.* Chicago: University of Chicago Press, 1968.

Neugarten, B. L., Wood, V., Kraines, R. J., & Loomis, B. Women's attitudes toward the menopause. In B. L. Neugarten (Ed.), *Middle age and aging.* Chicago: University of Chicago Press, 1968.

Parlee, M. Psychological aspects of menstruation, childbirth and menopause: An overview with suggestions for further research. Paper presented at conference *New Directions for Research on Women*, Madison, Wisconsin, 1975.

Radloff, L. Sex differences in depression: The effects of occupation and marital status. *Sex Roles*, 1975, *1*, 249–265.

Rotter, J. B. Generalized expectancies for internal versus external control of reinforcement. *Psychological Monographs: General and Applied*, 1966, *80*, 1–28.

Sears, P. S., & Barbee, A. H. Career and life satisfaction among Terman's gifted women. In J. Stanley, W. George, & C. Solano (Eds.), *The gifted and the creative: Fifty-year perspective*. Baltimore: Johns Hopkins University Press, 1977, in press.

Seligman, M. Depression and learned helplessness. In R. J. Friedman & M. Katz (Eds.), *The psychology of depression: Contemporary theory and research*. Washington, D.C.: Winston, 1974.

Sherman, S. R. Labor-force status of nonmarried women on the threshold of retirement. *Social Security Bulletin*, September, 1974, DHEW Publication No. (SSA), 75–11700.

Van Keep, P. A., & Kellerhals, J. M. The aging woman. *Acta Obstetrica et Gynecologica*, Scandinavica Suppl., 1975, *51*, 17–27.

Warren, R. B. *The work role and problem coping: Sex differentials in the use of helping systems in urban communities*. Paper presented at the meeting of the American Sociological Association, San Francisco, 1975.

Weiner, B., Frieze, I., Kukla, A., Reed, L., Rest, S., & Rosenbaum, R. *Perceiving the causes of success and failure*. New York: General Learning, 1971.

Weiss, R. S., & Samuelson, N. M. Social roles of American women: Their contribution to a sense of usefulness and importance. *Journal of Marriage and Family*, 1958, *20*, 358–366.

Weissman, M. M., & Klerman, G. L. *Sex differences and the epidemiology of depression*. Unpublished manuscript, Yale University.

Mental Illness or Social Problem?

Women as Psychiatric and Psychotherapeutic Patients

Phyllis Chesler

I would like to thank Elizabeth Friedman, Dr. Roger Zimmerman, and Kathy Borkin for their invaluable assistance in phases of the data collection and analysis.

Bart, P. 1971. "The myth of a value free psychotherapy." In Wendell Bell and James May (eds.), *Sociology and the Future*. New York: Russell Sage Foundation.

Bettelheim, B. 1965. "The commitment required of a woman entering a scientific profession in present day American society." In J. Mattfeld and C. Van Aken (eds.), *Woman and the Scientific Professions*. Cambridge, Mass.: MIT Press.

Broverman, I. K. *et al.* 1970. "Sex role stereotypes and clinical judgments of mental health." *Journal of Consulting and Clinical Psychology 34*.

Buhn, A. K., M. Conwell and P. Hurley. 1965. "Survey of private psychiatric practice." *Archives of General Psychiatry 12*.

Dayton, M. A. 1940. *New Facts on Mental Disorders*. Springfield, Ill.: Charles C. Thomas.

Engels, F. 1942. *The Origins of Family, Private Property, and the State*. New York: International Publishers.

Erikson, E. H. 1964. "Inner and outer space: Reflections on womanhood." *Daedalus 93*.

Foucault, M. 1967. *Madness and Civilization*. New York: Mentor Books.

Freud, S. 1953. [Fragment of an analysis of a case of hysteria.] (Dora) In J. Strachey (Ed. and trans.), *The Standard Edition of the Complete Psychological Works of Sigmund Freud 7*. London: Hogarth Press. (Originally published, 1905.)

———. 1957. [On the history of the psychoanalytic movement.] In J. Strachey (Ed. and trans.), *The Standard Edition of the Complete Psychological Works of Sigmund Freud 14*. London: Hogarth Press. (Originally published, 1914.)

———. 1961. [Some psychical consequences of the anatomical distinction between the sexes.] In J. Strachey (Ed. and trans.), *The Standard Edition of the Complete Psychological Works of Sigmund Freud 19*. London: Hogarth Press. (Originally published, 1925.)

———. 1964. [New introductory lectures on psychoanalysis.] In J. Strachey (Ed. and trans.), *The Standard Edition of the Complete Psychological Works of Sigmund Freud 22*. London: Hogarth Press. (Originally published, 1933.)

Gilbert, G. M. 1957. "A survey of 'referral problems in metropolitan child guidance centers'." *Journal of Clinical Psychology 13*.

Goffman, E. 1961. *Asylums*. New York: Doubleday-Anchor.

Gurin, G., J. Veroff and S. Feld. 1960. *Americans*

View Their Mental Health. New York: Basic Books.

Horney, K. 1967. "The flight from womanhood." In H. Kelman (Ed.), *Feminine Psychology.* New York: W. W. Norton. (Originally published, 1926.)

MacFarlane, J. et al. 1954. *A Developmental Study of the Behavior Problems of Normal Children Between Twenty-One Months and Thirteen Years.* Berkeley: University of California Press.

Maltzberg, B. 1959. "Important statistical data about mental illness." In S. Arieti (ed.), *American Handbook of Psychiatry.* New York: Basic Books.

Masters, W. H. and V. E. Johnson. 1970. *Human Sexual Inadequacy.* Boston: Little Brown.

Petersen, D. R. 1961. "Behavior problems of middle childhood." *Journal of Consulting Psychology 25.*

Phillips, D. L. and B. E. Segal. 1969. "Sexual status and psychiatric symptoms." *American Sociological Review 34.*

Phillips, L. 1956. "Cultural versus intrapsychic factors in childhood behavior problem referrals." *Journal of Clinical Psychology 12.*

———. 1969. "A social view of psychopathology." In P. London and D. Rosenhan (eds.), *Abnormal Psychology.* New York: Holt, Rinehart and Winston.

Pollack, E. S., R. W. Redick and C. A. Taube. 1968. "The application of census socioeconomic and familial data to the study of morbidity from mental disorders." *American Journal of Public Health 58.*

Rheingold, J. 1964. *The Fear of Being a Woman.* New York: Grune and Stratton.

Scheff, T. J. 1966. *Being Mentally Ill: A Sociological Theory.* Chicago: Aldine.

Schofield, W. 1963. *Psychotherapy: The Purchase of Friendship.* Englewood Cliffs, N.J.: Prentice-Hall.

Simon, L. J. 1970. "The political unconscious of psychology: Clinical psychology and social change." Unpublished manuscript.

Srole et al. 1962. *Mental Health in the Metropolis: Midtown Manhattan Study.* New York: McGraw-Hill.

Steinem, G. 1970. "Laboratory for love styles." *New York Magazine* (February).

Szasz, T. T. 1961. *The Myth of Mental Illness.* New York: Harper and Row.

Terman, L. M. and L. E. Tyler. 1954. "Psychological sex differences." In L. Carmichael (ed.), *Manual of Child Psychology.* New York: John Wiley and Sons.

U.S. Department of Health, Education and Welfare. 1970. *Selected Symptoms of Psychological Distress.* Washington, D.C.: U.S. Department of Health, Education and Welfare, Public Health Services, and Mental Health Administration.

U.S. Department of Justice. 1970. *Uniform Crime Reports—1969.* Washington D.C.: U.S. Department of Justice.

Zigler, E. and L. Phillips. 1960. "Social effectiveness and symptomatic behaviors." *Journal of Abnormal and Social Psychology 61.*

Masochistic Syndrome, Hysterical Personality, and the Illusion of a Healthy Woman

Betsy Belote

Bardwick, J. 1971. *Psychology of women.* New York: Harper & Row.

Beller, E. K., & Neubauer, P. B. 1963. Sex differences and symptom patterns in early childhood. *Journal of Child Psychiatry* 2: 414–33.

Bergler, E. 1949. *The basic neurosis.* New York: Grune & Stratton.

Bieber, I. 1966. Sadism and masochism. In S. Arieti (ed.), *American handbook of psychiatry* 3. New York: Basic Books.

Bieri, J.; Bradburn, W. M.; & Galinsky, D. M. 1958. Sex differences in perceptual behavior. *Journal of Personality* 26: (1), 1–12.

Brim, O. G.; Glass, D. C.; Lavin, D. E.; & Goodman, N. 1962. *Personality and decision processes.* Stanford: Stanford University Press.

Broverman, I. K.; Broverman, D. M.; Clarkson, F. E.; Rosenkrantz, P. S.; & Vogel, S. R. 1970. Sex-role stereotypes & clinical judgments of mental health. *Journal of Consulting and Clinical Psychology* 34 (1) 1–7.

De Beauvoir, S. 1970. *The second sex.* New York: Bantam.

Deutsch, H. 1930. The significance of masochism in the mental life of women. *International Journal of Psychoanalysis* 11: 48–60.

Deutsch, H. 1944. *The psychology of women: A psychoanalytic interpretation* Vols. 1 & 2. New York: Grune & Stratton.

Diagnostic and statistical manual of mental disorders. Committee on Nomenclature and Statistics, Washington, D.C.: American Psychiatric Association, 1968.

Easser, B. D., & Lesser, S. R. 1965. Hysterical personality: A reevaluation. *Psychoanalytic Quarterly* 34 (3) 390–405.

Freud, S. 1953. [Three essays on the theory of sexuality.] In J. Strachey (Ed. and trans.), *The Standard Edition of the Complete Psychological Works of Sigmund Freud* (Vol. 7). London: Hogarth Press. (Originally published, 1905.)

Freud, S. 1955. [A child is being beaten.] In J. Strachey (Ed. and trans), *The Standard Edition of the Complete Psychological Works of Sigmund Freud* (Vol. 17). London: Hogarth Press. (Originally published, 1919.)

Freud, S. 1957. [Instincts and their vicissitudes.] In J. Strachey (Ed. and trans.), *The Standard Edition of the Complete Psychological Works of Sigmund Freud* (Vol. 14). London: Hogarth Press. (Originally published, 1915.)

Freud, S. 1961. (a) [Libidinal types.] In J. Strachey (Ed. and trans.), *The Standard Edition of the Complete Psychological Works of Sigmund Freud* (Vol. 21). London: Hogarth Press. (Originally published, 1931.)

Freud, S. 1961. (b) [Female sexuality.] In J. Strachey (Ed. and trans.), *The Standard Edition of the Complete Psychological Works of Sigmund Freud* (Vol. 21). London: Hogarth Press. (Originally published, 1931.)

Horney, K. 1966. *New Ways in Psychoanalysis.* New York: W. W. Norton. (Originally published, 1939.)

Horney, K. 1967. *Feminine Psychology.* (H. Kelman, Ed.) New York: W. W. Norton. (Originally published, 1923–1937.)

Horney, K. 1967. "The problem of feminine masochism." In H. Kelman (Ed.), *Feminine Psychology.* New York: W. W. Norton. (Originally published, 1935.)

Kagan, J. & Moss. H. A. 1962. *Birth to maturity.* New York: John Wiley.

Krafft-Ebing, R. 1937. *Psychopathia sexualis.* New York: Physician and Surgeons Book Co.

Maccoby, E. 1966. *The development of sex differences.* Stanford, Ca.: Stanford University Press.

Marmor, J. 1953. Orality in the hysterical personality. *Journal of the American Psychoanalytic Association,* 1: 656–71.

Martin, P. A. 1971. Dynamic considerations of hysterical psychosis. *American Journal of Psychiatry 128:* 6.

McGuire, C. 1961. Sex role and community variability in test performances. *Journal of Educational Psych. 52.*

Parsons, T. 1955. Family structure and socialization of the child. In T. Parsons & R. F. Bales (eds.), *Family, socialization and interaction process,* Glencoe, Ill.: Free Press.

Rado, S. 1933. Fear of castration in women. *Psychoanalytic Quarterly 2:* 425–75.

Rado, S. 1956. *Psychoanalysis of behavior.* New York: Grune & Stratton.

Reich, W. 1949. *Character analysis.* New York: Farrar, Straus and Giroux.

Reik, T. 1941. *Masochism in modern man.* New York: Farrar & Rinehart.

Sears, R. R.; Whiting, J.; Nowlis, V.; & Sears, P. 1953. Some child rearing antecedents of aggression and dependency in young children. *Genetic Psychology Monographs 47:* 135–234.

Spangler, D. P., & Thomas, C. W. 1962. The effect of age, sex, and physical disability upon manifest needs. *Journal of Consulting Psychology 9:*313–19.

Thompson, C. 1964. *Interpersonal psychoanalysis.* (M. R. Green, Ed.) New York: Basic Books. (Originally published, 1931–1961.)

Vaught, G. M. 1965. The relationship of role identification and ego strength to sex differences in the rod and frame test. *Journal of Personality 33:* 271–83.

Witkin, H. A.; Dyk, R. B.; Faterson, H. F.; Goodenough, D.; & Karp, S. A. 1962. *Psychological differentiation.* New York: Wiley.

Wolowitz, H. M. 1972. Hysterical character and feminine identity. In R. Bardwick (ed.), *Readings on the psychology of women.* New York: Harper & Row.

Sex Differences in Depression in Relation to Learned Susceptibility

Lenore Sawyer Radloff and Sue Cox

Abraham, K. [Notes on the psycho-analytical investigation and treatment of manic-depressive insanity and allied conditions.] In Ernest Jones (Ed.), *Selected Papers of Karl Abraham.* London: Hogarth Press, 1948. (Originally published, 1911.)

Abramson, L. Y., Seligman, M. E. P., Teasdale, J. D. Learned helplessness in humans: Critique and reformulation. *Journal of Abnormal Psychology,* 1978, *87,* 49–74.

Akiskal, H. S., & McKinney, W. T. Jr. Overview of recent research in depression. *Archives of General Psychiatry*, 1975, *32*, 285–305.

Altemeyer, R. A., & Jones, K. Sexual identity, physical attractiveness and seating position as determinants of influence in discussion groups. *Canadian Journal of Behavioural Science*, 1974, *6*, 357–375.

Bart, P. B. Depression in middle-aged women. In V. Gornick & B. K. Moran (Eds.), *Women in sexist society*. New York: Basic Books, 1971, 163–186.

Bart, P. B. *Unalienating abortion, demystifying depression and restoring rape victims*. Paper presented at the meeting of the American Psychiatric Association, Anaheim, 1975.

Beck, A. T. *Depression*. New York: Harper & Row, 1967.

Beck, A. T. *Cognitive therapy and the emotional disorders*. New York: International Universities Press, Inc., 1976.

Bernard, J. *The future of marriage*. New York: Bantam Books, 1974.

Bernard, J. *The future of motherhood*. Baltimore: Penguin, 1975.

Block, J. H. *Another look at sex differentiation in the socialization behaviors of mothers and fathers*. Paper presented at Conference on New Directions for Research on Women, Madison, Wisconsin, May, 1975.

Bowlby J. *Attachment and loss, I: Attachment*. New York: Basic Books, 1969.

Bowlby, J. *Attachment and loss, II: Separation*. New York: Basic Books, 1973.

Brenner, B. Depressed affect as a cause of associated somatic problems. *Psychological Medicine*, 1979, *9*, 737–746.

Brown, G. W., & Harris, T. *Social origins of depression*. New York: The Free Press, 1978.

Campbell, A., Converse, P., & Rogers, W. *The quality of American Life*. New York: The Russell Sage Foundation, 1976.

Chodoff, P. The depressive personality: A critical review. *Archives of General Psychiatry*, 1972, *27*, 666–673.

Clancy, K., & Gove, W. Sex differences in mental illness: An analysis of response bias in self reports. *American Journal of Sociology*, 1974, *80*, 205–216.

Costrich, N., Feinstein, J., Kidder, L., Marecek, J., & Pascale, L. When stereotypes hurt: Three studies of penalties for sex-role reversals. *Journal of Experimental Social Psychology*, 1975, *11*, 520–530.

Feather, N. T., & Raphelson, A. C. Fear of success in Australian and American student groups: Motive or sex role stereotype? *Journal of Personality*, 1974, *42*, 190–201.

Feather, N. T., & Simon, J. G. Reactions to male and female success and failure in sex-linked occupations: Impressions of personality, causal attributions, and perceived likelihood of different consequences. *Journal of Personality and Social Psychology*, 1975, *31*, 20–31.

Freud, S. [Mourning and melancholia.] In J. Strachey (Ed. and trans.), *The Standard Edition of the Complete Psychological Works of Sigmund Freud* (Vol. 14). London: Hogarth Press, 1957. (Originally published, 1917.)

Friedman, R. J., & Katz, M. M. (Eds.) *The psychology of depression: Contemporary theory and research*. Washington, D.C.: Winston, 1974.

Frieze, I. H., Fisher, J., McHugh, M. C., & Valle, V. A. *Attributing the causes of success and failure: Internal and external barriers to achievement in women*. Paper presented at Conference on New Directions for Research on Women, Madison, Wisconsin, May, 1975.

Goldberg, P. A. Are women prejudiced against women? *Transaction*, 1968, *5*, 28–30.

Gove, W. R. The relationship between sex roles, marital status, and mental illness. *Social Forces*, 1972, *51*, 34–44.

Gove, W. R. Sex, marital status and mortality. *American Journal of Sociology*, 1973, *79*, 45–67.

Gove, W. R., & Tudor, J. Adult sex roles and mental illness. *American Journal of Sociology*, 1973, *78*, 812–835.

Holmes, T. H., & Masuda, M. Life change and illness susceptibility. In J. P. Scott and E. C. Senay (Eds.), *Separation and depression: Clinical and research aspects*. Washington, D.C.: AAAS Publication No. 94, 1973, 161–186.

Horner, M. S. *Sex differences in achievement motivation and performance in competitive and non-competitive situations*. Unpublished doctoral dissertation, University of Michigan, 1968.

Latane, B., & Dabbs, J. M. Sex, group size and helping in 3 cities. *Sociometry*, 1975, *38*, 180–194.

Lavach, J. F., & Lanier, H. B. The motive to avoid success in 7th, 8th, 9th, and 10th grade high-achieving girls. *Journal Educational Resources*, 1975, *68*, 216–218.

Lewinsohn, P. M. The behavioral study and treatment of depression. In M. Hersen, M. Eicler, & P. M. Miller, (Eds.), *Progress in Behavioral Modification*. New York: Academic Press, 1975, 19–64.

Maccoby, E. E., & Jacklin, C. N. *The psychology of sex differences*. Stanford: Stanford University Press, 1974.

McLean, P. Therapeutic decision-making in behavioral treatment of depression. In P. O. Davidson (Ed.), *The behavioral management of anxiety, depression and pain*. New York: Brunner/Mazel, 1976, 54–83.

Mendelsohn, M. *Psychoanalytic concepts of depression*. Springfield, Illinois: Chas C. Thomas, 1960.

Paykel, E. Life events and acute depression. In J. P. Scott and E. C. Senay (Eds.), *Separation and depression: Clinical and research aspects*. Washington, D.C.: AAAS Publication No. 94, 1973, 161–186.

Pearlin, L. I., & Lieberman, M. A. Social sources of emotional distress. *Research in community and mental health*. R. Simmons (Ed.), J. A. I. Press, 1977.

Radloff, L. S. Depression and the empty nest. *Sex Roles—A Journal of research*. In press.

Radloff, L. S. Sex differences in depression: The effects of occupation and marital status. *Sex Roles*, 1975, 1, 249–265.

Radloff, L. S. The CES-D scale: A self-report depression scale for research in the general population. *Applied Psychological Measurement*, 1977, 1, 385–401.

Radloff, L. S. Risk factors for depression: What do we learn from them? In M. Guttentag, S. Salasin, & D. Belle (Eds.), *The Mental Health of Women*. New York: Academic Press, 1980.

Radloff, L. S., & Monroe, M. M. Sex differences in helplessness: With implications for depression. In L. S. Hansen, & R. S. Rapoza (Eds.), *Career development and counseling of Women*. Springfield, Illinois: Charles Thomas, 1978, 199–221.

Radloff, L. S., & Rae, D. S. Susceptibility and precipitating factors in depression: Sex differences and similarities. *Journal of Abnormal Psychology*, 1979, 88, 174–181.

Radloff, L. S., & Rae, D. S. Components of the sex difference in depression. R. G. Simmons (Ed.), *Research in Community and Mental Health*, Vol. III, JAI Press. In press.

Rizley, R. Depression and distortion in the attribution of causality. *Journal of Abnormal Psychology*, 1978, 87, 32–48.

Rubin, J. Z., Provenzano, F. J., & Luria, Z. The eye of the beholder: Parents' views on sex of newborns. *American Journal of Orthopsychiatry*, 1974, 44, 512–519.

Scott, J. P., & Senay, E. C. *Separation and depression: Clinical and Research aspects*. AAAS Publication #94, Washington, D.C., 1973.

Seligman, E. P. *Helplessness: On depression, development and death*. San Francisco: W. H. Freeman, 1975.

Sergin, L. A., O'Leary, D. K., Kent, R. N., & Tonick, I. J. A comparison of teacher response to problem and preacademic behavior of boys and girls. *Child Development*, 1973, 44, 796–804.

Silverman, C. *The epidemiology of depression*. Baltimore: The Johns Hopkins Press, 1968.

Spitz, R. A. *The first year of life*. New York: International Universities Press, 1965.

Unger, R. K. Male is greater than female: The socialization of inequality. *The Counseling Psychologist*, 1976, 6, 2–9.

Weissman, M. M., & Klerman, G. Sex differences and the epidemiology of depression. *Archives of General Psychiatry*, 1977, 34, 98–111.

Weissman, M. M., & Paykel, E. S. *The Depressed Woman*. Chicago: The University of Chicago Press, 1974.

Williams, T. A., Katz, M. M., & Shield, J. A. (Eds.), *Recent advances in the Psychobiology of the Depressive Illnesses: Proceedings of a Workshop Sponsored by the Clinical Research Branch Division of Extramural Research Programs, National Institute of Mental Health*. Department of Health, Education and Welfare Publication # (HSM) 70-9053, 1972.

Winchel, R., Fenner, D., & Shaver, P. Impact of Coeducation on "Fear of Success" imagery expressed by male and female high school students. *Journal of Educational Psychology*, 1974, 66, 726–730.

Wolman, C., & Frank, H. The solo woman in a professional peer group. *American Journal of Orthopsychiatry*, 1975, 45, 164–171.

Mental Illness and Psychiatric Treatment Among Women

Walter R. Gove

The research for this paper was supported by NSF Grants #SOC73-05455-AOc and SOC76-15103.

I would like to thank Antonina Gove for reading an earlier draft of this paper.

Abernathy, V. Cultural perspectives on the impact of women's changing roles in psychiatry. *American Journal of Psychiatry*, 1976, *133*, 657–661.

Abramowitz, C. V., & Dokecki, P. The politics of clinical judgment: Early empirical returns. *Psychological Bulletin*, 1977, *84*, 460–476.

Abramowitz, S. I., Roback, H., Schwartz, J., Yasuna, A., Abramowitz, C. V., & Gomes, B. Sex bias in psychotherapy: A failure to confirm. *American Journal of Psychiatry*, 1976, *133*, 706–709.

American Psychiatric Association. *Annual Report, 1967*. Washington, D.C.: U.S. Government Printing Office, 1968.

Angrist, S. The study of sex roles. *Journal of Social Issues*, 1969, *25*, 215–232.

Bagley, M. A preliminary look at female sex role learning and mental illness. Presented at the Annual Meeting of the Southern Sociological Society, Atlanta, Georgia, 1977.

Bernard, J. The paradox of the happy marriage. In V. Gornick & B. Moran (Eds.), *Women in sexist society: Studies in power and powerlessness*. New York: Basic Books, 1971. (a)

Bernard, J. *Women and the public interest*. Chicago: Aldine, 1971. (b)

Blumenthal, M. Sex as a source of heterogeneity in a mental health survey. *Journal of Psychiatric Research*, 1967, *5*, 75–87.

Bohn, A., Gardner, E., Alltop, L., Knatterval, G., & Solomon, M. Admission and prevalence rates for psychiatric facilities in four register areas. *American Journal of Public Health*, 1966, *56*, 2033–2051.

Broverman, I., Broverman, D. M., Clarkson, I. E., Rosenkrantz, P. S., & Vogel, S. R. Sex role stereotypes and clinical judgments of mental health. *Journal of Consulting and Clinical Psychology*, 1970, *34*, 1–7.

Brunetti, P. M. Prevalence des troubles mentaux dans une population rurale du Vaucluse: Donnees nouvelles et recapitulatives. *L'Hygiene Mentale*, 1973, *62*, 1–5.

Chesler, P. Women as psychiatric and psychotherapeutic patients. *Journal of Marriage and the Family*, 1971, *33*, 746–759. (a)

Chesler, P. Patient and patriarch: Women in the psychotherapeutic relationship. In V. Gornick & B. Moran (Eds.), *Women in sexist society: Studies in Power and Powerlessness*. New York: Basic Books, 1971. (b)

Chesler, P. *Women and madness*. New York: Doubleday, 1972.

Clancy, K., & Gove, W. R. Sex differences in respondents' reports of psychiatric symptoms: An analysis of response bias. *American Journal of Sociology*, 1974, *78*, 205–244.

Davidson, C. V., & Abramowitz, S. I. Sex bias in clinical judgment: Later empirical returns. *Psychology of Women Quarterly*, 1980, *4*, 377–395.

Dohrenwend, B. The problem of validity in field studies of psychological disorder. *Journal of Health and Social Behavior*, 1975, *16*, 365–392.

Dorn, H. The incidence and future expectancy of mental disease. *Public Health Reports*, 1938, *53*, 1991–2004.

Dunham, W. *Social theory and mental disease*. Detroit, Mich.: Wayne State University Press, 1959.

Fink, R., Shapiro, S., Goldensohn, S., & Daily, E. The "filter-down" process in psychotherapy in a group medical care program. *Journal of Public Health*, 1969, *59*, 245–257.

Geerken, M., & Gove, W. R. Instrumental activities and family functioning. Mimeographed, 1978.

Gomes, B., & Abramowitz, S. I. Sex-related patient and therapist effects on clinical judgment. *Sex Roles*, 1976, *2*, 1–13.

Gove, W. Sex roles, marital roles, and mental illness. *Social Forces*, 1972, *51*, 34–44. (a)

Gove, W. Sex, marital status, and suicide. *Journal of Health and Social Behavior*, 1972, *13*, 204–213. (b)

Gove, W. Sex, marital status and mortality. *American Journal of Sociology*, 1973, *79*, 45–67.

Gove, W. R. Deviant behavior, social intervention, and labelling theory. In L. Coser & O. Larsen (Eds.), *The uses of controversy in sociology*. New York: Free Press, 1976.

Gove, W. R. Sex differences in mental illness among adult men and women: An evaluation of four questions raised regarding the evidence of the higher rates of women. *Social Science and Medicine*. 1978, *12*, 179–186.

Gove, W. R. Sex differences in the epidemiology of mental disorder. In E. Gomberg & D. Franks (Eds.), *Gender and psychopathology: Sex differences in disordered behavior*. Brunner/ Mazel, 1979. (a)

Gove, W. R. Sex differences in mental illness: Some

evidence on the learned helplessness hypothesis. Mimeographed, 1979. (b)

Gove, W. R. Sex, marital status, and psychiatric treatment: A research note. *Social Forces*, 1979, *58*, 89-93. (c)

Gove, W. R. & Geerken, M. Response bias in surveys of mental health: An empirical investigation. *American Journal of Sociology*, 1977, *82*, 1289-1317. (a)

Gove, W. R., & Geerken, M. The effect of children and employment on the mental health of married men and women. *Social Forces*, 1977, *5*, 66-75. (b)

Gove, W. R., & Herb, T. Stress and mental illness among the young: A comparison of the sexes. *Social Forces*, 1974, *54*, 256-265.

Gove, W., McCorkel, J., Fain, T., & Hughes, M. Response bias in community surveys of mental health: Systematic bias or random noise? *Social Science and Medicine*, 1976, *10*, 497-502.

Gove, W., & Style, C. The role of marriage in American society. Paper presented at the meeting of the National Council on Family Relations, San Diego, Calif., 1977.

Gove, W., & Tudor, J. Adult sex roles and mental illness. *American Journal of Sociology*, 1973, *77*, 812-835.

Gove, W., & Tudor, J. Sex differences in mental illness: A comment on Dohrenwend and Dohrenwend. *American Journal of Sociology*, 1977, *82*, 1327-1336.

Gurin, G., Veroff, J., & Feld, S. *Americans view their mental health.* New York: Basic Books, 1960.

Kazdin, A., & Wilson, G. T. Criteria for evaluating psychotherapy. *Archives of General Psychiatry*, 1978, *35*, 407-416.

Kellner, R. Psychotherapy in psychosomatic disorders. *Archives of General Psychiatry*, 1975, *32*, 1021-1028.

Klein, D., & Davis, J. *Diagnosis and drug treatment of psychiatric disorders.* Baltimore: Williams & Wilkins, 1969.

Kolb, L. *Modern clinical psychiatry* (8th ed.). Philadelphia: Saunders, 1973.

Kramer, M. Psychiatric services and the changing institutional scene, 1950-1985. (Series B, No. 12.) Washington, D. C.: National Institute of Mental Health, 1977.

Kramer, M., Pollack, E., & Redick, R. Studies of the incidence and prevalence of hospitalized mental disorders in the United States: Current status and future goals. In P. Hock & J. Zubin (Eds.), *Comparative epidemiology of the mental disorders.* New York: Grune & Stratton, 1961.

Levin, S., Kamin, L., & Levine, E. Sexism and psychiatry. *American Journal of Orthopsychiatry*, 1974, *44*, 327-336.

Malan, D. The outcome of psychotherapy research: A historical review. *Archives of General Psychiatry*, 1973, *29*, 719-729.

Mander, A., & Rush, A. *Feminism as therapy.* New York: Random House, 1974.

McKee, J., & Sherriffs, A. The differential evaluation of males and females. *Journal of Personality*, 1957, *25*, 356-371.

McKee, J., & Sherriffs, A. Men's and women's beliefs, ideals and self-conceptions. *American Journal of Sociology*, 1959, *64*, 356-363.

Moss, L., & Sachs, N. Feminist therapy. Paper presented at the Annual Meeting of the American Orthopsychiatric Association, Washington, D.C., 1975.

Murphy, J. Psychiatric labeling in cross-cultural perpective. *Science*, 1976, *191*, 1019-1028.

Northby, A. Sex differences in high school scholarship. *School and Society*, 1958, *86*, 63-64.

Pearlin, L. Sex roles and depression. In N. Datan & L. H. Ginsberg (Eds.), *Life span developmental psychology: Normative life crisis.* New York: Academic Press, 1975.

Phillips, D., & Clancy, K. Response biases in field studies of mental illness. *American Sociological Review.* 1970, *35*, 503-515.

Phillips, D., & Clancy, K. Some effects of "social desirability in survey studies." *American Journal of Sociology.* 1972, *77*, 921-940.

Phillips, D., & Segal, B. Sexual status and psychiatric symptoms. *American Sociological Review*, 1969, *34*, 58-72.

Radloff, L. Sex differences in depression: The effects of occupation and marital status. *Sex Roles*, 1975, *1*, 249-265.

Robbins, L. A historical review of the classification of behavior disorders and one current perspective. In L. Eron (Ed.), *The classification of behavior disorders.* Chicago: Aldine, 1966.

Rose, A. The adequacy of women's expectations for adult roles. *Social Forces*, 1951, *30*, 69-77.

Scheff, T. *Being mentally ill: A sociological theory.* Chicago: Aldine, 1966.

Scheff, T. Reply to Chauncey and Gove. *American Sociological Review*, 1975, *40*, 252–257.

Seligman, M. Depression and learned helplessness. In R. Friedman & M. Katz (Eds.), *The psychology of depression: Contemporary theory and research*. Washington, D.C.: Winston and Sons, 1974.

Sherriffs, A., & McKee, J. Qualitative aspects of beliefs about men and women. *Journal of Personality*, 1957, *25*, 450–464.

Smith, M., & Glass, V. Meta-analysis of psychotherapy outcome studies. *American Psychologist*, 1977, *32*, 752–760.

Szalai, A. *The use of time: Daily activities of urban and suburban populations in twelve counties*. The Hague: Houghton, 1972.

Szalai, A. Women's time: Women in light of contemporary time-budget research. *Future*, 1975, October, 385–399.

Taube, C., & Redick, R. Provisional data on patient care episodes in mental health facilities 1977. (Statistical Note #139) Washington, D.C.: National Institute of Mental Health, 1977.

Tudor, W., Tudor, J., & Gove, W. R. The effect of sex role differences on the social control of mental illness. *Journal of Health and Social Behavior*, 1977, *18*, 98–112.

Tudor, W., Tudor, J., & Gove, W. R. The effect of sex role differences on the societal reaction to mental retardation. *Social Forces*, 1979, *57*, 871–886.

Weissman, M., & Klerman, G. Sex differences in the epidemiology of depression. *Archives of General Psychiatry*, 1977, *34*, 98–111.

Zeldow, R. Sex differences in psychiatric education and treatment. *Archives of General Psychiatry*, 1978, *35*, 89–93.

Toward Change and Liberation

Raising Consciousness About Women's Groups: Process and Outcome Research

Alberta J. Nassi and Stephen I. Abramowitz

Abernathy, R. W., Abramowitz, S. I., Roback, H. B., Weitz, L. J., Abramowitz, C. V., & Tittler, B. Impact of a consciousness-raising curriculum on adolescent women. *Psychology of Women Quarterly*, 1977, *2*, 138–148.

Acker, J., & Howard, M. On becoming a feminist. Paper presented at American Sociological Association, New Orleans, 1972.

Allen, P. *Free space: A perspective on the small group in women's liberation*. New York: Times Change Press, 1970.

Aries, E. J. Interaction patterns and themes of male, female and mixed groups. Unpublished doctoral dissertation, Harvard University, 1973.

Barrett, C. J., Berg, P. I., Eaton, E. M., & Pomeroy, E. L. Implications of women's liberation and the future of psychotherapy. *Psychotherapy*, 1974, *11*, 11–15.

Bergin, A. E., & Strupp, H. H. *Changing frontiers in the science of psychotherapy*. Chicago: Aldine-Atherton, 1972.

Brodsky, A. M. The consciousness-raising group as a model for therapy with women. *Psychotherapy*, 1973, *10*, 24–29.

Broverman, I. K., Broverman, D. M., Clarkson, F., Rosenkrantz, P., & Vogel, S. R. Sex-role stereotypes and clinical judgments of mental health. *Journal of Consulting and Clinical Psychology*, 1970, *34*, 1–7.

Burr, R. L. The effects of same-sex and mixed-sex growth groups on measures of self-actualization and verbal behavior of females. Unpublished doctoral dissertation, University of Tennessee, 1974.

Carlson, R. Understanding women: Implications for personality theory and research. *Journal of Social Issues*, 1972, *28*, 17–32.

Cherniss, C. Personality and ideology: A personological study of women's liberation. *Psychiatry*, 1972, *35*, 109–125.

Chesler, P. Patient and patriarch: Women in the psychotherapeutic relationship. In V. Gornick & B. K. Moran (Eds.), *Women in sexist society*. New York: Basic Books, 1971.

Dorn, R. S. The effects of sex role awareness groups on fear of success, verbal task performance, and sex role attitudes of undergraduate women. Unpublished doctoral dissertation, Boston University, 1975.

Eastman, P. C. Consciousness-raising as a resocialization process for women. *Smith College Studies in Social Work*, 1973, *43*, 153–183.

Hanisch, C. The personal is political. In J. Agel (Ed.), *The radical therapist*. New York: Ballantine, 1971.

Hurvitz, N. Psychotherapy as a means of social control. *Journal of Consulting and Clinical Psychology*, 1973, *40*, 232–239.

Kincaid, M. B. Effects of a group consciousness-raising program on the attitudes of adult women. Unpublished doctoral dissertation, Arizona State University, 1973.

Kirsh, B. Consciousness-raising groups as therapy for women. In V. Franks & V. Burtle (Eds.), *Women in therapy*. New York: Brunner/Mazel, 1974.

Kravetz, D. F. Consciousness-raising groups and group psychotherapy: Alternative mental health resources for women. *Psychotherapy*, 1977, *13*, 66–71.

Krug, T. Consciousness-raising in Montreal. On file at the Montreal Ethnographic Data Bank, Sir George Williams University, Montreal, Canada, 1972.

Lieberman, M. A., & Bond, G. R. The problem of being a woman: A survey of 1,700 women in consciousness-raising groups. *Journal of Applied Behavioral Science*, 1976, *12*, 363–380.

Mander, A. V., & Rush, A. K. *Feminism as therapy*. New York: Random House, 1974.

Micossi, A. L. Conversion to women's lib. *Trans-Action*, November-December 1970, pp. 82–90.

Mitchell, J. *Women's estate*. New York: Vintage Books, 1973.

Mitchell, J. *Psychoanalysis and feminism*. New York: Pantheon Books, 1974.

Newton. E., & Walton, S. The personal is political: Consciousness-raising and personal change in the women's liberation movement. In B. G. Schoepf (Chair), *Anthropologists look at the study of women*. Symposium presented at the meeting of the American Anthropological Association, 1971.

Rice, J. K., & Rice, D. G. Implications of the women's liberation movement for psychotherapy. *American Journal of Psychiatry*, 1973, *130*, 191–196.

San Francisco Redstockings. Our politics begin with our feelings. In B. Rozak & T. Rozak (Eds.), *Masculine/feminine: Readings in sexual mythology and the liberation of women*. New York: Harper and Row, 1969.

Sargent, A. G. Consciousness-raising groups: A strategy for sex role liberation. Unpublished doctoral dissertation, University of Massachusetts, 1974.

Sprinthall, N. H., & Erickson, V. L. Learning psychology by doing psychology: Guidance through the curriculum. *Personnel and Guidance Journal*, 1974, *52*, 396–405.

Striegel, Q. B. Self-reported behavioral and attitudinal changes influenced by participation in women's consciousness-raising groups. Unpublished doctoral dissertation, University of Kansas, 1975.

Warren, L. W. The therapeutic status of consciousness-raising groups. *Professional Psychology*, 1976, *7*, 132–140.

White, H. R. Becoming a feminist. Unpublished honors thesis, Douglass College, 1971.

Whiteley, R. M. Women in groups. *Counseling Psychologist*, 1973, *4*, 27–43.

Woman's body, woman's mind: A guide to consciousness-raising. *Ms.*, July 1972, pp. 18, 22–23.

Feminist Psychotherapy: The First Decade

Ellyn Kaschak

Armstrong, L. *Kiss Daddy Goodnight*, New York: Pocket Books, 1978.

American Psychological Association. Task Force on Sex Bias and Sex Role Stereotyping in Psychotherapeutic Practice. *American Psychologist*, 1975, *30*, 1169–1175.

Association for Women in Psychology, Division 35 Committee on Consumer Issues in Psychotherapy. *Women & Therapy*, 1979.

Barbach, L. G. *For Yourself: The Fulfillment of Female Sexuality*, Doubleday, Garden City, & Ca., 1975.

Bart, Depression in middle aged women: Portnoy's mother's complaint. *Trans-Action*, 1970.

Brodsky, A. M. *AWP Feminist Therapist Roster*. Pittsburgh: KNOW Press, 1972.

Brodsky, A. M. The consciousness-raising group as a model for therapy with women. *Psychotherapy: Theory, Research and Practice*, 1973, *10*, 24–29.

Brodsky, A. M. A decade of feminist influence in psychotherapy. *Psychology of Women Quarterly*, Spring, 1980, 4:3, 331–334.

Broverman, I. K., Broverman, D. M., Clarkson, F. E., Rosenkrantz, P. S. & Vogel, S. R., Sex role stereotypes and clinical judgments of mental health. *Journal of Consulting and Clinical Psychology*, 1970, 34:1, 1–7.

Brownmiller, S. *Against Our Will: Men, Women and Rape*, New York: Simon & Schuster, 1975.

Chesler, P. Patient & patriarch: women in the psychotherapeutic relationship. In Gornick, V. and Moran, B. K. (Eds.) *Woman in Sexist Society*. New York: Basic Books, 1971, 363–392.

Chesler, P. *Women and Madness,* New York: Doubleday and Company, 1972.

Chodorow, N. *The Reproduction of Mothering: Psychoanalysis and the Sociology of Gender,* Berkeley: University of California Press, 1978.

Confal, J. *Preventive-therapeutic programs for mothers and adolescent daughters: skills training versus discussion methods.* Unpublished dissertation, The Pennsylvania State University, 1976.

Davidson, T. *Conjugal Crime: Understanding and Changing the Wife Beating Pattern,* New York: Hawthorn Books, 1978.

Fabrikant, B., The psychotherapist and the female patient: perceptions, misperceptions and change. In Franks, V. & Burtle, V. (Eds.), *Women in Therapy,* New York: Brunner/ Mazel, 1974.

Feminist Studies, Toward A Feminist Theory of Motherhood, 4:2, 1978.

Friedman, S. S., Gams, L., Gottlieb, N. & Nessebson, C., *A Woman's Guide to Therapy,* Englewood Cliffs, New Jersey: Prentice-Hall, 1979.

Griffin, S. Rape: The all-American crime. *Ramparts,* 1971.

Herman, J. & Hirschman, L. Father-daughter incest. *Signs,* 1977, 2:4, 735–756.

Kaschak, E. Sociotherapy: an ecological model for therapy with women. *Psychotherapy: Theory, Research & Practice,* 1976, 13:1, 61–63.

Koedt, A. The myth of the vaginal orgasm. *Notes from the Second Year,* 1970.

Leidig, M. W. Feminist therapy. Boulder, Colorado, 1977, unpublished manuscript.

Leidig, M. W. Violence Against Women: a feminist psychological analysis. In S. Cox (Ed.) this Volume, 1981.

Lerman, H. What happens in feminist therapy? In symposium, Feminist Therapy: In Search of a Theory, APA, New Orleans, La., 1974.

Mander, A. V. & Rush, A. K. *Feminism As Therapy.* New York: Random House, 1974.

Marecek, J. Powerlessness & women's psychological disorders. *Voices,* 1976, 12(3), 50–54.

Martin, D. *Battered Wives.* San Francisco, Ca.: Glide Publications, 1976.

Martin, D. and Lyon, P. *Lesbian Woman.* San Francisco: Glide Publications, 1972.

Masters, W. H. & Johnson, V. E. *Human Sexual Response.* Boston: Little, Brown & Co., 1966.

Mondanaro, J. F. Lesbians and therapy. In Rawlings, E. I. & Carter, D. K. *Psychotherapy for Women: Treatment Toward Equality,* Illinois: Charles C Thomas, 1977.

Moore, D. Assertiveness training: a review. In S. Cox, (Ed.), this Volume, 1981.

Murray, S. R. Who is that person? Images and roles of black women. In S. Cox, (Ed.), this Volume, 1981.

Nowacki, C. M. and Poe, C. A. The concept of mental health as related to sex of person perceived. *Journal of Consulting and Clinical Psychology,* 1973, 40(1), 160.

Polk, B. B. Male power and the women's movement. *Journal of Applied Behavioral Science,* 1974, 10:3, 415–431.

Radloff, L. & Monroe, M. K. Sex differences in helplessness—with implications for depression. In Hansen, L. L. & Ragoza, R. D. (Eds.), *Career Developments & Counseling of Women.* Springfield, Illinois: Charles C Thomas, 1978.

Rawlings, E. I. & Carter, D. K. *Psychotherapy for Women: Treatment Toward Equality,* Illinois, Charles C Thomas, 1977.

Russell, D. E. H. *Politics of Rape: The Victim's Perspective,* New York: Stein & Day, 1974.

Senour, M. N. Psychology of the Chicana. In J. L. Martinez (Ed.), *Chicano Psychology.* New York: Academic Press, 1978.

Steinberg, J. A. *Climbing the ladder of success—in high heels.* Unpublished dissertation, the Ohio State University, 1978.

Tennov, D. *Psychotherapy: The Hazardous Cure,* New York: Anchor/Doubleday, 1976.

Thomas, S. A. Theory & practice in feminist therapy. *Social Work,* 1977, 22:6, 447–454.

True, R. H. The profile of Asian American women. In S. Cox (Ed.), this Volume, 1981.

Walker, L. E. *The Battered Woman,* New York: Harper & Row, 1979.

Weisstein, N. Psychology constructs the female. In Gornick, V. and Moran, B. K. (Eds.), *Women In Sexist Society,* New York: Basic Books, 1971, 207–224.

Witt, S. H. The two worlds of Native women. In S. Cox (Ed.), this Volume, 1981.

Assertiveness Training: A Review

Donna M. Moore

Adler, R. B. *Confidence in communication: A guide*

to assertive and social skills. NY: Holt, Rinehart & Winston, 1977.

Agel, J. (Producer), The radical therapist. NY: Ballantine Books, 1971.

Alberti, R. (Ed.) Assertiveness: Innovations, applications, issues. San Luis Obispo: Impact Publishers, 1977.

Alberti, R. & Emmons, M. Your perfect right. San Luis Obispo: Impact Publishers, Third Edition, 1978.

Alberti, R. E., Emmons, M. L., Fodor, I. G., Galassi, J., Galassi, M. D., Garnett, L., Jakubowski, P., & Wolfe, J. L. Principles of ethical practice of assertive behavior training. Assert: The Newsletter of Assertive Behavior, June 1976.

Bem, S. L. & Bem, D. J. Case study of a nonconscious ideology: training the woman to know her place. In D. J. Bem, Beliefs, attitudes, and human affairs. Belmont, Calif.; Brooks/Cole, 1970.

Bloom, L. Z., Coburn, K. & Pearlman, J. The new assertive woman. NY: Delacorte Press, 1975.

Bodner, G. E. The role of assessment in assertion training. Counseling Psychologist, 1975, 5(4), 90–96.

Bower, S. A. & Bower, G. H. Asserting yourself: a practical guide for positive change. Reading, Mass.: Addison-Wesley Publishing Co., 1976.

Broverman, I. K., Broverman, D. M., Clarkson, F. E., Rosenkrantz, P. S. & Vogel, S. R. Sex-role stereotypes and clinical judgments of mental health. Journal of Counseling and Clinical Psychology, 1970, 34, 1–7.

Butler, P. A. Techniques of assertive training in groups. International Journal of Group Psychotherapy, 1976, Spring, 361–371.

Cheek, D. K. Assertive black . . . Puzzled white. San Luis Obispo, Calif.: Impact Publishers, 1976.

Chesler, P. Women and madness. NY: Doubleday, 1972.

Cotler, S. B. Assertion training: A road leading where? Counseling Psychologist, 1975, 5(4), 20–29.

Deaux, K. The Behavior of Women and Men. Monterey, Ca.: Brooks/Cole, 1976.

Eisler, R. M., Miller, P. M. & Hersen, M. Components of assertive behavior. Journal of Clinical Psychology, 1973, 29, 295–99.

Eisler, R. M., Hersen, M., Miller, P. M., and Blanchard, E. B. Situational determinants of assertive behaviors. Journal of Consulting and Clinical Psychology, 1975, 43, 330–40.

El-Shamy, S. E. The effects of time-spacing on outcomes in assertion training for women: The effectiveness of a workshop model. Dissertation Abstracts International, 1977 (February), 37 (8-A), 4861–62.

Fersterheim, H. & Baer, J. Don't say yes when you want to say no. NY: Dell Publishing, 1975.

Fiedler, D. & Beach, L. R. On the decision to be assertive. Technical Report 76-5, October 1976, Department of Psychology, University of Washington, Seattle, Washington. Office of Naval Research Contract N00014-76-C-0193.

Flowers, J. V., & Booraem, C. D. Assertion training: The training of trainers. Counseling Psychologist, 1975, 5(4), 29–36.

Flowers, J. V., Cooper, C. G., & Whiteley, J. M. Approaches to assertion training. Counseling Psychologist, 1975, 5(4), 3–9.

Flowers, J. V. & Goldman, R. D. Assertion training for mental health paraprofessionals. Journal of Counseling Psychology, 1976, 23, 147–50.

Flowers, J. V. & Guerra, J. The use of client coaching in assertion training with large groups. Community Health Journal, 1974, 10, 414–17.

Friedman, P. H. The effects of modeling and role-playing on assertive behavior. In R. D. Rubin, H. Fensterheim, A. A. Lazarus & C. M. Franks (Eds.) Advances in Behavior Therapy, 1969. NY: Academic Press, 1971, pgs. 149–169.

Galassi, J. P., DeLo, J. S., Galassi, M. D. & Bastien, S. The college self expression scale: A measure of assertiveness. Behavior Therapy, 1974, 5, 165–71.

Gormally, J., Hill, C. E., Otis, M., & Rainey, L. A microtraining approach to assertion training. Journal of Counseling Psychology, 1975, 22, 4, 299–303.

Grodner, B. S. Assertiveness and anxiety among Anglo and Chicano psychiatric patients. Dissertation Abstracts International, 1975 (December), 36 (6-B), 3042.

Hall, J. R. & Beil-Warner, D. Ordinal position, family size, and assertiveness. Psychological Reports, 1977, 40, 1083–1088.

Hollandsworth, J. G. & Wall, K. E. Sex differences in assertive behavior: An empirical investigation. Journal of Counseling Psychology, 1977, 24, 217–222.

Jakubowski, P. Assertive behavior and clinical problems of women. Chapter 8 in Rawlings, E. I. and Carter, D. K. *Psychotherapy for Women.* Illinois: Charles C Thomas, 1977, pp. 147–167. (a)

Jakubowski, P. Self-assertion training procedures for women. Chapter 9 in Rawlings, E. I. and Carter, D. K. *Psychotherapy for Women.* Illinois: Charles C Thomas, 1977, pp. 168–190. (b)

Jakubowski, P. & Lange, A. J. *The assertive option: Your rights and responsibilities.* Champaign, Ill.: Research Press, 1978.

Jakubowski-Spector, P. *An introduction to assertive training procedures for women.* American Personnel and Guidance Association, Washington, D. C., 1973.

Kazdin, A. E. Assessment of imagery during covert modeling of assertive behavior. *Journal of Behavior Therapy and Experimental Psychiatry,* 1976, *7,* 213–219.

Kazdin, A. E. Effects of covert modeling, multiple models, and model reinforcement on assertive behavior. *Behavior Therapy,* 1976, *7,* 211–222.

Lange, A. J. & Jakubowski, P. *Responsible assertive behavior: Cognitive/behavioral procedures for trainers.* Champaign, Ill.: Research Press, 1976.

Lazarus, A. A. *Behavior therapy and beyond.* NY: McGraw-Hill, 1971.

Linehan, M., Goldfried, M. R. & Goldfried, A. P. Assertion therapy: Skill training or cognitive restructuring. Paper presented at the Association for the Advancement of Behavior Therapy, San Francisco, 1975.

Mander, A. V. & Rush, A. K. *Feminism as therapy.* NY: Random House, 1974.

McFall, R. M. & Lillesand, D. B. Behavior rehearsal with modeling and coaching in assertion training. *Journal of Abnormal Psychology,* 1971, *77,* 313–23.

McFall, R. M. & Marston, A. R. An experimental investigation of behavior rehearsal in assertive training. *Journal of Abnormal Psychology,* 1970, *76,* 295–303.

McFall, R. M. & Twentyman, C. T. Four experiments on the relative contributions of rehearsal, modeling, and coaching to assertion training. *Journal of Abnormal Psychology,* 1973, *81,* 199–218.

Mehrabian, A. *Nonverbal communication.* Chicago: Aldine/Atherton, 1972.

Moore, D. M. *Assertiveness: An annotated bibliography.* San Luis Obispo: Impact, 1978.

Orenstein, H., Orenstein, E. & Carr, J. E. Assertiveness and anxiety: A correlational study. *Journal of Behavior Therapy and Experimental Psychiatry,* 1975, *6,* 203–207.

Phelps, S. & Austin, N. *The assertive woman.* San Luis Obispo: Impact Publishers, 1975.

Phelps, S. & Austin, N. The assertive woman: Developing an assertive attitude. In Alberti, R. *Assertiveness: Innovations, Applications, Issues.* San Luis Obispo: Impact Publishers, 1977, pp. 151–162.

Radloff, L. S. & Monroe, M. K. Sex differences in helplessness—With implications for depression. In Hansen, L. S. and Rapoza, R. S. (Eds.), *Career development and Counseling of Women.* Springfield, Illinois: Charles C Thomas, 1978, pp. 199–221.

Rathus, S. A. An experimental investigation of assertive training in a group setting. *Journal of Behavioral Therapy and Experimental Psychiatry,* 1972, *3,* 81–86.

Rathus, S. A. A 30-item schedule for assessing assertive behavior. *Behavior Therapy,* 1973, *4,* 398–406.

Rich, A. R. & Schroeder, H. E. Research issues in assertiveness training. *Psychological Bulletin,* 1976, *83,* 1081–1096.

Rimm, D. C. & Masters, J. C. Assertive Training. Chapter 3 in *Behavior Therapy: Techniques and Empirical Findings.* NY: Academic Press, 1974, pp. 81–124.

Rimm, D. C., Snyder, J. J., Depue, R. A., Haanstad, M. J., & Armstrong, D. P. Assertive training versus rehearsal and the importance of making an assertive response. *Behavior Research and Therapy,* 1976, *14,* 315–321.

Rock, D. Interscale variance analysis of three assertiveness measures. *Perceptual and Motor Skills,* 1977, *45,* 246.

Rosenthal, T. L. & Reese, S. L. The effects of covert and overt modeling on assertive behavior. *Behavior Research and Therapy,* 1976, *14,* 463–69.

Salter, A. *Conditioned reflex therapy.* NY: Capricorn Books, 1949.

Schultz, D. P. *A History of Modern Psychology.* NY: Academic Press, 1969.

Schwartz, R. & Gottman, J. Toward a task analysis of assertive behavior. *Journal of Consulting* and *Clinical Psychology*, 1976, *44*, 910-20.

Shelton, J. L. Assertive training: consumer beware. *Personnel and Guidance Journal*, 1977, *55*, 465-468.

Weissman, M. M. & Klerman, G. L. Sex differences and the epidemiology of depression. *Archives of General Psychiatry*, 1977, *34*, 98-111.

Wolfe, J. L. & Fodor, I. G. A cognitive/behavioral approach to modifying assertive behavior in women. *The Counseling Psychologist*, 1975, *3*, 45-52.

Wolfe, J. L. & Fodor, I. G. Modifying assertive behavior in women: A comparison of three approaches. *Behavior Therapy*, 1977, *8*, 567-574.

Wolpe, J. *Psychotherapy by Reciprocal Inhibition*. Stanford: Stanford University Press, 1958.

Wolpe, J. & Lazarus, A. A. Assertive training. In *Behavior therapy techniques: A guide to the treatment of neuroses*. NY: Pergamon Press, 1966, pp. 38-53.

Sex Role Identity, Androgyny, and Sex Role Transcendence: A Sex Role Strain Analysis

Linda Garnets and Joseph H. Pleck

We wish to thank Bettie Arthur, Nancy Conklin, Jere Johnston, Anne Peplau, Paul Suslowitz, and reviewers for this journal for their helpful comments on an earlier draft. The order of authorship was determined randomly. Requests for reprints should be addressed to Joseph H. Pleck, Center for Research on Women, Wellesley College, Wellesley, MA 02181.

Bem, S. L. *Psychology looks at sex roles: Where have all the androgynous people gone?* Paper presented at the U.C.L.A. Symposium on Sex Roles, May, 1972.

Bem, S. L. The measurement of psychological androgyny. *Journal of Consulting and Clinical Psychology*, 1974, *42*, 155-162.

Bem, S. L. On the utility of alternate procedures for assessing psychological androgyny. *Journal of Consulting and Clincal Psychology*, 1977, *45*, 196-205.

Berzins, J. I., & Welling, M. A. The PRF ANDRO Scale: A measure of psychological androgyny derived from the Personality Research Form. Unpublished manuscript, 1974. (Available from J. I. Berzins, Department of Psychology, University of Kentucky, Lexington, Kentucky 40506.)

Berzins, J. I., Welling, M. A., & Wetter, R. E. *Androgynous vs. traditional sex roles and the Interpersonal Behavior Circle*. Paper presented at the Annual Meeting, American Psychological Association, Washington, 1976.

Biller, H. *Father, child and sex role*. Lexington, Massachusetts: Heath Lexington, 1971.

Block, J. H. Conceptions of sex role: Some cross-cultural and longitudinal perspectives. *American Psychologist*, 1973, *28*, 512-516.

Brown, D. G. Masculinity-Femininity development in children. *Journal of Consulting Psychology*, 1957, *21*, 197-202.

Brown, D. G. Sex-role development in a changing culture. *Psychological Bulletin*, 1958, *55*, 232-242.

Hefner, R., Rebecca, M., and Oleshansky, B. Development of sex-role transcendence. *Human Development*, 1975, *18*, 143-156.

Heilbrun, A. B., Jr. Measurement of masculine and feminine sex role identities as independent dimensions. *Journal of Consulting and Clinical Psychology*, 1976, *44* (2), 183-190.

Kelly, J. A., & Worell, L. Parent behaviors related to masculine, feminine, and androgynous sex role orientations. *Journal of Consulting and Clinical Psychology*, 1976, *44* (5), 843-851.

Komarovsky, M. *Dilemmas of masculinity: A study of college youth*. New York: W. W. Norton, 1976, 274 pp.

Lynn, D. B. *Parental and sex role identification*. California: McCutchan Publishing Co., 1969.

Miller, D., & Swanson, G. *Inner conflict and defense*. New York: Henry Holt, 1960.

Rebecca, M., Hefner, R., & Oleshansky, B. A model of sex-role transcendence. *Journal of Social Issues*, 1976, *32* (3), 197-206.

Rogers, C. R. *Client-centered therapy*. Boston: Houghton Mifflin Co., 1951.

Rogers, C. R., & Dymond, R. F. (Eds.) *Psychotherapy and personality change*. Chicago: University of Chicago Press, 1954.

Secor, C. Androgyny: An early reappraisal. *Women's Studies*, 1974, *2*, 161-169.

Spence, J. T., & Helmreich, R. *The psychological dimensions of masculinity and femininity*. Austin: University of Texas Press, 1978.

Spence, J. T., Helmreich, R., & Stapp, J. The Personal Attributes Questionnaire: A measure of sex role stereotypes and masculinity-femininity. *Journal Supplement Abstract Service Catalog of Selected Documents in Psychology*. 1974, 4, 43.

Spence, J. T., Helmreich, R., & Stapp, J. Ratings of self and peers on sex-role attributes and their relation to conceptions of masculinity and femininity. *Journal of Personality and Social Psychology*, 1975, 32, 29–39.

Turner, R. H. *Family interaction*. New York: Wiley, 1970 (Ch. 1 and 2).

Wetter, R. E. Levels of self-esteem associated with four sex role categories. In R. L. Bednar (Chair), *Sex roles: Masculine, feminine, androgynous or none of the above?* Symposium presented at the Annual Meeting, American Psychological Association, Chicago, 1975.

Woods, M. M. The relation of sex role categories to autobiographical factors. In R. L. Bednar (Chair), *Sex roles: Masculine, feminine, androgynous or none of the above?* Symposium presented at the Annual Meeting, American Psychological Association, Chicago, 1975.

Male Power and the Women's Movement: Analysis for Change

Barbara Bovee Polk

De Beauvoir, S. *The second sex*. Trans. by H. M. Parshey. New York: Alfred A. Knopf, 1953; first published in 1949.

De Beauvoir, S. *Force of circumstances*. London: Andre Deutsch, 1965.

Burris, B., in agreement with K. Barry, T. Moon, J. DeLor, J. Parent, and C. Stadelman. *The fourth world manifesto: An angry response to an imperialist venture against the women's liberation movement*. New Haven, Conn.: Advocate Press, 1971.

Chafetz, J. S. *Masculine/feminine or human?* Itasca, Ill.: F. E. Peacock Publishers, 1974.

Chesler, P. *Women and madness*. New York: Doubleday & Company, 1972.

Epstein, C. F. *Woman's place*. Berkeley: University of California Press, 1971.

Firestone, S. *The dialectic of sex*. New York: William Morrow, 1970.

Grimstad, K., & Rennie, S. (Eds.), *The new woman's survival catalogue*. New York: Coward, McCann and Geoghegan/Berkley Publishing Corporation, 1973.

Millett, K. *Sexual politics*. Garden City, L.I., N.Y.: Doubleday & Co., 1970.

Mitchell, J. *Woman's estate*. New York: Random House, 1971.

Reed, E. *Problems of women's liberation: A Marxist approach*. New York: Merit Publishers, 1969.

Reynolds, J. *Rape as social control*. Unpublished paper presented at the Michigan Sociological Association meetings, Detroit, 1971.

Safilios-Rothschild, C. (Ed.), *Toward a sociology of women*. Lexington, Mass.: Xerox College Publishing, 1972.

Solanas, V. *The scum manifesto*. New York: Olympia, 1968.

APPENDIX B: Three Feminist Views

	Conservative	Socialist	Cultural
Goal	to obtain within the existing system political, economic, and social rights and privileges equal to those of men	to facilitate an economic revolution as a necessary precondition for the establishment of equality between the sexes	to abolish sex and class distinctions and to create a new culture based on a more balanced synthesis of Female and Male modes
Power	men are seen as more powerful materially. Women want to share this power equally with men	a few wealthy white men are seen as controlling material power. Redistribution of the material basis of power is sought	men have consolidated a material advantage invariant of economic structure. Matriarchal and Patriarchal modes of power deserve equal respect
Activities	intervenes at the institutional and organizational levels of society where inequities occur. The major current focus is the Equal Rights Amendment. Other activities include, for example, class action lawsuits and abortion law reform	educates people about the relationship of women's oppression and economic class oppression. Women are exploited as workers, earning even less than men, and provide unpaid labor in the basic economic unit, the family. Women are organized around these issues as well as better health care and community child care	educates and raises consciousness regarding current conditions. "The personal is political" refers to this process. Change is sought on many levels, both personal and institutional. Grassroots organization permits actions in diverse areas such as education, media, health care, child care, and building an alternative culture
Change in Sex Roles	there may be "innate" psychological differences between the sexes. Greater flexibility and modernization of sex roles are desired. Men suffer as much as women from the rigidity with which sex roles have been defined	there may or may not be psychologically "innate" sex differences. Some psychological differences may result from the economic structure. The "system" creates men's sexist attitudes, which are difficult to overcome due to their social conditioning and the present economic structure	there are no "innate" psychological sex differences. Sex roles at present are an artifical bipolarization of human psychological traits and are due to inequalities of power. Elimination of sex roles is sought. Though men may gain they have much to lose and would resist were women to support such changes

	Conservative	Socialist	Cultural
Constituency	tends to be middle-class and upper-middle-class professional and career women; some men in the organization	tends to be working class and middle-class, students, workers, women from the (male) Left (SDS, civil rights)	tends to be middle-class, students, workers, women from the (male) Left, women never before involved in politics
Sources and Further Readings	Bird, Caroline, *Born Female*, New York: Pocket Books, 1969; Friedan, Betty, *The Feminine Mystique*, New York: Dell, 1964	Eisenstein, Zillah R. (ed.), *Capitalist Patriarchy and The Case for Socialist Feminism*, New York: Monthly Review Press, 1979; Kuhn, Annette and Wolpe, AnnMarie (eds.), *Feminism and Materialism: Women and Modes of Production*, Boston: Routledge and Kegan Paul, 1978	Firestone, Shulamith, *The Dialectic of Sex*, New York: William Morrow, 1970; Koedt, Anne, Levine, Ellen, and Rapone, Anita (eds.), *Radical Feminism*, New York: Quadrangle, 1973

ACKNOWLEDGMENTS (cont'd)

3, No. 3, Spring 1979, pp. 270–283. © 1979 by Human Sciences Press. Reprinted by permission.

"Male Power and the Women's Movement: Analysis for Change" by Barbara Bovee Polk. Adapted with special permission from *The Journal of Applied Behavioral Science*, originally titled "Male Power and the Women's Movement" by Barbara Bovee Polk, Volume 10, Number 3, pp. 415–431, copyright 1974, NTL Institute. This version of the article first appeared in *Women: A Feminist Perspective*, ed. by Jo Freeman. Reprinted by permission of the author and NTL Institute.

POETRY

Excerpt from "Kathe Kollwitz" by Muriel Rukeyser from *Speed of Darkness*, © 1960, 1961, by Muriel Rukeyser. Reprinted with permission of International Creative Management, agent for the Estate of Muriel Rukeyser.

"Stepping Westward" by Denise Levertov from *The Sorrow Dance*. Copyright © 1966 by Denise Levertov. Reprinted by permission of New Directions and Laurence Pollinger Limited.

"Women" by May Swenson. From *New and Selected Things Taking Place*, by May Swenson. Copyright © 1968 by May Swenson. First appeared in *New American Review #3*. By permission of Little, Brown and Company in association with the Atlantic Monthly Press.

"Relationships" by Mona Van Duyn. From *To See, To Take*, by Mona Van Duyn. Copyright © 1966 by Mona Van Duyn. Reprinted by permission of Atheneum Publishers and the author.

"The Difference" by Grace Wade, from *This Is Women's Work*, copyright 1974 by Panjandrum Books, Los Angeles, CA. Reprinted by permission.

"Nikki-Rosa" from *Black Feeling, Black Talk, Black Judgement*, by Nikki Giovanni. Copyright © 1968, 1970 by Nikki Giovanni. "Poem for a Lady Whose Voice I Like" from *The Women and the Men* by Nikki Giovanni. Copyright © 1970, 1974, 1975 by Nikki Giovanni. By permission of William Morrow and Co.

"Too Much to Require" by Janice Mirikitani. © by Janice Mirikitani. From *Third World Women*, 1972. Reprinted by permission of the author.

"The Black Latin & the Mexican Indian" by Avotcja, from *Third World Women*; © 1972, Third World Communications, San Francisco. Reprinted by permission of the author.

Excerpt from "Snapshots of a Daughter-in-Law" by Adrienne Rich is reprinted from *Snapshots of a Daughter-in-Law, Poems, 1954–1962*, by Adrienne Rich, by permission of W. W. Norton & Company, Inc. and Chatto & Windus, Ltd. Copyright © 1956, 1957, 1958, 1959, 1960, 1961, 1962, 1963, 1967 by Adrienne Rich Conrad.

"The Process of Dissolution" by Susan Efros, from *This Is Women's Work*. Copyright 1974 by Panjandrum Books, Los Angeles, CA. Reprinted by permission of the publisher.

"Women's Laughter" by Marge Piercy first appeared in *Elima 1973*, from the book *To Be Of Use*, by Marge Piercy. Copyright © 1969, 1971, 1973 by Marge Piercy. Reprinted by permission of Doubleday & Company, Inc., Wallace & Sheil Agency, Inc., and the author.

"A Work of Artifice" by Marge Piercy first appeared in *Leviathan*, 1970; excerpt from "Doing It Differently" first appeared in *Anon* 1973, from *To Be of Use*, by Marge Piercy. Copyright © 1969, 1971, 1973 by Marge Piercy. Reprinted by permission of Doubleday & Company, Inc., Wallace & Sheil Agency, Inc., and the author.

Excerpt from "Letter to a Sister Underground," from *Monster: Poems by Robin Morgan*, by Robin Morgan. Copyright © 1972 by Robin Morgan. Reprinted by permission of Random House, Inc. Excerpt from "Lesbian Poem" and "The Invisible Woman" by Robin Morgan. Copyright © 1970 by Robin Morgan. Reprinted from *Monster: Poems by Robin Morgan* by permission of Random House, Inc.

"Rape Poem" by Marge Piercy from *Living in the Open*, by Marge Piercy. Copyright © 1976 by Marge Piercy. Reprinted by permission of Alfred A. Knopf, Inc., Wallace & Sheil Agency, Inc., and the author.

"Housewife" by Anne Sexton. From *All My Pretty Ones*, by Anne Sexton. Copyright © 1961, 1962 by Anne Sexton. Reprinted by permission of the publisher, Houghton Mifflin Company and The Sterling Lord Agency, Inc.

"Ghost of a Chance," "Trying to Talk With a Man," and "Prospective Immigrants Please Note," by Adrienne Rich. Reprinted from *Poems, Selected and New, 1950–1974*, by Adrienne Rich, with the permission of W. W. Norton & Company, Inc. Copyright © 1975, 1973, 1971, 1969, 1966, by W. W. Norton & Company, Inc. Copyright © 1967, 1963, 1962, 1961, 1960, 1959, 1958, 1957, 1956, 1955, 1954, 1953, 1952, 1951 by Adrienne Rich.

"Distances" by Linda Pastan from *A Perfect Circle of Sun*, by Linda Pastan, published by The Swallow Press, copyright 1971 by Linda Pastan. Reprinted with the permission of the Ohio University Press, Athens, the Jean V. Nagger Literary Agency, and the author.

"Woman" by Nikki Giovanni from *Cotton Candy on a Rainy Day*, by Nikki Giovanni. Copyright © 1978 by Nikki Giovanni. By permission of William Morrow & Company.

"You Say I am Mysterious" by Elsa Gidlow reprinted by permission of the author and by Druid Heights Books, publisher of *Makings for Meditation* in which this poem originally appeared.

"Untitled," poem by Nina Sabaroff, which originally appeared in *Amazon Poetry*, Joan Larkin and Elly Bulkin (eds.), published by Out and Out Books, 1975. Reprinted by permission of the author.

"A History of Lesbianism" by Judy Grahn from *The Work of a Common Woman*, by Judy Grahn. © 1980 by St. Martin's Press, Inc. Reprinted by permission of St. Martin's Press, Inc.

"Sappho's Reply" by Rita Mae Brown from *The Hand That Cradles the Rock*, by Rita Mae Brown. Copyright 1971 by New York University Press. Reprinted by permission of the author.

"Notes From the Delivery Room" by Linda Pastan from *A Perfect Circle of Sun*, by Linda Pastan, published by The Swallow Press, copyright 1971 by Linda Pastan. Reprinted with the permission of Ohio University Press, Athens, Linda Pastan, and John Murray (Publishers) Ltd., and the author.

"She Doesn't Want to Bring in the Tides Anymore" by Ruth Whitman. Copyright © 1966 by Ruth Whitman. Reprinted from her volume *The Marriage Wig and Other Poems* by permission of Harcourt Brace Jovanovich, Inc.

"Gesture" by Beverly Dahlen, reprinted from *Out of the*

CONTRIBUTING AUTHORS

Stephen I. Abramowitz is Associate Professor of Psychology and Director of Research in the Department of Psychiatry at the University of California School of Medicine, Davis. His major interests are group psychotherapy and the politics of clinical practice. With Howard B. Roback and Donald S. Strassberg, he has coedited *Group Psychotherapy Research: Commentaries and Readings,* and with C.V. Davidson, "The Woman as Patient," a special issue of the *Psychology of Women Quarterly.*

Rosalind C. Barnett received her Ph.D. in Clinical Psychology from Harvard University and has devoted her professional life to clinical practice and research concerning female development over the life span. Formerly a research associate at the Radcliffe Institute and Brandeis University, Dr. Barnett currently is a research associate at the Wellesley College Center for Research on Women. Together, Dr. Barnett and Grace K. Baruch, Ph.D., have published several academic works, including *The Competent Woman.* Their latest book, written for a general audience with Caryl Rivers, is *Beyond Sugar and Spice.*

Grace K. Baruch is a developmental psychologist specializing in the study of sex roles. She received her Ph.D. in Child Development and Education at Bryn Mawr and has taught at the University of Massachusetts. Formerly a research associate at the Radcliffe Institute and Brandeis University, Dr. Baruch currently is Program Director in Aging and Adult Development at the Wellesley College Center for Research on Women. She is the author of numerous academic articles and has coauthored *The Competent Woman* with Rosalind C. Barnett, Ph.D. Their most recent book, written for a general audience with Caryl Rivers, is *Beyond Sugar and Spice.*

Betsy Belote received her Ph.D. in Clinical Psychology in 1974 from the California School of Professional Psychology. She has worked in the field of mental health for fifteen years and currently is in private practice in San Francisco. She also is a licensed General Building Contractor, with an all-women crew.

Jeanne H. Block is an Adjunct Professor in the Department of Psychology and Research Psychologist at the Institute of Human Development at the University of California, Berkeley. Dr. Block holds an NIMH Research Scientist Award which has supported her research activities for a number of years. For the past 12 years she has been engaged in a collaborative study in which personality and cognitive development is being studied longitudinally from early childhood through late adolescence. Dr. Block's research also includes studies of gender role development, ego development, and parental socialization practices.

Phyllis Chesler received her Ph.D. in Psychology from the New School for Social Research in New York City. Currently she is an Assistant Professor in the Psychology Department at Richmond College of the City University of New York, has a small private practice, and lectures in the U.S. and Canada. She is author of several books including *Women and Madness, About Men,* and *With Child: A Diary of Motherhood,* and coauthor of *Women, Money and Power.*

Nancy Chodorow is an Associate Professor of Sociology at the University of California, Santa Cruz. She is the author of *The Reproduction of Mothering: Psychoanalysis and the Sociology of Gender* and of numerous articles in the areas of psychoanalysis and feminist theory.

Sue Cox received her Ph.D. in Psychology in 1972 from the University of Cincinnati and M.P.H. in 1978 from the University of California, Berkeley. She has taught Psychology of Women courses for several years at City College of San Francisco and San Francisco State University. She is currently engaged in research on depressive states at University of California, San Francisco, and is in private practice in San Francisco.

Jo Freeman is the author of *The Politics of Women's Liberation* (Longman, 1975), winner of an American Political Science Association prize, and editor of *Women: A Feminist Perspective* (Mayfield, 1975, 1979). She holds a Ph.D. in political science from the

University of Chicago (1973) and is currently completing an anthology on *Social Movements of the Sixties and Seventies* while attending New York University School of Law.

Linda Garnets received her doctorate from The University of Michigan in Clinical Psychology in 1978. Her current positions include: Core Faculty member and Director of Clinical and Community Placements at The Wright Institute, Los Angeles; and Research Coordinator of a NIMH-funded research and demonstration project—Southern California Rape Prevention Study Center. She is coediting a forthcoming book entitled: *Androgyny and Sex Role Transcendence: An Interdisciplinary Perspective.*

Walter R. Gove is a Professor of Sociology at Vanderbilt University. He is presently on the editorial boards of *The Journal of Health and Social Behavior, Social Psychological Quarterly, Social Science and Research,* and *Women and Politics.* He has previously been on the editorial boards of *Social Forces* and the *American Journal of Sociology.* Dr. Gove has published extensively in the areas of mental illness, sex roles, and crime. He is the author of a book on labelling theory published by Sage and has books on household crowding, living alone, and mental illness in press.

Helen Mayer Hacker is currently Professor of Sociology at Adelphi University, where she has pioneered courses in gender roles, non-ethnic minorities, sexuality, and most recently, women and religion. She has published a module, *The Social Roles of Men and Women: A Sociological Approach* (1975), contributed chapters entitled "Class and Race Differences in Gender Roles" and "Gender Roles from a Cross-Cultural Perspective" to Lucile Duberman's *Gender and Sex in Society* (1975), and authored a number of widely reprinted articles on gender roles.

Nancy M. Henley is an Associate Professor of Psychology at the University of Lowell, Massachusetts. She has worked with the Association for Women in Psychology and with *State of Mind* (formerly *Radical Therapist/Rough Times*), a journal of alternatives in and to psychology. Her research in recent years has focused on women and communication, both verbal and nonverbal. Dr. Henley's published works include "Politics of Touch" (*Berkeley Journal of Sociology*, 1973), *Body Politics: Power, Sex, and Nonverbal Communication* (1977), and coedited with Barrie Thorne, *Language and Sex: Difference and Dominance* (1975).

Judith Herman is a psychiatrist and a member of the Women's Mental Health Collective in Somerville, Mass., a woman-controlled, nonprofit mental health clinic. She received her medical degree at Harvard Medical School and her psychiatric training at Boston University School of Medicine. She is currently at work on a book on father-daughter incest, to be published in the fall of 1981 by Harvard University Press.

Lisa Hirschman is Assistant Clinical Professor in the Department of Community Medicine at University of California, San Diego, and is in private practice with The San Diego Family Institute. She is continuing to work on the effects of sexual abuse in childhood on adult women. She received her Ed.D. in 1979 from the Department of Counseling, Boston University.

Carol Nagy Jacklin received her Ph.D. from Brown University in 1972 in Experimental Child Psychology. She is currently Senior Research Associate in the Department of Psychology at Stanford University. She is coauthor of *The Psychology of Sex Differences* (1974) and has published extensively in the areas of sex differences and child development. She is an editor for several professional journals and has actively engaged in public feminist activities and in the dissemination of scientific developmental information.

Ellyn Kaschak received her Ph.D. in Clinical Psychology from Ohio State University and is currently Associate Professor of Psychology at San Jose State University. She was affiliated with the Women's Counseling Service of San Francisco from 1972 to 1978 and is presently in private practice in San Jose and Oakland, California. She has published several articles on feminist psychotherapy.

Marjorie Whittaker Leidig, Ph.D., is a feminist clinical psychologist in private practice in Boulder, Colorado. She is also on the faculty of the Psychology Department at the University of Colorado, teaching Psychology of Women to undergraduates. She has been active in theory construction, research, and service delivery with women victims of violence since 1974—primarily with rape victims, battered women, and more currently, retrospective incest victims.

Eleanor Maccoby received her Ph.D. in Psychology in 1950 from the University of Michigan. She is currently Professor of Psychology at Stanford University. She has published extensively in the areas of social psychology and child development. She is the editor of *The Development of Sex Differences* (1965) and coauthor of *The Psychology of Sex Differences* (1974). Her most recent book is *Social Development: Psychological Growth and the Parent-Child Relationship* (1980).

Kristiann Mannion received an M.S. in Clinical Psychology in 1975 from the University of Idaho. She has worked in all areas of outpatient services for the State of Idaho Regional Mental Health Center and has worked as a Staff Psychologist at the Idaho State School and Hospital with the developmentally disabled. She has specialized in feminist therapy including groups, assertiveness training, sexual therapy and crisis counseling with sexual assault victims. Currently she is Director of a program for displaced homemakers at a Y.W.C.A. in Idaho.

Martha T. Shuch Mednick received a Ph.D. in Clinical Psychology from Northwestern University in 1955. She is currently Professor of Psychology at Howard University and has been Professor of Psychology and Director of Women's Studies Program at University of Connecticut (1976–1978). She is on the editorial board of several journals, has been the Chair of the Committee on Women in Psychology of the American Psychological Association (APA) (1973–1975), and President of the Division of the Psychology of Women of the APA (1976–1977). She is the author of several publications and has lectured frequently on the psychology of women.

Donna M. Moore, Ph.D., is the Human Resources and Affirmative Action Officer at Montana State University in Bozeman, Montana. She is the editor of *An Annotated Bibliography of Assertiveness Materials* (Impact, 1978) and *Battered Women* (Sage, 1979) and has written articles on psychology and feminist issues. She is a feminist psychologist who has given over 200 speeches on women's issues and has helped organize women's centers, sexual assault centers, and centers for battered women. An active feminist, her major areas of interest include changing sex roles, self-esteem, assertiveness, and violence against women.

Saundra Rice Murray received a Ph.D. in Psychology from Howard University in 1976. She is currently Project Director for the National Evaluation of the PUSH for Excellence Project at The American Institutes for Research in the Behavioral Sciences. She has been an Assistant Professor of African American Studies and Psychology at the University of Maryland. She has several publications in the areas of achievement motivation and the psychology of black women and has co-edited a special issue of the *Psychology of Women Quarterly* on black women.

Alberta J. Nassi received her B.A. in psychology in 1974 at the University of California at Berkeley and her Ph.D. in clinical psychology in 1979 at the University of California at Davis. She is currently an Assistant Research Psychologist in Psychiatry and Family Practice and Visiting Assistant Professor in Psychology at the University of California at Davis. Her research interests include the adult development of political activists of the sixties and the psychosocial aspects of primary medical care.

Joseph H. Pleck, Ph.D., a sociologist and clinical psychologist, is a Program Director at the Wellesley College Center for Research on Women. He is the author of *Psychology Constructs the Male* (MIT Press, 1981), and coeditor of *Men and Masculinity* (Prentice-Hall, 1974); *Male Roles and the Male Experience* (Journal of Social Issues, 1978); *Men's Roles in the Family* (Family Coordinator, 1979); *The Male Role: An Annotated Research Bibliography* (NIMH, 1979); and *The American Man* (Prentice-Hall, 1980).

Barbara Bovee Polk is a policy analyst at the University of Hawaii, Honolulu. She holds a Ph.D. in Social Psychology from the University of Michigan, and has taught Sex Roles and methods courses in sociology and social psychology. Several of her articles have appeared in professional journals and published anthologies.

Lenore Sawyer Radloff is a research psychologist/statistician/psychiatric epidemiologist at the Center for Epidemiologic Studies at the National Institute of Mental Health. She received her graduate training at the University of Minnesota. She has presented and published several papers in the area of sex differences and depression. Her current research interest is the mental health of children.

Susan Carol Rogers received her Ph.D. in anthropology in 1979 from Northwestern University. Her research on French peasant women began in 1971 and she has published her work on sexual stratification. She lived for a number of years in France where she taught and was a consultant at UNESCO and OECD. She is currently a Visiting Assistant Professor in the School of Human Resources and Family Studies at the University of Illinois—Urbana, and is beginning ethnological research on Illinois grain farmers.

Nancy Felipe Russo received her Ph.D. from Cornell University in 1970. She is currently first Administrative Officer for Women's Programs of the American Psychological Association (APA), and President of the Federation of Organizations for Professional Women. She has been a past president of the Division of Population and Environmental Psychology of the APA and is a former member of the Subpanel on the Mental Health of Women of the President's Commission on Mental Health. She has also published extensively and lectured frequently in the field of social psychology and the psychology of women.

Maria Nieto Senour received her Ph.D. in Guidance and Counseling in 1972 from Wayne State University. She is currently Associate Professor in the Counselor Education Department at San Diego State University and Psychologist at the San Diego State University Center for Counseling Services and Placement. She is engaged in research on sex roles and the Mexican American woman and has served as a consultant to numerous institutions on bilingual education, cross-cultural counseling, the Mexican American cultural experiences, educating the Chicano, and women's issues.

Mary Jane Sherfey received her B.A. from the University of Indiana, where she studied with the late Alfred Kinsey, and her M.D. from the University of Indiana Medical School. She interned at Payne-Whitney, at Cornell Medical School, where in 1955 she was appointed Assistant Professor of Psychiatry.

She is author of *The Nature and Evolution of Female Sexuality*.

Leonore Tiefer originally trained as a physiological psychologist, but recently changed her focus of interest to human sexuality. She has taught in universities and medical schools, and has written both for professional and popular audiences. She is the author of *Human Sexuality: Feelings and Functions* (Harper & Row, 1979). She lives in New York City and is affiliated with Downstate Medical Center, Brooklyn, N.Y.

Reiko Homma True received her Ph.D. in psychology in 1975 from California School of Professional Psychology. She is currently Deputy Director of the Community Mental Health Services for the city and county of San Francisco and Lecturer at the University of California, Berkeley. She is also Chairperson for the Task Force on Asian American Women in Psychology for the American Psychological Association and has been a member of the Task Panel on Special Population, President's Commission on Mental Health (1977–78).

Shirley Hill Witt specialized in biosocial anthropology and genetic demography at the University of New Mexico and received a Ph.D. there in 1969. She is currently director of the Rocky Mountain Regional Office of the U.S. Commission on Civil Rights. She has been an Associate Professor of Anthropology at Colorado College and has taught at the University of North Carolina—Chapel Hill. Dr. Witt is an Akwesasne Mohawk and has devoted herself to civil, tribal, and human rights, and has worked with a variety of communities.